LABOUR AND THE GULAG

LABOUR
AND THE GULAG

RUSSIA AND THE SEDUCTION
OF THE BRITISH LEFT

GILES UDY

Biteback Publishing

First published in Great Britain in 2017 by
Biteback Publishing Ltd
Westminster Tower
3 Albert Embankment
London SE1 7SP
Copyright © Giles Udy 2017

ISBN 978-1-78590-204-8

10 9 8 7 6 5 4 3 2 1

A CIP catalogue record for this book is available from the British Library.

Set in Times New Roman

Printed and bound in Great Britain by
CPI Group (UK) Ltd, Croydon CR0 4YY

MIX
Paper from
responsible sources
FSC® C020471
FSC
www.fsc.org

CONTENTS

PREFACE

This book began ten years ago as one that was very different. I was researching the history of the labour camps in Norilsk, a city so high in the Siberian Arctic that it experiences six weeks of total darkness each winter and temperatures that fall as low as -50°C (-58°F). It is so isolated that the nearest road system is 800 miles south and the only way in for the prisoners was a 1,200-mile journey north on the river Yenisei in the summer months when the river was not icebound. Because of the rich mineral wealth that lies deep beneath its permafrost, the city began life as one of the most notorious of the Stalin-era gulag camps. It was a prison city. My intention was to tell the back-story of the 300,000 prisoners who passed through the camps, and the different nations and groups from which they came, each with its own testimony of suffering and oppression.

Many of the first Norilsk prisoners had been transferred from the White Sea labour camps on the Solovetsky Islands in anticipation of the outbreak of the war. Solovki, as they were collectively known, was the prototype Soviet concentration camp group. Solzhenitsyn likened it to the original cancer tumour which metastasised to become the Gulag Archipelago, the title of his famous trilogy.

The White Sea region's only resource was timber, which, I discovered, was imported into Britain in vast quantities in the early 1930s. In 1930, the total value was over £9 million, equivalent to more than £530 million today, and it amounted to well over a million tons each year. It was cut by hundreds of thousands of gulag slave labourers, working in terrible conditions, and as a consequence, an extraordinary campaign arose to persuade the British

Labour government to halt the trade and protest to the Soviets about the slave labour that generated it. To my astonishment, I found that Labour had persistently refused to do so – and had even blocked attempts to launch an inquiry into the conditions in the camps.

I assumed that other historians would have noticed these events and written about them. I was surprised to find that no such writings existed. With the exception of passing mentions of just a few pages in one or two other works on the period, at least one of which was full of mistakes, there was nothing. This was a totally new, untold story. It had to be written. My original project was put to one side, to be taken up at another time, and the result is this book.

Because of my background in gulag research I came to this part of British political history from a completely different direction to those of most other historians of the period. I am not, and do not pretend to be, a historian of the Labour Party or of British Communism, unlike the academics who form the vast majority of those who have written about British inter-war politics. Instead I came with an intimate knowledge, gleaned from countless prisoner memoirs, of the actual experience of those who suffered under Soviet oppression.

I knew what really happened to those hundreds of thousands in Russia whose plight so many in the British Labour movement had casually dismissed. I had followed the route on which some of those early prisoners were taken, sailing for almost a thousand miles on one of the last river ferries going north before the winter freeze set in. I had seen for myself the vast expanse of the Siberian wilderness, and as my ferry had moored at small riverside villages along the way, I knew the stories of those who were sent as exiles to those villages, those who, even though they had escaped the fate of the prisoners sent to the camps further north, had still experienced devastating trauma. Many did not survive to return to their homes in the post-Stalin thaw. Little physical evidence remains of their stories, but in Norilsk, where the permafrost is like concrete and graves dug by weakened inmates were sometimes sunk too shallow, seasonal ground movement still brings bones to the surface. Others lie deeper, their remains mummified beneath the ice. Tens of thousands died in Norilsk alone.

I had stood in a gulag punishment block, the inner prison of a punishment camp to which prisoners from 'normal' labour camps were sentenced, sometimes for the most minor of infringements. It was the very worst of the worst and only by some miracle it was still standing; even today the authorities prefer such things not to be known. I had seen the refinement of cruelty with which the cells had been designed: the 'dark' isolation cell, scarcely longer than a man's height, sealed with double doors and no window, so neither light nor sound would penetrate; 'open' cells with no roof, where prisoners were exposed to the elements and in the Arctic winter would quickly succumb. The metal sheet which lined the inside of these cell doors was studded all over with multiple piercings, a grim addition which meant that those who, in their final despair, tried to bang on the doors to be let out, would only shred their hands. I had seen what became of the gulag system in this, its pinnacle, even though eminent British Labour figures had praised Russian prisons as being more humane than our own and turned a blind eye to appeals on behalf of the thousands who were consigned to them.

I had walked in Bykivnia Forest just outside Kiev, in Ukraine, among trees planted by the NKVD, the People's Commissariat of Internal Affairs, to hide the mass graves of over 100,000 of its victims. Kept secret until the fall of Communism, the forest now holds a sacred place in Ukrainian national memory. Just one of many sites that form the Soviet killing fields – some known, others still to be found – Bykivnia keeps alive the story of suffering, even as the photos of the dead, pinned to trees by surviving relatives, begin to fade. And yet, in the 1920s, George Bernard Shaw, less known today than he was then as one of Labour's most charismatic public speakers, commended the Soviet executions that filled mass graves such as these as a necessary 'weeding of the garden'.

In spite of all this, I have tried to remain as objective as possible, though at times that has been hard. To those readers who feel that my passion still intrudes too much, I apologise. Eighty years ago a large proportion of Britain's political intelligentsia closed their ears to appeals on behalf of these people. Those appeals still demand a hearing.

The structure of the book

The structure of the book follows a chronological pattern but still needs some explanation. It became apparent in dealing with the events of 1929–31 that they could not be discussed without regard for the earlier context from which they arose. Additionally, they provoke many questions. How could all of this have come about? What was the emotional connection between British inter-war Socialism and communist Russia? For that matter, what *was* Labour Socialism in those days? What was Communism? Were the excesses of Soviet Communism the product of Stalin's later corruption of Lenin, or were they present from the start, for all those who were prepared to look, to see?

From a willingness to give the benefit of the doubt to the British political movement which sprang from compassion for the poor and the marginalised, further specific questions arise: Was Labour's apparent callousness an aberration? Did Labour's Soviet enthusiasts form only a minority of the party, an extreme fringe? Perhaps there really was so little information available that they could not have known what was happening in Russia. Was this why they were so silent? If they did not respond when appeals were made on behalf of those in the camps, when did they wake up to what was going on in Soviet Russia? What did they do then?

And what of attitudes at the time to religion, the plight of whose Russian adherents first inspired the British protests? Marx was bitterly hostile towards it, as was Lenin. What was the Labour movement's actual attitude towards religious belief at a time when it expressed so much admiration for Marx? Did that colour its reaction to the protests? Could residual prejudice against religious belief be one of the reasons for which historians of the period appear to have neglected these events even though, at one point, the protests involved over a million people around the globe?[1]

The need for these questions to be addressed widened the scope of the book, which grew to include a study of the impact of British Labour attitudes towards Soviet Communism throughout the whole of the inter-war period. While the central events of 1929–31 are covered by Parts III and IV, Parts I and II examine the context from which they emerged.

Part I therefore reviews the tumultuous years in Britain and Europe after 1917, when revolutions and attempted coups shook European capitals and, as public calls for a British socialist revolution grew and clandestine plans were drawn up for the formation of a revolutionary British Red Army, even the future of parliamentary government in Britain appeared to be under threat. It looks at the founding of the Labour Party and the political philosophy which directed the two figures who tower over its early history, Keir Hardie and

Ramsay MacDonald (whose reputation then was very different from the one that it became after 1931), examining the extent to which their enthusiastic endorsement of Marx's analysis of history convinced them of the inevitability of the coming world Socialist revolution. Both men fully intended that Labour would bring about such a revolution in Britain. It continues with an account of British radical sentiment and Soviet enthusiasm in the Labour Party and trades union movement through the General Strike of 1926 and the Arcos Raid of 1927. In passing it covers the lesser known story behind the infamous Zinoviev letter and fall of the 1924 Labour government – showing that the government's fall came because of an act of deliberate political suicide by Ramsay MacDonald, so that the government's interference to halt the prosecution of a communist agitator would remain hidden. Finally, this first part also reveals the previously untold story of a leading Labour MP's links to Soviet money laundering and Stalin-supported IRA gun-running.

Part II moves to Russia and Stalin's war against the twin 'dark forces' of the kulak peasant smallholders on the one hand, and religious believers on the other. It describes the deportation of the kulaks, when 30,000 were shot and over a million more were taken off their land and shipped north and east in cattle trucks. In the Russian north, where the kulaks were put to work cutting timber for the export market, conditions were appalling: over 20,000 children died in the first year, even as Labour hailed the Soviet 'economic experiment' that had caused those deaths. The book then turns to the plight of religious believers, rounded up alongside the kulaks, and traces the persecution of the Russian Church from 1917 to 1929 when churches were closed or destroyed, priests shot or forced into hiding, and even parishioners who tried to protect their churches and mosques were sent to the camps. Because the British Labour movement seemed impervious to their plight, the book considers in greater detail the attitudes of Soviet Communism and Labour towards religious belief and believers. Marx, Lenin and Stalin were all deeply hostile to religious belief, and the Soviets' 'socialist morality' treated with contempt the principles which Western European morality had derived from its Judaeo-Christian heritage. Having considered the philosophical foundations of Soviet Communist anti-religious sentiment, this part then considers the extent to which Labour's admiration for Marxian Socialism led it to share that hostility and either downplay or sympathise with the Soviet suppression of religion. The oft-repeated insistence that inter-war Labour was 'more Methodism than Marx' is examined and found to be wanting.

Parts III and IV deal with the years 1929 to 1931, when Labour was in government under Prime Minister Ramsay MacDonald. They form the central part of the story. Part III spans the period from when Labour took office in the spring of 1929 to the summer of 1930. After considering the role of the Christian Protest Movement, little-known today but so important then that ministers feared its protests might bring the government down, the book turns to a detailed examination of the conduct of the Cabinet and the Foreign Office, drawing upon the original documentary record in Cabinet minutes, Hansard and diplomatic dispatches. These records reveal that, while believing themselves to be objective, an underlying sympathy with Soviet Communism led Labour ministers to manipulate diplomatic appointments to the Moscow embassy and to deny reports from elsewhere which did not fit with their preconceptions. The widespread acceptance of Soviet propaganda by British left-wing commentators served to reinforce ministers' misconceptions and bolster the Labour movement in its rejection of the protesters' appeals. Further material is drawn from the papers of Cosmo Lang, the Archbishop of Canterbury. These form one of the most important archives on Soviet persecution in this period and confirm that, in spite of Labour denials, it was possible, based on reports available in the West at the time, to obtain an accurate assessment of the true and harrowing state of affairs in Russia.

Part IV continues until the fall of the Labour Government in the crisis of August 1931. It begins at the point when the initial protests over the widespread arrest and persecution of religious believers broadened into protests about the timber gulag and attempts to halt the import of timber cut by its inmates. In reality these were not two protests, but one, the first condemning the only arrests known about until the summer of 1930 (those of religious believers), and the second coming as news emerged of the deportation, and incarceration, of an even larger number of kulaks. These had been arrested at the same time as the religious believers, but their fate had not been known in the West until then. This part develops the theme begun in Part III of the unwillingness of the Cabinet to act and the studied refusal of the British Left to believe that the stories of human rights abuses were anything other than a Tory fabrication, invented in an attempt to bring down the government.

As the narrative develops, we see civil servants begin to voice their unease with Labour's stance, even as the Cabinet refused to hold an inquiry into the camps in the fear that this would confirm evidence of Soviet brutality, thus forcing them to ban gulag-cut timber. The role of the leading British timber traders, many of whom discounted the accounts of conditions in the camps and continued to trade with Russia, is then also examined.

The historical narrative is interrupted at this point to include detailed eye-witness testimony from an inmate of the timber camps who saw the events discussed in Britain at first hand. Serving as a clerk with access to regional camp returns, he records that in his area the rate of mortality among the prisoners in 1929–30 was 22 per cent per annum.

In the months leading up to the final collapse of the Labour government in August 1931, evidence continued to emerge to contradict Labour denials. Most important was a special inquiry by the Anti-Slavery Society; the society's report and Labour's refusal to acknowledge its contents are discussed in some detail.

Part V, 'Fellow Travellers', follows the course of events, in so far as they relate to Labour attitudes towards Russia, from the disaster of the 1931 election through to the late 1930s, when light finally began to dawn that Soviet Russia was a terror state. It traces how the Labour Party, as well as the Independent Labour Party which split from Labour in 1932, both shifted still further to the left, adopting policies so radical that even Philip Snowden, the former Labour Chancellor, dubbed them 'Bolshevism gone mad'. The remaining chapters then go deeper into the pro-Soviet attitudes and writings of some of Labour's major pre-war figures than was possible to do earlier in the book without breaking the flow of the historical narrative. These six individuals, Sidney and Beatrice Webb, George Bernard Shaw, Harold Laski, G. D. H. Cole and, to a lesser extent, Stafford Cripps, while representative of a much larger number of Labour figures, represent some of the key opinion formers and political theorists of the period. The Webbs' influential *Soviet Communism: A New Civilisation?* has become infamous for its uncritical adoption of Soviet propaganda, but most critics have gone no deeper than a few quotations. The book is so intellectually flawed that it merits a much fuller treatment. Shaw's writings on Socialism and Soviet Communism, which included proposals for British labour camps, the invention of poisonous gas to execute economic 'exploiters' (capitalists) and the state confiscation of the children of religious parents, are so shocking and unbelievable that they too deserve a more detailed consideration – as does the point that Shaw was looked on as a superstar of the British inter-war Left rather than as an extreme, embittered eccentric. Cole and Cripps both advocated the suspension of Parliament, a British dictatorship of the proletariat, and Cole stated that Stalin would be preferable as the ruler of the United Kingdom (*even with* Soviet repression, which Cole freely acknowledged) than a return to the pre-war status quo. Laski was Professor of Political Science at the LSE for twenty-five years, but his influence went far beyond British shores: Labour Prime Minister James Callaghan wrote that wherever he went in the world he was 'bound to meet a distinguished academic, administrator, or politician who would boast that he had been taught by Laski'. A committed supporter of the Soviet Union for most of that time, Laski was still praising the Russian Revolution in 1947 as the 'greatest' and 'most beneficent' event in modern history since the French Revolution, even as the Labour Party itself was finally beginning to move away from such a position.

Finally, the book closes with the complete reversal in Labour attitudes towards Soviet Communism, a change pioneered in the late 1940s by Foreign Secretary Ernest Bevin, whose confidential memoranda to the Attlee Labour Cabinet more closely reflected the position of his pre-war Conservative predecessor Lord Curzon than that of his own party at the same time.

I do not expect this book to go unchallenged. It reveals things about a British political party whose supporters have long claimed the moral high ground (and, it has to be said, not always without good cause). It contains some less than complimentary revelations about figures who are revered for their part in that party's history – a history that, the book asserts, may not be quite as glorious as some have taken it to be. People need a cause to rally behind and, once committed to it, are not easily shaken in their faith. In the 1920s Labour supporters believed so passionately that Soviet Russia was the new utopia that they would not hear any ill of it. Some who have invested their belief as passionately in 'Labour' today (however they interpret that concept) will also find it hard to hear ill of their party. They may prefer to shoot the messenger rather than to consider the message seriously. Perhaps the truth is not so much that one party is right and another wrong as that there are many more greys in politics – and life – than the blacks and whites we would prefer there to be.

In relation to this, I must therefore add some further comments. First, there are some matters I have left out for lack of space or personal expertise. Any detailed discussion of the Communist Party of Great Britain (CPGB) and its leading figures has been deliberately avoided. CPGB history has been exhaustively examined by numerous scholars at a depth which I could not possibly equal. I also have no need to do so: membership of the CPGB was much smaller than Labour's, and it was a minority party that slavishly followed Moscow's line, and had little impact upon government. I do mention individual CPGB members where they were part of the leadership of the trade union movement or where they were at some time also members of the Labour Party or Independent Labour Party.

I also have gone 'light' on the wider domestic issues which preoccupied the MacDonald government – the crash of 1929, the unemployment crisis that followed, and all that that entailed. I believe that I have covered these adequately enough to give some understanding of the atmosphere in which the Cabinet found itself. But in any book you have to stop somewhere: there are other and better histories of the second MacDonald government. This does not need to be one.

Secondly, a word needs to be said about the number and length of the quotations which appear throughout the book. An often valid criticism of quotations used to 'prove' a point is that they are used selectively, out of context, or even inaccurately reported. It is my firm belief that none of mine have been. It may be that, in spite of my intensive checking, I can be pulled up on the detail of one or two and I will happily correct any mistakes that are found in any subsequent editions. But the vast majority will stand. I make no apology for the extent of the documentary material presented here. It forms the basis on which every conclusion in the book is drawn. Without so many examples taken from contemporary sources, my conclusions would merely be a matter of opinion and rightly contestable for that.

'*Gulag*' – The Bolsheviks used concentration camps from the very beginning. As early as 1918, Lenin issued orders for the regime's opponents to be sent to work in the mines. Within five years, there were over 300 such camps, containing as many as 70,000 inmates.[2] Collectively, the Soviet prison system begun by Lenin and Trotsky has become known as 'the gulag' even though the state organisation 'The Chief Administration of Corrective Labour Camps and Colonies', the Russian acronym of which (GULAG) gave the system its name, was not founded until 1929 under Stalin. The sense in which the term is used in this book (and in its title) is the former – the penal system that existed from 1917 right through the period covered by this book. It includes every variety of prison camp, from the most severe 'corrective labour camps' to the kulak 'colonies', as well as the more conventional prisons such as Butyrka in Moscow. In each case, they were places where inmates were taken, held against their will under armed guard, and punished if they tried to escape.

'*Russia*' and '*Russian*' – From 1917 to 1922, 'Russia' denoted the 'Russian Soviet Federated Socialist Republic' (RSFSR) and, from 1922, on its founding, one component of the USSR. For much of the USSR's existence (1922–91) it was commonly referred to in the West as 'Russia' and where 'Russia' is used in this book it is used in that sense. The choice of the word 'Russian' to describe the nationality of those believers and citizens referred to in this book also requires some explanation. 'Soviet' is not always accurate because the persecutions began in 1917 before the Soviet Union was established. 'Russian' is used in the sense that it includes all those who lived within the borders of the Russian Empire as it existed at the outbreak of the Great War in 1914, excluding Finland and Poland, or alternatively those who would have been described as 'Soviet' after 1922 when Russia was just one part of the USSR. Citizens of today's independent nations of Belarus and Ukraine might rightly feel that being described as 'Russian' is at best misleading and at worst insulting. The most accurate description of these people would be the phrase 'Belarusian, Ukrainian and Russian' but that is clearly too unwieldy. Shortening that to 'BUR' is out of the question as that was the Russian name for the punishment block in a gulag camp!

'*Labour*' – The Labour Party was itself a federation founded by three different groups – the Independent Labour Party, the Fabian Society, and the Trade Unions. The 'Labour movement' comprised all three.

Currency values – Where modern equivalents are shown they have been calculated by reference to the Bank of England online calculator.[3]

I have looked forward to the opportunity to thank those who have in some way, either by concrete assistance or simple encouragement, helped me in the process of writing this book. I am delighted to be able to express my gratitude to:

David Aikman, Jonathan Aitken, Charlie Arbuthnot, Claire Berlinski,

Jenny Boughton, Revd. Canon Michael Bourdeaux, Vladimir Bukovsky, Lady Margaret Bullard, Miranda Carter, Nicholas Chance, Julian Dee, Xenia Dennen, Martin Dewhirst, Dr Dominic Erzdoain, Kim and Masha Eremenko, Prof. Anthony Glees, Lord (Brian) Griffiths of Fforestfach, Prof. Paul Gregory, Mark Kessler, Zhenya Koslova, Tim Lawson-Cruttenden, Al Lewis, Dr Victor Madeira, Prof. David Northrup, Cristina Odone, Andrey O., Melanie Phillips, Katerina Porter, Ann and John Pugh-Smith, Simon Marquess of Reading, Marina and Pavel S., Ayda and Colin Scott, Andrew Selous MP, Pavel Stroilov, John Sweeney, Count Nikolai Tolstoy, Hon. Michael Trend, Rev. Dr Kevin Tyson, Prof. Lynne Viola, Fr George Volkovinsky, Diane Walker, Dr David Wilmot and Michael Wright. My thanks to those mentioned above in no way implies their responsibility for its contents, for which I alone am to blame. I welcome information about mistakes of fact which I will be happy to correct in any future edition.

Olivia Beattie, Bernadette Marron, Namkwan Cho, and Gillian Pink at Biteback Publishing have gone to extraordinary lengths to wrestle with my manuscript, improving the text, spotting inconsistencies and alerting me to errors. Their contribution has been invaluable.

Malcolm Muggeridge's letter to James Maxton, the illustration of the Albert Hall 'Slavery in Russia' rally, and A. T. Cholerton's notes on William MacDonald are reproduced with the kind permission of Rev. Sally Muggeridge, Sir Richard Paget and Mrs Katerina Porter. I would also like to express my thanks to Lady Margaret Bullard for permission to view the full typescript of Reader Bullard's Russian diaries, which form one of the most fascinating and complete insights into life in Leningrad in the early 1930s.

This book would not have been possible without the generous and kind support of Sir Paul Marshall.

My greatest debt of thanks is reserved for my wife Sheila and our children Rebecca, Philippa, Benjamin, Daniel and Samuel. Their patience, encouragement and support over the many years it has taken to write this book have been immeasurable. Without their partnership it would not have seen the light of day.

Giles Udy
January 2017

North-west Russia, 1930

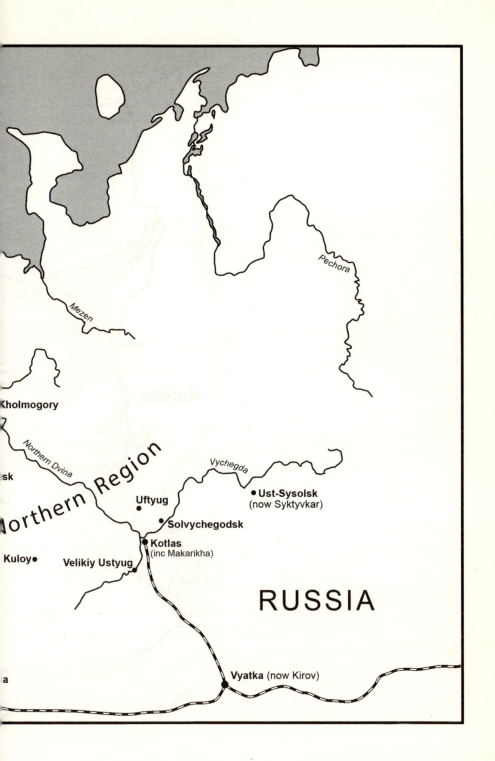

Kholmogory

Northern Dvina

sk

Mezen

Pechora

Karelia

Vychegda

Northern Region

Uftyug

● Ust-Sysolsk
(now Syktyvkar)

●Solvychegodsk

●Kotlas
(inc Makarikha)

Kuloy●

Velikiy Ustyug●

RUSSIA

a

Vyatka (now Kirov)

FOREWORD

THE PHIAL OF TYPHOID

Lenin was sent into Russia by the Germans in the same way that you might send a phial containing a culture of typhoid or of cholera to be poured into the water supply of a great city, and it worked with amazing accuracy.

No sooner did Lenin arrive than ... he gathered together the leading spirits of a formidable sect, the most formidable sect in the world, of which he was the high priest and chief.

With these spirits around him he set to work with demoniacal ability to tear to pieces every institution on which the Russian state and nation depended. Russia was laid low. Russia had to be laid low. She was laid low to the dust.
Winston Churchill, House of Commons, November 1919[1]

In the late afternoon of Easter Monday 9 April 1917, two officers of the German Imperial Army stood on the solitary platform of the little railway station at Gottmadingen, a small town which lies just inside the German-Swiss border. They were waiting for a train to arrive from Zurich. It was the hope of General von Ludendorff, the Chief of Staff on the Eastern Front, who had personally briefed them for this mission, that this train would change the course of the war.

Europe had just seen one of the severest winters in living memory. In the trenches of the Western Front the bitter cold had sapped morale. The replacement of the French commander-in-chief, Joffre, by General Robert Nivelle, had done nothing to turn the fortunes of the allied armies. Nivelle's new offensive had come to nothing. In the French ranks there was talk of mutiny.

At home, governments on both sides were struggling to maintain the war effort. Joffre had been dismissed on 3 December 1916. On 7 December, amidst much criticism of his handling of the war, Herbert Asquith, the British Prime Minister, was forced to stand down, and his place as leader of the wartime coalition was taken by David Lloyd George. Only a few days later in St Petersburg, a group of nobles led by Prince Felix Yusupov, despairing at Rasputin's influence over the royal family, had assassinated the Siberian monk. Disenchantment was growing throughout Europe.

Over that winter the Germans had dug a vast new network of trenches and defensive fortifications, the Hindenburg Line, to the rear of their existing positions. Thirty miles shorter than the current front, it needed fewer troops to defend, and a tactical withdrawal behind the Line began on 15 March 1917, freeing thirteen army divisions for service elsewhere. Five days later, the British began the initial bombardment that was the build-up to a major new assault – the Battle of Arras. In keeping with accepted military wisdom they began with a massive bombardment spread over a number of days. The bombardment was followed by a 'creeping barrage', a rain of shellfire that moved slowly ahead of a ferocious infantry attack against what, it was hoped, would by then be a demoralised and confused enemy. The attack was scheduled for Sunday 8 April, Easter Day, but delays by the French meant that it was postponed until 5.30 a.m. on the next day.

The contrast between Arras and the peaceful foothills of the Swiss Alps could not have been greater. On the afternoon of Easter Monday, as the German officers, Hauptman von Planetz and Leutnant von Burhing, were waiting alone in the quiet of Gottmadingen station, the Canadian army, 320 miles to the north west, was taking Vimy Ridge, one of their greatest battle honours. The assault cost the lives of 11,000 Canadians but crowned a day which saw some of the greatest gains of the war so far. There were to be a further 300,000 casualties and over 2.6 million more artillery shells fired before the war was over.

Events in the East had brought about the circumstances whereby the two officers were waiting on the station platform that day. From the beginning, the Germans had tried to avoid fighting a war on two fronts – against the Allies in the West and the Russians in the East. Their efforts had failed. And yet they had hopes that political and military disintegration inside Russia might be forthcoming and achieve what their campaign so far had not – the removal of Russia from the war.

By the autumn of 1916, the Russian army had lost a million men. More than three million more had been taken prisoner. The Germans halted their offensive as the signs grew that political unrest was destabilising the country. In February 1917, strikes in St Petersburg were followed by rioting, anarchy, and looting. Troops sent to quell the riots deserted and, on 2 March, Tsar Nicholas II was forced to abdicate. This first of two Russian revolutions in 1917 did not, however, bring the end to the war on the Eastern Front that the Germans had hoped for. To the relief of the Allies, the new Russian government, an alliance of liberals and socialists headed at first by an aristocrat, Prince Georgy Lvov, and then by the more bourgeois Alexander Kerensky, a brilliant orator and the son of a school headmaster, announced its intention of continuing the war against Germany.

In Switzerland, the news of the February Revolution was greeted with enthusiasm by the community of Russian refugees and exiles who had sought sanctuary there from the Okhrana, the Tsarist secret police. But in at least one of them, Vladimir Ulyanov, now better known by his revolutionary pseudonym Lenin, enthusiasm quickly turned into anger and frustration as rumours emerged that his fellow Bolsheviks in St Petersburg were about to reach an accommodation with some of the other parties involved in the new Provisional Government. Lenin was purist, a revolutionary to whom such compromises were anathema. He *had* to return to Russia to restore revolutionary discipline in the party he had helped to found. But how?

Lenin considered his options carefully. Germany was at war with Russia, and he would have to travel far to go round enemy territory. His idea of travelling through Germany disguised as a Swede was instantly dismissed by Nadezhda Krupskaya, his wife, on the grounds that as he spoke no Swedish the pretence would soon be discovered. One option was to go back through England, but the British were only too well aware of the danger posed by returning revolutionaries who considered that the war was a capitalist affair that was no concern of theirs: on the matter of the war, if on little else, Lenin was a pacifist. If the Bolsheviks were successful in taking Russia out of the war, the Germans would be able to concentrate all their forces on the Western Front, with potentially disastrous results. Stories of British obstruction of other Russians seeking to return home had filtered through to Switzerland. He had to find another route.

About this time, Lenin realised that if the British thought that their return to Russia might endanger the Allied war effort, the Germans might have reached the same conclusion. Would *they* be willing to grant him and his companions safe passage home? Accordingly, with the help of a Swiss communist, Fritz Platten, Lenin approached the German legation in Berne and asked for help to get back to Russia.

The German Foreign Secretary, Arthur Zimmermann, had only been in his job since November but he was working hard to promote his country's cause. Alarmed by the prospect of America joining the war, he had already secretly offered the Mexican government financial support to launch an attack against the United States to reclaim territory in New Mexico, Texas and Arizona.* To Zimmermann, the international schemer, the prospect of removing Russia from the war altogether was even more enticing.

Lenin knew that he was running a risk. Travel through Germany was tantamount to high treason. He had to appear to be innocent of colluding with the enemy and he needed guarantees that the party would be safe. He therefore set out a number of conditions, which Platten passed on to the German Foreign Ministry: there was to be no examination of passports or questioning of the travellers, whose names would not be revealed; the Russians would pay for their own railway tickets, a gesture which was devised to counter any later accusation that their return had been financed by the Germans; the train carriage was to be treated as if it were 'sealed', having a quasi-diplomatic status of foreign territory which no German national could enter. The Foreign Ministry agreed to all his demands and cabled its approval to the Berne Legation on 5 April. That same day, the British ambassador received reports of the negotiations from his agents and passed these on to London, where developing events were watched with increasing alarm.

---

* The offer was to backfire spectacularly. The coded telegram, dated 19 January 1917, was intercepted by British cryptanalysts, decoded, and passed to President Wilson. It was revealed to a stunned American public on 1 March and played a major part in drawing America into the war a month later.

As word went out to Bolsheviks across Switzerland to join Lenin and his wife for the return home, pleas to exiles from other opposition parties to join the expedition, to bolster its claim to legitimacy, were declined. When the party finally left Zurich, delayed by their unsuccessful efforts to recruit more passengers, those Russians remaining behind descended upon the station to voice their disapproval, banging on the railway carriages with sticks and jeering at the occupants. Lenin would not forget the slight.

Three quarters of an hour's travel from Zurich, the party of thirty-two men, women and children, reached the border. After sparring with the Swiss customs, which confiscated much of their food (there was wartime rationing and the export of food from Switzerland was forbidden), the train finally crossed the border and steamed round the bend into Gottmadingen, where von Planetz and von Burhing were waiting. At Gottmadingen the party transferred to a single German rail car, their baggage in a small wagon at the rear. Scrupulous in their observance of the agreement, the Germans took the last compartment and drew a chalk line on the floor corridor. Only Fritz Platten, as intermediary, was permitted to cross the line.

After travelling another 600 miles, the party reached the coast. They crossed by ferry to Sweden and thence by rail to Finland. At that time, Finland was part of the Russian Empire and, by agreement with its allies, Great Britain was assisting Russia with its border control. So it was British officers who greeted the party as they assembled at the border. Hostile though they were, they could hardly prevent Russians from entering their own country. Lenin had been away for almost ten years. Russia's suffering had already been immense; it was about to increase.

PART I

<u>REVOLUTION!</u>

We are perishing! The coming dawn of liberation is not yet in sight. Many of us are no longer capable of passing on to posterity the terrible experiences we have been through.

Learn the truth about us, write of it, you who are free, that the eyes of this present generation and those that are to come may be opened.

Do this – and it will be easier for us to die.

If our voice beyond the grave is heard by you, we bid you listen, read and ponder what we say. You will then follow the line laid down by our great author – L.N. Tolstoy – who in his own time cried out to the world: 'I cannot be silent'.

'To The Writers Of The World'
Letter from a group of Russian writers, 1927[2]

"Red wins – but the game is not yet over". Punch cartoon, January 1920. Bolshevik intrigue
and violence threatened the stability of many European governments.

CHAPTER 1

'THE RED FLAG WAVES'

Peace! Thrones are everywhere crashing and the men of property everywhere secretly trembling. How soon will the tide of revolution catch up with the tide of victory? That is the question which is exercising Whitehall and Buckingham Palace and causing anxiety even among the more thoughtful democrats.[1]
(BEATRICE WEBB, ARMISTICE DAY, 11 NOVEMBER 1918)

In Europe we are now faced with very serious conditions. Russia has gone almost completely over to Bolshevism. Even in Germany prospects are very black. Bavaria is already in chaos, and the same fate might await Prussia. Spain seems to be on the edge of upheaval. In a short time we might have three quarters of Europe converted to Bolshevism. None would be left but France and Great Britain.[2]
(DAVID LLOYD GEORGE, MARCH 1919)

Even after six decades, there were memories that 76-year-old Alexander Chernykh could not erase. It had been the winter of 1930 in Kotlas, a small town deep in the far north-western forests of Russia. Young Alexander was on his school holidays, but in those bleak years after the Revolution there was little time for leisure. He and some teenage schoolfellows were conscripted to work on the local farm. In those days in that region, where the winter temperature falls below -20°C (-4°F) and the snow lies on the ground for many months, the most common form of transport was the horse-drawn sleigh. One day, Alexander was ordered to report with his sleigh to the local railway station. When he got there, he found a detachment of soldiers waiting for a train. After an interminable wait, long after dark, the silence of the night was finally broken by the distant sound of an approaching steam train. As it drew alongside the platform, soldiers rushed forward to the doors of its freight wagons. When they were unbolted and the wagons spilled their contents onto the platform, Alexander saw to his surprise that they had been filled with people – men, women, and children, of all ages. Many wore only the lightest clothes, as if dressed for summer. These were kulaks, peasant smallholders from Ukraine and the surrounding regions, some of the hundreds of thousands of unfortunates summarily thrown out of their homes on Stalin's orders and dispatched to labour camps.

On the platform there was pandemonium: guards were shouting, babies were crying, old women were weeping. Eventually the women and children were loaded onto sleighs, the men formed into a column and the party headed out into the snowy night. Ten miles and many hours later they reached a small village. There, the exhausted group was finally allowed to rest. But there was no lodging prepared for them and they were forced to find shelter wherever they could – in doorways, barns, anywhere which gave some relief from the bitter cold. The next day the column reformed and pressed on deeper into the forest, where it finally reached an isolated group of barrack huts. They had reached a labour camp.

It was not that harrowing journey which still haunted the old man as he told his story many years later. It was what he encountered on his way back home. On the outward journey, with soldiers as his passengers, he had not seen the stragglers at the rear of the column and had little idea of the toll which the march had taken on the exiles, already weakened by many days locked in freight cars on their journey north. As he reached the place where they had spent their first night, Alexander saw a terrible sight. Coming towards him was a sleigh laden with corpses. Every so often, the sleigh driver would stop, stoop down and pick up another body from the side of the road, and sling it 'like a tree log' on top of the others. 'There were so many bodies,' he later recalled, remembering that day. The surviving marchers, lacking warm clothes of their own, had stripped the dead and dying even as they fell. It only added to the horror. 'Some were completely naked, others had only their outer clothing removed. So many people had perished from hunger and cold at that place where we had stopped.' It did not end there. The weakest had succumbed on that first night's march before they even reached the village. All the way back along the road home, the scene was repeated: 'On both sides of the sleigh there were corpses, corpses, corpses...'[3]

Although the gulag, the Soviet prison system, gets its name from the administrative body which was set up by Stalin in 1930,[4] its foundations were laid in the early days of the Revolution by Lenin, his predecessor, and Felix Dzerzhinsky, the head of Lenin's secret police, the *Cheka*. Both Lenin and Dzerzhinsky had few qualms about taking the most ruthless action against their enemies. 'There is nothing more effective than a bullet in the head to shut people up', Dzerzhinsky had written to a subordinate in May 1918.[5] Lenin ordered the same punishment for 'speculators'.[6] The future was still bleak for those whose lives were spared. For them there was mass arrest and imprisonment. In August 1918, writing to regional Bolsheviks, Lenin ordered the internment of 'kulaks, priests, White Guards, and other doubtful elements in a concentration camp'.[7] Both Dzerzhinsky and Trotsky had called for similar action only a few days earlier.[8] And, by September 1918, the process of setting up labour camps to intern counter-revolutionaries was well advanced. The *Cheka* ordered

> the arrest, as hostages, of prominent representatives of the bourgeoisie, landlords, factory owners, merchants, counter-revolutionary priests, all officers hostile to the Soviet government, and to confine this entire public in concentration camps, having set up the most reliable guard, compelling these gentlemen to work under escort. In the event of any attempt to organize, to rebel, to assault the guard – execute [the offender] at once.[9]

From that point, the early gulag expanded fast. In May 1919, every provincial city was ordered to establish a concentration camp that could hold a minimum of 300 inmates.[10] By October 1923, there were over 350 camps in existence, holding around 70,000 prisoners, many women and children among them. Conditions for inmates were terrible, especially in the famine years of 1921–22 when cholera and typhus were rampant. At its height, the mortality rate was running at 15–20 per cent a month.[11] In a few camps it was even higher, though in those cases it was by design rather than accident. At Kholmogory, not far from Arkhangelsk (Archangel) on the White Sea, the requisitioned monastery became a death camp. Between 1919 and 1922, over 25,400 of its inmates were shot.[12]

In November 1918, the Great War drew to a close, but the end of hostilities did not signal peace. Europe was in turmoil. In Berlin, on 15 January 1919, Communist leaders Rosa Luxemburg and Karl Liebknecht were lynched by right-wing paramilitaries. Communists under Béla Kun took power briefly in Hungary between March and August. A further Communist revolution in Bavaria was put down in May 1919. Communist uprisings broke out elsewhere too – in Alsace, Finland, Latvia, Estonia, Saxony, Bessarabia, Persia, Galicia, and Czechoslovakia.

British soldiers, back from the front and marked by their experiences, were emboldened in their own demands for social change. For some, the Russian Revolution had set an inspiring precedent and strikes and civil unrest spread in Britain too. On Thursday 13 January 1919, a columnist in *The Times*, writing of the Communist 'revolutionary movement' centred on the Clyde in Glasgow, described it as 'a powder magazine' where there was 'more explosive material than in any other area in the country'.[13] A fortnight later the spark was set. A strike for shorter working hours began and, by the end of the week, 100,000 Clydesiders were on strike. Demands were made for government intervention with the employers, accompanied by threats of 'non-constitutional' action if the demands were not met. On Friday 31 January, 10,000 of them descended upon the centre of Glasgow to hear the government's reply. When they discovered that their demands had been turned down, there was mayhem. Bottles were thrown, shops looted and the police made baton charges to dispel the crowds. A red flag was run up on the city flagpole.[14] The strike leaders were arrested and charged with inciting a riot. One, the communist William Gallacher, was additionally charged with assaulting a policeman. The Secretary of State for Scotland, Sir Robert Munro, told the Cabinet that 'it was a misnomer to call the situation in Glasgow a strike – it was a Bolshevist rising'.[15] Tanks and troops were sent north; by Monday morning thousands of soldiers were patrolling the streets.

In Belfast, shipyard workers formed their own 'Soviet', or workers' committee, to run their strike. It even issued permits to allow local traders to continue to operate. In London, a strike was threatened on the Underground. On the railways 400,000 members of the National Union of Railwaymen

(NUR), 40,000 engineers and 70,000 railways clerks threatened walkouts. Industrial unrest was reported among London and Welsh ship repairers, West Lothian and Lanarkshire miners, power station workers (including those of Chelsea Power Station), dairy workers, hotel and restaurant employees, Goole boilermakers and shipwrights, and Manchester engineers. In Calais, there was further trouble among returning soldiers awaiting demobilisation.

Talk of revolution was spreading. On 20 January the press reported that a secret conference of 'Bolshevists' arranged by the 'Hands Off Russia' Committee had taken place in Farringdon Street in London, and the possibility of engineering a general strike 'as the first definite step towards the Revolution' had been discussed. Handbills distributed at the meeting declared:

> ...the Red Flag waves intermittently in Berlin, in Budapest, and Vienna. And ere long, perchance, it will float from the clock tower at Westminster, and from the flag staff at Windsor Castle. To the strains of 'The International' as the movement pushes ever westward the only flag that matters will be raised successively in Dublin, in New York, in San Francisco, and maybe at no distant date in Tokyo and in Peking, in Delhi, and in Teheran. The revolutionary movement initiated in Petrograd during November 1917 will circle the world. The Workers International shall be the human race.[16]

'Hands Off Russia' was to become a familiar refrain. When the Bolsheviks* took Russia out of the war with Germany in March 1918, a million German troops, freed from the Eastern Front, transferred to the West to launch a vigorous new offensive against the Allies. Already reeling from the military consequences of the Russian capitulation, the British Government and Royal family were deeply shocked when the tsar, King George V's cousin, and his family were shot in July 1918. To prevent the Allied military supplies which had been sent to the Eastern Front from falling into the hands of the Germans, and to support the beleaguered Russians, Allied troops were landed in Archangel in August 1918. For the British Left, this was an assault upon

---

* 'Bolshevism' was the variant of Communism adopted by the Bolshevik party in the early revolutionary period. Over the course of time the use of the term 'Bolshevism' was gradually replaced by 'Communism', though the two were often used interchangeably. In Britain in the 1920s 'Bolshevism' was the term most commonly used.

Russian workers, struggling to be free from Tsarist oppression. From then on, the withdrawal of British troops from Russia became a unifying cause for socialists across all parties of the left, rallying under the cry of 'Hands Off Russia', the slogan which became the name of their campaign.

At that time, the dividing line between the Labour Party and British Communists was far from clear. Many British socialists moved freely between the Labour Party (founded 1900), the Independent Labour Party (ILP, founded 1893), from which it sprang, the British Socialist Party (BSP, founded 1911), which included a number of former ILPers, and the BSP's post-1920 incarnation, the Communist Party of Great Britain (CPGB). It was the BSP and the new 'Hands Off Russia' Committee which took the Royal Albert Hall, one of the largest and most prestigious concert halls in the country, with a capacity of over 5,000, in February 1919 to protest against British intervention in Russia and to demand the withdrawal of the Allied troops. Messages expressing sympathy with the object of the meeting were read from men who were or would be eminent Labour Party members – Bertrand Russell*, the future Labour minister and peer Arthur Ponsonby, and George Bernard Shaw. Neil Maclean, who sat as a Labour Member of Parliament from 1918 to 1950, first for the ILP, then for the Labour Party, spoke from the platform, as did John Maclean, the 'Bolshevist Consul in Glasgow'. When, as a result of his speech that night, one of the other speakers, William Foster Watson, was imprisoned for six months for sedition (his words were said to have included the call 'arm yourselves'[17]), George Lansbury, already one of the most popular figures in the party and future party leader, appeared in court to speak in Watson's defence. Ponsonby, Shaw, Maclean and Lansbury were all to be outspoken supporters of the Soviet Union† in the years to come. Although these rallies were called with the British withdrawal from Russia as their ostensible object, the agenda was wider; the protesters were concerned to defend the Russian Revolution as much as they were to achieve peace between the nations.

---

* Russell's enthusiasm for the Revolution waned after a visit to Russia the following year, when he professed himself 'profoundly impressed with the defects of the Bolshevik leaders [and] with the tyranny of their rule'. TNA, CAB 24-109, CP 1694, 26 July 1920. *The Russian Situation*, 'Memorandum by Dr H. A. L. Fisher (President, Board of Education) on his conversation with Mr Bertrand Russell'.

† The title 'Soviet Union' was not adopted until December 1922. For further discussion on the use of 'Soviet' and 'Russia' see the Preface.

Labour Party support for the 'Hands Off Russia' protests was made unambiguously clear by the party secretary Arthur Henderson at the Labour Party conference later that year, in June 1919. Henderson was already a senior party figure, having served two terms as party leader (1908–10 and 1914–17). He was to become Foreign Secretary in the 1929–31 Cabinet and party leader for the third time from 1931–32. Addressing the conference, his speech was a clear statement of Labour's support, not only for the withdrawal of British troops, but for the Revolution and its underlying political aims:

> The working-class … welcomes the revolutions which have destroyed the old order in Russia, Germany, Austria-Hungary, and elsewhere, and declares that the association of the Governments now engaged for hostilities against and in equipping with arms and munitions the leaders of the counter-revolutions in these countries will, if successful, wrest from the working-classes the social and political gains won by these revolutions, and are inspired by the interests of capitalism and monarchy.
>
> … It is the duty of the working-classes in every country to demand that military operations against socialist republics of Europe should be stopped … they should be left free from interference to settle for themselves the forms of government which they wish to adopt and which should then be recognized by the other Governments. To this end it is the further duty of the working-class movement to demand action in the various Parliaments and to bring whatever pressure it can command in view of its national circumstances upon the governing authorities of the various countries.[18]

The conference then passed a motion calling for strike action. To the consternation of those who feared the spread of revolution to Britain, it was not for the purposes of bettering the work conditions of its members, but for the explicit purpose of enforcing its will on British foreign policy:

> [Delegates] have considered the situation and declared a general working-class demonstration should be made as an evidence of their determination to prevent the Governments adopting a reactionary policy … The working-class must protest in particular against the help given to the reactionary elements in their attempts to triumph over the revolutions and over the new democracies.

> This conference ... denounces the assistance given by the Allies to reactionary bodies in Russia as being a continuation of the war in the interests of financial capitalism which aims at the destruction of the Russian Socialist Republic and as being a denial of the rights of peoples to self-determination and it instructs the National Executive to consult with the Parliamentary Committee of the Trades Union Congress with a view to effective action being taken to enforce these demands by the unreserved use of their political and industrial power.[19]

George Lansbury

George Lansbury's unsuccessful appearance in court on Watson's behalf is evidence of the standing in which he was already held in the Labour movement. His stature in Labour history, both then and now, is immense. In the mid-1920s, a semi-official history of the party declared him to be 'one of the most beloved men in the Labour Movement ... a man with the frame of a giant, the heart of a lion and the soul of a child'.[20] A modern biographer describes him as 'one of the most attractive and appealing personalities that the British Left has ever produced'.[21] Harold Laski wrote of him: 'He is the incarnation of the fellowship in the Labour Movement. Day in, day out, he has preached it is gospel. He has lit a flame in thousands of hearts; in others, it has burnt more brightly because he has been alive.'[22]

In the 1920s the flame that Lansbury lit was that of Soviet Communism. A well-known campaigner in his native Poplar, Lansbury launched the *Daily Herald* as a daily socialist newspaper in 1912, during the time that he was an MP. The *Herald* welcomed the Russian Revolution in 1917 and, as the years progressed, it maintained its vigorous and vocal support. Such was Lansbury's popularity that when he returned from a trip to Russia in March 1920, thousands filled the Albert Hall to welcome him home. The event was conducted with the fervour of a revivalist meeting:

> On his return from his visit to Russia Mr George Lansbury was accorded a welcome home by thousands of his admirers, who held a demonstration in the Albert Hall last night. Bouquets were presented to Mr Lansbury from the staff of the Daily Herald, from the National Federation of Women Workers, and from the Herald League.
>
> The hall, which accommodates 10,000, was packed, and before the proceedings

opened the great audience sang the 'Red Flag,' the Russian National Anthem, and other songs. Mr Tom Mann* presided, and when he led Mr and Mrs Lansbury onto the platform the audience rose and greeted them with rousing cheers.

In his speech of welcome Gerald Gould, associate editor of the *Daily Herald* said Mr Lansbury, whom he described as the ambassador of their movement, had brought back from Russia a message of inspiration from the first great Socialist Republic the world had ever seen.

Mr Lansbury said that he had never been so happy and so proud as when he crossed the frontier into Russia and was received among men and women who were his friends.

The Central Government of Russia and the Extraordinary Commission of Russia† had done more to put down on terrorism and keep down murder than any other Government in similar circumstances could be expected to do.[23]

Lansbury, the revival's evangelist, boldly proclaimed the new faith, declaring: 'I see the Socialists of Russia as a band of men and women striving to build the New Jerusalem.'[24]

He was quite candid about the degree of his support for the Bolsheviks too:

It is no part of my business as a Socialist to search out and strive to discover material for criticism or denunciation … I do not propose to be an apologist. I do not consider Lenin or his comrades need me or anyone else to act as such. In my judgement, no set of men and women responsible for a revolution of the magnitude of the Russian Revolution ever made fewer mistakes or carried their revolution through with less interference with the rights of individuals, or with less terrorism and distraction, than the men in control in Russia.

---

* Tom Mann (1856–1941) became a communist after reading the *Communist Manifesto* in 1886. After a time acting as Labour leader Keir Hardie's election manager, he moved to London and became a member of the Fabian Society Executive in 1896. By the 1920s, he had become a leading Communist organiser. As the British representative on the ten-member executive of the Red Trades Union International, he spent three months in Russia in June–September 1920. He was a member of the presidium of the CPGB through the 1930s. Too old to fight on the Republican side in the Spanish Civil War, he was honoured by having his name given to a Republican unit, the 'Tom Mann Centuria'.

† The *Cheka*, the Revolutionary secret police. Later known as the OGPU, NKVD, and KGB.

And, deftly, he then extricated himself from one of the most striking inconsistencies in the statement he had just made, continuing: 'When I speak of
the rights of individuals I exclude property rights, for the one object of the
revolution was to abolish for good and all the "right" of one set of individuals
to exploit the life and work of their fellow men and women.'[25]

Those of a less naive persuasion saw what was going on in Russia in a very
different light.

Bolshevism and the destabilisation of the British Empire

The years that immediately follow a major war are a time when bold governments can make daring foreign policy moves. Even victorious nations are
morally and economically exhausted, their leaders often unable to command
enough domestic support for robust responses to new threats from abroad.
Tired countries want only peace.

The Bolsheviks saw this clearly. The British Empire extended over one
fifth of the world's population and, as the 'Great Game', the nineteenth-century rivalry between the British and Russian Empires, took on new clothes
with Lenin in place of the tsar, it was the Bolsheviks who were bold and
David Lloyd George, the British Prime Minister, who was tired and indeci-
sive. On 3 March 1919, Lloyd George shared his fears with the Cabinet:

> In Europe we [are] now faced with very serious conditions. Russia has gone almost
> completely over to Bolshevism, and we have consoled ourselves with the thought
> that they are only a half-civilised race; but now even in Germany, whose people
> are without exception the best educated in Europe, prospects are very black. Ba-
> varia is already in chaos, and the same fate might await Prussia. Spain seems to be
> on the edge of upheaval. In a short time we might have three quarters of Europe
> converted to Bolshevism. None would be left but France and Great Britain.[26]

Lloyd George had ended the war as a hugely popular national leader, but his
Liberal Party was so divided that it fought the 1918 election as two rival parties.
He presided over a Liberal–Conservative coalition Cabinet that, on Russia, was
no less split. Lord Curzon, the Foreign Secretary*, Winston Churchill, who was

---

* Curzon was appointed Foreign Secretary in October 1919. Before that he had been Air Minister and
Lord President of the Council.

then the Secretary of State for War, Austen Chamberlain, the Chancellor of the Exchequer, and Walter Long, the First Lord of the Admiralty (a significant role at the height of British naval power) saw Bolshevism as a rising menace, potentially equal to Prussian militarism, that had to be confronted. By contrast, Lloyd George, supported by Sir Robert Horne, the president of the Board of Trade, and Conservative Andrew Bonar Law (who would succeed him briefly as Prime Minister in October 1922) clung to the belief that the answer was not confrontation but trade: trade with Russia, they reasoned, would bring prosperity to ordinary Russian people, and this in turn would weaken the appeal of the Bolsheviks and lead to their downfall. It was a vain hope, which proved wrong on all counts, but it served to provide a narrative to justify their tolerance of Bolshevik-initiated subversion in Britain and the empire.

Of the threat both at home and abroad there could really be no doubt: Bolshevik leaders had stated it openly. The Congress of the Third International, known as the Comintern, the international arm of Bolshevism and self-styled 'engine room' of world revolution, met in July 1920, and its international ambitions were quite plain:

A whirlwind of revolution has banished the faded illusion of compromise from the minds of millions. Gradually the masses are awakening to class consciousness and the international proletariat is awakening to class hatred of the world bourgeoisie. By powerful efforts it is advancing toward the realisation of the marvellous teachings of Karl Marx.

The Congress of the International has assembled in Russia, the centre of the Revolution, in order to map out for the peoples of the entire world the way of rebellion and victory.

The Third International [will lead to] the world dictatorship of the proletariat. Through the dictatorship of the proletariat [will come] the complete abolition of classes and the liberation of humanity.

A fierce struggle is raging through the world ... Colonial slaves, peoples crushed by the International Imperialist war, workmen who have penetrated into the bowels of the earth, workmen who have conquered the air by the power of machinery! The Third International will unite the force of your sufferings, the magnificence of your victories and the power of your energy, for the purpose of defeating the enemy of humanity – capital.[27]

In an attempt to convince the Cabinet that a firm response was called for, Churchill sent a copy of this declaration to his Cabinet colleagues. There was no shortage of corroboration of the threat Russia posed to British interests, either, and it was outlined in further briefing notes distributed to members of the Cabinet. Lenin himself had made it clear that the British Empire was his target:

> A very important factor for the development of world revolution is the awakening of millions of workers in the colonies and dependencies. This fact presents us with a most important task, which consists in helping these enormous masses of backward individuals on the road to world revolution.[28]

Stalin, still just one of the wider Bolshevik leadership group under Lenin, was no less direct, declaring that, 'the problems of the West would be incomparably easier of solution if the external power of France and England could be undermined',[29] and the Indian Communist leader Mahendra Nath Roy* reinforced the importance of a dual attack against Britain both at home and through its empire:

> A vast Oriental Empire enables British capital to maintain its position at home and to increase its international power. Its destruction is a vital factor if capitalist order in Europe is to be overthrown. The advanced proletariat of Europe cannot achieve this overthrow alone. It must be helped by colonial and subject countries like India, whose great economic, industrial and political development render them the principal economic and military support to the imperial capital.[30]

Bolshevik imperial ambitions were no less defined than British ones, except that they met with the approval, rather than disdain, of British socialists.

---

*   M.N. Roy was a protégé of Lenin's, founder of the Mexican Communist Party and, in 1920, the Communist Party of India. After travels in the Far East and Tashkent on Comintern business, he returned to Moscow in 1927 but fell into disfavour with Stalin on the latter's rise to power and was expelled from the Comintern. On his return to India in 1930, he was arrested and imprisoned. His return probably saved his life: many of his Comintern contemporaries perished in the purges of 1937–38.

Lenin's Trojan horse – the Russian Trade Delegation

When the Bolsheviks sought to reopen trade links between Russia and Britain, it was in the context of furthering these ulterior aims, with the active support of their British friends and any others they could deceive. In Cabinet, those who lacked the foresight of Churchill and Curzon grasped at the straw that was held out to them, believing that accommodating Moscow would reduce the Bolshevik threat. Churchill and Curzon felt that it was more likely to feed the monster than to starve it.

Lenin needed trade with Britain. Trade was essential to strengthen the Russian economy. On a practical level, Russian industry was bankrupt and ailing: the Red Army was so short of equipment that it could not exert control over the country, let alone extend its influence beyond its borders. It needed clothing and boots, none of which were available in sufficient quantities domestically; there were not even enough trains and rolling stock to move troops across the country. Britain could supply all these.

The Bolsheviks had two other equally important aims: diplomatic recognition and subversion. Diplomatic recognition by the world's foremost trading nation was essential. The regime had seized vast amounts of wealth, nationalising banks and taking over private property on a massive scale. With few resources to trade beyond the gold and the other assets it had sequestered, it was presented with a second problem, which only an official trade agreement could overcome – the legitimisation of those seizures so that they could be used in exchange for purchases made on the world market. But thousands of Britons had lost money or assets in Russia; property or businesses they owned had been nationalised without compensation; international debts incurred by Russian companies or the Tsarist government had been reneged upon. The total was believed to be in the region of £300 million (£12.1 billion today).[31] Until the revolutionary government was recognised as the lawful government of Russia, any gold it shipped abroad was not safe from claims by British creditors, one of the chief of which was the Bank of England. Recognition legitimised Bolshevik ownership of what had been taken by deeming the seizures to be those of a lawful government; and it set a legal distance between the pre- and post-revolutionary governments. Without it, Russian overseas trade was paralysed.

There was also a more sinister reason for which the Russians wanted a trade agreement. A trade agreement would enable them to establish offices (eventually employing 600 people) in London, at the heart of the empire, which could then be used as a cover for espionage and subversion. Weakening the power of its enemy by supporting and encouraging British domestic revolutionary elements was a key part of the wider Bolshevik project to destabilise the empire.

Negotiations

The sophistication with which the Bolsheviks conducted their negotiations, exerting pressure upon the British government over multiple fronts (not least by bringing the British Labour movement on board as an ally), was remarkable. Equally effective was the degree to which they proceeded incrementally to achieve goals which would have been impossible if pursued outright: each concession obtained, or deception successfully achieved, became the platform for the next. By this process they outwitted Lloyd George and succeeded in advancing all their political goals. Churchill and Curzon saw through it all and watched, frustrated and overruled in Cabinet, as their weak Prime Minister was manipulated and outmanoeuvred: 'Since the armistice', Churchill wrote to Lloyd George in March 1920, 'my policy would have been "Peace with Germany, war on the Bolshevik tyranny!" Willingly or unavoidably you have followed something very near the reverse.'[32]

The first Russian move came in January 1920 with a proposal to open trade negotiations between the elected leaders of the private Russian Co-operatives and the British. This both appealed to Lloyd George's belief in the power of trade to filter down to ordinary Russians and turn them against the Revolution and gave the appearance that the British were negotiating with the Co-operatives, not the regicidal regime with which the Allies were still (given the Archangel expedition) virtually at war. The British were outwitted from the start: as soon as it was agreed to begin talks, the Russian Co-operative leaders were replaced by senior Bolsheviks, including the man who was to become the Bolshevik spy chief in Britain, Nikolai Klishko. In reality, Klishko was the first Soviet intelligence resident (head of station) in London, though he posed as the secretary to the delegation; his nominal boss Leonid Krasin was actually his subordinate.[33] Born in Vilnius in 1880, Klishko had lived in London as an exile from 1907 to 1918, marrying an Englishwoman, Phyllis Frood.[34] Fellow exile and future Soviet Foreign Minister Maxim Litvinov was a frequent guest at their home in Hampstead, accompanied by his British wife, Ivy. Klishko was interned in August 1918 and subsequently deported, before returning to London in May 1920.[35]

So, in one simple move, the Russian Co-operative delegation became a Bolshevik government one. Once the format for talks was reached and the delegation's acceptance by the British thus confirmed, the deposed Co-operative leaders were thrown into jail. Lloyd George would never have agreed to negotiate directly with a Bolshevik delegation, but the Russians gambled that, once committed, he would not pull out because of a few arrests in Russia. They were right. Emboldened, they continued to press their advantage by whatever subterfuge they could employ.

The Danes were more strong-minded. The arrests took place in the middle of similar Russian–Danish trade negotiations and, as soon as the Danes heard what had happened they called the talks off. Undaunted, the Bolshevik party left Copenhagen and simply sailed on to London. There they met a much less determined response.

Frank Wise

It was unfortunate for British interests that E. F. 'Frank' Wise, the civil servant who was not only appointed by Lloyd George to lead the British team at the negotiations but became his trusted advisor on Russian trade, was also a closet Bolshevik sympathiser. Wise was so supportive of the Bolshevik cause that in 1923, once trading links were firmly established, he resigned from the British civil service and took Soviet government employment as a director of their new London-based trading company, Centrosoyus (the Soviet Russian Central Union of Consumers' Co-operative Societies), the organisation which his negotiations from the British side had been responsible for establishing.

The extent to which Wise was the Bolsheviks' man *before* the negotiations, or only became progressively so as they proceeded, cannot be determined, though even while he was leading the British negotiations in October 1920, *The Times* was prepared to risk a libel action when it described him as a man whose 'pro-Bolshevik sympathies are notorious'.[36] The accusation seemed to make no impact upon Lloyd George: two years later, Wise was still acting as his personal advisor on Russian trade and accompanied him in that capacity to the international conference in Genoa in 1922 to discuss the recognition of the Bolshevik government.[37]

Wise had been a member of the ILP since 1914[38] but, as a civil servant, he would have had to keep his political affiliation quiet until his controversial resignation in 1923. The position of the ILP, his party, on the Revolution was clear and there is no reason to suppose that Wise did not support it. In 1918 the ILP had committed itself to the establishment of a 'Socialist common-wealth' defined as 'the collective ownership and use of land and capital for the common and equal welfare and happiness of all'.[39] At its conference that year, it had affirmed its support for the 'workers of Russia' and, pledging to confront the 'lies' told about the horrors going on in Russia, 'to do all in its power to inform the people of Britain of the truth of the position adopted by Russian comrades in the interests of International Socialism'.[40] The following year, in a motion which was very similar to the one passed at the Labour Party conference, the ILP welcomed the revolutions that had established republics in Germany, Austria and Hungary and had overthrown their former ruling dynasties.[41] In 1924 and 1929, while in Soviet employ and while this was still ILP policy, Wise stood for election as an ILP MP. After the 1931 election, he became a leading member of the Socialist League, which attempted to repair the breach between the ILP and the Labour Party when they fell out.

Of Wise's subsequent activities in Britain on behalf of the Soviets more will be said later. At the time, Lloyd George not only trusted him as an ad-visor but appointed him to chair the British side of negotiations with the Russians – and it was in that capacity that he was in Copenhagen in May 1920 as a preliminary to the opening of London talks, just as the Danes called off their own talks. If his appointment had been fortuitous, the Russians would hardly have believed their luck. If Wise had already gone over to their cause and then lobbied for the post to further it, it was an extraordinary coup.

Had Wise's sympathies been more widely known it is unlikely that he would have been permitted to attend Cabinet meetings over the summer (three in total) where he was let into ministers' confidence about the negoti-ations and their concerns over the Bolshevik delegation.* We do know that by November, a month after *The Times* questioned Wise's allegiance, Austen

---

* Wise was present at Cabinet meetings on 28 May, 3 June, and 10 June 1920. Strictly speaking, they were 'Conferences of Ministers' not Cabinet Meetings but to all intents and purposes the same as Cabinet meetings, presided over by the Prime Minister with other senior ministers present. Two of the three were at Downing Street and one was in Bonar Law's rooms at the House of Commons.

Chamberlain, the Chancellor of the Exchequer, was forced to take him aside to reprimand him: the Treasury had complained that he was not keeping them properly informed nor adequately protecting Britain's interests in the talks.[42]

Whether or not Wise had already gone over to the Bolsheviks, his arguments for pursuing a trade agreement did more to serve their cause, not least by convincing Lloyd George along the way, than to represent the agreement's likely outcome. His early insistence that a deal with Russia would secure vast quantities of grain and commodities, without which Europe would starve, sounded enticing. Significantly, he argued for the Russians' ultimate objective, diplomatic recognition, suggesting that the humanitarian dividend would even make the cost of recognition worth the price:

> We want Russian grain; the Russians want British locomotives. The resumption of commerce between England and Russia would in the course of time involve virtual de facto recognition of the Soviet government, and perhaps some kind of 'peace negotiations'...
>
> Can we afford to do without Russian grain, or must we have it even at the cost of recognition? ... I know of no evidence to show that the economic position of Russia is deteriorating. As hostilities against the Soviets grow less intense, it improves ... There are not enough bread stuffs in existence to feed the world till [the following year's harvest] and the first people to starve will be those in the distressed areas of central Europe ... We must decide which is the most dangerous to the existing order of society in Europe and to the security of the United Kingdom, namely, virtual recognition of the Soviet government or starvation and disease in Europe on an unprecedented scale.[43]

Churchill was appalled. He rebuked Wise for raising 'an altogether false issue' to justify a rapprochement that he, Churchill, deeply opposed: the Russians, he insisted, had no grain to trade; their transport infrastructure was so destroyed that they had nothing on which to run locomotives – so that, even if the grain existed, they would be unable to move it to the ports. As for other commodities which could be used to pay for British exports, there were none: their industry was close to collapse and they had nothing 'apart from the gold which they have seized',[44] against which there were thousands of potential British claims already and which various other governments, including the Americans, had refused to handle.

As Wise was assuring the Cabinet that the plentiful supplies of Russian wheat, ready to feed Europe, justified even diplomatic recognition, Foreign Office information was totally at variance with this. Ministers were told that the Soviet economy was so weak that 'they know that if they are to save themselves it is a race against time ... the Reds themselves are now so short of grain that they are forced to requisition it to feed the cities'.[45] The first signs of famine had appeared in Russia as early as 1919. By then the total area planted with crops had shrunk by 25 per cent. It was reduced still further to 50 per cent of the original area in 1921. The famine which raged as a consequence in 1922–23 killed around three million people.[46]

Wise was a food procurement specialist. He had been a member of the Anglo-Russian supplies committee of the War Office during the war, rising to be assistant director of army contracts for clothing and raw materials in 1915 and ending the war as principal assistant secretary at the Ministry of Food. How, with that expertise, he could be so mistaken is a mystery; by August the following year the Cabinet were discussing ways to get aid to Russia's starving millions rather than the import of its crops. Wise's promise of overflowing Russian grain was an illusion, his assurance of its abundance either a result of a gullible readiness to accept Russian propaganda or deliberate misinformation.

Undaunted by his failure to convince the Cabinet to proceed straight to full diplomatic recognition (something that he would pursue successfully over a longer timescale, eventually negotiating it for Ramsay MacDonald in 1929), Wise proposed an alternative way to help the Soviets trade with the security against the seizure of their gold which diplomatic recognition would otherwise have afforded them – by setting up an offshore trading arm in Europe through which the gold could be channelled without it being detained by British creditors.[47] Churchill was appalled by this suggestion too: 'Here is a perfectly unblushing proposal by a Committee of British Government officials to enter into collusion with the Bolsheviks in order to "evade" the action of the Courts in this country and deny to British subjects who have been robbed by the Bolsheviks their ordinary remedies at law'.[48]

Propaganda and subversion

In contrast to Wise's real or assumed naïveté, Churchill and Curzon were deeply suspicious of the Trade Delegation – with ample cause. The delegation had been permitted to come to Britain on the clear understanding that its members would 'abstain from propaganda and other hostile action during their stay in this country'.[49] Within a few weeks of Krasin and Klishko's arrival in May 1920, it was apparent that they had no intention of keeping to that commitment. In the first nine months of 1920, money flooded in from Moscow. 'There is probably no extremist organisation in England which has not received financial assistance from Russia', the Home Office Directorate of Intelligence informed ministers the following month, estimating that the Soviets had donated around £100,000 (£4 million today) to revolutionary causes in Britain over that period.[50]

Bolshevik-inspired subversion in Britain did not begin with the arrival of the Russian Trade Delegation, though they developed it considerably. Many revolutionaries had fled to Britain to escape the Tsarist authorities before 1917 and some remained to aid the cause after that date. Theodore Rothstein was one of these. A Russian radical exile who had arrived in London in 1890, he knew Lenin, who had stayed with him in London, and was a friend of fellow exile Maxim Litvinov, who would later become the Soviet Foreign Minister. After the Revolution, Rothstein took on the role of the Bolsheviks' unofficial British ambassador and clandestine paymaster until his expulsion in August 1920. It was he who had provided the £500 (£20,100 today) to pay for the February 1919 Albert Hall protest meeting which demanded the withdrawal of British forces from Northern Russia. He also regularly acted as intermediary for payments to British revolutionary groups and individuals.

The 'Hands Off Russia' Committee was one such group. Formed just a month before the Albert Hall meeting, it was one of the very first Soviet front organisations in Britain. Its initial members included identifiable Communists such as William Gallacher, a CPGB founder member and later a Communist MP, and Harry Pollitt, who was general secretary of the CPGB from 1929, but as the committee repositioned itself in 1920 to appear more representative of mainstream Labour and trade union opinion, Gallacher and Pollitt withdrew. One consistent figure and driving force from its foundation until his death in 1960 was W. P. Coates, the national organiser of the British Socialist Party, who was 'lent' by the BSP to the 'Hands Off Russia' campaign. Coates was not only a founder member of the CPGB; his wife Zelda Kahan was Rothstein's sister-in-law.

The fact that the 'Hands Off Russia' Committee has been largely neglected by historians is tribute to its success as a front organisation. Having appeared initially as a protest organisation, it took on a new guise as the 'Anglo-Russian Parliamentary Committee' (ARPC) in 1924, acquiring an official-sounding status to which it had no claim, by presenting itself as a British forum of Russia-interested Labour MPs and trade union figures. In fact, from the very beginning, it seems to have been little more than a Soviet propaganda vehicle which used British voices to speak on Russia's behalf.

Their tactics did not always escape discovery. In a debate on 15 May 1923, Ramsay MacDonald, Labour leader, was downplaying the opposition's criticism of Soviet religious persecution. He urged members instead to 're-member Rasputin', and thus to accept that the Russian Church needed to be 'thoroughly renovated from top to bottom'. He then added that a Quaker minister who had recently been in Russia reported 'isolated cases of persecution of priests ... but to blazon to the world that a general persecution was under way is not only ridiculous but either a cruel malicious lie or cheap sensationalism of journalistic imagination'. A Conservative MP challenged him: 'Is the Hon. Gentleman reading from a personal letter addressed to himself, or do I seem to recognise a printed circular which has been addressed to many Hon. members?' The record shows that this was greeted by 'ministerial cheers'. MacDonald replied that he understood the circular 'had been addressed to a number of members'. Opposition MPs were fully alert to the real origin of MacDonald's alleged account.[51]

While the source of the longer-term funding of the committee can only be guessed, we know that Coates was in receipt of a weekly wage from Rothstein in 1919, and in 1920 the committee also received a subsidy from the Russian Trade Delegation – yet another direct contravention of their 'no propaganda' agreement.[52] More remains to be uncovered about this shadowy organisation, but given the substantial Soviet funding of the CPGB after its foundation in 1920, it is probable that, with no obvious other source of income, the committee continued to receive direct or indirect funding from Russia until its demise with Coates's death in the 1960s.

Even though it was funded by the Soviets and was founded directly by the party which became the CPGB, the 'Hands Off Russia' Committee, particularly in its second incarnation as the ARPC, was not ostensibly an organisation of fringe extremists. Its fortnightly circulars to MPs and regular output of pro-Soviet books and pamphlets, often countering issues on which Moscow was being criticised, carried the endorsement of a heavyweight British committee – five of whom were, or became, presidents of the TUC. Two others were to hold positions, both as Labour ministers and as chairmen of the Labour Party. One of those, George Lansbury, became Labour leader in the 1930s.[53] In the 1930s, it was the ARPC which took a leading part in refuting allegations of slave labour and religious persecution in Russia.[54]

'Active measures' (Soviet aims in Britain)

In the medium to long term, the Bolshevik goal in Britain was to bring the Labour movement on board in support of the world socialist revolution. More immediately, the task that faced Rothstein and the Trade Delegation was to build out of the British Labour movement so powerful and dominant a domestic pro-Soviet front that, by the threat of mass boycotts and strikes at home, it would both deter the British government from confronting Russia, and keep up the pressure on said government to establish full diplomatic and trading links between the two nations. The aim was to co-opt the British Left into becoming the Bolsheviks' agent in support of Russian foreign policy aims.

Many historians have remarked upon the fact that the course of relations between Labour and the Soviets in the 1920s was far from smooth. This is not as significant as it might seem at first sight. For the Russians, success was not defined by the extent to which Labour men and women became wholehearted enthusiasts for all things Soviet (though many did) but by the degree to which they were persuaded to support their *two lesser aims* – neutralising British government opposition to the new revolutionary government and establishing full relations between the two nations. In this, the Russians had considerable success.

Lenin believed that victory in war was achieved by far more than military action alone. Subversion played an important part too. Subversion has, as its object, the aim of causing political, economic, military, or moral damage to an enemy state by non-military means. During the Cold War, the tools by which the Soviet intelligence services realised their goals against hostile nations and individuals were known as 'active measures' (*aktivnyye meropriyatiya*).

Although the phrase was not used until later, its three main techniques – disinformation, influence operations, and the use of front organisations – were evident in Bolshevik activity in Britain from the earliest days.

Disinformation is the deliberate attempt to deceive public or government opinion. It can be employed to discredit individuals, political parties or national governments; it can also be used to generate alarm and fear about the impact of their policies upon the targets of the disinformation. Disinformation ensured that the British Left remained convinced that the British government and its allies were making active preparations for a new war against Russia that would include mass conscription at home; it fostered the belief that world peace was under threat from capitalist governments unless Russia's friends abroad joined it to stop them. Disinformation created the conviction that the thousands of Bolshevik executions and massacres were a propaganda myth created by Western capitalists and that the 'few' that were undeniable were the understandable consequence of a nation placed on a war footing by the actions of hostile capitalists abroad. In the 1930s, disinformation even persuaded some Labour MPs and supporters that the Soviet penal system was humane and its victims were not innocent slave labourers but the fortunate recipients of justice under a regime that was far more merciful and compassionate than its Western counterparts.[55] This deception was supported by guided tours for foreign visitors round specially prepared Russian prisons, where 'prisoners' told their gullible listeners that they were so content with their conditions that they wanted to stay in jail after the end of their sentences.

Political influence operations employed 'agents of influence' who disguised their Soviet connection while taking an active role in their nation's governmental, political, press, business, labour, or academic affairs. The object was to convert their influence in these different arenas into real policy gains for the Soviet Union.[56] Agents of influence also included those individuals whose sympathy for the principles and goals of Soviet Communism was so strong that they willingly acted in support of the Soviet cause without ever seeing themselves as having been co-opted by Soviet intelligence. Frank Wise was one of these. As the rest of this book will show, the Labour Party was home to many others.

The third means by which the goals of Soviet subversion in Britain were pursued was through the use of *front groups and friendship societies*. As with agents of influence, these organisations could either be overt or covert about the degree to which their activities were directed by the Soviet Union. Sometimes there was no obvious connection at all, as in the case of non-governmental, non-political organisations engaged in promoting ostensibly desirable goals such as world peace. In a nation so traumatised by war, the pursuit of peace had become a driving force. Soviet Communism held that peace could 'only be guaranteed through the ultimate triumph of Communism worldwide' and that peace was the 'main objective and supreme principle of Soviet foreign policy'.[57] Moscow's hand in the world peace movement throughout the Cold War years is now well documented, but it has a far older provenance. For the British Left between the wars, their fear, stoked by disinformation, coupled with the Soviets' declared support of world peace, gave their cause and the pursuit of world socialist revolution an unquestionable moral authority. The make-up or funding of any British organisation that appeared to pursue the same goal as the Russians, perhaps in friendly cooperation with a Soviet counterpart, was not examined too closely.

Even when the connection was more obvious, the degree of Soviet involvement could be hidden, as in the case of the 'Hands Off Russia' Committee when it evolved by shedding its more identifiable CPGB members and campaigning name to become the Anglo-Russian Parliamentary Committee – a title which models the use of disinformation because it gave the organisation an appearance of credibility, as if it had been sanctioned in some way by Parliament or was an official All-Party Parliamentary Group.

Agents of influence and front groups could be 'black' (clandestine), 'grey' (open about their allegiance but believing themselves to be independent of any direction from the Soviet Union) or 'white' (acting as open, admitted, propaganda vehicles employed by the Soviets for Soviet interests), and in the game of deception the line between these could be far from clear too. It was not unknown for a 'grey' group to be infiltrated and unwittingly taken over by 'black' agents.

Moscow's friends in Britain came in all types – from naive individuals who believed that Soviet Russia was the new utopia, pursuing a model for society that could be peacefully copied in Britain, to those on the other end of the spectrum who embraced violent revolution and fully accepted that bloodshed was likely to be an unavoidable part of establishing a proletarian dictatorship in Britain. One recurrent feature of Labour's Soviet supporters in the 1920s and 1930s is that, into whatever category they fell, the beliefs of these men and women were generated and constantly reinforced by Soviet active measures; they clung to them with a conviction which disregarded all evidence to the contrary for long past the time when intelligent men and women would normally be expected to have accepted it. The consequences for those in Russia whose appeals they dismissed were catastrophic.

CHAPTER 2

POLAND AND
THE CRISIS OF 1920

If the Red Armies are once allowed to overrun Poland they are quite strong enough to set all Germany aflame and to bring the fabric of civilisation in central Europe to the ground.[1]

BERTRAND RUSSELL, JULY 1920

The *Jolly George*

In April 1920, tensions between Poland and Russia escalated into open war. Only the year before, British troops had been engaged in operations in Archangel, and the Russians were now desperate to prevent British military support for the Poles in this new conflict. Pro-Bolshevik sentiment among the British Left, encouraged by Rothstein, was already strong. The Russian Trade Delegation arrived in Britain a few weeks later and at that point Klishko and his associates added their own efforts to Rothstein's.

C. T. Cramp, the industrial secretary of the National Union of Railwaymen (who also became Labour Party chairman in 1924), called upon workers to down tools on 1 May in support of the Bolsheviks.[2] On 20 May the *Daily Herald* published an appeal from the 'Hands Off Russia' Committee to the 'organised workers of Great Britain' to 'strike for peace' with Russia.[3] Meanwhile dockers discovered that the S.S. *Jolly George*, berthed at the East India docks in London, was loading cargo, presumed to be munitions, for Poland. The 'Hands Off Russia' Committee stepped in to coordinate support for the *Jolly George* to be embargoed and for other similar cargoes to be blocked. Their handbill made clear that support for Soviet Russia, not pacifism, was the ultimate aim: 'Keep a sharp eye on all cargoes. No munitions must sail. No guns, aeroplanes, shells, bombs. Take no heed of cowardly politicians. With peace, Russia will light a beacon for the world. This world over, the workers' cause is one. And murder is murder! Dockers, you will not fail.'[4]

The *Jolly George* was forced to sail without its munitions. Buoyed by their victory, the protesters broadened the scope of their protests to include campaigning for the boycott of other nations struggling to put down their own Communist revolutions.

Ernest Bevin is today remembered partly as a notable anti-Communist Foreign Secretary in the 1945 Labour Government,[5] but in 1920 his call for support for the cause of Communist revolution was firm. Bevin was the architect behind the formation of the Transport and General Workers' Union, founded in 1922, and was its first general secretary. The TGWU combined fourteen unions and with its 300,000 members, including the dockers, stevedores and lightermen, soon became the country's largest union. He was a powerful union man and a director of George Lansbury's pro-Soviet *Daily Herald* newspaper.

In 1920, Bevin called for the boycott of Hungary (then in the aftermath of the bitter civil war which had been provoked by a Bolshevik coup d'état), ignoring the contradiction raised by the fact that the 'Hands Off Russia' campaign was decrying a similar blockade of the Bolsheviks:

> No train should pass the Hungarian frontiers, no ship enter its harbours [*sic**], and no letters or telegrams from or to Hungary be dispatched. All traffic must be stopped ... and no coal, raw materials, or foodstuffs must enter the country. This weapon must be used as a means for putting a stop to the bloody regime of the Hungarian Government.[6]

By June 1920, the Labour Party conference extended the call still further to demand the diplomatic recognition of the Bolshevik revolutionary government and the establishment of full trading relations. Tom Shaw MP, a minister in both the 1924 and 1929 Cabinets, moved the Executive Committee's resolution, calling upon

---

*   Hungary lost its only seaport, Fiume (now Rijeka), under the Treaty of Trianon, signed a day before Bevin's speech.

Allied Governments to recognise the existing Government of Russia, to abstain from all direct or indirect attacks, and to offer every encouragement to the free development and exchange of her natural resources ... [The conference] welcomes the Russian Economic Mission now in London, and expresses its heartiest wishes for its complete success.

Tom Shaw (not to be confused with G. B. Shaw who was an even more vociferous supporter of the USSR) had just returned from Russia where he had been part of a Labour delegation sent by the TUC to make a first-hand study of the Soviet experiment. The delegation was headed by Ben Turner (TUC president 1928, Labour executive member in 1931), and included Shaw, Ethel Snowden (whose husband Philip was Chancellor in the 1924 and 1929 Cabinets), Robert Williams (party chairman 1925), Margaret Bondfield (TUC president 1923, Minister of Labour 1929), and A. A. Purcell (TUC president 1924). Leslie Haden-Guest, later a Labour peer, was one of the delegation secretaries.

This was the first visit to Russia by a delegation from the British Labour movement, and Lenin attached great importance to it. He instructed the All-Russia Central Council of Trade Unions to give them a hearty welcome and to acquaint them with the life of the Soviet people, 'so that they could tell the truth about Soviet Russia when they returned home'. Meetings were held and there was a great rally in the Bolshoi Theatre; a parade of the Moscow Garrison was held in their honour. Lenin needed the British Labour movement to put pressure on the British government not to intervene in Poland. Whatever reservations one or two delegation members had,* the rest were on side with the Bolshevik message and reported on their return that: 'The delegation members expressed their determination to strengthen fraternal solidarity between British and Soviet working people, and voiced a protest against any aid, whether overt, or covert, given by Britain to the Polish Government in the new offensive, and against any threat to force Russia to meet Polish demands'.[7] A few weeks later, A. G. Cameron, the chairman of the

---

* Ethel Snowden was a minority dissenting voice. She and her husband were later to clash over Russia with Sidney and Beatrice Webb, the leading British Soviet enthusiasts, and part company with the Labour Party in 1931.

Labour Party since the June 1920 conference, backed this up with a challenge to Parliament which came close to a threat of home-grown revolution:

> If the powers that be endeavour to interfere too much, we may be compelled to do things that will cause them to abdicate, and to tell them that if they cannot run the country in a peaceful and humane fashion without interfering with the lives of other nations, we will be compelled even against all constitutions, to chance whether we cannot do something to take the country into our own hands for our own people.[8]

The Council of Action

On 31 July 1920, the British Socialist Party, at a convention in the Cannon Street Hotel, London, established the Communist Party of Great Britain (CPGB). The party was financed by Moscow, which granted it £46,000 (rising to a total of £55,000, £2.2 million today, by the end of 1921).[9] The Russian Trade Delegation facilitated the transfer of the funds. Delegates to its founding convention included W. P. Coates, Robert Williams, a member of the Labour Party Executive, Cecil L'Estrange Malone, a Communist then Labour MP, who was appointed a Labour parliamentary private secretary in 1931, A. A. Purcell, and George Hicks and, who like Purcell also became a TUC president and Labour MP. Even though the Labour Party consistently refused to allow the CPGB to affiliate with it, the crossover in the membership of the two parties over the next few years was to be considerable.

Some days later, Purcell and Williams were among those who attended a special emergency meeting of the Parliamentary Committee of the Trades Union Congress, the National Executive of the Labour Party, and the Parliamentary Labour Party at the House of Commons to discuss the Polish-Russian crisis. Of the British government's hand in the looming crisis they were in no doubt, and they threatened to call a general strike to stop it:

> This joint conference feels certain that war is being engineered between the Allied Powers and Soviet Russia on the issue of Poland and declares that such a war would be a crime against humanity. It therefore warns the Government that the whole industrial power of the organised workers will be used to defeat this war.[10]

As 4,000 demonstrators gathered in Hyde Park, waving flags to the cry of 'Hands Off Russia!',[11] the meeting appointed a 'Council of Action' to lead the Labour movement's opposition to the government.* The following day, the council went to Downing Street to present their demands. Arthur Henderson had already cabled every local Labour party in the country to alert members to the seriousness of the situation: 'Extremely menacing possibility extension Polish war. Strongly urge local parties immediately organize citizen demonstrations against intervention and supply men and munitions to Poland. Demand peace negotiations, immediate raising blockade, resumption trade relations.'[12]

On 13 August a special conference was convened in Central Hall Westminster. It was attended by 689 trade union representatives and 355 representatives of local Labour parties. The conference instructed the Council of Action 'to remain in being until they have secured ... the recognition of the Russian Soviet Government and the establishment of unrestricted trading and commercial relationships between Great Britain and Russia'. At the end, the delegates rose to their feet and stood in silence for one minute in solemn affirmation of their belief in the integrity of 'the Russian Government's declaration in favour of the complete independence of Poland'.[13]

Of their certainty that the Bolsheviks' promise on Poland's independence could be trusted, they were in no doubt. As Tom Shaw told the conference, the Russian Bolsheviks were 'immensely superior to our Government in candour, truth, and in doing things in the light of day.'[14] The reality was that, in its naive enthusiasm, the Labour movement had once again allowed itself to be duped. A British government intercept of a cable between Moscow and the Trade Delegation made it clear that the Soviets' intentions were far more

* Members appointed on 10 August were: from the Parliamentary Labour Party: W. Adamson MP, J. R. Clynes MP, J. O'Grady MP, John Robertson MP, Colonel J. C. Wedgwood MP; from the parliamentary committee of the TUC: Harry Gosling, A. A. Purcell, A. B. Swales, R. B. Walker, Margaret Bondfield; from the Labour Party executive: A. G. Cameron, Frank Hodges, C. T. Cramp, Robert Williams, J. Bromley. Additional members were appointed a few days later: Ernest Bevin, J. H. Thomas, Robert Smillie, Ben Turner, George Lansbury, John Ogden, A. E. Holmes, W. H. Hutchinson, J. E. Bowen. Secretaries (in addition to Ernest Bevin, already included above) were F. Bramley, H. S. Lindsay, J. S. Middleton. Of these members, Bevin, Hodges, Turner and Williams were directors of the *Daily Herald*; Purcell, Bromley, Turner and Williams either were or were to become members of the 'Hands Off Russia' Committee or its later incarnation, the Anglo-Russian Parliamentary Committee. 'Report of the Special Conference on Labour and the Russian-Polish War on Friday August 13th, 1920', *Warwick Digital Collections, University of Warwick.* <htttp://contentdm.warwick.ac.uk/cdm/ref/collection/russian/id/594>, accessed 19 January 2017.

malign and that they were committed to assist 'in the arming of the Polish workers under the control of representatives of the trade unions of Russia, Poland, and Norway'.[15] But Lev Kamenev, the senior Bolshevik who had joined the delegation over the summer, softened the wording of the cable before passing a copy to the Council of Action so that in translation it now appeared to assure its readers that Moscow's intentions in Poland were peaceful.

Convinced of the Soviets' goodwill, in contrast to the British government's supposedly aggressive objectives, the Council of Action issued instructions to all regional councils to gather reports on the production or movement of munitions and other military equipment thought to be 'capable of being used for war purposes' or unusual mustering of troops.[16] With hundreds of union members now acting as observers, the national council received their reports and then passed them to the Russian Trade Delegation with whom they met regularly. British trade unionists had, in effect, become an unwitting arm of Bolshevik military intelligence.[17]

The Council of Action Conference, Central Hall, Westminster, 13 August 1920. Labour and trades union leaders, joined by over 1,000 delegates, demand the recognition of the Russian revolutionary government. The posters read 'Would you fight for Warsaw?' and 'Down tools for peace'.

At the brink

As the weeks passed, the Council of Action grew increasingly bold. When their deputation went to Downing Street on 10 August to meet Lloyd George, they asked him for a statement on Poland which they could publish after the meeting. Conscious of how this would play with their members and appear to strengthen the council, Lloyd George refused, saying that any statement on Poland would be made to Parliament first and not to them; there was no 'soviet' (in this sense, a communist committee) running Britain. Brazenly, one of the members retorted: 'unless you take the deputation this morning as the Provisional Government'.*[18]

On 16 August, the council began daily sittings, and pronounced 22 August as a national 'Peace with Russia Sunday', calling for mass demonstrations throughout the country. Robert Williams declared that it might be necessary for the council to sit regularly and publicly as a 'Committee of National Security'.[19] Echoes of the French Revolution's Committee of Public Safety were unmistakable. George Lansbury called for local 'soviets' to be established throughout the country.[20] Around 300 local and regional Councils of Action were quickly established. In Coventry, the local Council of Action proposed to abolish all elected local authorities and replace them with soviets.[21] The Lambeth Council of Action petitioned the national council to establish a 'civil guard', the nucleus of which would be drawn from members of the police and prison officers' union.[22] The north-eastern district Council of Action called on the national council to stay in place 'until universal peace had been secured in Europe', and all British troops had been withdrawn not just from Russia but from Ireland, Egypt, India and Mesopotamia'.[23]

Some were in no doubt as to where they wanted the protests to lead. G. D. H. Cole, writing from the Labour Party headquarters to the journal *Labour Leader*, was quite clear about the movement's revolutionary ambitions:

> Let us make no mistake about what we are in for. We are co-ordinating the forces of Labour not simply in order to increase Labour's strength in negotiations, strikes and elections, we are marshalling our battalions for an actual assault upon Capitalism, to be followed by an actual assumption of power.[24]

---

*   The Russian 'Provisional Government' had taken power on the abdication of Tsar Nicholas in March 1917.

A. A. Purcell, a member of the council, was just as forthright:

> Some of us are of the opinion that we should have done in this country very
> much like what the Russians have done in Russia. I believe in the dictatorship
> of the proletariat, but if the workers of this country overthrow Capitalism, they
> must set up an armed proletariat. If there is bloodshed it will be because the
> capitalists resist. We have sent a message to the Russian people that we are
> trying to overthrow our own Government.[25]

Warsaw was close to falling to the Red Army. Had it done so and had the
British government remained determined to support the Polish government,
its assistance would necessarily have been increasingly overt. The chances of
a national strike and further agitation for the overthrow of the government in
Westminster would only have increased.

In Russia, Lenin also believed that the Council of Action's campaign was
the prelude to a British Communist revolution:

> Bolshevism is spreading among the British workers. The old leaders of the
> British workers have begun to waver and have changed their minds. They
> were opposed to the dictatorship of the working class, but now they have come
> over to our side. They have set up a Council of Action over there in Britain.
> This is a radical change in British politics ... a tremendous turning-point ... Its
> significance to Great Britain is as great as the revolution of February 1917 was
> to us. ... The Council of Action has presented an ultimatum to the government
> on behalf of the workers. This is a step toward [proletarian] dictatorship.[26]

Just as events at home were reaching an apparently alarming climax, a turn
of events in Poland took the heat out of the crisis. On 14 August the Polish
Army counterattacked. The collapse of the Red Army was so sudden and so
complete that it became known thereafter to the Poles as the 'Miracle on the
Vistula', the river where the battle turned. By 16 August the Soviets were in
full flight, retreating at thirty kilometres per day. British government intervention was not needed. At home, Labour moderates began to have second
thoughts about the direction that some of their more hot-headed colleagues
were taking them. On 18 August, the Council of Action was reported to be

reconsidering its call for a general strike.[27] British government intervention in Poland might justify a general strike, perhaps even the overthrow of the government, but diplomatic recognition of the Bolsheviks hardly did so.

The news of the battle on the Vistula took time to arrive and the planned 'Peace with Russia' rallies still went ahead a few days later. In Trafalgar Square, the main speakers were Margaret Bondfield and George Lansbury himself. Lansbury told the crowd how he had met Lenin and found him 'a pure-hearted, noble-souled man'. The rally's closing resolution was infused with revolutionary solidarity:

> We pledge ourselves loyally to support the National Council of Action in whatever steps it deems necessary to prevent war – open or otherwise – between the British Government and the Socialist Republic of Russia, and to secure an honest peace and the frank recognition of the Soviet Government. Fervently desiring peace everywhere, we send fraternal greetings to all the workers of the world, and we appeal to the peoples of all lands to join together and make triumphant the fundamental principles of the International Labour and Socialist movement.[28]

The *Daily Herald* and 'Moscow gold'

A large part in the collapse of the Red Army campaign in Poland had been due to the breaking of Soviet ciphers. The British government had also been able to crack the codes in Russian cables and, in a move to block the momentum that the 'Hands Off Russia' campaign was building, the government decided to leak other intercepted telegrams to *The Times*. Its main target was George Lansbury, whose influential *Daily Herald*, with a circulation of about 300,000 copies, was at that time playing a leading part in building support for the Bolshevik cause among British workers.

On 19 August, under the headline 'The Daily Herald. Bolshevist Help Sought. Promise of Paper and Subsidy. Lansbury's Orders from Moscow', *The Times* printed exchanges of telegrams between Georgy Chicherin, the Soviet Commissar for Foreign Affairs, Maxim Litvinov, his deputy, and Krasin, the leader of the Russian Trade Delegation. These revealed that, after discussions with the Soviets during his Russia trip earlier in 1920, Lansbury had received significant amounts of Russian financial support for his paper. Part came as shipments of tons of Scandinavian newsprint, paid for at source by the Soviet government so that their identity, as purchasers, could remain hidden; yet more came in parcels of cash and jewels smuggled in by the Russian Trade Delegation.[29]

One of the cables confirmed that on 9 June, three weeks after Krasin arrived in the UK, he and Klishko met with Lansbury and Francis Meynell, one of the other directors of the *Herald*, to arrange for a further subsidy for the paper. When Krasin returned to Moscow on 2 July to report on progress in the trade discussions, Klishko remained behind and a lively exchange of coded dispatches then followed between Klishko in London, Litvinov in Copenhagen, and Chicherin in Moscow. Diplomatic cover was seen to be the safest route for bringing the money, and so Klishko cabled Litvinov on 10 July with instructions that 'help for Francis* should be sent with Krassin, who is leaving Moscow about 12 July'.[30] Litvinov then discussed the details with Chicherin the following day:

(Litvinov to Chicherin, July 11, 1920): If we do not support the Daily Herald, which is now passing through a fresh crisis, paper will have to turn 'Right'… *In Russian questions it acts as if it were our organ*… After Lansbury's journey [to Russia], it has gone considerably more to the 'Left,' and decidedly advocates 'direct action'.[†] It needs £50,000 for six months, then it hopes again to be on firm ground. I consider work of Daily Herald is especially important for us. I advise therefore that this help be afforded from funds of (? Commissariat) for Foreign Affairs, not from those of International Commission, and that it be payable in several instalments. (My italics.)[31]

On 14 July, Klishko wrote directly to Chicherin in Moscow to assure him that the money would be well spent: 'We are making use of the "Daily Herald" for the purposes of information and agitation, and in so far as we are able to do this, public opinion is responding in our favour. The working classes are on our side.'[32]

Monitoring these communications, British intelligence established that the Trade Delegation had handed over £40,000 to the *Daily Herald*,[33] and that Krasin and Kamenev expected to raise another £50,000 (£2 million today) of which a further £10,000 was to be paid to the newspaper.[34] On 23 July,

---

*   Francis Meynell, through whom the negotiations had been conducted.
†   Strikes in support of Russia.

Klishko cabled Litvinov that 'Francis has already received £10,000', and confirmed that the paper was responding in kind: 'our note was published yesterday by the *Daily Herald*'.[35]

Realising usable bank notes from the assets brought in by the delegation posed some problems. All gold sales had to be made through the Bank of England and so could be monitored by the authorities: although Soviet funding for British radical political groups is known collectively as 'Moscow gold', gold was at this time the least easy vehicle to use. Convertible bonds were a safer option, and Litvinov gave instructions that some Chinese bonds which had formerly been in the possession of the Russian Imperial treasury[36] should now be handed over to the paper.[37] Smuggled jewels were another way of bringing in money and, by October 1920, Scotland Yard had tracked the sale on the London market of almost £2 million (£80.6 million today) worth of unset Russian diamonds, much of these paid for in untraceable French notes, which could then also be re-exported 'clean' for further use abroad.[38] The quantities released by the Russians so flooded the market that the London diamond price was halved.[39]

When *The Times* broke the story, there was panic at the *Herald*. Francis Meynell, fearing arrest for treason, was rumoured to be making plans to escape London at the earliest opportunity.[40] The paper flatly denied the story, insisting that 'we have received no Bolshevist money, no Bolshevist paper, no Chinese bonds'.[41] These protestations were soon seen to be unsustainable: very few, even on the left, believed them. In their place, an alibi was concocted, but British intelligence, still decrypting Russian transmissions, traced every development of its creation. Even as Moscow was instructed by Kamenev to assist in fabricating it, it only served to further highlight the close cooperation between the senior members of the Trade Delegation and the directors of the *Herald*.

On 4 September, Kamenev and Krasin sent a coded cable to Chicherin in Moscow: 'On receiving this telegram please send immediately en clair* the following message: "Inform Meynell that his communication together with the valuables has been received. Klinger, Secretary to the Third International." The matter is urgent and important. The reasons will be sent by courier.'

---

* i.e. without encryption, in plain prose.

The message was a smokescreen designed to fool British intelligence, a preamble to the new alibi which was about to be put out by the *Herald*. But because the instruction to send it had already been deciphered, the British authorities were fully in on the deception when it was published.

On 10 September, the newspaper admitted that the money *had* been received – but insisted that it had only been received by Francis Meynell and that the other directors of the paper knew nothing about it. It was further explained that it had been 'gradually collected' over the course of time (i.e. it comprised multiple small donations from supportive individuals, not a lump sum from Moscow) and that Meynell was only holding it to send on to the Third International (the Comintern) with the possibility that, if it was needed, the Comintern might offer to loan it to the *Daily Herald*.

Four days later, the board of directors of the *Daily Herald* – Bevin, Lansbury, Frank Hodges, Ben Turner* and Robert Williams – issued a further statement flatly denying that they had had any knowledge of any financial discussions with the Russians, and that their fellow director Francis Meynell had been acting alone. They insisted that Meynell had only taken money on trust for transmission to the Comintern and that he had now offered to resign, a resignation which had been accepted. They then added that they had decided not to accept the Russians' offer of a loan, and would be returning the money.[42]

The paper had been in a financial crisis and threatened with closure for months, something all the directors would have been well aware of. In spite of their protestations of innocence, it seems almost impossible that the directors – a group of very able men who comprised a future Labour Party Minister and leader (Lansbury), one of the most powerful union men in Britain and a future Labour Foreign Secretary (Bevin), the general secretary of the Miners' Federation and First Lord of the Admiralty in the 1924 Labour Cabinet (Hodges), a Labour MP and future president of the TUC General Council (Turner), and a future chairman of the Labour Party (Williams) – were wholly ignorant of so important a bail-out for their floundering newspaper. Moreover, the Soviet money alone had kept the paper afloat since February

---

* Turner told a gathering of Yorkshire miners that the charges were a 'fabrication', and offered to pay £100 to a local hospital if any of them could be proved. Either he had been deceived by Lansbury or he was lying. TNA, CAB 24-111, CP 1908, 30 September 1920. RROUK no. 74.

of that year, a fact of which they can hardly have been unaware. Intelligence sources had already confirmed that, at the very least, the Lansbury family had been intimately involved in the Russian money laundering: 'It appears that the diamonds brought by Kamenev were disposed of by Mrs Glassman, the mother-in-law of Edgar Lansbury,* and that they were actually displayed in Edgar Lansbury's house. As George Lansbury breakfasts with his son every morning it is inconceivable that he was ignorant of the transaction.'[43]

On 15 September, faced with the *Daily Herald*'s continued denials, the government issued its own statement to the press.[44] It revealed that Lloyd George had personally confronted Kamenev over his involvement in the sale of the jewels which had realised the money given to Lansbury, and that this had contributed to the government's decision to expel him. Turning the heat on the *Herald*, it insisted that the paper's directors had only been forced to speak out because they knew that the police had traced bank notes from the sale of Russian jewels in London to Edgar Lansbury's bank account. As the spotlight turned on the younger Lansbury, Edgar, who had just been part of the founding conference of the CPGB, admitted that he had been in possession of the incriminating notes, but insisted that he had passed them through his bank only to 'oblige' his friend Francis Meynell, and that his father had had no knowledge of the transaction at all.[45] Few were convinced. Instead, Ramsay MacDonald and other supporters of the *Daily Herald* rallied to the paper's defence, claiming that if it had accepted Russian money 'it would be no worse than "The Times" or other papers that accepted foreign subsidies for special supplements', a somewhat disingenuous argument which overlooked the difference between taking paid advertising and secretly selling one's editorial position to a foreign power bent on destabilising an elected government.

The Trade Delegation shifts its focus

Over the summer, the Trade Delegation worked hard to firm up the pro-Bolshevik front in the Labour movement. Delegation members met frequently

---

* Edgar Lansbury, son of George, and later father of actress Angela, was a member of the CPGB from its foundation in August 1920, eventually becoming a member of its central committee and mayor of Poplar in 1924. He was jailed in 1921 for his part in the protests against the levying of an increase in local 'rates' or taxes.

with senior members of the Council of Action.[46] On 1 July, Chicherin instructed Krasin to place various pieces of disinformation damaging to British foreign policy in the British left-wing press. One of these fabrications was the story that, using Pyotr Wrangel, a general in the Russian 'White Army', as a proxy, the British had annexed Crimea – by implication, as a prelude to an all-out war with Russia. These were to be planted in the press 'for the purposes of agitation among labour organisations', and then developed further by Krasin in his 'conversation with labour organisations'.[47]

Cables also revealed that by mid-August the Russians were concerned that the more moderate members of the Council of Action might be dragging their feet. To prevent this, Chicherin suggested that 'some Communist' on the council should write a statement on Poland and invite the other members to sign it.[48] Any members who refused to sign would therefore be identifiable and action could be taken to neutralise them. He proposed Robert Williams for this ruse. He knew Williams through their joint membership of the British Socialist Party in London and had met him again a few weeks earlier when Williams, together with other future Council of Action members, Turner, Bondfield, and Purcell, had been in Russia as part of the British Labour Delegation. In addition to behind-the-scenes subterfuge, there were more open exchanges too: Lev Kamenev met members of the Council of Action (W. Adamson, J. H. Thomas, Robert Williams, Ernest Bevin and J. S. Middleton) in the third week of August.[49] All these activities were a clear breach of the Russians' 'no propaganda' commitment.

By early September, there were over 300 regional Councils of Action in place. The more extreme voices suggested that if the government did not make peace with Russia by a specific (as yet unfixed) date, there should be a general strike until the government changed its position. When the constitutionality of such a call, accompanied by a threat even to overthrow the government, caused some consternation, Ramsay MacDonald was unrepentant:

When people talked of this Council as being unconstitutional, they talked nonsense. Everything necessary to protect the Constitution is constitutional, if constitutional means anything at all except passive obedience to any outrageous acts done by men who happened to be Ministers. And that Ministers should secure majorities by fraud and use them to act without reference to the National will and govern as though public affairs were their personal and private concern is the very antithesis of constitutional government.[50]

It was an extraordinary statement for a man who would be Leader of the Opposition in Parliament within two years: a general strike was justified because the actions of ministers of an elected government were, in the opinion of their political opponents, 'unconstitutional'.

The defeat of the Soviet Army in Poland dulled the enthusiasm of the more moderate members of the national Council of Action for extreme measures. The revelations about Moscow's use of the *Daily Herald* took time to sink in but, as they did, they added to a growing suspicion felt in some parts of the Labour movement that they were being manipulated. Some members began to have second thoughts. Rivalry and turf protection surfaced too, as some union leaders took exception to the 'Hands Off Russia' Committee issuing calls for strike action directly to their members without consulting them first.[51]

The change of mood was not lost on the Russians. Theodore Rothstein, now in Moscow after having been declared *persona non grata* by the British government, continued to direct events as if he had never left London:

[Chicherin, Moscow to Krassin, London, 9 September 1920] Rothstein desires me to transmit to you the following:-'I notice in the papers an inclination on the part of the Council of Action toward the side of agreement with and adaptability to the policy of the British Government. This is unavoidable, having regard to the present composition of the Council, and, therefore, I should consider necessary the energetic continuation of the agitation among the masses themselves through the committees of "Hands off Russia" and the ruthless exposure of the traitorous tendencies of the Council through the Communist Party. Communicate this view of mind to Kamenev for transmission to my son,* and instruct Kamenev to offer £500 for the use of the [regional Hands Off Russia] committees indicated.' Rothstein.[52]

Over the next few weeks, watched by Scotland Yard, the national 'Hands

---

* Andrew Rothstein was a founder member of the CPGB (a member of the executive in 1923) and became press officer to the Russian Trade Delegation in 1921. Elected to the executive of the CPGB in 1923, he remained for many years a correspondent for the Soviet press agency TASS.

Off Russia' Committee, with the encouragement of the Trade Delegation, manoeuvred itself to eclipse the national and local Councils of Action, and take control of the protest movement. In some cases, local 'Hands Off Russia' committees had already infiltrated regional Councils of Action;[53] at a national level the committee addressed the Councils of Action directly, assuming an authority which would become familiar in later Soviet propaganda and which, consistent with that genre, made no concession to bad news (in this case the rout of the Red Army in Poland):

> The National Hands Off Russia Committee ... has issued a circular, dated yesterday, to local Councils of Action, [asserting that] the peace terms offered by Soviet Russia to Poland are so generous that the worst enemies of the working-class Government of Russia are astounded at their leniency ... French financiers do not deny the magnanimity of Russia's terms, but their thirst for the life's blood of Russia's manhood, and their fiendish desire to starve Russian women and children, is insatiable. French financiers are the foulest gang of child murderers that have yet cursed the earth. Compared with them Herod of the New Testament was a kind-hearted old gentleman.[54]

The committee then demanded a stoppage of all British coal supplies to France until France withdrew its aid from Poland, made peace with Russia, and recognised the Soviet government.

Theodore Rothstein

Theodore Rothstein's expulsion (of his own accord he temporarily left London for Moscow on 11 August 1920 but was refused permission to return) was hardly a surprise. After taking over as the Bolsheviks' unofficial representative in London on Litvinov's earlier return to Russia, the Home Office had watched as Rothstein acted as the paymaster of a wide variety of revolutionary groups and causes. Payments made or authorised by Rothstein supported Sinn Fein extremists in Ireland,[55] first-class fares for British delegates (including future Labour Cabinet minister Ellen Wilkinson*) to the 1921 Red Trade Union International conference in Moscow,[56] the 'Hands Off Russia'

---

*   Wilkinson was a founder member of the CPGB, from which she resigned in 1924, being voted onto the Labour Executive in October 1927.

rally at the Albert Hall in February 1920 (Rothstein paid the cost of £500),[57] and the salary of his brother-in-law C. P. Coates, the secretary of the 'Hands Off Russia' Committee. Rothstein also acted as conduit for Bolshevik funds sent into Europe, which included a payment of 25,000 francs to the organisers of a rail strike in France.[58]

He also was involved with Sylvia Pankhurst and her Workers' Socialist Federation. Famous as suffragette icons, the revolutionary tendencies of some of the Pankhurst family are now often overlooked. While Adela, one of Emmeline Pankhurst's three daughters, went on to found the Australian Communist Party, her sister Sylvia was the most extreme (and eventually fell out with her mother for this reason). In her attempts to position the Workers' Socialist Federation as the pre-eminent British Communist Party, appealing even to Lenin himself for funds, Sylvia alienated many on the left. Given her character, it is not surprising that her relationship with Rothstein was not always good but, nonetheless, Rothstein provided her with financial support, at one time paying for two of her employees and subsiding her paper, by now renamed the *Workers' Dreadnought*.[59]

While admitting Rothstein's part in the bankrolling of 'revolutionary groups and movements in Britain', Marxist historian Keith Neild insists that 'the amounts have often been wildly exaggerated [and] the total amount during just over two years [1919–20] was about £15,000'.[60] Aside from the fact that £15,000 (£605,000 today) was no small sum, this would be mis-leading if it was intended to imply that the overall level of Bolshevik fund-ing of subversion in Britain was in any way inconsiderable. Once the Trade Delegation had arrived, Rothstein was no longer the only courier. The *Daily Herald* publicly admitted to receiving an 'offer' of £75,000 (£3.02 million today) and certainly received £50,000; the CPGB received £46,000 in 1920, rising to £55,000 by the end of 1921.[61] London was also used by Moscow as a clearing house for laundering much larger amounts for onward dispatch to Europe and the empire.

Rothstein's son Andrew, a British citizen, remained active on behalf of Soviet interests after his father's departure. A notable British communist and a founder member of the CPGB, he became British correspondent for the Soviet press agency TASS, and president of the Foreign Press Association, from 1943–50. He was also a British recruiter for Soviet intelligence.

CHAPTER 3

'HANG CHURCHILL'

We are soldiers of the International Red Army who fight or soon will fight in every country over the five Continents of the earth. We shall not lay down our arms before the world is ours, before the dark night of oppression and the blood-red stormy dawn of revolution has changed it into the glorious day of Freedom and Communism. A grim struggle lies before us. Down with our enemies, the Churchills, the Capitalists, the Imperialists and all their lackeys. Long live the Red Army!
CECIL MALONE, MP, *RED OFFICER COURSE*, 1920[1]

The events of the summer caused considerable alarm in the Cabinet. At a meeting of ministers in Lloyd George's absence, Sir Robert Horne, president of the Board of Trade told his colleagues that the damage which was being done by the 'Russian agitators was of so grave a nature that it was most important to get them out of the country immediately'. They agreed with him that 'the time had now come to request the Russian Trade Delegation to leave'.[2] A few days later, displaying a hesitation which exasperated Churchill almost to the point of resignation, Lloyd George postponed the decision: a miners' strike threatened and he did not want to inflame radical tempers.[3]

Curzon lobbied the Cabinet at least to expel Klishko, whom he described as 'an unprincipled agitator'.[4] Churchill wholeheartedly agreed, adding that in his view 'the entire Bolshevik Delegation in this country should be invited to leave as speedily as possible'. If they remained, he warned, 'the only use they will make of their stay here is to work us injury by every means that still remain open to them'.[5] At the Admiralty there was similar high feeling. In Walter Long's view:

> It is impossible to exaggerate the danger of keeping Krassin & Co. here. There is no doubt that propaganda work among the sailors and employees in the dockyards has been increasing... So long as we keep them here, it is very difficult for us to check the spread of this pernicious form of revolutionary movement.[6]

Alarm of a different nature was expressed by the City as suspicions arose (correctly) that Lloyd George was planning to push through a trade agreement with Russia without firm assurances regarding British compensation claims and debt settlement. The Governor of the Bank of England urged him to insist upon formal recognition by the Russians of all classes of debt.[7] Similar appeals came from the insurance industry[8] and the chambers of commerce.[9] They were ignored: at another meeting at which the majority of hardliners were absent, Frank Wise was instructed to proceed with the negotiations with a view to *concluding* an agreement.[10]

When Curzon, Churchill and Long heard what was happening, their objectives became even wider than just the expulsion of some of the Bolsheviks. On 27 September, Long wrote:

> I understand that the Russian Trade Committee under Mr E. F. Wise has been instructed to proceed ... I must record my opinion that the Committee's proposals are, in the present circumstances, premature: and I earnestly hope that no active steps towards the resumption of trade will be taken while we are neither at peace nor war with Soviet Russia ... There is a grave danger that the goods Russia receives from Britain will simply be used to reequip the Red Army for the purpose of attacking our friends and allies in Europe and in embarrassing our Empire in the East.[11]

Field Marshal Sir Henry Wilson, Chief of the Imperial General Staff, had watched Lloyd George's weakness towards the Bolsheviks with growing unease, confiding in his diary that he even wondered if 'L.G. is allowing England to drift into Bolshevism on purpose'.[12] The Trade Delegation was already placing initial orders for uniform and equipment and Wilson's office sent Churchill a note for the Cabinet in which his concerns were expressed in more concrete military terms:

> The supply of clothing to the Russian Army is far more important to Soviet interests than the supply of arms, for the army is already practically without uniforms and boots, and during the coming winter will, if unclothed, be impotent [...] To assist the Soviet Government to reclothe its armies on such a scale as these contracts make possible, is calculated to encourage them not only to continue their efforts to destroy Poland, but also to further their declared policy of attacking the British Empire in the East.[13]

The coal strike preoccupied minds through October and postponed any action but once it was over, Curzon issued another stern warning: Bolshevik subversion was continuing unabated both at home and in the Empire. Furthermore, decrypts of Russian cables clearly showed that the Trade Delegation had not only flagrantly broken the initial 'no propaganda' condition on which they had been admitted to Britain, but had no intention of keeping the same commitment which was already in the draft treaty. 'We refuse the literal interpretation of the point as to propaganda and hostile activities', Chicherin had written to Krasin, instructing him that the previously agreed points on propaganda should be postponed to a later 'political conference' at which the Bolsheviks planned to press for full recognition of the Soviet government. The plan was to draw the British into a prospective trade deal and for it to be withheld at the last minute to put leverage on the British government to commit to talks on full diplomatic recognition.

As Foreign Secretary, Curzon refused to step back from his responsibility:

> The duty of my office is to see that we do not allow ourselves to be duped, and that whatever we gain by the transaction commercially (and it will in my opinion be very small – for I am unaware of anything but gold and diamonds which Russia is in a position to export) we do not lose politically.

His Majesty's Government demanded that the Russians should refrain from official propaganda, direct or indirect, against British institutions and more particularly from military action or propaganda against British interests or the British Empire. This was described as 'the *fundamental condition* of any trading agreement between Russia and any Western Power.'

If anything, Curzon added, the situation was now getting worse, not better:

Since the Russians 'accepted' our 'conditions' they have continued and even increased their hostile activities. [Their behaviour] diminishes the value of [their] guarantee that, if the Trade Agreement is concluded, the hostile activities will be brought to an end.

They [have exchanged] the attitude of hair-splitting, recrimination, and evasion which they have hitherto adopted, for one of open and truculent menace [and] the merry game in the Middle East of intrigue, propaganda, bribery on a colossal scale, military assistance to our enemies, political treaties (with our enemies), and a stream of agents pouring into India from every side, [and] will go on while we are discussing exactly what the legal interpretation of propaganda is …

As things are at present [the Foreign Office] sees itself expected to enter into relations with a State which makes no secret of its intentions to overthrow our institutions everywhere and to destroy our prestige and authority, particularly in Asia.

I should decline, therefore, to conclude the trading agreement until we are satisfied that the political activities of the Bolsheviks against us are not merely going to cease at some indefinite moment in a distant future, but have ceased here and now.[14]

Curzon's memorandum provoked an extended discussion in Cabinet running over two days, 17–18 November 1920. A former Viceroy of India, Curzon was quite clear on the danger that he felt now faced Britain: 'The Russian menace in the East is incomparably greater than anything else that has happened in my time to the British Empire'. But it became apparent from the outset that the threats from the 'Hands Off Russia' movement had left their mark on Lloyd George; timidity ruled the day. To the frustration of the hardliners – Curzon, Churchill (who came close to resigning over the issue), Long, Chamberlain, and Edwin Montagu the Secretary of State for India – the Prime Minister abandoned the Cabinet's previous insistence that Soviet propaganda cease *before* an agreement was signed and now suggested that it should only cease *once* the agreement was signed. If the Russians were shown to be in breach after the agreement had been signed, he reasoned, then the agreement could be cancelled.

Curzon knew (as Lloyd George probably did too) that if the Soviets were confronted they would deny, prevaricate and deceive; even if they admitted a charge, they could insist that the breach had ended, whether or not it had; at any moment they could close down the operation in question and open up another elsewhere. Finding sufficiently concrete proof to cancel the trade agreement once it had been signed would be like trying to catch a shadow. His frustration was evident:

> Why am I concerned about this? Because the whole of the evidence is that from Moscow to Tashkent conspiracies worked by Bolshevik agents and paid for by Bolshevik gold are going on. Let us assume the agreement is concluded. What is going to happen? They do not intend to desist from propaganda. The purport and pith of their Government is propaganda throughout the world. You conclude an agreement with them. The same business will go on at Teheran, Baku, etc. You will be in the midst of negotiations here which you cannot break off. You will find that after the trading agreement all this will go on just the same.

Churchill also had little time for compromise: Wise's promises of food and commodities had evaporated; the Soviets had 'nothing to offer but gold and precious stones, acquired by naked robbery';[15] the eventual trade would be so small as to make little difference to Britain's economy. Austen Chamberlain added that he was concerned that Wise had been too soft in defending Britain's interests in the talks.

The warning fell on deaf ears. The majority supported Lloyd George, a number of them repeating his assertion that Bolshevism could only be weakened by trade. Wise's committee was then instructed to conclude the trade agreement *without* any prior requirement on propaganda. Russian debts were ignored and left out of the agreement altogether. Instead the British government agreed that they would lay no claim to any Russian gold that came into Britain.

The hardliners realised that they had been defeated. As the conversation drew to a close, Churchill spoke up angrily: signing the agreement in no way altered the general position that the government had taken up as to the Bolsheviks, namely, 'that Ministers shall be free to point out the odious character of their regime. It seems to me you are on the high road to embrace Bolshevism. I am going to keep off that and denounce them on all possible occasions'. And that is exactly what he did, here addressing a lunch meeting in London:

> The deadly disease which has struck down Russia should not be allowed to spring up here and poison us as it is poisoning them ... In every city [in Britain] there are small bands of eager men and women, watching with hungry eyes [for] any chance to make a general overturn in the hopes of profiting themselves in the confusion, and these miscreants are fed by Bolshevist money. They are ceaselessly endeavouring by propagating the doctrines of Communism, by preaching violent revolution, by inflaming discontent, to infect us with their disease.
>
> There is developing a world-wide conspiracy against our country, designed to deprive us of our place in the world and to rob us of the fruits of victory. They will not succeed. They will fail. We must be ready: we must be on our guard to recognize every symptom of danger, and to act with strong conviction against it. Having beaten the most powerful military empire in the world, having emerged triumphantly from the fearful ordeal of Armageddon, we will not allow ourselves to be pulled down and have our Empire disrupted by a malevolent and subversive force, the rascals and rapscallions of mankind who are now on the move against us.[16]

Curzon had predicted that he would be back in Cabinet in six weeks with further evidence of the Bolsheviks' bad faith. He was back in four. Deciphered intercepts confirmed that Moscow now intended to refuse the propaganda clause closer to the signing date and then insist that the subject should be postponed for discussion at an international conference after the agreement had been concluded. On 13 December 1920, he wrote another memorandum for the Cabinet, confirming that his previous suspicions, which the Lloyd George faction had overridden, were proving to be correct.

I once again plead with my colleagues not to allow ourselves to be cheated by these tactics … On the former occasion I pleaded that the fulfilment of the political conditions should be anterior to the conclusion of the Trade Agreement. The Cabinet decided it should be simultaneous. It is now proposed [by the Bolsheviks] that it should be indefinitely subsequent. I hope that this stratagem may be defeated and that our preamble will be retained.[17]

The Anglo-Soviet Trade Agreement was signed on 16 March 1921.[18] Curzon's paper, written in December, was not even acknowledged in Cabinet until two days before that.[19]

'Hang Churchill'

Over the autumn of 1920 Bolshevik sympathisers suffered a number of setbacks as the police closed in on the wilder elements. Sylvia Pankhurst was arrested on 21 October and sentenced to six months' imprisonment for inciting sedition and mutiny in her paper, the *Workers' Dreadnought*.[20] A few days after her arrest, the police raided the flat of the Communist MP Cecil Malone. Malone was away but they found and arrested Erkki Veltheim, a Finnish Comintern courier who was staying there.[21] Veltheim was in possession of letters from Pankhurst to Lenin and Zinoviev decrying the softness of other British Communists and appealing for more funds for her own party. He was also found in possession of a copy of a British 'Red Army' instruction manual. Called as a witness in Veltheim's court hearing, Malone denied all knowledge of him and insisted that he must have broken into the flat. Veltheim, meanwhile, had already admitted to police that he knew Malone. Alerted, the police kept a close watch on Malone, around whom the net was also closing.

On 7 November 1920, the increasingly powerful national 'Hands Off Russia' Committee joined with the CPBG to hire the Albert Hall for a rally to commemorate the third anniversary of the Revolution. Resolutions congratulated the Soviet government, protested against the current policy of the British government towards Russia, and called upon the national Council of Action:

to send an ultimatum to the Government declaring that, unless the Government raised the blockade, abstained from all interference in Russian affairs, established full trading relations, and recognized the Soviet Government by a specified date, the Council of Action should call for a national 'down tools' policy [a general strike].

But it was the speech given by Malone which caused the biggest stir. In it, he declared that the hanging of a few 'Churchills or Curzons' from lampposts was a price worth paying for revolution. The authorities could not allow such comments to pass unchallenged. Malone was arrested. Police agents present at the meeting took the speech down in shorthand, but it was Malone's own notes, which he followed closely, which were read in court:

> Mr Malone spoke against a number of leading members of the Government [and urged delegates] to leave no stone unturned in preparing for social revolution. The day was not far distant, he hoped, when they would meet in the Albert Hall to bless the British revolution. (Cheers.) When that day came, 'woe to those people who get in our way.' They were out to change the present constitution, he declared, and if it was necessary to save bloodshed and atrocities, they would have to use the lamp posts or the walls. What were a few Churchills or Curzons on lamp posts compared with the massacres of thousands[22] of Indians at Amritsar, or compared with condemning the harmless Egyptians, or the reprisals on hundreds of Irishmen in Ireland? What were the punishments of those world criminals compared with the misery they were causing to thousands of men, women, and children, in Russia?

Robert Williams was lucky to escape a similar charge for comments that were scarcely less seditious:

> The revolution would not be achieved when they witnessed spectacles like that of a few weeks ago, when 15,000 men, who had risked their lives in the war, were kept back in Whitehall by 150 police. Even that vast audience could be held by one machine gun and two men outside the Albert Hall. They should realise the gravity of the facts, and get hold of the machine guns and the places where they were made.[23]

The meeting ended with three cheers for 'The Soviet Republic' and

'International Communism,' and the singing of 'The Red Flag'. The furore it created had only just begun.

The Malone trial

Malone was charged with sedition. In his subsequent court appearance it became apparent that his extremism went further than mere oratory. When the police came to his flat to arrest Veltheim, they found an envelope addressed to him which contained two railway cloakroom tickets wrapped in a sheet of plain unmarked paper. Further investigation revealed that each cloakroom ticket matched a parcel of a dozen copies of a booklet which appeared to be military training instructions for revolutionaries.

According to its preface, the booklet, most probably written by Malone, a former army officer, was a training manual ('Red Officer Course') for the officer corps of a new underground Communist British 'Red Army'.[24] Given that there remains a tendency to minimise the extremism of British revolutionary sentiment in the 1920s and to make light of the threat posed by its proponents, the document merits more extended mention. Here follow some excerpts:

We put this book in your hands, comrades. Use it to the best advantage in our fight against the capitalist classes. It is a weapon wrested from the hands of the bourgeois-militarists. We are soldiers of the International Red Army – that army of Proletarians and Workers led by the Communists, who fight or soon will fight in every country over the five Continents of the earth. We shall not lay down our arms before the world is ours, before the dark night of oppression and the blood-red stormy dawn of revolution had changed it into the glorious day of Freedom and Communism. A grim struggle lies before us in our section of the international front. Down with our enemies, the Churchills, the Capitalists, the Imperialists and all their lackeys. Long live the Red Army!

This course is intended for comrades of a determined revolutionary spirit, comrades who do not ask why armed insurrection must be used in our fight against capitalism, but how it is to be applied.

[The object of the course is:] to train a number of men into conscientious Communists, and to give them sufficient knowledge about the different sides of military work, in order that they may be able, in the near future, to carry out the duties of (1) organisers of the British Red Army; (2) officers of the British Red Army; (3) Communist military commissaries to control the non-Communist technical officers and staff which may be employed by the Revolutionary Authority.

… For the present the work must be carried out 'Underground', and under strict secrecy, but it is also of absolute importance that this body of Red Army leaders does not regard itself as an independent, fighting, terroristic, or similar organisation. It is not a body of plotters or riot makers, but of future Red Army leaders and officers, who act closely and loyally in line with the Communist mass movement …

Some comrades, quite in earnest and keen on the job, may have doubts as to the possibility of getting anything really efficient done, compared with the Regular Army, when we have to work in such difficult conditions. Well, it is difficult, but it is not hopeless by any means, if we consider the following points:-

(1) The efficiency and discipline of the Regular Army can be practically broken by propaganda, and parts of it may come over on our side.

(2) We shall have to fight, mainly, against people who are more or less trained and organised like ourselves, viz. bourgeois White Guards. They may have more skilled officers, but it is up to us to show that they have less morale, less determination, less endurance.

(3) The Revolutionary Civil War will, at any rate in the beginning, have largely the character of improvised guerrilla warfare, street fighting, and so on. Although we must be prepared to meet tanks, aircraft, flame-throwing, and even gas here, it will not be quite the same as the gigantic skilful murder engineering of the imperialist war.

(4) In the time shortly after the revolution, which may have been comparatively bloodless in its first stage, even the mere existence of a Communist Red Army and its armed demonstrators in the streets may be enough to impose the will of the revolutionary proletariat and keep down counter-revolutionary aggressiveness.

(5) In a revolutionary war more depends on the highly personal quality and spirit of each fighter than on his technical equipment …

Persons who act as provocateur or with malicious intent betray their comrades and organisation may be punished with death.

Among other more detailed instructions were the following:

Barricades: Overturned buses, trams, carts, form a good framework for a barricade.

Seizure of a bank: Evict occupants. Locate the bullion. Every entrance seal. In big towns, if a central branch, prepare for defence, strengthen windows and doors (vide Manual of Field Engineering). Await instructions from Central Revolutionary Party.[25]

There were also lessons entitled 'Machine Gun Drill', 'Use of Bombs' and 'Use of Revolvers'. Other pages contained instructions for the 'Defence of a Factory', 'Defence of a Mine' and for seizing post offices and telephone exchanges.

Malone was almost certainly its author. In a speech in the North of England a few days before his flat was searched, he had already made a public appeal for recruits for a British Red Army.[26] The typeface on the pamphlets matched a typewriter found at his flat (which turned out to have been stolen from a government office). It seemed that the original had been typed on his machine, sent off to be duplicated, and these tickets were the printer's way of delivering the finished brochures without them being traced to their source. Only the inability of the prosecution to prove in a criminal court that there was a conclusive connection between Malone and the finished brochures saved him from the more serious charge of high treason, which at the time could even carry the death penalty. He was jailed and stripped of his OBE.

It is said that Malone made a break with Communism after his imprisonment.[27] He certainly moved to the ILP when the CPGB failed to gain affiliation to the Labour Party, but the willingness of the ILP to accept him without reservation is an illustration of how little concern was felt about his revolutionary sentiments. It is a graphic illustration of how the ILP's own sympathy with Soviet Communism enabled it to overlook the extent to which one of its candidates had been an advocate of violent revolution. Malone failed to win a seat for the ILP in the 1924 election, but was returned to parliament in the 1929 general election, and became a parliamentary private secretary to the Labour Minister of Pensions, Frederick Roberts. In the 1929–31 parliament he continued to ask questions and to make speeches which were hostile to the opponents of religious persecution and slave labour in Soviet Russia.[28] To that extent he had not changed.

What is also surprising, given the content of Malone's speech at the Albert Hall and the Red Army manual found in his flat, was the presence of so many prominent Labour figures alongside him on the stage, and later in court, where he was supported by Neil Maclean MP, Robert Williams and George Lansbury, in spite of the latter's avowed rejection of violence.

George Lansbury. © National Portrait Gallery, London.

Moderates

It would be misleading to imply that the admiration of many Labour figures for the Bolsheviks' revolutionary Socialism went unchallenged, even by eminent figures in the party. J. R. Clynes was one of these. Clynes had begun life in absolute poverty, the son of an illiterate immigrant Irish gravedigger. By determined effort, educating himself, he had risen to become an MP, party chairman in 1921 and leader of the parliamentary party in 1922. In June 1919, when the Labour Party conference voted two to one in favour of a national strike if British troops were not withdrawn from Russia, Clynes unsuccessfully tried to persuade the conference that strikes should not be threatened for solely political aims.[29]

Although he would eventually sit in Cabinet alongside Lansbury, his views on Soviet Communism could not have been more different:

> I detest the idea of Bolshevism, and its methods are as reprehensible to me as anything can be ... The leading Bolshevists are not working-class represent-atives, but are self-appointed persons ... pursuing ... the attainment of their views by domination, and by the extermination of the classes who differ from them. The more the working classes understand how vicious, unjust, tyrannical, and dictatorial Bolshevik methods are, the more unitedly will they reject them.[30]

J. H. 'Jimmy' Thomas, like Clynes, was a member of both the 1924 and 1929 Cabinets. The illegitimate son of a domestic servant who was brought up by his widowed washerwoman grandmother, he had also risen through his own ability to a position of political prominence. He became general secretary of the National Union of Railwaymen in 1916 and remained on its leader-ship until 1931 when the union stripped him of both his membership and (unjustly) his pension for refusing to abandon Ramsay MacDonald when he formed the National Government. Thomas had been a leading member of the Council of Action in 1920 (as had Clynes), hardly a moderate body, but in the spring of 1921 when another miners' strike was threatened, a promise of supportive industrial action by the rail and transport workers fell through at the last minute. This 'Triple Alliance', as it was called, would have brought the country to a standstill. Thomas came down on the side of conciliation rather than conflict and thus made himself an enemy of many on the left. Those who were pressing for a strike blamed him for deserting the cause. He further fell out with the militants by supporting the idea that safety officers should still be allowed into the mines during the strike to monitor gas build-ups or flooding damage – both of which could have damaged or closed mines for good, putting miners out of work and adding to their hardship.

Francis Meynell, after his embarrassing resignation from the *Daily Herald*, moved on to become editor of the CPGB's *The Communist*. In this post, he did little to restrain the belligerence and hostility often expressed by the CPBG towards any in the Labour movement whom they thought were too politically soft. *The Communist* turned on Thomas and condemned him as a 'traitor'. When, over successive editions, the insults showed no sign of abating, Thomas sued for libel. A jury found in his favour and awarded damages of £2,000 against *The Communist's* publishers National Labour Press, Francis Meynell and Arthur MacManus, the CPGB chairman.[31] In the light of the abuse, Labour's continued refusal to let the CPGB affiliate to the Labour Party was scarcely surprising.

The authorities' position on political extremism was straightforward. The expression or promotion of alternative political views was legitimate, no matter how radical, and the state had no place to interfere unless those views were accompanied by incitements to enforce them by violence. If the incitement to violence was made with the intent of influencing the government, it became sedition and was illegal.[32] In that case, the government would no longer stand by, but would take action. The Malone prosecution was one such case. A crackdown on the CPGB office was another. The CPGB's printed output had become so inflammatory that the police raided the CPGB offices in May 1921. Among the materials which had prompted the raid was a section in *The Communist* which called for soldiers to 'turn your bayonets upon the bourgeoisie', an incitement to mutiny. Albert Inkpin, the CPGB secretary, was charged with procuring the service of the National Labour Press (NLP) for the purpose of printing and distributing seditious material. George Lansbury stood bail for Inkpin, but when the verdict was returned, Inkpin was sentenced to six months in prison. Costs were awarded against the party, which was forced to find £1,000 to pay these in addition to the £2,000 it paid on losing the libel case.

In the course of the investigation, the police needed to show that Inkpin had personally commissioned the print runs. It was discovered that the party had written cheques to the NLP for £2,781 (£122,800 today) in the first few months of 1921 alone. The party membership was only about 5,000, half of whom were unemployed and paid no membership fees. The obvious question was: where had the party been getting so much money? Seized minute books gave the clue and mentioned 'large sums from abroad' which had been received. It was obvious that the money had come from Moscow.

A separate inquiry later in the year traced the movement of funds through bank accounts held by Klishko which, by mid-1921, contained no less than £1.65 million (£73 million today). A trail of money laundering was uncovered:

Russian gold was being re-melted in Sweden, stamped by the Swedish Mint, shipped to America, and then sold there as if of Swedish origin. The proceeds were sent to London, where the money was either disbursed or shipped out again, 'clean', for use elsewhere. Of the British disbursements, one particular set of complex payments proved to be particularly incriminating: £800 (£35,300 today) from Russian sources had been sent through various intermediaries to pay miners during the strike of April 1921.[33] This was just one payment; it was suspected that there were many others. Further raids and inquiries over the next seven years would continue to shed light on the Soviet funding of British revolutionary groups and causes, funded at least in part by Russian money laundering in London (see Chapter 9).

CHAPTER 4

LABOUR SOCIALISM AND THE RUSSIAN REVOLUTION

[Marx's] memory is a consecrated treasure enshrined in the hearts of millions of the best men and women of all lands.
KEIR HARDIE, 1910[1]

The Russian Revolution is the greatest and the most beneficent event in modern history since the French Revolution.
HAROLD LASKI, 1947[2]

Redistribution of the national income by communal ownership and workers' control is an urgent and inevitable economic necessity. We have a plain choice. We can accept the redistribution, and have a peaceful revolution. We can, by illegitimate and violent means, resist the redistribution, and have bloody revolution. There is no third way.
GERALD GOULD, 1920[3]

Hardie and MacDonald

The origins of the modern Labour Party lie in the foundation of the Independent Labour Party in 1893 as the political expression of the British trade union movement. Two ILP men tower over the early days of the Labour Party – J. Keir Hardie (1856–1915) and James Ramsay MacDonald (1866–1937).

Keir Hardie was the ILP's first chairman (1893–1900); Ramsay MacDonald joined the ILP the year after its foundation. In 1899 the Trades Union

Congress formed the Labour Representation Committee (LRC), which linked the unions, the ILP and the Fabian Society, the three pillars on which the Labour Party was built.* MacDonald was unanimously elected as its first secretary. Then, in 1906, the LRC became the Labour Party and Hardie the new Labour Party's first chairman. Hardie resigned in 1907. MacDonald, meanwhile, took on Hardie's earlier role as leader of the ILP from 1906 to 1909 and followed him as chairman of the Parliamentary Labour Party from 1911–14 before becoming Leader of the Opposition in 1922. In 1924, he rose to heights that Hardie had not reached, becoming Prime Minister in the first Labour government, a feat he repeated in the second Labour government of 1929.

History has dealt with Hardie more kindly than MacDonald; Hardie remains commonly regarded as the founder of the Labour Party and one of its greatest figures. MacDonald, by contrast, has been vilified, particularly by the left of the party, for his supposed betrayal of the party in 1931, and dismissed as a vain social climber and 'traitor'. Modern historians are beginning to salvage his reputation and show that his achievements were greater than his detractors have previously allowed. His early contemporaries certainly would not have recognised that picture: in the first decades of the century, he was said to be one of the most inspiring platform speakers of his generation and in 1922, when he was returned to Parliament as Labour leader, the ILP paper the *New Leader* described him as one who would 'infallibly become the symbol and personification of the party'.[4]

Labour Party Socialism

When the British Labour Party restyled itself as 'New Labour' in the 1990s, it signalled the party's transition from Socialism to the centre ground of social democracy. The politics espoused under Tony Blair were so different from the Socialism of its founders that some disputed that Labour still was really socialist even if it called itself a socialist party. Whether or not it returns to those roots in the future, it is hard, looking at the party in the Blair era, to

---

* The Social Democratic Federation (SDF) was also involved, but it broke off links with the LRC within a year, before joining forces with left-wing members of the ILP in 1911 to form the British Socialist Party (BSP). In turn, the BSP merged with a number of small left-wing groups in 1920 and together they founded the CPGB.

appreciate how radical Labour Party Socialism was in the first half of the twentieth century and how distinct and articulated, as a political theory, its Socialism was at the time.

Labour Socialism from the 1890s onwards was inseparable from Marx, and it was no less a figure than Keir Hardie who summarised that succinctly in a series of articles written in 1910:

> Socialism is without exception, the greatest revolutionary ideal that has ever fired the imagination, or enthused the heart of mankind ... The Socialist state is the end [and] Marx knew of only one way [to get there]: the organisation of a working class movement, which would in the process of time evolve [into] the Socialist state.
>
> The Trades Union movement is the real movement of the working class, and the ILP is its advanced wing. That was what Marx intended the Socialist movement to be.
>
> Marx illustrates the methods to be employed for bringing Socialism into being ... the first step is to raise the working class i.e. form a Labour Party so as to make the workers the 'ruling class'. He goes on to say that this new ruling class 'will use its position of supremacy to wrest, by degrees, all capital from the capitalist class' [and that would be by]
>
> 1. Abolition of property in land, and the application of all rents of land to public purposes.
> 2. A heavy progressive or graduated income tax.
> 3. Abolition of all right of inheritance.
>
> Socialism will abolish the landlord class, the capitalist class, and the working class. That is revolution: that the working class by its actions will one day abolish class distinctions.[5]

Marx had been an observer at the ILP's founding conference in 1893, and Hardie's debt to, and admiration for, him were beyond question:

> Marx's real title to greatness and certainly his greatest claim upon the gratitude of the working class, rests on his discovery of the truth that history is but

the record of class struggles … With each succeeding struggle the bounds of human freedom have been enlarged [and now] the final stage of the struggle of freedom has been entered upon.

It was the inspired vision of Karl Marx, which first formulated as scientific fact the inevitable coming of that glorious time. Little wonder that his memory is a consecrated treasure enshrined in the hearts of millions of the best men and women of all lands.

Hardie's view was one widely held: British Labour saw itself as a *Marxist* party, as four leading figures in the first fifty years of the Party – Aneurin Bevan,[*] James Maxton,[†] Harold Laski[‡] and George Bernard Shaw[§] – all make quite clear. Bevan wrote in 1920:

The Communist Manifesto stands in a class by itself in Socialist literature. No indictment of the social order ever written can rival it. The largeness of its conception, its profound philosophy and its sure grasp of history, its aphorisms and its satire, all these make it a classic of literature, while the note of passionate revolt which pulses through it, no less than its critical appraisement of the forces of revolt, make it for all rebels an inspiration and a weapon.[6]

James Maxton declared, in 1933: 'The only teaching which I know which gets anywhere near to providing intelligent explanations and intelligent solutions of the troubles of the world is the Marxist teaching',[7] while Harold

---

[*]   Aneurin 'Nye' Bevan (1897–1960), MP (1929–60), Minister of Health (1945), Minister of Labour (1951), shadow Colonial Secretary, shadow Foreign Secretary (1956), party treasurer (1956), deputy leader of the Labour Party (1959). He sat on the Board of Tribune (1936), and was a supporter of the Unity Campaign of 1937, which sought to bring about a united front between Labour, the ILP and the CPGB.

[†]   James Maxton (1885–1946), MP (1922–46), ILP member of the Labour Party Scottish executive, and the NEC, ILP chairman (1926–31, 1934–39).

[‡]   Harold Laski (1893–1950), academic political theorist and politician. Unofficial assistant to Prime Minister Ramsay MacDonald (1924), Labour Party NEC (1936–48), Labour chairman (1945–46); professor of political science at the London School of Economics (1926–50), leader writer for the *Daily Herald* (1914), executive member of the Fabian Society (1921–36), president of the Rationalist Press Association (1930), co-founder of the Left Book Club (1936), supporter of the Socialist League (1932) and of the Unity Campaign (1937).

[§]   George Bernard Shaw (1856–1950) is known today for his work as a playwright (uniquely winning both a Nobel Prize for literature in 1925 and an Oscar for the screenplay of *Pygmalion* in 1938), but from the late 1890s he was also one of Labour's most widely known figures. An early leader of the Fabian Society and contributor to its *Fabian Essays in Socialism* (1889), Shaw also played a part in the part formation of the ILP in 1893.

Laski, as Labour Party chairman, wrote in 1948: 'The Labour Party regards [*The Communist Manifesto*] as one of the great historical documents in socialist history ... The Labour Party acknowledges its indebtedness to Marx and Engels as two of the men who have been the inspiration of the whole working-class movement. Who can doubt our common inspiration?'[8] For his part, George Bernard Shaw still held the same beliefs in 1950:

> What was it that saved Russia from ruin after 1917? – her adoption of British Communism, made constitutional and practicable by myself, Sidney Webb, and our fellow Fabians ... Marxism, a British Museum export, was set on its feet by Fabianism, another British export. We are the spiritual fathers of modern successful Communism.[9]

James Maxton

Socialism and Communism

In *The Communist Manifesto* and his other writings Marx developed a theoretical framework for interpreting the evolution of history. He saw history as an unstoppable process arising out of conflict between classes. As each new dominant class arose it would create an underclass. Conflict would then break out between the two. Out of that conflict a new class would arise. In turn that would create a new underclass and the process would continue. The final end, Communism, would be a classless society of such universal brotherhood that the constraints of government would no longer be needed. The state would 'wither away'. Marx was to economics and to politics what Darwin was to nature, the discoverer of previously hidden mechanisms which explained the course of history.

Marx believed that these inexorable shifts had taken place intermittently over hundreds of years and that the stage was now set for the final conflict, the overthrow of capitalism. But he did not see the immediate advent of Communism. A transitional phase, the 'dictatorship of the proletariat' or 'Socialism' would be required first. During this time, the new ruling class, the proletariat, would deprive capitalists of their wealth and nationalise all productive assets – factories, utilities, land, banks and so on.

This principle was enshrined in 1918 in the Labour Party's new constitution, 'Labour and the New Social Order', drafted by Fabian member Sidney Webb, the fourth clause of which affirmed the party's aim:

> To secure for the workers by hand or by brain the full fruits of their industry and the most equitable distribution thereof that may be possible upon the basis of the common ownership of the means of production, distribution and exchange, and the best obtainable system of popular administration and control of each industry or service.

'Clause four' was so central to the party's identity that it has been fought over repeatedly. Party leader Hugh Gaitskell's attempt to delete it was defeated by the left of the party in 1959, and that tussle resulted in it being printed on the back of party membership cards. When that was reversed in the Blair reforms of 1995, many believed it showed that the party had finally abandoned its socialist roots.

Even in the inter-war years, when Socialism as a political philosophy was much more clearly defined and better understood, the terms 'Socialism' and 'Communism' were capable of different uses. To many, Socialism was considered to be the first phase and Communism the higher phase of Marx's final class conflict. Lenin used them both in that sense and that was why in 1922 the new Russian nation was called the 'Union of Soviet *Socialist* Republics'. But Marx himself had said that 'Communism is not for us a state of affairs still to be established, not an ideal to which reality will have to adjust. We call Communism the real movement which abolishes the present state of affairs',[10] and so even among its leading proponents, therefore, there was no clarity. Mostly, however, the terms 'Communism' and 'Socialism' were used interchangeably throughout the late nineteenth and early twentieth centuries, as their respective entries in the 1929 edition of *Encyclopaedia Britannica* show:

Communism ... is a term originally used as almost synonymous with Socialism ... The words 'Socialism' and 'Communism' [denote] those systems and movements which aim at communalizing the means of production, justify the pursuit of this end by a scientific analysis of the capitalist system of economics and in the efforts to reach it count principally on the support of the masses of industrial workmen, the proletariat, and the numerous classes of lower clerks, etc. ...

Socialism is essentially a doctrine and a movement aiming at the collective organisation of the community in the interests of the mass of people by means of common ownership and collective control of the means of production and exchange.[11]

British Communists

Relations between the CPGB and the Labour Party were often fractious. Although the CPGB's forerunner, the BSP, had been affiliated to the Labour Party since 1916, in 1921 the Labour NEC refused the CPGB's application to affiliate.

On an individual level, things were more fluid, and members moved freely between the two parties. In the December 1923 election, seven of the nine CPGB candidates stood under the Labour Party banner. There were 430 communist delegates in attendance at the 1923 Labour Party conference. Though Labour's 1921 rejection of CPGB affiliation had been carried by a large majority at the party conference, it remained opposed by some influential figures within the party. In 1925, James Maxton, George Lansbury, A. B. Swales the TUC chairman, A. A. Purcell MP, the TUC vice-chairman, and a number of others all appealed to the Labour conference for the CPGB to be affiliated. They were unsuccessful. Even so, Harry Pollitt of the CPGB was permitted to address the conference on the same issue.

Antagonism between Labour and the CPGB, usually triggered by the CPGB's inept, Moscow-provoked, belligerence towards Labour, was also a constant feature of this period. But, though vocal, the CPGB was not a large party: by the end of 1929, its membership stood at around 3,500; Labour polled over eight million votes in the 1929 general election, the Communists just 50,000. And while Labour's relations with the CPGB were difficult, its warmth towards Communists grew in proportion to their geographical distance from Westminster, so that it could still sympathise with the philosophy's Soviet incarnation, particularly as the 1920s progressed and earlier protests by the British left about the persecution of non-Bolshevik Russian socialists were forgotten. As one commentator has remarked, 'It would be a mistake to regard the Labour Party's attitude towards the CPGB as a reliable barometer of its attitude to Russia.'[12]

Besides, in Britain in the early 1920s, Labour supporters often described Russia (and themselves) as socialist rather than communist.[13] To complicate matters, the use of the two terms has changed over time. John Strachey was elected a Labour MP in 1929 but in the 1930s was one of the most articulate proponents of Communism in Britain. In 1935, speaking in an American court after his arrest while on a lecture tour of the United States, he explained his definition: 'I describe myself as a Communist. What I mean by this description is that while I am not a member of the Communist Party I do hold views which can be described as Communist in general principle and I hold the economic theories of Marx are true.' And he then also called those who were like him 'fellow travellers', people 'who accept the Communist principles in general but who are not members of the party'.[14]

In Britain in the *second* half of the twentieth century, 'communist' became more often used to describe members of the CPGB or other Leninist, Trotskyite or Stalinist factions. Thus, former Prime Minister Gordon Brown could insist that ILP leader James Maxton, one of Brown's personal heroes, 'was no Communist' in the sense that he was not a member of the CPGB, while Maxton definitely *was* a communist in Strachey's terms, as these comments of his (Maxton's) in 1935 make clear:

The Marxian theory is that social progress throughout the ages has proceeded as a result of struggles between classes and that the last class-struggle which remains to be fought out is the struggle between Capitalism and the proletariat. When that struggle has been fought out to its final conclusions, the working-class will assume power and proceed to construct a Socialist Commonwealth.

It is the period of transition from Capitalism to Socialism – the intervening period when the working-class has assumed power and must maintain it – which is described by Marx as the period of the 'dictatorship of the proletariat'. Notice – not the power of an individual over the community, but the definitely established power of the overwhelming majority constructing a new social order over the minority who are the remnants and relics of the dying social order. In fact, that type of dictatorship will be a freer and greater democracy than has ever been known in any land under Capitalism.

When the transition period from Capitalism to Socialism has been passed we shall go forward into a classless society in which the use of government to suppress class by class will come to an end and the function of government will be the co-ordination of things for the benefit of all, rather than the direction, the dragooning, and the drilling of men.[15]

Russia, Bolshevism and the British left

The association between the British left and Russian revolutionaries dated back to before 1917. When Hardie wrote his commentary on Marx in 1910, Marxism was captivating radicals everywhere, but the socialist state was still only a dream, nowhere seen in practice; in reality, the decade before the Great War was such a troubled time for European monarchies that Socialism's advocates were already feared and persecuted.

London became a magnet for these idealists. The city, particularly the East End, had long been a haven for refugees. Its Jewish community contained many who had escaped the pogroms of Eastern Europe, and in the early years of the twentieth century their numbers were supplemented by new arrivals who had fled the Tsarist secret police, the Okhrana. Trotsky escaped from exile in Siberia and arrived in London in 1902, settling there for a while and was joined by Lenin in editing *Iskra* ('Spark'), the revolutionaries' journal. Lenin passed through London a number of times between 1902 and 1911 and was in London for the 1902 congress of the Russian Social Democratic

Labour Party (RSDLP), the Russian Marxist party which split in 1912 into the Bolsheviks and Mensheviks. Stalin himself came to Whitechapel for the 1907 RSDLP congress.

Once in London, foreign radicals such as Theodore Rothstein and Nikolai Klishko met and mixed freely with their British counterparts. Maxim Litvinov, Soviet Foreign Minister from 1930, was typical of many. Litvinov had fled to London in 1906 and remained there until he was expelled by the British government in 1918. Like Klishko, he married an English wife – in his case a British woman named Ivy Lowe, whose family were friends with H. G. Wells and who was related by marriage to Leslie Haden-Guest.*

The problem of violence

The problem for socialists was that the goal they sought, the establishment of a utopian socialist state, could only be achieved by 'expropriation'. Very few would give up their wealth and property voluntarily. Hardie had affirmed in 1910 that the Labour Party's aim was to 'wrest, by degrees, all capital from the capitalist class'. The following year, Hardie's ILP published *The Case for Socialism* by Fred Henderson (no relation of Arthur Henderson, sometime party leader and Foreign Secretary), which made this quite clear. The book was first published in 1908 by the Clarion Press and was reprinted by ILP in 1911 (the year after Ramsay MacDonald chaired the party) and again in 1924. In 1933 the Labour Party published its own edition. As such, it can be considered as produced very much under the Party's imprimatur. Its tone is unmistakable:

> Socialism is an attack upon the institution of private property in land and capital. We Socialists advocate the expropriation of the landed and capitalist class; their deprivation of their present way of living; and the organisation of the wealth-producing activities of the nation by the nation itself.
>
> Definitely and clearly, our purpose is to deprive these people of their way of living, and to make the wealth which now passes into their possession

---

* Haden-Guest (1877–1960) was on the executive of the Fabian Society in 1907–11 and was elected MP in 1923. He was created Baron Haden-Guest in 1950. His relationship with Ivy Lowe was tenuous – he divorced her aunt Edith in 1909 – but illustrates the social connections between Bolshevik émigrés and the British left. Haden-Guest was a member of Labour's first fact-finding delegation to Russia in 1920.

available for the national life ... Private ownership and control of land and capital is only a different form of slave-owning ... to put an end to that is not confiscation, but the prevention of confiscation ... The end it has in view ... is the wiping out of private property in land and capital.[16]

The Fabian Society had been no less explicit in its ultimate goal – the nationalisation of all land and industry:

The Fabian Society consists of Socialists. It therefore aims at the reorganisation of society by the *emancipation of Land and Industrial Capital from individual and class ownership*, and the vesting of them in the community for the general benefit ... The Society accordingly works *for the extinction of private property in Land* ... for the transfer to the community, by constitutional methods, of all such industries as can be conducted socially; and for the establishment [of] the regulation of production, distribution and service, [for] the common good instead of private profit. (My italics.)[17]

Marx had not been silent on the subject of force, telling one interviewer towards the end of his life that 'no great movement has ever been inaugurated without bloodshed',[18] a sentiment he had expressed in even more forceful terms thirty years earlier: 'There is only one way in which the murderous death agonies of the old society and the bloody birth throes of the new society can be shortened, simplified and concentrated, and that way is revolutionary terrorism'.[19]

It was hard to see how compulsory expropriation, if resisted, could be achieved without force, and how its enforcers could be kept from thinking that violence was justified. That conundrum remained a matter of theoretical debate until, in 1917, a group of revolutionaries in Russia put the theory into practice. The world looked on in shock as the Russian tsar was first overthrown and then, with his family, murdered in a cellar in Yekaterinburg.

Marx in the Russian context

Writing in mid-nineteenth-century industrial Europe, Marx pictured the final conflict as the mass of industrial workers rising up against their capitalist masters. But in Russia, there was no industrial working class to be radicalised, only a conservative peasantry. Lenin's contribution was to develop Marx's theories to encompass the Russian context. With no mass of workers to form the core of a revolution, a comparatively small elite band of professional revolutionaries, the Bolsheviks, were to take power instead and carry out the revolution themselves, imposing their will by ruthless force. Bolshevism freed Russian Marxists from the otherwise apparently necessary precondition of having mass support from the people for their revolution (at the outset, there were probably no more than 20,000 Bolsheviks in a population of 160 million). Since then, Marxism-Leninism has provided the rationale for minority revolutionary groups around the world to resort to terrorism to overthrow their governments. Throughout the twentieth century, sponsored by Moscow as official (though clandestine) Soviet foreign policy, the doctrine had devastating consequences and blighted the lives of millions.

The eventual cost of the 'great experiment' (as Labour supporters called it) of Socialism in Russia was to be horrendous. Between 1917 and 1922, in the Revolution and its aftermath, nine million Russians died from violence or famine provoked by the Civil War,[20] about the same number as total military fatalities on all sides in the 'Imperialist' Great War. During the years covered by the main portion of this book, 1929–31, when the second Labour government was in power, another quarter of a million Russians were shot or died as a result of their imprisonment. Through the 1930s, the numbers would climb still further. At the height of the Great Terror, in 1937–38, executions ran at over 10,000 each week. By 1953, the year of Stalin's death, Soviet Communism had been responsible for over twenty million deaths, almost three million of them in the gulag. Many of the fourteen million who survived the camps were so emotionally or physically damaged that they never fully recovered. The impact of major trauma travels through generations of a family. Hundreds of thousands were left with nightmare memories that did not lose their power – a parent or sibling taken, never to return, a sudden arrest in the night which changed lives for ever, children left behind and dispatched to barbaric state orphanages. Sometimes a survivor came home from the camps so scarred that life was never the same for the family to whom they returned. Psychologically disturbed parents raise damaged children who then become dysfunctional parents themselves. There are thousands alive today, in Russia and in the other countries of the former USSR, who never knew the gulag era but have inherited its scars and still live with its wounds.

A NICE DISTINCTION.

"Moderate" Socialist (to Communist). "I DISAPPROVE OF YOUR WEAPONS OF VIOLENCE. I PREFER THIS SIMPLE METHOD OF STRANGLING THE NATION'S LIFE."

["There are many of us whose connexion with key-industries has brought us, and may bring us again, into collision with Governments as well as employers. If that time comes, we shall be with the organised workers whatever may be the path they follow."—*Chairman of the Labour Party Conference*.]

"A nice distinction". Punch *cartoon, October 1925. Critics highlighted Labour's inconsistency – commending the Bolsheviks as fellow socialists, advocating compulsory expropriation, but still insisting that the party was committed to non-violence and democracy.*

British reaction

It was not long before stories of widespread atrocities began to filter out of Russia with fleeing refugees. Accounts of the Bolsheviks' 'Red Terror', the mass reprisal shootings of hostages, and stories of the rape, torture and murder of priests and nuns all struck horror into the hearts of British readers.[*]

---

[*] The Red Terror (1918–22) refers to the period of savage repression by the Bolsheviks of those who were suspected of being opponents of the Revolution or, by their class origins, deemed to be potential opponents. Summary arrest, torture and execution without trial were widespread. Between 10,000 and 15,000 people were executed within the span of two months at the end of 1918, and by 1920 executions were still running at 1,000–2,000 per month. 'Blood? Let blood flow like water!' proclaimed the Kiev *Cheka*'s newspaper *The Red Sword*, 'Let blood stain forever the black pirate's flag flown by the bourgeoisie, and let our flag be blood-red for ever'. Courtois et al., *The Black Book of Communism*, pp. 78, 102, 106.

Violence was met with violence and 'White' Russians fought back against the 'Reds' in the vicious Civil War which followed. As Allied governments sent ships to the Black Sea to rescue dispossessed Russian nobility and an expeditionary force to Archangel in support of the 'White' Russian forces of Admiral Kolchak and General Denikin, British socialists, who shared all the Bolsheviks' hopes of a new socialist world order, were confronted with the challenge of how to respond.

The political reaction of the British left – the protests, strikes, demands for Allied withdrawal and the campaign for recognition of the new revolutionary government – has already been considered; the challenge for the Labour Party was to develop a theoretical response too. Questions were being asked of a British party which had expressed its own 'revolutionary' agenda for Britain: What did Labour think about what was going on in Russia? Was Labour on the Bolsheviks' side or not? How did the two differ? Did Labour condemn or applaud the violence? Would it do the same if it took power in Britain? What did it mean when it called for socialist revolution at home? In 1919, Ramsay MacDonald, soon to be Labour's first Prime Minister, took to print to explore that theme.

CHAPTER 5

'PARLIAMENT AND REVOLUTION'

The Socialist spirit knows that there are various roads leading to the same trysting place; that the Russian comrades may come one way and the British come another way.[1]

RAMSAY MACDONALD, 1919

Ramsay MacDonald, in common with a number of his ILP colleagues, had taken the pacifist line in the Great War. It had cost him his seat in Parliament and, for a while, much of his popularity. His marriage to the daughter of a theoretical chemist had given this illegitimate son of a Scottish farm girl the security of a private income, and the time he now had before his return to Westminster enabled him to write a detailed response to the Russian Revolution, *Parliament and Revolution*.[2] As Keir Hardie's writings on Marx define Labour's view of Socialism at the time of the party's founding, so MacDonald's 100-page book defines the party's view on the Russian Revolution, Russian Communism, and Labour's thoughts on the role of Parliament in achieving socialist goals in Britain.

Although the book was written in 1919, its perspective on the Russian Revolution was the one generally agreed upon by Labour for the next two decades. Given MacDonald's eminence in the party and his leadership in the events of 1929–31 which are the main subject of this book, *Parliament and Revolution* is extremely important in illustrating the Labour Party mindset which was to undergird its future relations with the Soviets. The position set out in his book helps to explain the party's otherwise illogical and inhumane refusal to respond to appeals to help those suffering in the Russian camps, and its continual turning of a blind eye to stories of crimes against humanity in the timber gulag, or to any other account which contradicted the benign picture it held of its fellow socialists in Russia.*

The book shows that MacDonald unambiguously supported the Revolution and that Labour was firmly on Lenin's side:

> The Russian revolution has been one of the greatest events in the history of the world, and the attacks that have been made upon it by frightened ruling classes and hostile capitalism should rally to its defence everyone who cares for political liberty and freedom of thought. ... Labour is drawn to Lenin ...† because he is fighting its battle, and because it is not deeply influenced by the accusations of tyranny and so on brought against him, for it knows that the accusers themselves have been guilty of the same faults.[3]

Those who read it to the end would have seen that, as far as the nationalisation of private property was concerned, there were ways in which MacDonald did not think the Bolsheviks had gone far enough: '[The Revolution's political] programme is such, on the whole, as any Socialist government would put into operation, though its land policy would be stronger in this country and, with some preliminary preparation, its proposals regarding wealth conscription would have been less crude'.[4] 'Wealth conscription' was MacDonald's delicate term to describe the Russian revolutionaries' theft and mass plunder.

In the book, to counter the stories of atrocities committed by the Bolsheviks, MacDonald produces a range of excuses: that most of the stories were untrue; that Lenin was totally opposed to terror; that those stories which were true were excusable under the circumstances; that, besides, the real people to blame for the horrors were capitalist governments which had

---

*   In the 1920s, it did protest the persecution of non-Bolshevik socialists, as will be shown, but these tapered off when the victims were of a different political persuasion.

†   The text here reads: 'not because it associates itself with all that Lenin does or stands for'. The reason for the omission is not to make MacDonald's words seem more damning but that MacDonald's perspective on the necessity for violence in Russia is discussed in Chapter 5 and does not alter his endorsement of Lenin.

sought to defend the Tsarist monarchy, not the revolutionaries carrying out the shootings:*

> I leave out of account the Terror and similar incidents, not only because most of them are mere fabrications … Besides, Lenin abhors them, whereas Koltchak glories in them. We know that some expedients† have been purely temporary; we know that others cannot bear close and detailed examination. For them a comprehensive excuse, which is a justification under the circumstances, can be made that they belonged to the stress of the revolution.[5]
>
> Had it not been for the attacks of the Allied Governments the earthquake stage of the Russian revolution would have been over by now, and the world would have had the advantage of witnessing the assimilation by Russia of the ideas of a Socialist Republic. The only effect so far of this Allied attack upon Russian Socialism has been to prolong their chaotic 'dictatorship' stages of the revolution. It created the Red Terror, it has maintained the revolutionary tribunals, it has been responsible for the executions of politicals. The Recording Angel, who sees more truly than men see, has put down the crimes of the past years in Russia not to the Soviet Government but to France, Great Britain, and America, and on their doorsteps will history lay them.[6]

And, in any case, MacDonald insists, capitalists had done the same and so their complaints were hypocritical:

> [The revolution] has aroused the fears and the enmity of the governing orders all over the world, and yet it has not applied a single principle but what they themselves applied – nor, on the other hand, committed an atrocity but what they themselves had committed or condoned … When the masters murdered the slaves no one troubled; when the slaves murdered the masters the world was shocked … Those of us to whom murder and starvation are always murder and starvation whoever may be the victims are alone entitled to condemn.[7]

---

* There are uncomfortable resonances between this argument and the frequent IRA claim during the Northern Ireland Troubles that its bombings and assassinations were the responsibility of the intransigent British government, not of its own members.

† I.e. executions and murders.

MacDonald's insistence that only Socialists had the right to criticise Bolsheviks and, later, Soviet Communists, is repeated elsewhere in his book ('We repudiate the right of the capitalist critics of the Russian revolution to condemn the dictatorship of the proletariat in Russia'[8]) and it became a recurring theme in Labour ranks throughout the 1920s and 1930s. It gave shelter against all unanswerable charges and laid suspicion upon the motives of everyone who raised them.

The doctrine was elaborated by figures such as George Lansbury. On Lansbury's return from Russia the following year, he declared: 'It is no part of my business as a Socialist to search out and strive to discover material for criticism or denunciation.'[9] A decade later, his perspective remained unchanged: 'The colossal task set themselves by the Russian Socialists is one which should be supported by all lovers of the race. We are not called upon to judge or accept all the means they adopt to attain their ends.'[10]

MacDonald was not blind to the abolition of liberty for which those pursuing revolution in Russia were responsible. Of the nature of its central mechanism, 'the dictatorship of the proletariat' (whose necessity 'no one is in a position to dispute except those who have taken the Independent Labour Party view of the war'[11]), he was quite clear: it was 'a knife [with which] the dictatorship prunes mercilessly the dead wood and the parasitic growths of Society and leaves only the branches which draw sap and contribute to life'.[12]

Of another of the revolution's restrictions, 'disenfranchisement' (the refusal to permit someone to be allowed to register to vote, which carried a number of other highly punitive associations, such as the refusal of food rations), he was equally candid. He defends this: '[Given] the tyranny of the ruling minorities [and] the conditions of Russia, freedom of election is out of the question.'[13] In conjunction with another passage, this is also significant because it admits, as early as 1919, that Labour was aware of the targeted persecution of priests, something Labour ministers were to deny in Parliament a decade later, at the height of the affair which is the main subject of this book:

> The [Soviet] Constitution states that 'it is impossible during the present decisive struggle to admit exploiters to any organ of government or authority.' Thus all parasites and non-producers are disenfranchised, all who employ others for

profit and those living on unearned incomes, together with members of what are considered to be useless professions, like that of a *priest*. (My italics.)[14]

Two pages later, MacDonald even endorses the Bolsheviks' sneering dismissal of the disenfranchised, a group in which he had just included priests, by uncritically repeating the Russians' description of them as 'parasites': 'A close examination of what has happened in Russia shows that it is not the disenfranchisement of the parasites that has consolidated the Soviet government, but the external conspiracies of Allied governments and the internal conspiracies of the counter-revolution'.[15]

What would Labour do?

The most important question was not what was going on in Russia, but how the British Socialists would respond. Central to MacDonald's and Labour's reaction to the dictatorship and the suspension of liberty in Russia, was the suggestion that the British and Russian situations were so different ('in order to understand revolutionary events, we have to discriminate between Russian political conditions and our own'[16]) that violent revolution was not on Labour's agenda. Leninism had arisen because there was no industrial working class to rise up and take over, but there was such a class in Britain. So, MacDonald reasoned, the British Socialist revolution could be achieved through the ballot box without the use of force: 'A Parliamentary election will give us all the power that Lenin had to get by a revolution, and such a majority can proceed to effect the transition from Capitalism to Socialism with the cooperation of the people and not merely by edict.'[17]

MacDonald was not disavowing Bolshevik violence (he had already excused this); instead, he was merely stating that violence would not be needed in Britain because Labour could pursue its goal of nationalisation and expropriation through Parliament. The inconsistencies begin to appear, however, when MacDonald reveals that his view of Parliament as an institution for introducing those reforms was distinctly jaundiced:

We have by experience found that Parliament can be manipulated, that election issues can be fraudulent, that executives can use Parliament for purposes that are not in accord with the will of the people, that cabinets can coerce

Parliament, and that the further removed from the electors the governing power is the more self-willed becomes that power.[18]

While he insisted, in the second half of *Parliament and Revolution*, that Parliament was the only route open to British socialists to achieve their ends, he had already put in Lenin's own mouth enough criticism to justify its virtual suspension:

> Parliamentary government has become a capitalist institution, and will remain a capitalist fortress. Its phrases are drawn from bourgeois conceptions of government. Revolution is therefore required to effect a real change in Society. Such in a few sentences is the doctrine which Lenin, the master mind of the Russian revolution, preaches. During the revolution the structure of capitalism is to disappear, and with it must go 'the whole ideology and phraseology of the bourgeois democracy.' Unless this is done the revolutionary conditions will pass and the people will still be in chains.[19]

Then, in his discussion of the British route to socialist revolution, MacDonald began to speculate about measures that might be needed to circumvent Parliament. Resonances with the organ of government of the French Revolution would not have been missed by his readers:

> Of course, if it came to be that we had a bankrupt country, a demoralised and disorganised people, and anarchy, either active or latent, from one end of a ruined nation to the other, a Committee Of Public Safety might well step into Whitehall and make up its mind to impose a New Order upon an Old Chaos.[20]

In this MacDonald was not alone; the idea was raised again by Robert Williams at the height of the Council of Action crisis in August 1920. It was dangerous ground; over a century later, the suspension of democracy for the sake of restoring order and confidence remains the standard defence of coup plotters and military juntas.

Most importantly, MacDonald explained, there was 'direct action', the strike weapon: 'When Parliament in dealing with Labour interests shows an unwillingness to act or a hostility … 'direct action' or the threat of it is necessary. It is political action in a form which has become necessary because the Parliament is bad.'[21]

After his insistence that Socialism could be achieved in Britain by parliamentary means, and his rejection of force, MacDonald's defence of the strike tactic was disingenuous: 'The argument that "direct action" is inconsistent with Parliamentary government is baseless, because such action can never come into operation whilst Parliamentary government is fulfilling its functions as representative government: it can only be used to support representative government.'[22] He also noted that its intention 'is not to take sovereignty from Parliament, but to limit its liberty to abuse its sovereignty'.[23] In other words, MacDonald asserted, Parliamentary government was acceptable only if it supported the Labour Party position. MacDonald saw himself as a democrat but his sentiment was one with which any nineteenth- or early twentieth-century autocrat would have been comfortable – if Parliament does not agree with you, shut it down.

Another option would be to manipulate the electoral roll. MacDonald's justification of the Bolsheviks' use of that tactic ('disenfranchisement') has already been remarked upon. In his book he went further and left the door open to justify its use by Labour:

If we compare the rationale of the Russian franchise with our own, it has no reason to be ashamed of itself ... If we are to have classed government, it is better to have the working-class in authority than the non-producing class. The very last people who are in a position to object to the Soviet franchise are, therefore, our own Conservative and Whig parties, because in condemning the Soviet principles they condemned their own ... The disfranchisement of the interests assailed by the revolution *may be necessary* and can be defended. (My italics.)[24]

In spite of all that he said, MacDonald genuinely believed that British Socialism was committed to non-violence. In many ways, he saw that the Labour Party (especially the ILP, his own party, which was then in the ascendant) was forging its own variant of Marxism for the British context, as Lenin had done in Russia: 'The Independent Labour Party is a product of British history and British conditions ... [drawing from] the radical movement ... Chartism and earlier Socialist thinkers ... [and] continental Socialists – especially Marx. It joins democracy to Socialism, carrying on in this respect the work of Marx.'[25] But alongside that commitment, MacDonald allowed a number of inconsistencies and contradictions: he excused or denied the extreme violence of the Bolsheviks, exemplified by the Red Terror and its extra-judicial killings; he absolved them of the responsibility for it and blamed capitalists for driving them to it; he justified a number of other Bolshevik anti-libertarian measures which fundamentally opposed the very freedom of the individual that his party stood for.

In all this he was not alone. *Parliament and Revolution* accurately reflected the views of the wider Labour Party, as their statements and actions over the next fifteen years were to bear out. And yet, by refusing to denounce these things as objectively wrong, MacDonald's and the party's reasoning allowed any Soviet atrocity to be justified. As the years passed, and as such a position became steadily more and more untenable, the more doggedly did Labour's Soviet friends cling to it.

If others in the party were conscious of the inconsistencies, they did not show it. At the Labour Party conference in 1918, Maxim Litvinov was given a standing ovation when he was welcomed as the new 'Plenipotentiary for Great Britain of the Russian People's Government'.[26] He was among old friends. At the ILP conference a few months earlier, the conference had placed on record 'its appreciation of the stand made for social and economic freedom by the workers of Russia', and pledged itself to do all in its power to inform the people of Britain of the secret treaties made against its 'Russian comrades' by 'capitalist imperialism' to overthrow the new regime.[27] The theory that the Allies were preparing for war against the Soviet Union had been implicit in MacDonald's book. It was a constant refrain from Moscow and was a belief from which the ILP never wavered either, as its conference minutes record in 1931, thirteen years later:

This Conference congratulates the Soviet Government and the whole of the working class of the USSR on the success of the 'Five-Year Plan' up to the moment, and it recognizes that the furious religious attacks, the cry of slave labour, the distortion of news about Russia, etc., is preliminary propaganda designed to prepare the way for a vast militarist attack on the workers of Russia.

This Conference, therefore, expresses its determination to oppose such war preparations and reassures the workers of Russia of our wholehearted support of the project they have undertaken.[28]

Hardie and MacDonald set the tone that others followed. Harold Laski, who was to become an eminent Labour political theorist of the inter-war years, wrote his own analysis of Marx, published by the Fabian Society, in 1922. While a reader of *Parliament and Revolution* might have thought that Mac-Donald believed that a violent interpretation of Marx was the development of the Bolsheviks, Laski left his readers in no doubt that the use of force was an essential ingredient of Marx's original thought:

Necessity of Revolution: The method by which the proletariat was to secure power lies at the very root of Marx's doctrine; and it has been in our own day, perhaps, the main source of his influence. The method was revolution, and a dictatorship of iron rigour would consolidate the new system until the period of transition had been effectively bridged. *Marx did not blind himself to what all this implied.* The history of capitalism was the history of a relentless defence of each phase of the rights of property.

The period of consolidation, moreover, must be a period of iron dictator-ship. *Marx had no illusions about the possibility of a democratic governance in such an hour.* The ideals of freedom were impossible to maintain until the ground so conquered had been made secure. Revolution provokes counter-rev-olution; and a victorious proletariat must be on its guard against reaction. Rev-olution, in fact, demands of the revolutionary class that it secure its purpose by every method at its disposal. It has neither time nor opportunity for compas-sion or remorse. Its business is to terrorize its opponents into acquiescence. It must disarm antagonism by execution, imprisonment, forced labour, control of the press. For as it cannot allow any effort at the violent overthrow of what it has established, so must it stamp out such criticism as might be the prelude to further attack. Revolution is war, and war is founded upon terror. The methods of capitalism must be used for the extinction of capitalism.

The end, in fact, is too great to be nice about the means employed.

In his view there is no place in history for the majority principle ... To introduce considerations of consent, to wait on in the belief that the obvious

rightness of communist doctrine will ultimately persuade men to its acceptance, is entirely to ignore reality. The mass of men will always acquiesce in, or
be indifferent to, whatever solutions are afforded. Communists must proceed
upon the assumption that nothing matters save the enforcement of their will.
(My italics.)[29]

It might be argued that Laski, in describing Marx's theories, was not endorsing them. If challenged, he would have denied it. And yet he was later to call
the Russian Revolution 'the greatest, and the most beneficent event in modern
history'[30] and describe *The Communist Manifesto* as 'one of the great historical
documents in socialist history'.[31] Laski exemplifies the problem faced by the
British left when it flirted with Revolution but still insisted that its own intentions were only humane. How could Laski show that Marx clearly endorsed
terror as an essential component of revolution and at the same time praise
Marx's most famous work and describe one of its consequences, the Russian
Revolution, as the 'greatest and the most beneficent event in modern history'?

Such logic, pursued, raised a number of troubling questions about a party
which so closely identified itself with Marx. Was Labour's disavowal of the
use of force believable if leading members of the party thought that it was integral to bringing in Socialism? What were they to think of such claims when
a man such as C. T. Cramp, speaking in 1924, the year he became chairman
of the Labour Party, declared: 'I am not interested in Parliament. I do not
believe that Parliament can do anything for the workers. Capitalism has got
to be smashed as it is smashed in Russia. Those of us who are revolutionaries
are determined to do it'?[32] What about Parliament? If in power, would it be
long before Labour took steps to suspend it? The ILP acknowledged that the
Bolsheviks had overthrown that key component of democratic government
and, from its tone, the ILP seemed to accept their reasons for having done so:

The Bolsheviks believe – apparently with good reason – that they alone are
able to secure a democratic peace. The Bolsheviks were, therefore, faced with
the alternative of dissolving the Constituent Assembly or allowing Russia to
give way to Germany and to compromise with the capitalist forces. They chose
the former knowing that it was a definite breach of the accepted standards of
democratic government.[33]

Regardless of what the party said now, would a time come when radical elements within it, justifying their actions by citing Marx, would push the Labour Party beyond that disavowal – if not into violence, then at least into the suspension of civil liberties? In fact, as will be seen in Part V, over time leading party members were to propose just that course of action. This issue dogged Laski's career too. In 1946, he lost a highly publicised libel action he took out against a newspaper which implied that he had supported violence in pursuit of Socialism in Britain.[34]

CHAPTER 6

THE 'GREAT GAME' CONTINUES (1921-23)

Back in Russia in the summer of 1922, famine was seriously taking hold. In London, Lloyd George received a request for a meeting from the Russian Trade Delegation to discuss aid for its victims. He met them on 5 August, accompanied only by Frank Wise and his private secretary, an indication of the trust that he still placed in Wise, even though the meeting itself was ample evidence that Wise's assurances on Russian grain supplies had been misguided. The Soviet delegation comprised just Jan Berzin, the new deputy Trade Delegation leader, and Klishko, the Soviets' London spy chief. The ostensible purpose of the meeting was to appeal for aid for Russian famine victims. In reality it was a ruse to extract trade goods on 100 per cent credit.

Under the watchful eye of his 'deputy', Klishko, Berzin carefully explained that those peasants who had grain surpluses could not be persuaded to part with them, and that the Moscow government therefore urgently needed clothing, boots and other goods in order to barter with the peasants in return for their grain. In practice the Soviet authorities thought nothing of imposing widespread grain seizures when it suited them. Such supposed gentleness was also scarcely believable in the light of the campaign to seize the treasures of the Orthodox Church that was about to begin on Lenin's instructions. That campaign was conducted with ruthless brutality: around 1,000 clergy were killed (one source suggests it was as high as 8,100)[1] and a further 20,000 clergy and laity were jailed.[2]

The goods requested included £2 million worth of cloth, £1.5 million of boots, £750,000 of agricultural machinery and tools, in addition to two million tons of grain and a million tons of coal. The sums involved, £10 million (£442 million today) were massive and the Russians wanted it *all* on credit. When the British suggested that payment could be made by contracts for future deliveries of timber from Russia's abundant forest reserves, the suggestion was dismissed. The only security the Russians would offer was their word that the debt would be repaid. Lloyd George understandably placed little faith in that. In return, he challenged them on the many breaches of their existing promise to halt anti-British propaganda. All were shrugged off and blamed on individuals acting 'on their own initiative'. The discussions progressed no further.

Just three weeks later, Curzon delivered yet another protest. Reminding the Russians again that the trade agreement had committed them to 'refrain from any attempt by military or diplomatic or any other form of action or propaganda to encourage any of the peoples of Asia in any form of hostile action against British interests or the British Empire, especially in India and in the Independent State of Afghanistan', Curzon detailed a succession of breaches which British intelligence had uncovered: the training and infiltration back into India of an explosives expert, now running a bomb-making operation; Comintern support for anti-British revolutionaries in Egypt; the provision of arms and ammunition to tribesmen in the Indian North West Frontier, shipped through Afghanistan; the activity of the Soviet mission in Teheran, staffed by over a hundred personnel under the leadership of Theodore Rothstein, channelling funds and communist infiltrators into India.[3] In short, the protest note concluded, 'His Majesty's Government are forced to the conclusion that the overthrow of British rule in India still constitutes the main object of the Soviet Government's eastern policy'. Calling upon the Soviet government to desist, Curzon added the warning that Britain would take 'all legitimate means' to defend itself. The Soviets once again came back with furious denials.

Lloyd George falls

In spite of the protests of his hardliners, Lloyd George continued to inch the Cabinet towards diplomatic recognition. Churchill reminded him that he had previously agreed that the trade agreement would be terminated if it were violated; and that it had been, without restraint. Curzon pleaded that no concessions should be made until Russian subversion in the empire had been shown to have ceased.[4] Lloyd George acknowledged their objections, but insisted that full trade was essential and that it inevitably had to include the presence of a Soviet chargé d'affaires in London.[5] His government, however, was not to last long enough to see his plans realised.

In November 1922, the Liberal-Conservative coalition fell and Lloyd George left high office for good. Churchill, at that stage still a Liberal, was out too, but he would have been heartened to see that the new Conservative Cabinet's attitude to the Soviets was hardening; the arrest, in late January 1923, of the British trawler *Magneta* off Murmansk, and its subsequent foundering with the loss of ten crew, stiffened the Cabinet's resolve still further. Earlier in the previous year, Lloyd George had taken Frank Wise as his personal advisor to the Genoa conference which discussed Russia's future status but Wise did not have the ear of Andrew Bonar Law, the new Conservative Prime Minister, in the same way. In March 1923, he resigned from the civil service and took Soviet employ as the director of the London office of Centrosoyus, their trading arm. The following year, now free of any obligation to observe an appearance of political neutrality, he stood as the ILP candidate for Bradford North. Though unsuccessful, his immediate selection as a parliamentary candidate indicated the respect in which he was already held by the party which had so resolutely expressed support for its 'Russian comrades' in their pursuit of 'International Socialism'.[6]

Budkevich and the Moscow Trial

The diplomatic spat generated by the loss of the *Magneta* was minor in comparison to the international outrage which was provoked only a few weeks later by the Soviets' arrest of a number of leading Roman Catholic clerics, including Archbishop Jan Cieplak, the leader of Russia's Catholics, and his Vicar-General, Monsignor Konstantin Budkevich.

The Bolshevik repression of the Catholic Church was as brutal as it had been towards other faiths and denominations. By 1926, 208 of the 473 Catholic priests in the church's three main jurisdictions in Russia had been shot; others were in prison and more than a third had fled the country. Of the 1,200 Catholic churches in Russia in 1917, only 50 were still functioning by 1935.[7] At Cieplak's trial in 1923, Nikolai Krylenko, the Soviet prosecutor, made little pretence of the real reason for the prosecution: 'The Catholic Church has always exploited the working classes', he declared in his summing up, before calling for the death penalty. 'No Pope in the Vatican can save you ... Your religion, I spit on it, as I do on all religions, on Orthodox, Jewish, Mohammedan, and the rest'.[8] Cieplak and Budkevich were sentenced to death while the other clergy were given long prison sentences.

The suppression of Cieplak and his associates had been ordered by Grigory Zinoviev, Lenin's close associate and the party boss in Cieplak's home city of Leningrad.* When the priests' sentences were announced, appeals for clemency came in from governments around the world. The British added their own voice to these, reminding the Soviets that 'the execution of the sentence cannot fail to produce throughout the civilised world a feeling of horror and indignation which the Russian government can hardly wish to invite'.[9] The Bolsheviks responded with insults:

Being an independent country and a sovereign state, [Russia] has the undeniable right of passing sentences in conformity with its own legislation on people breaking the law of the country, and that every attempt from outside to interfere with this right and to protect spies and traitors in Russia is an unfriendly act and a renewal of the intervention which has been successfully repulsed by the Russian people ... The representative of the Irish Republic in France, on the same subject, in asking for mercy on behalf of Cieplak, ... says that he is doing so 'in spite of the hypocritical intervention of the British Government, which is responsible for the assassination in cold blood of political prisoners in Ireland, where 14,000 men, women and young girls are treated in a barbarous and inhuman fashion in conformity with the will of Great Britain, while British control over cables prevents the civilised world from learning the horrible details of these atrocities.' If similar facts which have taken place under British rule in India and Egypt are taken into consideration, it is hardly possible to regard an appeal, in the name of humanity and sacredness of life, from the British government as very convincing.[10]

---

* In 1936, in a grim irony typical of many of the period, Krylenko would be in place as People's Commissar of Justice at the time of Zinoviev's own trial. Zinoviev was shot; Krylenko himself was shot just two years later.

Budkevich was shot on Easter Sunday, 1 April 1923, a calculated affront to the worldwide Christian community which was at that time praying for the priests' safety.* Cieplak was sentenced to ten years' solitary confinement. The fifteen other defendants were also sentenced to prison terms.†

British friends of the Soviets were in some confusion, defending the principle of the trial while pleading for leniency for the accused. But some did not even support the calls for mercy. The *Daily Herald*, now run by the Trades Union Congress (which finally had bailed out Lansbury and taken over the paper), defended both the trial *and* the sentence. World protests, it insisted, were driven not by humanity but by class prejudice:

> We are justified in demanding that, so long as the death penalty is inflicted, it shall be inflicted without respect of persons. We in this country have executed bishops, and even an archbishop, for treason. Why should there be such an outcry over the execution of this Russian Roman Catholic priest?
>
> He has been found guilty of treasonable correspondence with the enemy in war-time. He was executed for that. To call his execution an attack on religion is nonsensical. The Roman Catholic Church enjoys wider liberty under the Soviets than it ever had under the Tsar and the Holy Synod. But religious liberty does not anywhere include exemption from the law.
>
> Governments are not wont to protest against executions for treason ... Why do they protest now? They are not moved by humanity, but by class feeling. Governments of the older order – gentlemanly governments – may butcher as they will. But if a new kind of government punishes for high treason a man who was a gentleman, a priest and a monsignor, the cry of 'barbarism' goes up.[11]

---

* The precise time is not known. It was either late on Easter Saturday or in the early hours of Easter Sunday.

† Many clergy were sent to the gulag camps in the Solovetsky Islands. In 1937 most of those who had survived were taken to the Sandarmokh ravine, near Medvezhiegorsk, in Karelia, 150 miles north of Leningrad, where they were shot. Although the Sandarmokh killings took place throughout 1937, the greatest numbers slain were on 11 March and 12 August. 'Among the Catholic dead were Georgian Byzantine Bishop Batmalashvili, Armenian Bishop Karapetian, Sister Kamilla Krushenyckaya – one of the last [Catholic] nuns in the USSR – of Moscow, and 32 priests. They were joined in death by four Russian Orthodox bishops, Archbishops Damian of Kursk and Peter of Samara, and Bishops Nikolai of Tambov and Alexey of Voronezh.' The massacres also claimed the head of the Baptist Union, Moslem imams and over one thousand others. Zugger, *The Forgotten*, p. 259.

As the sentence on Budkevich was being carried out, the Soviets seized another British trawler, the *James Johnson*, off Murmansk. On 5 April they made two further attempts to arrest British ships while their naval protection vessel was refuelling. Both were unsuccessful.

The 'Curzon Ultimatum'

After only seven months in office, Bonar Law's health was failing. Increasingly absent from Cabinet meetings, he was finally forced to resign, which he did in May. He died on 30 October that same year. While Bonar Law had had some sympathy with Lloyd George's approach, his successor, Stanley Baldwin, was inclined to be much more robust. Besides, as Churchill had correctly predicted two years earlier, the trade agreement had brought no substantial trade to Britain.[12] There was little to lose.

The contempt in the Soviet reply to the British appeal on behalf of Cieplak and his colleagues, the attacks against British fishing vessels, and reports of increasing subversion all stretched the government's patience to its limit. With his Indian experience, Curzon understood full well the implication of the reports coming into the Foreign Office of hostile Soviet action in the empire, and pressed for action to be taken. In Baldwin, he found a receptive listener.

On 2 May 1923, with the Cabinet's full support, he issued the strongest protest yet to Moscow, soon known as the 'Curzon Ultimatum':

His Majesty's Government [cannot] with due self-respect continue to ignore the repeated challenges which the Soviet Government has thought fit with apparent deliberation to throw down. ... [The trade agreement] has from the start been consistently and flagrantly violated by the Soviet Government...

[Although for a while propaganda was lessened] more recently these pernicious activities have been vigorously resumed. It would be easy to fill many pages with a narrative of these proceedings resting upon an impeachable authority. Such a narrative would doubtless provoke, as it did before, an indignant denial from the Soviet Government with allegations as to false information and spurious documents. His Majesty's Government have no intention to embark upon any such controversy. They are content to rely exclusively upon communications which have passed in the last few months between the Russian Government and its agents, and which are in their possession...

The ultimatum then detailed a number of examples of propaganda and hostile action overseas. These included details of deliveries of weapons and money to anti-British groups in Afghanistan, and extensive activity by the Soviet mission in Persia to foster anti-British intrigue in India. But most incriminating of all was evidence which directly implicated the London Trade Delegation in the financing of Indian subversion:

> A number of Bank Notes of £100 each, issued through Lloyd's Bank and the Russian Commercial and Industrial Bank in London to Nikolai Klishko ... were cashed in India on behalf of a revolutionary Panjabi in touch with other Indian seditionaries who are known to have been closely associated with the Russian representative in Kabul. ... It is [further known that] the sums of £80,000 and £120,000 were allotted to the British and Indian Communist parties respectively [by the Third International].

Religious persecution

In the context of the events discussed later in this book, the directness of the Curzon/Baldwin Cabinet's protest about the persecution of religious believers is most notable. In 1929–31, the Labour government refused to raise any but the most muted token complaint at the widespread arrest of clerics and religious believers, hiding behind the Soviets' insistence that these were internal matters over which the British had no right to interfere. The same defence was raised by the Bolsheviks in 1923, but the Conservatives, even allowing for the niceties of diplomatic correspondence, would have none of it:

> *Return of notes relating to religious persecution.*
>
> In July 1922 the Metropolitan Benjamin of Petrograd and ten other priests were tried and condemned to death, and, it is believed, executed for opposing the confiscation of church property. At the end of March 1923 Archbishop Cieplak and Monsignor Butkevitch were condemned, the former to ten years' solitary confinement and the latter to death, the sentences being duly carried out...
>
> His Majesty's Government have refrained from expressing an opinion upon the nature or validity of the charges brought against these ecclesiastics, conceiving that that is a matter on which they are not called to pronounce.

No attempt, however, is made in Russia itself to deny that these prosecutions and executions are part of a deliberate campaign undertaken by the Soviet Government, with the definite object of destroying all religion in Russia, and enthroning the image of godlessness in its place. As such they have excited the profound consternation and have provoked the indignant remonstrance of the civilised world. It was in sympathy with this outburst of the affronted moral sentiment of mankind that on 30 March the British representative at Moscow, acting under the instructions from His Majesty's Government, approached M. Chicherin with a 'submission that the execution of the sentence cannot fail to produce throughout the civilised world a feeling of horror and indignation which the Russian Government can hardly wish to invite' and 'with an earnest and final appeal to that Government for a stay of execution.'

On the following day Mr Hodgson received a reply from M. Weinstein claiming the undeniable right of Russia to pass sentences in conformity with its own laws, and declaring that 'every attempt from outside to interfere with this right and to protect spies and traitors in Russia is an unfriendly act.' Further, M. Weinstein proceeded in the same letter to make an irrelevant and insulting reference to a communication received by M. Chicherin from the alleged representative of a so-called Irish Republic in France. This note was at once and rightly returned by Mr Hodgson … On 4th April Mr Hodgson received a further reply from M. Weinstein couched in terms even more offensive.

This is only the latest incident in a long series of studied affronts which have been recorded in this memorandum, [and] it seems difficult to arrive at any other conclusion than that the Soviet Government are either convinced that his Majesty's Government will accept any insult sooner than break with Soviet Russia, or that they desire themselves to bring the relations created by the trade agreement to an end.

It is not possible for [the British Government] to acquiesce in a continuance of the treatment that has been summarised in this memorandum and which is incompatible alike with national dignity and with mutual respect.[13]

The ultimatum demanded that all the propaganda and hostile action detailed in the memorandum cease, that the Soviet government release the British ships which had been seized, and that the insulting replies sent to London in response to their appeal on behalf of the Catholic clerics be 'unequivocally withdrawn'.* This time, they meant it. The Russians were given ten days to comply and were told that if they did not, the British mission in Moscow would be withdrawn and the Russian Trade Delegation sent home from London.

The Soviets came back with the usual denials and counter-accusations, but the seizure of yet another British trawler, the *Lord Astor*, strengthened the Cabinet's resolve still further. Within a month, the Soviets had given in on all but some minor face-saving points.[14] The forthrightness that Churchill and Curzon had urged from the beginning was now shown to be the only approach which would produce results. It was a marker for the future. The expulsions which followed the Arcos affair in 1927, and the suspension of trade after the arrest of the Metropolitan-Vickers engineers in 1933 (both bitterly opposed by Russia's British friends) followed the precedent set by Curzon's 1923 ultimatum (see Chapters 8 and 35). By contrast, Lloyd George's optimism and MacDonald's naïveté were, like Neville Chamberlain's appeasement of Hitler, a triumph of hope over reality, and doomed to failure.

---

* A further demand was added for compensation for the widow of a British man shot by the Bolsheviks in Petrograd in 1920, and for a Canadian female journalist falsely detained and only released after a harrowing time in prison.

CHAPTER 7

THE RISE AND SWIFT FALL OF THE FIRST LABOUR GOVERNMENT (1924)

The pompous folly of standing aloof from the Russian Government will be ended – ended, not because we agree with what the Russian Government has done. That is not our business.

RAMSAY MACDONALD[1]

Given Britain's imperial prominence, Baldwin's determination to stand up to Moscow could have set the tone for a determined international response to the Soviets' overseas ambitions, of which the British were not the only victims. It would have been a propitious time to trim Moscow's sails: Lenin had been incapacitated by a stroke in 1922 and died in January 1924. Internal difficulties increasingly preoccupied the remaining Bolshevik leadership and weakened their ability to sustain their destabilisation of other nations abroad. A number of attempted communist coups in Europe had failed and been brutally suppressed. The predicted uprising of the international proletariat and overthrow of worldwide capitalism had not happened. Back in Russia, an alternative doctrine of 'Socialism in one country' was being developed to cover up for the failure of the spread of worldwide revolution. One of its central principles, which Stalin was to elaborate on in a later speech to the party Central Committee, concerned the duty of socialists everywhere to support the USSR while it developed Socialism: 'An internationalist is one who is ready to defend the USSR without reservation, without wavering,

unconditionally; for the USSR it is the base of the world revolutionary movement, and this revolutionary movement cannot be defended and promoted
without defending the USSR'.[2]

Baldwin, with the support of Curzon, might have led the way, but at that
moment he made a big political miscalculation, calling an unnecessary general election at the end of 1923. The Conservatives lost their majority and
the election resulted in a hung parliament. The Conservatives took 258 seats,
the Liberals 158, and Labour, in their most successful election to date, came
second with 191 seats. H. H. Asquith, the Liberal leader, offered his support
to Ramsay MacDonald, and Britain's first Labour government took office.

The new government would take a wholly different perspective on Russia.
Lloyd George saw Bolshevism as a threat and hoped that trade would emas-
culate it; Baldwin agreed with his verdict but confronted it; MacDonald
believed its aims were fundamentally benign and tried to befriend it. Whereas his predecessors had sought to curb its influence in Britain, MacDonald
instead suspended the Home Office monthly intelligence reports to Cabinet
on revolutionary activity in Britain, sniping that the right-wing *Morning Post*
merited just as much examination.

For Churchill, a Liberal for over twenty years, Asquith's support for a So-
viet-friendly Labour administration was anathema. He was so appalled that
he cut loose from the party for good and stood in a subsequent by-election
as an independent 'Constitutionalist and Anti-Socialist', before finally joining the Conservatives, the party he was eventually to lead. Asquith's gamble
was to backfire disastrously: in the next election the Liberals lost two thirds
of their seats to the Conservatives and they have never formed a majority
government since.

The arrival in Downing Street of Ramsay MacDonald as Britain's first
Labour Prime Minister was a momentous occasion for British Socialists. A
euphoric George Lansbury told a post-election meeting that they now had the
chance to lead the country 'from the inferno of capitalism to the cooperative
commonwealth'.[3] Although the election took place on 6 December 1923, it
was not until 21 January that Baldwin, unable to command a majority in the
Commons, was forced to resign. Domestic concerns were naturally Labour's
greatest priority, but MacDonald, who had appointed himself Foreign Secretary in addition to his duties a Prime Minister, acted quickly on Russia.

Ten days later, even before Parliament could reassemble to oppose such a step, MacDonald granted full legal ('de jure') recognition to the Soviet government.

Correspondence between Christian Rakovsky, Krasin's successor at the Russian Trade Delegation, and Chicherin, in Moscow, shows that Frank Wise, once again with the ear of a British Prime Minister, had been at the centre of it. Wise, now on the Soviet payroll, had persuaded someone dubbed 'X' in the cables to grant immediate and unconditional recognition to the Soviet government. 'X' had asked for his identity to be kept out of all correspondence so that news of his meeting with Rakovsky would remain secret. Historian Victor Madeira has identified 'X' as none other than Ramsay MacDonald.[4] Records show that at MacDonald's behest Rakovsky and Wise had even drawn up the actual terms of the recognition agreement.

The *Daily Herald* was ecstatic, declaring it 'a triumph for International Labour', before going on to praise the contribution of Frank Wise (in his earlier public role, unaware of the part he had just played in more current events), concluding by 'paying tribute to the work of Mr. Coates and his fellows of the "Hands Off Russia" Committee'.[5] Amidst a flurry of self-congratulation the 'Hands Off Russia' Committee, its first task now completed, gave itself a new identity as the official-sounding 'Anglo-Russian Parliamentary Committee'.

Wise had arranged with MacDonald that the next step would be to set up an Anglo-Soviet Commission to discuss all the outstanding debt and political issues between the two countries. The Soviet delegation arrived in April, and fractious discussions progressed through the summer. The Russians did not enamour themselves to MacDonald, but by September 1924 a deal, part of which included granting Russia a substantial loan, was ready to put to Parliament. When the House of Commons baulked at the size of the loan and the lack of security offered by the Soviets, MacDonald refused to back down on that part of the agreement. The stage was set for a showdown in Parliament at the very moment when another scandal broke and took the Government down.

The government falls (the Campbell case)

The reasons for the fall of the Labour government in October 1924 have largely been obscured by the controversy that surrounded the publication of the 'Zinoviev letter' in the general election that was called as a result of its collapse. The idea persists that an innocent Labour government was brought down by what was, in all probability, a forgery put out by monarchist Russian exiles. In reality, the cause was very different – and Labour's hands in the matter were not entirely clean.

John Ross Campbell was a Glaswegian communist. After three years as editor of a Clyde radical paper called *The Worker*, he came to London in 1924 and, in July of that year, became acting editor of the CPGB's *Workers' Weekly*. On 25 July, *Workers' Weekly* carried a call to those serving the British Armed Forces to mutiny:

> Soldiers, sailors, airmen, flesh of our flesh, and bone of our bone, the Communist Party calls upon you to begin the task of not only organising passive resistance when war is declared, or when an industrial dispute involves you, but to definitely and categorically let it be known that neither in the class war nor in a military war will you turn your guns on your fellow workers, but instead will line up with your fellow workers in an attack upon the exploiters and capitalists and will use your arms on the side of your own class.
>
> Form committees in every barracks, aerodrome, and ship. Let this be the nucleus of an organisation that will prepare the whole of the soldiers, sailors, and airmen not merely to refuse to go to war, or to refuse to shoot strikers during industrial conflicts, but will make it possible for the workers, peasants and soldiers, sailors and airmen to go forward in a common attack upon the capitalists and smash capitalism for ever and institute the reign of the whole working class ... Turn your weapons on your oppressors.[6]

The Director of Public Prosecutions consulted Sir Patrick Hastings, the Attorney-General (the Labour government's law officer), about the article and Hastings confirmed that it constituted a breach of the law. Campbell was arrested and appeared in court on 6 August, charged under the Incitement to Mutiny Act, 1797, with having 'feloniously, maliciously and advisedly endeavoured to seduce divers persons unknown, then serving in His Majesty's Navy, Army, and Air Force, from their allegiance to His Majesty'.[7] He was released on bail, the surety of £100 each being put up by Edgar Lansbury, George Lansbury's son and member of the CPGB Central Committee, and

Alex Gossip, the general secretary of the National Amalgamated Furnishing Trades Association and a member of the ARPC.

That evening, prompted by the alarming way in which events were developing, the matter was raised in Cabinet.[8] The Cabinet were in no doubt that the article was seditious: Henderson called it 'criminal'; Stephen Walsh, the Secretary of State for War, under whom the servicemen to whom it was addressed served, called it 'atrocious', the 'worst article I've ever read' and recommended the prosecution go ahead. But then other members rounded on the Attorney-General. Lord Parmoor blamed Hastings for not having consulted the Prime Minister before going ahead with the prosecution. Even though Hastings repeatedly defended his position, saying it was an 'exceptionally bad case', J. H. Thomas agreed with Parmoor and, as the conversation widened, Thomas put a motion before the meeting that 'no prosecution of a political character take place without the prior sanction of cabinet'. It was passed unanimously.

Hastings then offered MacDonald a way out: 'Inasmuch as it transpired that the person charged was only acting temporarily as editor and was prepared to write a letter to that effect, steps could be taken not to press the prosecution in the circumstances against this particular offender, *if the cabinet so desired*'. (My italics.) The minutes concluded with the record that the Cabinet agreed 'that in the particular case under review the course indicated by the Attorney-General should be adopted'. It amounted to political interference in a criminal prosecution. Thomas remarked at the close of the meeting 'the real fight will start two months hence' (Parliament was then in the middle of the summer recess). He was right. It did.

In a highly unusual move, MacDonald later challenged Sir Maurice Hankey, the Cabinet Secretary, over the accuracy of the Cabinet minutes for the 6 August meeting. He insisted that a correction be added,[9] but when the case next came up in court, on 14 August, the action taken was consistent with Hankey's original text. The barrister appearing for the Director of Public Prosecutions (DPP) withdrew the charges, stating that it had not been known at the time that Campbell was only the temporary editor, that the article was copied from another journal (in other words, that Campbell was hardly responsible for it) and that he was otherwise a young man of 'excellent character'. The barrister continued that 'it has been represented that the object and intention of the article in question was not to endeavour to seduce men in the fighting forces from their duty and allegiance, but that it was a comment upon armed military force being used by the State for the suppression of industrial disputes'. The charges were dropped. Campbell walked free from the court.

It was far from over. The CPGB, which had no love for the MacDonald administration, began mischief-making at once. It disavowed the DPP's statement: the CPGB had made no such 'representation', its spokesman said, and it had not come from them. They had planned to fight the case and subpoena MacDonald, Henderson and J. R. Clynes to appear for the *defence*, having amassed quotes from speeches and articles by them which they alleged supported their views. They went on to claim that this 'victory for the workers' had come about because of pressure by Labour supporters such as George Lansbury (who had offered to give evidence in Campbell's defence) and James Maxton.

Ramsay MacDonald's minority administration was only kept in power due to the sufferance of the Liberals. Over the summer, the Liberals had begun to share the Conservatives' increasing alarm at MacDonald's plans to push through the new treaty with Russia, part of which would release British loans of £35–50 million to the Soviets on very little security and with only limited prospects of any substantial knock-on benefit to British exports. Increasingly speaking with one voice, the Liberals and Conservatives began systematically to dismantle Labour's defence of its conduct in the Campbell trial. The prosecuting barrister had told the judge that it had 'been represented' that the object of the article was less than had first appeared. The obvious question was: represented by whom? If the CPGB now denied their hand in it, was it the government? Had they interfered with a criminal prosecution? Was there any connection between the fact that the negotiations for the new Russian trade treaty had broken down just as the case was about to come to court? Was the government trying to avoid upsetting the Soviets at the very moment that they were trying to bring them back to the negotiating table?

As for the implication that Campbell, 'a young man of excellent character', was virtually an innocent bystander, facts soon appeared which told a very different story – and the truth of Campbell's significance within the Communist movement both at home and internationally became apparent: he was British secretary of the Red International, an organisation established by the Comintern to coordinate international communist trade union activity, and had travelled to Moscow in June of the previous year as a delegate to the Red International conference. He was important enough to have been proposed as a CPGB parliamentary candidate in the January election.[10] He was not new to radical journalism either, and he had been editor of a similar communist paper in Scotland, *The Worker*, for three years – so was hardly inexperienced.[11]

And then there was the most obvious discrepancy of all: how could a call to servicemen '*not merely* to refuse to go to war, or to refuse to shoot strikers during industrial conflicts' (my italics) but to 'turn your weapons on your oppressors' really be presented in court as only a 'comment upon armed military force being used by the state for the suppression of industrial disputes'? Now that Cabinet records for the period are open, we can see that even members of the Labour government did not take that view.

One of the central principles of the British constitutional and legal system is the separation of the executive (the government) from the judiciary. As *The Times* put it, when discussing the case:

> The most valuable and dearly prized of our liberties [are] the purity of the administration of justice and the equality of all before the law. [They have been] the rights of British citizenship, hardly and slowly acquired after generations of persistent and resolute effort. They are our proudest boast; they have been the admiration and special envy of all other civilised peoples; they are the bulwark of all other rights, and particularly of those least able to defend themselves.[12]

The government now stood accused of halting, for its own political advantage, the criminal prosecution of someone who seemed to be guilty of sedition. In spite of the vigorous denials it issued at the time, the minutes of the Cabinet meeting on 6 August show clearly that this was *exactly* what it intended to do – and, indeed, passed a motion to ensure it would do so in the future, too.

The matter came to a head in Parliament on 8 October 1924.[13] The Conservatives had put down a motion to censure the government. The Liberals were not minded to topple the government and called only for an inquiry. The Cabinet were determined to resist even the latter, insisting among themselves that it could not 'put the honour of the Government in the hands of

a partisan [select] committee composed of seven opponents on the government and only three supporters', a fine-sounding defence whose hollowness
became apparent when, later in the same meeting, Hastings's suggestion that
the government should offer 'some less partisan form of alternative inquiry
by a Royal Commission, by the Judicial Committee of the Privy Council, or
by a Judge' (which would have at least partially cleared him) was dismissed.
He was so bitter about this that he asked for his dissent to their refusal to be
recorded in the minutes.

In a later biography which made extensive use of his papers, Hastings is
said to have insisted that he had been pressured by MacDonald to take the full
blame and save the government. In return, MacDonald offered that he and
other ministers would come to speak for Hastings in his constituency at the
next election.[14] It did not save them. The Conservative censure motion failed,
but the Liberal motion to appoint an inquiry was successful. In his final plea
to MacDonald to let the inquiry go ahead, Sir John Simon for the Liberals
voiced his incredulity at MacDonald's intransigence:

> I do not in the least care how such a tribunal is composed. I do not make the
> slightest attempt to put the Government at a disadvantage or in a minority, but
> I know this, that if, indeed, the proposal for a fair and impartial inquiry in some
> form or other is resisted by this Government, then it is not because this is an
> issue which is adequate for a General Election, but it is because the Govern-
> ment, if they were to resist such an inquiry, would be in the position of the man
> who is asked to produce a document from his desk but prefers to burn down
> his house rather than produce it. Whether it is a man or a Government that
> does that, it is equally obvious in either case that they have something to hide.

MacDonald chose to burn his house down. The Labour government resigned
rather than be subject even to an independent inquiry. A general election was
called for 29 October 1924.

The Zinoviev letter

Just four days before the election, the *Daily Mail* published a letter purporting to be from Grigory Zinoviev of the Comintern, containing a call for the
agitation of the British proletariat in preparation for revolution.[15] There is

reasonable cause to believe that the letter was forged by White Russian émi-grés. To Labour supporters, the notorious 'Red Letter' was responsible for toppling the first Labour government, and was evidence that no depths were too low for capitalists to employ in their efforts to destroy Socialism. It fur-ther cemented the place of the *Daily Mail*, which published the letter, at the head of that pantheon of villains. Undoubtedly, the right welcomed it without searching too far into its origins, but for both right and left the letter and the affair which followed only confirmed their preconceptions about each other.

Labour had been in an extremely precarious position. It led a minority government, holding fewer seats than its Conservative opposition, and had only been put in power by the Liberals when Asquith refused to join Baldwin in a coalition after the December 1923 election. It had never been likely to last long, and in fact gained votes at the subsequent election – up from 4.2 million in 1923 to 5.2 million in 1924.[16]

What brought Labour down in 1924 was its interference in the process of a criminal prosecution and its decision to lose power rather than have it exposed by an impartial inquiry. Labour was not a victim of assassination by forces of the right so much as brought down by an act of political suicide. And what lost it the subsequent election was not the letter, but the desertion of two million Liberal supporters who went over to the Conservatives. Mac-Donald, with or without the 'Red Letter', never stood a chance of getting back into power.

While historians agree with that assessment,[17] the urban myth persists that it was the combined skulduggery of MI5 and the *Daily Mail* that brought down the Labour government.[18] Such an assertion is not made any truer by its constant repetition over the ensuing decades. Moreover, though it probably was a forgery, the contents of the letter differed *so little* from the reality of Comintern sentiment, that Moscow initially took it at face value and sent a stiff reprimand to the London office of the CPGB for handling such contro-versial material so carelessly,* a fact missed by a number of Labour histori-ans and commentators today.[19] Even the Labour Party's official account of

---

* Aino Kuusinen, the wife of Otto Kuusinen, president of the Comintern, who was working in the Moscow Comintern headquarters at the time, also tells of how Comintern files were hastily cleansed of incriminating information before the TUC delegation came to inspect them. The deception worked and the delegation reported back that the Comintern were innocent of any malign intent towards Britain. Aino Kuusinen, *Before and After Stalin* (London: Michael Joseph, 1974), p. 51.

the affair contains inaccuracies which perpetuate the myth, such as that the letter 'alleged there were links between Russian Communists and the British Labour Party'.[20] Their narrative implies that the letter played a part in Labour's subsequent defeat ('With an atmosphere of fervent anti-Communism, Labour lost 40 seats and the Tories were returned to power') and yet we know that the Labour vote held up. It was the Liberal vote that collapsed.

Furthermore, the letter only appeared to confirm links between Moscow and the CPGB (of which British intelligence was already fully aware), *not* the Labour Party. It was scathing about the Labour leadership, calling them 'leading [puppet] strings of the bourgeoisie' and dubbed Labour's foreign policy an 'inferior copy' of the Conservatives'. It accurately stated that there was a 'group in the Labour Party sympathising with the [Anglo-Soviet commercial] Treaty', but that was hardly controversial; even Liberals supported closer trading links with Russia.

The letter's instruction to the CPGB to agitate for 'armed insurrection' would have been scandalous if it had been unique, but the events that had led to the fall of the MacDonald government began with a *genuine* appeal by J. R. Campbell for members of the Armed Forces to do just that. The year before, Cecil Malone had been imprisoned for expressing the same sentiments in the Albert Hall. The letter called for the leadership of the 'British Red Army' to be strengthened; Malone's trial heard of his involvement in just that enterprise.

Moscow's aggression towards British interests abroad was also beyond dispute: the Conservative Cabinet had heard evidence only twelve months earlier of widespread attempts to provoke an uprising against the British in India, and of Stalin's call for the 'destruction' of the British Empire in order to hasten the overthrow of the 'capitalist order in Europe'.[21]

We now also know that the year after the 'Red Letter' scandal, Stalin concluded a secret agreement with the IRA according to which Russia provided the bulk of their funding so that they could continue their campaign against the British, more of which follows in Chapter 9.

Anti-socialists

Anti-socialists did not leave the pro-Soviet left a clear field when it came to political agitation, and two organisations in particular rose up to challenge it.

The British Empire Union (BEU) had been founded in 1915, and the Middle Classes Union (renamed the National Citizens Union, NCU, in 1922) was founded in March 1919. By the early 1920s public alarm over strikes at home, revolution abroad, and fear of it in Britain, had reached considerable proportions. The BEU and NCU became the voices of public disquiet and acquired a strong following across the country. Their speakers drew large crowds and their publications were widely distributed; the BEU claimed that 25,000 had attended its meetings in 1924 and 150,000 leaflets had been distributed.[22] It became the 'leading anti-communist organisation in Britain by the mid-1920s',[23] and its petition to ban 'seditious and blasphemous teaching' by Communists to children in Communist and Socialist Sunday Schools (see Chapter 13) was signed by an astonishing total of over seven million supporters.[24]

Hostility between the BEU/NCU and the British left was inevitable. G. D. H. Cole, branded the NCU as an 'auxiliary of the richer classes in the community against the manual workers'.[25] The ILP described them as 'a blackleg corps for fighting organised Labour, inspired and supported by Big Capital, though recruited mainly from the hirelings and hangers-on of capitalism'.[26] When strikers raised the red flag over Glasgow City Hall in January 1919, it was not an isolated incident, but one of many identical attempts by pro-Soviets to assert their dominance. BEU supporters resisted them wherever they could (such incidents were recorded at Edmonton and Croydon, for example[27]) but they were not always successful; 'outrage' was recorded when Communists managed to storm the platform at a BEU rally at Central Hall Westminster in October 1921 and tear up the Union Flag.[28]

The General Strike

In the years since the General Strike of 1926, it has acquired mythic status. Important though it was, it lasted just nine days and was a failure for its chief participant, the miners' union, the Miners' Federation of Great Britain (MFGB). In June 1925, high unemployment and an ongoing financial crisis led mine owners to give notice that they were going to cut wages and add an hour to each working day – drastic measures which were understandably rejected by the miners. When it looked as if wide sections of the trade union movement would support them in a strike, the government offered a temporary wage subsidy and a commission to review the matter. When that commission found in favour of the mine owners the following year, the TUC pledged its support to the miners and they went on strike on 3 May 1926.

In anticipation of the disruption a general strike might cause, the government had established the Organisation for the Maintenance of Supplies (OMS) the year before. The BEU and NCU had already been inspired by the example of Italian Fascists in their creation of a patriotic national citizens' force, capable of stepping in to fill the gap left by strikers, in order to keep essential services running during a major strike. Early on, both organisations came fully behind the OMS and their members made a major contribution when the strike came.

The fact that 'fascist' has become such a pejorative term should not mislead us in our assessment of the BEU and NCU and the nature of British 'fascism' in the mid-1920s, almost a decade before Oswald Mosley (who parted company with Labour, not the Conservatives, to set up his fascist party). As historians Ian Thomas and Thomas Linehan have shown,[29] many British people who called themselves 'fascists' in the 1920s initially thought of fascism as little more than a patriotic anti-Bolshevik 'predominantly middle-class defence force'. Indeed, when it became apparent that ideological Italian Fascism was much more than that, the NCU made it clear that it would have nothing to do with it:

> Although Mussolini certainly broke the Communist movement in Italy, the Fascist activity was entirely a lawless undertaking, accompanied by much bloodshed and even murder. Its tyranny would never appeal to Englishmen for long, and rightly so, on the principle that two wrongs never made a right. Further, the time for violence or harsh action has not arrived and probably never will, because the more reasonable methods of education, propaganda and debate will achieve the desired object in our country, and civil war or class murder will neither be tolerated nor necessary.[30]

Linehan identifies three marks of authentic fascism, in all of which the BEU and NCU failed to qualify: a leadership cult, a 'desire to overthrow the existing order and replace it with a new type of state based on the myth of a revitalised national community', and preparedness 'to embrace a culture of political violence'.[31] Thomas points out that, by contrast, 'the BEU and NCU saw their role primarily as defending the existing order and preventing its overthrow',[32] and in incidents such as the pitched battle to hoist the Union Jack rather than the red flag over Edmonton Town Hall, the violence grew out of the right's determination to *defend* its platform from left-wing attacks. He concludes: '"Fascism" in its British context thus centred on the defence of the Empire from those alien forces allegedly at work trying to undermine Britain's pre-eminence at home and abroad. Paramount among these forces was Bolshevism, which was widely believed to be behind both domestic industrial unrest and nationalist insurgency.'[33]

The strike fails

At least 1.5 million people came out on strike in May, and the strike was successful in closing mines, power stations, newspapers and the docks. But thanks to the OMS, supported by the BEU and NCU, its impact was blunted. The TUC, meanwhile, alarmed that the strike's failure might lessen its own future authority, entered into negotiations with the government. The miners refused to join those, and when the strike ended with the negotiating committee broadly accepting the original commission's recommendations, the miners stayed out on strike until November. The hardship among them was considerable. Recrimination within the Labour movement was bitter. Ramsay MacDonald condemned the use of the general strike as a 'clumsy and ineffectual' weapon.[34]

When Soviet miners (commonly assumed to be the Soviet government) donated £250,000 (£11 million today) to their British comrades, the British government formally complained at Russia's support of an 'illegal and unconstitutional act constituting a serious threat to established order'.[35] Mikhail Tomsky, Chair of the All Russian Central Council of Trade Unions, had been an honoured guest at the Congress in 1924 and 1925. Now, he bitterly criticised the TUC General Council's handling of the strike. As the wedge between British Labour and the Soviet government grew, a second offered Soviet donation of £26,000 (£1.1 million today) to the TUC was refused.

Political prisoners – the non-Bolshevik socialists

Amidst the warmth that the Labour movement expressed towards its socialist cousins in Russia, one unsettling fact kept surfacing: the Bolsheviks were not just pursuing counter-revolutionary monarchists and social parasites, something which could be overlooked as unfortunate but unavoidable; they were also rounding up non-Bolshevik socialists – Mensheviks, Social Revolutionaries and others. Some had undoubtedly been shot; many more were in prison. None of this fitted the narrative that the British left had persuaded itself to believe – that Lenin was a benign character who had tried to keep violence to a minimum, and that the Russian Revolution was one of all socialists against the forces of monarchist tyranny. How could socialists now be the enemy?

It was all the harder to process because many Labour men and women had emotionally invested so heavily in the belief that Socialism was the answer to mankind's problems and that Soviet Russia was providing the evidence which proved it. So strong was that psychological investment, and so reinforced was it by the mutual self-persuasion of fellow party members and the Labour press, that very few had the strength to abandon it. Bertrand Russell, George Orwell, and Malcolm Muggeridge (whose stance ended his job as the *Manchester Guardian*'s Moscow correspondent) were among those who did. For some, such as Ethel Snowden, disillusion set in quickly; for others, of whom Walter Citrine of the TUC was one, it grew over time.

Many preferred to believe that the repression of the non-Bolshevik socialists was an aberration from, rather than a manifestation of, Soviet Communism; or that they actually were closet counter-revolutionaries. When the revolutionaries turned upon their own, first with the overthrow of Kamenev, Zinoviev and Trotsky in 1927–28, and then in the show trials of the 1930s, counter-revolution was the official script which seemed to explain it all, and many in Britain found that to be a more attractive and much less troubling answer than the real one. For many on the left, reality would not dawn until the late 1930s.

In the post-revolutionary years, the subject perplexed many. At the 1922 Labour Party conference, an emergency resolution was carried in response to the threat of executions of these socialists. It condemned 'the harsh and unjust treatment of Russian Social Revolutionary prisoners by the Government of Russia', regarding the situation 'as nothing short of scandalous' and warned that 'the execution of any of these comrades would be an outrage to the working-class sense of justice, and a tragedy which Socialist and Labour supporters could only remember with shame and horror'.[36]

The following year, conference again voiced its opposition to the persecution, but the resolution began with a statement of support which illustrated the conflicted feelings within the party:

> The Congress considers it to be the duty of the world's workers to combat with all their strength the endeavours by the imperialist powers to intervene in the home affairs of Russia or to cause a fresh civil war in that country. Therefore, in the name of millions of Socialist proletarians which support it, and in the interest of the Russian, as well as the entire international working classes, the Congress declares that it opposes the violent intervention of imperialism by the moral intervention of the international proletariat.

Conference then counter-balanced this with a plea on behalf of the persecuted:

> In order to preserve Russia as a support for the Revolution, and to prevent it becoming a focus of the international reaction, the Congress supports the following demands to the Soviet government (which calls itself a workers' government)
>
> (1) the immediate cessation of the outrageous persecution of Socialists and workers of different opinions in Russia and in those parts of Georgia occupied by Russian troops, immediate release of all such persons as have been convicted, condemned or exiled for the propaganda of their political convictions.
>
> (2) complete abandonment of the system of terroristic party dictatorship and the adoption of a regime of political freedom and democratic self-government of the people.
>
> The Congress expresses to the Socialist victims of Bolshevist terror in Russia and Georgia its warmest sympathy and declares it to be the duty of all affiliated Labour and Socialist Parties to give every moral and material support to all those Russian Socialists who work in the spirit of this resolution.[37]

These appeals achieved nothing; the Bolsheviks' repression of all opposition continued unchecked. In September 1924, the TUC received a plea on behalf of over a hundred Mensheviks held on the Solovetsky Islands, who were now on hunger strike. A joint TUC/ILP/Labour Party delegation (Fred Bramley, C. T. Cramp, William Gillies and Fenner Brockway of the ILP) went to see Jan Berzin, now secretary to the Soviet chargé d'affaires. They were met in this and subsequent exchanges with assorted denials, admissions and contradictions and, finally, an assurance that the prisoners were well-clothed, fed and warm and that there was no cause for concern.[38]

The matter was again raised at the October 1924 Labour Party conference. Unlike in 1922, the hostility was absent. The tone was understanding and conciliatory and reflected the only interpretation of events that Britain's Soviet friends could hold without abandoning their belief in the Bolshevik project, expressing:

Appreciation of the conditions under which the Soviet Government was obliged to maintain its existence in the past, and their recognition of the fact that during a period of civil war the civil and political rights of the individual were inevitably interfered with or even suspended; and further ... the hope that normal conditions are now being established in the internal life of the Russian people and, in particular, that very soon there will be opportunities for free and unfettered expression of the minority thought within the working class and Socialist movement.[39]

When one delegate complained that even this mild admonishment was 'a gross and unwarrantable interference with the affairs of the Russian government', Robert Williams, replying on behalf of the Executive, replied that, 'for their friend to describe this as an attack on the Russian regime was a figment of his imagination'.[40] Things were getting back on course.

The following month, an official British trade union delegation visited Russia. While avowing that they were unprejudiced, even critical, observers, the delegation, wanting to believe the best of their charming hosts, were out-manoeuvred and duped. The delegates praised the Soviet system for providing greater religious liberty than in many European countries',[41] assuring the readers of their report afterwards that 'there appears to have been no actual persecution of the clergy as such, but those who have thought fit to take political action against the State have met with exactly the same treatment as any other political agitator who infringes State regulations'.[42] At the very same time that their report was being finalised, the Orthodox Patriarch Tikhon told a visitor that, 'according to the best information he could obtain', about a hundred bishops and 10,000 priests were in prison or exile.[43]

The plight of the prisoners in the Solovetsky Islands concentration camps was obviously a topical issue. The delegation asked to be able to visit Solovki and were pleased to report that their suggestion 'met with no opposition'. It cost the Russians nothing to be so amenable, for, as the delegates added in their next sentence, 'it was found to be a season at which the island was inaccessible' and they were invited to return another time to visit the camp. Instead, they were taken to meet some opposition Socialist leaders held in Butyrka prison in Moscow. There they concluded that the prisoners were held in conditions that were 'as good as those of first-class misdemeanants in England', and reported that prisoners themselves said that their conditions were better than they would have been in Tsarist times. The impression that the visitors took away was that they were quite comfortable. Apparently their only difficulty was they could get nothing but 'bourgeois' foreign papers, not international Labour ones. The British put in a plea for this on their behalf and were assured it would be attended to.

But they offered the prisoners no other support. The Soviets had defended the socialists' imprisonment on the grounds that if they were released, there was a likelihood of bloodshed. Tragically, the British trade unionists took this smokescreen at face value. When the prisoners told them that they would not agree to restrictions on their liberty if they were released, 'the Delegation did not feel, in the circumstances, that it could take the responsibility of pressing for the release of such irreconcilables'.[44] The most that they were prepared to do was recommend that the Soviets send them into exile, the standard punishment for political opponents in hated Tsarist times, rather than set them free.[45] It was a bizarre outcome, but one that could only be explained by the inverted reasoning on repression which foreign supporters now had to adopt if they were to keep intact their faith in Soviet Communism. Gulag memoirs abound with the same phenomenon – devout Communists on their way to the camps or execution still insisting that if only Stalin himself knew of their plight the mistake would be remedied and they would be set free.

The report's conclusion summed up these mental gymnastics well: the great successes achieved by the Bolshevik government had 'reconciled all but a very small minority to renouncing the rights of opposition that are essential to political liberty elsewhere' and this position had been accepted by the populace (and, by inference, should be by British trade unionists) 'because these rights have been replaced by others of greater value'. Eight years later, G. D. H. Cole would imply his approval of just the same trade-off in a future British socialist state.[46]

A greater cause

The fact was that there was a greater cause on which Labour and the Soviets were united, and which demanded that their differences be put aside – world peace and liberation, phrases that were to become totemic for revolutionary socialists and those they influenced in the second half of the twentieth century. It was urgent, too. As A. B. Swales told delegates in his presidential address to the 1925 Trades Union Annual Congress in September, there were 'clear indications of a world movement rising in revolt and determined to shake off the shackles of wage slavery'.[47]

As the left saw it, the issues at stake were enormous. Convinced by Soviet scaremongering, they had persuaded themselves that the world stood at the brink of Armageddon. Some months earlier, in April 1925, Tomsky and a delegation of Soviet trade unionists had met with senior TUC figures to discuss mutual cooperation. In the end, their joint declaration went far beyond matters of trade union cooperation. It was both paranoid and Messianic in equal measure:

A new war, more terrible, more monstrous than anything known hitherto is being prepared. New weapons of destruction are being devised; the chemists and scientific thinkers of European countries are devoting their knowledge and skill to the task of inventing new weapons of torture and destruction for use not only against the soldier but also against the civilian ... So-called disarmament conferences are merely encouraging dangerous illusions. They are being used to deceive the workers and lull them into a sense of false security ...

There is but one power that can save mankind from being plunged into another catastrophe. There is but one power which can defend the workers of all countries against political and economic oppression and tyranny. There is but one power which can bring freedom, welfare, happiness and peace to the working class and to humanity. That power is the working class.[48]

Ben Tillett, Fred Bramley and A. A. Purcell were among the British signatories. All three had been in the delegation to Russia only a few months earlier. Tillett, who had just lost his seat as an MP and was to become president of the TUC and an MP once again in 1929, had been so enthused by his trip to Russia that he produced his own book of reflections.[49] He assured his readers that in Russia 'the whole administration of the law is humane [and] prison is more like a hospital than a place of detention'. Furthermore, he continued, 'religious, social and political freedom, with economic security is now established in Russia. Never before could the individual be free to worship as he chose'.[50] Tillett's book was published in March 1925. In May, just two months later, all 'servants of religious cults for whom this service is a profession' (clergy, monastics, mullahs etc.) were disenfranchised. This measure, stipulated in Article 69 of the Constitution of the Soviet Union not only banned them from voting (the least of their concerns) but, far more seriously, removed their entitlement to ration cards and other state benefits. This left them with no option but to renounce their vows and leave the priesthood.

Tillett's enthusiasm was unbounded, and in his final remarks he stretched poetic licence painfully to its limit:

Nothing like this Russian miracle of change and magic of adaptation was ever conceived by us in our wildest dreams and fancies. An oriental morning twilight has come to the long dark night of Russia's agony and crucifixion.

The Heaven's shaft of light that transfixed St Paul in fright and shock and illumination could not have been more appalling in its suddenness than this great change and conversion to high civilisation. Yet it has come.

Those of us who have hungered in our soul for a message, we have seen, we have heard the sights and sounds of the awakening of a vast conglomeration of tongues and nations aglow, alert, with a new zest for life.[51]

CHAPTER 8

LABOUR'S ROAD BACK
TO POWER (1927–29)

The Arcos raid

On 12 May 1927, under the authorisation of the Conservative Home Secretary, Sir William Joynson-Hicks, police raided 49 Moorgate in London, the building jointly occupied by the Soviet Trade Delegation and the All-Russian Co-operative Society, otherwise known as Arcos. An informer had told the police that the Russians had obtained a copy of a British military manual and the raid was launched to find it. Although it failed in that respect, it uncovered other incriminating material which confirmed that both organisations had been actively involved in espionage and subversion in Britain.[1]

Labour and the Soviets were close; on hearing of the raid, the Soviet chargé d'affaires, Arkady Rosengoltz, rushed to the House of Commons to consult with Arthur Henderson, the shadow Foreign Secretary. Labour and the unions immediately rallied to the Soviets' defence, vigorously condemning the government's action. While many Labour MPs and party members refused to believe that the Russians were guilty of any wrongdoing, some made it clear that, even if they were, their own support would be undiminished. James Maxton, the ILP leader, was one:

Let me leave the House under no delusions. My sympathies are absolutely with the ultimate aims and objects of the Russian Soviet Government. Make no doubt about it, that if their powers of propaganda in this country have been

injured in any way by this attack on the part of the British Government, I will
do my personal best to make up for it.

I believe that the capitalist system of society makes for nothing but poverty
and degradation. I believe that before there is a possibility of world peace, of
world comfort, of world security, capitalism has to be overthrown in every country in the world. I believe that most profoundly and most sincerely, and I will
work for it with all the power I possess ... The fact that these men stand for a
different social order, the fact that they push their propaganda for that new social
order in every corner of the globe, just as Great Britain preaches British Imperialism in every corner of the world, does not justify this action [the police raid].[2]

When the government announced that all Soviet diplomats and trade officials
were to be expelled, Labour MPs responded by organising a lunch in their
honour in the House of Commons. The gesture did not go unchallenged, but
Conservative MPs who found out about it were unable to prevent it taking place.

Among the fifty guests and hosts, there to express their solidarity with the
Soviets, were MPs James Maxton, Richard Wallhead (chairman of the ILP
1920–22), Arthur Greenwood (a minister in the 1931 Cabinet), Ellen Wilkinson
and R. A. Taylor. The trade unions' representation at the lunch could not have
been more solid: George Hicks, TUC president, presided over the lunch; also
present were Walter Citrine, General Secretary of the TUC 1925–46, as well as
past and future TUC presidents A. A. Purcell MP (1924), A. B. Swales (1925),
Ben Tillett (1929) and John Bromley MP (1932). Tillett had been an MP until
1924 and was returned to Parliament in 1929. Many of the same individuals
were also at Victoria Station a few days later, on 3 June, to bid farewell to the
chargé d'affaires. This time they were joined by Arthur Henderson, George
Lansbury (whose daughter Violet was then living in Moscow with a Russian
Communist Party official) and Robert Williams. Two years later, as Foreign
Secretary, Henderson was to reverse the expulsion and give full diplomatic
recognition to the Soviet Union. The 1929 treaty also carried a 'no propaganda'
clause which the new Soviet delegation just as consistently ignored.

Reprisals

After these expressions of support and respect from British Labour, it might
have been expected that Labour-Soviet relations (which had not been easy

since the collapse of the General Strike the previous year) would have remained on a friendly footing but it was not to be. A series of events, beginning with the assassination of a Soviet diplomat in Poland, were to place the relationship under severe strain.

On his way home, Rosengoltz stopped off at Warsaw railway station to consult with Pyotr Voikov, the Soviet ambassador. Voikov had been a leading Bolshevik in Yekaterinburg at the time of the execution there of the tsar and his family and he had been closely involved in the killings. For this reason, his appointment to Warsaw had been controversial. As Rosengoltz and Voikov returned to the railway carriage, a young Russian monarchist leapt out and shot Voikov six times. Voikov died shortly afterwards.

Bitterness over the Arcos expulsions, coupled with paranoia about a world conspiracy to overthrow Bolshevism, brought out the worst in the Kremlin. Two days later, on 9 June, in a savage and pointless reprisal, twenty former officers and members of the old aristocracy were taken from their cells in Leningrad and shot.[3] A number of them were accused of spying for Britain and planning the assassination of other Soviet diplomats abroad. On 10 July, twenty-five more 'British agents' were arrested.[4] Fantastically, one was accused of masterminding the Sofia Cathedral bombing in 1925 – which had actually been carried out by local Communists, reportedly under instructions from the Bulgarian communist Georgi Dimitrov, who took over the leadership of the Comintern a few months after the Arcos raid.[*]

By the end of July, there had been reports of over a hundred further executions around Russia.[5] On 30 August, another 'great trial' of British spies was announced, as a result of which nine more people were shot.[6] In a further trial in late September four more spies were condemned to death.[7] Five had been shot 'resisting arrest' before it began.

One of the most shocking of these reprisals was the execution of a 'Mme Kelpikov', the wife of an officer who had been shot a few weeks earlier for 'espionage in favour of England'. Kelpikov had been sentenced to death on 16 June, and his wife had been given a three-year prison term. The Soviet

---

[*] In 1925, in an attempt to assassinate the entire Bulgarian royal family and government, Bulgarian Communists planted a bomb in Sofia Cathedral. The Cathedral was almost destroyed and over 120 people were killed and 500 injured. In its primary aim it failed: all of the most important government targets survived or were absent. King Boris would have been present on the afternoon of his intended assassination, but was away attending another funeral.

authorities had then ordered her re-trial 'under conditions involving the death penalty'. She was executed a short while after the new sentence was announced on 12 July.[8]

When the verdicts of the first spy trial were carried out in mid-June, some Labour MPs rallied to the defence of the Soviet government, implying that, as the British embassy must employ spies, the charges could be valid.[9] A. J. Cook, the miners' leader, sending off a party of children of British Communists to Russia that summer ('every child of twelve in Russia knew twice as much as a child in this country,' he had said) still declared his support:

> I am proud of Russia, and I owe more allegiance to Russian workers than to Mr Baldwin and his government. The Labour Party and the trade union movement is out to do what Russia has done. It is not for me to say just how it will be accomplished, for the necessities of the moment will decide what action we shall take to achieve that end, but undoubtedly it will be accomplished.[10]

While Cook's enthusiasm for Soviet Communism in general was shared by many, disillusion over the Soviet response to the Arcos expulsions was beginning to spread. On 23 June, a joint committee of the TUC and Labour Party issued an official protest against the 9 June executions.

> While recognising the exceptional difficulties and dangers of the political situation in Russia, and fully appreciating the justifiable indignation of the Russian Government at the assassination of M. Voikoff, [the Labour Party and the TUC] feel obliged to protest against the policy avowedly adopted by the Soviet Government of executing persons innocent of the murder of M. Voikoff as a reprisal for murder.[11]

At this point, Labour-Soviet relations deteriorated. The CPGB, speaking as one with Moscow, condemned this statement as 'treachery to the workers' and 'sickening hypocrisy'.[12] Nikolai Bukharin added fuel to the fire by describing the British trade union leaders as 'treacherous rascals'.[13] Tomsky, who had been welcomed as an honoured guest at the TUC in 1924 and 1925, demanded a meeting with TUC president George Hicks and General Secretary Walter Citrine in Berlin. He was unrepentant over the executions and indignant at the protests. 'Instead of receiving co-operation from the [TUC] General Council', Tomsky complained, 'the Soviet workers received a telegram protesting against the shooting of enemies of the working class.'[14]

On 30 August the USSR Central Council of Trade Unions wrote to the TUC. It accused TUC leaders, led by 'traitors Thomas and his followers Hicks and Purcell' of crimes against the British working class, charging them with betrayal for not supporting the General Strike. On the trade unions' response to the Arcos raid, the Soviets insisted that the Tories had now 'begun openly to prepare war against the First Socialist State', and blamed the British unions for refusing to take adequate measures 'to avert the danger of a most frightful cruel and frankly counter-revolutionary war', presumably having expected them to call a general strike until the Russians had been allowed back.[15] This response was not only arrogant and delusional, but extremely short-sighted. Insulting British trade union leaders served only to unite them against the Soviet attacks. The disagreement suited the government well, and Joynson-Hicks's refusal to allow Tomsky a visa to attend the Edinburgh conference prevented any opportunity to heal the rift.[16]

The Soviet letter was discussed at the TUC conference in September and it did not go down well. As a report of the conference sent to the Cabinet observed, 'the Russians appeared utterly unable to conceive of any policy except their own ... and resorted to abuse and violent disagreement if other nations failed to accept their views'.[17] Even so, conference still accepted a motion from Harry Pollitt of the CPGB deploring the breaking off of diplomatic relations and instructing the General Council to press for a Commons Select Committee to investigate the matter. It was passed unanimously.

The Labour Party conference in September voted to cease its discussions with the Russian trade unions, but made it clear that the obstacle was the tactics of the Soviet Government, not their political ideals. J. R. Clynes insisted that 'the congress showed undiminished friendship for the people of Russia' and its 'resentment [was] at the impertinence of Russian leaders'.[18] On behalf of the ILP, James Maxton, George Lansbury, and Fenner Brockway telegraphed Alexei Rykov, chairman of the Council of People's Commissars of the USSR, appealing for the executions to be stopped. But even this appeal must be seen in the context of Lansbury's own article in the ILP's *New Leader*, published on the same day that Clynes addressed the Labour conference (Lansbury was chairman of the Labour Party at the time):

> The capitalist press is jubilant because after much harsh and useless talk the Trades Union Congress has suspended negotiations between itself and the Russian Trade Unions … It would be a mistake to imagine there is anything but goodwill in the minds of British workers toward their fellow workers in Russia … No matter what our views on tactics and policy may be, every Socialist and Labour man and woman in Britain and throughout the world will rejoice that in spite of enmity and hatred and the most venomous and vicious opposition, the Soviet Union has not only lasted till now, but is marching onward from strength to strength.[19]

Fenner Brockway, secretary of the ILP (who was to be elected to Parliament in 1929 and to become ILP chairman in 1931), declined to go to Moscow to join the celebrations of the tenth anniversary of the Revolution, but he supported a delegation of trade unionists who did, and the delegation was sent off in October by TUC General Council members Ben Tillett and A. J. Cook.[20] Brockway's open letter of 4 November 1927, also published in *New Leader*, leaves the reader in no doubt not only of where his sympathies lay but of his desire to be able to give the cause of Soviet Communism his wholehearted support:

> Dear Comrades, I greatly appreciate the invitation which the Society for Cultural Relations in Moscow has given me to visit Russia for the 10th anniversary of the establishment of the Soviet Republic. I wish I could come. You will be celebrating the greatest event in working class history. It would be an unforgettable privilege to be present.
>
> And yet I do not feel I can accept the invitation, any more than I have felt able to accept previous invitations to visit Russia as the guest of Soviet organisations. I think it best to state the reason frankly.
>
> You will not suspect me of lacking sympathy with Soviet Russia … I admire beyond measure your heroic achievements in building up the Workers' State despite the antagonism of Capitalist enemies on every side. It has been an epic of creative courage … There has not been a finer achievement in recorded human history.

But, still, I cannot accept your hospitality. The reason is this: I know that amidst all this triumph, there are hundreds of Socialists lingering in your prisons and exiled from civilisation, whose devotion to the working class, whose love of social justice and human freedom, has been proved by courage and sacrifice no less than yours...

I am glad that the working class delegation is on its way to Russia from Britain. When I found that its expenses were to be met by contributions from this country, I did not hesitate to associate myself with it. I hope someday to come to Russia under similar conditions. It is disagreeable and seemingly ungracious to reject friendly and generous invitations to come at your expense. But not even my admiration for your wonderful achievements, my realisation of the immense significance to the world of the maintenance of the Workers Republic for ten years, can close my ears to the cry of the Socialists in prison and exiles in Russia. I know what imprisonment means, and I cannot do other than associate myself with those who, for their convictions, are undergoing imprisonment now.

Fraternally yours,

Fenner Brockway[21]

In the same issue of *New Leader*, the ILP journal, which carried Brockway's letter to Rykov, James Maxton, the party's then chairman, could still write:

To build a Socialist Commonwealth out of the chaos left by war and the tyranny of the Tsar ... was a stupendous task, for the pre-war rule of Russia had left a huge mass of the Russian people illiterate ... To create out of these conditions a conscious working class, controlling its own political and economic destinies, was a giant's task; but when to these difficulties were added the bitter enmity of the other nations of the world, aiding counter-revolutionary plotters within, and the famine and pestilence which stalked the land, it is not an exaggeration to regard the men and women who carried on as lionhearted heroes, who deserve praise and honour from the people of the world...

The attainment of the 10th Anniversary of the revolution is a tremendous achievement ... Ungrudging praise and thanks goes out to the men and women, previously inexperienced and unskilled in the work of government, who have accomplished this task.[22]

These two pieces amply illustrate the tortuous path that Soviet Communism's British friends forced themselves to tread. A protest made in such meek terms by the secretary of the ILP while at the same time its chairman was describing the Bolsheviks as 'lionhearted heroes who deserve praise and honour from the people of the world' was hardly likely to be listened to. Indeed, it was not. Within a year or two, a selective amnesia seems to have stolen over the minds of many Soviet enthusiasts among the British left. Its protests died away even while the Russian socialists for whom they had spoken up remained in prison. It was to take ten more years before they finally spoke out, and by then most of those on whose behalf they had actually protested would be dead (see Chapter 34).

Nothing could dampen Lansbury's optimism for the great experiment. The following year, in his autobiography, he wrote in glowing terms of his meeting with Lenin in 1920:

> I have met all the men and women of my time considered great in the world of religion, literature, and politics: none compares with Lenin. He was a great man in every sense of the word ... I shall always esteem it the greatest event in my life that I was privileged to see this fine, simple, wise man and speak with him, learning from him how a human can occupy the leading position in a nation and yet remain simple, unaffected, and without personal pride.[23]

And in the same year of 1928, he gave the chairman's address at the Labour Party conference. On Russia, he was upbeat, condemning the Conservatives for breaking off relations with 'that great nation' as 'folly of the worst description', before continuing:

> It was Charles James Fox, 130 years ago, who said of the French Revolution: 'How much is it, by far, the greatest and best thing that has ever happened in the history of the world?' I would repeat those words today in reference to the great Russian Revolution which every one of us hailed with great enthusiasm.
>
> The fearful autocracy which ruled with an iron rod from the Baltic to the Black Sea and from the Volga to the Pacific, has gone never to return. Its influence, like that of Kaisers, has gone for ever. Because this is so we rejoice. The peasants and workers of that great nation, encircled by implacable foes

who unceasingly intrigue, conspire and work to restore the Czardom, need our sympathy and help, and we need theirs.

Labour when in power will again, as it did in 1924, hold out the hand of friendship to the people of Russia, and do all possible to establish mutually honourable, diplomatic and full trading relationships. It is easier, as Ramsay MacDonald has said, to discuss disagreements face-to-face than pelt each other with dispatches, theses, and manifestoes.[24]

CHAPTER 9

GUN-RUNNING AND MONEY LAUNDERING: THE LABOUR CONNECTION

Two discoveries (March 1928)

In 1925, a delegation from the IRA visited Moscow to appeal for Soviet financial support. In return, they offered to supply the Russians with intelligence about the British. While both sides viewed each other with a great deal of suspicion, a meeting with Stalin, then still just one among the group of Bolshevik leaders, resulted in a promise to the Irish of regular funding of £500 a month (£22,000 today). For the next two years this provided the bulk of the IRA's income and enabled it to rebuild after its defeat in the Irish Civil War two years earlier.[1]

Stalin became concerned that the British would find out about the deal and the Soviets' support was greatly reduced in late 1926. This so alarmed the IRA leadership that it sent senior members to meet Soviet intelligence officers in London to plead for the decision to be revoked. Though unsuccessful, they did manage to extract a single final payment of £1,000. This payment was made in May 1927, the same month that British police raided the Arcos building, an action which, the British left complained, was groundless and driven purely by anti-socialist prejudice. The IRA transactions were to remain secret until the fall of Communism.

The same year that the Irish first travelled to Moscow, 1925, British police raided the headquarters of the CPGB in King Street, Hammersmith. British intelligence already knew about Moscow's funding of the CPGB, though only in broad terms; the CPGB had even admitted it themselves. One of the documents seized confirmed the details, noting that in 1925 the party had been 'allocated' just over £16,000 (£877,400 today).[2] Half of their members were unemployed and paid no subscription; the other half did not pay anything like enough to amount to this. It must therefore have come from the Soviets; but how was the money finding its way from Moscow into CPGB hands in Britain?

The answer to that question was revealed by a fortuitous coincidence in March 1928, when Stalin's fears of discovery were realised. Three men were seen loitering near Goodge Street in central London, each carrying a brown paper parcel. When police approached them, they tried to escape, but were caught and arrested. Their parcels and a suitcase found in their lodgings were revealed to contain a total of thirty-five revolvers. The men were IRA gun-runners. But they were not only carrying weapons. At the time, British banks kept a note of the numbers of all bank notes they issued and, in many cases, the organisation or person to whom those notes were given. One of the IRA men had two bank notes in his possession which matched notes that had been obtained by the London branch of the Bank of Russian Trade (formerly named the Arcos Bank Ltd). The Moscow-IRA funding link had been uncovered.

News of the discovery leaked quickly. When questions were asked in Parliament on 19 April, Joynson-Hicks made it clear that he was quite satisfied that the notes were ones that could be traced back to the bank. Joynson-Hicks had already ordered a full inquiry, and further questions were forestalled by the government's announcement that it intended to publish material which gave more information about the employment of Soviet funds for subversive purposes in Britain.

In follow-up questions, Labour MPs attacked the government, seeking to deflect attention from the Soviets by accusing the Conservatives of impropriety and unwarranted suspicion. Hugh Dalton sought assurances that there would be 'no more interference with persons who are desirous of carrying on trade between this country and Russia for the benefit and employment of people in this country'; Labour 'red Clydesider' Tom Johnston and ILP MP Wilfred Paling both sought to smear the Conservative MP who had first raised the question, accusing him of improperly obtaining the information linking the gunmen to the bank notes. This question, which raised the link, constituted the first public exposure of the affair.[3] Joynson-Hicks, confident of the facts which his investigators had already uncovered, shrugged them all off.

These two discoveries – the details of the CPGB's funding and the IRA link to a Soviet-owned London bank – prompted further investigation. Over the next few months, police dug deeper into the affairs of the British branches of two Russian banks, the Bank for Russian Trade and the Moscow Narodny Bank. What they found was not only evidence of Soviet funding of subversion in Britain, but an uncomfortably close link with a man who was already, and would continue to be, an important member of the British Independent Labour Party, E. F. Wise.

Money laundering

Police investigation revealed a complex money laundering operation involving Russian banks and front companies in Berlin and London. Its aim was to convert Russian money into untraceable British currency. The scheme failed because the Soviets and their British associates were mistaken on the central idea on which the deception was based – that bank notes issued by the Bank of England could be traced by their number but that different notes issued by the Treasury could not.[*] In fact, the numbers on Treasury notes *were* recorded.

The police established that the IRA man's Treasury notes had passed through the Bank for Russian Trade in London and that they had been sent, by registered post, to a Soviet bank in Berlin on 9 November 1927. Though the subsequent movements of the two notes were unclear, they had turned up, four months later, back in London in the pocket of an IRA gun-runner.

As the inquiry widened, it revealed that two British employees of the London office of Centrosoyus, Frank Quelch and F. Priestley, had been responsible for depositing £16,000 in the London branch of the Moscow Narodny Bank (MNB). The deposits were made into the account of a Berlin-based engineering company, and the Soviet commercial attaché in Britain had the authority to make withdrawals from that account. The match between that sum and the £16,000 annual subsidy to the CPGB strongly hinted that the

---

* Treasury notes were issued between 1914 and 1928 and remained legal tender until 1933.

Berlin transfers were being used to hide the ultimate source of the CPGB's funds.

Though a number of bank messengers and employees had been involved, the central figures had been Quelch and Priestley, the two Centrosoyus employees, and W. B. Duncan, a clerk in the foreign exchange section of the MNB. Between them, they had laundered £27,998 in the ten months between 5 July 1927 and 20 April 1928. The police report said that their investigations left little doubt that 'the whole of this money found its way into the hands of Communist organisations in this country'.[4] The value of those transfers today would be around £1.6 million. The three men had proven Communist connections: Duncan was twenty-six years old, a clerk who had been with the bank for three years. He was a member of the Communist Party and his reference for the bank had been supplied by Andrew Rothstein. Priestley and Quelch were also known Communists; Quelch was sufficiently important to be chosen as one of the forty-eight members of the 'British Workers Delegation' which sailed to Russia on 29 October 1927 to attend the tenth anniversary celebrations of the Revolution in Moscow.[5] Furthermore, Quelch and Priestley had received some of their Bank of England notes from a third man, Squair, the treasurer of the London District Communist Party Committee, a known associate of Andrew Rothstein.

The Wise connection

When the Arcos raid took place on 12 May 1927, it was launched to find evidence that the Soviets were conducting subversion and espionage in Britain. The extent to which the documents obtained in that raid were incriminating has been disputed by some – usually Labour – historians, but affirmed by others.[6] When the raid took place, Labour protested vigorously that Soviet commercial operations in Britain had no involvement in Communist subversion. They were completely mistaken. The evidence uncovered by the police shows that over the ten months in question the laundering continued on a massive scale. Some of the money found its way into the hands of the IRA and it is not inconceivable that the two notes found in the gun-runner's possession were the remainder of a wad of Soviet-originating notes which had just been used to pay for the pistols.

By the summer of 1928, it was clear that the MNB was heavily involved in the money laundering. That, in turn, implicated Frank Wise. The exact timing of Wise's first association with the MNB is not entirely clear. He did co-author a book with a director of the bank which was published by the bank in 1926.[7] We know that he was described as 'a member of the Council' of the bank by 27 April 1928 and was present at two board meetings in May 1928.[8]

Ironically, in the aftermath of the Arcos raid, Wise had accompanied Arthur Henderson to see the Home Secretary William Joynson-Hicks in an attempt to limit the number of Russians included in a secondary list of expulsions. In a meeting on 26 July 1927, he rallied to the defence of the MNB board, assuring Joynson-Hicks that the directors of the bank 'would have been far too competent to allow any members of staff to engage in illegal activities', a protestation which the subsequent police investigation showed to be hardly credible. He similarly defended a director of Arcos, Litinsky, saying that he 'would stake his reputation that Litinsky was politically innocuous'.[9] Joynson-Hicks disagreed.

Wise had also been a director of the London branch of Centrosoyus since he had so controversially resigned from the civil service in 1923. There was a close link between Centrosoyus, Arcos and the MNB, too: Centrosoyus (Центросоюз) was the Russian acronym for the Central Union of Consumers' Co-operative Societies. Arcos was its English-language equivalent, the All-Russian Co-operative Society, established in Britain as a limited company in 1920, separate from its Russian parent. Even though the Moscow Narodny Bank London Ltd was, like Arcos Ltd, legally separate from its Russian counterpart, one of its shareholders was Centrosoyus.

Wise had therefore been a director since 1923 of a company which was a major shareholder in the Moscow Narodny Bank, as well as being on the council of the bank himself. In addition to being an employee of the Soviet Government, and through one or both of these firms reputedly earning a very handsome £5,000 a year (£220,000 today),[10] he was connected twice over with the Moscow Narodny Bank at a senior level.

As the police investigation began to focus on the responsibility of the directors and senior officers of both Centrosoyus and the MNB, the two organisations tried to make it seem as if the responsibility for events lay with junior employees. In a move to justify this, they began to dismiss those involved. The bank sacked three of its messengers. At a meeting of the board of Centrosoyus on 7 May 1928, Quelch was sacked for 'engaging in private business whilst in the employment of the Company'.* Priestley suffered the same fate four days later. The bank also dismissed Duncan. Throughout the investigation, the bank directors insisted that they had had no knowledge of any of the transactions. The police were unconvinced: 'It seems to us remarkable that a series of transactions running into thousands of pounds and extending over nearly ten months, in which three cashiers, a clerk in the Foreign Exchange Department, and five messengers were concerned, should have been conducted without having come to the knowledge of any responsible official'.[11]

Frank Wise stands close to the centre of all these events. His importance within these organisations is made all the more clear from the fact that he was one of just three people who attended the Centrosoyus board meeting on 7 May which sacked Quelch – A. B. Gourevitch (in the chair), Wise and a Russian secretary. Less than a fortnight earlier, on 27 April, Wise had also been present, also with Gourevitch, when the police met with the directors of the MNB and, furthermore, Gourevitch's presence at meetings of both organisations further illustrates their closeness.

A number of interesting connections also link Quelch and Wise. Quelch was a reasonably senior Centrosoyus employee: according to Priestley he was 'in charge' of the London building. They had had little conversation, Priestley merely obeying orders to make payments on Quelch's instructions. When Quelch travelled to Moscow for the celebration of the tenth anniversary of the Revolution, Wise was in Moscow. He wrote about it in the ILP's *New Leader*[12] and his article indicates that he travelled *with* the British delegation,† which therefore included Quelch, his office manager. Once in Moscow, the delegation was hosted for the duration of their three-week stay by none other than the Moscow branch of Centrosoyus. Beyond these facts, any further speculation (on conversations they might have had with each other or with others while in Moscow, for example) must remain in the realm of conjecture.

---

* Memories were probably too short to recall that when the *Daily Herald's* Soviet funding had been uncovered in 1920, Francis Meynell was also declared to have been acting entirely on his own account and was duly sacked.
† The delegation left London docks in late October on board the S.S. *Soviet*.

What are we to conclude? How much did Wise know? There are three options – first, that Wise was a willing conspirator in the affair, fully aware of all that his employees both at Centrosoyus and at the bank were doing; second, that the operation was conducted without Wise's active involvement, that he had some suspicion of what was going on, but that his sympathy for the cause of Soviet Communism in general was such that he deliberately turned a blind eye to the possibility that money laundering was going on and preferred not to know. The third option is the one which makes him the least culpable of illegality but still guilty of both naïveté and gross irresponsibility as a company director – that he thought so highly of the Soviets' integrity that he would never have considered them capable of such widespread and deliberate deception, that he was unaware of the widely published rumours that they had been heavily funding communist subversion and propaganda in Britain, and that he was so deficient in his duties as a company director and a member of the council of the bank that it never occurred to him to check that there was adequate oversight of employees to prevent their involvement in corrupt currency transactions. Willing co-conspirator, aware onlooker choosing to look the other way, or credulous dupe, all three reflect the spectrum of positions held by many on the left on Soviet Communism until the late 1930s and, in some cases, well beyond.

●   ●   ●

The years immediately following the October Revolution and the end of the Great War were a time not just of political turmoil throughout Europe but emotional uncertainty. The trauma of the war had a profound impact upon every section of British society, not least the left. A number of Labour supporters had been pacifists; some had been jailed as a result, often in conditions of great hardship. Arthur Henderson lost his eldest son on the Western Front and this undoubtedly inspired his work with the Geneva Disarmament Conference for which he was to receive the Nobel Peace Prize in 1934. After two world wars, the Gulag and the Holocaust, we forget today how unprecedented were the losses of the Great War and how deeply they affected British society and political life: approximately 4,500 British soldiers and sailors were killed in action in the Crimea; 5,700 in the Boer War. By contrast, 20,000

British and Allied troops died on the first day of the battle of the Somme in 1916 and a further 50,000 were wounded. By its end, five months later, the Somme had claimed one million casualties. Henderson's son was one of those who died there.

The British left were not solely driven by a determination to prevent a repetition of the tragedy of those four years; in their view the capitalist powers had been responsible for a world war of unparalleled devastation. Socialism, dethroning the very ruling class which had been responsible for that war, and replacing it with an international brotherhood of the working class, seemed to be the only viable alternative. And in Russia in 1917, that new world order began to take shape for the first time. As the 1920s progressed, parties of British enthusiasts, trade unionists and politicians flocked to the Soviet Union to see the new utopia for themselves. On their return, they wrote articles, pamphlets and books which were eagerly devoured by the thousands who had not been able to travel to see the miracle at first hand. While they may have thought of themselves as level-headed and objective, when it came to Russia, many were romantic idealists.

Russia was the new hope of the world, the physical embodiment of the utopia the British left had long imagined and, by leading the cause of a united international working class, it was providing a bulwark against future wars. It demanded their support, and their enthusiasm for that cause allowed them to ignore or excuse its excesses.

The mental gymnastics required to support a dictatorship even as it repressed their own Socialist brethren were considerable. For a while in the 1920s, the non-CPGB left's resolve nearly broke. And it is possible to argue, as some have done, that Labour understood what was happening in Russia but trod a pragmatic path of condemning Soviet brutality while seeking to keep the USSR within the comity of nations. Two factors contradict this explanation. The words of the many significant Labour figures quoted so far belie any claim to general objectivity: dewy-eyed admiration and gullibility might be a more appropriate description. Where reality dawned, it was expressed selectively: the real tragedy behind the protests on behalf of the non-Bolshevik socialists in the mid-1920s, which Harold Laski went as far as to call 'tyrannical suppression',[13] is that, on other matters of equal horror in Russia, they were silent. Secondly, when, during the 1929–31 MacDonald administration, overwhelming evidence emerged of an even greater repression, this time of kulaks (peasant smallholders) and religious believers, two groups for which Labour felt no sympathy, and over 1.5 million people were dispatched to concentration camps in cattle cars, the British left offered no protest at all. No voice was raised on behalf of the hundreds of thousands who were shot or died as a consequence of their privation. The contrast between that silence and the 'warmest sympathy' expressed by the 1923 Labour Party Conference for the far fewer 'Socialist victims of Bolshevist terror' is striking.[14] Where voices were raised, it was more often to deny, excuse, justify, or even praise what was happening.

In *Doctor Zhivago*, Boris Pasternak tells of how Strelnikov, Lara's gentle lover, is transformed over time into a brutal revolutionary. 'His madness', Pasternak writes, 'does not spring from theories but from the ordeals he has gone through'.[15] It is possible that the extent of the Great War's slaughter had desensitised them and that they had lost the sense of value which a society born in gentler times places on each individual life. Soviet Socialism demanded that the rights and lives of individuals be subordinated to the demands of the state. The same tension was never far from the surface in its British counterpart. If the European monarchies had taken the world into a war which had cost millions of lives, they reasoned, it might be that, to save future millions from a similar fate, the sacrifice of a smaller number would be unavoidable in the making of a new world. How else could someone like David Kirkwood MP stand up in the House of Commons and declare:

> You can depend upon it that I shall use all the power I have, physical and mental, and every ounce of energy that I have to fight on [the working classes'] behalf. It is in order to let the British ruling classes understand that the Socialist movement is prepared to fight, and will fight, until we carry the Socialist Republic – if necessary at the point of the bayonet.[16]

In May 1929, Ramsay MacDonald led the Labour party to its second election victory. In its first term, in 1924, the party did not even have the largest number of seats. Now, the result was only slightly better. Labour gained more seats in Parliament than the Conservatives (Labour 287, Conservatives 260), though they had polled fewer votes (Labour 8.37 million, Conservatives 8.66

million). Without an outright majority, it was once again dependent on the Liberals. Even so, Labour was back at the helm, not just of a nation, but of an empire. In just under twenty-five years since its foundation, the party had come a long way.

It is true that the majority of British socialists abhorred violence, but they nonetheless endorsed a philosophy which allowed those who had no such compunction to thrive, and made themselves wilfully blind to the full extent of the violence meted out to those considered enemies by the Soviet regime. That would have mattered less if they had been carefree young student activists, but they were not; they were the intellectual and ruling elite of the British Labour movement, now a national political party in government, leading a world superpower. They bore a responsibility towards the millions of their own supporters who were convinced by their propaganda on behalf of the Soviet Union, for the foreign policy of the nation they governed, and for the impact of that policy upon an empire which stretched around the globe and held one fifth of the world's population.

PART II

RUSSIA: 'BLOODSUCKERS' AND 'PARASITES'

Near Novo-Sibirsk, having lost my way in the forest one night, I unexpectedly struck the Trans-Siberian railway line, which I followed for several miles. After a while my attention was attracted by the sound of an approaching train. As the ponderous locomotive thundered slowly by, throwing a shower of sparks into the night, I noticed that it was drawing a great number of cattle trucks.

I was surprised to see that the little barred windows of the high trucks were crowded with the grey faces of men and women. The distracted, almost demented, appearance of these poor wretches, gazing disconsolately out into the silent forest, sent a cold shiver into my very soul. There were over fifty of these trucks, each carrying the same load of human suffering. Huddled together as they were, shoulder to shoulder, there must have been fully a thousand of these reluctant passengers.

At the tail of the train on an open platform two soldiers sat with their rifles slung over their shoulders laughing and smoking in the light of the lantern. The crude contrast between the deathly intentness of the prisoners and the boisterous joviality of the guards is strangely symbolic of the relationship between rulers and ruled in Russia today – callous indifference on the one hand, resignation and despair on the other.

COL. CHRISTOPHER FULLER, SIBERIA, 1931[1]

CHAPTER 10

WAR ON THE COUNTRYSIDE: THE LIQUIDATION OF THE KULAKS

In sheer size, there was nothing compared with it in all Russian history. It was the forced resettlement of a whole people, an ethnic catastrophe.
ALEXANDER SOLZHENITSYN [1]

There is no reason to tolerate these spiders and blood-suckers any more.
STALIN

The hammer and sickle, the ubiquitous symbol of Communism, is still to be seen on thousands of buildings and monuments in Russia. The walls of the Lubyanka, the Moscow headquarters of the Soviet secret police in all its incarnations*, are studded with it, all round, at regular intervals. It remains on either side of the gates through which the newly arrested prisoners of the NKVD were driven. In the West, for a while, it became a fashion item, adorning bags and T-shirts, a meaningless logo with 'exotic' associations that most of its wearers would not attribute to its Western European equivalent, the swastika. As the symbol of the unity of purpose of the urban industrial class (the hammer) and the country peasant (the sickle), it represented wishful thinking rather than accomplished fact. The countryside did not embrace

---

*   The Soviet *Cheka*, GPU, OGPU, NKVD, NKGB, MGB, KGB and now the Russian FSB.

Bolshevism. The stupefying death toll in the Civil War and famine of the early 1920s ensured that.

The Soviet countryside held the key to food production. Without food, the cities faced starvation, and the civil unrest which would inevitably follow risked increasing popular support for counter-revolution. When agricultural production faltered because of the Civil War, Lenin was forced to backtrack. In 1921, his New Economic Policy (NEP), permitted peasants to sell their surplus on the open market. This nod to the free market did what free markets tend to do – stimulated production. Food began to reappear in the cities. But it was always a compromise, a doctrinal fudge. Even as the more enterprising peasants began to build up their smallholdings again, they did not see that their prosperity remained dependent on their leaders' pragmatism. The NEP had been a tactical withdrawal, not a retreat. The Revolution in the countryside was still to be completed. A combination of circumstances over the winter of 1927–28 tipped the balance.

Makeshift kulak shelters. Northern Region, 1930. "There are no floors, the roofs are made of poles and loosely sprinkled hay and crumbled mud. As a rule, the temperature does not go above 4 degrees. [Everything] is lice-ridden. Along with the miserly feeding, and for many almost nothing, all this creates colossal [rates of] illness, and death among children." A rare, poor quality photograph from a damaged negative, showing the terrible conditions in which some deported kulaks were forced to live.

The struggle for power within the Central Committee peaked in November 1927. Trotsky, Kamenev and Zinoviev, together with hundreds of their supporters, were expelled from the party. Trotsky went into exile, to be assassinated in Mexico in 1940; Kamenev and Zinoviev would have to grovel to be re-admitted to the party. Stalin, in temporary alliance with Bukharin, was now in control.

At exactly the same time, a grain crisis was looming. The problem was not with the harvest, but with the supply to the towns. Faced with a state buying price that was between a quarter and a third of the price on the open market, farmers simply chose to stockpile their grain rather than sell it. Grain production (as defined by deliveries to the market, not the actual harvest) dropped by almost a third (from 6.8 to 4.8 million tons). To the countryside, ravaged by years of hardship and persecution, it was an act of self-preservation. To Stalin, it was an act of political defiance, home-grown capitalism that was confronting and obstructing the party and the Revolution itself, a cancer to be cut out before it spread.

In January 1928, Stalin made a rare trip to Siberia and the Urals to investigate the situation at first hand. Already convinced that the NEP had been a compromise too far, he issued orders (tellingly, without reference to his nominally equal colleagues in Moscow) for the compulsory seizure of private grain stockpiles. It was the opening salvo in a war on the countryside. Throughout 1928, the seizures continued. As poorer peasants were encouraged to unmask richer households hoarding grain in return for a share of the grain recovered, the process turned nasty. Settling old scores against more prosperous neighbours was to become a constant feature of the campaign to come.

When the NEP was abandoned, private businesses that had reopened or started up under it collapsed. As the next planting time drew near, it became obvious that the farmers were not going to submit meekly to the forceful requisition of their produce or to the implicit demand that they become the unpaid (or poorly paid) slaves of the state: they planted less, harvested less, and sold less. Although no one would have realised it at the time, things were about to change for the worse. From where we stand today, looking back over that period and knowing what was to come, there is a sense of sickening anticipation. This is the product of hindsight, of course. At the time, the people would not have known what the future held. '1937 began in 1934', it is said, meaning that the Great Terror, the purges of 1937–38, had their origin in the (probably Stalin-inspired) assassination of Leningrad party boss Sergei Kirov in 1934 and the initial purges that immediately followed. And yet, the development of Stalin's repression actually begins with his assumption of power in 1928, and grows with him, in tandem with his control over the country. In 1928, the axe was poised to fall.

Kulaks, Velikiy Ustyug, 1930. In the north, churches were used as temporary housing for kulak deportees. Even though they are only four hundred miles south of the Arctic Circle, some of these children have no shoes.

Stalin's problem was twofold: to ensure the food supply, and to neutralise the countryside as a potential base for future revolt. The enforced solution of the first (seizing peasant grain) only increased the risk of the second. His solution was both ambitious and brutal: to seize all farm land, machinery and livestock for the state; to deport, imprison, or shoot all smallholders and middle-ranking peasants ('dekulakisation'); and to transfer the remaining poorer peasantry in newly established state-owned collective farms ('collectivisation').

The human cost was staggering. Between twenty-five and thirty-five million people (including women, children and old people) were forced to join collective farms and surrender their homes and land to the state. A further 1.8 million were deported, hundreds of thousands of whom died over the next few years or in the purges of the Great Terror in 1937–38. A few years later, the resulting disaster in agricultural production brought famine, which led to a further three to five million deaths from starvation. For these, Stalin and the Politburo bear direct responsibility. Historians have made a strong case to suggest that the famine deaths were wholly preventable (if not deliberately inflicted), not least because the Soviet Union was earning foreign currency by exporting 'surplus' grain even as millions of peasants were dying of starvation in Southern Russia and Ukraine.

The kulaks

The word 'kulak' literally means 'fist'. In the sense that it was applied, it described a class group of tight-fisted, money-grubbing landlords and oppressors of the poorer peasantry. After the bloodletting of the Revolution and Civil War, it is not known how many of these characters survived into the late 1920s, even if they had existed outside myth – in the form in which they were portrayed – in the first place. In fact, by 1927–28 those classed as kulaks were generally smallholding farmers who were then demonised by the Soviet leadership for political ends – initially to shift the blame for food shortages from the government and then, as they began to resist the compulsory seizure of their grain and property, as an excuse for a widespread attack upon all actual or potential opposition to the government in the countryside.

In May 1929, as Stalin's own views on the solution to the problems of the countryside were hardening, the first Five-Year Plan announced a target of five million households (twenty-five to thirty-five million people) to be 'collectivised' by 1932–33. Significantly, it was nowhere stated whether the five million were intended to agree voluntarily to relinquish their land and allow it to be merged into state-owned collective farms ('kolkhoz'), or if this was to be forced upon them. The issue of compulsion was to provoke heated debate within the leadership, which, in turn, triggered the downfall of Bukharin and, according to some, Stalin's wife Nadezhda's suicide in 1932.[2]

In the same month that the Five-Year Plan was published, the government issued a decree *On The Characteristics of Kulak Farms Subject to the Labour Code*, which set out the criteria to be used for defining kulaks.[3] A kulak was deemed to include any one of the following: someone who regularly employed hired labour; owned a mill, complex equipment, or a complex machine with a mechanical motor; who systematically let agricultural machinery or facilities for rent; or had involvement in commerce, moneylending, commercial brokerage or other non-manual occupation, which included all ministers of religion.

In practice, when the campaign of dekulakisation was under way, these definitions were stretched almost beyond recognition. 'Regular employment of hired labour' could mean paying a neighbour to come over to help gather the harvest for a few days; 'ownership of a complex machine with a mechanical motor' was used to deport a family who owned a sewing machine; 'involvement in commerce' included selling surplus grain on the market, something permitted, encouraged even, under Lenin's NEP. In short, the authorities could find a pretext to take anyone they wanted or, when arrest quotas were issued, anyone they needed to make up numbers. This definition of a kulak household was a preliminary for the campaign that was to come. The attack on the kulaks represented a new development in Soviet repression. Formerly, people's class determined what action the state took against them (priests and nobility were irredeemable and were therefore shot or imprisoned, and so on); now the state first decided who it wanted to repress and then created a class analysis to justify that action.[4]

Over that summer and autumn, the May 1929 decree on kulak farms provoked the first expulsions of kulaks from their homes by zealous party workers, but it was not until the end of the year that Stalin announced the mantra for the coming campaign – 'the destruction of the kulaks as a class' – that was to signal an all-out assault upon them. A complete social class, real or imaginary, was to be eliminated.

'Spiders and bloodsuckers'

The brutal intent behind the proposal is clear from Stalin's own words, in speeches between December 1929 and mid-1930. The first, delivered at a conference of Marxist Agronomists on December 27, 1929, formalised the anti-kulak campaign (the italics are mine in each of the following extracts):

We have passed from the policy of restricting the exploiting tendencies of the kulaks to the policy of *eliminating the kulaks as a class* ... To launch an offensive against the kulaks means that *we must smash the kulaks, eliminate them as a class*. Unless we set ourselves these aims, an offensive would be mere declamation, pinpricks, phrase-mongering, anything but a real Bolshevik offensive. To launch an offensive against the kulaks means that we must prepare for it and *then strike at the kulaks, strike so hard as to prevent them from rising to their feet again*.[5]

Kulaks were to be forbidden from joining the collective farms, depriving them of their only possible source of employment once their own land had been taken from them: '[Should] kulaks be permitted to join the collective farms? Of course not, for they are sworn enemies of the collective-farm movement.'[6] It was not only the kulaks' land and homes that were to be expropriated. In many capitalist nations, even a bankrupt cannot be deprived of the tools of his trade; in Soviet Russia, the kulaks were to be stripped of even those:

> In order to oust the kulaks as a class, the resistance of this class *must be smashed in open battle* and it must be *deprived of the productive sources of its existence and development* [free use of land, instruments of production, land-renting, right to hire labour etc.] ... without [this], talk about ousting the kulaks as a class is empty prattle ... Without it, no substantial, let alone complete, collectivisation of the countryside is conceivable.[7]

And Stalin clearly understood how vast were the numbers of those who were about to be repressed:

> Measures of repression in the sphere of socialist construction are a necessary element of the offensive ... *You may arrest and deport tens and hundreds of thousands of kulaks*, but if you do not at the same time do all that is necessary to speed up the development of the new forms of farming ... the kulaks will, nevertheless, revive and grow ... The kulaks are doomed and will be eliminated.[8]

Stalin authenticated the attack upon the kulaks by reference to Lenin himself – no matter that Lenin's kulaks, even if they had existed in the form that he described, could not possibly have survived intact in the countryside after ten years of Bolshevik persecution:

> The kulak is *an enemy of the Soviet regime*. There is not and cannot be peace

between him and us. Our policy toward the kulaks is to eliminate them as a class ... Here is what Lenin says about the kulaks:

'The kulaks are most *bestial, brutal and savage exploiters*, who in the history of other countries have time and again restored the power of the land-lords, tsars, priests and capitalists. The kulaks are more numerous than the landlords and capitalists. Nevertheless, the kulaks are a minority of the people ... These *blood-suckers* have grown rich on the want suffered by the people during the war; they have raked in thousands and hundreds of thousands of rubles by raising the prices of grain and other products. *These spiders have grown fat* at the expense of the peasants who have been ruined by the war, and at the expense of the hungry workers. *These leeches have sucked the blood of the toilers* and have grown the richer, the more the workers in the cities and factories have suffered hunger. *These vampires have been gathering* and are gathering the landed estates into their hands; they keep on enslaving the poor peasants.' ...

We tolerated these *blood-suckers, spiders and vampires*, while pursuing a policy of restricting their exploiting tendencies. We tolerated them, because we had nothing with which to replace kulak farming, kulak production ... There is no reason to tolerate these spiders and blood-suckers any longer ... these spiders and blood-suckers, who set fire to collective farms, murder per-sons active in the collective farms and try to disrupt crop-sowing.[9]

Although they were the main target, Stalin extended the campaign against the kulaks to other groups, such as engineers, intellectuals and religious believ-ers. In March 1928, a group of engineers at the Shakhty coal mine were put up for trial on trumped-up charges of involvement in a counter-revolutionary plot. Confessions were beaten out of them; there was a widely publicised show trial; five were shot; others were given lengthy prison terms.

Stalin had a purpose in spreading such venom, in speaking, as the leader of the nation, so openly in terms of hatred that it became acceptable for all to hate, in dehumanising neighbours alongside whom people had lived for decades. Genocide – or more accurately 'democide' as this genocide by class has been called – requires many thousands of ordinary people to assist it. The tragedies of Kristallnacht and Rwanda were preceded by such language too.

The author Vasily Grossman, saw the parallels clearly. It was the villagers who would unmask the kulaks in their midst. As he later wrote, in a novel which drew on his own first-hand experience, in the villages they were

> ... all people who knew one another well, and knew their victims, but in carrying out this task they became dazed, stupefied ... They would threaten people with guns, as if they were under a spell, calling small children 'kulak bastards', screaming 'bloodsuckers!' ... They had sold themselves on the idea that the so-called 'kulaks' were pariahs, untouchables, vermin. They would not sit down at a 'parasite's' table; the 'kulak' child was loathsome, the young 'kulak' girl was lower than a louse. They looked on the so-called 'kulaks' as cattle, swine, loathsome, repulsive: they had no souls; they stank; they all had venereal diseases; they were enemies of the people and exploited the labour of others ... And there was no pity for them. They were not human beings; one had a hard time making out what they were – vermin, evidently.[10]

Grossman continues:

> Who thought up this word 'kulak' anyway? Was it really a term? What torture was meted out to them! In order to massacre them it was necessary to proclaim that kulaks are not human beings. Just as the Germans proclaimed that Jews are not human beings, thus did Lenin and Stalin proclaim, 'kulaks are not human beings'.[11]

Deportations

After Stalin's speech to the conference of Marxist Agronomists on 27 December 1929, the sporadic outbreaks of anti-kulak activity of the second half of 1929 gelled into a systematic campaign of 'dekulakisation'. Throughout January 1930, the OGPU carried out an assessment of the numbers of kulaks likely to be involved in a mass deportation, and on 30 January 1930 a special commission headed by Vyacheslav Molotov (later Soviet Foreign Minister, but at that time chairman of Sovnarkom*), issued instructions about what was

---

* The Council of People's Commissars (Совет народных комиссаров, shortened to Совнарком) was the main organ of Soviet government, whereas The 'Central Committee' was the Central Committee of the Communist Party.

to be done with the kulaks in *Measures to Liquidate Kulak Households in Regions of Total Collectivisation.*[12] It was to be repression by quota.

The kulaks were split into three categories. The 60,000 'worst' kulaks were designated 'first category' and were to be 'immediately eliminated by confinement in concentration camp, *including the death penalty when necessary'.* (My italics.) In fact, though the quota for arrests of 'first category' kulaks had been set at 60,000, the zeal of functionaries on the ground ensured that that target was vastly over-fulfilled – the final total of 'first category' arrests in 1930–31 was 283,717, of which 124,889 were kulaks and 149,395 other individuals (including over 5,000 clergy) who were swept up under the measure.* About 30,000 'first category' kulaks never made it to the trains. In accordance with instructions given before the arrests began, they were shot.[13] In one Kiev jail it was reported that 70–120 men were shot each night. And accounts even remain from those who did the killing:

> By my personal count, I shot thirty-seven people and sent many more to the camps. I know how to kill quietly. Here's the secret: I tell them to open their mouth, and I shoot them close up. It sprays me with warm blood, like *eau de cologne,* and there's no sound. I know how to do this job – to kill.[14]

Their families and other kulaks were deemed to pose less of a threat and were designated as 'second category' and deported to labour 'colonies', under a less strict regime than those in labour camps, but still subject to military discipline, OGPU control, and compulsory labour. Turned out of their homes with only a few hours' notice, many deportees were never to return:

> From our village … the 'kulaks' were driven out on foot. They took what they could carry on their backs: bedding, clothing. The mud was so deep it pulled the boots off their feet. It was terrible to watch them. They marched along in a column and looked back at their huts, and their bodies still held the warmth from their own stoves. What pain they must have suffered! After all, they had been born in those houses; they had given their daughters in marriage in those cabins. They had heated up their stoves, and the cabbage soup they had cooked

---

* The annual figure was 140,724 in 1930 and 142,993 in 1931

was left there behind them. The milk had not been drunk, and smoke was still rising from their chimneys. The women were sobbing – but were afraid to scream. The Party activists didn't give a damn about them. We drove them off like geese.[15]

The remaining 'third category' kulaks, all those not in the first two categories, were not deported but had their land and homes seized and forcibly incorporated in collective farms. Those who remained fared little better, however. In one village in the Poltava province, 300 'third category' kulaks who had escaped deportation, including thirty-six children and twenty old people, were expelled from their homes in March 1930 and dumped in caves three miles away. The remaining villagers were forbidden to offer them help. Only 200 were still alive a month later when it was decided to round them up too and ship them to the far north.[16] There, they would be someone else's problem. Over the next two years 1.8 million kulaks were arrested, loaded onto cattle trucks and deported to the far north and Siberia. By the end of 1932, an estimated 240,000 kulaks had perished.[17] Those who survived, now logged on police records, remained vulnerable; a further 370,000 were rounded up and shot in the purges of 1937–38.

The Northern Region timber camps

The expulsion of kulaks dovetailed with plans to develop Soviet timber exports to earn foreign currency – plans that could not be pursued unless labour could be found to work in the harsh and under-populated northern forests. Dekulakisation solved that problem. The deportations began almost immediately. By the end of the year, 230,000 had been sent to the Northern Region, 132,000 to Siberia, and 145,000 to the Urals.[18]

The Northern Region, *Severny Krai,* was a newly defined administrative district[19] encompassing an area of north-west Russia the same size as Spain and France combined (or three times the size of California). Containing dense and commercially valuable forest, it was deeply inhospitable country, cold and sparsely populated, with typical mid-winter temperatures of -20°C (-4°F) and snow cover from October to April. To the west lay the Karelian Region of Scandinavian Russia and to the east, the Urals. To the north, it was bordered by the Barents Sea and Arctic Circle. It was very cold.

The first settlers arrived in February 1930. By the middle of March, 134,000 people had been dumped in transit centres in the region, a further 29,000 were on the way, and 70,000 were in camps in the south awaiting transport. By the end of the first week of April, the total number of arrivals had reached 204,927, with 10,673 en route, and 26,500 awaiting transport.[20] The deportees arrived in special trains, roughly 1,700 people per convoy, loaded forty to a wagon or cattle car.[21] Forty per cent of them were children. In common with prison train convoys throughout the Stalin era, conditions on board were terrible and the callous indifference of the guards was almost beyond comprehension. On journeys lasting five or more days, there was sometimes no food, or water, and on the occasions when the limited water provided was not boiled, there were outbreaks of dysentery. Few wagons had toilet facilities, and those that did only had holes in the floor. With so many children and old people among the deportees, deaths were inevitable.

On arrival, it was found that many deportees were inadequately clothed; some even had no shoes. The transit centres in which they were held were massively overcrowded. In one place a local jail housed 3,500 settlers; in another a monastery was used to accommodate 7,500.[22] In Vologda, forty-seven churches were taken over and filled with deportees.[23] One report speaks of piles of human excrement and another of one small well being hopelessly inadequate to supply the needs of hundreds of people.

> In Archangel all the churches were closed and used as transit prisons, in which many-tiered sleeping platforms were put up. The peasants could not wash, and were covered with sores. They roamed the town begging for help, but there were strict orders to locals not to help them. The residents, of course, dreaded arrest themselves. Even the dead could not be picked up.[24]

With a small population and virtually no transport infrastructure, the Northern Region was totally ill-equipped to handle such vast numbers of exiles, even given a year's notice. As it was, they had only a few weeks. The original quota of 100,000 families (around 500,000 people) provoked frantic correspondence between the regional party secretary and Moscow.[25] It led to the intervention of, and a rebuke from, Stalin himself, but in the end the quota was reduced to 50,000 families – still a quarter of a million people.

There was very little accommodation waiting for them and it was months before any was built. In the first year of the quota- and target-obsessed first Five-Year Plan, the regional administration, the OGPU and the timber companies squabbled among themselves until mid-summer over who was to pay for it. From the beginning, food supplies were so low that malnutrition quickly began to take its toll – in deaths from both actual starvation and epidemic diseases which the already weakened settlers, particularly the children, were unable to resist. Exposure took still more.

> In ... the district capital, in a little park by the station, dekulakised peasants from the Ukraine lay down and died. You got used to seeing corpses there in the morning; a wagon would pull up and the hospital stable-hand, Abram, would pile in the bodies. Not all died; many wandered through the dusty mean little streets, dragging bloodless blue legs, swollen from dropsy, feeling out each passer-by with doglike begging eyes, they got nothing; the residents themselves, to get bread on their ration cards, queued up the night before the store opened.[26]

Measles, whooping cough and other diseases swept through the overcrowded transit camps. In early April, typhus appeared. Even government observers spoke of the death rate as 'colossal'.[27] In the camp at Makarikha (see map), 1,277 children died in the four months to July 1930.[28] In Solvychegodsk, with a population of 5,100 deportees, 418 of the 2,170 children died between 19 March and 21 July 1930.[29] In another unnamed kulak settlement it was reported that all but six of the 690 children under twelve died of hunger or disease.[30] By the end of the year, over 21,000 Northern Region deportees, mostly children, had died.

The kulaks' suffering did not end at the transit centres. They had been sent north to cut timber – and the timber was out in the forests. The unluckier kulaks, particularly the first category ones destined for hard labour rather than the 'milder' regime of the labour colonies, were sent straight to the forests. There, many were forced to build their own shelters, sometimes dug in the snow, as they arrived. Pasternak, in an account which is obviously drawn from eyewitness testimony, describes the establishment of such a camp:

We got off the train. – A snow desert. Forest in the distance. Guards with rifle muzzles pointing at us, wolf-dogs. At about the same time other groups were brought up. We were spread out and formed into a big polygon all over the field, facing outward so that we shouldn't see each other. Then we were ordered down on our knees, and told to keep looking straight ahead in front on pain of death. Then the roll-call, an endless, humiliating business going on for hours and hours, and all the time we were on our knees. Then we got up and the other groups were marched off in different directions, all except ours. We were told: 'Here you are. This is your camp.' – an empty snow-field with a post in the middle and a notice on it saying: "Gulag 92 Y.N.90" – that's all there was. First we broke saplings with our bare hands in the frost to get wood to build our huts with. And in the end, believe it or not, we built our own camp. We put up our prison and our stockade and our punishment cells and our watch towers, all with our own hands. And then we began our jobs as lumberjacks.[31]

These two accounts are from letters smuggled out of Russia to the West, the first dated 18 February 1931:

Eighty per cent are already unable to work. Numbers [of us] have frozen hands and feet [frostbite which, without amputation, can be fatal]. Many run away from the work as they have no warm clothing and are starving. When caught, they are locked up and have to lie on the cold ground without food, and thus they remain until the Almighty releases them from this world. Many die of hunger in the woods and are simply buried in the snow without clothing. Some are seen lying on the roads too weak to move off. Try to work day and night on 300 grams of bread a day, without rest! Drops of our blood are on every log. In our barracks we have 11 cases of typhoid and no medicine. Please, please help us...[32]

Three hundred grams of bread equates to about 400 calories. The optimum intake for a manual worker in the Arctic is 5,000–6,000 calories per day. The second letter is undated:

[A party of timber workers] met, coming through the forest, two children of 10 and 12 years of age, who were both utterly exhausted. They said they were just wandering on. Their mother had died at 'R' and their father at 'Y'. They could get no more bread where they had come from so they had left to go just anywhere. They were already in the depths of the forest, far away from any roads. There are many berries in the forest now, blackberries among them, so they may manage to keep alive on these...[33]

Reading these accounts, it takes little imagination to appreciate the misery experienced by so many defenceless and innocent people: a father or son shot, others arrested and sent to an unknown prison camp while the remainder of the family, deprived of their breadwinner, is turned out of the only home and living they have ever known, from which they may never have strayed more than a few miles. Then, carrying their few remaining possessions, they face a long journey in an unheated cattle truck, sometimes with no food or water for days and the only sanitary facilities being a hole in the floor. On the journey, the weakest – an aged relative or a young baby – succumb and die; at the end, a long walk through the snow with small children inadequately clothed or shod, to an overcrowded barn or leaking barrack hut; then, over the next weeks, no end of misery – scant food, growing starvation and, in many cases, the deaths, one by one, of the children in the family.

Kulak children, Northern Region (possibly Makarikha) 1930. The sign reads 'Children's Barrack'. These would have been either orphans, abandoned children or those separated from their parents.

Meanwhile, British Labour enthusiasts overlooked the horror stories and hailed the Soviet reformation of agriculture as a tough but necessary reform in the construction of the new Socialist utopia. The severity of the measures against the kulaks was clear from the start. As early as January 1930 the left journal *New Statesman*, describing it as a 'cruel experiment', reported that 'by banishment, confiscation, and if necessary, *imprisonment and execution, they are now being driven out of their farms and dispossessed of their be-longings'*[34] (my italics). But the ILP's James Maxton had nothing but praise for the programme in his chairman's speech to the party conference in April 1930:

> The great agricultural experiment which the Russian people have been en-deavouring to put through – to transform its agriculture from a primitive peas-ant basis to a large-scale communal basis – has attracted the attention of the world, and all who appreciate courage, as well as well-wishers of Russia, will hope that complete success may crown their efforts.[35]

In the ILP journal *New Leader*, H. N. Brailsford described the crushing of 'rich individualist peasants' as 'the excess of a great quality', excusable from men working under 'the spur of a lofty social ambition'.[36] Under the pen of Sidney Webb, the deportations would later be spun not as they really were, ethnic cleansing by class, but as a benevolent gesture by the state to save them from starvation and give them a way to earn a living (Webb got the dekulakisation and the famine which was its consequence the wrong way round). Shocking though these statements are, there was an aspect of this which brought the issue far closer to home. This was not just a problem in a distant country: Britain was intimately involved. It was the largest customer for Soviet timber exports, and the timber shipped to the UK was worth about £9 million a year, £530 million at today's prices.[37] It was cut and loaded onto ships by gulag slave labour.

CHAPTER 11

THE SAMILENKO STORY:
AN EYEWITNESS ACCOUNT

O ne eyewitness to the kulak deportations was Ivan Samilenko, who gave evidence to a United States Government Commission of Investigation in 1988. His family were deported and his father died of malnutrition in the camps. His mother escaped, but Ivan was captured when he returned to try to rescue his father. He was sent to a prison camp from which he himself escaped a year later. He was lucky to survive. In his camp in the winter of 1930–31 around 1,800 prisoners died. Ivan's story is worth telling at some length because it illustrates the tragic consequences of dekulakisation for millions.

The Samilenko family were farmers in Pryluky, in Ukraine. One of the innovations of the New Economic Policy had been the creation of 'model farms', part of a programme to stimulate the agricultural sector of the economy. The family built up one such model farm and had been official-ly recognised for their success in doing so. Unfortunately, such recognition marked them for repression when the official mood in favour of the NEP was reversed. Samilenko senior had successive, punitive, grain quotas imposed upon him. Many kulaks, under similar pressure, sometimes accompanied by equally impossible tax demands, sold up.

Then, in 1929, Samilenko's two oldest sons, Ivan and Grigor, were ex-pelled from their higher education colleges. Their 'class origins' were deemed incorrect. Ivan was studying to be a teacher; Grigor had only two months left before his graduation. Ivan fled to East Ukraine, and managed to lose himself in the factories of the Donbas industrial region, hoping to take up his education again at a later date and, in the meantime, to escape the attention of the authorities as they purged the countryside.

One night in December 1929, the final blow fell upon the family. Vasil, Ivan's and Grigor's young thirteen-year-old brother, recalled that night and the subsequent events before a U.S. Congressional Committee in 1988.[1]

It was in the evening when the OGPU came in a wagon to my home. Inside my house was my mother and my whole family. The senior OGPU officer took out papers and read before my entire family this order. Take only what you can wear and take something to eat. You are under arrest. And, they took us all outside and placed us in the wagon. They took us to the railroad station far away called Ichniya. We rode the entire night. At the station there were cattle cars used for loading cattle and other types of domestic animals. They opened the doors and shut us all in. They didn't tell us – they shut the doors – didn't tell us where they were going. There was no air, except from tiny vents on the roof of the cars. We rode for a little over a week. Nobody was permitted to go out. Nobody could relieve themselves outdoors. Everything, all the refuse, was discharged through the windows.[2]

As well as his parents, the OGPU took two uncles and his brother Grigor. It was December.

On our way to Arkhangelsk, we stopped at a station called Lepsha, and this is where we were told to disembark. When the people who were in the cattle car came out, they told them to separate into two groups. The men on one side, the women and the children on the other side, and we were told that our fathers were leaving to do work – to do forest labour – and that they would return in a week or so. The children and mothers were led along a snowy path. They were beaten to make them hurry along, and they were taken to a place where some barracks were standing and also some were under construction. In the barracks there was only one stove for all the people who had arrived by cattle cars. It was impossible to get any more heat. There were beds. People were all over the place. Some lay on top of the stove. Some were scattered all over the place. There was no food. They didn't give us any food. We were forced to subsist on the food which the women had brought with them to finish that off, and they gave us some liquid food, some soup and some sardines once in a while. A week passed and people began to fall sick. And because the barracks were not heated, children began to die. A week passed, longer – but our fathers did not return. When we questioned what had happened to them, we were denied answers.[3]

Vasil survived only because he and his mother managed to escape:

After some time, some of our relatives arrived with false documents indicating that my mother was not a prisoner, but in fact had come to visit a relative who was in prison in that place. With those false documents, she was able to escape. There were no false documents for me and I was forced to travel the entire way in a large bag my mother made. All throughout the train ride, I was forced to lie under the seat where my mother was sitting. She fed me scraps until we got out of the danger zone in about three or four days.[4]

Back in Ukraine, Ivan, who had so far remained free of the authorities' attention, learned not only that his father was seriously ill in a camp at Lepsha, near Kotlas, but that there was a regulation that permitted close relatives to apply for the release of seriously ill or disabled prisoners. Ivan determined to rescue him and took the long journey north to find his father. He later recalled that first meeting:

[The camp] was wired all around, guarded all around. I found many barracks … finally I reached barrack No.8. … It was about eight o'clock, quiet. Finally, a voice: who is that? It was voice of my father. It was difficult to see, and I found he could stand and walk on his feet. He was filled up [swollen by malnutrition]. Finally, when I picked up my matches and tried to find a candle to light the room. I found in this section of the barracks seven bodies on a bench, a wooden bench [camp barracks sometimes had a single shelf running the length of the barrack instead of bunks]. Three of them were dead; four had already lost consciousness.[5]

And on another occasion:

Everywhere at the camp I saw emaciated dead bodies lying with arms and legs in the air, half buried in the snow. In a conversation with a camp official,

I explained I wanted to take my father away because he was disabled and dying. But this man angrily replied, 'But he still has teeth, doesn't he? We will force him to work with his teeth, but remember, his bones will remain here forever!'[6]

Ivan was told that if he wanted to obtain a permit to take his father home he would need to travel to Arkhangelsk, almost 200 miles further north. To do that, he first needed to get to Plesetskaya Station, five miles away, and obtain a pass to travel. The journey did not begin or end well: 'There was the station, you couldn't go inside. There were a thousand people; they stayed in line two, three days to get permission to go to this headquarters. Finally, on the third day I received permission to go to this headquarters.'[7]

In Arkhangelsk, he had to get confirmation of his father's details from the OGPU records department before seeing a more senior officer for the permit to remove his father. He did not know that the detailed questions that the records official asked about his family would reveal his relationship to his mother, who, the OGPU already knew, had escaped from her camp.

The chief ... asked me one thing. He took a look at this, at the yellow record that was given by [the records officer] Mr. Kuzmin, and asked me, where is your mother? Where is your brother? Now, he said, you have a special assignment, you are illegally taking prisoners from the concentration camp ... He arrested me and sent me to a special cell for investigation.

Ivan was sent to a labour camp on the North Dvina river. He never saw his father again. In the new camp, he met an old friend from home who had been transferred from the Lepsha area, where Ivan's father had been. He brought the news that his father was dead. After just under a year in camp, Ivan himself managed to escape. He was lucky to have survived long enough to make his escape attempt; 1,800 prisoners died in the camp that winter.

Back in Ukraine, those who had evaded arrest thought they were lucky. They were not. The 1932–33 famine, which followed the chaos of dekulakisation, claimed the lives of millions of those who had been left behind.

CHAPTER 12

OPIUM OF THE MASSES: SOCIALIST MORALITY AND RELIGION IN RUSSIA

Communism abolishes eternal truths, it abolishes all religion, and all morality.
MARX AND ENGELS, *THE COMMUNIST MANIFESTO*, 1848[1]

The Christian world order cannot be taken any further ... it must collapse under its own weight and make way for a humane, rational order.
ENGELS, 1844[2]

Every religious idea, every idea of God, even flirting with the idea of God, is unutterable vileness.
LENIN, 1913[3]

The Party cannot be neutral toward the bearers of religious prejudices, toward the reactionary clergy who poison the minds of the toiling masses. Have we suppressed the reactionary clergy? Yes, we have. The unfortunate thing is that it has not been completely liquidated.
STALIN, 1927[4]

'Socialist morality'

Crimes against humanity, mass deportations and genocides, particularly those sanctioned at the highest level by the authorities of the state, seldom, if ever, occur without an underlying philosophical rationale. The demonisation of a perceived enemy, sufficiently developed to ensure the compliance of junior functionaries in carrying out mass killing or repression, has to be justified if it is to be sustained. Otherwise the latter cannot be induced to set aside the natural revulsion that resides in all humanity against the taking of the life of another, the revulsion which many would take as being one defining quality of being fully human. The one exception is the psychopath, who lacks all empathy and in whose psychological make-up the switch of compassion appears to be permanently turned off. Dictators attract and exploit them; indeed, dictators will often be psychopaths.

Western society has at its roots the Judaeo-Christian concept of the sanctity of human life. It is a value so basic that has been inherited without question by Western secular humanism. In fact, it was so widely seen as natural that most observers of the Soviet Union, particularly its friends on the British left in the inter-war years, assumed that it was central to the mindset of the Soviet leadership too. In this, they made a fundamental mistake. It was not.

It is still hard to appreciate how far-reaching the difference was between Western morality (whether secular or religious) and the socialist morality espoused by Bolshevism's two leading figures, Lenin and Trotsky. Gone were Judaeo-Christian absolutes, the idea that there were some things – good and evil, justice, murder, deceit, theft, and hate, for example – which were objectively always right or wrong. Socialist morality's ultimate point of reference was not the Bible, or secular principles descended from it, but the impact of an action *upon the working class*, the proletariat. Theft and killing were therefore quite acceptable if they were in support of the working class, but not if the reverse was true. To the question 'Who is God?' Engels had declared 'God is man',[5] and he made it clear that socialists would not accept the validity of a moral system that claimed a non-material justification: 'We reject any attempt to impose on us any moral dogma whatsoever, as an eternal, alternate and for ever immutable moral on the pretext that the moral world too has had its permanent principles which transcend history and the differences between nations.'[6]

It was obvious too that the Church, as the most resolute defender of that morality, had to be got out of the way. As Trotsky put it, 'As for us, we were never concerned with the Kantian-priestly and vegetarian-Quaker prattle about the "sacredness of human life."'[7]

Lenin made this clear in a speech to the Young Communist League, the Komsomol, in 1920:

Is there such a thing as communist ethics? Is there such a thing as communist morality? Of course, there is. It is often suggested that we have no ethics of our own; very often the bourgeoisie accuse us Communists of rejecting all morality. This is a method of confusing the issue, of throwing dust in the eyes of the workers and peasants.

In what sense do we reject [traditional] ethics, reject morality?

In the sense given to it by the bourgeoisie, who based ethics on God's commandments. On this point we, of course, say that we do not believe in God, and that we know perfectly well that the clergy, the landowners and the bourgeoisie invoke the name of God so as to further their own interests as exploiters ... We do not believe in an eternal morality, and we expose the falseness of all the fables about morality ... We reject any morality based on extra-human and extra-class concepts. We say that this is deception, dupery, stultification of the workers and peasants in the interests of the landowners and capitalists ... There is no such thing as a morality that stands outside human society; that is a fraud ...

Our morality is entirely subordinated to the interests of the proletariat's class struggle. Our morality stems from the interests of the class struggle of the proletariat. Morality is what serves to destroy the old exploiting society and to unite all the working people around the proletariat, which is building up a new, communist society.[8]

It was no coincidence that Lenin should have spoken so directly to the conference of the Young Communist League. Marx had called for the abolition of the family in *The Communist Manifesto*. It was the family which transmitted counter-revolutionary bourgeois concepts to the next generation. Old minds were more set and harder to change, but young ones could be moulded. The family had to be overthrown. Western onlookers, titillated by the looser sexual morality which was one consequence of this, ignored the chilling conclusion of the new morality so explicitly detailed in one of the Komsomol's own publications, *The Young Guard: the Life of the Komsomol* (1927) even when excerpts were reprinted in the West:

We are against God, that advocate of exploitation in all forms ... The 'thou shall not steal' of the bible of the exploiters has long been replaced by the ethical formula of Comrade Lenin: 'steal what has been stolen'.

[On the commandment 'Honour thy father and thy mother'] No! ... We recommend the young to honour only those fathers who have a revolutionary proletarian point of view, who knowingly and energetically defend the class interests of the proletariat; the other parents must be educated by communist children.

[On 'Thou shall not kill'] This commandment was for the bourgeoisie a rule of bigotry. The proletariat is the only class in history which has never recourse to bigotry. If an individual is excessively harmful, if he is dangerous to the revolutionary fight, you have the right to kill him, obeying the order of your legal class organ.* In moments of danger it is useless to thwart this order. The murder of an incorrigible enemy of the revolution is a legal ethical murder, a legal death sentence, for Communism does not recognise the metaphysical value of human existence.[9]

Class analysis as the basis of summary justice became the hallmark of the Red Terror. It was not random but deliberate. 'The Red Terror is a weapon utilised against a class, doomed to destruction, which does not wish to perish', Trotsky had written in 1922.[10] Martin Latsis, a top official in the *Cheka*, the secret police, concurred:

We are out to destroy the bourgeoisie as a class. Hence, whenever a bourgeois is under examination the first step should not be to endeavour to discover material proof that the accused has opposed the Soviet government, in deed or word, but to put to the witnesses the three questions: 'To what class does he belong?' 'What is his origin?' 'What is his upbringing, education and profession?' And it is solely in accordance with the answers to these three questions that his fate should be determined.[11]

Misunderstanding the amorality of Soviet ethics tripped up gullible Westerners for years. British Labour politicians optimistically negotiating with

---

* A national, regional or local agency or body that is an authorised representative of the proletariat – a local council, workers' soviet, workers' court, etc.

Russian fellow socialists over trade agreements or diplomatic relations would have done well to heed the words of Trotsky:

> Official morality is a bridle to restrain the oppressed. In the course of the struggle the working class has elaborated its own revolutionary morality, which began by dethroning God and all absolute standards. But we understand [morality to be] honesty ... of words and deeds before the working class, checked by the supreme end of the movement and of our struggle: the liberation of humanity through the social revolution.
>
> *We do not say that one must not deceive and be cunning, that one must love one's enemies, etc... We hate or despise our enemies, according to their deserts; we beat them and deceive according to circumstances*, and, even when we come to an understanding with them, we are not swept off our feet by a wave of forgiving love ... One may play a double game with the enemies of the proletariat, but not with the proletariat itself. (My italics.)[12]

This naïveté resulted in some almost laughable statements by committed fellow travellers. One such was Lord Marley who, when speaking for Labour in the House of Lords, was challenged that some Soviet figures he was using in a debate could be untrue. He replied that it was impossible: 'Think how ashamed the Soviet government would be if their figures were proved to be false'.[13]

All Russian quotations cited so far in this chapter pre-date the rise to power of Stalin, who is often blamed by Western Communists for corrupting the 'purer' principles of Lenin. Such an assertion is a convenient way to salvage some honour for Soviet Communism and the Revolution from what we now know of the gulag and the Great Terror. But as a sleight of hand it does not stand up to examination. Solzhenitsyn insists that responsibility for the millions of deaths in Russia lies as much with Lenin and Trotsky, the architects of the anti-morality of the Revolution (who also directly sponsored killing on a mass scale), as with Stalin, who operated according to its principles. It is a disputed view, challenged over the years by many on the European left, and still challenged today but, considering these statements, it is a hard position to hold.

Communism and religion

Although Communists despised religious believers for their ethical views, it was the Church's belief in an afterlife, the consolation for all the suffering of the earthly one, which particularly made it an enemy of the revolutionaries. Marx had famously likened religion to a drug used by the ruling classes to stupefy the working class and neutralise any ambition of theirs to throw off their slavery. Lenin agreed: 'Religion is the opium of the people. Religion is a sort of spiritual booze in which the slaves of capital drown their human image, their demand for a life more or less worthy of man.'[14] That sentiment fuelled bitter hatred for religion and religious believers from all three of Soviet Communism's leading figures. Marx had written that 'the abolition of religion as the illusory happiness of man is a requisite for their real happiness'.[15] Engels articulated the same idea: 'We want to sweep away everything which claims to be supernatural and superhuman ... For that reason we have once and for all declared war on religion and religious ideas.'[16] And this is also from Lenin, who famously wrote to Gorky that: 'Every religious idea, every idea of God, even flirting with the idea of God, is unutterable vileness [and religion] consists of filth, prejudices, sanctification of ignorance and stupor on the one hand, and of serfdom and monarchy on the other.'[17] Andrew Rothstein's translation is the most commonly known but, unsurprisingly, Rothstein does not convey the full strength of Lenin's offensiveness, as Bertram D. Wolfe explains:

> Except in the words *bogostroitelstvo* 'god-creation' and *bogoikatelstvo* 'god-seeking' which were technical terms of contemporary intellectual discussion, Lenin refused to use the word *bog* (god), substituting [the word] *bozhenka*, which defies translation by any English term which would convey his contempt. The nearest I could come to it ... in English [is] ... 'Every *bloody little god*'.[18]

A few lines earlier Lenin expresses this contempt in words even more direct and obscene, the closest rendition of which would be: 'All pursuit of little (pathetic, puny) God is akin to having sex with a corpse.'*

The Bolsheviks maintained publicly that their actions against the Russian Orthodox Church were a response to its corruption under the tsar. It was an

---

* My translation based upon the context of the Russian text *vsjakij bozhen'ka est' trupolozhstvo* (всякий боженька есть труположство) which literally reads 'every god is necrophilia'.

excuse taken up by supporters in the West. Further details from Lenin's letter is revealing because it shows that actually he feared a strong, devout and pure Church far more, and it was this that drove his anti-ecclesiastical campaign:

> A million sins, filthy deeds, acts of violence and physical plagues are much less dangerous than the subtle, spiritual idea of a god dressed up in the smartest intellectual costumes. A Catholic priest who seduces young girls ... is far less dangerous for democracy than a priest without a crude [i.e. corrupted] religion, a principled and democratic priest who advocates the construction and creation of a 'bozhenka'.

The Bolsheviks viewed the Church as standing in the way of the Revolution, as an enemy force which had to be eliminated. They wanted class war, fought ruthlessly until all enemies of the Revolution had been eliminated. The Church, by contrast, believed in the brotherhood of man, forgiveness instead of violence, and urged pity for those suffering and in need, such as the kulaks, even if they had been denounced as enemies of the state. Such ideas were 'counter-revolutionary' indeed.

CHAPTER 13

LABOUR: MORE METHODISM THAN MARX?

Religion has always been the instrument of the possessing class by which the dispossessed have been reconciled to their fate.
NEW LEADER (THE ILP JOURNAL), JANUARY 1929[1]

As Marx, Engels, Lenin and Stalin were totally opposed to religious belief, this was, by the late 1920s, a point of view shared by many in the Labour Party, as well as across the wider British left, and their hostility was particularly directed towards organised religion and the established Church. In turn this clouded their view of religious persecution in Russia. This is not the traditionally held view of Labour's relationship with religion. The idea, cited earlier, that the party 'owes more to Methodism than Marx' has become part of Labour mythology,[2] and Tony Blair is one of its most recent proponents.[3] Mention is often made of the faith of Keir Hardie and George Lansbury, and of Arthur Henderson's former role as a Methodist lay preacher. One author even claims that Ramsay MacDonald was a leading Christian socialist.[4]

The problem with taking the Christian faith of individual Labour MPs as evidence to refute the party's indifference or hostility to religious belief (and to the plight of Russian believers) in the late 1920s is fivefold:

First, in the *definition* of 'Christian' and 'Methodist':* some would have claimed to be members of a particular faith, but owed it no more than a tribal allegiance and allowed it little impact upon their own ethical outlook or

---

* 'Methodism' provides an alliterative counterpoint to 'Marx', but Labour Nonconformists could as easily be Congregationalists or Baptists. Many were.

decision-making. It is a mistake to confuse belief in the historical Jesus with religious faith – even atheistic revolutionaries have claimed Jesus's opposition to Roman rule as their example. Theology was significant too. Atheism looked very different in the late nineteenth century. A number of 'religious' organisations with which Labour men were associated had the trappings of churches (Sunday meetings in halls, a strong emphasis on the brotherhood of man and high moral standards), but could either only loosely be described as 'Christian', or not at all* – something that did not escape the notice of a number of Nonconformist theologians. While Keir Hardie is claimed by many as Labour's pre-eminent Christian, a closer examination of his beliefs shows that he 'progressively narrowed attention on only those parts of the New Testament that were applicable to economic factors',[5] with the result that his perception of the Kingdom of God was not so much a spiritual phenomenon as a worldly state of brotherhood and the abolition of private property that was virtually indistinguishable from the communist utopia. Ramsay MacDonald held a position of some responsibility in the South Place Ethical Society and attended meetings at the South Place 'Chapel', but it was not a Christian body, more an imitation of one which promoted secular ethical excellence. Lansbury, who is often mentioned, was not a Low Church Nonconformist but a High Anglican and quite atypical. More on him later.

Second, *the period* for which an influence of religion in the Labour Party is claimed. The strength of that influence varied over time – from the founding of the ILP in 1893, to Hardie's death in 1915, or to the events with which this book is concerned, almost forty years after the party's founding. Similarly, a moment of religious enthusiasm in the 1870s (when Hardie professed his conversion, for example) was no determinant of the strength with which that faith was held three or more decades later.

Third, the existence of a genuine religious belief by an individual does not automatically imply that its holder will not subordinate it to other things – pragmatism, peer pressure, the prospect of promotion or the fear of ostracism. Moreover, the fact that a number of leading Labour figures had had a religious upbringing was in itself no guarantee of sympathy towards the cause of religion, either. Some of the most militant Labour atheists and supporters of

---

* E.g. the Labour Church, the Pleasant Sunday Afternoon Association, the Brotherhood, the Ethical Churches.

Russia were children of the manse or parsonage, among them H. N. Brails-ford (ILP writer, son of a Wesleyan Methodist preacher) Fred Bramley (General Secretary of the TUC, son of an itinerant preacher) Fenner Brockway of the ILP (son and grandson of missionaries) and rector's or vicar's sons Cecil Malone (Communist, later Labour, MP), Lord Olivier (Fabian leader), and Graham Wallas (LSE and president of the anti-religious Rationalist Press Association). A. J. Cook, the miners' leader, was said to have been strongly influenced by the Welsh revival of 1904–05, but too much should not be read into that connection either. One characteristic of the Welsh revival had been its support and public prayer for the tsar in the 1905 revolution. Cook celebrated the tsar's overthrow in 1917, and by 1920 was a founder member of the CPGB, which was totally opposed to religion in all its forms.

Fourth, the strength of hostility among Nonconformists to the established Church should not be discounted. Arthur Henderson, whose personal faith is undeniable, seems to have been privately strongly anti-Catholic.[6] Nonconformists' defence of the continued power of the Russian Orthodox Church, undeniably corrupt in parts, was by no means automatic.

Fifth, there needs to be evidence that there were any Labour MPs who professed a Christian allegiance (there is no denial that some MPs did) and then *acted on* that loyalty by acknowledging and standing up for the plight of persecuted Russian believers. Of that there seems to be very little.

Some point to the 'Labour Church Movement' as evidence of a uniquely Labour Nonconformist voice, but this is unconvincing. In fact it was probably the reverse. It was not significant numerically; the movement began in 1891 but by 1895 had peaked at fifty branches. By 1902 there were only twenty branches and 'had ceased to be an effective force'.[7] Henry Pelling, the Labour historian, says that 'this gospel was one of social amelioration and not of religious salvation', and suggests that the movement 'must accordingly be considered not as a purely religious manifestation, but rather as a symbol of religious decline, of transference of religious enthusiasms to the political sphere'.[8] It is a telling observation and reflects the wider climate of the day.

In all, quite a number of historians challenge the 'more Methodism than Marx' tradition, and it is against their expertise that the legend needs to be tested. Henry Pelling is one of these. A fellow of St John's College, Cambridge, Pelling was the author of two leading histories of the party.[9] Born in

1920, he was close to his subjects chronologically, and writes with an authority that comes from that. He disputes the strength of the Labour-Nonconformist link by the end of the nineteenth century. By this time, he suggests, 'the enlistment of Nonconformity as a whole [was] behind the banner of the *Liberal* Party'. (My italics.)[10]

The eminent Communist historian E. P. Thompson concurs, insisting that 'the attempt to suggest that the ILP was founded by a slate of Methodist parsons and local preachers is even more wildly inaccurate than the attempt to attribute it to the single-handed efforts of Engels and Aveling', and that the Nonconformist establishment 'fought the ILP every inch of the way'.[11] Leonard Smith insists that Nonconformism's 'historic alliance with the Liberal Party prevented close relations with the Labour movement'.[12] And it appears that the trend continued into the twentieth century: as late as 1910, the *British Congregationalist* claimed that if it 'avowedly identified itself with the Liberal Party', 90 per cent of its readers would be in agreement.[13] Some said, however, that Nonconformists were leaving the chapels for politics, rather than taking their faith with them into politics. Another historian, Graham Johnson, summarises the situation by observing that in the late nineteenth-century Labour movement, 'despite Christian members and favourable attitudes, Christianity on the whole was attacked, criticised and [only] occasionally considered in a sympathetic light before being rejected.'[14]

Whether the Nonconformist chapels made a significant contribution to the early philosophy of the Labour Party, or merely provided a training ground for oratory and the awakening of a social conscience for those who later moved away from their early faith (what E. H. Hobsbawm calls 'a training ground for labour cadres'[15]), there seems to be agreement that by the end of the first decade of the twentieth century, political nonconformity 'largely ceased to count'.[16]

Labour and the Catholic Church

Catholic-Labour associations were just as tenuous, even though the large numbers of Irish immigrant labourers might have been expected to support the workers' party.[17] Although the 1891 papal encyclical 'On the condition of workers' (*Rerum Novarum*) had come out strongly against the Socialism of its day, the Catholic hierarchy in Britain remained circumspect in its attitude towards the Labour Party in the early years of the twentieth century.[18] The 1917 Revolution and the formal adoption of socialist principles in the party's 1918 Constitution the following year made prevarication much harder. The Church watched Labour's convolutions on Russia through the early 1920s with growing alarm, and the Catholic journal *The Tablet* was forced to ask 'whether the British Labour Party is whole-hearted in its repudiation of Communism and', it added tellingly, 'of the kinds of Socialism which are almost indistinguishable therefrom'.[19] The General Strike in 1926 added to its unease and increasing numbers of Labour Catholics announced that they were leaving the party. As one observed, 'The extremists are gradually getting hold of the machinery ... the controllist and secularist tide is gradually coming in.'[20]

The official parting of the ways came in 1931 with the Pope's robust condemnation, not just of Communism, but also of Socialism. *Quadragesimo Anno*, published forty years after *Rerum Novarum*, was, however, far from an endorsement of the status quo.[21] In a detailed examination of Catholic teaching on the nature of labour and employment, liberal economics, capital ownership and the family, it recognised 'the huge multitude of working people, oppressed by wretched poverty' and the social irresponsibility of those who left others 'bound to perpetual want, to the scantiest of livelihoods'. It called for a new social order which recognised the 'the worker's human dignity' and ended the exploitation of labour but it reaffirmed the right of individual property ownership and inheritance, two totemic targets of *The Communist Manifesto*.

Unsurprisingly, given the Bolsheviks' devastating assault on the Catholic Church and the murder of priests such as Budkevich in 1923, its verdict on Communism was uncompromising:

Communism teaches and seeks two objectives: Unrelenting class warfare and absolute extermination of private ownership. Not secretly or by hidden methods does it do this, but publicly, openly, and by employing every and all means, even the most violent. To achieve these objectives there is nothing which it does not dare, nothing for which it has respect or reverence; and when it has come to power, it is incredible and portent-like in its cruelty and inhumanity. The horrible slaughter and destruction through which it has laid waste vast regions of eastern Europe and Asia are the evidence.

Far more serious for the Labour Party was its equally resolute rejection of Socialism. While it accepted that Socialism was 'more moderate' and 'professes the rejection of violence', at its heart, *Quadragesimo Anno* insisted, 'it does not reject entirely the class struggle and the abolition of private ownership'. The Vatican had also noted its ambiguity on the role of compulsion: 'Society, as Socialism conceives it, can on the one hand neither exist nor be thought of without an obviously excessive use of force.' And those writers and theorists who sought to hide Socialism's more uncomfortable features were said to be peddling 'an alluring poison which many have eagerly drunk whom open Socialism had not been able to deceive'.

In conclusion, 'Socialism, if it remains truly Socialism, cannot be reconciled with the teachings of the Catholic Church because its concept of society itself is utterly foreign to Christian truth.' Any attempt to synthesise the two was similarly rejected: 'Religious Socialism, Christian Socialism, are contradictory terms; no one can be at the same time a good Catholic and a true socialist.'

A parliamentary voice?

One litmus test of the strength of the voice of Labour Christian, particularly Nonconformist, MPs by the time of the 1929–31 parliament might have been their response to appeals made in the Commons on behalf of the hundreds of Russian Baptist leaders who had been shot or had disappeared. There was none. It was Liberal MPs Geoffrey Shakespeare[22] and Ernest Brown,[23] supported by a number of Tories, who urged the government, in parliamentary questions, to protest on behalf of their fellow Nonconformists in Russia. Labour backbenchers heckled or denied there was any persecution, their comments going unchallenged by their fellow MPs.[24]

On the government front bench, Arthur Henderson, the former Methodist lay preacher and the senior Labour figure with overtly Nonconformist origins, insisted that he could not 'question the right of the Soviet Government to exercise jurisdiction within their own territory',[25] in marked contrast to the precedent set by his own party in its vigorous protests on behalf of imprisoned Russian socialists at Labour Party conferences in 1922 and 1923 (as already discussed in Part I). His apparently conciliatory offer to enquire about the persecuted Baptists eventually resulted in Foreign Office enquiries with the

British Embassy in Moscow concerning just eleven individuals. Even this modest gesture came to nothing when, seven months later, Henderson told the House that the ambassador had not been able to obtain any information about them and that further action was therefore neither 'expedient [nor] possible'.[26]

This was not the only appeal made to the government by Nonconformists which was ignored. On 29 April 1930, the General Body of Protestant Dissenting Ministers (representing the combined Congregationalist, Baptist and Presbyterian denominations) expressed their 'indignant reprobation of the persecution of Christian and other religious bodies by the Soviet authorities in Russia' and 'trusted the Government would urge upon the Soviet Government its imperative duty to bring this treatment to an end'.[27] In the Commons, Henderson was asked by Sir William Davidson – a Tory MP – for the government's response to the appeal. Two months earlier, Henderson had been told by the British Baptist leader J. H. Rushbrooke that 'there has not been in history so widespread, carefully organised and resolute attack upon religion, and especially upon Christianity' as that in Russia,[28] but he sidestepped Davidson's question, saying that he had not read it.[29]

If there was no significant Nonconformist voice in the Labour Party by the late 1920s, and British socialists were predominantly both warm towards Soviet Russia and disinterested in the plight of Russian believers, this did not preclude individual Labour MPs from holding a religious faith, as has already been suggested. Undoubtedly, valid claims for religious belief or affiliation can be made for a number of Labour MPs, of whom George Lansbury is one of the best known.

While Lansbury was certainly a man of faith, a number of qualifying observations need to be made to the implication, drawn by some, that his faith indicates that the Labour Party was welcoming to mainstream Christians at that time.[30] Moreover, Lansbury was a High Anglican, not an evangelical Nonconformist, and his faith has little relevance to the subject of Nonconformist influence in the 1929 party or its role in the founding of the party. Even in his Anglicanism, Lansbury was something of a maverick, and it may not be appropriate to describe his faith as 'impeccable', as some have done.[31] He was a member of the humanist Ethical Union in the 1890s;[32] in 1914 he joined the Theosophical Society,[33] an occult pantheistic sect, and he remained sympathetic to theosophy until the end of his life.[34] In the 1930s, he became

British president of the World Fellowship of Faiths, a body whose ecumenism was at that time increasingly influenced by Hindu mysticism. Theosophy is fundamentally incompatible with orthodox Christianity: it denies the key Christian doctrines of atonement, the existence of a personal, infinite God, and the divinity of Jesus Christ. It also teaches reincarnation and karma. In reality, all three organisations would have been regarded with considerable suspicion by theologically orthodox Christians.

Theology apart, it is hard to resist the conclusion that, on many occasions, Lansbury's enthusiasm for Soviet Russia trumped some of the imperatives of Christian morality: he excused the executions and atrocities committed by the *Cheka* in the Red Terror of 1917–22,[35] and the killing of thousands of Orthodox clergy and monastics;[36] he handled stolen Russian gems and cash smuggled by Bolshevik agents into Britain for the support of revolutionary causes, with few apparent qualms as to the manner in which they had been acquired;[37] he denied that there was any repression of religious believers[38] and dismissed reports of Russian slave labour as 'grossly distorted', insisting that the Soviet experiment was 'wonderful' and that it was not for socialists 'to judge … all the means they adopt to attain their ends'.[39]

Within the wider Anglican Church, of which Lansbury was a member, it would be a mistake to attribute too much influence to pro-Soviet left-wing clerics. The insistence by a small number of British clergy, such as the Labour-appointed pro-Communist Dean of Canterbury Hewlett Johnson and Anglo-Catholic Conrad Noel, that Stalin was merely enacting the Christian doctrine of 'love thy neighbour' was not representative of the position of the Church of England which, even at the time, dismissed them as fringe lunatics. In spite of attempts to do so, the laxity of the ecclesiastical disciplinary process prevented their removal from their posts.[40]

Labour hostility

In practice, many in the Labour Party looked on the Church (Anglican, Catholic and even Nonconformist) as a reactionary force to be neutralised, and they would have sympathised with Eric Hobsbawm's observation that Christian teaching 'remains an obstacle to the construction of a consistently social-revolutionary doctrine'.[41]

Many in the Labour movement agreed, among them Sidney Webb, George

Bernard Shaw, H. N. (Henry) Brailsford, Harold Laski, and James Maxton – all eminent figures in the movement. Sidney Webb, early Fabian leader and architect of the 1918 Labour Party Constitution, expressed the view of many when he described the clergy of the Church of England as 'a mere appanage of the landed gentry'.[42] In 1928, George Bernard Shaw, one of the most famous men in England and a revered elder statesman of both the Labour Party and the Fabian Society, declared that a future socialist state should remove all children from parents who taught them the church catechism, adding for good measure, that he hoped to see prosecuted anyone who preached about blessings to come in an afterlife.*

In the ILP journal *New Leader*, Labour notables such as H. N. Brailsford decried the Church as 'an organised conspiracy to perpetuate all the evils of ignorance and poverty under which men labour here below'.[43] In the same journal, Harold Laski, one of the most eminent Labour political theorists of the day, summed up the general view that religious faith could be tolerated only if it remained a private affair and took no place in the public square:

> Whatever comfort religion may bring to the individual, considered as an organised body of ideas which the churches exist to promote, its influence … has been distinctly hostile to truth … The churches are definitely hostile to social experiment, and they must be taken to represent one of the major armies in the force of reaction.[44]

James Maxton, chairman of the ILP, who was offered a seat on the Labour shadow front bench by George Lansbury in 1931, was even more unequivocal: 'The only teaching which I know which gets anywhere near to providing intelligent explanations and intelligent solutions to the troubles of the world is the Marxist teaching, which includes within it the destruction of the idea of a supernatural God'.[45]

Socialist hostility to religion took a number of practical forms, one of them being the campaign to remove religion from all state-funded schools.[46] The Secular Education League was formed in 1907 and claimed support from many in Labour ranks.[47] A motion in support of the cause was put forward

---

*   See Chapter 37.

at the TUC congress in 1908 (and contested by Catholic delegates[48]) and by 1910 had the support of the Labour conference.[49] In the face of Catholic opposition, MacDonald dropped it from the parliamentary programme in 1911.[50]

Even though the cause never gained enough traction at Westminster, the left continued to campaign for it, and hostility to religious influence remained. Sir Charles Trevelyan, the president of the Board of Education, made this plain in 1929: 'I am absolutely determined that the Labour Party shall not get into the hands of any religion, least of all the Catholics. I represent a constituency swimming with Irish Catholics. I would rather lose the seat than give the priesthood a bigger power in the schools.'[51]

And in 1932 the ILP conference passed a resolution, by a large majority, which reaffirmed its belief that 'the only logical settlement of the education question lies in the adoption of secular education in all schools supported by public funds, and that ILP members [must] be instructed to vote for secular education'.[52] One delegate, a teacher, seconding the motion, added that he believed that 'religious education had a bad effect both on the teacher and children [and] contributed to a system of fear and false respect incompatible with Socialism'.

Socialist Sunday Schools

Socialists took their opposition to religious education further by providing their own alternatives – Socialist Sunday Schools, and the more radical Proletarian Sunday Schools.

The first Socialist Sunday School was set up in 1892. A national movement, the National Council of British Socialist Sunday Schools Union, was formed in 1909. Its president, the trade union leader Alex Gossip, was also a member of the committee of the Anglo-Russian Parliamentary Committee. He visited the USSR the same year and, at the height of the purges in 1937 was as enthusiastic about Soviet Communism as ever: 'The establishment of the USSR is undoubtedly the greatest event the world has yet witnessed, and one can have no patience whatever with those carping critics who are continually trying to belittle the splendid efforts of our Russian comrades.'[53] Within twenty years, there were at least 120 and possibly as many as 200 Socialist Sunday Schools throughout the country; twenty of them in London. Avowedly secular, they had their own 'hymn' (song) book, and their own version of the Ten Commandments, the 'Socialist Precepts', which included statements such as:

> Love your schoolfellows, who will be your fellow workmen in life ...
> Honour good men, be courteous to all men, bow down to none ...
> Remember that all good things of the earth are produced by labour ...
> Look forward to the day when all men and women will be free citizens of one fatherland and live together as brothers and sisters in peace and righteousness.[54]

They were unashamedly intended to be the schools of the alternative secular 'religion', Socialism:

> Socialism has been termed the greatest religion that ever stirred mankind because there can be no greater religion than that which seeks the upliftment [*sic*] and perfection of men and women ... *Socialism is essentially a religion*, using the term in its strict sense of service and love to humanity ... The purpose of the schools is to impart the idealistic and religious conception of our great cause ... Just as the orthodox Sunday Schools exist in order to inculcate in the young the supernatural or social conceptions contained in orthodoxy; so we of the Socialist faith have founded our schools in the desire to promulgate in our young people the ideas and principles relating to Socialism. And in like manner as the orthodox Sunday Schools serve as a training and recruiting ground for the churches of all creeds, so will the Socialist Sunday Schools become the chief recruiting ground for the adult Socialist organisations in the future. (My italics.)[55]

If the Socialist Sunday Schools were secular but were not vocally hostile to Christianity, the Proletarian Schools, led by Glasgow communist Tom Anderson, were. Anderson began them as Socialist Sunday Schools but renamed them and took them even further left along the political spectrum.* They also had their own songs, a parallel baptism (a 'naming ceremony', infused with revolutionary phrasing), and a membership oath which ran 'I swear that I will

---

* Those who campaigned against them were not always clear about the difference, and it does appear that the dividing line was not always clear either. Some individual Socialist Sunday Schools seem to have had links with the Proletarian School movement.

be faithful and bear true allegiance to my Class, their heirs and successors, according to the Class Struggle, without any God'.[56]

In Anderson's instruction booklet, *How to Open and Conduct a Proletarian Sunday School* that sentiment was reinforced:

> Christ on the cross dying for sinners is so ridiculous that one despairs at the hold this superstition has on the minds of the working class ... To teach the children the ideal of the revolution should be the primary end of a Socialist Sunday School; all other teaching is of no avail.[57]

Anderson's 'Ten Proletarian Maxims' were far more fiery than the socialist ones, though perhaps a little challenging for younger minds and vocabularies:

> Thou shalt not be a patriot, for a patriot is an international blackleg. ...
>
> Thou shalt teach Revolution, for revolution means the abolition of the present Political State, and the end of Capitalism and the raising in their place an Industrial Republic. ...
>
> Thou shalt demand, on behalf of your class, the complete surrender of the capitalist class and all the means of production, distribution, and exchange, with the land and all that it contains, and by doing so you shall abolish class rule. ...
>
> Thou shalt wage the class war, by pointing out that the history of all recorded societies is an history of the Class Struggle, and that the emancipation of the working class from wage slavery must be brought about by themselves.[58]

Although little is known of these schools today (though Tom Anderson is beginning to emerge as a left folk hero[59]), they were deeply controversial at the time. The British Empire Union and the National Citizens Union both campaigned vigorously for the suppression of Socialist and Proletarian Sunday Schools. A public petition launched in 1922 by Sir John Butcher, Conservative MP for York, to ban the schools drew an astonishing 7,012,143 signatures. Butcher's bill in Parliament to enforce the ban ran out of time before the Government changed.[60] The BEU was successful, however, in provoking the authorities to investigate Tom Anderson's material on sex, and he was subsequently charged with publishing and selling obscene literature.[61]

Rationalists

No review of Labour perspectives of religion in this period could be complete without a passing mention of the curiously named Rationalist Press Association, founded in 1899, which was the leading 'freethinking' or 'rationalist' organisation of its day. The association in this period was not just passively atheist but actively opposed to religious belief and the continuance of the Church. Although RPA members were drawn from all political persuasions, it had a number of eminent members drawn from the British left – and it is indicative of their personal strength of feeling against religion that two of its leaders, successive presidents in the 1920s, were leading Fabians and fellow professors at the London School of Economics, Graham Wallas and Harold Laski. Two editorials from the equally curiously named RPA journal, *The Literary Guide*, one from each of their tenures, are representative of their views. In 1924, the journal dismissed reports of widespread religious persecution in the Soviet Union in the years immediately following the Revolution:

> If it be true that the million wasted candles once burning before wooden images have fallen to a hundred, this is certainly alarming news for the Churches, but joyful news for humanity. It is certainly to the good. There is no reason why any Rationalists in this country should weep over those missing candles.[62]

By 1930, Laski had replaced Wallas in the editor's chair. That April, Stalin's new campaign against believers, with its shootings, deportations and destruction of churches was provoking revulsion in many Western nations – but not in pages of *The Literary Guide*:

> To an onlooker the spectacle of the Christian Churches of Europe – Catholic, Protestant and Nonconformist – organising days of prayer in order to instruct the Almighty and All Wise on his duty toward Russia is both amusing and interesting. It is, in fact, a large-scale confession that the Christian belief is a thing of vanity and emptiness, sheer 'make-belief,' and nothing more. If these pious people really believe that the Deity is all-powerful to save, they must also believe that he is all-powerful to slay. If in his perfect wisdom he chooses the latter course, it is not for his puny creatures to demur his will.
>
> But there is a further aspect of this protest against 'the persistent persecution

of the faithful in Russia' which does not seem to have occurred to these virtuous protesters, and that is that those who live in glass houses should be the last to throw stones.

There are few among us who are not familiar with the terrible records of the Holy Inquisition and its thousands of tortured victims. Whatever may be the truth as to the alleged persecutions of the Soviet Government, the worst charges against it fall short of the ruthless cruelty of this infamous ecclesiastical tribunal.[63]

One insight into the strength of Laski's animosity towards religion can be found in a letter which he wrote to Oliver Wendell Holmes Jr. in 1927. While in America at the end of the War, he had struck up a friendship with the much older, famous Supreme Court judge. Their friendship continued through extensive correspondence until Holmes's death in 1935.

The context was the now notorious Supreme Court decision in *Buck v. Bell* (May 2 1927) which upheld the principle of applying compulsory sterilisation to the 'feeble minded' … 'for the protection and health of the state'. Carrie Bell was an intellectually disabled teenager, and the Virginia State Colony for Epileptics and Feebleminded proposed compulsorily sterilising her. Carrie's cause was taken up by religious groups, and a defence was launched to overturn the decision. Over the next three years, the case moved higher and higher through the American court system, finally arriving in the Supreme Court in 1927. There, by a vote of eight to one, the Court agreed to her sterilisation. Holmes, who had said in the hearing that 'three generations of imbeciles are enough', wrote the Court's ruling. The case set a precedent and over 60,000 compulsory sterilisations followed in the United States until the practice was abandoned in the 1960s.

Holmes wrote to Laski about the furore surrounding the case, complaining that 'the religious' were 'all astir' over the decision. Laski's reply was blunt: 'Sterilize all the unfit, among whom I include all fundamentalists'.[64]

•   •   •

By the time Labour took office in 1929, sympathy for Soviet Communism had become an integral part of its political outlook. Fellow travellers dominated every important Labour institution and journal; hundreds of Soviet enthusi-asts filled the worlds of politics, journalism, universities and the arts. While there cannot be said to have been a single British socialist viewpoint on reli-gion at the time, any more than there was a single British 'left', there was a general consensus: many agreed with Lenin that the Church was a negative force in society, a symbol of, and dominated by, the ruling classes, and an ob-struction to socialist revolution. This natural antipathy meant that they were unconcerned over stories of the suppression of religion in Russia. Socialists believed that its influence needed to be curbed. Once again, the difference between most British socialists and Bolsheviks became one of method, not of principle. If British socialists made mildly dissenting noises at the *idea* of brutality in religious persecution, many still applauded its aims.

CHAPTER 14

THE PERSECUTION OF
THE RUSSIAN CHURCH

The Bolsheviks and the Church (1917–25)

The clash between Bolshevism and religion was inevitable. When it came, it led to the destruction of thousands of churches and the 'liquidation' of hundreds of thousands of religious believers. From the Revolution onwards, the Russian Church suffered successive waves of violent persecution. Over time the violence spread to all other religions (Judaism, Islam, Buddhism, and even native Shamanism were all repressed) as well as to other Christian denominations but initially it was the Russian Orthodox Church that was the target of the revolutionaries' anger.

The Bolsheviks' contempt for the Church became tangible in a succession of acts of unprecedented savagery. During the 1917 Revolution and the subsequent Civil War, thousands of bishops, clergy, monks and nuns were tortured and slaughtered – mutilated, raped, disembowelled, buried alive, crucified, forced to take communion with boiling lead, castrated or, in mid-winter, drenched with water and frozen to death as macabre statues. Then in 1922, under the pretext of raising famine relief, Lenin launched an attack to finally break the Orthodox Church, ordering the seizure of the many treasures that it held.

The Russian Orthodox Church's veneration of sacred objects and relics had brought about a tradition of fine craftsmanship in jewels and gold and it possessed many beautiful treasures. Before the Revolution, the Bolsheviks had financed themselves by robbing banks, an occupation at which Stalin himself had tried his hand. Confronted with national economic and agricultural disintegration, the regime turned its gaze upon the treasures of the Church and planned new robbery on a grand scale.

Lenin was aware that the Church still had a strong following, particularly in the countryside, and could not be attacked head-on. In March 1922, he wrote a secret directive to members of the Politburo, the heads of the OGPU, the People's Commissariat of Justice, and the Revolutionary Tribunal which revealed that his true goal was not just plunder ('we must lay our hands upon a fund of several hundred million gold roubles, perhaps even several billion'[1]), but the destruction of the Church:

> On the subject of the seizure of the Church's valuables: the conference is to reach a secret decision to the effect that the removal of valuables, and especially those in the wealthiest abbeys, monasteries, and churches, must be carried out with merciless determination, stopping at nothing whatever, and in the shortest possible time. Therefore, the more representatives of the reactionary clergy we manage to shoot, the better. We must give these people, right now, such a lesson that for decades to come they will not dare even to think of resistance.[2]

In specific instructions about the suppression of protests in Shuia, a town 150 miles (250 km) north-east of Moscow, he made it even clearer that his intention was to strike a mortal blow to the Church across the whole nation:

> For us this moment is not only exceptionally favourable but generally the only moment when we can, with ninety-nine out of a hundred chances of total success, smash the enemy* and secure for ourselves an indispensable position for many decades to come ... We must give battle ... in the most decisive and merciless manner and crush [the Church's] resistance with such brutality that it will not forget it for decades to come ...
>
> Arrest as many representatives of the local clergy, petty bourgeoisie and bourgeoisie as possible, no few than several dozen ... [Their trial should] ... end in no other way than execution by firing squad of a large number of the

---

* In the context of the memorandum, 'enemy' refers specifically to the Church, not just to the Church as one of a number of counter-revolutionary forces.

most influential Black Hundreds* in Shuia and to the extent possible, not only in that city but also in Moscow and several other clerical centres.[3]

Lenin was well aware of the sensitivity of expressing such brutal views in print, and ordered all copies of his letter to be returned by his colleagues uncopied. The letter remained secret until Gorbachev ordered it to be made public in 1990, though *samzidat* (underground) versions had been circulating in the émigré Russian community abroad for some years.[4]

Meanwhile, for public consumption, the assault was passed off as a philanthropic measure to save lives, opposed by a callous Church hierarchy indifferent to the suffering of the masses:

> The government has no thought of persecuting believers or the church in any way ... Valuable objects are created by the people's labour and belong to the people. The conduct of religious services will not lose anything from the substituting of other, plainer articles for precious ones. But the valuable items make it possible to buy enough grain, seeds, cattle, and equipment to save not only the lives but the households of the peasants of Povolzhya and all other famine-stricken areas of the Soviet federation ...
>
> Only a clique of the princes of the church, accustomed to luxury, of gold, silk, and precious stones, does not want to part with these treasures to save millions doomed to die. In its greedy desire to hold on to its valuables at any cost, the Church's privileged clique does not shrink from criminal conspiracies and incitements to open rebellion. While committed as always to full understanding and tolerance of believers, the Soviet government will never, not for one minute, permit the privileged ringleaders of the Church, garbed in silk and diamonds, to create a special government of Church princes within the government of workers and peasants.[5]

Lenin's subterfuge was laid bare when the Patriarch offered to raise the equivalent value in cash if the Church were allowed to keep its treasures. The offer was refused. Lay believers came out onto the streets. In Petrograd, it was rumoured that over 200,000 turned out to protest. In retaliation, clergy

---

*   I.e. the clergy.

were taken away and shot. Patriarch Tikhon was himself arrested and only escaped execution because of an international campaign on his behalf.

Before long, religious persecution spread beyond the Orthodox Church, belying claims by Western communist sympathisers that the repression of the Church was motivated solely because of the Orthodox Church's association with the former tsar. A campaign against the Catholic Church and a show trial of leading Catholic prelates resulted, as already mentioned, in death sentences and terms of long imprisonment.

The Church was cowed. Before he died in 1925, Tikhon estimated that 10,000 priests were either in prison or in exile, often in the most isolated and impoverished circumstances. By the end of the decade, 20 per cent of the inmates of the notorious Solovetsky Islands labour camps, the prototype from which the gulag system grew, were believed to be in prison because of some connection with the Orthodox Church.[6] Over 150 bishops were in prison or exile. Over 15,000 clergy, monks and nuns had perished.[7] The violence subsided during the second half of the 1920s, but as many clergy remained in the camps, the reality is that there were simply fewer potential targets at liberty. Then, as the decade drew to a close and Stalin's hold on power grew stronger, a new wave of terror began.

The persecution grows (1925–29)

The persecution of religious believers of all faiths and denominations was more and more strictly enforced by Soviet law as the 1920s progressed. In May 1925, article 69 of the constitution stipulated that 'servants of religious cults for whom this service is a profession' were to be disenfranchised. The measure did not distinguish between faiths and therefore equally applied to priests, pastors, rabbis, and mullahs. In itself, given their antipathy towards the Bolsheviks, those singled out by the measure might not have cared to vote in the first place but, once singled out, the disenfranchised (*lishentzi*) became an identifiable group against whom severer measures of repression were taken.

One of the most drastic consequences of being classified as *lishentzi* was that this group was no longer entitled to ration cards. In a time of severe food shortages, that meant that clergy were forced to buy bread at vastly inflated black market prices. Given the extent of the increasing financial penalties being imposed upon them, the price of basic foods were beyond their reach; it was a life-threatening prohibition. And the Soviets fully understood its bleak consequences – starvation. As one official callously told the British ambassador, Sir Esmond Ovey, in February 1930, 'There is not enough food to go around, so we cannot do anything for them, as we have to consider first and foremost those who are helping to build up our new system.'[8]

Even though article 69 of the constitution had already excluded 'servants of religious cults', instructions about elections published on 4 November 1926 banned an even wider group of individuals associated with any church, synagogue or mosque:

> Monks, novices, priests, deacons, psalm readers, mullahs, muezzins, rabbis, cantors, RC priests, pastors, elders, and people under other names performing the same duties regardless of whether they receive pay for their services.[9]

A later declaration expanded the list still further, naming:

> Choir singers, choirmasters, organists, readers, shamans, rezhniks,* muezzins, teachers of church schools, heads and teachers of various circles run by religious societies, members of parish councils, different officials and personnel of parish councils and religious societies, [and even] artists who execute work by order of parish councils and religious societies.[10]

In April 1929, the most draconian measure of all was introduced, one which would remain in place as the backbone of the Soviet state's repression of religious belief for decades to come. The 'law on religious association'[11] outlawed almost all but the performance of religious ritual within the confines of a church building. Religious organisations were forbidden to raise funds or organise Bible studies; all other meetings of Church members (even purely social ones), charitable work or medical aid, meetings for children, and material aid to fellow Church members were banned. Further decrees outlawed sermons, evangelism, religious publishing and the distribution of literature. The enforced closure of churches, punitive taxes on remaining

---

* These are Jewish butchers who kill meat in accordance with the Levitical law.

church buildings (closed if the faithful could not find the money to pay for them), and even taxes on the use of candles, followed. And the threat of arrest for counter-revolution was ever-present:

> In March 1930 44 priests were arrested in Petrograd, on the pretext that they were hoarding small silver change which had at that time disappeared from circulation. If over 10 roubles in small coins was found in a church money box the clergy were accused of 'counter-revolutionary designs'. In many cases the penalty for this was death. I have been told that in Petrograd alone 17 priests were shot for this offence.[12]

It is only in the detail of these regulations, and other measures passed around the same time,[13] that the true severity of the attack upon religious believers becomes clear:

- On collectivisation, clergy were refused permission to join co-operatives and collective farms, were classified instead as 'private entrepreneurs' and thus liable to pay income tax at up to 81 per cent. Similarly, their right to an allocation of land for growing their own food was severely curtailed. What little land they could be allocated was then taxed.
- As *lishentzi*, clergy were banned from serving in the army, but were then penalised for not doing so. The rate for this tax was 50 per cent of the income tax they had already paid, rising to 75 per cent on higher incomes. Officially, the total of non-military service tax was not meant to exceed 20 per cent of a person's income but if one had already paid 81 per cent income tax, such a concession was meaningless. Inability to pay or delay in paying was punishable by imprisonment.
- Further penalties included a 100 per cent levy on income they received as a result of carrying out their clerical ministry and an additional tax, effectively an ongoing fine, on account of their disenfranchised status.
- A number of measures made it almost impossible for clergy to obtain or keep a home. All Church property had been nationalised in 1918. In 1929, it was decreed that all clergy with an income in excess of 3,000 roubles were to be evicted immediately. From that date also, clergy were not permitted to rent state property, whatever their income. For those on low

incomes living in Church property after the regulations came into force, further punitive measures were introduced to force them out. Their rent was set at ten times the rate of a worker. As the actual rate was determined by the local authorities' valuation of the property (priests paid 10 per cent of the value in rent, workers 1 per cent or 2 per cent), clergy were at the mercy of officials who could (and did) arbitrarily and maliciously inflate their calculation.

- Until August 1929, church councils could insure their clergy for medical care and pensions. The state then expropriated these funds, deprived clergy of all state health care, and cancelled the pensions of retired priests. The only medical care that clergy could obtain was by approaching doctors privately, to be charged whatever rate the doctor demanded. Many thus lost access to all medical care.

- To keep their place of worship open, parishioners had to pay an annual tax of 0.5 per cent of the market value of the church building. The valuation, also made by state officials, was often arbitrary and could not be challenged. If it was not paid, the building was seized.

As one scholar has observed, the only places left for clergy to live were in private houses, of which, after collectivisation, almost none but semi-rural cottages remained. Moreover, in the climate of enhanced religious persecution, not many laymen dared to offer housing to members of the clergy. This measure forced many priests to 'un-frock', conceal their former vocation and take on civilian jobs.[14] Those who supported homeless and starving priests and their families were in turn persecuted by the authorities, as one priest explained:

> The woman who rents me a room (the hut has been bought with my money in her name, because I have no right to buy it for myself) and who owns about an acre of land which has been given this year 4 'measures' of wheat (about 640 kg)* and was required to give 50 pud (800 kg) to the 'grain collector'. When the woman, after the manner of women, began sobbing in the office of the village Soviet, and asking for an explanation of this unjust assessment, she

---

* I.e. was assessed for tax or grain requisition purposes as able to produce 640 kg of wheat.

was publicly answered: 'drive out the priest from your hut, then we shall not demand this grain from you.'[15]

The personal impact of the crushing burden caused by these arbitrary and punitive taxes is vividly and movingly illustrated elsewhere in the same letter quoted above, which was smuggled out of Russia and published by Orthodox exiles in Paris in July 1930:

> Our existence is most pitiful, and each year it is growing worse and worse. The year 1929 has heaped misfortunes on us surpassing all the preceding years; this is especially the case for the clergy and the Church. I did not write to you about this so far because I know how hard it was for you to have to know of the painful state of my soul. But now the cup of suffering is full to overflowing and every minute it threatens to gush forth. I have no strength to hide it in my heart. Somebody has to hear of my suffering, so to whom, if not to you, will I make my sorrow known.
>
> Wherein to our misfortunes consist? The chief and most unpleasant misfortunes are the heavy blows on our pockets. It is growing impossible for the clergy to pay the unbearable and progressively increasing taxation. For instance, I have had to pay a certain sum annually for various taxes, increased from year to year, but not unreasonable. This year however I have had to pay with the greatest difficulty (I am in debt to the limit) a sum which is seven times larger than last year. This so-called 'voluntary assessment' alone amounted to 22.70 roubles last year; this year it has been fixed at 155.30 roubles. My yearly income amounts to 560–575 roubles. As I have no family it suffices for my needs. Now as always I have been content with what my parishioners give me voluntarily for my services. But in the books of the Finance inspector my yearly revenue was first fixed at 600 roubles; after two years it was raised to 800 roubles; after two more years to 1,000 roubles; then 1,200 roubles. On my protesting (with others) against such unjust taxation, it was raised to 1,500 roubles, and as a result all kinds of taxes are poured out on us, as from the Treasury house of Sin. Our 'supposed' revenue increases from year to year, till it reaches unheard of proportions, notwithstanding declarations of actual amounts received. These declarations are simply not believed, though they are still officially demanded of us; and we are heavily fined (1

rouble to 200 roubles) for failure to submit them or even for being one day late with them …

Life is growing unbearable … We cannot buy any products whatever; we are obliged to send someone to buy for us. I find it difficult even to explain so strange an order of things. If you are boycotted on all sides – despised, people refuse even shaking hands with you, they hate you, turn away from you, laugh at you, turn you into ridicule, curse you and spit at you – why should you also be deprived of procuring food? Soon, perhaps very soon, priests have to lodge under some fence.[16]

Propaganda and the League of the Militant Godless

Legislation was but one aspect of the state's repression of religious believers; virulent anti-religious propaganda was another. As Stalin made clear in a meeting with American trade unionists:

The Party cannot be neutral toward the bearers of religious prejudices, toward the reactionary clergy who poison the minds of the toiling masses. Have we suppressed the reactionary clergy? Yes, we have. The unfortunate thing is that it has not been completely liquidated. Anti-religious propaganda is a means by which the complete liquidation of the reactionary clergy must be brought about.[17]

Under slogans such as 'Let us deal a crushing blow to religion!' and 'We must achieve liquidation of the Church and complete liquidation of religious superstitions!', the League of the Militant Godless (LMG) was chosen to lead the propaganda assault, campaigning for the destruction of all religious activity. Membership of the LMG grew from 87,000 in 1926 to 500,000 in 1929 and at its highest it was over five million – though many of those were compulsorily enrolled through their school or local party organisation. By 1931, its newspaper *Bezbozhnik* ('The Godless') had a circulation of 500,000. The leader of the LMG, Yemelyan Yaroslavsky, was outspoken in his hatred of religious belief. 'We ought to wage pitiless war against religion, not only in our schools, but in the bosom of the family', he declared at a league youth congress in August 1929. His words were echoed by education minister Anatoly Lunacharsky in support of the LMG newspaper: 'With all my heart I wish *Bezbozhnik* every success in the fight against the repugnant spectre of God'.[18]

In 1928, in a move that opened the way for their destruction, Lunacharsky removed 6,000 of the 7,000 churches from the list of protected buildings. Resolutions at the LMG congress in June 1929 called for the cessation of all private donations to churches, for members of trade unions to refuse to do any work for the Church, whether printing, repairs, or new building, and for nothing short of the complete social isolation of all priests and other clergy. Press attacks on religion appeared every week. *Bezbozhnik* not only played a leading part in these, but approvingly reported accounts of arrests and shootings, inuring the general population to the repression by the very regularity and volume of reports such as this, in *Bezbozhnik* on 18 August 1929:

> At the trial of the so-called 'Vavilov Dol' case* the court has decided that preachers Turanin and Molodikh are to be considered as socially dangerous and parasitical elements. A former monk of the Athos monastery has also to be considered as a parasitical element. Further the court has decided that the counterrevolutionary sermons of the priests Juravlev and Prakhin have to be considered as an extremely serious but cunningly masked crime committed during a period of acute class struggle.
>
> Taking into consideration the social danger represented by the prisoners under trial and the degree of guilt of each of them, the court has sentenced: Dorofeev one of the founders of the community, priests Juravlev and Prakhin, 'elders' Molodikh and Turanin are to be shot and all their property confiscated.[19]

Or this news item, from *Bezbozhnik* on 6 February 1930:

> The meeting of the peasants decided to close the church and invited the peasants of the neighbouring villages of Peskovka and Bashtanovka to follow their example. In a meeting of the collective farmers and the active members of the Communistic Party it was decided to close the church and to arrange an anti-religious demonstration. On the day of the demonstration the priest Pavlenko made the service last till 2 p.m. while usually he finished it at 10 a.m. with

---

* The Vavilov Dol monastery in the Saratov region was formed from a number of caves dug into the hillside. They were blown up and the monastery was destroyed in 1929. Many of the monks were shot.

the purpose that the anti-religious demonstration should meet the believers. When the place was overcrowded and the demonstration of the schoolchildren and pioneers arrived carrying the slogan is 'instead of the church let us build the school', 'down with the priests!', Buyan and Karpenko, being incited by the priest and the kulaki [kulaks], started to shout: 'Why are you silent? They take away the church! Beat them.' The kulaki and the priest started to beat the school children and the peasants. Several children and peasants were severely beaten. Priest Pavlenko, psalm-reader Didenko, Buyan and Klimenko were sentenced to be shot. The Superior Court of the USSR confirmed the sentence.[20]

These two excerpts are typical. There is no evidence that cases such as these are reported with anything other than approval. Because of these articles, the Russian Orthodox Church today knows of the martyrdom of Dorofeev, Juravlev, Molodikh, Turanin, Pavlenko, Didenko, Buyan and Klimenko. The names of many hundreds of other victims will never be known. In Ukraine alone in 1928–38, thirteen archbishops and bishops, 1,150 priests and 20,000 members of parish and district church councils were executed or died after arrest in camps.[21]

The liquidation of believers had its counterpart in the destruction of their places of worship. Those buildings which were not destroyed were turned into factories, stables and warehouses, their treasures plundered and their frescoes defaced. The most infamous case, captured on film, was the dynamiting of the Moscow Cathedral of Christ the Saviour in 1931, but it had been preceded by the wholesale destruction of some of the most precious landmarks of Russian Christianity, buildings such as the fourteenth century Simonov Monastery whose destruction was so lightly dismissed in the press reports reproduced at the beginning of Part III of this book. 1929 and 1930 were years in which the closures accelerated, even as Western fellow travellers such as geneticist J. B. S. Haldane, brother of writer Naomi Mitchison, denied what was happening:

It is ridiculous to describe the present state of affairs in Russia as 'almost the worst record of religious persecution that the world has seen ... Christianity is no more persecuted in Russia today than was Atheism in England 80 years ago ... Very powerful groups who wish to overthrow the Russian Revolution are seeking a new weapon against it. As a recent visitor to Russia I know how misleading are their statements on many points which I was able to verify. I trust that Rationalists in Britain will be very cautious in accepting them.[22]

Of 60,000 Russian churches known to exist in 1917, only 100 were functioning by 1939. Of Moscow's 500 churches, 224 were still open on 1 January 1930, and only eighty-seven two years later.[23] According to one researcher, 'in one region alone, Bezhetsk, 100 of the surviving 308 churches were shut in 1929–30, while only twelve had been closed between 1918 and 1929. In the Tula diocese 200 out of 760 churches were closed at this time.'[24]

It was not just the Orthodox Church which was under attack. There were four million Protestants in Russia. Their churches and seminaries were closed, their pastors arrested and their denominations branded as 'counter-revolutionary kulak organisations'. By 1930, 10,000 of 12,000 mosques had been closed, their imams as ruthlessly persecuted as Christian clergy.[25]

The final blow – classification as kulaks

By now, religious believers were under acute pressure. Clergy were being evicted and faced starvation. Arbitrary and punitive taxes left many destitute. There was more to come. In May 1929, a decree, *On the Characteristics of Kulak Farms Subject to the Labour Code* set out categories of people who would be subject to the mass repression which (though they did not then know it) was to begin the following year. The decree defined as a 'kulak' anyone 'having any other income obtained not through labour (*included in this category are members of the clergy*)'. (My italics.)[26]

Every blow that fell upon the kulaks was now to fall too upon priests, pastors, rabbis and imams – from the initial shooting of the most 'dangerous' 30,000 to the deportation of the remainder, in cattle trucks, to forced labour in the camps of Soviet Karelia, the Northern Region, and Siberia. In the dekulakisation and anti-clerical campaigns of 1929–31, 60,000 religious believers were arrested and 5,000 of these were shot. As the persecution increased through the 1930s, a further 200,000 were arrested. It is estimated that 100,000 Russian believers perished for their faith.

PART III

PERSECUTION
(MAY 1929–JULY 1930)

THE DESTRUCTION OF THE SIMONOV MONASTERY

Founded in the late fourteenth century, the ancient Simonov Monastery on the southern approaches to Moscow was once reputed to be the richest in the region. Its famous white stone cathedral was built between 1379 and 1405. In 1930 it was blown up to make way for a car factory.

On 22 January at nine a.m. in the Lenin district a great Saturday voluntary work will be arranged on the occasion of the demolition of the Simonov Monastery. During the preceding night part of the walls and foundations of the bell-tower will be blown up and afterwards the bricks and stones will be sorted and piled up. Over 5,000 people will participate in the work. The work will be filmed. After the end of the work at two p.m. a meeting will be organised and it is expected that the members of the Government and of the Party will speak. *Izvestia*, 19 January 1930[1]

There was plenty of bustle. In order to put piroxelene [explosive] in the walls it was necessary to work with electrical drills, with compressors. But they penetrated very deep – to the very heart – no possible means of escape …

'You are not afraid of God, comrade Kondakoff? He may be angry with you for such work of destruction.' The Commander of the Explosion Battalion is laughing. Red soldiers are laughing. Workmen are laughing.

A lantern is dancing in the hands of someone – it snatches out of the darkness cheerful faces... They put piroxelene tablets into the walls of the first class Stavropigiate Simonov Monastery... They are blowing it up... Quickly, back! Run...

A clean lustrous white sharp-pointed mountain steeply ascends. One has the desire to run up this mountain... Lo! This is really remarkable! The Cathedral is broken up into quite separate, complete, intact bricks. They lay as a hill of sugar lightly sprinkled with limy powder, ready this very moment to be used for a new building.

'EXPLOSIONS AT DAWN', *PRAVDA*, 22 JANUARY 1930[2]

Our atheism is – and here it differs from bourgeois atheism – a fighting one. It attacks all the fortresses of the old world as well as its ideology. The task is not peaceful cooperation with the church, but pitiless war against religion.

SCHEINMANN, *THE GODLESS*, c.1929[3]

This Conference congratulates the Soviet Government and the whole of the working class of the USSR on the success of the 'Five-Year Plan' up to the moment, and it recognizes that the furious religious attacks, the cry of slave labour, the distortion of news about Russia, etc., is preliminary propaganda designed to prepare the way for a vast militarist attack on the workers of Russia.

This Conference, therefore, expresses its determination to oppose such war preparations and reassures the workers of Russia of our wholehearted support of the project they have undertaken.

INDEPENDENT LABOUR PARTY CONFERENCE, APRIL 1931[4]

CHAPTER 15

THE ANTI-PERSECUTION CAMPAIGN BEGINS (MAY–DECEMBER 1929)

Labour's first months

The British general election took place on 30 May 1929. In 1924, the previous Labour administration had fallen because of Russia, and new Foreign Secretary Arthur Henderson would have been dismayed but not surprised when Russia cropped up on the very first day of Foreign Office questions in the new parliament, 15 July 1929.

Carlyon Bellairs, the Conservative MP for Maidstone, setting the tone that government and opposition exchanges would take over the next two years, challenged Henderson about the use of forced labour in the cutting and shipping of the Russian timber which was being imported into the United Kingdom. The re-establishment of Anglo-Soviet diplomatic and trading relations, broken off by the Conservatives in the wake of the Arcos affair in 1927, had been a Labour manifesto pledge. Henderson stalled, replying that it was not possible to obtain any information until diplomatic relations with the Soviet government were fully restored – a neat riposte to a member of the party which had broken off relations in the first place. When Bellairs then suggested that the government could make enquiries straight away from British shippers and merchants already trading in Russian timber, his question was ignored.

Two weeks earlier, the Baptist Union had passed a resolution condemning the widespread arrests of Russian Baptist pastors, many of whom were now in prison and some of whom, it was understood, had been shot. On 17 July, Geoffrey Shakespeare, the Liberal MP for Norwich, asked Henderson if the release of the 'hundreds' of imprisoned Baptist pastors and leaders could be discussed during the negotiations to restore relations. As Shakespeare was a Liberal, the party supporting Labour's minority Government, Henderson's reply had to be more accommodating, but he still fell back on the defence which Labour would use to deflect all appeals in the coming months – the British government could not interfere in the internal affairs of a foreign state: 'I cannot question the right of the Soviet Government to exercise jurisdiction within their own territory. I would, however, in the event of the machinery of diplomatic relations being re-established be prepared to make an appeal to the Soviet Government in the cases referred to by the Hon. Member.'[1]

The Labour Cabinet, 1929. © *National Portrait Gallery, London*

When diplomatic relations were restored, no such appeal was forthcoming.

Only ten days later, Parliament rose for the summer recess, the long break during which the business of government continued but the House of Commons did not sit. Between mid-July and 28 October, when MPs returned, little more was heard in public about the re-establishment of diplomatic relations. Negotiations between the two countries were conducted in secret and, by the time Parliament returned, a preliminary protocol (agreement) between the two governments had been signed.

Compensation for British assets seized after the Revolution had been a persistent sticking point in negotiations between the two countries for a decade. Claims by the British for recompense for the millions of pounds of investments and industrial assets seized after the Revolution were met with similarly vast counterclaims for compensation by the Soviets for damages alleged to have arisen from British support of the anti-Bolshevik White forces in the years after the Revolution. As Labour's vocal support for the Revolution had included constant accusations about Winston Churchill's 'warmongering' in Russia after 1917, the British side was hobbled, being in no position to now deny what they had already so publicly condemned.

Henderson was under pressure from many quarters. He expected to be hounded by the Conservatives when the draft treaty was published, but his backbenchers, many of them keen supporters of the Soviet Union, were pushing him to conclude an agreement from the moment the party had come to power, *without* conditions, trusting the Soviets would come good in the follow-up negotiations. Their naïveté was not matched by the Soviets, whose approach to the negotiations (and view of the British sympathisers who were so enthusiastically aiding the discussions) was both cynical and suspicious, as Stalin made clear in a letter to Molotov:

> Henderson needs a restoration of relations more than we do ... We have pushed him to the wall ... In short, no backing down from our position. Remember we are waging a struggle (negotiation with enemies is also struggle), not with England alone, but with the whole capitalist world, since the MacDonald government is at the vanguard of the capitalist governments in the work of 'humiliating' and 'bridling' the Soviet government.
>
> We really would be worthless if we couldn't manage to reply to these arrogant bastards briefly and to the point: 'You won't get a friggin' thing from us.'[2]

The Soviets had a very different perspective on propriety in diplomatic exchanges – none. This was the government which had retaliated after the Arcos expulsions by the mass execution of 'British spies'. It had no concerns about how it might offend Western sensibilities. Sensing the weakness of Labour's position, and that its desire for the restoration of relations was driven as much by emotional as by practical motives, the Soviets were quite brazen.

They demanded the *immediate* restoration of diplomatic relations *before* the discussion of any outstanding debts. They felt they were on strong ground and pushed hard.

As well as its outstanding debts, Soviet propaganda in Britain and the empire was still a serious issue. The British wanted a commitment that it would cease. But here also they failed to achieve the assurances they sought; the Russian government once again insisted that it bore no responsibility for the activities of the Comintern. In the end, Labour's capitulation was almost total. A clause recognising mutual respect for the sovereignty of each other's *internal* affairs – notably, not those of overseas territories, for the Soviets refused to make any commitment to refrain from propaganda in the empire – was in the final treaty, but whenever the Conservatives subsequently challenged Labour on the frequent and substantial breaches of it, the response was always that the example was not sufficiently serious to warrant investigation.[3]

Russian friends on the British side

Two Labour men who played a part in the negotiations were both in the pay of the Soviets – one openly, the other secretly. As we have already seen, Frank Wise was employed by Moscow to represent Russian trade interests in the UK in addition to his responsibilities as an MP. William Ewer was ostensibly the foreign editor of the pro-Soviet *Daily Herald*. He had also been a Soviet agent since 1919 and was the leader of a Soviet intelligence ring based in London.[4] As the summer progressed, Ewer made himself an energetic contributor to the process and a frequent visitor at the Foreign Office. Hugh Dalton, Henderson's junior minister, perhaps more forthright in the privacy of his diary than he would have been in person, described him as a 'tiresome busybody'.[5]

When Frank Wise had pressed Henderson to allow him to be involved in the negotiations, Henderson gave in, but was vexed by his 'indiscretion and self-importance'.[6] As Lloyd George's former aide, Wise had more credibility than Ewer: he had a long history of involvement in Anglo-Soviet negotiations at the highest level; he was a frequent visitor to Russia and had good working relationships with a number of senior Soviets. Henderson dispatched him in July to begin secret discussions with the Soviets in Germany.[7] Even so, both

Henderson and Dalton, who referred to the former as 'Uncle' in his diary, were under no illusions as to Wise's loyalties: 'Uncle asks my view of W's reliability. I say that he's all right if you want him to leak to the Russians, but not otherwise.'[8]

Restoration of relations – the first Commons debate

Although the protocol was signed in October 1929, the government, to the dismay of its more pro-Soviet backbenchers, promised Parliament that diplomatic relations would not be restored without the matter being brought before the House of Commons. On 5 November, the first important parliamentary debate on Anglo-Soviet relations took place. The debate, which was comfortably won by the government, rehearsed arguments that were to be much heard in the coming months.

Given Wise's track record, it was not going to be likely that the British side would succeed in extracting many concessions from the Soviets. Stanley Baldwin, now Leader of the Opposition, charged Henderson with 'the most humiliating surrender' on the subject of propaganda pledges.[9] Fellow Conservative, Edward Marjoribanks, decried the Bolsheviks' persecution of religion and then embarrassed Ramsay MacDonald by quoting from a speech in which MacDonald had stated:

> I have the greatest sympathy for the Russian Government … Those of us who take the world into account when we make our promises can now take the Moscow Soviet Communist Revolutionary Government under our wing and clothe it with the furs of apology to shield it from the blasts of criticism.[10]

Labour MP John Bromley of the Anglo-Russian Parliamentary Committee, whose pro-Soviet contributions would become a feature of the coming parliament, joined in to deny the allegations of Soviet persecution of religious believers. Contradicting the assertions of the British Baptist Union, he insisted that the Baptist Church in Russia had 'increased out of all proportions of what it was in the old days' before reverting to the defence which Henderson had used when first challenged on the subject: 'the internal affairs of Russia are nothing to do with us'.[11] He flatly denied that religious instruction of children was now forbidden, even though in reality those found doing so were punished severely. Another Soviet sympathiser, Labour MP Alexander Haycock, welcomed not only the treaty but the Revolution twelve years earlier, declaring, 'I rejoice that the Bolsheviks were successful … it is a good thing for the world that the Soviet Government are there'.[12]

A week later, the Cabinet privately acknowledged the failure of its negotiations on the propaganda issue. Although the Soviet government *refused* to do so, ministers concluded that they would still interpret the recent treaty to include the activities of the Comintern but that the question should be left 'until a specific case of propaganda should arise, when it would at once be taken up with the Soviet government'[13] – by whom, the Conservatives would have pointed out, had they known of the decision, it would no doubt be ignored. In the end, no case of propaganda brought to the government's attention by the opposition over the next three years was ever taken up with the Soviets.

On 3 December, Henderson reported to the Cabinet that the Soviet government had also refused the British request that the anti-propaganda pledge should also include the Dominions.[14] He would have been hard put to deny a Conservative taunt that the government had been trounced by the Russians, who had obtained all they had sought from the rapprochement at no cost to themselves.

Ambassadors were exchanged at the beginning of December and, in the Commons, Conservative Carlyon Bellairs pursued the timber question once again, this time in questions to the president of the Board of Trade, William Graham. Was Graham aware that part of the Russian timber exports was produced by large prison camps? What was he going to do to stop 'the illegal importation of these products of prison labour' into this country? Graham dodged the question, saying he had no information about it.[15] In return, Labour MP John Beckett protested to the Speaker about Bellairs – was it in order, he asked, for a member of the House 'to make insulting insinuations about Russia'?[16]

A few days later, on 16 December, when the Foreign Secretary was back at the dispatch box answering questions, Bellairs raised the matter with him too: would Henderson obtain copies of sworn affidavits, now available, from those escaped prisoners who had fled to Finland from Russian labour camps? Henderson sidestepped once again and ignored the question.[17]

Archbishop Lang – the House of Lords

The Archbishop of Canterbury, Cosmo Lang, had already received a number of letters urging him to intervene on behalf of persecuted Russian religious believers. Although he was unhappy about the renewal of relations with the Soviets, he was reticent about doing anything that might make the situation worse for those who were already suffering.[18] He was not averse to the principle of intervention, though: in 1923, Russian Orthodox Patriarch Tikhon had been under threat of execution and Lang had been close to the then Archbishop of Canterbury, Randall Davidson, during British protests on Tikhon's behalf. Those protests had probably saved Tikhon's life.

In the House of Lords, the Earl of Birkenhead had already put down a motion for 4 December, condemning the diplomatic recognition of the Soviet government. Given his position and longstanding interest in Soviet religious persecution, Lang was expected to speak. In preparation for this, he wrote to the former official representative of the Russian Orthodox Church in Britain, Fr. Basil Timotheieff, now in Paris, asking for 'recent, reliable' information on the state of the Church in Russia.[19] Soviet supporters frequently accused campaigners of rehashing the genuinely appalling atrocity stories from the early period of the Revolution and the Civil War, and Lang wanted to be sure that his sources would stand up to examination. Unfortunately, Timotheieff's reply reached Lang too late for the debate and the consequences of that delay were to cause Lang considerable embarrassment.

In his speech, Lang voiced his doubts that public statements of protest would be as effective as action by the British government through 'ordinary diplomatic means', but gave the government notice that he felt bound to maintain 'the closest vigilance' on the matter and would not hesitate to make representations to the government if it appeared that there had indeed been a resurgence of the injustices of the past. He kept steadfastly to this position throughout the coming months.

His next comment, however, was unfortunate and was to be much criticised. He stated that he believed there had been 'a cessation of those more flagrant violations of the elementary principles of justice that led to the protests some time ago'[20] – words which he was to regret over the following days, especially when Timotheieff's reply from the Russian Orthodox émigré community in Paris arrived to contradict them. Lang's assertion was immediately challenged by Viscount Brentford, the former Conservative Home Secretary William Joynson-Hicks, who had ordered the Arcos raid in 1927. Brentford quoted numerous examples of hostile Soviet remarks which contradicted the impression Lang had given that the persecution was dying down. He gave an extract from a speech by Yemelyan Yaroslavsky, the leader of the League of the Militant Godless at a youth congress in August 1929, a few months earlier: 'We ought to wage pitiless war against religion, not only in our schools, but in the bosom of the family', and followed with the words of Education Minister Anatoly Lunacharsky in *Bezbozhnik*: 'With all my heart I wish the godless every success in the fight against the repugnant spectre of God'.[21]

Just a year later, in 1931, the ILP's *New Leader* carried a series of interviews with Lunacharsky. *New Leader* might have been writing about a different person. The article spoke of a cultured man, of 'courtly manner and much personal charm', 'one of the foremost writers on philosophy, and author of a number of works on European and Russian literature, art and the theatre' and possessor of a 'thoughtful cast of face' which 'radiated optimism'.[22]

The transcript of the debate was published in *The Times* the next day, and immediately Lang began to receive letters which showed that the picture in Russia was far grimmer than he had suggested. Metropolitan Eulogius, the leader of the émigré Russian Orthodox Church in Western Europe, wrote to him on 22 December. The persecution, he insisted, was now 'especially intensive'.[23] J. H. Rushbrooke of the World Baptist Alliance wrote that any change in the persecution was 'one of method [only, and that] violations of elementary principles of justice appear even more widespread'.[24]

Realising his mistake, Lang replied at once, urging Rushbrooke to send him more information. It was the first of many enquiries he would make over the next few months which would result in a detailed and stark assessment of the dire conditions under which religious believers lived and worshipped in Soviet Russia. The information Lang obtained through these enquiries would eventually far exceed that supplied to the government by the British Embassy in Moscow, and give a picture very different from the one which ministers were being given by their Moscow embassy.

The day after the debate, the *Morning Post* newspaper sent a telegram to the Archbishop of Canterbury, asking him to join their national campaign against religious persecution in Russia. Hesitant about the political implications of associating himself with a campaign run by any newspaper, particularly the right-leaning *Morning Post*, Lang declined. The following day, the paper carried three pages of articles on the religious persecution issue, including some stinging criticism of Lang and his House of Lords speech (which it 'deplored'). It then announced the public launch of a 'Christian Protest Movement'.

Alfred Gough

Prebendary Alfred Gough (1862–1931) was born in Hartshill, Staffordshire. He was the son of a clergyman and, after a degree in modern history at Oxford, he entered the Church too, serving mostly in parishes in the north of England. In 1895, he moved to the north London parish of St John's Highbury Vale and there built up the congregation from 150 to 500 in four years. Seeing his success, the Bishop of London asked him to take over the almost empty Brompton parish church of Holy Trinity. By 1929, it was so popular that, on a Sunday morning, there were queues to get in.

Preb. Alfred Gough.

Gough was reputed to be one of the finest preachers in London, an energetic and inspirational figure. His bishop called him a 'fiery and affectionate' man. But he was no stranger to the world of politics and campaigning either. As a vicar in Hull in the early 1890s, he became active in the Saturday Half Holiday Movement for shop assistants. He was even asked to become chairman of the local branch of the Shop Assistants' Union and, so powerful were his efforts on behalf of his members, that one local newspaper predicted that in time 'Gough Thursday' might become a household word in the shop assistants' homes.[25] One description of his early days, probably referring to this time in Hull, calls him a 'Labour leader' and reports that, in his later years, 'he would say that he had sacrificed more to the cause of Labour than many Labour leaders of his time'.[26]

Gough's faith fired his social conscience, both in his activities in support of shop assistants and in his sense of Christian mission to the larger world, in a way which would be deeply unfashionable today:

> Gough did not believe that one fourth of the human race lived under our Sovereign by chance, but that this was the plan of Providence and that the British were stewards entrusted with the solemn duty of Empire Building. To him the men who went out to serve England in the distant parts of the world were in fact missionaries of the Christian faith and he believed that the carriage of our laws, based upon the Ten Commandments, to backward races was in fact pioneer work for propagation of the faith in which he so passionately believed … He believed that the British races had a mission and that our people were the banner bearers of a civilisation based upon justice and truth.[27]

Whatever one's view of the imperialist mindset, it was this which made him also a passionate campaigner against injustice.

Gough had published a book, *The Lure of Simplicity*, in July the year before. While praising the social conscience of many earlier Socialists (with whom he identified), he was forthright in criticising the current state of the movement which, he felt, had grown so close to Soviet Communism as to be little short of 'a plan for systematised and authorised burglary'.[28] Ramsay MacDonald, George Bernard Shaw and Henry Brailsford all came in for sharp criticism within its pages. Gough had played a notable part in the

British Empire Union, even speaking from the platform, and he had worked alongside many of the leading anti-Bolshevik campaigners of the day. His popularity as a speaker, combined with this, was probably what prompted the *Morning Post* to invite him to lead their new campaign.

If the paper thought that they were going to get someone to head up a political agitation against MacDonald's administration, they were mistaken. Gough was emphatic: he would accept on one condition – 'on the understanding that I might change the basis of its action from a largely political one to one of a definitely religious character'.[29] 'The work in which we are engaged', he wrote to his parishioners, 'is an appeal to the conscience and religious sense of our country to apply the almost untried – or only sporadically tried – engine of spiritual power to support the sufferers with fellowship and to co-operate with the spiritual world in a crusade of faith.'[30]

Remarkably, the *Morning Post* agreed: 'The editorial staff accepted my proposal, and while promising to give me every assistance in its power – a promise which it has loyally fulfilled – left me free to follow the policy which I put before them.'[31] Under Gough's leadership, a remarkable and unique national movement was born. Over the next few months, it was to attract hundreds of thousands to join its protests and take the campaign against Soviet persecution worldwide.

Not without some justification, Lang was hurt by the *Morning Post*'s criticism. He had tried to obtain reliable information on conditions in Russia before his Lords speech and had only been thwarted in that by Timotheieff's absence from Paris. Gough wrote to him separately, apparently unaware of the *Post*'s invitation, asking him to be president of the campaign. Lang refused, expressing misgivings about the apparent political nature of the campaign, unaware of the assurances Gough had obtained before accepting the *Post*'s offer.[32] Instead, he wrote to a number of bishops and urged them to have nothing to do with Gough's campaign. Whether because of differences in churchmanship or simple jealousy at his prominence and success, Gough did not have the natural sympathy of the more middle-of-the-road bishops and archbishops (Lang included). One of those, the Bishop of Ely, Leonard White-Thompson, agreed with Lang: 'the chairman of the Protest Committee [is] not a man whose lead I should willingly follow'.[33] White-Thompson did, however, add that he felt uneasy that diplomatic relations had been resumed without the preliminary condition that the persecution should cease.

One feather in the campaign's cap had been to obtain the support of Charles D'Arcy, the Archbishop of Armagh. When Lang heard that D'Arcy had joined, he was dismayed: 'If you had consulted me on the matter I might have been able to give you some good reasons for my declining to involve myself.' As Primate of Ireland, the archbishop was of equal rank to Lang, and could be his own man. He tactfully declined to adopt Lang's position:

> I'm quite sure that you, in the office you hold, have to be very sure of your ground before you take action. This Russian horror has been on my mind for a long time and I have felt as if we were all blood-guilty for silence and slackness ... We are, I suppose, helpless in this matter of Russia. But, after all, moral indignation at gigantic evil is never surely quite without effect. The Protest Committee made an effort to get me to take the office of President and this I declined, but they are putting my name on the list of vice presidents. With thanks for telling me your position on the matter.[34]

Lang's ambivalence was short-lived. He soon became convinced of Gough's determination not to allow the campaign to be hijacked by political concerns and, as the months passed, worked increasingly closely with a number of the campaign's leading supporters.

Lang stirred

Although initially refusing to associate with the Christian Protest Movement, Lang was challenged by it and by the reports and testimonies of persecution that were now coming regularly across his desk. He wrote privately to the Foreign Secretary, urging him to raise the matter with the new Soviet ambassador when he arrived. The letter also contained a warning: Lang was not going to let the matter rest if the government refused to take any action, and he challenged Henderson not to sacrifice morality for trade:

> I am ... gravely concerned about the duty of this country in the matter. Indeed the very fact that I have not opposed your policy and have hoped that once we were in direct communication with the Soviet government we might be able to

do more than has been possible in the past to alleviate the lot of those who are cruelly and unjustly suffering make me all the more anxious to press on you the duty of making representations at an early stage with the Soviet Ambassador. ... I cannot think we would be justified in entering into relations with the Soviet Government for the purposes of trade, or even the cause of world peace, without using this position to do the utmost to see that the Government is one which observes the elementary principles of justice in which, as I said in a recent public letter, the intercourse of civilised nations must be based.

I am trying to keep informed, from sources I can trust, of the actual condition of things in Russia in this matter of religious persecution, and if I find that there is no mitigation of the present policy I may feel obliged to raise the matter publicly in the House of Lords but at present I am only writing to you confidentially but with the earnest hope that you may deal with this matter at the earliest stage with the Soviet Ambassador. I think you can point out to him (and that is where the present [Gough's] national protest may be of real service) that he cannot be blind now that he is here to the indignation which is widely felt in this country, and that if he wishes to be on friendly terms much will depend on the attitude of his Government towards these principles of elementary justice.[35]

Cosmo Gordon Lang, Archbishop of Canterbury. © National Portrait Gallery, London.

The former lay preacher Henderson could have been expected to be among the most sympathetic members of the government towards the cause of religion, but his apparently conciliatory reply made no concrete assurance that he would do anything that might prejudice the progress of the rapprochement between the two nations:

> No one could be more desirous than I am to use any influence I can to further the cause of religious liberty in the Soviet Union. ... It is certainly my intention, when a suitable opportunity arises, to point out to the Ambassador the intense feeling which the anti-religious policy is arousing in this country. I do not however think it is desirable when the ambassador has been here so short a time, to take up as one of the first questions the discussion of a matter which his Government will certainly regard as a matter of their own internal policy.[36]

A careful reader will have noted that drawing the ambassador's attention to the feeling that Soviet policy aroused in the *country* fell far short of an expression of disapproval of the British *government*, and that there was no commitment expressed to do so within any particular timescale.

The launch of the Christian Protest Movement

The launch of the new movement was announced by Gough in the press in characteristic fashion:

> A Union Jack has flown on the tower of Brompton Parish Church since the early days of the War. As flag after flag has worked ragged with the weather during these years another has always been ready to take its place.
>
> Yesterday this flag was flown at half-mast in token of mourning for the Russians who have suffered for their faith, and, especially, those who have died during the summer and autumn of this year. Tonight the Cross of St George will be hoisted at topmast and will take its place as the emblem of a spiritual crusade.[37]

The first major event of the new movement took place that night, 19 December 1929, at a mass meeting in the Royal Albert Hall. The left-leaning *Manchester Guardian*, which at that stage had not yet developed its strong opposition to the movement, headed its report 'Russia's Campaign Against Religion – World Crusade Started' and, as well as quoting the meeting's insistence that it had 'no political motives', the newspaper left no doubt that religious fervour, not just political protest, infused the gathering:

> Viscount Brentford moved the following resolution: 'That this meeting of worshippers of Almighty God vehemently protests against the persistent and cruel persecution of our fellow-worshippers in Russia and calls upon believers in God and lovers of liberty throughout the world to pray and work unceasingly for the religious freedom of the people of Russia.'[38]

Those who watched it would have been mistaken if they had dismissed this gathering, and the movement that sprang from it, as comprising just a group of mild-mannered churchgoers. The organisers made it clear that they would not stop at prayer alone. Two other motions showed that the campaign intended to flex both material as well as spiritual muscle, agreeing: 'that the British Government be urged to make the strongest possible representations to the Soviet Government to bring this persecution to an end [and] that copies of this protest be forwarded to the heads of all civilised Governments'.[39]

It was an era in which spiritual leaders carried far greater respect than they do today and the campaign committee was drawn from a wide and influential spectrum of Church and secular leadership; Gough was chairman. He and the Archbishop of Armagh, already mentioned, were joined by, among others, the Bishops of London, Gloucester and Chelmsford, former Home Secretary Viscount Brentford, the Earl of Glasgow, Lord Clifford of Chudleigh, and a number of leaders of the Free Churches. The Chief Rabbi was one of the vice-presidents.

After the Albert Hall launch, the Christian Protest Movement spread rapidly throughout the country. By March 1930, Gough was speaking at over fourteen meetings a month.[40] The campaign held 270 meetings in its first year of operation, an average of five a week. By December 1933, it had distributed 220,000 leaflets, articles and booklets, and hosted over 800 meetings.[41] Spurred by the establishment of the British movement, similar organisations sprung up in France, Belgium, Holland, Germany, Sweden, Norway, Switzerland, Finland, Bulgaria, Hungary, Italy and Yugoslavia.[42]

The public meetings and publicity generated by the Christian Protest Movement provided the national backdrop against which subsequent events would be played out in Parliament, Downing Street, Lambeth Palace and the British Embassy in Moscow. It was the pressure generated by the campaign that kept the subject alive even when ministers and civil servants were desperately trying to bury it. The responsibility for that must go in no small measure to Alfred Gough, who worked so tirelessly to promote the cause of persecuted Russian believers that it eventually led to a breakdown in his health and brought on the heart attack from which he finally died.[43]

CHAPTER 16

THE FOREIGN OFFICE
(JUNE 1929-MARCH 1930)

Clashes at the Foreign Office

The relationship between a British socialist administration which was broadly sympathetic to the Soviet Union, and a Foreign Office, many staff members of which represented the class that was the target of Socialism, was always going to be challenging. Henderson set about stamping his authority upon the ministry at once.

His first obstacle was Sir Ronald Lindsay, the Permanent Under-Secretary, the senior civil servant at the Foreign Office. Lindsay was an aristocrat, the son and brother of an earl. After their first meeting, Hugh Dalton described him as 'sly and reactionary'.[1] Within a fortnight, Dalton had recorded in his diary Henderson's 'first row' with Lindsay and a number of clashes with more junior members of staff.[2] By November, Henderson was so fed up with Lindsay that he had decided to move him out of the way and appoint him, to the relief of both parties, as the new ambassador to Washington. Lindsay left in January 1930 and was replaced by the more amenable Sir Robert Vansittart, who had been Permanent Private Secretary to Prime Minister Ramsay MacDonald the previous year.

The Northern Department of the Foreign Office was responsible for the Soviet Union, as well as for the Baltic States, Scandinavia and Poland. At its head was Horace Seymour, a diplomat with twenty years' experience who had served in Washington, Rome and The Hague, but who had only been promoted to head of the department in April 1929, a month before the election. Perhaps because this was his first post at this level and he had had no previous experience of working with the government as the head of an important Foreign Office department, Seymour exhibited less reluctance than others might have done where the government's pursuit of policy seemed to be at the expense of principle. As the religious persecution crisis developed and as evidence mounted of widespread human rights abuses in Soviet Russia, Seymour's department, in cooperation with the Moscow embassy, created a wide-ranging defence against the Church and opposition human rights protests, such as devising a tortuous redefinition of 'persecution' to absolve the Soviets of the charges and to justify the government's non-intervention. When other members of his department began to alter their perspective on Russia, it was Seymour who remained the most firm.

Henderson was determined that the newly appointed ambassador to Moscow should be a diplomat, not a politician (a number of whom had in-dicated they would like the post), and someone who had a good working knowledge of Russian. This seemed both reasonable and uncontroversial. In the end, however, the result of the selection process had dire consequences for those suffering under the Soviets. The final choice fell on Sir Esmond Ovey, former ambassador in Mexico. Although he had not been to Russia since 1900, he had spent four years in the Northern Department between 1920 and 1924.

In the end, though, it was less the relationship of the Foreign Secretary and the Permanent Under-Secretary which was to be so influential in determin-ing British responses to Soviet persecution than that between Henderson's number two, Under-Secretary of State Hugh Dalton, Ambassador Ovey, and Northern Department head Horace Seymour.

Appointments vetoed

As Henderson's junior minister with day-to-day responsibility for Russian affairs, Hugh Dalton's role in the events of 1929–31 was central. Brought up at Windsor Castle, Dalton (1887–1962) was the son of the Anglican clergy-man who was tutor to the two sons of the Prince of Wales, Eddie and George (later George V). In 1906, after Eton, he went up to Cambridge and there his politics moved to the left (as would happen, with far different consequences, with Philby, Blunt, Maclean and Burgess in the 1930s). He joined the Fabian Society, where he came to the attention of Beatrice Webb, one of the founders of the LSE. After being awarded his doctorate at the LSE in 1921, he lectured there from 1922–25, publishing a polemical call for a wealth tax in 1923.[3] An unsuccessful attempt to enter Parliament followed in 1924 before he was finally elected as MP for Bishop Auckland in 1929. As a radical economist, he watched the development of a planned socialist economy in Russia with great interest and some sympathy, though his view of the Soviets themselves was more circumspect. That played out in his handling of Russian affairs in the Foreign Office.

It began with the selection of staff for the new embassy in Moscow. In a highly unusual move, he overruled Foreign Office selections for staff for the embassy and vetoed those who seemed anti-Bolshevik in order to ensure that the embassy was firmly 'on side' with the Labour view on Russia. Ovey met with Dalton's approval. 'He doesn't want anyone on his staff who will abuse the Bolsheviks if he has had a couple of glasses of port after-dinner', he wrote in early November, adding his own view, that 'we do not require people at Moscow should be pro-Bolshevik but at least they should be objective'.[4] In another context, both remarks might seem to exhibit sensible prudence. In fact, 'objective' meant that any candidate who did not share Dalton and Ovey's minimum requirement of sympathetic neutrality was weeded out:

December 4. At the office I exercise my veto for the fourth time on a proposed appointment on Ovey's staff for Moscow. This time of Waite, a consul, who was there with Hodgson, was attacked in the Bolo press when the mission left, & has a White Russian wife … Before, it was Osborne, proposed as councillor, who admitted to hating Bolo principles and practice so much that the idea of going to Moscow seemed to him a nightmare; Cave, also with Russian wife, who was there before, and sees no hope in the Five-Year Plan, hopelessly biased; [name illegible] … who is described in the Foreign Office list as having been arrested and imprisoned by the Bolos in 1918! The fifth item was stopping the appointments committee from sending Hodgson as minister to Riga, of all places! No gumption at all in these suggestions.[5]

Such interference in Foreign Office overseas appointments by a government minister was highly unusual.[6]

The blocking of Sir Robert Hodgson's appointment to Riga in neighbouring

Latvia was even more a case of political prejudice overruling common sense. Hodgson was ideally suited to the post. He had been chargé d'affaires in Moscow until the breach of relations under the Conservatives in 1927; and he had extensive experience not only in Moscow but also in Vladivostok in the Russian Far East and Omsk in Siberia. As one of the closest foreign capitals to the Russian border, Riga was the main conduit for good intelligence on the situation in Russia. But therein lay the problem. Labour politicians did not like the reports which came out of Riga and complained so frequently about 'biased' anti-Soviet reporting by Western correspondents there that, for many on the left, 'Riga' had become synonymous with 'reactionary fabrication'. The British representative had to be someone who, in Labour terms, was 'objective' on Soviet affairs. Hodgson's perspective had been formed by intimate first-hand experience of Soviets, something of a rare commodity at the time, but the end result was that, in Labour eyes, he was suspect.

Dalton's concern about how Hodgson's appointment might play with Moscow displayed an accommodation for Soviet sensitivities which was in stark contrast to the Soviet proposal, greeted with great consternation by the Cabinet,[7] to send Lev Kamenev as ambassador to London. Kamenev, one of the old Bolsheviks and a leading trade negotiator, had been expelled from Britain in 1920 because of his involvement with the 'Hands Off Russia' campaign and the Council of Action.[8] In the end, Moscow's choice was to be less inflammatory with the appointment of Grigori Sokolnikov, one of the group who had accompanied Lenin on his return journey from Switzerland.

Ovey's bias

Sir Esmond Ovey met with the approval of Sidney and Beatrice Webb when they made their pilgrimage to Russia in June 1932, Beatrice finding him full of 'mostly favourable' views about the Soviet government and 'indignant with the constant libelling of the Soviet administration in the British press'.[9] Those who met Ovey or worked alongside him in Russia were much less complimentary. One Western visitor to Moscow reported that the rest of the foreign diplomatic community thought he was 'a fool'.[10] Reader Bullard, the Leningrad consul, was far from being a Tory. It was perhaps because Bullard had been mildly supportive of the Soviet Communism that he had managed to make it past the shortlist to be appointed in the first place. He changed his mind when he saw it at close quarters. He wrote in his diary that Ovey was 'rather disgustingly pro-Soviet',[11] and 'never seems disgusted or horrified by anything the Russians do',[12] adding on another occasion:

> The Ambassador is not quite honest – not positively dishonest, but not honest enough to feel disgust at the Soviet lies and humbug ... Sir Esmond tried to draw the deduction that all nations are very much alike, and in particular that we should not act as though the Bolsheviks were any worse than ourselves. The fact is that Sir Esmond is morally lazy and the dishonesty of the Soviet leaders does not disgust him.[13]

Ovey's attitude changed markedly in late 1932 after the arrest of the British Metropolitan-Vickers engineers. When Bullard recorded this, it only highlighted what Ovey had been like for the previous three years:

> The Ambassador is a changed man. The ordinary observer would say that he was pro-Bolshevik [until recently]. But he has changed. Only a month ago ... he was trying to persuade me that the Soviet officials were about as honest as those in the United Kingdom, and now he is cursing them. ...
>
> Foreigners who were at first enthusiastic or at any rate favourable observers of the Russian scene are becoming increasingly disillusioned both here and in Moscow. I have already spoken about the Ambassador. One day he remarked that probably a couple of million people will die of hunger this winter but that the authorities wouldn't mind that. He would not have said that a year ago, nor would he have let anyone else say it without criticism.[14]

Bullard was not the only one who bemoaned Ovey's views in the early years. Gareth Jones, the Welsh journalist who exposed the Ukraine famine, spoke also of how Ovey was 'prejudiced in favour of the Soviet Government' and was 'pro-Bolshevik'.[15] The first secretary in the embassy, E. A. Walker, noted how Ovey disapproved of one particular report which was critical of the Soviets, saying that he was 'usually somewhat put out when awkward facts crop up as to the shortcomings of the Bolsheviks'.[16]

Col. William Osbaldeston-Mitford, Ovey's private secretary and attaché, who had been on his staff in Mexico and was his best man when he got married later that year, was no different. When Mitford came over to London on leave in March 1930 singing the praises of the Bolsheviks, Dalton was delighted:

> Col. Mitford, Ovey's private secretary and honorary attaché, blew in today …
> He is impressed of the five-year plan. The Russians will certainly make good.
> The stuff about religious persecution is all moonshine. The priests whom he sees all look fat. They have shut up a lot of churches of course. But no one ever went to them except a handful of old people. Weren't a lot of City [London] churches shut up a few years ago? … Our embassy are a united party, except Patrick who is a bit of a die hard.* Mitford ought to run about the West End talking this stuff. It's grand![17]

The King had heard about Mitford's remarks too, and was upset – understandably, given that the Bolsheviks had killed his cousin, the tsar, and his family, only a decade earlier. This pleased Dalton even more:

> Jebb [Henderson's Private Secretary] tells me that K-Hugessen,† who kissed hands on appointment to Riga, reported that the King had heard that Mitford had been telling everyone at St James's Club that the Bolsheviks were very good fellows. The King was displeased at this and would have preferred more impartiality … Good old Mitford![18]

King George and Dalton obviously had different views on what impartiality looked like in a member of the Moscow embassy staff.

Postscript – old school ties?

While there had been a social clash between Henderson and Lindsay, it is incorrect to assume that there was a distinct class divide between Foreign Office staff and Labour politicians. In fact, it is quite possible that the closeness of the two had far-reaching repercussions.

---

* Colin Patrick (1893-1942) left Moscow and resigned from the diplomatic service the following year. He became a Conservative MP and was a forceful critic of the Soviet regime (see Chapter 12).
† Hughe Knatchbull-Hugessen (1886–1971) was later British ambassador to China, Turkey and Belgium.

The dual role of civil servants is to serve and to advise the elected government. At times, there will be a tension between these two functions. One curious feature of the events of 1929–31 is that, in spite of abundant evidence of the Soviets' repression of human rights, Foreign Office officials gave their politicians far more credibility and for longer than logic or deference alone dictated. It was quite some way into Labour's tenure that the evidence became so overwhelming that the staff of the Foreign Office broke ranks and challenged the government's interpretation of events, i.e. that the stories of persecution had been exaggerated by Tory diehards to attack the Labour government. One factor has emerged which may partly explain this: a number of officials and Labour politicians, Dalton, Ovey and Seymour among them, had been to the same school, Eton. As with the national position in which the Church was held at that time, we have to appreciate the contemporary context of this circumstance to see its significance – the mutual understanding, solidarity, sense of trust and connection that there was between former pupils of the same public school, particularly one such as Eton, in Britain in the early 1930s.

On 23 November 1929, just before Ovey left for Moscow, Dalton entertained Ovey to dinner at the House of Commons. Of the eight dinner guests, four were Old Etonians – Dalton, Ovey, Hughe Knatchbull-Hugessen, who was appointed ambassador to Estonia, Latvia and Lithuania in April 1930, and John Strachey MP. Strachey had spent five weeks in Russia the previous year and had returned with glowing reports of its progress and of the character of its newly emerging leader, Stalin.[19] Although an Old Etonian from a privileged background, Strachey would go on to become one of the most prolific and widely read British Communist theorists of the 1930s.

At the dinner, Ovey, the newly appointed Moscow ambassador of the British Labour government, would have heard two of its members, Dalton and Strachey, declare that, beyond doubt, the Soviet Communism was fundamentally benign. Dalton and Strachey were not among the rough working-class radicals who could also be found in Labour's ranks. They were members of the same privileged elite as Ovey, and for that he would have found their assertion all the more persuasive. It may indeed have been a contributing factor to Ovey's naive faith in the Soviets' goodwill, which was to become notorious among the expatriate Moscow community.

Dalton and Strachey were not the only influential Old Etonian Labour politicians sympathetic towards Soviet Communism. While Ovey had been serving in the Northern Department in 1924, Labour's negotiations with the Soviets were overseen by one of the party's most enthusiastic Soviet supporters, Dalton's predecessor Arthur Ponsonby, also an Old Etonian. As Ovey moved on to Moscow, Ponsonby was made a peer and became Labour Deputy Leader in the House of Lords. There, he continued to be one of the most outspoken Soviet apologists in Parliament.

Given that Ovey was to show himself almost wholly persuaded of the good intent of the Soviets, one might imagine that there could have been challenges to this view from staff in the Foreign Office or embassy. Once again, however, the Eton connection may have come into play. Seymour, the department head, was six years younger than Ovey. Public schools were rigidly age-structured, 'fagging' (the system of a junior pupil acting as unpaid servant to a senior boy) was the norm, and deference to those a few years higher up in the school was instilled into younger boys, often by beating. The deference of a younger former public schoolboy to an older one remained into adult life. Seymour, newly in post, serving the older Ovey, who had taken up one of the most important and sensitive ambassadorships in the British diplomatic service, as well as Under-Secretary Hugh Dalton, and another Old Etonian, Permanent Under-Secretary Sir Robert Vansittart, remained compliant.

In the embassy, the ambassador's will was supreme but, once again, the old school tie would have ensured an even greater degree of compliance than usual when Ovey's reports seemed over-generous to the Russians. Two of the three senior embassy staff were Old Etonians, all junior in age to Ovey. The return of one of them, F. T. Ashton-Gwatkin, to the UK in April 1930 then in turn all ensured that the majority of Northern Department staff were Old Etonians, once again all younger than Ovey.

None of this is to say that *all* Foreign Office Old Etonians were pro-Soviet, only that their mutual connections might well have delayed the point at which they were willing to admit to themselves that their superiors were wrong and that the Soviet regime was in fact a perpetrator of crimes against humanity on a massive scale – a phenomenon which becomes apparent as the events which followed unfold. When Vansittart decided that he had had enough and spoke out, he did so forcefully.

CHAPTER 17

THE PROTESTS GO NATIONAL (JANUARY 1930)

The Christian Protest Movement (CPM) gathered momentum quickly and public meetings continued throughout January. Even though it had been launched with the help of the right-wing *Morning Post*, reaction to the campaign across the wider political spectrum was not initially hostile. When the Labour-supporting *Manchester Guardian* reported on the CPM rally in the Free Trade Hall (Manchester) on 24 January, its reference to the Russian persecutions did not carry the epithet 'alleged'. That neutrality was not to last long: within weeks, it would accompany all references to religious persecution made by the Labour press, the Cabinet and the Foreign Office.

Ovey had arrived in Moscow to reopen the embassy in December 1929. Within days, he was being asked to report on the situation for religious believers in Russia but Ovey and his staff (for they, as much as he, were responsible for the intelligence passed on to London) actually had very little idea of what was going on in Russia. There had been no British mission in the capital for two years; there was none of the residue of general background understanding which would have accumulated among the staff of an embassy over a longer period of time. Ovey himself had spent the previous four years in Mexico. Furthermore, Russian nationals were often too frightened to associate with foreigners. This was no idle fear: arrests were common and the announcement of shootings of Russians found to be 'foreign spies' was frequent. When diplomatic relations had been broken off in 1927, some local Russian embassy employees had been imprisoned or shot.

Information gathering expeditions outside Moscow by journalists or embassy staff required official permission, were rare and were closely controlled by the OGPU. Even journalists admitted to relying heavily on the official Soviet press for information. Malcolm Muggeridge, correspondent for the *Manchester Guardian* in 1933, described the life of a Western observer in Moscow as being like looking out from inside a goldfish bowl.[1]

Whether from pride or professional insecurity, Ovey would not admit directly that he was hard put to obtain *any* detailed information at all in response to the enquiries put to him by the Northern Department, beyond translations of Russian decrees and regulations and snippets of news gleaned by conversations with foreign journalists. At one point (to be discussed shortly), he apologised to the department for the delay in reporting on religious persecution because he had to wait for a Soviet government specialist to advise him.

The limited extent of Ovey's ability to obtain useful information on religious persecution is highlighted by a comparison between the volume of material produced by the Moscow embassy for the Foreign Office in 1930 and that produced by the supporters of the campaign. They drew on numerous sources in the Baptist Church worldwide, the Orthodox expatriate community (mostly based in Paris, whose information bureau was partly financed by Gough's CPM), and the Vatican, as well as press correspondents based outside Russia and who were free not only from censorship but also from the fear that critical reporting would lead to a revoking of their press credentials and expulsion from the country. The British Embassy produced no more than fifteen pages of reports on religious persecution in 1930, excluding translations of Soviet legislation. By contrast, the three most significant reports produced by Lang and the CPM stretched to a total of over 130 pages. Those campaigning on behalf of the persecuted were far better informed than the Foreign Office.

Ovey's first response

When the protests first began, Ovey insisted that any approach to the Soviet Foreign Ministry on behalf of those suffering 'alleged' persecution would only make matters worse for them. It would also be seen as interference in the Soviet Union's internal affairs and hinder the development of Anglo-Soviet friendship which Ovey had been sent to Moscow to facilitate. Henderson was concerned by the reports of persecution and, on 10 January, asked Ovey what would be the Soviets' likely reaction should there be a representation by the British on behalf of persecuted believers. Ovey was unequivocal: any approach by the British would draw the response that it was in breach of the treaty signed between the two parties 'scrupulously to respect the undoubted right of a State to order its own life within its own jurisdiction in its own way'.[2] This was the downside of the 'no propaganda' part of the agreement by which the British government had bound themselves, even though the Soviets were to display little intention of abiding by it themselves. Ovey advised strongly against making any complaint.

Ovey's scruples could not merely be ascribed to following the accepted course of British diplomacy to human rights abuses abroad, as might be assumed. For a start, repression of their citizens by tyrannical regimes is always cited as an 'internal' matter – that is their nature; to protest none would be to leave repression unchecked around the globe. Ovey's position was in sharp contrast to the attitude of the Conservative government towards the Soviets six years earlier. In March 1923, they had not hesitated in joining protests at the arrest and imprisonment of the two leading Russian Catholic prelates, Archbishop Cieplak and Monsignor Budkevich, and their colleagues who had been put on trial for counter-revolutionary activity. The Soviets had at the time told Ambassador Hodgson (the same man whom Dalton had blocked from Riga) that his appeal was 'an entirely inadmissible attempt at interference in the internal affairs of the independent and sovereign RSFSR' (the acronym later changed to USSR).[3] The protests had not prevented Budkevich from being shot, but other condemned men, including Cieplak, had undoubtedly been saved by the international protests that Britain had joined – at the risk of the same accusation that Ovey now feared. The Conservative government of the day (and many other Western governments) had felt that there was an overriding moral imperative to protest.

With the assistance of Frank Wise, who was back in Moscow and an old acquaintance of Litvinov, now Soviet Foreign Minister, Ovey met first Anastas Mikoyan, the Trade Commissar, on 13 January 1930 and then Litvinov himself on 31 January. His report on the second meeting is important, not least because it shows the part that Ovey played with the Foreign Office in developing a misleading and artificial distinction between degrees of religious persecution in order to downplay its significance – one which was to surface later in Parliament in attempts to minimise the severity of the persecution.

Litvinov flatly refused to discuss any Soviet responses to British complaints of religious persecution, so Ovey took another approach:

> As he declined to suggest even informally any step which his government
> could take I had recourse to asking him to confirm certain views *I had already*
> *formed* ... which may perhaps (a) tend to disprove the case of 'cruel persecu-
> tion' and (b) to explain the real attitude of the Soviet government as regards
> 'suppression of religious education'. (My italics.)[4]

Ovey hoped, he wrote, that this would 'help to deal with the technical accusation of cruel persecution and disprove that all religious teaching is actually
prohibited by law'. The Soviet government, Litvinov assured Ovey, never
closed churches except at the request of local authorities (a defence which
was to be repeated by Labour fellow travellers). On the subject of the religious education of children, Litvinov declared that there was nothing to
prevent any adult Russian from receiving religious education or from sending
his children for instruction. In fact, as Ovey admitted in a later report,[5] any
adult discovered doing so would have lost his job. As for executions, Ovey
assured Henderson there had been 'no cases whatsoever of shooting or persecuting priests on account of their religious beliefs'. Litvinov conceded that it
was true that everyone in the service of the Church was deprived of his right
to vote, but remarked that the penalty was no different from that extended to
certain other classes. No mention was made of the real impact of disenfranchisement upon those who were marked by it, by further persecution.

Back in London, Horace Seymour's reaction was revealing: 'to press the
matter further would be to court a serious rebuttal, which could be very un-
desirable at the present stage of the negotiations'. Negotiations for a new Anglo-Soviet Trade Agreement were currently in progress.[6] The success of those
negotiations could not be jeopardised; it had only been a few months since
the Wall Street Crash, and British unemployment was rising at an alarming
rate. Any possibility of using the negotiations as leverage for human rights
improvements in Russia was out of the question.

Ovey sent a second telegram on the same day to qualify the remarks by
Litvinov which he had reported in his first telegram.[7] In an attempt to convey
the truth accurately while still providing the government with a way out of

its implications, Ovey then proceeded to qualify Litvinov's comments with a series of remarks which alternately confirmed and mitigated the severity of the religious persecution: 'It cannot of course be denied that strong moral and economic pressure is brought to bear ... on people who continue openly to profess their faith ... but ... it is primarily by propaganda that the Soviet government hope to achieve their object.' 'Moral and economic pressure' actually meant the denial of ration cards, medical treatment, housing and employment – in other words, destitution and starvation. He was wrong too; as has been seen, around 60,000 religious believers were arrested directly because of their religious activities between 1929 and 1931.[8] Ovey continues: 'all sermons, Litvinov added, would technically be religious propaganda but sermons and services continue to be permitted in Russian churches although I am told that in practice in only about 150 churches in Moscow out of possibly over 1,000 [are] services still held'. Being illegal, any preacher was liable to arrest and imprisonment at any time that the authorities wished to have an excuse to remove someone. Many were. Ovey's account of 85 per cent of Moscow churches being closed down makes the difference between 'cruel persecution' and 'persecution' academic. Finally: 'It is probably true that priests like many other persons have been arrested, exiled and even killed in the course of police clashes in connection particularly perhaps with the present agrarian struggle but I have no proof of any such action being taken on purely religious grounds.' Ovey is ignorant (unlike Russian émigrés reporting on the matter at this time) of the inclusion of all religious personnel in the definition of kulaks in the Soviet decree of 21 May 1929. Conceding that the stories of the execution of priests were 'probably true', but then downplaying it by suggesting that they were shot for counter-revolution, is disingenuous.

Direct confirmation of the shootings of priests arrived in the Foreign Office on 10 February 1930 in a note from Henry Chilton, the British Ambassador to the Holy See in Rome. Chilton reported that the Vatican Secretary of State had discussed with him the shooting of priests in Russia and spoken 'with great bitterness', then showing him a list of clergy who had 'recently been condemned to death or shot'.[9] Chilton's dispatch was printed and circulated to the King and Cabinet (and to the Moscow embassy). One has to question whether or not, so soon after Ovey's dispatch, any pretence that priests were being shot on account of anything other than their status was possible.

In the same telegram, Ovey advised London that he was preparing a report on the whole question of religious persecution – but, surprisingly, *with* Soviet assistance. 'Litvinov offered to put me in touch with an expert on the matter', he wrote, blithely ignoring the likelihood that what he would get from this offer was disinformation rather than fact. In the end, he depended so much upon Litvinov's expert that his subsequent report had to be held up because Litvinov's expert had been 'delayed'. It is astonishing that a British ambassador should have relied so heavily upon the evidence of a specialist offered by the very government that was under investigation.

No further mention is made in any of Ovey's correspondence about the Soviet expert on whom he clearly depended for information about the allegations of persecution. What is significant about this omission is that at least some of his future dispatches were likely to have been compiled with that expert's assistance. These communications were extraordinarily influential in determining the government's response to the British protest campaign and were even circulated to Buckingham Palace (where they met with the approval of the King). When Ovey's main report was delivered a few weeks later, the fact that he asked for it to be kept secret to protect his position in Moscow implied that its contents were exclusively his own. In reality, parts reflect the Soviet propaganda line so closely that they seem to betray the hand of the nameless expert.[10]

CHAPTER 18

THE CABINET DECIDES...
TO DO NOTHING

O n the morning of 12 February 1930, the Cabinet met to decide how to respond to the growing demands for it to join appeals to the Russian government to cease its persecution of religious believers. A major debate on the subject was to take place in the House of Lords the following day. It decided to take no action. Minutes of that meeting record the decision that 'as regards the alleged religious persecution His Majesty's Government could not interfere in the internal affairs of a foreign state'.[1]

This was an important moment. Henceforth, whatever personal doubts Henderson might have felt (Dalton and Ovey appear to have had none), he was bound by the doctrine of Cabinet collective responsibility to follow the government's line. Challenged to intervene by Conservatives in the Commons the very next afternoon, his vague assurance of action was actually empty of all meaning, especially in the context of the Cabinet decision the previous day: 'His Majesty's Government will, when possible or compatible with the interests of those affected, use all its influence in support of the cause of religious liberty and the freedom of religious practice'.[2] In the House of Lords on 13 February, Lord Parmoor, the Labour leader, repeated Henderson's statement.[3] Having also sat in the Cabinet meeting the day before, he would also have known that the assurance was worth very little.

The first major Lords debate
With Liberal cooperation, the government had a majority in the Commons and were able to block difficult debates on Soviet affairs. They could not do

so in the Lords. Even in the 1930s, there was strong pressure from the left to abolish the House of Lords. Perversely, it was just the House of Lords' unrepresentative nature which enabled it at this time to reflect national unease and speak up for the oppressed in Russia. If the government had had its way there would have been no discussion of the subject at all in either House.

The debate places on record the depth of revulsion held on the matter outside government, and the moral imperative that many felt obliged Britain to take a stand. The Foreign Office case, made all the more persuasive by the Russian trade negotiations then going on, was that any action by the government was futile and therefore pointless. Speaking for the bishops, the Bishop of Norwich addressed this point directly, answering also the charge that the Church should keep out of the business of government and foreign policy:

> It is not for us who sit on this [bishops'] Bench to interpose in strictly political issues. That perhaps has kept some of us silent longer than otherwise would have been the case. There are always those who say: 'It is not your business.' But I emphatically feel to-day that this is not a political issue but a grave religious issue. What we are speaking of is the casting to the winds of all the restraints and the decencies of humanity. Such persecutions as we are hearing of to-day would have been denounced in heathen Rome long ago as against the very standards of civilisation. And I claim that we are entitled to protest when we hear of these things going on almost before our eyes.
>
> 'But what good would come from such a protest?' people ask. Well, I think that stronger than law is public opinion ... and the pressure of public opinion can be felt from one country to another. Why, then, should we despair of the expression of public disgust in England doing some good over there in Russia? This public opinion, informed not by diplomacy but by Christianity, is a rising tide denouncing all this cruelty and savagery, this persecution and debauchery and the defiance of all that is best and uplifting in human nature and the affairs of men. Every atom of respect for things human and things divine urges us to lift up our voice in this dreadful hour, to lift it up in compassion and appeal among men and in prayer to God.[4]

The debate also introduces us to one of the most disturbing characters in the whole affair – Charles Cripps, Lord Parmoor, the Labour leader of the

House of Lords. Parmoor (1852–1941) was an ageing former lawyer. His late wife had been Beatrice Webb's sister, and he was therefore brother-in-law to fellow Cabinet member Sidney Webb. A second brother-in-law, through another of Beatrice's sisters, was Labour MP H. T. Muggeridge, father of journalist Malcolm Muggeridge. His son was Stafford Cripps, the MP. A wealthy landowner, the war had turned Parmoor, according to Beatrice Webb, 'into something very like an international socialist'.[5] More accurately, Cripps appears drawn to the left by pacifism rather than Socialism.

Unlike Dalton, Ovey, or more extreme fellow travellers John Strachey, George Lansbury, James Maxton or even Lord Ponsonby, his deputy leader and eventual successor in the Lords, Parmoor appears to have had no conviction whatever that the Soviets were innocent of the charges laid against them. What makes Parmoor's defence of the government seem all the more unprincipled, is that he had been a leading layman in the Church of England, chancellor and vicar-general of York province from 1900 to 1914, and from 1902 to 1924 vicar-general of Canterbury province. In 1924, MacDonald, short of Labour peers, offered Parmoor a seat in the Cabinet and he resigned his Church positions.

To put it at its most uncharitable, Parmoor was a true lawyer, a mouth for hire. As a lawyer, it was his custom diligently to argue the case, without scruples, of those who employed him – in this instance the Cabinet, his worldly masters, in opposition to his former masters, the Church, and their spiritual brethren in the Soviet Union. Parmoor's speeches on Russia in the House of Lords make no moral case but turn upon small points of argument. His technique was to appear to agree wholeheartedly with an opposition speaker and then introduce so many qualifications and doubts that he ended up all but withdrawing his own agreement.

Parmoor's speeches give the impression that he knew he could not win the argument on Russia, but recognised that his function was to stall political and ecclesiastical opposition in the face of evidence which would have forced a government with a greater moral conscience to intervene. In his terms, success was defined not by being able to refute opposition claims (that would have been impossible) but merely by introducing enough points of doubt that government inaction or delay seemed justified.

In this debate, Archbishop Lang announced that he had formed a committee to enquire into the Russian persecution and then report back to him.* Now, faced with expressions of moral outrage and calls for government action, Parmoor chose to fall back on propaganda supplied by the shady Anglo-Russian Parliamentary Committee. He did not need to say that he *believed* their propaganda (put out in weekly newssheets to all MPs), only that it justified inaction:

> Only to-day I received a message from the Anglo-Russian Parliamentary Committee – I have no special knowledge of them myself – enclosing a note of an official statement made in Russia by a spokesmen of the Government only last Sunday, February 9. I am not asking your Lordships to accept as truth any statement of this kind, but it emphasises my point that the whole truth must be sought for and studied. It cannot be got from the statements which we see from day to day in the newspapers.
>
> This is what the note says. This is an official statement made in Russia last Sunday, February 9: – To this day tens of thousands of churches of all denominations function in the U.S.S.R. – that is the Union of Soviet and Socialist Republics – and priests who refrain from counterrevolutionary activities are allowed to conduct religious services unmolested. As I say I am not asking your Lordships – of course no one who is accustomed to deal with matters of evidence would ask it – to accept a statement of that kind without further inquiry, but what I say is that there are statements on both sides and if by means of such an inquiry as has been indicated into what appears, at the present time, a horror to our whole Christian civilisation we can find the truth, an enormous step in advance will have been made.

The fact that Parmoor coupled his stalling with a rare admission of the 'horror' of the persecution further took the wind out of the opposition's sails. No other members of his party would have used such a word as 'horror' to describe *any* aspect of Soviet policy. On the surface it seems to indicate a man of moral perception. In practice, Parmoor's stance was as amoral as those

---

*   When Lang eventually brought those findings to the House of Lords that April, Parmoor said that he accepted Lang's report in its entirety, but then suggested that Lang could not have meant by the words that he used the meaning commonly ascribed to them. We shall return to that debate in Chapter 22.

who were so enamoured by Soviet Communism that they denied its reality, if not more so; those in leadership who refuse to believe in the existence of crimes against humanity because of their political prejudice bear one form of responsibility for their inaction; those who admit them but then justify a refusal to respond, bear another.

Parmoor was challenged by Lord Hayter (George Chubb of the lock-making firm), who asked if the British government had called the attention of the Soviets to the deep concern which was being felt in the country. 'No,' he replied. When Lord Danesfort followed by asking if the government were taking steps to ascertain the truth of the matter with a view to taking action, Parmoor's answer, once again, was 'no'. Both peers were over-optimistic to hope that the government would do anything; the day before, let us remember, Cabinet had decided to take no action. Parmoor merely repeated (twice) Henderson's fine-sounding but empty promise from the day before that the government would 'when possible or compatible with the interests of those affected, use all its influence in support of the cause of religious liberty and the freedom of religious practice'.

Ovey asked for a full report

On Saturday 15 February 1930, Ovey telegraphed the Foreign Office to advise them that he had sent a summary of some aspects of Soviet legislation on religious practice in the diplomatic bag. But, he feared, it would 'not help much to alleviate the situation'. He continued by offering some suggestions as to how the wording of legislation might be used to defend the government's position, to offer his

> case against accusation of 'cruel persecution' although clearly may be difficult or inadvisable to use, may be summed up as follows
> 1. Existence of 69 articles in the decree regulating conditions under which religious services are permitted.
> 2. The absence as far as this Embassy knows of any statement by the government of their intention to destroy religion.
> 3. That destruction of churches occurs either for utilitarian purposes such as widening streets and demolition or utilisation for secular purposes at the request of local committees.[6]

Ovey was not the only one who was hesitant about using these arguments. Fellow Northern Desk official C. H. Bateman agreed:

> The only safe thing to do is to rely on the technical provisions of the [Soviets'] decree [prohibiting religious practice] and not to engage (publicly at any rate) in any discussion as to their scope. It is pretty clear from article 18, in any case, that the limits within which religion can be preached is the affair of the Soviet Government and that in spite of the 69 articles, they are very narrow indeed.

Arthur Henderson's Nonconformist background was well known and J. H. Rushbrooke, of the Baptist World Alliance, used that to appeal to Henderson on behalf of imprisoned Russian Baptists when the two met privately on 18 February. Later the same day, a Foreign Office telegram was dispatched to Moscow, asking Ovey for a 'comprehensive' and 'impartial' report on the situation. Tragically, Ovey's reply, compiled with the assistance of the Soviet 'expert', was neither, and the opportunity that might have been presented by his correctly supplying the information for which he had been asked slipped by.

The wording of Henderson's telegram was very different in tone from previous messages sent to the Moscow embassy. Of all the Foreign Office correspondence written in this period, it alone seems to have been written by someone with an understanding of the nuances of persecution beyond 'atrocities'. It was signed by Henderson (as were all dispatches to Moscow), but the tone indicates that it had been written on his instructions, perhaps even using his words, rather than by a civil servant:

> It is essential that I should receive comprehensive report from you reviewing so far as you are in a position to do so not only theoretical attitude of Soviet Government to religion in general, and freedom of worship in particular, but also treatment by judicial or economic pressure of ecclesiastics or worshippers in the Soviet Union.[7]

Not only did Henderson understand that persecution consisted of far more than spontaneous mass shootings (a point which Rushbrooke had emphasised when they met) but he also showed his personal acknowledgement that the

matter was more than a political storm whipped up by the Conservatives and
right-wing newspapers:

> present feeling here not merely agitation engineered by political opposition
> [and] emphasises brutal treatment, and even torture, of priests etc., but actual
> dates of such incidents are rarely recorded ... Your report should be as com-
> prehensive and impartial as possible.

Hugh Dalton appears to have shared few of Henderson's concerns, but he was
present on the day the telegram was dispatched, and wrote his observations of
Henderson's mood in his diary:

> 'Religious persecution' stunt worrying Uncle a great deal. Ovey and his offi-
> cials want to do nothing. But the Wesleyan and the politician combine to make
> him try to do something. In the last resort, he and I agree, we may have to
> choose between sending Sokolnikov away or seeing the government go down.
> If that wretched choice comes, we shan't willingly choose the latter. But we
> aren't there yet.[8]

Henderson was clearly shaken, and at least partially convinced, by what he
had heard from Rushbrooke. And yet, he was in a difficult position. He was
bound by the Cabinet's decision that taking action on religious persecution
was an 'inadmissible interference in the internal affairs of the USSR', and he
was pressed by Dalton, backbenchers in the Labour Party and by Seymour
and others in the Foreign Office to brazen out the storm.

On Rushbrooke's return to his office, he compiled a report for Henderson
summarising their conversation on the plight of Russian Baptists, naming
some of the hundred or so leaders who had been imprisoned or had disappeared. Rushbrooke's conclusion was unequivocal: 'In my judgement, it is
correct to say that there has not been in history so widespread, carefully organised, and resolute attack upon religion, and especially upon Christianity'.[9]

A couple of days later, a memorandum arrived in the Foreign Office from
Labour MP Philip Noel-Baker which boded ill for any hopes that the report
that Henderson had asked Ovey to produce would be of any objective value.[10]
It also confirmed that Rushbrooke's allegations of intense persecution against

Russian Baptists were correct. Noel-Baker had been invited to dine with the Soviet ambassador Grigori Sokolnikov[11] by the Webbs (Lord and Lady Passfield) at their Hampshire home. They were at the beginning of the long infatuation with Soviet Communism which was to result in their great book on the subject, *Soviet Communism: a New Civilisation*. He sat next to Sokolnikov, and recorded their conversation in his memorandum: 'I dined with Lord Passfield on February 19th and sat next to M. Sokolnikov, with whom I had a long conversation. In the course of a talk he spontaneously raised the question of the alleged persecutions in Russia.'[12] On the persecution of Russian Baptists, Noel-Baker pressed Sokolnikov for more detail:

> In reply to my question whether they had been particularly severe against the Baptists, he explained that the Baptists were a special case, because they were an international organisation and therefore brought in foreign influence which was regarded as being anti-Soviet. This perhaps amounted to an admission that special measures against the Baptists had been taken.

Sokolnikov also held out no hope that Ovey's report would shed any light upon the situation:

> He also expressed mild surprise that the Secretary of State had said that he would ask for the report from the British Ambassador in Moscow. He said that in his view Ovey would be in an impossible position for making such a report. He must get his information from government or from private sources. If he sought to get it from government sources, he would receive the answer that they could give him no information if it was not the business of the British government. If he sought it from private sources, it would probably be inaccurate and in any case inadmissible that it should be used in an official report.

Horace Seymour agreed with Sokolnikov's assessment: 'I think that M. Sokolnikov describes correctly the conditions in which Sir E. Ovey's report must necessarily be produced'. In spite of this recognition, Ovey's report, when it arrived and appeared virtually to absolve the Soviets of all wrongdoing, was universally accepted as accurate in the Foreign Office and the government, though Henderson, personally, must have had some doubts about it.

CHAPTER 19

OVEY'S SECRET REPORT (MARCH 1930)

Antipathy at the Foreign Office

'Ovey and his officials want to do nothing', Dalton had noted in his diary when discussing Henderson's concerns after the latter's meeting with Rushbrooke. In fact, as more rumours and reports of persecution arrived, Dalton and the civil servants dug in their heels still further. The antipathy of senior officials in the Northern Department to the idea of protest in support of those suffering persecution of any sort in Russia is nowhere more clearly illustrated than in their response to a letter which arrived at the Foreign Office just after Henderson's meeting with Rushbrooke. The desperate plight of religious Jews under the Soviets is not given much prominence today. Tsarist pogroms and the Nazi Holocaust are better known. Moreover, at this time the discrimination did not affect all Jews (many leading Bolsheviks were Jewish themselves) – only religious ones. They were repressed with the same severity as the kulaks and members of other religious groups.

News had reached London that a number of rabbis in Minsk had been arrested when they protested the forced closure of their synagogue. Because they had appealed to foreign 'co-religionists', they now faced the death penalty. Even the pro-Soviet chairman of the US Senate Foreign Relations Committee, Senator Borah, had personally appealed to the Soviet government to release them. The head of the British Jewish Board of Deputies now wrote to Hugh Dalton, to suggest that the British government 'may be able to convey to the Moscow authorities the indignation and horror with which … [their execution] … would be regarded in this and other countries'.[1] At the foot of the memorandum with the letter, Northern Department counsellor W. H. Montagu-Pollock commented: 'I do not think this letter calls for any further reply'. In another hand at the foot of the attached note is written: 'the information is all so vague'.

While Henderson may have had some sympathy for the Russian Baptists, the wider business of politics was far more pressing. He faced many responsibilities, particularly working towards the world disarmament conference for which he was eventually awarded the Nobel Peace Prize. The day-to-day management of Foreign Office business in connection with the Soviet Union was run by Dalton, Horace Seymour and his subordinates in the Northern Department. While Dalton and his civil servants may have acknowledged the constraints under which Ovey was required to operate, Dalton particularly refused to admit as legitimate any sources of information about Russia which might contradict views that Labour already held.

The Berlin dispatch

This approach by Dalton was made particularly clear when a dispatch arrived from Sir Horace Rumbold, the British ambassador in Berlin.[2] Dated 1 April 1930, Rumbold attached a startling five-page eyewitness account of the privations which religious believers were experiencing. Rumbold supplied a detailed provenance of the letter: it had come to him via a German magistrate who was a personal friend of the writer, whose name and address were provided in confidence alongside the document. The writer, named as Wassil Kotschubey of the small town of Lochwiza in the Ukrainian province of Poltava, had been a moderately wealthy lawyer before the Revolution. The magistrate added that Kotschubey was a man of 'honourable, truthful, and disinterested character and deserving of the fullest confidence'.

Kotschubey told how members of one parish council in Poltava province were summoned by the local OGPU commander. Rapping his revolver menacingly on his desk, this commander demanded that 'of their own free will' they give up their church building or be condemned as counter-revolutionaries. The councillors called a meeting of the parishioners, but when the parishioners refused to give up the church, the OGPU commander informed the council leaders that a patent on candles existed and told them they had been illegally selling them to parishioners (in the Orthodox Church, as in the Catholic Church, the lighting of candles by the faithful is a common practice). The tax that was then levied was applied retrospectively and directly upon the council members themselves. The sums were so vast that the council members were required to sell their homes in order to pay them or face imprisonment – an option of destitution or incarceration. Kotschubey concluded:

> Priests are being thrown into prison where hundreds of unhappy persons now sit, or rather stand, for there is no longer any room to sit ... simple faced peasant women are summoned to the courts with their little children in their arms and are then condemned for their religious activities ... I feel I cannot be silent. I beg you my dear Christians to save oppressed religion and your persecuted brothers who have no one to whom they can turn for assistance.

By chance, we have direct confirmation of one part of Kotschubey's account, a report of conditions in Poltava prison that same year:

> One 'kulak' sent to Poltava prison in 1930 tells typically of 36 prisoners in a cell built for seven, then of one for 20 holding 83. In prison, rations ranged from 100 grammes to 150 grammes of 'doughy black bread' a day, with about 30 dying every day out of the prison total of some 2,000. The doctor would always certify 'paralysis of the heart'.[3]

Laurence Collier, the number two in the Northern Department, was first to comment on the internal memo which circulated with the Berlin document. He was clearly convinced of its authenticity ('this seems a genuine letter'), but his remark was followed by a very different one from his superior, Seymour. Seymour's comment displayed indifference, if not callousness: 'I do not quite understand whether the writer meant us to pass his letter to the Christians of England. In any event, I don't see what we can do with it – if that was his intention'.[4] Such a comment, as the preamble of a further observation, might be benign. As it was, that was Seymour's only response to the letter before it went into the files.

Dalton was even more dismissive, condemning the messenger who sent the unpalatable news as well as the message he brought:

I have observed that [the British Embassy in] Berlin sends us a good deal of information about Soviet affairs and that it is consistently anti-Soviet in tendency. It is interesting to receive it, but Sir E. Ovey and his staff are in a better position to inform us accurately than persons in Berlin.[5]

As we now know, Ovey, in his Moscow goldfish bowl, dependent on a Soviet expert feeding him disinformation, was virtually incapable of knowing what was really happening around him. The most accurate reports were ones like these, which were smuggled out or came from refugees.

A few days earlier, the British ambassador to the Holy See passed on a warning from the Vatican that the anti-religion campaign was part of a larger political threat against British interests, particularly in Africa, which its observers had seen at first hand. The full text of the document, including the comments on the attached memorandum, is revealing:

British Legation to the Holy See
Rome, March 27, 1930
Sir,
A day or two ago Mr Randall, secretary to this Legation, had occasion to speak to Monsignor Marchetti, secretary of the Congregation of Propaganda. In the course of conversation Monsignor Marchetti, speaking, of course, unofficially and personally, raised the question of the Soviet anti-religious campaign. He said that, receiving reports on this from all parts of the world, he found himself constantly wondering whether the extent and seriousness of the Soviet or, at least, Soviet-approved propaganda were completely realised in England. It was at work in all kinds of places, even remote parts of the British Empire. The anti-God campaign was not directed merely against religion in a general way; it had a political aim; it was meant to discredit Christian culture, and that meant, very largely, British culture. There was plenty of evidence of this. In his two years journeying in Africa, for example, Monsignor Hinsley had come across, even in remote colonies, 'anti-God' missionaries, who are working for the subverting of British prestige and influence.

I have ventured to report these remarks as Monsignor Marchetti is the efficient secretary of a Congregation which, dealing as it does with Catholic missions all over the world, is constantly receiving reports on general conditions in European colonies and possessions. He has also shown himself consistently friendly to British interests so far as has lain within his power.

I have, etc.

H. G. Chilton

The Foreign Office internal memorandum attached to the letter reads:

(distribution:) The King, Cabinet, Dominions

Communism, of course, has its anti-British side; but I doubt if its anti-religious side has any *special* connection with its anti-British side. Copy to Moscow. (L. Collier April 1)

The Monsignor's remarks are interesting. L.O. 3 Apr

Rival propagandists seldom love one another! H.D. 9/4[6]

'L.O.' is Sir Lancelot Oliphant, Assistant Under-Secretary (one of three, one rank down from the Permanent Under-Secretary, Vansittart). 'H.D.', who dismissed the Vatican's helpful and sound advice as 'rival propaganda' was of course Hugh Dalton. In fact, the Vatican, with its extensive worldwide network, was one of the best sources of information on life inside the USSR and on the impact of Soviet influence further afield. The threat to British interests was very real, as the history of complaints by the Conservative Foreign Secretary Lord Curzon had made clear. But Dalton, even though he was the Foreign Office minister, was so convinced of the underlying soundness of the Bolsheviks' socialist ideals that he dismissed the Vatican's clear warning.

One interesting example of the very circumstance against which Mgr. Marchetti was warning was recorded by Hensley Henson, Bishop of Durham. Henson, whose intervention in the debate in the Lords on Soviet slave labour the following year was to be widely praised, had been in conversation with Sir Reginald Wingate, the former High Commissioner in Egypt. Wingate told him of his experience of Soviet attempted subversion there:

Under pretence of raising a sunken Russian warship, a Russian Commission secured permission to enter Egypt, then a British Protectorate. The immense quantity of baggage passed unexamined until, by accident rather than design, the contents of one box were disclosed & found to be nothing but Bolshevist

propagandist pamphlets printed in all languages. Further investigation revealed the representative character of this box: and the project of infecting the
merchant navies of the world* with Communism lay unmasked. The fiction of
raising the warship was abandoned and the Commission returned to Russia.[7]

The report arrives

The detailed report that Henderson had commissioned from Ovey arrived on
3 March 1930.[8] Dalton declared it 'a first class document, blowing up all the
atrocity stories'.[9] In fact, subsequent research has revealed, as we have seen,
that it contained a combination of incorrect facts, inadequate analysis and
outright bias.

In an effort to take control of the mounting crisis, the Cabinet had ordered
Henderson 'to resist demands for the publication of despatches already received from the Ambassador'.[10] When Ovey's report arrived, the ban was
extended to that too. The document which was to determine the course of
British foreign policy with respect to Soviet persecution for the duration of
the Labour administration was therefore never subject to critical examination.
With its arrival, the government closed its ears to all further appeals for intervention, and stories of persecution were dismissed. Even though Noel-Baker
had warned them that the Soviet ambassador himself had indicated that the
contents of the report would be untrustworthy, they accepted it without question. The report had such an important impact on the government that it needs
to be examined in some detail.

Changed brief

The first liberty taken by Ovey was to change his brief and, with it, the whole
tenor of the report. Henderson's original brief had allowed for there to be
more to persecution than 'atrocities':

> It is essential that I should receive comprehensive report from you reviewing so far
> as you are in a position to do so not only theoretical attitude of Soviet Government
> to religion in general, and freedom of worship in particular, but also treatment by
> judicial or economic pressure of ecclesiastics or worshippers in the Soviet Union.

---

* The Suez Canal was a major conduit for merchant traffic.

Instead, Ovey offered the following as his introduction: 'In compliance with your request for a comprehensive report of the alleged atrocities against priests and adherents of the Orthodox Church and other Churches in Russia ...'.

He had been asked for a comprehensive report on the *attitude* of the Soviet government towards religion and its treatment of believers, but what he supplied was a 'comprehensive report on the *alleged atrocities*'. Henderson had made no mention of atrocities. Answering a question that had not been asked, Ovey then insisted (near enough correctly, if going by his own definitions) that no 'massacres' or 'atrocities' had taken place since the early 1920s, and ignored the persecution, imprisonment and executions which were still widespread:

> I wish to premise with, some confidence, that the anti-clerical attitude of the Government and even the anti-religious propaganda of the Communist party do not connote 'atrocities' in the physical sense. I have no evidence of any general shootings of priests, or massacres of religious congregations. There has been no return to the thumbscrew-and-rack period of religious persecution. As recent questions in Parliament convey an impression that such 'atrocities' have taken place, it would be of great assistance to me if I could be put in possession of the material facts in individual cases.

An extensive review of Hansard for the period reveals little or no evidence of allegations by MPs of ongoing 'atrocities' as Ovey defined them. MPs realised, like Henderson, that there was more to the issue than that.

Persecution downplayed

Throughout the report, Ovey consistently interpreted events to make them seem less extreme, and rephrased the vocabulary of repression to make it seem less serious. Under Ovey's pen, religious believers were not suffering 'persecution', but 'disabilities and disqualifications' and were said to be under 'severe pressure'. They were victims not of physical ill-treatment (the arrests, imprisonments or shootings that were actually taking place), but of an 'anti-clerical *attitude*' and 'anti-religious *propaganda*' (my italics), which 'do not connote "atrocities" in the physical sense'.

Moreover, he implied, the Russian Orthodox Church to some degree deserved to be repressed. 'Full allowance,' he informed his readers, must be made for the 'great ignorance and corruption' in the pre-revolutionary Orthodox Church, for the fact that priests spied on parishioners and were regarded as an instrument of Tsarist rule, and that Orthodox monasticism was 'a decadent institution' which had 'outlived its period of utility for the people'. The persecution (rephrased as 'reforms') was then downplayed by being likened to Henry VIII's dissolution of the monasteries.

There was also a major inconsistency in Ovey's use of the Orthodox Church's past shortcomings to imply that resentment against the Russian Church was justified. There were four million Protestants in Russia; they had particularly suffered under the Tsarist regime and could in no way be described as decadent or corrupt. There were also around half a million Catholics, particularly in the western provinces. Later on in his report, Ovey himself admitted that the Soviet measures against religion were against all paid or unpaid religious officials of *all* religions and denominations. It was disingenuous to use this argument to pass over the impact upon all of them.

In some places, Ovey's rephrasing of simple vocabulary was so contorted that he seems to have been reproducing Soviet propaganda verbatim. Priests and other Church officials, disenfranchised, were refused ration cards. If unable to buy food at extortionate black market prices, they starved. In a previous dispatch, Ovey had described their lack of this essential as merely being 'deprived of the *advantage* of ration cards'. In his report, he continued in the same vein: 'They are not allowed ration cards and other arrangements made for the regular and organised provision of food to persons employed, directly or indirectly, in State reconstruction.' 'State reconstruction' meant that ration cards were only given to a select group and priests simply did not qualify.

Ovey let slip to a bishop passing through Moscow that summer that he had little sympathy for religious belief,[11] and his rationalist outlook, which many in the Labour government shared, meant that he presented Marx's view of the Church, and the Soviet policy which derived from it, as quite reasonable. Marx had been against religion, Ovey observed, so it was '*logical* for the Soviet Government to regard the Church as nucleus of opposition' (my italics). The Church was 'not merely a harmless eccentricity, but a definite handicap to [the] full development of the reasoning powers of man'. In reality, the Church was a threat not because it hindered so noble a concept as the 'full development of the reasoning powers of man', but because it preached the brotherhood of all of humanity, something that was fundamentally unacceptable to Soviet Communists, whose whole raison d'être was built on the principle of class war and the superiority of the proletariat.

Ovey insisted that priests were not deliberately singled out for persecution. Instead, he asserted, they were *accidental* victims because as a 'friend of the kulak … some of the blows of the Communist drive inevitably fall upon [their] shoulders':

> The impression which seems to be pervading Western Europe that a wave of intensified religious persecution is sweeping over Russia, appears to me to have arisen, not so much as a result of specific instance, but as a distorted (or rather incomplete) reflection of this latest phenomenon. The real objective of the new campaign in Russia is the kulak, not the priest; but since the priest is often the friend of the kulak, some of the blows of the Communist drive inevitably fall on his shoulders. When kulaks are shot for opposing the government's policy, it may be that priests are shot, too; but in such a case they will be suffering from their political errors and their economic fallacies, rather than for their religious faith.

Once again, Ovey's conclusion was far from the truth. It was true that Budkevich had been shot in 1923 for 'counter-revolutionary espionage', not for being a priest – yet not one of the Western governments who joined the international protests then believed the charge was anything other than a cynical cloak for a political execution. And priests were not 'accidental' victims, as Ovey maintained. They had been included in the kulak definition in the May 1929 decree, and so, in law, they were identified as the direct and deliberate targets of persecution.

The Law on Religions
Ovey's defence of the draconian Law on Religions of April 1929 echoed the claims, made by fellow travellers and Soviet apologists throughout the period, that Soviet law was designed to *permit* rather than restrict religious practice:

The government have not, as will be seen, issued decrees or laws designed to render the practice of religion a criminal offence. On the contrary, however restrictive legislation may be, it is actually designed so as to permit the continuance of religion under certain very definite conditions.

Ovey's statement in support of this ('A proof of this exists in the fact that a considerable number of churches are open, and services are legally, freely and regularly held therein') is surprising in light of the fact that only three weeks earlier he had reported that 85 per cent of the 1,000 Moscow churches had been closed, and in a subsequent section of his report he told of how priests living in Moscow had been forced to give up their vocation or leave the city.

A comparison between Ovey's defence of the 1929 Law on Religions and the comments of three modern Soviet scholars is startling. Rev. Michael Bourdeaux is the founder of the Keston Institute (formerly Keston College), which was for many years the leading organisation dedicated to the study of religion in Communist countries; Robert Conquest's ground-breaking book *The Great Terror* established him as one of the world's foremost experts on Soviet repression; Dimitri Pospielovsky was an Orthodox academic, whose study of the Soviet persecution of the Orthodox Church is the most complete in the English language to date.

Bourdeaux describes the law which Ovey makes light of as 'catastrophic ... It introduced, as intended, a period of the most intense persecution'.[12] Robert Conquest makes it clear that the law banned almost all religious activity:

> The law of 8 April 1929 forbade religious organisations to establish mutual assistance funds; to extend material aid to their members; 'to organise special prayer or other meetings for children, youths or women, or to organise general Bible, literary, handicraft, working, religious study or other meetings, groups, circles or branches, to organise excursions or children's playgrounds, or to open libraries or reading rooms, or to organise sanatoria or medical aid.' In fact, as an official comment put it, 'church activity was reduced to the performance of religious services.'[13]

Dimitri Pospielovsky reaches the same conclusion and confirms the devastating consequences of the law, as it 'deprived the church of all rights except the holding of liturgical services within the church walls. [And thereafter] the closing of churches, mass arrests of the clergy and religiously active laity and the persecution of people attending church reached unprecedented proportions.'[14] Pospielovsky estimates that 60,000 believers were sent to the camps and 5,000 shot during this period.

The closure of churches

When he turned to the widely reported phenomenon of the Soviet closure of churches, Ovey's comments reflected even more closely the Soviet line; phrases like 'the Soviet reply would be' and 'a Soviet spokesman might add' indicate that these passages were probably near verbatim extracts taken directly from the material provided by his government expert.

To an enquiry why so many churches had been closed, the Soviet reply would be that their number was clearly superfluous, and that sufficient had been left open to supply the needs of those desiring to exercise their religion. A Soviet spokesman might add that churches are closed for two reasons:-

1. As may occur in any country when the site is required for purposes such as street-widening; and
2. When a report is received from local Communists to the effect that, whereas the church as a religious building is only used by quite a few people, it would, if secularised and used as a club or meeting-place, be of great advantage to the majority of the commune.

… It would be as difficult as it would be invidious for me to attempt to lay down any opinion as to the extent to which these local communities act entirely on their own volition in demanding the secularisation of the churches. In some cases, however, it is reasonable to suppose that the majority of the people definitely desire the change.

[Where churches are closed] I understand, the evicted congregation are free to hire other premises for the purposes of devotion. For instance, at Minsk, which has a considerable Jewish population, I am informed that the principal synagogue has been secularised because the local authorities considered it to be unnecessarily large for its religious purpose, but that the Jewish community is not prevented from hiring a room for the practice of their cult.

Ovey's mention of the Minsk synagogue case, in support of the reasonableness of these closures, was unfortunate in the extreme. Just two weeks earlier, as has already been mentioned, the Foreign Office had been approached because the Minsk rabbis were under sentence of death for opposing the closure of their synagogue. It is quite clear that, whatever Ovey believed, in this case it was quite incorrect to say that 'the majority of people definitely desire[d] the change'. Minsk was such an important Jewish centre that it was known as the 'Jerusalem of White Russia', with a Jewish population at the end of the 1920s of over 50,000.[15] It is extremely unlikely that lack of demand rendered the synagogue redundant.

'Nothing new'

By referring earlier to the British dissolution of the monasteries, Ovey implied that the Soviet 'reforms' were not unique. As the report progressed, he continued to build the impression that what was happening was neither unique, nor new:

> As regards the purely religious side of the question, there is really no change to record. The disabilities and the disqualifications of the clergy are long-standing. ... anti-Christmas demonstrations have been going on since 1922 ... the blatant ridicule showered on religion in ... newspapers ... and antireligious museums ... is nothing new...

Referring again to the destruction of churches, he continued in the same vein:

> One well-known monastery was blown up last January for propaganda effect ... two other famous monasteries have recently been closed ... [church] bells have been melted down ... and churches have been turned over to secular purposes...

Once again, the language is important: 'turned over to secular purposes' means in reality that the congregations were thrown out; the blowing up of a monastery 'for propaganda effect' was still a manifestation of the persecution of religion. 'But this is a process which has been continuing over a series of years, and is not without its counterpart in the history of other countries, including our own.' So, Ovey implied, it was not that significant.

The disenfranchised

Ovey was at his most accurate when he moved on to describe the plight of the disenfranchised:

> [Concerning] the legislation specifically aimed at the control of religion, it should be observed that priests and church officials have been assigned to that class of community which is known as the 'Lishienchi', or those deprived of civic rights.
>
> Such persons are deprived of the right of voting. Further, they are not allowed ration cards and other arrangements made for the regular and organised provision of food to persons employed, directly or indirectly, in State reconstruction. This latter disability has been imposed upon them, so I am informed, for about a year and a half. It implies that they have to buy all food and provisions at the highest prices, or go without. This disability has, within the last few months, been extended to housing, at any rate in Moscow, where the housing question is very acute. Here the 'Lishienchi' are deprived of the right to a given area of dwelling room to which all other citizens are entitled. Further (by ordinance of the Presidium of the Moscow Soviet of the 31st of July, 1929, dealing with the ejection from their dwellings of non-workers and former house owners), they are liable to be turned out of rooms actually inhabited by them, if the space is required by citizen of the privileged classes.
>
> As a result, I am informed that about half of the 'Lishienchi' class have left Moscow, drifting either into the country or to other towns where the pressure is less severe. About half have made their peace with the Soviet authorities by being able to prove that they are engaged in activities useful to the State. But very few priests are to be found in this latter category since, in order to make terms with the authorities, they would probably be required to abjure their religious faith and find secular employment. This means that in all probability a number of priests have had to leave Moscow, since there is no place where they can find lodging.

This should have been enough to alert an objective reader to the drastic consequences of such measures on their victims, but Ovey immediately downplays it: 'I am told, however, that some of them are living in their church buildings, and that some are taken in as guests in the rooms of charitable people. This is not illegal.'

Ovey's conclusion

The report then reached its climax with the most important section – Ovey's conclusion, which would confirm the British government in its policy of non-interference. The distinction which Ovey himself had developed between ordinary persecution and 'atrocities' and 'medieval' persecution was crucial to the argument:

> I think it may be fairly adduced from the foregoing paragraphs that, although special regulations have been made for the control of religion this country, yet churches are open, services are held, priests function and even preach sermons, and the faithful may freely attend; also that, although priests and other ministers of religion suffer from serious disabilities, their treatment is not wholly discriminatory, since they form but one part of a whole class of disenfranchised and disqualified persons; and, finally, that there are no 'atrocities,' no massacres and no religious persecution in the mediaeval sense of the term.

Sir Esmond Ovey, British Ambassador in Moscow. © National Portrait Gallery, London.

Ovey then made the extraordinary assertion that all executions of priests and believers in Russia were taking place because of their political crimes, and that it was not for the British government to judge the legitimacy of sentences passed by another government upon its citizens. In the light of events which were about to unfold in Nazi Germany, such an attitude is dismaying:

> The oppression and suppression of religion has (in recent years, at least) been of a slow motion character, and the executions of priests and believers which have from time to time taken place have been punishment for the political intrigues against the state, the justice of which is hardly the business of another State officially to appraise.

In his final paragraph, Ovey went even further in absolving the Soviets. The persecution was not just 'not mediaeval' – it was not even violent:

> The present government and its supporters are convinced that the material disadvantages of religious faith outweigh its spiritual consolations, that their policy is to secularise the thought of the people, that they unquestionably exert to this end a degree of pressure which offends our modern ideas of tolerance, but that *they stop short on the fringe of persecution by violence*. (My italics.)

The impact of the report

By early March 1930, less than a year since it had taken office, the Labour government was not doing well. Hugh Dalton, recording a near defeat in the Commons in December 1929, had written in his diary: 'Today the Gov't all but fell … Shall we last out 1930?'[16] On 11 March 1930, he wrote of an 'awkward' defeat by eight votes on the Coal Bill.[17] In the week that Ovey's report arrived, gloom was spreading throughout the Cabinet:

> A tired, frightened snob, our Great Prime Minister … Our cabinet is full of overworked men, growing older, more tired, and more timid with each passing week. High hopes are falling like autumn leaves. There is a whisper of spring in the air but none in the political air.[18]

The Conservatives harassed the government constantly on Russia. It came off badly in a debate in the House of Commons on 5 February and in two Lords debates on 13 and 20 February. Russia came up in debates and questions (usually more than one question per sitting) in the House of Commons on twelve of the nineteen days of that month in which the House sat. Henderson had been particularly targeted at weekly Foreign Office questions. In the Commons on 3 February, Henderson remarked that he had answered 101 parliamentary questions on Russia since 24 October 1929.[19] On the Russian question alone, the Cabinet were desperate for something to give them breathing space.

The report provided it. Ovey's assurances helped to steady nerves. The government took it as justification for their stance. In the Foreign Office, Dalton had good reason to be delighted. In fact, he and Henderson initially wanted to publish it, but Vansittart convinced them that it was not a good idea and would make Ovey's position very difficult. Ovey had pleaded for confidentiality on the same grounds and the King agreed, adding that 'Sir Esmond Ovey would be irreplaceable.'[20]

The impact of the report's absolving of the Soviets was not only felt at home. Britain was an imperial power and the governments of South Africa and Australia both made contact with London, seeking more information. Both were receiving Soviet exports. In Australia's case significant timber shipments were arriving from Vladivostok, and stories of persecution there were being reported in Australian newspapers. South Africa asked to be allowed to see a copy of the report. The Soviets could not have wished for a better person to be in place as Secretary of State for Dominion Affairs (the Minister responsible for relations with Australia, Canada, South Africa, New Zealand and the Irish Free State) than Sidney Webb, who had just entertained Sokolnikov, the Soviet ambassador, at his home for the weekend. Webb allayed all their fears.

When the Cabinet had determined that not even the report's conclusion would be made public, it was put beyond challenge. Those who were permitted to read it saw in it only what they looked for – support for their own predetermined views. Had it been made public, its weaknesses and inconsistencies would quickly have been exposed. With its arrival and acceptance by the government, the possibility of any form of official intervention ended. From that moment on, the prevailing view was that the affair was little more than the creation of a hostile opposition and press, out to make mischief at the government's expense and to exploit gullible British churchmen.

CHAPTER 20

EMPIRE PROTEST

Within a month or two of its founding, the Christian Protest Movement (CPM) had generated a considerable following. Newspaper coverage of disruptions of its meetings by communist protesters only heightened public interest. And as its impact grew, the government noted its rise with some concern. Fearful of the damage which the campaign might do to the smooth development of Anglo-Soviet relations, Henderson and Dalton sent Vansittart and Seymour to speak to Archbishop Lang and S. M. Dawkins (the CPM secretary) respectively, in an attempt to moderate their calls for the British government to intervene. Their efforts were successful. Insisting that, at this juncture, it might hinder rather than help the cause of those they supported, Vansittart and Seymour obtained the agreement of both men not to publicly press for government intervention on the religious persecution issue, which had been CPM's call at its inaugural rally.[1]

Lang's compliance was conditional. The day after he met with Vansittart, Lang spoke to the Anglican Church Assembly (predecessor of the Anglican Synod). The Pope had just appointed 19 March as a Catholic day of prayer on behalf of the persecuted Russian believers[2] and the archbishop announced a similar call to the Anglican communion, to take place on Sunday 16 March. He also made it quite clear that, whatever government supporters might say to deny the persecution, he was in no doubt about its reality or severity:

I feel bound, at the opening of this Convocation, to refer to a matter which lies heavy on our conscience and stirs our strongest feelings. It is the cruel and persistent persecution of all forms of religion which continues to be waged by the Soviet

Government in Russia … It is not easy to get accurate information about anything which happens in Russia. But no one can question the truth of a long and shocking tale of the imprisonment, the exile, the deliberate doing to death of prelates and parish priests, of monks and nuns, and of the humblest folk. It is a record almost unparalleled in the pitiful history of religious persecution … I had hoped that there had been some mitigation of this cruel and barbarous policy. But alas! it now seems to be continuing as before, even in some ways to be more relentlessly pursued.

This seems to be a public acknowledgement by Lang that his comments in the first Lords debate on 4 December 1929, about a 'cessation' in Soviet religious persecution, were mistaken. He continued:

I am sure that already from many hearts and in many churches … prayers are being, and will continue to be, offered. But the time seems to have come when the Church should express its corporate sympathy by a united act of intercession. I venture to hope that your Lordships may be willing to request that prayer should be offered in all the churches of your dioceses at celebrations of the Holy Communion and that morning and evening prayer on Sunday, March 16, the second Sunday in Lent. We know that during that week multitudes of our fellow-Christians throughout the world, at the bidding of his Holiness the Pope, will be joining in prayer.

Then he turned his attention to the more political aspect of the matter:

At the risk of being misunderstood, I have carefully waited before making the protest I have made today until it could be clearly disassociated from any political issues in this country; and I have kept apart from any movements which might be regarded as propaganda against the present political regime in Russia* … But the fact that diplomatic relations with Russia have been

---

* When Prebendary Gough approached Lang to ask for his support for the Christian Protest Movement, Lang had sought an assurance from Gough that the movement was not politically motivated. In spite of Gough's assurances, he still refused to associate himself with it. His initial hostility to the CPM was driven in part by his reaction to the *Morning Post*'s attack upon him for his 4 December Lords speech, coupled with its sponsorship of the CPM. Over the course of the first four months of 1930, that hostility waned: Lang even welcomed Gough to Lambeth Palace to discuss the publication of a speech that Lang made in the House of Lords in support of the Russian Church. Moreover, Sir Bernard Pares, one of Lang's report committee, joined the CPM, and the CPM sponsored Klepenin and the Orthodox research bureau in Paris which became an important source of information for Lang on the persecution in Russia.

resumed lays upon this country responsibilities which in loyalty to all its best traditions it cannot ignore. And the Soviet Government has a representative in this country. Let it take note that a strong public opinion is rising, shared by persons of every class, party, and creed, which will insist that satisfactory diplomatic relations must depend, not on material advantages only, but also and even more on the common acceptance of those principles of justice, liberty, and humanity which are the basis of all international intercourse.

Lang may have agreed not to call upon the British Government to act, but his mention of the country's 'responsibilities' came close to doing so, as was his next threat to take the matter up in Parliament if nothing changed:

I am taking steps to have a careful enquiry made into the present facts about religious persecution in Russia, and unless there is evidence of real improvement I may feel bound to deal with the matter in Parliament, not as a matter of politics, but as a matter which concerns the honour of a Christian people and the demands of our common civilisation.

I beg to move from my place here:- 'That this House records its indignant protest against the persecution of all who profess any form of religion in Russia; offers its most deep and heartfelt sympathy to those who are suffering through this persecution; calls upon all members of the Church tonight in prayer to God on their behalf; and expresses its conviction that if the Soviet Government desire satisfactory relations with this country to be maintained it must observe the principles of a just and humane civilisation'.[3]

Lang's call, published in *The Times*, was taken up by other denominations. The Methodists were as unequivocal as the archbishop in their assessment of events in Russia:

An invitation has already been issued to all Christian people, by persons of high authority in the Christian churches, to join in prayer and intercession on Sunday, March 16, for all the persecuted Christians in Russia. We write this letter to call on all Methodists to take their part in this urgent duty.

Exact details as to the extent and severity of the sufferings inflicted on Christians by the Russian Government, we know, are hard to come by; nor is it easy to say how far the victims are being attacked because of their loyalty to their religion, or for real or alleged opposition to the party now in power in Soviet Russia …

At least two things have become clear, from the statements of the authorities themselves: First, that Christians are being widely and severely penalised not only for their political actions but for their religious beliefs; and, secondly, that the Soviet State has deliberately committed itself to a campaign against all religion as such; not simply against the Russian Orthodox Church, but against all belief in God. This is a new thing in the history of any nation.

We would therefore urge that March 16 should be kept as a day of prayer for the members of Christian communities in Russia who are enduring sufferings from which, whatever their exact nature, the bravest of us would shrink … We would also urge that such prayers should not be postponed till March 16 or discontinued afterwards … And however some among us may desire or shrink from any form of political action, all human needs (and where are they more intense than in Russia today?) call for prayers to the Disposer Supreme and Charge of the Earth; and they also demand a constant renewal of our own obedience to His eternal laws of justice, self-abnegation, and goodwill.

Signed

W. F. Lofthouse (President, Wesleyan Methodist Conference),

R. H. B. Shapland (President, United Methodist Conference),

J. G. Bowran (Acting President, Primitive Methodist Conference).[4]

Vansittart, Seymour, Dalton and Henderson, reading *The Times*'s report of Lang's speech the next day, would have been wise to take heed of the archbishop's warning 'to deal with the matter' in Parliament unless there was 'real improvement'. Had they done so, they might have been able to head off the storm which was about to break.

The Cabinet bans prayers

Many in the Labour Party regarded the Anglican Church as a reactionary body largely drawn from the upper classes, hostile to Socialism. Sidney Webb had dismissed the Anglican clergy as the 'appanage of the landed gentry'.[5] Already opposed to the CPM, they interpreted the archbishop's call as a hostile gesture. When the Cabinet met next, on 19 February, concerns were voiced about the proposed day of prayer. Cabinet members were largely powerless to prevent it – except in the Armed Forces, where service personnel attended compulsory weekly church parades. They promptly banned members of the Armed Forces from taking part in the planned Russian prayers.[6] It was an ill-thought-out and over-hasty decision and it provoked the biggest Church/state crisis of the inter-war years.

Forces chaplains were under both military discipline and the authority of the archbishop of Canterbury. Now one superior was countermanding the other. The Chaplain General of the Army, A. C. S. Jarvis flatly refused to issue the order (an unprecedented step), until it had been reworded to make it clear that it came from the War Office, not the archbishop. 'My conscience is clear', he wrote to Lang's chaplain, Mervyn Haigh, 'and I have washed my hands of this dreadful business. The order is going out tonight. It will come to nothing but various trouble I fear.'[7]

"The Holy Father with his Holy Son". Izvestia cartoon, 1930. The editor of the Morning Post *kneels before the Pope for a blessing. The cudgel is labelled 'Anti-Soviet propaganda'. It is a measure of the impact of the British protest campaign that Russian propagandists felt it necessary to lampoon it.*

Reaction

Anglicans were not the only ones to be deeply upset by the interference with their religious practice. The leaders of all the main Nonconformist denominations – the Baptists, Methodists and Congregationalists – had also called their members to prayer on the same day. As church parades were Anglican, Nonconformist soldiers, sailors and airmen left their bases each Sunday to worship at civilian chapels nearby. The government had no jurisdiction over what took place in these chapels. Now the government appeared to be interfering with Nonconformists too, by banning some of their congregation members from attending church on that Sunday. They were outraged. After years of state persecution and discrimination, the Nonconformist denominations guarded their independence fiercely. Alienating them only further illustrated the political ineptness of the decision – which now united all British Churches against the government.

The newspapers rounded on the Cabinet. *The Times* insisted that 'nothing but the necessities of the government's position requires, in the face of unanswerable evidence to the contrary, the official view that the purpose of religious intercession is political intervention' and accused the government of 'embarrassing a religious occasion with those very political entanglements which they profess to condemn'.[8] The *Daily Telegraph* announced, 'Cabinet and Russian Persecution – Constitutional Crisis Through Prayer Ban', and its leader comment spoke of the Cabinet's 'ignoble order'.[9]

As a furious storm blew up, MacDonald was forced to call an emergency meeting with the leaders of the other two parties to try to find a solution. William Temple, Archbishop of York, wrote in a private letter to Lang that the government's interference was 'offensive'.[10] Lang told Temple that he had telephoned the Prime Minister and that MacDonald had agreed to meet with the two Leaders of the Opposition, Lloyd George and Stanley Baldwin, to try to settle the matter.[11] MacDonald refused to back down and, in Parliament, he insisted the problem had been created by hostile newspapers. Lloyd George, for the Liberals, would not let that pass: 'I assure the Prime Minister that it is not a newspaper agitation. I have received a very many letters from leaders not unfriendly to the Government – communications which show very great concern.'[12]

Statements in the Lords

In the House of Lords on 6 March, the Duke of Atholl, in a twist which could only have heightened the government's embarrassment, now accused the *Cabinet* of religious persecution, tabling a motion calling for the government 'to state on what grounds they justify the abrogation of religious freedom for British subjects'. In his own speech to the House of Lords, Lang reminded the government of the words which he had used at the Anglican Church Assembly a week earlier, in which he had specifically disavowed a political subtext:

> In the very speech delivered in the Convocation of Canterbury in which I called for the observance of this day of prayer I used deliberately these words:- 'I have carefully waited before making the protest I have made today until it could be clearly disassociated from any political issue in this country…His Holiness the Pope has asked all those who owe allegiance to him to join with him in these intercessions for those who are suffering oppression in Russia. It will not, I think, be supposed that His Holiness is actuated in this matter by political motives. No, my Lords, this call for prayer has not arisen, and never did arise, out of political controversies. It has arisen from the instinct which impels men, in the stress of great sympathy with suffering and anxiety for the sufferers to pray; and this instinct in our country and elsewhere on the Continent of Europe and in the United States of America is so deep and widespread that it has demanded this expression in common prayer.

Then, sentence by sentence, he went through the proposed form of prayer, no doubt to the growing discomfort of Lord Thomson, the Air Minister, who was speaking for the government in the debate.

> Is there anything that suggests political propaganda or political controversy in such a summons as this? –
>
> 'Let us, in common with multitudes of our fellow Christians throughout the world, make remembrance in our prayers of those in Russia who are suffering oppression of their faith.'
>
> I do not think there can be the slightest doubt about that: they are suffering from oppression.
>
> 'Let us commend them to the mercy and protection of Almighty God our Heavenly Father. Let us pray that the power of His Spirit may uphold them in their sufferings, strengthen their faith, and give them fortitude and hope. Let us pray that the hearts of their oppressors may be changed' –

I wonder whether even the noble Lord would hesitate to express such a prayer as that –

'That they may be delivered from fear and peril, and that the Church in Russia, purified by its affliction, may arise to fulfil its mission to the people with new zeal and power.'

Is there anything political in such a request for prayer, or is there anything in which the officers and men of His Majesty's Forces might not have been permitted to join?

Lang's conclusion was a clear rebuke to the government:

I think I have made it clear that, in my judgement, the whole of the action of the Government has really been superfluous, and that it has been extremely confused and unfortunate in the way in which it has been carried out ... I wish it had never occurred; I think it need never have occurred.[13]

Lang's goodwill, so skilfully obtained a week earlier by Vansittart, had been squandered. What little that remained was completely lost when MacDonald, furious with Lang for his speech, wrote on 7 March an extraordinarily intemperate letter in which he accused Lang of stirring up the affair for political ends, interfering in government foreign policy before ending with a threat to retaliate by banning all forces church parades. It should be noted that, in the first paragraph, the cause of the protests – the physical persecution of religious believers and the destruction of their places of worship – becomes, under MacDonald's pen, as it had under Ovey's, something far more benign: 'the *attitude* of the Soviet government and its agents to religious *observances*.'

I cannot allow the speech which you delivered in the House of Lords yesterday to go without a word of protest. When the church authorities decided that a form of prayer was to be used regarding the attitude of the Soviet government and its agents to religious observances and when without consultation with me or so far as I know with anyone responsible for the diplomatic handling of the situation, when they decided to use for their purposes the official arrangements for worship in the Navy, Army, and Air Force, they committed a blunder of very great consequence.

Had you informed me precisely what your intention was, I should have been very glad to have discussed it with you and to put the full issues before you ... The next appearance of the affair in public was when a newspaper, which had been deeply committed to making political propaganda out of the persecution, used the church as a stick with which to beat the Government. I cannot believe that you and those who had been acting with you have been unaware of the fact that this agitation has had far more of the Morning Post in it than the Gospels and that its devotion to prayer is much less conspicuous than its desire to produce political results.

Indeed, as things have turned out your day of intercession will be much more profitable for the party in opposition to us than it will be for the promotion of religious toleration in Russia. For that the church is solely to blame.

I have done my best to prevent evil following up on your action and I was hoping yesterday you would have seen your way to have supported me. ... you are not only interfering in a secular policy of government, but strengthening those in Russia who are responsible for the persecution* ... I want to make it perfectly clear to you that whilst I decide to unsettle nothing that has been established by practice, neither the government nor myself personally will allow ecclesiastical authorities to interfere with the political policy of the country and that whatever the immediate consequences may be we shall oppose most strenuously the attempts now being made by papers like the Morning Post and the Daily Telegraph to use religious sentiments in order to create a European situation which will play into the hands of the enemies of good international feeling or of settled civilization.[14]

It was an astonishing letter from a Prime Minister to an Anglican Primate. Lang's riposte showed that he was the bigger man and the greater diplomat: 'When I asked for a day of prayer in the convocation of Canterbury and the bishops concurred with my request it did not occur to me that on such a matter it was necessary to discuss the matter with the government.'[15]

The day of prayer

When the day of prayer itself came, the controversy achieved the opposite end to the one the government had hoped for. The event was now reported

---

* An interesting admission by MacDonald that he accepts that the persecution is real.

widely in the newspapers and prominence was given to bishops and other clergy who spoke to support the claim that there was widespread persecution of religious believers in the Soviet Union – and to their thoughts on the government's interference.

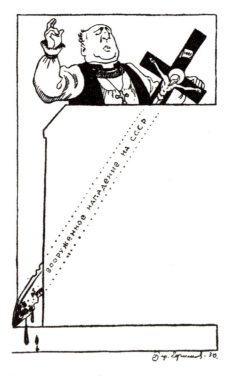

"The Assailants of the Crucifix". Archbishop Lang's hidden sword reads 'Armed aggression against the USSR'. Izvestia cartoon, 1930.

The Bishop of London, Arthur Winnington-Ingram, preaching at St Matthew's, Bayswater insisted that 'there is nothing political about this. This is one part of the Church of Jesus Christ praying for succour and sympathy for the other, and indeed we should be craven and heartless if we did nothing of the kind.'[16]

The Bishop of Durham, Herbert Hensley Henson, speaking in Newcastle Cathedral, joined others in rejecting the government's charge of political partisanship: 'If it is suggested that the action of the Christian church in organising concerted prayer for the victims of Bolshevist persecution … is designed to assist one political party and injure another, I think it is sufficient reply that all British parties are agreed that religious persecution is truly abominable'.[17]

It was certain, he continued, that the policy of rooting out religion in Russia 'recently had been carried out with accentuated cruelty and in meticulous detail'. In Ilkley Parish Church, the Bishop of Bradford unwittingly addressed one of the most indefensible statements in Ovey's report: 'It may be said that [clergy] have been put to death for political reasons, but if you mix up politics and religion and you cannot help it sometimes – they are really martyrs to the Christian faith.'[18]

Criticism did not only come from Anglicans. In the leading Church of Scotland church south of the border, St Columba's in Pont Street, London, the minister Dr Archibald Fleming addressed the issue of the reality of the persecution:

> Of the reality and terrible character of the persecution to which Christians in Russia have been subjected there should be no doubt. Persecution and the war to the death on religion have been acknowledged and gloried in by those who perpetrate them, and it is with painful amazement that we hear denials of the existence in certain quarters among ourselves.[19]

Dr J. C. Carlile was a former chairman of the Baptist Union, which had been pressing Henderson for nine months to intervene on behalf of persecuted Russian Baptists. His chapel in Folkestone was usually attended by servicemen from the RAF base nearby. He spoke for many Nonconformists when he said that 'we will have nothing to do with the political side of the issues involved. We do not recognize the right of the secular authority to order prayers or to forbid prayers.'[20]

In an article in the *Manchester Guardian*, the Rev. E. L. Macassey, wrote that it was characteristic of the present government's inability to discern signs of the times that they should have forbidden the fighting forces to pray for 'persecuted Russian brethren', continuing that it was 'sheer nonsense to assume that our fighting men share the government's fear of Russian susceptibilities'. Many would have agreed with his final comment: 'It is the genius of the present government to come to grief every time it touches Russian affairs'.[21]

The press not only reported the reaction to the ban, but contributed their own comment. Many clergy read out in their services an article from *The Times* the day before. Under the heading 'The Call To Prayer', the newspaper took the opportunity to urge those of its readers who had a religious faith to support the intercession:

> In our churches and chapels tomorrow prayer will be offered on behalf of those who are suffering oppression in Russia through loyalty to their faith. News from that country leaves no doubt as to the reality of the persecution there taking place against all who profess their belief in God ... Christians can have no doubt that they ought to join in intercession for those who are being oppressed, and not seldom treated with violence, for no other reason than that they are true to the faith they profess.

And, in a comment that directly contradicted the definition of persecution which Ovey had used in his report to the government, *The Times* restated the most commonly accepted understanding of the word:

> Persecution is the infliction of penalties or pains in restraint of freedom of conscience, the refusal of liberty to live according to rules of life and worship which express and assist men's religious belief ... There is nothing in the Bolshevist theory which runs counter to the spirit of persecution. It is perfectly at home in such an enterprise of relentless extermination.[22]

The day of prayer was the biggest single act of protest against Soviet Communism in history, if a united day of world prayer counts as 'protest', something upon which MacDonald and Lang would have disagreed. The day (or two days – the Catholic version being three days later) was observed by millions around the world. Fifty thousand people attended the Vatican mass in St Peter's Square in Rome,[23] though Western diplomats, including the British, stayed away.[24] They were joined by many of the 350 million Catholics around the world. The Lutheran World Convention called their 81 million members to prayer too.[25]

In New York, 3,500 people attended a service of prayer at the Anglican Cathedral of St John the Divine. Metropolitan Platon, primate of the Russian Orthodox Church in America and Canada, Archbishop Alexander, of the Greek

Church in North and South America, as well as Methodist and Presbyterian clergymen, and the secretary of the Greater New York Federation of Churches were in attendance. The Catholic churches of the Archdiocese of New York had chosen to adopt the day themselves and prayers were said in each of their 445 churches. In New York, 3,000 worshippers filled St Patrick's (Catholic) Cathedral, while in the city's Free Synagogue, rabbi Stephen Wise preached on 'Russia's crime against religion'. Elsewhere in the city, a public meeting was arranged by the American Jewish Congress, and on the streets there were marches and demonstrations. The communist 'Friends of the Soviet Union' held an opposing rally at the Bronx Coliseum. When a group of White Russians demonstrated outside the offices of Amtorg, the Soviet trade agency, to protest at the arrest of four bishops and thirty clergyman of the Orthodox church in Kharkov, a group of communist counter-demonstrators arrived on the scene. Punches were thrown and arrests were made.[26]

ANYTHING BUT QUIET ON THE EASTERN FRONT !!

"Anything but quiet on the Eastern Front". Arthur Henderson, weathering the Russian storm. Cartoon from the ILP's New Leader, *March 1930.*

Meetings and services were held across Europe. In Munich, the Cardinal archbishop was joined by the Bavarian Premier; the Coptic Patriarch ordered prayers in Cairo, as did the Patriarch of the Serbian Orthodox Church in Belgrade.[27] In France, in addition to the widespread observance of the prayer day by Catholics, the Fédération protestante (the national body of French protestants) held their own service. It was attended by Eulogius, the Russian Orthodox Metropolitan of Paris, the leading Russian Orthodox bishop in exile. The Grand Rabbi of France sent a representative.

The Archbishop of Canterbury's call was widely supported throughout the empire and dominions. The line-up of bishops on the platform at a CPM Albert Hall rally, held a few months later to coincide with the ten-yearly Lambeth Conference of Anglican bishops, shows how extensive that support had been. The Archbishops of Armagh, Australia and New Zealand were joined by bishops from Africa (Grahamstown, Johannesburg, Lebombo [Mozambique], Pretoria, Uganda, Zanzibar), Asia (Fukien, Kataria [India], Mauritius, Singapore, South Japan), Australia (Ballarat, Bathurst, Goulburn, Willochra), Canada (British Columbia, Caledonia, Cariboo, Moosonee, Quebec, Saskatchewan, St John's), Honduras and the United States of America (Erie, Maine, West Michigan) as well as three Irish bishops and the Bishop of Europe. Also present were the Pope and the Patriarch of the Coptic Orthodox Church of all Africa, and metropolitans and bishops of Greek, Polish, Romanian, Eastern and Serbian Orthodox Churches.[28]

The two days of prayer were a remarkable and unprecedented display of the global revulsion felt at the Soviets' abuse of human rights. Gough had previously approached Francis Bourne, the Cardinal archbishop of Westminster, to get Vatican support for his own campaign (Catholic, Jewish and Muslim representatives were involved with the CPM), and the extent to which his unceasing work over the previous three months had contributed to the worldwide success of the prayer day can only be guessed at. He undoubtedly deserves some of the credit.

CHAPTER 21

COUNTER-ATTACK: DISINFORMATION AND PROPAGANDA (FEBRUARY–JUNE 1930)

As soon as the British day of prayer was announced, on 12 February 1930, the Russian government repeated its denial that there was any religious persecution in the Soviet Union. Alexei Rykov, the chairman of Sovnarkom, the Council of People's Commissars, insisted that Soviet legislation ensured that its citizens enjoyed complete religious freedom, and that there was no persecution of anyone because of their religious beliefs. The report in *The Times* of the speech followed with a list, in detail, of those Soviet measures and decrees which directly contradicted Rykov's claims.[1]

In Minsk, where the main synagogue's rabbis' appeal to foreign supporters to save their synagogue from closure had resulted in arrests and death sentences, the same rabbis, no doubt under pressure and fearing for the safety of their own families, put their names to a new statement, reprinted in the *Manchester Guardian*, which insisted that:

> no rabbi has ever been shot under the Soviet regime, and that certain rabbis recently arrested in Minsk were quickly freed … 'We cannot be silent regarding the fact that neither the Pope nor the Archbishop of Canterbury undertook measures when the Jews were persecuted by Tsarist Russia. We categorically protest against the Pope's crusade against the Soviet Union.'[2]

Hundreds of thousands of demonstrators poured onto the streets of other Soviet cities to protest; the Soviet press claimed a million had turned out in Moscow and half a million in Kharkov.[3] British Communists came out too (in much smaller numbers): protesters interrupted church services; demonstrators were arrested outside Ebury Barracks in central London; and agitators descended upon garrison towns, such as Aldershot, where they distributed leaflets exposing 'lying and hypocritical anti-Russian services':

> Comrades … if the priests introduce the abominable slander about the Russian workers at services which you are forced to attend make a joint protest with your mates … remember that the Russian workers' fight is your fight. Stand with them against the dirty lies of the Christian Protest Movement.[4]

Andrew Rothstein, reporting from Britain for *Izvestia*, told his readers that the British government was readying for a military attack on the Soviet Union 'which is being prepared amid the clanging of church bells'.[5]

On 17 February, the beleaguered Russian Orthodox Patriarch Sergius was brought out in Moscow to deliver a prepared statement to the world press which declared that stories of persecution were slander which 'had nothing in common with the true facts'. Although he refused or was not permitted to answer foreign journalists' follow-up questions, his denial was enthusiastically seized upon by Western supporters. The *Manchester Guardian* reported it with the sub-headline 'Pope Reminded of Catholic Torture and Burnings', a classic *tu quoque* ('you too') attack, evading the issue in question by challenging the integrity of the accusers and, consequently, their right to accuse.

Propaganda war

In an age when information took time to surface and its sources were much fewer, the press carried great authority and influence. As pressure mounted on the government, the British Socialist press – The *Manchester Guardian*, *Daily Herald*, *New Statesman* and *New Leader* – rallied to its support. The *Manchester Guardian* quoted Secretary of State for War, Tom Shaw, who sided with the Communists and accused the CPM of making up its stories: 'We have no right to interfere in the internal affairs of any other country …

Those of you who read the Manchester Guardian will have already found what a campaign of lying – it is no use mincing words – has been conducted.'[6] Home Secretary J. R. Clynes, Shaw's ministerial colleague, took a similar line, saying that he 'could not believe the stories of physical persecutions, executions and deaths which, it was said, were occurring because of the practise of religious beliefs in Russia.'[7]

Casting doubt on the motives of opponents and portraying all of them, even moderates, as extremists, were standard disinformation techniques and were employed frequently. The *Manchester Guardian* thus ignored the widespread support for the protest campaign from people like (distinctly non-Tory) British Baptist leader J. H. Rushbrooke, and instead reported without reservation *Pravda*'s insistence that the movement for the protection of religious against the 'alleged' (always 'alleged') persecution was the work of 'diehard' Conservatives acting from purely political motives, a sentiment it echoed in its own leader column.[8]

Not every action by the pro-Soviet press was successful. The *Daily Herald* had attempted to smear the CPM and intimidate its backers, but when it accused one high profile contributor, Lady Houston, of being a 'Tory plotter' against Russia, she took them to court for libel. They lost and were forced to pay her damages.[9]

The ILP and the *New Leader*

In the response of the left-wing press, the role of the *New Leader*, the ILP journal, was significant. The journal was widely respected: Otto Bauer, the Viennese socialist leader, believed it to be 'the best Socialist publication in the world';[10] in the opinion of Kingsley Martin, the famous editor of the *New Statesman*, 'between 1922 and 1926 the *New Leader* set a literary standard which no socialist paper in England has been able to match'.[11] During the persecution crisis, the journal played its part in bolstering the determination of Labour MPs to ride out the storm (142 of the 288 Labour MPs elected in 1929 were claimed as members of the ILP[12]), and also reinforced the party's position with activists and supporters in the country.

By the time Labour took office in 1929, the stance of the *New Leader* on the Soviet Union was unambiguous. An editorial in December 1927 spoke of Lenin as 'enshrined in the hearts and thoughts of most of us as the world's greatest revolutionary leader'. The editorial board had no reservations about accepting contributions from leading Bolsheviks, like Karl Radek, and in 1931 they published four articles by him. Radek, who had been responsible for a failed communist coup in Germany in 1923, was described in the accompanying biographical note as 'one of the most gifted and brilliant writers in the world press on international affairs'. Well-known pro-Soviets such as Anna Louise Strong and W. P. Coates of the Anglo-Soviet Parliamentary Committee were also to be found in its pages (where Coates dismissed the allegations of religious persecution as 'fairy tales').[13]

The *New Leader* also published anti-religious articles by leading atheists such as C. E. M. Joad, the famous philosopher,[14] and Harold Laski on a regular basis, and supported a generally militantly atheistic line in comment columns. Religion was portrayed as a force for harm ('the breeding ground for intolerance'[15]), in contrast with the promise for peace that Socialism held. When stories of persecution became harder to deny, the paper slightly modified its tone, but not its sympathies. When the Pope appealed to the world community to call upon the Soviets to halt the terror, the paper adopted the *Manchester Guardian*'s *tu quoque* approach, and pronounced that 'if what is written about persecution in Russia is true, it would pale into insignificance before the record of Rome itself'.[16] 'No one', the editor wrote a week later, 'who watches the anti-religious campaign can doubt that a political purpose inspires it'.[17]

Communist Labour MP John Strachey was another regular contributor to the *New Leader*. After his trip to Russia, he wrote a series of complimentary articles on the Soviet Union which were published in the journal in March 1928. These were followed by a sympathetic portrait of Stalin later that year. In February 1930, at the height of the religious persecution controversy, Strachey wrote in another paper that 'the miracles predicted under Lenin and Trotsky are now being seen under Stalin'.[18] Strachey's sister Amabel was married to the famous architect and founder of Portmeirion, Clough Williams-Ellis. Both were Soviet admirers; in 1935, Amabel contributed a glowing introduction to the English edition of Gorky's *The White Sea Canal*, a book which eulogised the Soviet penal system, portraying it as noble and redeeming. The canal was dug virtually by hand by over 100,000 slave labourers, 10,000 of whom died in the process.[19]

H. N. Brailsford

The editor of the *New Leader* from 1922 to 1926 was Henry 'H. N.' Brailsford, (1873–1958). A leading member of the ILP, Brailsford is described as having a place 'among the giants of the Labour movement',[20] someone who today is 'widely recognized as one of the greatest journalists of his generation and as one of the outstanding socialist political writers of the century'.[21]

Brailsford had expressed unease at the Soviet persecution of fellow socialists in the mid-1920s, but those expressions of concern diminished with time, as the victims changed. When it came to the persecution of religious believers, Brailsford and the *New Leader* rallied to the Soviets' defence. He still acknowledged that there was repression, but by now his former distaste had been replaced by admiration; thousands were dying or being killed, but Brailsford excused the Soviets' actions as being 'the excess of a great quality' about which 'we can afford to be tolerant'. Here some extracts from his article of 7 February 1930, written as the religious persecution affair was taking off:

Russia is moving again to a revolutionary tempo. The programme which she has set herself in the Five Year Plan calls for an effort so intense, on a scale so colossal, that it demands a united will, such as nations rarely show in time of peace ...

Every sceptic, every critic, is suppressed. She silences, first on the Left and then on the Right, almost every man of distinction in the ruling Party. She crushes the opposition of the rich individualist peasants, and faces all the consequences of village mutinies and Cossack discontent. She falls pitilessly upon the few surviving partisans of the old regime, and offends with complete recklessness the religious sentiment of the older generation. *This rashness and severity is the excess of a great quality.* Russia is displaying in its constructive tasks the same indomitable will which inspired her throughout the civil war ...

We can afford to be tolerant if men working at this pace, under the spur of a lofty social ambition, express themselves roughly. And equally we can understand why the enemies of Russia, and of every Socialist effort, redouble their attempts to isolate and to thwart her. We have a great responsibility to discharge while we hold office. It is not enough to foil this Tory scheme of a rupture. Our aim must be to make the relationship so mutually helpful that rupture in the future shall be unthinkable ...

> The International* exists to carry on the class war on a worldwide scale …
> It is well that we should remember that we are also Socialists and belong to an
> International. (My italics.)[22]

When it came to religion, whatever credence Brailsford gave in 1925 to those
protesting at the persecution of non-Bolshevik socialists was not extended to
those campaigning on behalf of those suffering persecution for their religious
faith. He not only insisted (incorrectly) the stories were long out of date, that
they had been effectively dismissed, but *applauded* the suppression of religion, accused Archbishop Lang and Prebendary Gough of lying, and those
who taught religion to children of committing an 'outrage' against them (a
stance shared, as will later be shown, by George Bernard Shaw):

> No one who watches the international religious campaign against Russia can
> doubt that a political purpose inspires it. The prime movers in this country are
> Die-hard Tories, who have used every other stick to beat the Soviets until it
> broke in their hands …
>
> Let us try, then, to arrive at the facts … With the tales of torture and massa-
> cre it is impossible to cope. For, as the 'Morning Post' prints them, they lack
> every detail by which they could be tested … Readers who have moderately
> good memories can recall that we read the same vague, but edifying, narra-
> tives a good 10 years ago. *In short, if there is a message of truth in them, they
> happened during the Civil War …*
>
> The Church in the Civil War ranged itself solidly on the side of the Whites,
> and undoubtedly many of the clergy were imprisoned for conspiracy, and some
> were shot. In at least one case a bishop was killed by an angry mob of work-
> ers. *But these tales (grossly exaggerated as they are) are doubly irrelevant.*
> They're out of date by ten years, and they do not prove religious persecution
> … The 'Manchester Guardian' has devoted much space to the dissection of
> these atrocities, and has effectively disposed of most of them. It is evident that
> Prebendary Gough has been misled by unscrupulous translators …
>
> [Religion] is the chief obstacle to every advance, even in such mundane

---

* 'The International' refers to the Labour and Socialist International (LSI), a federation of national
socialist parties founded in 1923 as the continuation of Marx's Second International (1889-1916).
The LSI executive committee's first chairman was Arthur Henderson.

matters as the adoption of rational methods of cultivation. [The Church] ... *is an organised conspiracy to perpetuate all the evils of ignorance and poverty under which men labour here below* ...

The Soviet method of handling the legal problem of its relations to organised religion is open to criticism, and I shall not shrink from it. But *it is grossly misleading, to speak, as the Archbishop of Canterbury has spoken, of 'the persecution of all who profess any form of religion in Russia.'* On the contrary, to the public exercise of religious rites, whether Orthodox, sectarian, Jewish or Moslem, *there is no hindrance whatever...* On the whole, the nonconformists and the Moslems have gained in freedom ... The churches are open and often crowded ... [The closing of churches] *is not the persecution of religion.* A priest may pray, or preach, or confess, or administer the sacraments as he pleases ...

[On the prohibition of religious instruction to children] *Personally, I think that a grown person commits an outrage on the immature mind of a child, who imposes any view of controversial questions upon it, whether in religion or politics* ...

[All] this is not religious persecution in the Archbishop's meaning: still less is it the nightmare of the 'Morning Post.' There is (to sum up) no trustworthy evidence of any recent aggravation ... *The open warfare on superstition I applaud.* (My italics.)[23]

Brailsford may have been one of the 'greatest' socialist journalists of the century but, in his denial of the repression of kulaks and religious believers, history has proved him wrong on every count – and reveals a very different picture of him than the 'intellectual disinterestedness and integrity' which Labour biographers claim for him.[24] But his influence and that of the *New Leader* was considerable; such bold dismissals no doubt convinced many.

'GBS' writes to *The Guardian*

Brailsford was not the only Labour 'giant' to come out to oppose the persecution protests. On 6 March the *Manchester Guardian* published a letter from some which gave the clearest indication that the loyalty of a substantial portion of the Labour movement lay with Russia and not with the campaigners at home. Signed by George Bernard Shaw and a number of leading MPs

and trade union leaders, it decried the 'false atrocity stories', calling the allegations of religious persecution 'malicious inventions', and attributed them
instead to the hostility of the British ruling class, cynically exploiting the
religious feeling of the British people for its own ends:

> We have witnessed during the last few weeks a fierce campaign on the part
> of the capitalist press, with one or two honourable exceptions, against Soviet
> Russia, with whom the Labour Government has just resumed normal diplo-
> matic relations. We note with satisfaction that the Labour Government has not
> been deceived by the Tory allegations of religious persecution, and has refused
> to be intimidated.
>
> The campaign of the press is not based on facts but upon malicious
> inventions.
>
> We are all most strenuously opposed to any kind of religious persecution,
> wherever such is taking place, but at the same time we are bound to express
> protest when we realise that the religious feelings of the British people are
> being cynically exploited in the interests of a class whose hostility to the
> Russian Government is precisely the same character as their hostility to the
> majority of the British people.
>
> We trust British public opinion to resist most emphatically any attempts to
> injure the development of friendly relations between these two great countries
> by means of false atrocity stories and malicious inventions.[25]

What is particularly notable about the letter is that among Shaw's eleven
co-signatories were some significant Labour and trade union leaders – five
presidents of the TUC, four MPs, two past and one future Labour Party chairmen, and the leaders of two of the largest national trade unions (miners and
railwaymen), with 1.5 million members between them. These were not fringe
characters. They included:

* George Hicks *(Labour MP 1931–1950, president of the TUC 1927)*
* Ellen Wilkinson *(Labour MP 1924–31, 1935–47, founder member of the
  British Communist Party 1920, Labour Party chairman 1944–45, Minis-
  ter of Education 1945–47)*
* Ben Tillett *(Labour MP 1917–24, 1929–31, president of the TUC 1929,*

international and political secretary of the Transport and General Workers' Union (TGWU))

- John Bromley *(Labour MP 1924–31, president of the TUC 1932, general secretary of the Associated Society of Locomotive Engineers and Firemen (ASLEF))*
- James Maxton: *(Labour MP 1922–46, chairman of the Independent Labour Party 1926–31, 1934–39)*
- A. E. B. Swales *(president of the TUC 1925, Amalgamated Engineering Union)*
- A. J. Cook *(general secretary of the Miners' Federation of Great Britain 1924–31)*
- C. T. Cramp *(Labour Party chairman 1924–25, general secretary of the National Union of Railwaymen 1931–33)*
- W. H. Hutchinson *(Labour Party chairman 1919–20)*
- Hicks, Bromley and Swales had all been members of the official TUC delegation to Russia in 1924.

Soviet disinformation

'We do not say that one must not deceive and be cunning, that one must love one's enemies … We hate or despise our enemies, according to their deserts; we beat them and deceive according to circumstances,' Trotsky had said.[26] True to this principle, the Soviets thought nothing of issuing public pronouncements which had little basis in fact and were designed solely to destabilise foreign protests.* Denials came first, followed, to cloud things still further, by partial admissions, blamed on the excesses of subordinates.

On 15 March, timed to defuse the day of prayer the next day, the Soviet Central Committee issued a statement which appeared to be a victory for the campaign:

The Executive Committee consider it necessary to take note of the absolutely indefensible departure from Party policy in the struggle against religious prejudices. We refer to the administrative closing of churches without the consent

---

* Stalin used a version of the technique himself against his opponents; often, just days or hours before an arrest of someone already earmarked for destruction, he would make an especially friendly or supportive gesture towards them – a private phone call or a public endorsement.

of the overwhelming majority of local populations. Such action usually leads to the strengthening of religious prejudices.[27]

It hinted at only a *limited* concession, and the results of this, on the ground, were indeed minimal. The destruction of churches continued unabated (the Cathedral of Christ the Saviour in Moscow was dynamited in December 1931) and, more importantly, none of the thousands of imprisoned religious believers were set free.

Stalin's famous 'Dizzy with Success' speech was published on 2 March 1930, halfway between the announcement of the day of prayer and the day itself.[28] Understanding the context provides a hitherto unremarked insight into Stalin's critical comments in that speech on the overzealous destruction of church bells.[29] It was part of the propaganda response that was intended for foreign consumption, deflecting the blame for what was state-initiated persecution onto overzealous party functionaries. Because Soviet historians have been largely unaware of the religious persecution affair, its significance has been missed.

The *Manchester Guardian* letter of 6 March 1930 signed by G. B. Shaw and others illustrates well how a partial admission of protesters' complaints could be used to water down the strength of the complainants' case. A few weeks later, some of the same men put their names to a statement issued by the Anglo-Russian Parliamentary Committee as one of their regular output of pro-Soviet press releases. Distributed to MPs and ministers, these news-sheets provided a constant background 'noise' in 1930–31 to chip away at the protesters' claims. In February, when Archbishop Lang had first raised the question of religious persecution in the House of Lords, it was an ARPC press release which Lord Parmoor had used to justify the government's inaction.[30]

On 10 April, just after Lang had delivered his report on the persecution to the House of Lords (see Chapter 22), a few weeks after the Soviet Central Committee proclamation which apparently criticised the closing of churches without local consent, the ARPC lent its support to the Soviets' defence that there had been excesses but that these were the work of rogue officials, not state policy:

No one has ever denied that in certain parts of the Republic local officials, whether from a desire to discredit the Soviet system, or from excess of mistaken zeal, had committed excesses or violated Soviet laws, not only with regard to religion but on a number of other subjects. But in every case where the attention of the Soviet authorities has been drawn to such abuses they had immediately taken steps to put the matter right. It is therefore not impossible that some of the cases cited by the Archbishop which quite evidently violate Soviet laws may actually have occurred somewhere in the USSR but we are perfectly certain that if in any of these cases the aggrieved persons have appealed to the Soviet authorities their grievances have been put right.[31]

It was a clever move (Stalin's aside about the church bells had made the same point), for the statement was impossible to refute and was all Soviet friends in Britain needed to rebut the charges. Moreover, the line-up of Labour figures in whose name this ARPC press release was issued was impressive. Four of them (Hicks, Maxton, Swales and Tillett) had already signed the *Manchester Guardian* letter. To these were added the names of others whose importance within the Labour movement has already been noted.[32] It would have been hard for any Labour sympathisers to doubt a statement issued on such impressive authority.

Blackmail

As well as denial and disinformation, the Soviets were not averse to using hostages. The sad story of an Englishwoman lost in Russia is one of the more unpleasant parts of this episode. When the British broke off diplomatic relations with the Soviets in 1927, one of the dozens of Russians executed in revenge was Vladimir Evreinov, an official in the Soviet State Bank, who was shot 'for being an agent of Sir Robert Hodgson, head of the British Mission to Russia'. Evreinov's British wife was thrown in prison and then disappeared into 'exile' in Turkistan.

The British Embassy spent months negotiating permission for her to leave the country. Unfortunately the negotiations coincided with the day of prayer in March 1930 and she was pointedly refused an exit visa. Even when the crisis subsided, the Soviets successively raised and dashed hopes for her release, finally increasing her exile term. Such vindictiveness on the part of Soviet officials was not at all uncommon. This is taken from the Foreign Office report, written the following year:

The case of Mme Evreinov, an Englishwoman by birth, who was imprisoned in 1927 when her husband was shot on a charge of espionage and who was afterwards exiled to Turkistan, formed the subject of private conversations with the Commissariat for Foreign Affairs throughout the year. On the 10th of March M. Litvinov informed Sir E. Ovey that the authorities had no objection, in principle, to her release, but thought that be 'a state of tension' at the moment made the granting of permission to return to the United Kingdom 'inadvisable.'

His Majesty's Chargé d'Affaires discussed the matter with M. Litvinov again on the 20th of September, reminding his Excellency that the tension no longer existed. The Commissar said the matter was beyond his competence, but promised to make enquiries. On the 22nd October the head of the Western Department stated that the Soviet authorities were definitely unwilling to permit Mme Evreinov to leave the Union. His Majesty's Ambassador therefore saw M. Krestinsky on the 15th of November and urged him to reconsider the matter.

On the 30th of November Mme Evreinov wrote to the Norwegian Minister at Moscow that she had been notified by the police on the 11th November that she would be allowed to leave the country. However, this permission was withdrawn without explanation on the 19th of November and Mme Evreinov's period of exile was, according to a statement, extended by three further years.[33]

This was not the only case of a British-born spouse or Russian married to a British subject who was refused permission to leave the country,[34] though, given her history, Mme Evreinov's story is one of the saddest. The last that is recorded of her is in 1932, five years after the execution of her husband, when she was still in Russia.

CHAPTER 22

ARCHBISHOP LANG AND
THE HOUSE OF LORDS

*If you only knew, our life is only moaning, tears and sighing. Happy those
who died before and do not see the ignominy, the desolation, and the persecution of us peasants ... We are terrified. They do not let us live. We tremble
like a leaf in autumn and life has lost for us all its charm.*
ANONYMOUS LETTER TO LANG, 1930

*We cannot go on indefinitely merely scraping some facilities for trade, and
paying no heed to these offences against the common order of civilisation.*
LANG, HOUSE OF LORDS, 2 APRIL 1930

In February, Archbishop Lang had told the House of Lords that he had
commissioned an inquiry into the allegations of persecution in Russia and
would be returning to the House to report when it was complete. Lang was
acutely aware of the need for accurate and up-to-date reports from Russia.
The common response by Soviet sympathisers to the stories of persecution
was that they were ten years out of date and rehashed by Tory diehards. He
knew that he could not speak with authority in either the House of Lords or
the nation until he had received properly authenticated information. In this,
Alfred Gough's Christian Protest Movement played an important part, both
directly and indirectly. Lang approached Lord Charnwood, a Liberal politician, biographer and former Oxford philosophy lecturer who also was on the
CPM committee. He asked Charnwood to assemble a confidential committee
to look into the claims of persecution and to draw up a report for him on the

subject. Charnwood immediately approached Sir Bernard Pares, the Director of the School of Slavonic and East European Studies (SSEES) at King's College London, who was one of the foremost British experts on Russia.

Klepenin and the Paris Bureau

One of the most important acts of the CPM had been to fund an information-gathering bureau set up in the Russian Orthodox Academy in Paris.[1] Paris was the home of a substantial proportion of the White Russian diaspora, and the bureau was probably the best informed group outside the OGPU in Moscow. The information which it obtained, collated and redistributed was far more detailed and accurate than anything coming out of Russia through press or diplomatic channels. The material went to both Lang (via Charnwood and Pares) and to the CPM.

The bureau's head was a Russian émigré, Nikolai Klepenin.[*] Klepenin knew Pares, who published a detailed article of his on the persecution in the SSEES academic journal, the *Slavonic Review*, a copy of which was forwarded to Lang.[2] A few weeks later, Pares brought Klepenin over to Lambeth Palace to meet the archbishop personally. After two meetings in early March, Lang was left in no doubt that the stories were true and that the persecution was intense and ongoing. He recorded their conversations in a memorandum:

[6 March 1930] [Klepenin] confirmed my view that the greatest possible difference exists between the formal laws or decrees of the Soviet Government and their administration ... I asked him about the treatment of clergy. He pointed out that they were not only deprived of civil rights but that the clergy had no right to food tickets which are necessary for obtaining food except at almost exorbitant prices, or the allotment of house room. They had to depend upon the hospitality of their people. I asked him about the actual oppression of religious people and he gave me an instance. His brother-in-law and aunt had joined with a small group of people in receiving Holy Communion. This was regarded as an unauthorised religious demonstration, though Mr Klepenin assured me from his knowledge that none of them had any political bias, and

---

[*] Klepenin, a former officer in the White Army, was finance officer of the Institut Théologique Saint-Serge in Paris, and secretary of foreign relations to Metropolitan Evlogie (Georgievsky), hierarch of the Russian Orthodox Church in exile.

they were all sent off to Solovetski Island on the White Sea where multitudes of similar persons have been sent, where conditions are most severe.

The memorandum continues with notes of the second meeting a few days later, which show that Lang's concern was not just with those who professed religious belief but all who were suffering oppression in the Soviet Union. The kulaks' plight was to become a major issue from the summer of 1930:

[11 March 1930] ... the kulaks [are] now being everywhere deprived of their property ... anyone accused of being a kulak is deprived of political rights, oppressed with taxes, and is under constant menace of the confiscation of his goods ... I pointed out to him how unsatisfactory it was to go on repeating statistics about executions and so forth which occurred during the Red Terror and asked him to give me instances of shooting of prisoners from religious grounds during the last few months.[3]

As a device to bring more notice to the matter, Lord Charnwood decided to press the government in the House of Lords to reveal more about the punitive April 1929 Soviet Law on Religions. His motion was greeted with dismay by Foreign Office officials, and the Lord Chancellor was co-opted to try to persuade Charnwood to withdraw the motion. Charnwood was invited to the Foreign Office, where Seymour explained how time-consuming it would be to provide the information he sought. Charnwood knew by then that the report of his research group had already gone to Lang and that Lang was preparing to use it in the House of Lords. With little to lose, he withdrew, knowing Lang could not be silenced so easily.

The Charnwood Report

In the third week of March 1930, Charnwood sent Lang a 42-page *Memorandum on Oppression of Religion in Russia*.[4] It left Lang in no doubt as to the severity of the conditions under which Russian believers currently languished. 'It is the settled and declared policy of those who control the government of Russia so far as possible to extirpate all religion,' the report began, before confirming that the suffering endured by the persecuted was both acute and extensive. It was true that the atrocities of the Civil War period (used in the sense of fatal torture) had ended but, the report insisted, 'it is on the other hand equally misleading to dwell upon the fact that horrors of this kind have ceased. The cruelty which is seriously alleged to be practised today is sufficient.'

Lang had also been taking soundings from a number of other sources and now was well briefed and confident that he had a full grasp of the true and harrowing situation in Russia. He had warned the government publicly and privately that he would raise the matter in the Lords; MacDonald's letter must have made him all the more resolute. Lang now put down a motion in the House of Lords for further debate on the persecution. The stage was set for just the type of scene which Vansittart had tried to head off ten weeks earlier. Before Lang left for the country to write his speech,[5] he wrote to the Prime Minister, with a copy to Henderson, to inform them of his intent and to assure them that he was not going to use the occasion to attack the British government.

My dear Prime Minister,

You may have seen that I have put down a Notice for the House of Lords on April 2nd to call attention to the present position of religious oppression in Russia. I ought to send you a word of explanation.

As you know, I stated some time ago that I was taking such steps as I could to make a full enquiry as to the actual facts and that it might be my duty to lay the results of this enquiry before Parliament and the country in the House of Lords. I have been busy myself in this task and I have also had the assistance of several men of knowledge and capacity and a full sense of responsibility. I therefore think it is my duty to tell the public what I've been able to estimate as to the real facts of the situation. I think this will serve good purpose and clear the air of a good deal of misapprehension.

I do not propose, I need scarcely say, to make any kind of attack or criticism of the government. I merely indulge in the hope (though it is not a very sanguine one) that such a statement may have some effect upon the mind and policy of the Soviet Government. By the technical terms with which the Notice concludes, 'to move for papers' – which, as you know, is the customary form of such Notices in the House of Lords – I do not mean to press the government to publish anything which is inconsistent with the public interest.[6]

Losing a motion 'to move for papers' in a debate compelled the government to make a specific response – by obtaining and publishing information further to the subject of the debate. It was not only time-consuming, but could accidentally provide the opposition with more ammunition to attack the government.

The royal card

Notwithstanding his placatory comments, Lang's action was not welcome. The very fact that the debate was to take place was an implied criticism of the government's inaction, as Henderson well knew. Campaigners had been unable to force the matter further in the Commons, but the press carried reports of parliamentary debates and this would now bring the issue before the nation once again.

The Foreign Office's immediate reaction was to see if the archbishop could be persuaded to back down. At the top of Lang's copy to Henderson, circulated to civil servants, is a comment from his secretary: 'Seen by Sec of State who thinks that the Archbishop should be sent a copy of Lord Stamfordham's letter at once before he puts in motion "moving for papers"'.[7] Stamfordham was the King's private secretary, and the letter in question was the one which had spoken of the King's approval of Ovey's report and of the decision to keep it confidential. Now it was hoped that the knowledge that the King himself approved of its secrecy might persuade Lang to think twice before raising the matter publicly.

In the end, Henderson decided not to pressure Lang to withdraw, possibly because he realised that Lang was not likely to back down and it might only make things worse. It still did not prevent him using his 'royal card' when he replied:

My dear Archbishop,

It was very good of you to send a copy of your letter to the Prime Minister … from my answers to questions in the House of Commons you will have seen that I have taken up the attitude that I could not publish the report of the Mission in Moscow in regard to the situation, nor make any statement on the basis of that report and I think that the overwhelming majority of the House were of opinion that I had adopted the right course. I might add, for your confidential information, that the line which has been taken in this matter has the approval of the highest authority.[8]

Dalton had commented wryly, a couple of weeks earlier, on the irony of the King's approval of the decision not to publish the reports enabling a socialist government to 'shelter behind the throne' against the attacks of the Tory party.[9] It was now trying to do the same with the Church. With no majority in the Lords, any vote was going to be lost. Alarmed at that prospect, Dalton and his civil servants now discussed steps that might be taken to mitigate any future damage. Their preferred solution was to put pressure on Lang to withdraw his motion at the end of the debate and not let it go to a vote. Without a vote, there would be no 'call for papers'. They also considered what 'papers' they could safely release without giving more ammunition to protesters. This is Dalton's comment of 29 March on the department memorandum:

> I agree with Mr Seymour that to publish any further regulations [some of the possible 'papers'], etc might restart the agitation, which is now dying down. On the other hand, to publish [some from] 1918 would have the advantage of showing that this is not a new problem, but that the situation has not changed fundamentally in the last 12 years.[*]
>
> Withdrawal of a motion, after debate, is a common procedure in the Lords and indicates that the mover is reasonably satisfied with the government's reply. I think we should try to get the Archbishop to withdraw at the end of Wednesday's debate. Acceptance of the motion by the government, especially if violent speeches are made in support of it, would look very like an official attack on the Soviet government.

As they were all aware, given that the contribution from other peers was likely to be far less measured than Lang's, it would look very like an attack upon the *British* government too.

The archbishop speaks

The government had not allowed so much as one debate in the House of Commons on persecution in the Soviet Union. While it was unable to silence the House of Lords, it had stalled calls for action with pleas that there was no clear evidence of human rights abuses. With Ovey's secret report to bolster

---

[*] The situation had in fact changed for the worse since April 1929, but Ovey had denied this.

confidence in its position, it hoped to ride out the storm. But Charnwood's report had put in the hands of a leading member of the House of Lords the first detailed and comprehensive confirmation of the Soviet oppression of religious believers. The debate took place on 2 April 1930 and Lang spoke for almost an hour.[10] As he reminded his listeners, the subject was one of concern far beyond Westminster:

> The matter is one which has so deeply touched the public conscience, and aroused the public feeling, that it seemed only right that some such inquiry should be made and its results should be stated. It is a matter so grave that it ought to be kept outside our Party controversies. It has been, it is, and will be my resolute intention so to keep it.

Even though he had not seen it, Lang immediately cast doubt upon the accuracy of Ovey's report and of Ovey's ability to be able to know from the seclusion of the Moscow embassy what was happening elsewhere in so vast a country:

> It seems to be impossible to expect any satisfactory report from our own Embassy in Moscow. Experience proves to us the uselessness of inquiries assisted by the Soviet Government, and to conduct inquiries apart from them would be obviously, from a diplomatic point of view, most difficult. Certainly I have reason to know that persons who were suspected of being in communication, or who were seen to be in communication with any representatives of our Embassy, would be placed in great embarrassment, if not danger.
>
> But after all, what can be told about Moscow and its neighbourhood is of little value in helping us to estimate what is happening in the vast territories of Russia.

By comparison with the ambassador's report, Lang told the House how widely sourced his research had been:

> I have done my best, my Lords, in the interests of truth. I have had the assistance of four responsible men—two of them closely acquainted with Russia, two of them accustomed as public men to weigh evidence. They have

conducted most elaborate researches into the official Press in Russia and I am grateful beyond words for the assistance they have rendered. I have had a mass of independent information given to me from leading representatives of the Orthodox Church, of the Baptist community, of the Jews. I have read many reports from eye witnesses who have just returned from Russia. I have had private letters sent to me from different parts of that vast country. I have read apologies for the religious policy of the Soviet Government.

Much of Lang's long speech reviewed the evidence which he now had, and which confirmed the persecution of religious believers in Russia, ground that has been covered here already. Other significant elements of the speech, and the government's replies, bear closer examination.

Lang countered the insistence of socialists that the tales of persecution were merely a rehash of stories from ten years earlier, acknowledging that mistakes had been made by some campaigners, but insisting that his report related only to events which had taken place within the previous twelve months. Cleverly, he sidestepped the 'cruel' persecution or 'atrocities' defence by stating that he had chosen to refer instead to 'oppression' in his motion. And of that, there was no doubt, he told the House: 'In Russia there is still deliberate, systematic and persistent oppression of religion.' He insisted that it was not valid to present the Soviet oppression of believers as a response to Orthodox association with the previous regime, as some had done (Ovey had used this explanation too). This persecution was against *all* faiths, not just the Orthodox Church:

The campaign ... is directed against every form of theistic religion. Church, Meeting House, Synagogue, Mosque, all alike are declared to be the enemies of social reconstruction. All alike are of their essence counter revolutionary agencies ... As to the Baptists, I have received very full information from the Secretary of the Baptist World Alliance. It is the same story. Their pastors and lay-officers are disfranchised, refused food tickets and subjected to special taxation. They, too, are forbidden to teach their children except in the house. They are forbidden to print or to circulate their Bibles. Their meeting-houses are being largely closed. I am told that the arrests of Baptists and other Evangelical Christians in 1929 extended to hundreds, mostly by administrative action without trial. The school for their preachers which existed up to March, 1929, was closed by the mere imprisonment of the teachers. For them also there is a racking anxiety of nerves.

There is a peculiar vigour of persecution against the Zionists, because they are described as agents of British Imperialism. Many of them have been imprisoned and sent to camps in the White Sea, even boys and girls of sixteen or seventeen.

George Bernard Shaw and the others who wrote to the *Manchester Guardian* had declared that the acting Patriarch Sergius's speech denying the persecution was 'not questioned by anyone' and was 'irrefutable' proof that 'the campaign of the press is not based on facts but upon malicious inventions'. It is clear, however, that Sergius only made these statements because his predecessor and his two other Patriarchal locums were in prison.* Lang, rightly understanding the intense pressure on Sergius, begged to differ:

Perhaps I ought at this moment to make a digression to refer to the statement some time ago published in his name, denying the reality of any persecution or oppression of religion in Russia. I have no doubt that the questionnaire submitted to the Metropolitan was so carefully framed that it was possible for him to make a conscientious answer, but no one knows what happened to his answers or under what pressure they were made.

Remembering, as I have reason to do, the pressure exerted upon his predecessor Tikhon, and the threats to himself or others which were brought against him, I have grave doubts about the genuineness of that document. I should like to know whether the members of the G.P.U. were present when it was drawn up. Certainly the language which was used, I am assured by those who know best the mind and character of the Metropolitan – especially the references to his Holiness the Pope and the Archbishop of Canterbury – would never have been used by him. The voice is the voice of Jacob but the hand is the hand of Esau.

---

* Metropolitan Peter was appointed Tikhon's successor in April 1925 but (rightly) fearing his own imminent arrest (which happened in December of the same year) he appointed three other locums to take his place if he were arrested. By December, only one, Metropolitan Sergius, was still free. Sergius thus became the de facto head of the Russian Orthodox Church. Peter remained in prison for twelve years until he was shot in 1937.

Drawing to a close, Lang was emphatic. In an unmistakable, though diplomatically worded, rebuttal of British government's denials, he concluded:

> I have only used fragments of the mass of information which has been put at my disposal. I have tried not to exaggerate and to keep strictly to the present situation. But I submit *there can be no question as to the rigour, the persistence and the cruelty of the oppression of religion in Russia at the present time.* (My italics.)

What was to be done? 'That is a question which is far more naturally asked than easily answered,' he admitted. He made a number of suggestions of changes to Soviet policy which London could press for. While he recognised the difficult situation in which the government found itself, he was not going to let it evade the moral ambivalence of the policy it had chosen:

> It is not for me to describe the difficulties of our own Government. They may take it from me that I most fully recognise them. I have no wish in any way to embarrass them. I know that men like the Prime Minister and Mr. Henderson, and the noble and learned Lord who will follow me [Lord Parmoor] detest oppression of religion and would most willingly abate it. They may have made some representations. I do not suppose this afternoon they can give us much information on the point, but sooner or later some representations must, I think, be made.
>
> I am not … questioning, the advantage, even for those that we wish to help, of having a representative of our own in Moscow, and a representative of the Soviet Government in London, but advantages carry with them special responsibilities. *We cannot go on indefinitely merely scraping some facilities for trade, and paying no heed to these offences against the common order of civilisation.* That would be like bartering for a mess of pottage the birthright of those principles for which this country has always desired to stand among the nations of the world. (My italics.)

Parmoor replies

Lord Parmoor's reply for the government was either masterful or appalling, depending on the sympathy of the listener. He opened by saying he wholly accepted Lang's account, only then to dismiss it as inaccurate:

My Lords, I am sure we have all heard with much emotion and with deep respect the very weighty and touching speech of the most rev. Primate. To a very great extent we shall all agree with him, and certainly there will be no dissentient voice from the present Government. At the same time when he traces, as he has traced with such care of statistics, the gross mechanical tyranny of the present Soviet Government in Russia, he cannot expect the Government, and I think he cannot expect the members of this House, to accept as accurate the whole picture and story as he has told it to us of the conditions in Russia ... He has warned us himself that accuracy is not possible. No one who listened to him can have failed to be impressed by his evident desire to give the most accurate account possible, but accuracy at the present time is beyond the scope of any individual or any Government.

Parmoor then deliberately misinterpreted a number of Lang's remarks and denied the misinterpreted version he had created – thus avoiding the main issues Lang raised. Finally, he attributed to Lang a conclusion which Lang had not reached (that the situation was improving) and then used that conclusion to justify the government's policy of inaction.

Lang had made it quite clear that the 'cruel' or 'medieval' persecution argument was irrelevant and insisted that there was still 'deliberate, systematic and persistent oppression of religion'. Parmoor paid no attention and went on to deny the medieval persecution as if Lang had claimed it:

To sum up, we all detest the systematic denial of religious tolerance. We all deplore the disabilities under which those who profess religious belief continue to suffer in Russia. But I doubt whether at the present time the violence of persecution in Russia makes it of the same character as that which was known in mediaeval times and of some of the worst persecutions of the Inquisition.

Like Ovey, Parmoor downplayed the language of persecution – as 'disabilities' arising from a 'denial of tolerance'. Parmoor appears to be the only government figure on record who identified and condemned even the Soviets lack of 'tolerance'. Elsewhere they were denied. But as with his remarks in a similar vein in the February debate, this admission was a device which served to put the opposition off their stride rather than to accept their case and respond.

When it came to action, Parmoor's intention was, as it had been from the first debate on 13 February, to stall. For the government to approach the Soviets, he insisted, required both proof of the persecution and an assurance that intervention would bring some result. Lang, he insisted incorrectly, had provided neither:

> What, then, should we do? – because, after all, that is the difficulty. So I come back to the question with which I started, and which the most rev. Primate asked me at the end of his speech. No outside Government could, I venture to say, rightly act in such a case unless two conditions were present, and they are very important conditions. First, it would need to have overwhelming accurate proof that great wrongs are being committed, wrongs so grave in their character and extent that they cease to be the concern of the country where they are committed, and become the concern of the whole civilised world ... And as I have indicated, we have no such proof that wrongs are being suffered to the extent that I have indicated.
>
> The second condition is that a Government should have good reason to hope that its action would really alleviate such wrongs, or at least not do more harm than good.

Brentford challenges Parmoor

The second main speaker, representing the opposition, was Viscount Brentford, who was also the joint president of the Christian Protest Movement. He was not going to let Parmoor get away with so casual a dismissal of Lang's points:

> After the most rev. Primate has summed up the result of his investigation in those remarkable words, a 'deliberate systematic and persistent oppression of religion' is still going on, and the Leader of the House [Parmoor], speaking on behalf of the Government, is asked what can be done, he informs your Lordships that there are two conditions upon the fulfilment of which only can the Government move. The first is that there should be overwhelming and accurate proof that great wrongs are being committed.
>
> Does the noble and learned Lord say that there is no overwhelming proof in the speech of the Archbishop, or does he say that though it is overwhelming it is not accurate?

Parmoor's reply was extraordinary:

> I do not think that the most rev. Primate himself would claim that in making the statement he was accurate in the sense that I have indicated. Of course, he was accurate in the sense that he gave us information, but that does not mean an accurate picture of what is going on in Russia.

Brentford had no time either for the idea that inaction was justified unless results could be guaranteed. By that principle the slave trade would never have been brought to an end:

> Practically the whole religious world is united in deploring the present position of affairs. Surely there is a responsibility upon the Government of a great country like this ... When the slave trade was rife in various countries, we did not stand back and say: 'We can do nothing.' We did not stand back and say: 'This is the domestic concern of other countries.' We at least tried, and in the end we succeeded in abolishing the evil of the slave trade. Whether we can succeed to-day I am not prepared to say, but we can try. Surely in the name of the civilised world, we can make an intimation in the most friendly manner to the Government of Russia, with which you are in friendly relations, asking them to consider whether they cannot carry out some of the suggestions made by the most rev. Primate.

And with all the CPM's resources to inform him, Brentford firmly rebutted Parmoor's pretence that Lang had declared that the persecution was dying down: 'There is no evidence whatever, in my possession at all events, and I imagine there is no evidence in the possession of the Government itself, that there has been the slightest cessation or modification of persecution.'

Lord Ponsonby

The second speaker for the government was Lord Ponsonby, an outspoken Soviet enthusiast, the deputy Labour leader in the Lords, who was to take over Parmoor's role in 1931. He accused the opposition of political bias, making a grudging exception in the case of Lang, but then, insultingly, implying that Lang had been manipulated by the Tories. Ponsonby insisted that the House of Lords had no right to condemn the Soviets, that no government had the right to dictate the political philosophy of another country, and any action or protest to the Soviets would be an unwarranted interference in the internal affairs of the USSR:

> If I might respectfully say so, I doubt if this House is the proper place in which to bring up a matter of this sort ... the most rev. Primate has undoubtedly been used outside by those who have whipped up this feeling with such strength, peculiarly enough in the last nine months while a Labour Government has been in office, in order to show the folly of having recognised and had diplomatic relations with the Government of Russia ... I doubt even whether this debate which has been held here this afternoon will do anything but harm.

Lang's reply

As the proposer, Lang was allowed to conclude the debate. He took issue with both Ponsonby and Parmoor:

> The noble Lord who has just sat down [Ponsonby] seemed to doubt whether your Lordships' House was a proper place in which a matter of this kind should be dealt with. I do not agree with him. I think the Parliament of this country is a place which has always been ready to speak out the heart of the British people when it is deeply stirred, and do not know what I am doing in this House as a Spiritual Peer unless my presence gives me the right, at all times, to raise any issue affecting the moral and religious life of our own country and indeed of the world.
>
> [One] condition laid down by the noble and learned Lord [Parmoor] was that the Government would have to be very sure that their action would not do more harm than good to those whom they wished to benefit. That is a very difficult matter, and I quite appreciate the difficulty of the Government in regard to it. I feel one takes a certain measure of responsibility in even advocating that the risk should be run, but I have in memory the effect of outside expostulation and interference in the case of the Metropolitan Tikhon in the years between 1921 and 1925, when he died, and it is, I should have thought, certain that it was those expostulations which did spare his life and secure his release at least from the worst incidents of imprisonment. Further than that I should have

thought that it was common knowledge that it was the expostulation of the whole Christian world expressed, among others, by my predecessor [Lord Davidson], by Cardinal Bourne, by leaders of the Free Churches, and most of all by His Holiness the Pope, that spared the Archbishop Cieplak from execution.

Parmoor's device was to stall, Ponsonby's to head off the prospect of a protest altogether. Lang would have neither:

What I said was that the inaction, however necessary it may be for the moment, cannot go on indefinitely. We cannot permanently acquiesce in the state of things in which we reap whatever benefits we are alleged to reap from this association with the Soviet Government, and yet make no kind of representations as to what the public opinion of this country feels so intensely.

Lang closed his speech with some words directly from Russia itself:

I ask you to listen to a cry from the heart of oppressed Russia. It comes in a letter sent to me by an exile from his niece, the daughter of simple peasants, in a remote village in Russia. I wish I could read the whole of it. It is to me a picture most convincing, because of its simplicity and its spontaneity, of the mingled social and religious oppression under which so many of the peasants are suffering. Let a few words make their own appeal to our hearts. I think it is strange that the letter of that remote Russian peasant girl should reach your Lordships' House in London to-day: – 'If you only knew, our life is only moaning, tears and sighing. Happy those who died before and do not see the ignominy, the desolation, and the persecution of us peasants … We are terrified. They do not let us live. We tremble like a leaf in autumn and life has lost for us all its charm.'

But, as Parmoor had made clear, the government's position was not going to change – whatever the archbishop had uncovered or confirmed.

Foreign Office reaction
When Lord Charnwood consented to withdraw his motion he urged Henderson to allow Lang's motion to be carried unopposed (without being put to a

vote), as a sign of goodwill. Civil servants were wary of this and counselled against it. The government was bound to lose the debate and be forced to provide 'papers' anyway, but it was a concession to the archbishop and protesters that the officials were unwilling to make.

In the end, to the officials' surprise, the government unexpectedly decided *not* to oppose the motion. 'I had been under the impression that the motion was to be resisted and I am not sure of the exact reasons for acceptance', Seymour wrote. H. L. Baggallay, another of the Northern Department staff, added that it was a 'rather unexpected conclusion' and 'some sort of explanation should be given to Sir E. Ovey'.[11]

The reason became apparent in Henderson's next dispatch to Ovey. From time to time throughout this affair, we have glimpses of Henderson's intervention, often opposed by Dalton.* This is one of those instances.

Your Excellency will observe that the motion of the papers was not resisted. This was partly because His Majesty's Government have already decided that there were certain papers, that is to say, translations of Soviet legislation dealing with the question of religion, which they could properly lay before Parliament. But this was only a technical consideration.

The real reason was that His Majesty's Government, although they do not accept much of what passes for evidence of religious persecution, and although they are aware that much that is called persecution does not, when properly understood, amount to persecution at all, are, none the less, unable to avoid the conclusion that the Soviet Government and the Soviet local authorities, in striving to secure the universal acceptance of beliefs which they had every right to hold or to propagate, are employing methods of discrimination which British and other opinion regards as substantially unjust.

To this extent His Majesty's Government do not disassociate themselves,

---

* The contrast between Henderson's moral perspective and Dalton's more cynical pragmatism is nowhere more evident than in an exchange between the two men, recorded in Dalton's diary, over the correct response to Russian wireless propaganda broadcasts, forbidden under the terms of the agreement between the two countries: 'Russia is a bloody hair shirt! As Uncle [Henderson] said, "if it wasn't for Russia we would be having quite a good time at the FO" ... I say "you are giving an answer that will please the Conservatives." He says, "Can't you look at the questions from a wider point of view than party? ... Can you deny this is propaganda? I can't understand why you always want to shield these people." ... The officials, I think, all agree with me in not wanting another protest. But Uncle has got a Soviet complex at the moment.' LSE/BLPES, Dalton, *Diary*, 3 December 1930.

and have no wish to disassociate themselves, from public opinion in this country. That this is their attitude has, in fact, been evident throughout the controversy from replies to questions in Parliament and other public utterances of
members of the Government. But His Majesty's Government differ from the
Lord Archbishop and others in his opinion as to the point at which they would
be justified in interfering in the internal affairs of another Government because
the methods of that Government do not comply with the standards which are
accepted in this country.

You may, if necessary, make any use you think fit of this explanation,
should the Acting Commissar for Foreign Affairs or any other member of the
Soviet Government question you about the debate.[12]

On the surface, it seemed to be a positive outcome from the Lords debate but
in practice diplomatic niceties in the language meant that it was sufficiently
hesitant and mild that it would have been greeted in Moscow with derision.
The statement said that the government did 'not accept much of what passes
for evidence' and agreeing that much of what was 'called persecution does
not … amount to persecution at all'. Reviewing the material brought into
the public domain by Lang, Brentford, Klepenin and others, it is hard to find
anything the government could dismiss, let alone 'much' of it.

Any impact upon the Soviet government would have been further neutralised by assurances that the British government felt that the Soviet had 'every
right to hold or to propagate' certain beliefs, which ignored the fact that those
beliefs included the principle that religion was counter-revolutionary and that
its professors could justifiably be shot.

The dispatch's final sentence, that the British government did not feel it
would be justified in interfering because the matter was an internal one, even
though the Soviets did not go along with 'standards which are accepted in
this country', implied that acts of repression were not wrongs which could
be defined as such by any objective measure, but depended upon the cultural
perspective of the nation committing them. Neither Gough nor Lang (nor
Wesley himself, the founder of Henderson's branch of the Church) would
have accepted such moral relativity.

This was the last concession that Henderson was to make, even though the
evidence mounted still further over the coming year of yet more widespread

oppression in the kulak deportations and the timber camps, the products of which Britain was buying. Dalton's opposition to further compromise by his superior and the constraints of the Cabinet decision on non-intervention a few weeks earlier prevented Henderson from doing more. In Parliament, Henderson's line was that conditions for persecuted believers were gradually improving. The only evidence to back that up was disinformation put out by Soviet officials, Stalin included, which was enthusiastically seized upon by British fellow travellers.

After the success of Lang's motion, the Northern Department was compelled to make arrangements for something to be published, but they naturally did what they could to publish nothing which might help the opposition:

> I have placed within the rough draft of a Command Paper containing the legislation which Lord Parmoor promised should be laid in the course of the debate on April 2nd [signed] L. Baggallay 11th April 1930 ... The Archbishop's motion for papers having been accepted we must publish something. I do not think the papers will add very much to the state of public information, *but they are harmless*. [signed] Seymour 12/4. (My italics.)[13]

Ovey's confirmation

Hansard extracts of Lang's speech were sent to Ovey for comment. On 19 May Ovey, normally sanguine on Soviet excesses, confirmed that Lang's speech presented 'a fair picture, not only of the actual definite results of the policy of the government, but the abuses which have undoubtedly arisen therefrom ... unbridled fanaticism and apparently unlimited power has been rife'.[14]

Baggallay added his own comment to the accompanying memorandum: 'It is apparent that the Archbishop's account of religious conditions in the Soviet Union was substantially correct, and indeed there has never been any reason to doubt that it was.'

This was not all, for Ovey continued by implying that protests *did* have some effect: 'I have always contended that the recent anti-Soviet campaign in Europe on the grounds of the alleged religious persecution has caused this government to pause and think.'

Baggallay noted:

Sir E. Ovey's remarks confirm in a striking manner the opinion expressed by Sir R. Hodgson in 1923 [in the campaign to free Archbishop Cieplak and Monsignor Budkevich] that a widespread press campaign in other countries was the most likely means of bringing about some relaxation in religious oppression in the Soviet Union.

Two of Parmoor's main arguments in the Lords debate – that Lang's assessment of the oppression was unconfirmed and that protests were futile – had now both been refuted by Ovey himself. Baggallay's comments were not challenged by any of the officials who subsequently initialled the memorandum as it was circulated around the department.

Whereas their previous efforts had been to defend the government's position, the sentiment of civil servants and the tone of their internal minutes began to change after Ovey's May 1930 dispatch, as one of their own confirmed that the archbishop's speech was substantially correct – even though, in spite of Ovey's assessment, the Labour government's own position did not alter. By the time the timber trade crisis blew up later in the year, civil servants had moved substantially from guarded scepticism to acceptance that there existed widespread repression in the Soviet Union. Their relationships with ministers changed correspondingly – from support in face of what at times they treated as their mutual enemy (Tory agitators) to damage limitation where they had come to believe the allegations of the opposition. But that change was a gradual one and only set in as the opposition campaign on religious persecution began to lose steam and regrouped around the subject of the timber camps.

CHAPTER 23

'SOVIET ABATES WAR ON RELIGION'

In the end, disinformation triumphed, though the victory was to prove only temporary. The Soviets' ability to manipulate information and propaganda was too sophisticated for their Western critics and their Labour sympathisers, who were consistently outwitted. The Christian Protest Movement allowed its hopes for improvement to persuade itself that the picture painted by the Soviets was real before the evidence confirmed it. If they were naive, they were only temporarily so and they were encouraged to be so by the Foreign Office. The *Morning Post*, enthusiastic for self-congratulatory headlines, bears a responsibility too, for it claimed a victory for itself when there was none. Further parts were played by a member of the embassy staff and a clever Soviet deception which targeted a senior churchman passing through Moscow.

The March Central Committee decree condemning the 'absolutely indefensible closing of churches without the consent of the overwhelming majority of local populations'[1] was pivotal in the disinformation process too, though it took time do its work.

Dawkins, Haigh, Temple and Embling
In the second half of June, S. M. Dawkins, the secretary of the CPM, met an unnamed member of the Moscow embassy staff who was passing through London and who assured him of a 'somewhat changed attitude of the Soviet Government'.[2] This was then reported to Gough and Lang. Additionally, Assistant Bishop Embling of Korea had passed through Moscow on the way

home. There, he had been targeted by Soviet officials and convinced not only that the British protests had been successful, but that they should now be abandoned before they did any harm. Embling convinced William Temple, the Archbishop of York, who then wrote to Lang:

> I have with me here Bishop Embling (Korea) who came through Moscow, spending some time there on the way. He is anxious for it to be known in England that (1) undoubtedly the Prayers for Russia and the protests such especially, as your speech in the Lords, have had great effect. More churches are open, more priests have received ration tickets, and it is possible to register as a congregation – for worship and instruction – a group of 20, whereas it used to be 200. (2) almost certainly any further action, such as might be regarded as 'nagging at them' would do harm, while some gesture of appreciation of what has happened might do great good.
>
> I thought this of sufficient interest to pass to you.
>
> Yours affectionately,
>
> William Ebor[3]

Lang was convalescing in the country, and his chaplain and personal secretary Rev. M. G. Haigh was handling his correspondence. During the Lords debate, Viscount Brentford had warned that no Soviet statements should be taken as fact unless *evidence* of a change had been forthcoming. Perhaps if Lang had seen Temple's letter first, Haigh might not have taken action on his own initiative. Handwritten on top of Temple's letter in Haigh's writing are the words 'I've already written to the Gough people *strongly* on these lines. M.G.H.' (emphasis as in the original).

What had given rise to Embling's view of developments in Russia only came to light when he visited Lambeth Palace a month later. Embling had managed to see (or it had been engineered that he see) Foreign Minister Litvinov, with whom even Ovey had had difficulty in getting an interview, and had spent time afterwards discussing the religious situation with his 'assistant'. He had come away convinced of the Soviets' good intent. Moreover, he had 'met' a group of young Communists on the Trans-Siberian express. They had happened to speak good enough English to converse with him. They, too, had impressed him. This is Lang's memorandum on the meeting:

I had a long talk with Bishop Embling, late assistant bishop in Corea [*sic*], on July 17, 1930. He had passed through Russia on his way from Corea. He took pains to become intimate with some young Communists in the train who were engaged in propaganda work in some of the more distant villages. He was much impressed by the fervour of their idealism. They described how completely religion as presented by the Orthodox Church in Russia had been identified with the Czarist regime, and how little it had to give to young and ardent people of social outlook and aspiration. He felt that it was not wholly their fault, in any need of some kind of religion, that they had betaken themselves to a religion without God.

At Moscow, he had an interview with Litvinov, the Foreign Minister of the Soviet government, at the British Embassy and was able to have much conversation with Litvinov's assistant who speaks both French and English. They felt that the adherents of the Orthodox Church were so instinctively reactionary that they were regarded with some suspicion. He also made the interesting point that there is great fear among the Soviets of the increase of power of the Roman Catholic Church.

He said that they did not speak at all bitterly of the Anglican Church or even of the appointment of a Day of Prayer or of my speech in the House of Lords of which they seem to know. But they did object to the announcement of prayers as on behalf of the persecuted Russians, instead of on behalf of the Church and People of Russia.[4]

How much this series of events was planned and how much accidental is hard to say, but it looked as though Embling had been specifically targeted; given Haigh's response, successfully so. The news passed from the CPM to the *Morning Post*, which trumpeted the news as a great victory for their campaign in a report which was full of mistakes and exaggerations:

SOVIET ABATES WAR ON RELIGION

Confiscation of Churches Stopped: Free Exercise of Faith – Change of Policy Now Reported – Swift Result of World-Wide Protest Started by Morning Post

The Morning Post learns that important information of undoubted authority and reliability has been received by those in London who are in closest touch with the Russian situation of a radical change in the policy of the ruthless persecution of religion which the Central Soviet Government in Moscow has hitherto pursued.

This information shows that the former policy of the Soviets has been reversed in the three following particulars, each of which is recognized as a major issue:

1. Churches and other places of worship are no longer being confiscated
2. Free exercise of religion is being allowed and official encouragement is no longer being given to the Bezbozhnik or the 'Anti-God movement'
3. Bread tickets are being issued to priests[5]

As evidence, the *Post* reprinted the Central Committee resolution of mid-March, in other words, of *three months earlier*:

> The following was the text of the proclamation: 'the Central Committee considers it necessary to take note of the absolutely indefensible departure from party policy in the struggle against religious prejudice. We refer to the administrative closing of churches without the overwhelming majority of local populations ... Resolutely discontinue the practice of the administrative closing of churches under the pretence that such closing is the voluntary desire of the local population ... For jeering at peasants and religious sentiments, prosecute the guilty with rigour.'

Gough wrote for confirmation to the Foreign Office, where the *Morning Post*'s triumphalism was already raising eyebrows. Ovey was asked for more information. His telegraphed reply was not encouraging:

> Any recent change has arisen from the gradual application of the concession made in March last ... I know of no new decree on the subject. It would appear therefore that [the] information is a re-hash of old news. Demolition of certain churches already planned in Moscow is proceeding and there is no evidence of any new move in this direction ...
>
> The principal advantages which clergy enjoy as a result of the March 'let up' are as follows:
>
> 1) Any citizen is now allowed to buy (at about double prices) in any shop, bread over and above [the] quantity of 500 grammes which he can buy on

his [ration] card. This concession in practice is of advantage only to priests and other disenfranchised as all cardholders … are entitled to an amply sufficient quantity twice as cheaply.

2) Private trading in market produce (being relaxed) … recognised clergy can buy food in the market … Now parishioners no longer have to feed them out of their insufficient rations but can give them money to buy provisions for themselves

3) Third important concession is that mere fact of being a son of a priest no longer automatically puts individual in class of disenfranchised

These three concessions … have improved the position of priests but it all dates from three months ago and [they] are so worded as to refer to the disenfranchised only without any mention of 'clergy'.[6]

The change amounted to the theoretical removal of one highly punitive measure against the children of priests and a general right to market traders to sell bread more freely, which by accident might lessen some of the misery of the clergy, if they had the funds to afford it. There were no other improvements. Disenfranchised priests were still not being given ration cards as the *Post* had suggested. Church closures and demolitions continued. The thousands of believers in prison remained there. Ovey did say that he had been told (we are not sure if it was by the same Soviet government-supplied 'expert') that the closure of some country churches had been reversed, but that he could not report it as more than hearsay. It was hardly a thaw, but Henderson helped it all along in the House of Commons a week later, in answer to a Tory question asking if he had had any further reports from the Moscow embassy: 'No further comprehensive report has been received but recent telegraphic correspondence appears to indicate that there has been some improvement following upon the gradual application of the decree of March last.'[7]

The Foreign Office replied to Prebendary Gough on the same day, 2 July, informing him of Ovey's comments, including his remarks about the limits of the concessions and their timing, but concluding that 'generally it may be said that the position of the priests has improved during the last three months'.[8] The letter was sent in Henderson's name and under his signature. It convinced Gough. He wrote enthusiastically in his parish newsletter that 'news has reached me today of a striking change of heart towards religion'.[9] Sadly, it was wishful thinking.

Had Henderson chosen to read a lengthy bulletin, sent to him by Sir Bernard Pares on 15 July, he might have found its contents challenging.[10] The bulletin had been edited by Nikolai Klepenin in Paris, and the first twenty-two pages were devoted to an examination of the situation after the Central Committee decree of 15 March. Nothing, Klepenin insisted, had changed. He quoted extensive Soviet press exhortations to continue anti-religious activity, of which one, in the *Red Evening Newspaper* a month later, was typical: 'We have not yet by a long way obtained victory on the anti-religious front. A cruel long fight is in front of us. It is the duty of Communists to be first in the skirmishes against Churchmen.'[11]

This was hardly the language of moderation. Klepenin's paper also recounted how, just one day after the March Central Committee decree which was now hailed as relaxing the pressure on believers, Sovnarkom passed a new measure which deprived all former (not just current) teachers of religion and seminary professors of the right to the pensions granted to all teachers.[12]

The day after Henderson's statement that things were getting easier for Russian believers, it was announced that, in an attempt by the Soviets to silence Metropolitan Eulogius, and in retaliation for his participation in the day of prayer services, acting Patriarch Sergius had dismissed him.[13] Meanwhile, in the Foreign Office, officials were noting that any relaxation was minimal, and one of the documents supporting it was 'solely connected with election [voting] rights'.

Lang's successful motion and call for papers meant that the Foreign Office was compelled to publish something on the latest information on religion in the USSR. But, concerned that the information might defeat the CPM's largely groundless optimism, Dalton ordered a delay. The memorandum concerned is marked with a secretary's comment that, 'Mr Dalton suggests that publication should be deferred until after Prebendary Gough's Albert Hall meeting'. The signatures of those who had seen this instruction (and in this case clearly endorsed it) include that of Ramsay MacDonald himself.[14] Although the papers had already been vetted to ensure that they were innocuous, nothing could be risked which might rekindle the agitation, particularly now that a new Anglo-Soviet trade agreement, secured on promises by the

Soviet ambassador of orders for £15–20 million of British goods, had been agreed. Correspondingly, publication was delayed until it could be done with minimal notice: it was released on 2 August 1930 in the middle of the parliamentary recess and summer holidays, two weeks after the CPM rally at the Royal Albert Hall.[15]

The Lambeth Conference rally

Every ten years, the Archbishop of Canterbury hosts a conference at Lambeth for bishops from the worldwide Anglican communion. By now, Gough and Lang were working well together, Lang's earlier suspicions overcome. No objections were raised therefore to the proposal that the CPM host a rally in the Royal Albert Hall on 14 July, to coincide with the Lambeth Conference. After just over eight months' work, the worldwide impact of the movement could be seen in the line-up of bishops on the platform (detailed above in Chapter 20).* It testified to the extraordinary success of Gough's campaign, and the deep feeling around the world for the plight of those suffering in Russia.

From the platform that night, Lord Brentford told the assembled prelates that 'there is today an intensive pressure on religion itself. The attempts which are being made to destroy all religion were more wholehearted than they were a year ago.' The Archbishop of Armagh, the Primate of Ireland, spoke too:

> Have you ever heard or read an account [like that of] the condition of things in that terrible island in the Arctic Sea all in the most bitterly frozen parts of Siberia, and of the tens of thousands who are sent there to perish of cold and hunger because of their faith? I do not know that in all the records of persecutions there has ever been anything more terrible. Even massacre would seem to be better.[16]

In spite of Brentford's rousing speech, it seemed that the Soviets, British fellow travellers, and the Foreign Office had fought off the campaign. The *Morning Post* had backed down after having claimed a non-existent victory. Dalton and his officials had good reason to think that the crisis had passed.

---

* Conscious that members of all religions were under threat, Gough had even invited a Muslim, Sooffee Abdul Qadeer Abdullah, to speak.

They were wrong. As information about the plight of the kulaks and priests *after* their arrest and deportation began to emerge from the Northern timber forests, the agitation was to intensify. It was around that cause that the campaigners were already re-grouping. The stage was set for the second act.

PART IV

SLAVE LABOUR (JULY 1930 – OCTOBER 1931)

DEAR SIRS, FELLOW HUMAN BEINGS, RULERS OF ALL THE WORLD,
The Russian Revolution is responsible for many a funeral pyre: first they went after the bourgeoisie, then, when they had been got rid of the intelligentsia, who were in part murdered, and in part gave into the Red Imperialism and tyranny. Then came the Middle Class, which forms the great mass.

And where is this class? In the midst of the forests of northern Russia, collecting wood for your coffins.

Shame on you, Europe, consider what you are doing!

America, far away, has already taken steps, she has protested and refused to take the timber stained with blood, tears, and sweat, and you, who ought to know better, strive in rivalry to strengthen commercial ties with us on every hand, and thus fulfil the Five-Year Plan. Consider, however, that you are preparing the noose for your own necks.

Open your eyes, O European politicians, before it is too late!

We have to work like beasts, without food, clothing, medicine, etc. We have to work for sixteen hours in the sweat of death in order to earn 700 grammes of bread, without a single day of rest, no fats, no meat – absolutely nothing.

We are distended already, and black with exhaustion and hunger. The husband no longer knows his wife, children do not know their parents, one man does not know the other. It is unbelievable, indescribable, and its parallel is not to be found in any fiction.

People eat the bark of trees and grasses. Children, women, and old men run and grovel about in the forest and feet like animals all wild beasts. Why are people [in the West] silent, together with the Commission of Enquiry into our timber trade?

Take steps on our behalf, help us for God's sake, for we are dying of hunger and oppression.

ANONYMOUS APPEAL, c.1931–32[1]

On the Friday afternoon, the 18th April, 1930, four members of the staff of the Embassy, during the course of a walk, reached Belkamemaya station on the Ceinture Railway. We saw standing there a train, composed of forty-eight goods wagons and four coaches, guarded by troops with fixed bayonets.

On approaching nearer, we saw that each of the good wagons had been converted into a prison van; the small ventilators near the roof had been barred over, and the doors fastened by the hasp, so they were open to the extent of about 6 inches.

At many of the ventilators were to be seen the faces of from three to five children, while at the narrow door opening was occupied from top to bottom by faces of men and women. It was difficult to judge but as other forms could be seen dimly, there would appear to have been from thirty to forty in each wagon – men women and children. All we could see were of the typical peasant type, and were evidently some of the so-called kulaks on their way to the great concentration camp at *Vologda*, and the forced forest labour of the Archangel province.

From one of the wagons, hands were extended, holding tin cups in a vain appeal for water. The few workpeople occupied in the vicinity appeared quite indifferent, while the troops were joking about the 'freight' they were conveying.

C. H. HARDY, MOSCOW, APRIL 1930[2]

In one kulak concentration camp near *Vologda*, barracks were built on swampy land for the wives, children and women folks of the exiled kulaks, while the males worked in the forests. In the summer of last year there were 690 children under 12 in these barracks.

By Fall there were only six children left, all the rest died of disease and hunger.

EDWARD L. DEUSS, LENINGRAD, FEBRUARY 1931[3]

CHAPTER 24

OPENING SALVOES

What a blot it will be on the Labour Party in the future, if they do nothing now.
FROM A PRIVATE LETTER TO ARTHUR HENDERSON, 3 FEBRUARY 1931[1]

The Prime Minister and His Majesty's Government have no intention of introducing elaborate legislation to meet a condition of affairs about which we have not any sure and authentic data.
LORD PONSONBY, 5 FEBRUARY 1931[2]

It is apparent that a considerable part of the cutting of timber and pulpwood in Russia and transportation and loading is done by convict labour under the most brutal conditions. It is a constant story of undernourishment, uninterrupted toil, misery and blood. Hundreds of thousands of aristocrats, former professional and businessmen, army officers, kulaks, and Social Democrats and other anti-revolutionaries have disappeared into the forests without leaving any trace.
REPORT TO THE UNITED STATES CONGRESS, JANUARY 1931[3]

When, on the first day of Foreign Office questions in the new parliament in July 1929, Carlyon Bellairs MP raised the topic of forced labour in the Soviet timber export trade, British campaigners were still unaware that many of the arrested priests and pastors who had escaped execution were being shipped north to the Northern Region timber camps or to their even more severe counterpart – the 'corrective labour' camps such as those on the Solovetsky Islands in the White Sea. It was to be many months before it became apparent that the plight of those suffering religious persecution and that of the deported kulaks in the Northern Region timber camps were intertwined.

Bellairs tried again in March 1930. On 26 March the Conservatives managed to squeeze Russia into another debate in the House of Commons. Bellairs took the opportunity to challenge the government once again about Russian prison labour. He reminded them that when he had raised the subject before he been told that action was not possible, first because no diplomatic relations were in place, and then because of the absence of information. Now, he informed the house, not only were ambassadors in place, but he had sworn affidavits given by escaped prisoners who had been employed in the labour camps preparing timber exports for Great Britain.[4] The Foreign Prison-Made Goods Act of 1897, he reminded ministers, prohibited the import of goods which had been 'made or produced wholly or in part in any foreign prison, gaol, house of correction, or penitentiary'. He continued:

> One cannot help finding it a little strange that in Great Britain more atten-
> tion has not been paid to conditions in Russia which are incompatible with
> the principles adopted by British trade ethics and sanctioned by the British
> Empire. Great Britain has never favoured products of forced labour and we
> do not believe a change in this respect is taking place ... In one camp alone,
> Solovjetsk Island, 45,000 prisoners are employed entirely on timber cutting
> and loading and so on.[5] Hon. Members object so much to stories of horrors
> being given and they pour disbelief on them, but from those given on the
> testimony of the prisoners it is perfectly clear that hundreds of them die. They
> have to submit to terrible privations, and in every respect the tales which are
> told of these prisoners' camps are tales which would excite the horror of the
> whole of Europe.[6]

Bellairs demanded that the government respond, but George Masterman Gil-lett MP, Hugh Dalton's deputy at the Foreign Office, was dismissive: '[Bellairs] told us that, in spite of all the questions which he had put to the Foreign Office, he had never got any answer ... At any rate, he will be none the worse off tonight when he has heard my speech.' Ministers refused to engage on the subject and continued to thwart every opposition attempt to raise it.

First stories emerge

The first cattle cars arrived in the isolated northern forests in February 1930 at the height of the British campaign against religious persecution. The Moscow authorities themselves had little idea of the chaos which had followed the kulaks' arrival. It took even longer for news to reach the West. Archangel, the White Sea ports and the rivers that fed them were all icebound until May each year, and the timber which was cut in the forests could not be floated downstream to the deep-water loading ports until the rivers had melted. It was only when foreign ships had arrived over the summer to load the timber that British seafarers became aware of the dockside camps and the appalling conditions in which the prisoners were being held. As revelations of slave labour in the timber camps from escaped prisoners and returned seafarers broke, the Christian Protest Movement, reinvigorated, took on their cause too.

Though they were later to downplay it, ministers knew early on that something was up in the Russian north. C. H. Hardy's account of the kulak train which he had stumbled across in Moscow arrived on the desks of the Northern Department in April 1930. Seymour remarked, in a note on the accompanying memorandum, 'It is clear we shall have to be very careful as to what we say in reply to questions about "forced labour" in the timber producing districts'.[7]

Then, on 11 July 1930, the Home Secretary, J. R. Clynes, told the Cabinet about the growing number of Russian prisoners who had escaped to Britain as stowaways on timber ships:

> [They] claim to be political prisoners and ask not to be sent back to Archangel, stating that they would be shot on arrival. One has said he would sooner commit suicide than return to Russia … [This is] the fate which they state, *no doubt correctly*, awaits them if they are returned to Soviet Russia. (My italics.)[8]

Ministers were sufficiently convinced to agree not to send the stowaways back.

Over the summer, William Strang, covering for Ambassador Ovey, who was on leave, sent two important dispatches to the Foreign Office, the conclusions of which both Henderson and Dalton would have seen or been made fully aware. On 19 August 1930, a representative of a leading British timber company in Archangel had reported to D. W. Keane, the Leningrad consul, that there was 'no doubt whatever' that about 10,000 prisoners were loading timber in the port.[9] Keane, passing this information on to Strang, added:

> As I understand the question may become important ... [I confirm that] 35,000–45,000 persons [are] engaged in forced labour in the Karelian forests ... At Kem on the White Sea there are some hundreds of forced labourers kept in a prison camp surrounded by barbed wire, who are employed in loading timber.[10]

On 22 October, Strang forwarded further confirmation from Keane:

> Late information bears out approximately the facts given in my last report. Toward the end of the summer the system was greatly extended throughout the White Sea area, little free labour being employed in cutting or handling timber. ... I learn on tolerable, though second-hand, authority that at Kem, 160 forced labourers were shot for failing to carry out their work conscientiously.[11]

There seemed little doubt that the Northern Region (with the port of Archangel) and neighbouring Soviet Karelia (the region occupied by the Solovetsky camps) had become a vast prison camp.

The first 'Slave labour' debate (20 November 1930)

The lengthy summer parliamentary recess had stretched through August, September and all but the last days of October, so it was only then that, as the new session began, concerned campaigners were able to raise the matter again. MPs being unable to voice their concerns in the Commons, the House of Lords once again became the only place in Westminster in which the horrifying stories, which were now beginning to emerge, could be discussed.

The first mention of the timber gulag in the Lords came from Viscount Brentford in a debate on Soviet propaganda on 12 November, 1930:

> A very remarkable letter from a British officer on one of our ships at Archangel appeared in the Daily Mail in August of this year – I have verified this letter – describing the loading of timber vessels by convicts, as he calls them, working on twelve-hour shifts, marched about in gangs of two to three hundred, and all of

them destitute. He says that they were not convicts in the ordinary acceptance of the term, not criminal convicts; they were slaves, pure and simple, and as slaves ninety-five per cent of them did not know why they were there. To see them hungrily watching our men going along the decks at meal time with their steaming soup, roast beef, vegetables and so forth would make a stone heart bleed.[12]

Brentford, the CPM president, then moved on to challenge the government by repeating, to the embarrassment of Labour peers, the Prime Minister's own condemnation of exploitative labour conditions, given the Labour Party Conference the previous year:

Speaking at Birmingham in October of last year, Mr. Ramsay MacDonald dealt with the question and said: 'Where there are glaring examples of sweated goods produced under conditions against which people could not compete without lowering their standard of living …' – Will any noble Lord deny that the goods produced in Russia today for the export trade are produced under conditions against which British people could not possibly compete without lowering their standard of living? They are produced under conditions of slavery, as the noble Lord knows. They are produced under conditions of poverty and hardship such as God forbid that our English workmen should ever be driven down to. What was the remedy mentioned by the Prime Minister? – '… the remedy is not safeguarding but prohibiting the entry of such goods.'

I again appeal to the Prime Minister. There is his statement, that the remedy for sweated goods pouring into this country is prohibition. What are the Government going to do about it? Are they going to adopt the Prime Minister's opinion of last year, that it is not a question of tariffs, but of prohibition?

Brentford then urged the British government to follow the example set by other nations – France, Holland, Belgium, Romania, Canada and America[13] – and take steps to prohibit or control the import of gulag-produced timber. The charge of hypocrisy was hard to refute, not least because MacDonald's remark was not made in isolation: no fewer than seven members of his present Cabinet had sat on Labour's 'Sweated Goods Committee' while in opposition in 1926. They had produced a strongly worded condemnation of such labour conditions and had recommended that 'sweated' imports' be banned:

Greater efficiency (from industrialism) will not enable British production to compete on fair terms with enterprises drawing upon inexhaustible supply of cheap and, it may be, semi-slave labour. The use of such labour, lowly paid and employed and conditions long since abolished in Western countries, is open to grave objection on both economic and moral grounds.

Our considered opinion is broadly that international standards should be worked out and embodied in Conventions and that the persistent refusal by a nation to adopt and carry into effect such Conventions ... should be followed by exclusion by all signatory states of the goods produced under 'sweated' conditions until the necessary conditions are established.[14]

On 20 November, eight days after Lord Brentford's challenge to the government to ban Russian timber, Lord Newton opened the first full debate specifically devoted to labour conditions in Russia, which he described as a 'slave state system'.[15] Newton's motion challenged the government to provide information to confirm or refute that allegation and, if it was confirmed, to ban the import of Soviet goods produced under that regime.

He told the House of Lords that many Russian peasants had been executed in the course of the previous winter and reminded the government for the second time in a fortnight of Ramsay MacDonald's declaration that 'sweated' goods should be banned. In the light of those, he insisted, the government was compelled to respond.

Strang, in Moscow, had already reported the mass shootings, adding that they had created an 'extraordinarily painful impression upon foreigners resident here',[16] but Labour peers were not going to concede anything. The Labour leader in the Lords, Lord Parmoor, deflected the question in his usual style by arguing about definitions, denying that Russia was a 'slave state' and quibbling over the degree to which it used forced labour.

Opposition and crossbench peers recognised his dissembling. Vere Frederick Bertie, Viscount of Thame (1878–1954), challenged Parmoor to admit that Soviet labour was 'sweated' and that Russian timber was *exactly* the type of produce that Ramsay MacDonald had said should be banned when he had been talking about it in 1928. To this Parmoor ingenuously replied, 'I do not know exactly what you mean by sweated labour,' and went off into a digression on the different definitions that could be put on the word 'sweated'.

Lord Darling, himself a High Court judge and well able to see through such evasion, would have none of it:

> The noble and learned Lord, Lord Parmoor, asked to be told what was meant by 'sweated.' Why, the Party to which he belongs uses the word constantly, I may say daily. There is not a trade unionist in the country who does not know what 'sweated' means. Instead of asking some noble Lord, who, of course, spends his time in idleness, like all of us, why not ask some hardworking trade unionist what 'sweated' is, and remain ignorant on that subject no longer?

As for the definition of 'slave', Lord Darling cut through the verbiage: Dr Johnson's dictionary defined a slave as 'one subject to compulsory labour'. There wasn't much confusion about that.

Parmoor's deputy, Lord Ponsonby, was even more dismissive. Ponsonby, who had been responsible for Anglo-Soviet trade negotiations during the brief Labour government of 1924, was an unabashed enthusiast for the Soviet 'experiment' and was not afraid to declare it:

> Anybody who has investigated this vast, this terrific, this perhaps savage experiment that is going on in Soviet Russia, must recognise that they are experimenting in a way that may open out an entirely new economic idea in the world, and that those of us who are going on with old systems may find that we shall have to revise our systems. It is a great experiment which may fail. On the other hand, it may, as generations pass, succeed. A new effort is always regarded with suspicion, and by those minds which cannot adapt themselves to anything new it is always condemned.

The debate was won by the opposition, as was to be expected. The Lords' powers were limited, but their victory compelled the government to 'publish papers'. The result was a White Paper on Soviet labour legislation which, when released a few months later, was to fuel the debate still further.

CHAPTER 25

THE AFFAIR GOES PUBLIC
(DECEMBER 1930–JANUARY 1931)

The Times correspondence

Eighteen months after Carlyon Bellairs's first parliamentary question about the source of imports of Soviet timber, Conservative MPs were still being stonewalled. It was at this point that the matter was taken up by Bellairs's parliamentary colleague Sir Edward Hilton Young and the story finally broke.

On 11 December 1930, Hilton Young wrote to the Prime Minister. This time, mindful of Bellairs's previous lack of progress, he sent a copy of his letter to *The Times*. Enclosed were three affidavits, which gave graphic accounts of the appalling conditions in which Russian prisoners – both political prisoners and exiled kulaks – were kept. The writers were three prisoners who had been loading timber onto a British ship and had stowed away, escaping to England, where they had made their statements in front of a lawyer. Hilton Young challenged MacDonald to take action under the Foreign Prison-Made Goods Act. If the act could not be used, he asked the Prime Minister what steps the government proposed to take 'to put a stop to a trade which is stamped with the worst features of servile labour. Trade carried on under such conditions … is a disgrace to civilisation, and it is not consistent with our traditional reputation for humanity that Great Britain should continue to engage in it'.[1]

Hilton Young's letter received only an acknowledgement from MacDonald's secretary, nothing more, so Bellairs himself wrote to MacDonald on 29 December 1930, also copying his letter to *The Times*. Referring to the secretary's assurance to Hilton Young that the matter was 'being looked into', Bellairs pointed out to the Prime Minister that ample evidence was *already* available on the existence and extent of prison labour in the Russian timber export trade through the testimony of refugees who had fled across the border to Finland. They would be able to supply all the eyewitness evidence that was needed. In fact, he added, the government could have enquired there months before, and need not have waited until an ambassador was in place in Moscow:

> We have a representative in Finland: let him obtain permission to visit one of the three Russian refugee camps there. I suggest the camp near Kotca (Kymil-linnan [*sic*] Pakolaishnostola), where there are over 235 occupants, of whom over 50 are escaped prisoners ... this means of acquiring information has always been open to the Government, but we have been met first by a refusal to enquire until we have a representative in Russia.[2]

Bellairs got only another brush-off. The Prime Minister's office replied that it was a matter for Customs, and that the letter had been passed to them.[3] Bellairs seized the moment and forwarded this correspondence to *The Times* together with a copy of his subsequent reply which included the following: 'Without complaining of the discourtesy, I accept the attitude as evidence that this terrible blot on the labour of the world is not being regarded seriously by the government, and one's only recourse is to appeal to the conscience of the nation'.[4]

Provoked by the publication of the letter, MacDonald himself finally replied to Bellairs, who sent that letter straight to *The Times* too. Ignoring the affidavits which Edward Hilton Young had sent him on 11 December, MacDonald insisted that Bellairs and his colleagues *still* had not produced sufficient evidence for action and then finished by accusing Bellairs of being driven by ulterior political, rather than humanitarian, motives:

> Complainants have been challenged repeatedly to lay the evidence upon which they base their questions before the Commissioners of Customs. In no case have they produced evidence which would enable action to be taken under the Prison Goods Act that would be sustainable if challenged in a court

of law. The request is still open and, unless something is done by you and the other accusers, it is not the indifference of the government, but your desire to make charges without adequate evidence, in order to start a political stunt for no higher motive than that you should cross the floor of the House of Commons.[5]

Bellairs's reply, also reprinted in *The Times* on 3 January 1931, must only have added to MacDonald's discomfort. The Prime Minister's letter had been weak, containing at least one untruth, an unnecessarily discourteous accusation, and a refusal to investigate a situation which was far more severe than the type of labour which his own party had already condemned as immoral. In that reply, Bellairs, once again, quoted MacDonald's 1928 condemnation of sweated labour against him:

[You said] at the annual meeting of your party that your policy was to prohibit all sweated goods coming in. When it comes to practice we cannot even induce you to make an enquiry into prison goods! ... I have no objection to the description of the political stunt, for the matter is gravely political and stunt is defined in the dictionary as 'a specified task.' We have to see that the Soviet Government does not defeat the clear intentions of Parliament. Wilberforce set out to alter the law and suppressed legalised slavery. I have no doubt his opponents said it was a 'political stunt.' I am merely asking that the law shall be enforced. If it is inadequate to meet the surprising conditions in Russia, then the government is asked to apply to Parliament to strengthen the law. At present we cannot induce you even to make enquiries.[6]

The Times joined in and came down firmly against the Prime Minister with a leader column titled 'The Retort Discourteous':

The Prime Minister has sent a reply at once ill-informed and ill-mannered to the request of Commander Bellairs that the obvious opportunities of checking conditions of prison labour in Soviet Russia should be utilised ... He charges Commander Bellairs with the deliberate manufacture of a 'political stunt.' The suggestions are untrue and the charge an unprovoked insult.

A Labour government, whose international and humanitarian proclivities had been so widely advertised, should be the first to investigate charges of this kind, quite irrespective of whether they can take any action under a particular Act or not ... The Prime Minister becomes his own worst enemy when he becomes the mouthpiece of those who see in [the affair] only the hallucination of opponents as bigoted as themselves.[7]

MacDonald's final reply to Hilton Young was published in *The Times* on 20 January. In it, the Prime Minister extended his previous justification for inaction still further. The Foreign Prison-Made Goods Act, he maintained, required that the evidence on which the government could act must be 'detailed and conclusive. It is, I think, clear that the law, as it stands, does not give the Government the power you wish it to exercise, and that therefore legislation would be necessary.' If legislation were introduced to enact a ban, he continued, it would result in the total exclusion of Russian timber:

> This would be a very serious step in view of world labour conditions and, after careful consideration of its bearing on our commercial relations, and not in present circumstances satisfied that such a measure (the only one which would satisfy the humanitarian feeling stirred up by this anti-Soviet campaign) is practicable.[8]

In other words, commercial reasons justified Britain's continued importation of Russian timber regardless of the conditions in which it was being produced. It was the exact opposite of the position which Labour had historically taken so firmly on such matters.

Bellairs's and Hilton Young's letters laid out the case that campaigners were doggedly to pursue over the following months: the importation of products of the Soviet timber gulag was immoral and was already prohibited in the spirit, if not in the letter, of British law. If the wording of existing legislation, the Foreign Prison-Made Goods Act, did not enable the Government to ban Soviet timber, the nature of the Act was consistent with such a ban. The Government should introduce an amendment to its wording, which would allow the ban to be enacted and the Conservative opposition offered its full support to the government to enable amended legislation to be swiftly put on the statute book.

Not for the last time, supporters of those in the Russian prison camps claimed the precedent of Wilberforce and the abolition of slavery. The Cabinet had no intention of doing anything to jeopardise its relationship with the Soviets but, like Wilberforce, the protesters were driven by a moral imperative on behalf of those it sought to protect, and would not be deterred. For them, this was not an abstract political issue; it was a humanitarian tragedy of immense proportions and they could not remain silent.

New witnesses come forward

With the publication of the correspondence in *The Times*, the matter was out in the open. It was quickly taken up elsewhere in the press, which in turn encouraged more witnesses to come forward. On 6 January 1931, *The Times* printed a letter from a Merchant Navy officer who had been on a ship loading pit props at Kem, the White Sea port which was part of the Solovetsky Islands prison camp complex. The loading had been done by about 150 prisoners, and the witness reported that they had appeared to be in very poor health and half-starved.

Responding swiftly to events, the Board of Trade, on 5 January, sent a detailed memorandum to the Foreign Office on the possible consequences of a ban on the import of Russian timber. Their opinion was that a breach of the Anglo-Soviet Trade Agreement could be defended on moral or humanitarian grounds and that its effect on imports from the Empire was likely to be very limited: 'It is no doubt true that the circumstance of goods being manufactured by forced labour *is not likely to occur in many, if in any, countries other than Soviet Russia*'.(My italics.)[9]

Laurence Collier, second counsellor at the Northern Department, added his own concurrence to the board's opinion:

As far as I can see [the political consequences of any such action] would not be particularly serious. The Soviet government ... require trade and goodwill more than we require theirs; and, though they would of course make a great outcry, I do not believe that they would go so far as to denounce the Trade Agreement, while the Scandinavian countries and Finland would probably be both able and willing, in their own interests, to make good the deficiency in our timber supplies at reasonable prices (though not, of course, at such completely unremunerative prices as those now obtained for Soviet timber).

Meanwhile, the evidence continued to mount. On 12 January 1931, a week before MacDonald's final letter published in *The Times*, a dispatch arrived from the British Embassy in Moscow which reported the estimation by the foreign diplomatic corps that around 50,000 people were cutting timber under punitive conditions of one form or another (hard labour camps or labour colonies). Another diplomatic source put the figure at closer to 170,000.[10] The same dispatch reported the remarks of a Soviet official that 400,000 kulaks were about to be deported to Turkistan. There was no doubt that a major campaign of arrests and deportations was going on in the Soviet Union.

A short while later, Keane's annual report from the Leningrad Consulate observed that forced labour in the timber industry 'is well-nigh universal in one form or another ... and the dispatch of convicts, political or otherwise, kulaks and priests to forced labour in the forests [is] now fairly well understood,' before adding, as if to confirm that the pressure on clergy remained intense, 'the Roman Catholic Bishop, Mgr. Malecki has been arrested and sent into exile somewhere north of Irkutsk'.[11]

On 27 January, the British Consul in Helsingfors (Helsinki) sent five new affidavits to the Foreign Office.[12] These were the most persuasive yet, especially considering their source – escaped Russian prisoners who had been interned in the labour camps. They confirmed the widespread use of prisoner labour in the export timber trade and the dreadful conditions in which they were held.[13] Two were from clearly educated men – a trained forest engineer and a pastor. The engineer's statement detailed the escalation of the use of prisoners in the 1929–30 felling season, including those from the Solovetsky Islands camp group. The pastor, a former Lutheran clergyman, Aatami Kuortti, in his statement bore out not only the allegations of prison labour but also gave details of his own arrest, which clearly confirmed that he had been persecuted and imprisoned *solely* on account of his status as a pastor, a state of affairs which Ovey and the British government had denied the year before.[14]

On 4 February, Horace Seymour, head of the Foreign Office Northern Department, noted on the Helsingfors copies that this was 'pretty conclusive as to use of prisoners in these camps'. Hugh Dalton's initials are next to the comment, dated '4/2', as is the remark from Henderson's private secretary 'S[ecretary] of S[tate] informed 3/2'.[15] On 16 February, the Swedish ambassador wrote personally to MacDonald with copies of the same five affidavits.[16] Arthur Henderson, Hugh Dalton and Ramsay MacDonald were all therefore fully aware of the contents of these sworn affidavits – at the latest on 3, 4, and 16 February respectively.

In spite of this, Lord Ponsonby, speaking for the government in a debate on the timber camps in the House of Lords on 5 February, still insisted that: 'we are bound to accept official statements that are brought before us, and His Majesty's Ambassador has been informed by the Soviet authorities that neither prison labour nor any general labour of sentenced persons is employed in the [export] branches of the timber industry'.[17] As further evidence, Ponsonby cited a Russian denial sent to the *Manchester Guardian*:

> That has also been further elaborated by Mr. Danishevsky, the Chairman of the Exportles* of the Soviet Republic, in a letter to the Manchester Guardian, from which I must give this quotation: 'These accusations endeavour to create in the mind of the British public that timber exported from the Soviet Union is produced by convict labour. This I can emphatically deny. As Chairman of the Exportles I am in possession of the most complete and up-to-date information, and I am in a position to state that not a single standard of timber exported from the Soviet Union is produced otherwise than on conditions established by collective agreements between trade unions representing the workers and the State timber-producing trusts.'[18]

When the Anti-Slavery Society published the results of its own inquiry a few months later, Danishevsky's and Ponsonby's claims that no prisoners were involved in the export trade were to be comprehensively dismissed – not least because the timber cut in the Northern Region forests was impossible to move except through the export ports of Archangel and Kem, the port at the centre of the Solovetsky labour camp group. Danishevsky's loyalty was not to be rewarded. In common with most of the senior Russian trade officials and diplomats who worked in or visited Britain, he perished in the Great Terror.[†]

Conscripted labour

In addition to the hundreds of thousands of deported kulaks held against

---

* Exportles was the organisation which, from 1926, controlled all Soviet timber exports.
† On the executions of Soviet trade officials and diplomats, see Appendix 1.

their will in labour colonies or with political prisoners in the tougher strict regime labour camps, Soviet desperation for foreign currency had resulted in the introduction of compulsory forced labour. Defenders of Soviet labour practices tried to make light of conscription in Russian villages and towns, but the reality was exceedingly grim. On 21 January 1931, *The Times*'s Riga correspondent, frequently maligned by Labour MPs for reprinting 'lies' about Russia, reproduced the wording of two official Soviet statements which unequivocally confirmed the use of conscripted forced labour in the northern timber industry.[19] The first, dated 26 November 1929, was published on 14 December 1929. It announced an eightfold increase in production in order that timber should become the leading Soviet export product. It ordered the recruitment of peasants into lumbering and the creation of the 'greatest discipline'. The second, dated 13 February 1930, and published in *Izvestia* on 15 February 1930, announced how the peasant 'recruitment' was to take place – by compulsion, with severe penalties following for those resisting it.

Each village was compelled to supply a certain number of workers. Individuals who refused to work in the forests would be fined up to five times the value of the work they had been ordered to do; groups of peasants who refused would be sent to do compulsory labour for one year, or could be imprisoned for two years, with the confiscation of the whole or part of their possessions and subsequent compulsory exile. Collective punishment would apply to the fellow villagers of those so convicted, taking the form of personal fines, and fines added to the village budget (taxes it was compelled to pay to the central government). The wording of the decree strongly implied that either minimal wages, or none at all, would be paid to the workers. The recruitment was termed 'voluntary self-imposed sacrifice', but it was quite obviously forced labour.

A further decree published in *Izvestia*, on 18 December 1930, confirmed that the accusations about Russia being a 'slave state' were not far off the mark: it stated that 900,000 labourers were to be recruited that winter, mostly from collective farms. Although once again it was called voluntary, the collective farming headquarters in Moscow set quotas for each collective farm to supply a certain number of workers, who would have no option as to where or for how long they would serve. The British Embassy in Moscow was sent further information anonymously from a village in the Perm region, a handbill, which informed villagers that anyone found evading the 'voluntary' conscription would be 'punished according to criminal law'. This meant imprisonment at the very least, and could even result in their being shot. The conscription was to include *every* person who had been disenfranchised, the result of which would be the compulsory conscription of every priest and pastor. The handbill also detailed reprisals to be carried out against any local officials who deliberately or accidentally failed in their duty to raise the conscription.[20]

The announcements reproduced in *The Times* also stated that the Commissariat of Agriculture, which had charge of the forestry industry, issued instructions in June 1929, 'on the use of convicts for lumbering', direct confirmation of a fact still being denied by some British friends of the Soviet Union. It was debatable that any beyond a very small proportion of workers in the two northern forest regions (Karelia to the west of the White Sea and the Northern Region to the east) were true volunteers, working in the timber industry entirely of their own volition.

'Fairy tales'

In Britain, Russophile MPs and union leaders still rallied to the Soviets' support. On 21 January, when Sir William Davidson pressed Ramsay MacDonald to accept the authenticity of the Russian eyewitness affidavits which had been published, there were typical interruptions by Labour MPs, in this instance from Jack Lees and Will Thorne. 'Is the Prime Minister prepared to give the pledge of the Government that they are prepared to prevent slave conditions for miners and railway-men in this country?', Lees interjected. Thorne attempted to divert the issue by making untrue smears against Finnish and Swedish timber producers: 'Is the Prime Minister aware that the timber produced in Finland and Sweden is produced under worse conditions than in Russia?'[21] Thorne's careless fiction won him no friends in the Cabinet and MacDonald and Henderson were forced to take steps to placate the Swedish ambassador, who complained to them that the Labour MP had been defaming his country.[22]

Soviet disinformation was supplemented by appeals to Western trade unionists to rally to the support of the Soviet Union. Notwithstanding *The Times*'s reproduction of the official Soviet statements confirming it, 'Comrade Bekker', the chairman of the Russian Timber and Woodworkers' Union, denied that forced labour was being used anywhere in the timber industry and called upon the workers of Europe and America to frustrate any attempt to prevent Soviet timber from reaching foreign markets. In Britain, the unions rallied to the cause. Thomas Barron, chairman of the Amalgamated Society of Woodworkers Union, wrote in the February 1931 edition of the Society's *Monthly Journal*:

> In the case of Russian timber … a statement was signed by the [Russian] State Department and by the workers engaged in the industry that the timber was produced under trade union conditions and that union rates were paid. Representatives of the Society who visited Russia were of the opinion that working conditions in the industry were satisfactory …
>
> Tory reactionaries, having failed in their other anti-Soviet stunts have discovered another mare's nest – joinery and timber cut and manufactured by 'forced labour, carried out under conditions of barbarity.' Our members do not need warning against accepting these yarns. They are fairy tales worked up for political purposes by the anti-trade union party.[23]

A few weeks later still more trade union leaders declared their support for the USSR in a booklet entitled *Forced Labour in Russia?* Among them were John Bromley MP, A. A. Purcell MP, George Hicks (all members of the ARPC) and Alfred M. Wall, secretary of the London Trades Council, the umbrella organisation of all London trade unionists. As secretary of the Amalgamated Union of Building Trade Workers, Hicks was at the head of a body of workers who were leading consumers of Russian wood products. These are extracts from their comments:

> [John Bromley:] The Soviet government has informed our Ambassador in Moscow that no forced or prison labour is employed in the preparation, sawing, or loading of timber for export. It is a matter of common knowledge that, as in this country, convicts in Russia have to work. It is possible that they are employed in felling timber for home purposes. Is that any worse than making mailbags in His Majesty's prisons in this country? …
>
> [George Hicks:] On what are the charges of 'slave' and 'forced' labour in the Russian lumber camps based? They are based on a series of affidavits each more ridiculous than the other. …

[A. A. Purcell:] The 'die-hards' are exploiting the bogus charge of 'convict and forced labour' for an ulterior object … the aim of the present anti-Soviet 'stunt' is the wrecking of the five-year plan. …

[Alfred Wall:] The 'die-hards' who are conducting this campaign against political and economic relations with Russia are not animated by any feelings of sympathy towards the Russian workers.[24]

All four represented a solid body of trade union opinion on Russia.

CHAPTER 26

THE 'BLUE BOOK' DEBATE (5 FEBRUARY 1931)

These things are a horror greater perhaps than anything in modern times.
LORD BRENTFORD, 5 FEBRUARY 1931

On 29 January 1931 the Foreign Office published the 'papers' it was compelled to produce following Lord Newton's successful motion in the 20 November House of Lords debate on the timber camps. Colloquially known as the 'blue book', its real title was *A Selection of Documents Relative to the Labour Legislation in Force in the Union of Soviet Socialist Republics*.[1] With its publication, the centre of the debate returned to the House of Lords, where the report prompted one of the fullest of all the parliamentary discussions on slave labour and the Soviet timber gulag.

The Foreign Office was obliged by Lord Newton's motion to produce papers (research and background reports) relating to *conditions* in the timber camps. Disregarding this major detail it published, instead, a set of translations of Soviet decrees on labour *practices*. In the end, these were damning enough, however, and on 5 February the House of Lords gathered to resume the discussion of Russia in the light of the information that the 'blue book' provided.[2] If the government had hoped to be able to limit discussion it failed. The public debate had gone too far for that. One after another, peers rounded on Labour, appalled by conditions in Russia and by the party's apparent indifference to the suffering there.

Lord Newton opened the debate and refused to be deflected by the Foreign Office's prevarication:

My satisfaction at the action of the Government is considerably diminished
by the fact that this collection of Papers does not contain in the least what
we asked for. What we asked for was an independent report by the British
representative of the conditions in Soviet Russia. Instead of receiving that, we
are presented with a collection of documents which embody the various laws
that have been recently passed by the Soviet Government.

   ... it does serve one purpose: *it firmly establishes the fact that we were
practically correct in asserting that free labour in Soviet Russia no longer
exists*, and that the State is practically, although not technically, a slave State.
(My italics.)

He then accused Labour and the unions of double standards:

The Labour Party and the trade unions in this country have always prided
themselves upon being champions of the oppressed and downtrodden, and one
would really have supposed that they would be the first to protest against the
condition of things to which the Russian proletarian is subjected, the cruelty,
oppression and privation.

Lord Phillimore* followed Newton and called the House to consider the humanitarian implications of the matter they were considering: 'By day and by
night these people have been haunting my mind ... I feel something must be
done for these poor people.'

   The most powerful speech in the debate came from Herbert Hensley
Henson, the Bishop of Durham, and was widely reported in the national and
local press the next day.[3] A past anti-slavery campaigner, Henson spoke of
how this was not just an economic and trade issue, but a 'moral question'
which the nation could not permanently leave unanswered 'without losing
our national self-respect'. He called upon the government to 'do something
to disassociate us as a nation and an empire from the abominable proceedings
going forward in Russia ... of slavery in the worst degree ... and the moral
disgrace involved in our indifference to these horrors'. Henson's speech

---

*   Godfrey Walter Phillimore MC, 2nd Baron Phillimore (1879–1947). The son of a British law lord
     and Privy Counsellor, Phillimore had been wounded in 1916 and was taken prisoner by the Ger-
     mans, from whom he had made a number of attempts to escape.

remains one of the most eloquent defences of those suffering under oppression in Russia, and merits quoting in some detail:

This is not only an economic issue of the utmost gravity to this country, but it raises a moral question which we cannot permanently or without losing our national self-respect leave unanswered ...

For a very few minutes I shall ask your Lordships to listen to me while I endeavour as far as one man can to associate the Episcopate with the expressions of sorrow, consternation and shame which the present relations of our country and Soviet Russia are stirring in the minds of considerate and informed citizens.

It does not appear to me that the Government realise the strength or the justice of those feelings which are thus finding expression. I will try to do what I can to impress upon them the obligation in which they stand ... even at the eleventh hour, to take some responsible action which will relieve our wounded national self-respect and do something to dissociate us as a nation and an Empire from the abominable proceedings which are now unquestionably going forward in Russia.

We maintain that the conditions of labour in the timber camps in Russia – and not there only – are conditions of slavery, slavery in the worst degree.

The whole theory of Communism, as it has been interpreted and applied in Russia, implies a brutal contempt of elementary individual rights. The very core and essence of slavery is precisely that contempt of individual rights. We maintain that as the conditions of labour are disclosed officially by Russia, and as a great mass of evidence authenticates them as existing at this moment – we maintain that all the worst elements of slavery are present in these labour camps.

The economic menace which this slave labour creates for this country is very grave ... As Bishop of Durham, I have to live in a community broken by economic distress, and I cannot be indifferent to the prospect looming dark on the national horizon of still worse pressure being brought to bear upon these distressed people in our mining areas ...

There is a greater question – the moral disgrace involved in our indifference to these horrors, and in being in any degree associated by the Government of this country with some kind of apology for them. That is too terrible for any self-respecting man to contemplate. I believe that there is a Nemesis upon the kind of moral indifference to which we are tending at this moment.

I hope very earnestly that His Majesty's Government will be able this afternoon … to remove the grave anxieties which are in all our minds, and do something which will begin to lift the great shadow of shame.

The moral force of Henson's speech was undeniable. Later in the day, he bumped into Lord Sankey, the Labour Lord Chancellor, who congratulated him on his speech 'and expressed agreement'. 'He is evidently very uncomfortable,' Henson later wrote.[4] Perhaps unsurprisingly, Sankey was one of those who was expelled from the Labour Party for staying with MacDonald after the 1931 crisis.

Viscount Brentford, freer than the bishop to directly upbraid ministers, pressed home the attack:

I should have thought that perhaps after what has been said the Government would have been prepared to admit the existence of these cruelties and these horrors … I do not know whether even at the eleventh hour the noble Lord [Ponsonby, who was due to reply for the Government] will admit the existence of these miseries and these horrors, of which, I venture to say to him, 90 per cent of the reading population of this country are already convinced.

We have read of the horrors of men who are ill and weak being compelled to work, of men being thrashed when they do not work, of their dying like flies of disease of every kind in these prison camps, of no wages, of little food, food consisting of 2½ lbs. of black or brown bread and a little soup made of mouldy or rotten fish. That has been said over and over again.

I do not know whether the noble Lord who is going to answer will say: 'I do not believe it. I am not prepared to admit it.' It has been stated in all these documents which have been produced and mentioned in the public Press. There are men working in extreme climatic conditions, without adequate clothing, sleeping on bare boards without any beds, in filth indescribable, no laundries, no sanitary conveniences, the place swarming with bugs and fleas and lice. Does the noble Lord agree or not? Does he agree that these things are taking place?

I am convinced, and I think most noble Lords who have read their newspapers in the last few months are and must be convinced, that these things are a horror greater perhaps than anything in modern times.

Brentford then yet again raised the embarrassing subject of Ramsay Mac-Donald's 1928 declaration on the prohibition of sweated goods and turned the quote against Lord Parmoor, who had tried to quibble over its definition in the original debate a few months earlier.

It seems to be a pity that the Lord President did not have in his mind the speech of the Prime Minister. The Lord President said: 'You cannot compare the labour in one country with the labour in another.' That is exactly what the Prime Minister said you must do, because he said that if the goods were produced under conditions against which British people could not compete without lowering their standard of living, the remedy was to prohibit the entry of those goods...

Surely the time has come for our Government to take its courage in both hands and to act upon the statement made by the Prime Minister to which I have alluded. The Labour Party appointed a Committee to deal with this matter, and they have stated as follows:- 'We do not suggest that cheap goods should be excluded because they are cheap,' – nor do I – 'but that goods, whether cheap or not, should be excluded if they are made under conditions which violate the world's standards.'

Brentford then turned on Sidney Webb (Lord Passfield), the Secretary of State for the Colonies, who was sitting on the Government front bench. Webb had been one of the original 1926 Labour Committee which had recommended the prohibition of sweated goods and was fast becoming one of the most public and staunchest British Soviet enthusiasts: 'I see that the noble Lord, the Secretary of State for the Colonies, is good enough to accept that. I go further, and say that these goods are produced under conditions which violate the world's standards. Does the noble Lord agree with that?' Hansard cannot indicate if Webb's reply was delivered boldly or as an embarrassed aside. It was certainly lame: 'I am not in a position to say.'

The government's reply

In Lord Parmoor's absence, the government's reply was given by Lord Ponsonby, his deputy. Ponsonby, who had published a virulently anti-clerical book in 1921,[5] began with an attack on the Bishop of Durham. Instead of responding to the substance of the bishop's speech he resorted to a *tu quoque*

– saying the Church had not complained of excesses during the Tsarist period and therefore had no moral right to complain now. He then rounded on both Newton and Henson with the accusation that their complaint against the Soviet government was tainted by 'class prejudice, class bias and Party feeling'.

In Henson, Ponsonby picked the wrong person to accuse; Henson was no defender of the status quo. He disapproved of blood sports, and gave guarded support to ideas as radical as the disestablishment of the Church of England and the abolition of Armistice Day.[6] In 1912, he had spoken up forcefully on behalf of the indigenous tribespeople of the Putumayo region in South America whose terrorisation and exploitation by the Peruvian Amazon Company had involved such appalling atrocities (there were allegations of rape, torture and murder) that the Commons Select Committee had felt unable to print some of the details in its report on the affair. The case was taken up in Britain by the Anti-Slavery and Aborigines' Protection Society and Henson was so appalled by the affair that he controversially named three directors of the company who were responsible from the pulpit of Westminster Abbey, risking a court action for slander by doing so.

Nor was it appropriate to accuse the Anglican Church as a whole of standing by in the face of slave labour elsewhere. The Church had lent its support publicly and forcefully to the campaign to halt the terrible cruelty inflicted on the inhabitants of the Congo by soldiers employed by King Leopold of Belgium in the last decade of the nineteenth century. One rally, organised in 1909 by the Congo Reform Association in the Albert Hall, had been chaired by the Archbishop of Canterbury, accompanied on the platform by eight bishops (including Canon Henson), while a further eleven bishops had sent messages of support. They had most certainly not defended the 'forces of reaction' represented, in this case, by the Belgian monarch.[7] Ironically, at another meeting the previous year, Ramsay MacDonald himself had called upon the British government to speak out forcefully to condemn the trade in rubber 'which pours out of the Congo stained with blood.'[8]

Whatever the truth about the Anglican Church's hesitation over Russia more than twenty-five years earlier, it was quite ludicrous to draw a parallel between the scale of injustices in Tsarist Russia before the 1905 Revolution and February 1931, though that was the smokescreen commonly put up by the

Soviets and their supporters abroad. On 1 January 1931 the prison population was 71,800 in the Solovetsky camps in Karelia, and 49,716 in the Northern Region (Archangel and other locations east of the White Sea).[9] Those numbers included only those in the strict 'corrective labour' camps. While many religious believers and 'worst' category of kulaks were among them, many more kulaks were held in 'labour colonies', still under military guard. By 10 December 1930, 230,065 kulaks and their families had been deported to the Northern Region, of whom approximately 10 per cent, mostly children, had already died.[10] At the time of the Lords debate at the beginning of February 1931, a further 50,000 kulaks were being evicted from their homes in the south and shipped north in cattle cars. The Tsarist prison system had known nothing like those numbers.[*]

Standing in for Parmoor, Ponsonby uncharacteristically adopted Parmoor's customary tactic to disarm the government's critics – at first appearing to accept the allegations made by the opposition, only to follow that with the voicing of such doubts over their accuracy as to render such an acceptance meaningless.

I do not dispute the evidence for one moment; I am not going to say a word against it. The noble Viscount assures us that the testimony that he has got is perfectly authentic, and I do not doubt it for a single moment. But when one does look through some of the evidence which is brought forward with regard to the conditions in Russia, it may be right or it may be wrong, but one very often finds that it is a little bit contradictory.

We have heard a great deal said by the noble Viscount with regard to these horrors. They may be true. I am not disputing the facts. They are very horrible. But, as we know, when one Government takes upon itself the task of looking into the horrors of the world it becomes rather a difficult one, and *when we are going to correct other nations because they do not observe the same standards of morality and social decencies that we do, I am afraid we shall find our hands very full. At any rate, before we embark upon a task of that sort, let us have authentic, indisputable evidence. And that we have not got.* (My italics.)

---

[*] 'In 1906, only about 6,000 katorga convicts [prisoners sentenced to forced labour] were serving sentences.' Anne Applebaum, *Gulag: A History of the Soviet Camps* (London: Penguin/Allen Lane, 2003), p. 17.

Ponsonby was insistent. No matter how many affidavits or witnesses the opposition produced, the evidence was insufficient:

> I am authorised to say that the Prime Minister and His Majesty's Government have no intention of introducing elaborate legislation to meet a condition of affairs about which we have not any sure and authentic data. We have grave suspicions but we have not any authentic data that we could put before Parliament in order to frame legislation.

In his discomfort, Ponsonby had made another mistake, a slip of the tongue, in referring to the government's 'grave' suspicions. The other peers pounced on it:

> Lord Phillimore: Did the noble Lord say: 'We have grave suspicions?' I did not quite catch the phrase.
>   Lord Ponsonby: I do not think I said that. I said: 'We may have suspicions.'
>   Viscount Hailsham: No; the noble Lord said: 'We may have grave suspicions.' That is what he said.
>   Lord Ponsonby: I might have said that; but we cannot legislate on suspicion.

Then, in spite of everything, Ponsonby returned to the government's statement in defence of the Soviets, quoted earlier: 'We are bound to accept official statements that are brought before us that 'neither prison labour nor any general labour of sentenced persons is employed in the branches of the timber industry for export'.

Viscount Hailsham spoke for many in the chamber when he concluded:

> I doubt whether in the records of this House there has been a speech which has been more equivocal, more inconsistent, more unsatisfactory, more deliberately evasive of plain questions than the one to which the noble Lord has just given utterance.
>   The noble Lord told us that they accepted the evidence which had been put before them. Your Lordships have heard extracts from that evidence. Having said that he accepted the evidence, he then proceeded to minimise its importance, and to sneer at its accuracy by suggesting that, for instance, numbers varied.

I do not suppose anybody knows with precision the number of unfortunates who have been herded into these prison dens in Northern Russia to starve and die, but because one man may know of more than another is that good reason for saying that either of them is saying what is untrue?

If the Government accept the truth of the evidence, as they say they do, then these facts at least are established, that in Northern Russia to-day there are hundreds of thousands of men, women and children who are being starved and tortured, ill-treated, bowed down, decimated by disease, used in the pursuance of a plan by which Russia at once destroys her own best citizens because they will not accept the cursed doctrines of Communism, and uses the product of their labour whilst they are worked to death, in the endeavour to destroy the economic system of this country. The noble Lord says that they are bound to accept official statements. I wonder why. Does the noble Lord himself believe them? I venture to suggest that not even the innocence of the Front Bench opposite would accept the official statement as being true – or would believe it to be true, at least.

The protesters raised the issues clearly, but the government was not to be moved. Trade continued unhindered.

CHAPTER 27

THE CABINET ADMITS THE TRUTH... AND DOES NOTHING (11 FEBRUARY 1931)

There [is] little doubt that an investigation would show that Russian timber was handled by forced labour.
CABINET MINUTES, 11 FEBRUARY 1931[1]

We all know perfectly well in all conscience that in parts at least conditions in the timber trade are inhuman.
SIR ROBERT VANSITTART, 24 FEBRUARY 1931[2]

At Archangel they use all convict labour for timber for loading under guard ... On board one of the German vessels loading wood pulp and timber [there] the cook had made an extra large pot of soup for the stevedores [prisoners] who were employed in leading the vessel. The captain, on consulting the Russian armed guards who were on board during the loading operations, asked them if it were possible for the cook to give up this soup to the stevedores. The armed guards said that this would not be allowed.

When the guards had left No.3 hatch and had gone forward, the cook gave two of the stevedores a bowl of soup, and they were drinking this when the Russian armed guard appeared. The stevedores who had been drinking the soup were immediately shot by the guard.
REPORT FROM THE AMERICAN CONSULATE GENERAL, HAMBURG, 21 FEBRUARY, 1931[3]

An early day motion

To reinforce the debate in the Lords, Carlyon Bellairs lodged a Commons' early day motion on the same day.* Bellairs and the other MPs concerned by the issue were not going to give up, even in the face of a government majority in the Commons to prevent a formal debate on Soviet slave labour, and the motion was signed by 117 MPs. Developments across the Atlantic gave the opposition a new reason to highlight the issue, as the motion explained:

> This House, having had its attention called to the unanimous Report of the Special Committee of the House of Representatives in Washington that the Treasury Department should prohibit the entry of Soviet pulpwood and lumber until such time as their agents are permitted by the Soviet Government to make a thorough investigation and report on the use of prison and forced labour, and believing in the imperative need of putting a stop to prison and compulsory labour, calls upon the Government to confer with the Government of the United States of America with a view to corresponding action.[4]

On the 6 February, spurred on by Ponsonby's insistence, the day before, that the evidence was insufficient, Bellairs wrote again to the Prime Minister, this time enclosing nine new witness statements. Once again, copies (with another eyewitness account from a British merchant naval officer) were sent to *The Times*.[5] These had been prepared in Finland and were even more detailed and conclusive than those which had previously been published. Downing Street passed them to the Foreign Office, but as Bellairs had not requested a reply, Horace Seymour thought it best not to do so: 'It would be going out of our way to create difficulties, if we attempted to compose an answer.'[6] The protesters' case was, increasingly, best answered only by silence.

On 10 February, another dispatch arrived from Ovey with a Soviet statement alleging that wages in the timber cutting areas were between two and five times the pre-Revolution rate. Seymour observed that, while professional lumber men may be better off than before, 'kulaks and others from warmer climates or with urban training, who are sent as exiles or convicts to the forests, are almost bound to succumb to the hardships and cold'.[7] It was another

---

*   Early day motions are formal motions submitted for consideration but which are unlikely to be debated. They are used to publicise a particular cause.

acknowledgement from within the Foreign Office that kulaks and others were likely to have perished in the forests. In his note on the minute, Dalton ignored Seymour's conclusion and, by way of an implied denial, instead drew his civil servants' attention to an 'important' article in the *Manchester Guardian* by J. F. Stewart. During Stewart's visit to the Northern timber areas, he had seen no forced labour but, crucially, he had been there a year before the kulaks were exiled – a fact which was consistently ignored by those who used his report to support their refusal to accept Conservative claims about the camps, even after the chronological discrepancy was pointed out to them.*

In the Commons, Conservative MPs continued to press government ministers for action, while Labour fellow travellers sniped from the sidelines. A comment by ILP leader James Maxton was typical: 'Is the Right Honourable Gentleman aware that the Russian Government are gravely concerned about conditions in the Lancashire cotton industry?'[8] Similar *tu quoques* were regularly used to interrupt and to attack Conservatives as they challenged ministers in parliamentary question times – for example, by Fenner Brockway ('Will the Right Hon. Gentleman consider the necessity of making similar enquiries about forced labour in Kenya and the Indian states?'[9]) and John Beckett ('Will the Right Hon. Gentleman ask the Soviet government to co-operate with him in an enquiry into the conditions of labour imposed by public assistance committees in London?'[10]).

Calls for an inquiry

There were two Russian questions down for Prime Minister's questions on 11 February 1931. Godfrey Locker-Lampson asked the Prime Minister if he had received any protests from trade unions about the import of timber. It would not have been likely, given the line-up of former presidents of the TUC who were on the pro-Soviet Anglo-Russian Parliamentary Committee.[11] The second, from his brother Oliver Locker-Lampson, also a Conservative MP, was more significant, echoing growing demands for a government inquiry.

Oliver Locker-Lampson asked the Prime Minister to appoint a small committee 'to take the evidence of certain persons who have lately been in Russia in regard to the Labour conditions prevailing in the Russian timber trade'.

---

* For more on the unreliability of Stewart and the other witnesses used by Labour supporters, see Appendix 2.

In the Foreign Office (to which the question would have been sent for a preliminary opinion), Bateman was not inclined to agree with the Conservatives about the usefulness of the affidavits they had so far produced:

> Nothing but an investigation by impartial people on the spot will get anywhere near the truth and this is rendered impossible by the attitude of the Soviet government [and, anyway, an inquiry would have no effect because] the President of the Board of Trade [William Graham] has stated definitely that *he does not intend to seek powers to interfere with the free import of Russian timber*. (My italics.)[12]

His comment about Graham's attitude is significant. If Graham was determined not to stop trade, at any cost, then no amount of evidence would alter the government's position.

At Henderson's request, Vansittart discussed the matter with Hugh Dalton, and afterwards wrote:

> I think and Mr Dalton concurs, that the appointment of a Committee would be bound in any case to lend *some* impetus to the clamour for legislation … if there was [*sic*] a committee it would have to be judicial, and I think there would have to be cross-examination of witnesses [and] I feel that the *bulk* of its findings would be bad.[13]

In the meantime, Vansittart suggested that the best reply that Henderson could give in the House would be to say that he did not think that any useful purpose would be served by the appointment of such a committee. 'That, I think, gives us the best tactical position, and also time for further enquiry, and reflection on the results of the enquiry before we are committed.'

The Cabinet decides

Lord Newton had called for an inquiry in the House of Lords debate on 5 February. Locker-Lampson's parliamentary question, demanding the same, had been tabled for an answer on the afternoon of 11 February. The Cabinet met that morning, and the minutes of that meeting reveal that, in the privacy of the Cabinet room, ministers not only conceded what they denied in public

– that the evidence for human rights abuses in the camps was very strong – but made it clear that they were determined to block any inquiry into the timber gulag:

> The Secretary of State for Foreign Affairs informed the Cabinet that the question had been addressed to him in Parliament asking if he was willing to appoint a small committee to examine into the conditions of labour in the Russian timber trade. He himself was opposed to the appointment of any committee.
>
> In the course of the discussion of the subject it was pointed out that the appointment of a committee would open up a very large question. *There was little doubt that an investigation would show that Russian timber was handled by forced labour* and it was imported at prices with which the United Kingdom industry could not compete ...
>
> The committee would then be likely to advise the extension of the Foreign Prison-Made Goods Act of 1897. In practice, however, it would be found impossible to confine the operation of such an extension to Russia, and that other countries were affected in varying degrees. The extension of the Acts to these countries would be found to conflict with our international obligations. (My italics.)[14]

The Cabinet's excuse was that the legislation used to ban Russian timber might also block goods produced under forced or indentured labour in the empire. In fact, this argument, which was to be repeated by the government a number of times during the affair, had already been demolished by the Board of Trade. As has been mentioned, a month earlier, the Board sent to the Foreign Office a memorandum on the legality and implications of banning Soviet timber imports. It stated that 'there would seem to be no doubt that such a prohibition could be defended under International Convention as one imposed for "moral or humanitarian reasons" '.[15]

In referring to 'international convention', the Board of Trade were highlighting the fact that, had the Cabinet decided to take a stand, such a position would have had considerable legal and moral support. Forced and slave labour had already been the subject of international treaties. Article 5 of the Slavery Convention (1926) committed contracting nations to bring forced labour to an end and ensure that, until then, it should 'always receive adequate remuneration, and [should] not involve the removal of the labourers from their usual place of residence'. In June 1930, the British government's own representative voted in favour of the Forced Labour Convention (1930), which committed it to work 'to suppress the use of forced or compulsory labour in all its forms within the shortest possible period'.[16] And, regardless of the feasibility of amending the Foreign Prison-Made Goods Act of 1897, the British government was already a signatory to one significant measure which should have compelled it to act, Article 23a of the Covenant of the League of Nations (1919) which declared: 'Members of the League ... will endeavour to secure and maintain fair and humane conditions of labour for men, women, and children, both in their own countries and in all countries to which their commercial and industrial relations extend'.[17]

On the threat to empire trade, an excuse for inaction which was to become a regular response by ministers, the Board stated: 'It is no doubt true that the circumstance of goods being manufactured by forced labour is not likely to occur in many, if in any, countries other than Soviet Russia', and that, in the event of a ban, 'practically no other goods would in fact be excluded'. According to qualified civil servants in the Board of Trade, therefore, the defence had no substance.

Cabinet minutes say almost nothing about the actual course of the conversations that take place during a meeting. The 'Conclusions' (decisions) that are eventually minuted are brief and bland. However, at least one of those present on that morning of 11 February appears to have been less than happy with the outcome, and asked if there was some way in which the existing output of Russian exported timber could indeed be classified as the product of a 'prison', in which case action could be applied under the existing Foreign Prison-Made Goods Act, without the need to extend the act and the complications for Britain's trade that would thereby arise. It was the simplest solution and would have required just a few sentences to amend the act. Those campaigning on behalf of the inmates of the timber gulag would have seen no logical reason for which such a suggestion could not have been pursued. Prisoners in the camps of Karelia and the Northern Region were held under punitive conditions behind barbed wire, under armed guard, were shot if they tried to escape, and were taken outside the camp under armed escort for the purposes of timber cutting. To all intents and purposes, the camps were indeed 'prisons'.

The unknown dissenter was unsuccessful. In the end, the Cabinet agreed that the Foreign Secretary should *not* appoint a committee, but that he should see the Soviet ambassador and impress upon him the growing seriousness of the situation in Parliament and the threat which the affair was posing to Anglo-Russian trade – not a complaint made about the morality of the camps or a plea on behalf of those held in them but an appeal to the Soviets to be as pragmatic in protecting their trading relationship as the British government were trying to be. Admittedly, William Graham, the president of the Board of Trade, *was* enjoined to consider whether any means could be found 'for bringing the question within the scope of the Foreign Prison-Made Goods Act 1897', but Graham had already made it clear that he had no intention of doing so and in the only House of Commons debate on the subject, six weeks later, he confirmed that position, saying he only wished the 'great experiment' well.

Six of those present at the 11 February Cabinet meeting had sat on the 1926 Labour Sweated Goods Committee* which had declared that the use of forced labour was 'open to grave objection on both economic and moral grounds', and recommended 'the exclusion of the goods produced under "sweated" conditions'. They were now pursuing a course of action which was the opposite of all that they had stood for a few years earlier.

The following day, news arrived from Washington that the American government had decided to impose a ban on Soviet timber imports after its Customs Department investigation had found that Soviet timber was cut and loaded by convict labour. 'This will mean a good deal of further trouble for us,' Vansittart noted.[18]

'The time is past for this Nelson touch'

Only the day after the Cabinet meeting, Baron Palmstierna, the Swedish ambassador, wrote to MacDonald with further copies of the affidavits from escaped prisoners which Carlyon Bellairs had sent to *The Times* a few weeks earlier.[19] The stream of evidence showed no signs of abating.

---

* The Labour Party Sweated Goods Committee comprised the following (titles in parentheses are those held by the members in the 1929–31 Cabinet): Philip Snowden (Chancellor of the Exchequer), Lord Arnold (Paymaster General), Arthur Henderson (Foreign Secretary), Tom Shaw (Secretary of State for War), Sidney Webb (Secretary of State for the Colonies), Arthur Greenwood (Minister of Health), Rt Hon. John Wheatley MP, V. Crittall, Thomas Johnson MP, George A. McEwan, Frank Varley MP.

In the Foreign Office, Hugh Dalton remained resolute. The Foreign Office received a copy of some articles from a recent visitor to the Soviet Union which were moderate in their criticism, but which had not been published because of some administrative mix-up between the author and *The Times*, for which they had been destined. 'Very interesting,' remarked Dalton, who saw the delay as part of a general anti-Soviet conspiracy, 'but not sufficiently one-sided to appeal to *The Times* which would dislike [any indications of] improvement since pre-revolutionary days. For *The Times* the psychological moment never slips by, if the material is sensationally and unconditionally anti-Bolshevik.'[20]

On 24 February 1931, the first eyewitness report of prison labour from a diplomat came through Reader Bullard, the British consul in Leningrad. He reported that the Norwegian consul at Archangel himself 'was frequently on board Norwegian ships which were loading timber, and he often seized the chance to speak to such Russians as were working on board', and confirmed that 'nearly always' the timber was loaded by prisoners.[21] For the first time, Foreign Office officials began to break ranks. Vansittart, commenting on the internal memorandum circulated with Bullard's report, took the first step: 'We all know perfectly well in all conscience that in parts at least conditions in the timber trade are inhuman ... the time is past for this "Nelson touch" of the blind eye. That is not our proper line of defence. It has been too far breached.'[22]

Dalton would have none of it, finding a minor detail in Bullard's account which he insisted provided 'evidence to show that there is some lying about the conditions of labour in Archangel by our Tory Wilberforces'. Laurence Collier, also in the Northern Department, emboldened by his senior's forthrightness, added his own comment:

Whether the workmen are guarded or not seems to make no difference to the question whether their labour is or is not forced ... all Soviet labour is forced, and there is no real moral distinction between labour in the timber industry and labour in any other industry under Communism. The labourers may be slaves in a good cause, in the opinion of their masters, and even sometimes in their own opinion ... but they are nonetheless slaves, if they are not free to leave their work.[23]

C. H. Bateman was the last to come round. It was his remark which had originally drawn the 'Nelson' rebuke from Vansittart. When, a few days later, Ovey referred as usual to 'so-called forced labour in the USSR', Bateman finally took issue with the ambassador's phrasing:

> If we take the definition of forced labour which appears in the US tariff law (viz work or service exacted under menace of penalty for its non-performance and for which the worker does not offer himself voluntarily) then I hardly see the necessity of referring to forced labour in Russia as 'so-called'.[24]

Dalton had had his civil servants' uncritical support since the beginning of the persecution affair in December 1929. They had gone along with dismissing the arrest of believers and the closure of churches as not being persecution 'in the mediaeval sense of the term'. Quite clearly, Vansittart was now signalling that, as far as the bounds of propriety and the duty of civil servants to their ministers would allow, enough was enough.

On 7 March, the *Manchester Guardian*, not usually given to negative reporting about the Soviet Union, carried an eyewitness account which spoke of 60–100 deaths per day in Solovetsky camps – of which the White Sea timber-loading port of Kem was part.[25] Two days later, Ovey reported that, in response to the foreign outcry and clamour for an investigation, 60,000 prisoners were being moved away from all forest areas and ports where they might be seen by visitors.[26] He also sent a copy of a Russian decree which explicitly threatened kulaks who did not fulfil their work norms, or spoke about conditions in the camps to outsiders, with execution. Dalton initialled the dispatch without comment.

Ovey's dispatch also included an extract from *Pravda Severa*, a newspaper from the Northern Region, which had come into the possession of an American journalist in Moscow. Dated 10 January 1931, it contained a decree by the Regional Procurator of the Arkhangelsk District, which among other things repeated that kulaks who 'sabotaged' the timber preparation were liable to be shot and those kulaks guilty of 'non-fulfilment of fixed tasks imposed upon the kulak class' (i.e. those who did not fulfil their forced labour quotas) were liable to up to two years' imprisonment and the confiscation of all their property. The 'counter-revolutionary sabotage' offences that would merit shooting were defined as 'agitation designed to create opposition to standards of output for timber workers and their entry into the forests', or 'agitation [to promote] the failure of timber preparation programmes'.[27] In other words, anyone talking to journalists or foreign ships' crews could be shot.

At home, the British trade union leaders continued to repeat Soviet denials and to insist that the Tories were just trying to find excuses to attack Russia. The day after Ovey's report arrived, the industrial correspondent of the *Daily Herald*, now owned by the TUC, rallied yet again to the Soviets' defence:

> British trade union leaders have no sympathy with the Tory campaign to keep Russian timber out. A joint committee of the Woodworkers' Union and the employers watches imports of made up woodwork.* No joinery is used unless that committee certifies that the conditions under which it is produced satisfactory. The unions have no evidence that forced labour is used in Russian camps. 'Ridiculous figures had been given,' said Mr R. Coppock, secretary of the National Federation of Building Trades Operatives, yesterday. 'It has been stated that there are 4,000,000 political prisoners at work felling trees.† And that number of men will clear a forest the size of the United Kingdom in two weeks.'[28]

Elsewhere in England, the reaction to allegations about the conditions in the timber gulag was not so emollient. The National Committee of the Catholic Women's League passed a resolution, which stated:

> In view of the pitiless cruelty of the present rulers of Russia toward the workers employed in the timber industry in Siberia [*sic*] as revealed by the sworn statements of escaped nationals now resident in England, the Catholic Women's League, representing the organised Catholic women of this country, calls upon His Majesty's Government to denounce these inhuman practices, and to use every resource available to procure an alleviation of sufferings unjustly inflicted upon helpless victims.[29]

---

* Some of the Russian timber imported was already made up into doors.
† The figure of 4,000,000 does not appear on any of the affidavits used by Conservative MPs, received by the Foreign Office, or sent to the Prime Minister. As an exaggeration, it made the claims of protesters appear ridiculous.

CHAPTER 28

'ECONOMIC WAR!'

[This] scarcely finds its equal in the dark and melancholy catalogue of human crime [and] today we find the Government of the day apologising for these villainies.
WINSTON CHURCHILL[1]

This is war, and the most terrible of all wars, economic war.
G. M. GODDEN[2]

Stories that have been circulated about slavery in the Russian camps are grotesque. To say that the people are 'slave driven' is a mischievous libel.
H. E. METCALF, ENGLISH STEEL CORPORATION[3]

The Bolsheviks' bitter hostility towards the Vatican, exemplified in the murder of Mgr. Budkevich on Easter Sunday in 1923, meant that British Catholics were more alert to threats from Russia than many others in Britain. Some of their own number were its current victims: at least fifty Catholic priests were still incarcerated in Solovki.[4] The Catholic weekly, *The Tablet*, had picked up on the timber issue early on, in November 1930. At that stage, less had been known about the conditions of the camps, but the economic threat which they presented was already plain to the paper:

Vast consignments of cheap convict-sawn timber, poured into England, means that 'something little short of ruin' would seem to be in store for the Scandinavian industries. And ruined industries are the most fertile of soils for the revolutionary Communism which the Soviet agents are constantly disseminating.[5]

The consciences of the British timber consortium 'should be pricking them', the paper added. It then proceeded to elaborate on the wider impact which Soviet exports, produced by low-cost forced and prison labour, were having on a continent already reeling from the financial collapse of the previous year.

It was not only anti-slavery campaigners who were becoming alert to the economic threat. On 9 December 1930, William Graham presented a paper on the subject to the Cabinet, containing figures drawn up by his civil servants at the Board of Trade.[6] It appeared that the story told by *The Tablet* three weeks earlier had been substantially correct.

"Slavery in Russia". Poster for the Albert Hall rally, March 1931.

In Britain, Russian fruit pulp was being sold to British jam makers at such low prices that some British growers had been forced to leave their fruit trees and bushes unpicked. Losses among East Anglia fruit farmers had been computed at over £13,000 (£766,000 today). There had been similar stories from Hampshire strawberry farmers. It looked set to get worse – imports being expected to rise the following year from 300 to 2,000 tons.[7] When a consignment of ninety tons of Soviet soap arrived in Cardiff in October 1930, British soap firms reduced their output accordingly. One manufacturer described the impact of the Russian imports on employment in home soap factories as 'disastrous'.

Britain was not alone. There were similar stories throughout Europe. *The Tablet* reported that cheap imports of Soviet matches had shut down three Belgian match factories. The German government responded to the threat to its own match industry by creating a state monopoly. In France, egg farmers were under threat from imported Russian eggs, some of which then found their way onto the British market labelled as French eggs. Soviet coal was being sold in Strasburg at a price under the cost of domestic pro-duction and transport, rates with which the French and Ruhr coalfields were unable to compete. Unrest in the mining industry was then being exploited by Communists.

Russian wheat, flooding into Europe, was causing the greatest concern. In Britain, imports had risen from 940,000 cwt. in the years 1929–30, to 11,277,000 cwt. in 1930, a rise from 0.9 per cent to 28.3 per cent of im-ports for the year.[8] In Romania, Bulgaria, Yugoslavia and Hungary, the price of local wheat had tumbled. So worried were the Romanians for their own peasantry, 'on the verge of starvation, in the midst of a glut of corn', that they raised the matter at the League of Nations. In Britain, the paper alleged, thousands of acres of Yorkshire wheat were left uncut by the farmers, who saw that employing workers to harvest it would only further increase their losses. In October 1930, 50,000 tons of Soviet wheat had been imported into Hull alone; millers were buying it at less than the cost of production of Eng-lish wheat.

It was the same story with Russian glucose, selling at 15 per cent below market price. Confectionery imports for the first nine months of 1930 were 8,962 cwt. (value £195,000, £11.5 million today), and these had been arriving at two-thirds of the price of similar commodities. Reporting these alarming figures to the Cabinet, William Graham added that stories had reached the Board of Trade that Russian trade officials were now offering cotton at up to 40 per cent below British prices.[9]

Ten years earlier, Europe had been rocked by a succession of attempted communist revolutions, in many of which the hand of Moscow had been clearly discerned. The financial collapse which began in October 1929 was already threatening economic stability and employment, fertile ground for new revolution, which Communists were only too willing to exploit. *The Tablet*'s verdict was clear. What was happening was: 'the creation of world-wide distress, the subsidising of chaos and unemployment in all industries, the impoverishment of workers, [and] the shattering of economic and political stability. This is war, and the most terrible of all wars, economic war, with its train of scarcity, unemployment, and mass discontent.'[10]

The article ended with a warning of remarkable prescience:

[There is another] point for the buyers of Soviet products to consider. Every ounce of foodstuff exported from Russia today brings the 170 millions of the Russian people appreciably nearer to famine. In the Russian famine of 1921–1922 it is estimated that 2,000,000 men, women and children perished. Already [there is] the threat of famine for this winter. At the same time the Soviet Government has exported over 5,000,000 quarters of wheat, oats, and barley. If the buyers of Soviet wheat wish to sleep quietly in their beds, they will be well advised to avoid recalling the cannibal horrors of the Russian famine of nine years ago. For their consciences will assuredly tell them that those who help to deprive a starving people of their food are accomplices of the criminal Government through whose acts famine is being created.

In the light of the famine which was to ravage the Ukrainian countryside in 1932–33, taking millions of lives, it was a prediction that was to prove entirely correct.

The timber consortium

For the British timber industry, the political controversy could not have come at a worse time. Erratic price-cutting by the Russians had destabilised the British softwood trade in 1928, with imports to one wholesaler being set at one price and then followed by others at lower prices. Then, in the crash of October 1929, timber prices fell by 30 per cent and those with stock which had been imported at higher prices were now forced to sell at a loss.

To regularise the trade, a consortium of all the British timber importers, the Central Softwood Buying Corporation (CSBC), was formed in 1929. The Russians disrupted the market again the following year, trying to sell timber at cheaper prices to non-consortium members but, by the end of 1930, the CSBC consortium brought some stability to the market by contracting to buy up all the Russian timber exports destined for the UK. The quantities involved were enormous: in a single season, the UK imported 949,000 tons of Russian pit props, 345,000 tons of railway sleepers and 50,000 doors.[11]

Although the contract had been signed for the timber exported in the 1931 season, the first deliveries on that contract could not be shipped until the late spring thaw in May opened up the rivers, allowing the cut logs to be floated down to the ports.* The British timber consortium was therefore at its most vulnerable in the months from January to April 1931, just as the polemic surrounding the timber camps was at its peak. An import ban would have been disastrous for the industry unless the government had been prepared to compensate the consortium and stand up to the Russians. There were no indications that it had any intention of doing so.

Carlyon Bellairs had written to the industry trade paper, the *Timber Trades Journal*, and had received a reasonably understanding response. In December 1930, the journal had printed an editorial which, after briefly outlining the contents of the affidavits which Bellairs had published, criticised the Foreign Secretary's silence on the matter. It continued:

In the face of such allegations it is absolutely impossible for the matter to be permitted to remain in its present state. If the Soviet authorities find it difficult to answer [the charges] with frankness, they can have no cause for complaint if the rest of the world feels justified in believing that the horrors depicted by the three refugees must be true in substance. In that case, even after making a liberal allowance for the imagination of men recounting ghastly experiences, the conditions under which they and their fellow victims had existed must have approached in brutality the atrocities of the Congo, which roused the indignation of the whole civilised world until they ceased.[12]

---

* Murmansk, further north, was open all year round, warmed by the tail end of the Gulf Stream, but the shipments from there were limited.

The article then urged that a full inquiry be made in order to put 'beyond the risk of reproach the body of British timber agents and buyers who, both within and outside the Central Softwood Buying Corporation, are honoura- ble, clean-handed businessmen'.

This was to be the last sympathetic editorial in the *Timber Trades Journal*. The very day on which it was published, Montague Meyer, chairman of the consortium and one of the most powerful timber men in the country, wrote to *The Times*. As far as Meyer was concerned, conditions under which the timber was produced were irrelevant in a commercial transaction: 'This company has no knowledge of the conditions which obtain in regard to production in Russia and as a trading organisation does not consider itself qualified or required to investigate this matter'.[13] Besides, he insisted, the evidence was insufficient.

Meyer's approach became the one adopted by the British timber trade for the duration of the affair. Importers consistently disputed and refused to believe evidence of brutal conditions in the timber camps, or to accept any responsibility for the trade it was sponsoring. Financial considerations ruled the day, as political considerations did in Westminster. It seemed that, for once, British capitalists and British socialists were on the same side.

Boycotts

Public opinion in Britain was coming out against the imports. On 7 February 1931, *The Tablet* added its voice to calls for a boycott of Russian timber:

> Every Briton who says to his architect, contractor, builder, or timber-merchant: 'I won't have a Russian door, a Russian window-frame, a Russian floor-board, a Russian lath, or a Russian pit-prop in my house, or garage, or shop, or mill, or colliery,' or whatever the place may be, is thereby reducing the demand for Bolshevist wood and may, therefore, be the cause of some poor Russian escap- ing the labour-levy [forced labour conscription] during the coming Summer.[14]

One week later, it reported with delight that W. H. Smith had joined the boycott – not only of Russian timber, but Russian grain too – and urged others to join:

> Railway travellers know how plentiful are the book-stalls and kiosks of timber which bear the name of W. H. Smith & Son. 'Old Morality' was the admiring

and affectionate nickname of a member of this famous firm in Late Victorian days; and we rejoice to hear that moral idealism is not regarded as out-of-date by his successors. Messrs. W. H. Smith have decided that they will buy no Russian timber for making or mending bookstalls and that no more Russian oats shall be eaten in their stables. Spurred by this example of a commercial firm, surely no one who has the power to keep Russian timber out of new churches, presbyteries and schools will refrain from action. In the event of a contractor grumbling that a veto on Russian timber is impracticable let him be told of Messrs. Smith's decision.[15]

Others joined the campaign. The Timber Trade Federation reported to its committee that a number of 'large consumers' were boycotting Russian timber.[16] A Rotherham miller, E. F. W. Mills, announced that it would boycott Russian grain.[17] Liverpool City Council instructed its committees not to buy Russian timber – to the fury of the leader of the Labour group on the council who denounced the move as 'an hysterical, childish, and futile stunt intended to interfere with the legitimate rights of the Russian people'.[18] When London County Council had passed a similar measure to prohibit the use of Russian timber in all its new housebuilding, Dimitri Bogomolov from the Soviet Embassy complained about this to Horace Seymour at the Foreign Office. On Henderson's instructions, he was given a sharp (and rare) rebuff.[19] Unlike the Soviets, it was made clear, the British government did not control the activities of civic bodies.

The *Daily Worker* responded in characteristic fashion with the headline 'SMASH 'EM ON MARCH 5!' before decrying the 'SLAVE COLONY OF THE LCC – Mr Dence (Chairman of the Housing Committee) has evidently quite forgotten the coercion and penal conditions which obtain in the forced labour camps maintained by the London County Council, to which they exile unemployed London workers'.*[20]

The Trade Defence Union

Many shared *The Tablet*'s view. On 11 February, Carlyon Bellairs issued a

---

* In 1929 the Ministry of Labour established a number of work camps throughout the country as places of residential training for the long-term unemployed. By the time the scheme closed in 1939 approximately 200,000 young men had been through the programme.

statement to the press that 'in consequence of the Government's persistent refusal to take action against Russian imports and slave made goods and in order to meet the menace of the Soviet Economic War, it has been decided to form a Trade Defence Union'.[21] Its chairman was Lord Brentford, who was also on the committee of the CPM, and the committee of the union included Bellairs, Sir Edward Hilton Young and a number of other MPs who had taken a close interest in the timber camps. A fortnight later, *The Times* gave notice of the organisation's first public meeting:

SLAVERY IN RUSSIA: An International Campaign against brutalities in the Soviet Prison Camps – to bring home to our people that the Communists are using Russia for an economic war on the world – to bring about a common front to the common enemy, Communism – will be opened by a MASS MEETING, Friday, March 6th, 1931 at 8 p.m. at the ROYAL ALBERT HALL[22]

Following on from the prayer day of the previous year, the Albert Hall rally was one of the most significant expressions of public opinion against Communist Russia in 1931. Reports do not indicate the number of attendees but it was described as 'a very large gathering' and there must have been thousands present. The CPM had been campaigning for over a year, and had held hundreds of meetings; public interest was high. The announcement that an escaped prisoner would be appearing on the platform would have only swelled the numbers. Although politicians were in evidence (Lord Brentford, Hilton Young, and the bête noire of Communists and fellow travellers, Winston Churchill), they were accompanied on the platform by clergy representing the complete ecclesiastical spectrum – from the Jesuit priest Arthur Day, to the general secretary of the National Free Church Council, Rev. Thomas Nightingale, both of whom addressed the meeting.

Soviet sympathisers were out in force too. Brentford's opening speech was interrupted a number of times while heckling protesters were ejected – in one case after 'brief fights' with stewards. In spite of those, he was still able to make his point:

Lord Brentford said that there was a camp in the North of Russia where one-fifth of the prisoners were women. 'I hardly know,' he said, 'whether I dare tell you in this mixed audience; but we have evidence that in the camp the women are habitually violated by the guards; ... Are we to stand up and see these things go on? Are we a civilised nation? A Christian nation? A nation which has a conscience? Are we to stand by while these things are being done in this world of ours? ...'

Continuing, he said, he would we had a Wilberforce today to go from one end of the land to the other to preach against the barbarities. Lord Brentford said he would we had a Gladstone. England in those days was not afraid to speak her mind to the nations of the world. She had a backbone then. She knew what was right, and stood for what was right in spite of any criticism that was made against.

Churchill was on sparkling form, sparring with protesters, as forthright as ever, robust in his condemnation of the timber camps and contemptuous of MacDonald's prevarication. His speech that night, reported in the press the next day, is a classic of his style and it deserves more consideration than a brief quotation – not least because it illustrates the degree to which the subject had penetrated and stirred the wider public conscience.

Mr Winston Churchill, who was received with loud cheers, interspersed with groans and 'boos,' said:- 'You have seen the carefully prepared organisation which is in action to prevent us from holding our meeting, and making protest. Here are miserable hirelings, poor wretched people paid with roubles for making trouble, brought here and forced to do their bit or they do not get their cash. (Cheers.) Cannot you see far better than any words we could put to you by this carefully staged demonstration that there are force and money behind the opposition? (Cheers.) But we shall succeed in this country in maintaining free speech and the rights of citizens to congregate together to express their opinions on great public issues. This issue is surely one which has claimed the allegiance and accord of those who agree about the decencies of civilisation. We have heard some amount of detail of the horrible conditions which prevail in the Russian timber camps.'

In all parts of the galleries there were now processions of both men and women disturbers being escorted from the hall, on which Mr Churchill remarked: 'We must make allowance for those who are earning their pay. They get a bonus for being thrown out.' (Cheers and laughter.)

'Look at the impudence of it,' continued Mr Churchill, 'coming here and interfering with our rights. Why don't they go to their Utopia in Russia? The conditions there were tantamount to slavery. That Government possessed despotic power, and used that power against their political opponents, and sent them in scores of thousands to those hideous places of punishment. Then we were told that in England we ought to receive the produce of their sweated labour because some persons or other here might grease their fingers with commission. That was a matter that had got to be dealt with according to the heart and conscience of the nation.' (Cheers.)

Mr Churchill said that if today we find the Government of the day apologising for these villainies in Russia and patting on the backs those who grease their paws (Cheers) – if today we found that situation, and if today we found a certain sluggishness in our life, that was because we were for the moment – let us frankly admit it – passing under a cloud of weakness and confusion; but behind it the strength and power of the British nation were gathering. (Cheers.)

'I know well,' said Mr Churchill, 'the English people, and I have never seen them fail when great issues are put to the test. They are gathering their strength day by day. This meeting filling this vast hall, of men and women who knew they would have to face opposition, is only one sign of the revival of a national strength and affection which, when it has reached its full vigour, will sweep away and drive away before it all who commit offences against the freedom and dignity of man.' (Cheers.)

By voting for the resolution which had been proposed, those present would record a definite protest against a system of convict and forced labour in Russia, which, to quote a phrase of Mr Gladstone, 'scarcely finds equal in the dark and melancholy catalogue of human crime.' (Loud cheers.)[23]

Men of business

Those with business interests in Russia were alarmed. One of these was Henry E. Metcalf, a businessman whose close involvement in trade with Russia meant that his own fortunes were bound up with progress of Anglo-Soviet relations. He had been a member of the British Industrial Mission to the Soviet Union in March 1929, and had visited the Soviet Union on a number of previous occasions.[24] One source describes him as employed by the English Steel Corporation.[25] He appears in Reader Bullard's diary a number of times, though not in an entirely complimentary light:

Joined at tea by Mr. Metcalfe [*sic*], a business man who is touring Russia. Much of what he says is more sensible than the anti-Russian stuff one reads in most English newspapers, but I don't trust him…

An Englishman called Metcalfe passing through … [he] is not a man I like, because he is always flattering the Soviet authorities in public in order to ingratiate himself to get business. I agree we should try to get business, and that the Soviet methods of government no concern of ours, but I dislike the licking of the comrades' boots.[26]

It is not clear if Metcalf felt any personal sympathy towards Soviet Communism, or merely cynically cultivated his relations with the Soviets and with Soviet supporters for financial gain. The relationship clearly continued for some years. In 1937, he chaired and opened the first session of 'For Peace and Friendship' at the National Congress of Peace and Friendship with the USSR.[27] The conference was staged by a British Soviet front organisation and was also addressed by leading Russophiles such as Hewlett Johnson, D. N. Pritt, G. D. H. Cole, and John Strachey.

Whatever his motives, it was in Metcalf's interest to damp down anything which might hinder Russian trade and he was active to that end.[28] He wrote regular letters to the press in support of the development of Anglo-Russian trade and, responding to the Trade Defence Union, he attacked the organisers of the Albert Hall rally, accusing them of:

Doing British industrial workers a great disservice by attempting to antagonise a powerful neighbour and a great potential customer, and at a time when the appalling conditions prevailing in England are causing untold suffering and embitterment. I say this even at the risk of being called cold-blooded as far as the Russian Timber Camp conditions are concerned.[29]

In late March 1931, a 47-page booklet, *Forced Labour in Russia: Facts and Documents*, was published by the pro-Soviet British trade journal *The British Russian Gazette and Trade Outlook*. It contained a comprehensive selection of the documents, statements, letters and articles which those who supported the Soviet position used to refute the evidence produced by the opposition and newspapers such as *The Times* and the *Morning Post*.

The introduction and foreword are dated 21 March 1931, four days before the only House of Commons debate on the timber camps, and it is likely that the booklet was published in order to get copies of those statements into the hands of sympathetic MPs before the debate. The foreword, written by Metcalf himself, is unambiguous – the stories of human rights abuses in the camps were 'grotesque' and a 'mischievous libel':

> It will be seen from this booklet that the stories that have been circulated about slavery in the Russian camps are grotesque. Nine-tenths of timber workers are seasonal hands, many of them coming up from their villages with their own horses; and their task is no harder than that of lumber men in other northern latitudes. The pay, even taking into consideration the higher cost of living, is better than it was formerly; the huts are solidly built and well heated and there are fairly well-equipped hospitals with competent medical attention, a thing unknown in these camps in pre-war days. In Russia life is terribly hard in many respects, but to say that the people are 'slave driven' is a mischievous libel.[30]

Alarm among the timber men

The Albert Hall rally and the success of the call for a boycott provoked an emergency meeting of the Executive Council of the Timber Trade Federation, 'to discuss the serious position that had arisen owing to some large consumers having decided to abstain from the purchase of Russian wood, owing to the campaign which was being directed against all Russian goods by the Trade Defence Union'.[31]

The meeting hammered out what was to become the federation's defence – that the timber camps and prison camps were different and that the latter had nothing to do with the export timber trade. E. P. Tetsall, the federation president, addressed the meeting:

> It was a complete misrepresentation to say that the goods handled [by the federation] were produced by forced or slave labour thus creating a strong

prejudice in the minds of all right-thinking people against Russian goods. The attempt to identify the penal settlements with the timber camps was an unfair method of attack.

Percy Meyer, Montague Meyer's brother, agreed: 'The examination by any sane person who was looking at the evidence without prejudice would show that the majority of the statements made were in regard to prison camps and did not particularly refer to timber camps.'[32] Both were wrong, but even that argument did not address the charge that prisoners were manning the vast majority of dockside sawmills, where timber was trimmed and cut, and were then loading all of the finished timber onto the ships.

Prisoners arriving at Kem prison camp on the White Sea. Kem was the port for onward transport to the Solovetsky Islands. A still from an early Soviet propaganda film. Note the timber stacks in the background.

A few days later, at the federation's annual dinner on 18 March, Karl Danishevsky, the president of the USSR Timber Export Corporation, was an honoured guest. In his speech, Tetsall told those present that to suggest that a system of convict labour was in operation in the export timber trade in Russia was 'a serious misrepresentation. The accommodation in the camps was satisfactory, and food supplies in those camps were better than in the towns.'[33] The federation then sent a lengthy memorandum (discussed at greater length in Chapter 29) to William Graham to brief him in advance of the debate.

The following week, the *Timber Trades Journal* reported 'No Slavery in Western Dvina', in an article by M. Bick, managing director of timber merchant Charles Boss and Co. In spite of the title, the article contained nothing to disprove the slavery claims, and in fact highlighted the 'dire' conditions ('in a desperate plight') in which those penalised by the loss of their civil rights existed: deprived of lodging and ration cards, they were forced to buy food on the black market at prices so inflated that they were beyond the ordinary pocket. But, Bick concluded, 'As far as I can ascertain no forced labour is employed.'[34]

At the end of June, Tetsall led a federation delegation to Russia to investigate conditions in the timber areas of Russia, particularly in the Archangel district. Considering the elaborate measures taken to deceive the press on another occasion (detailed in Chapter 30), the delegation cannot really be blamed for being duped. Seeing only what the Soviets wanted them to see, they came back glowing with enthusiasm for the 'experiment'. The *Timber Trades Journal* printed Tetsall's report and, carrying the authority of an eye-witness account by the federation president, most people in the industry were convinced, and thus prepared to accept the Labour accusation that the affair was a Conservative 'stunt':

It is a new Russia we see today ... A new force with which we have to reckon – virile and courageous. Russia is looking her immense problems square in the face, determined that she will take her place in the sun, though perhaps a little headlong in her impetuosity to reach the goal. There are so many urgent problems, so much that cannot wait; and she is bravely tackling so many of those at one and the same time that one wonders if the energy and power needed to drive it all through with the pace she has set herself can be sustained. You may or may not like their system of government; but I verily believe she is working to raise the standard of life of her people. Everywhere we found the same energy and determination and record of progress in the provision of facilities which add to the comfort of life. There are improvements in quays and yards to be seen everywhere, besides several completely new mills. Interested and energetic workers can be seen everywhere [and] the system goes with a quiet and forceful efficiency belying all suggestion of anything but voluntary and satisfied labour.[35]

In conclusion, Tetsall added a fellow delegation member's outright denial that prisoners in Solovki (the Popov Island camp was part of the Solovki group) had ever been engaged in timber work. The comment had been made by William Thompson JP, head of a timber firm in King's Lynn:

We saw only *one* prison-camp, and found that it is on Popoff Island (Kem) and we found nothing unusual about it. It appeared to compare favourably with our own convict prisons, and the inmates looked reasonably comfortable. We established as a fact beyond dispute that no prisoners are ever engaged in timber loading or lopping, and *we could not discover that any had ever been so engaged!*[36]

The *Daily Worker* was delighted: 'Three Capitalists Look at Russia: They Saw No Forced Labour', it declared, before reproducing most of the article verbatim.[37] In December 1931, the same month in which a further delegation of British timber men travelled to Russia, the Duchess of Atholl published a photograph of a handbill from the OGPU ordering the authorities of Solovki to step up timber production by 300 per cent in one year. It was headed: 'Declaration of measures for the stimulation officials and prisoners engaged in the timber camps'.[38] Thompson had clearly been fooled. Perhaps Reader Bullard spoke with some insight when he wrote in his diary:

Timber curing is very unpopular work and the peasants who don't run away from it adopt passive resistance and do as little work as possible. Last year a group of English timber merchants reported that conditions in the timber camps they visited were very good, but they had just been let off part of a contract with the Soviet Government which was becoming onerous, so they can hardly be considered unprejudiced observers.[39]

A postscript: Montague L. Meyer Ltd and Harold Wilson

The involvement of the Meyers' firm in the import of Soviet timber has an interesting postscript in the post-war period. The company continued to prosper under the chairmanship of Montague's son and grandson and remained a leading importer of timber, specialising in Russian softwood. Today, under new ownership after a management buyout, it remains one of the largest UK importers of Russian panel products.

The firm had contacts with the British government which stretched back to the Great War. There were rumours that their dealings had not been entirely honest. Montague and Percy Meyer had been employed by the Board of Works and had gone from there to set up their own timber business. At one point, Percy Meyer was still a civil servant placing timber orders for the government while Montague had set up the business, in part fulfilling contracts for the government or buying surplus government stock. Questions over the probity of their dealings caused a number of questions to be asked in Parliament in 1920, the very clear inference of which was that their business activities were suspect.[40] Certainly, when the questions drew too much attention, Montague was forced to pay back his profit to the Board of Trade. This was not the first time doubts had been raised about the brothers either. In 1915, they had been the subject of parliamentary questions no fewer than nine times.[41]

After the Second World War, Ernest Bevin, who had known Montague Meyer in the 1930s, introduced Tom Meyer, Montague's son, to Harold Wilson. Wilson entered Parliament in the 1945 election and was appointed Parliamentary Secretary to the Ministry of Works. Only two years later, in 1947, he was made president of the Board of Trade. At the age of thirty-one, he was the youngest Cabinet member of the twentieth century. He remained in government until he suddenly resigned in May 1951. Only three weeks later, he joined Montague L. Meyer Ltd as a consultant. Meyer particularly valued the contacts Wilson had made with the Russians while at the Board of Trade, and on the firm's behalf, Meyer commissioned Wilson to travel to the USSR to do business. He made his first trip to the Soviet Union in May 1953, and over the following twelve years, before he returned to politics, he made a further eleven trips to Russia for the firm.

In the years of post-war reconstruction and currency controls, the import of heavily rationed materials was closely restricted. Those who could obtain import licences (from the Board of Trade) had the opportunity to create considerable wealth. Montague L. Meyer Ltd. was one company which had prospered. Its friendly relations with the Labour Party, forged at the time of the 1930s Russian timber affair, probably also helped when it came to pitching for the contract to handle timber clearance in the unsuccessful ground-nut-growing scheme in Africa, overseen by another former close friend of the USSR, John Strachey, now Minister of Food. Montague L. Meyer Ltd was awarded the contract.

Wilson's time at the Board of Trade, the manner of his leaving, and his contacts with Montague Meyer generated a stream of rumour and innuendo. Hartley Shawcross, who succeeded Wilson in 1951 as president of the Board of Trade, wrote to *The Times* in 1974 about the corruption which he had discovered when he arrived at the Board of Trade, and said that it involved 'one individual occupying an exalted position'. Wilson's enemies, aided by *Private Eye* magazine, took this to be a reference to Wilson himself.

Meanwhile, the Security Service had become alarmed at the frequency of Wilson's trips to Russia. It was the height of the Cold War; the success of *any* British business venture in the USSR could not have been achieved without the tacit approval of senior members of the Soviet government. The Security Service feared that Wilson had been compromised and blackmailed to work covertly for the KGB, then given the contracts to keep him useful for Meyer, and thus able to keep returning to handlers in Moscow. He would not have been the first; businessmen visiting Russia were regularly targeted by the KGB. Given the atmosphere at the time, the hypothesis was not without some logic, though when the rumour finally leaked, after his retirement, that a British Prime Minister had been spied on by his own security service, there were howls of outrage from those on the left who saw it as evidence of an overbearing security service which had very much overstepped its brief.[42]

Wilson did not help himself. While his sympathy for the Soviet Union undoubtedly helped his work for Meyer, it did not endear him to moderates in his own party. David Leigh writes:

Wilson certainly did not go out of his way to appear anti-Soviet. In 1956 he declined to sign a letter sent to *Pravda* by five impeccably left-wing colleagues to protest about the Soviet crushing of the Hungarian uprising. And in 1961, as Labour's foreign spokesman on the Berlin Wall, we find him arguing that the

West should make it 'clear by word and deed that we are prepared to renounce the use of West Berlin as an advance battle headquarters and centre of provocation in the Cold War. The price we pay, in terms of suspicion and ill will for insisting on keeping West Berlin for Radio Free Europe and similar organisations, and as a centre for spies and provocateurs, is out of all proportion to any value that may be thought to derive from these activities.'[43]

The post-war Anglo-Soviet timber trade was therefore not free from controversy either, and the 'blind eye' allegations over gulag labour first made in the 1930s resurfaced. One correspondent wrote to the *Daily Telegraph* in 1950 (while Harold Wilson was still in his post as president of the Board of Trade, before he joined the Meyers' company) that Britain should inspect the 'slave labour areas of Siberia' where the timber was cut: 'It would do the Ministry of Supply no harm to know how Soviet timber is cut.'[44] It would have been very surprising if Wilson had not known.

CHAPTER 29

'LET THE EXPERIMENT CONTINUE': THE ONLY COMMONS DEBATE (25 MARCH 1931)

There are none so blind as those who are determined not to see.
ANTHONY EDEN

The government could not indefinitely stall opposition pressure for a Commons debate. On 25 March 1931, a debate on the Consolidated Fund (the government's general bank account at the Bank of England) provided a pretext for the matter to be raised, albeit against the government's wishes.[1] Carlyon Bellairs had used the same debate, the year before, to raise the subject of the timber camps.[2] One year on, this was to be the sole House of Commons debate on Russian timber imports, and thus gives us a uniquely detailed insight into the wider views of Labour and Liberal MPs on the subject.

As a minority government, Labour relied upon the Liberals for support and, on the subject of Russian forced labour, the Liberals rallied firmly behind the government and its silence on the human rights abuses in the timber camps. While it is important that Labour and Liberal dismissals of the protesters' claims not be judged according to our knowledge today of conditions in the camps but in the context of the evidence that was available at the time, the debate nevertheless shows that it was overwhelming even then.

A 'welter of evidence': two briefs

It was not only socialists who were alarmed by the widespread protest campaign: the Timber Trade Federation became increasingly nervous as 25 March, the date set for the debate, drew near. The federation sent a lengthy memorandum to William Graham, who was to speak for the government in the debate. Part of their defence was the well-publicised 'reliable and independent evidence' by the timber expert J. F. Stewart. Stewart's report was completely invalidated by the fact that it derived from time spent in the timber areas a year *before* the kulak deportations began. In spite of this, his report still included the telling observation that 'if weakly townspeople are suddenly dumped into logging in such a hard country as North Russia, I can quite imagine they would quickly succumb under any conditions'. 'Succumb' could only mean one thing – death – but that still did not stop defenders of the trade, whether in business, politics, or the left-wing press, from using Stewart's report as evidence that totally absolved the Soviets. The Northern Department's own brief, written for Graham to accompany the Timber Trade Federation memorandum, contradicted the federation's assurance that all was well:

> It is quite true that, as the Federation point out, there have been overstatements and exaggerations in the evidence of escaped prisoners and renegade Soviet officials published in the British press, but in the opinion of the Foreign Office it would be wrong to place too much importance on that side of the question. The plain fact is that, despite inaccuracies and over statements, there cannot but be some truth found in the welter of evidence available.[3]

On Stewart's report, the department emphasised, once again, that his evidence was invalid:

> *It is clear that he knows nothing whatever of conditions in Russia since the end of 1929.* The whole point of the present agitation is that the allegations of prison labour, forced labour, and harsh and brutal treatment refer simply and solely to the drive which has been set on foot since the beginning of 1930. Thus what may have been true in 1929 is not necessarily true in 1930 or 1931. In fact it is quite clear from the Blue Book, published by the Foreign Office,

that there has been a complete change in the extent to which forced and prison labour is used in order to increase the output in timber. (My italics.)

Although the Board of Trade officials had just stated that the massive influx of kulak exiles and the increase in the prison population had invalidated Stewart's report, Dalton still added his own final comment to the memorandum: 'Nonetheless, [Stewart] is a witness with expert knowledge, whose evidence should not be wholly disregarded.' Dalton was determined to believe whatever supported his own view.

The Board of Trade also provided William Graham, as its president, with its own briefing document. This stated:

Even presuming that the evidence of escaped prisoners is somewhat biased, the volume of evidence is so great that it may well be that abuses have been and are taking place. The Soviet Government maintain that convict and forced labour are not used on timber for export, but it seems almost incredible that they should be able to keep the different classes of timber separate, and there is no evidence apart from their own statements that they attempt to do so.[4]

Graham was therefore fully briefed by both the Foreign Office and his own ministry as to the facts of the existence of the timber gulag. He also could not have avoided being aware of the conditions in the camps from the publication in the press of the statements of escaped prisoners and British merchant seamen who had loaded timber in Kem and Archangel. While many of his more junior parliamentary colleagues may have chosen to disbelieve the eye-witness accounts, Graham had been advised by the Northern Department of the Foreign Office that, whatever their minor discrepancies and errors, they were, in the main, correct. He had also been present at the 11 February Cabinet meeting at which it was acknowledged that an inquiry would be likely to find that conditions in the timber camps were so bad that the government would have no option but to ban Soviet timber imports.

This was the state of the government's and Graham's own understanding on the morning of 25 March 1931 and yet, in the House of Commons debate, Graham would insist that '*no evidence of any kind* has been tendered' (my italics) to confirm the allegations of the campaigners.

'Unspeakable misery': the opposition opens

The debate began with pleas for government action by the men who had led the campaign from the opposition benches – Edward Hilton Young, Godfrey Locker-Lampson and Carlyon Bellairs. Locker-Lampson confronted the government with the moral case:

> Timber in Russia is produced under what I believe, and what my hon. friends believe, to be conditions utterly alien to our notions of civilisation ... We believe that slavery exists there in all but in name. We believe that this forced labour, living in unspeakable misery, is being used for the export of goods to this country, and we do ask the Government once again to press the Soviet to allow an investigation, and if the request is once more refused, to institute their own enquiry here and elsewhere.[5]

For Hilton Young, the evidence was now too great for the government to continue to deny:

> We suggest that there is *prima facie* evidence which no candid man can reject that timber and wooden products are being produced in Russia under conditions which in the first place are an outrage to the standards generally accepted in any civilised country ... That is our appeal to the Government tonight: we put the case of humanity before them, a case in which they ought to spare no pains to find out whether they may not be encouraging a great wrong.[6]

When he came to reply, 'the case of humanity' got very little response from Graham, whose one concession to the facts put before him in his briefing documents was, in the same sentence, immediately downplayed:

> There is no doubt that the evidence before us shows that there may be a certain amount of prison labour employed, but I am afraid that some of the statements which have been made will not bear investigation because they seem to indicate that people are felling trees right and left day and night. I think we can disregard a good deal of extravagant material of that kind.[7]

From the opposition benches, Anthony Eden, who was to have Dalton's job by the end of the year, unknowingly echoing both of the briefs given to Graham, insisted that the 'large volume of evidence' was undeniable:

> It is no answer to our case to say [that the charges] cannot be proved. I can only tell the House that there is a very large volume of evidence, and we ask our Government to follow the example of other Governments in this matter and to institute an enquiry. There is nothing so very preposterous in a suggestion of that kind.[8]

Eden's conclusion was one with which many by now agreed: 'The only inference that one can draw from their attitude is that they do not wish to know any more than they can possibly help about these matters. There are none so blind as those who are determined not to see.'[9]

'Better than English prisons' – Labour replies

Labour MPs, seemingly oblivious of the moral compromise, rallied to the defence of the Soviet and British governments. George Strauss, a future Labour peer and Father of the House, gave the opening speech for the government. He admitted the existence of forced labour in the Russian timber camps, but insisted that conditions for Russian prisoners were not appalling and in fact were 'very much more favourable than in our English prisons' and that the labour was not used to export timber. Furthermore, he attacked the campaigners:

> What has not been yet been proved is that this labour is used for export and that these appalling conditions really do exist ... I think we are justified in a close examination of the *bona fides* of the accusers ... The humanitarian side of the case which has been presented by the Rt. Hon Gentleman opposite is a cloak to support the economic aspect of the situation which they want to put forward ... I think the evidence supports me that the stories of brutality now put forward in connection with Russia, like the atrocity stories during the war, were put forward on political grounds with political motives.[10]

In support of his case, Strauss devoted considerable portions of his speech to the evidence which had been published by the *Manchester Guardian* to refute the claims of human rights abuses in the timber camps. The flaws in these statements are examined in Appendix 2.

Morgan Philips Price, the Labour MP for Whitehaven, had visited Russia in the early days of the Revolution and had spent three and a half months working for the Soviet Foreign Ministry, writing English-language propaganda for the new government. He was firmly convinced that the allegations made against the Soviets were all false, declaring: 'I have it on quite definite authority that no convict labour is employed in the export timber industry.'[11]

Frank Wise spoke up too. He had no time for Eden's complaints, and instead rebuked the Conservatives with another *tu quoque*:

> I can only contrast his [Eden's] zeal for this enquiry with the attitude which was adopted by members of his party some time ago when it was proposed there should be an enquiry into the Indian prisons ... The only evidence of British subjects, both of whom have been in the Northern timber districts, entirely contradicts most of the allegations which have been made ... I have not been in the timber districts of the North, but I was in the timber districts of the South a year and a half ago, and the only complaint made there was that the wages paid were so high that the peasants were being drawn away from all other sorts of occupations.[12]

It was not only Labour members of the Commons who were deaf to pleas to stop the trade. Their minority government could not survive without Liberal support. This was forthcoming. Dr E. Leslie Burgin spoke for the Liberals, and opened with an extraordinary assertion about the unreliability of the eyewitness accounts:[13]

> Great credence has been attached to evidence of escaped prisoners ... I do not think that anybody who has had any experience on the bench of magistrates, or in the law, is required to be told that there is no evidence quite so untrustworthy as that of the dismissed servant or the discharged employee, for there is a feeling of resentment and bitterness which naturally discolours the narration, even the simple set of facts. So although there has undoubtedly been suffering of a great and most distressing character, we must be a little careful in accepting evidence from these escaped prisoners in Finland or elsewhere.[14]

Burgin then suggested that many of the affidavits, some of them sworn before British officials, were forgeries. In fact, the story of the forgery, said to have been revealed by White Russians (and therefore presumed to be credible) was itself a forgery. It had been put out as disinformation by the Anglo-Russian Parliamentary Committee in its newsletter to MPs. Providing an intriguing insight into the tactics of the ARPC, it is discussed further in Appendix 3.

With Burgin's final comments, protesters were forced to abandon all hope that the Liberal Party might use its influence to persuade the government to adopt a more compassionate approach towards those in the Russian camps:

> I am satisfied that a large number of the complaints genuinely and honestly put forward as complaints of brutal conditions would be common to the lumber industry in most northern latitudes. The evidence so far produced, and which has been examined by some of us who are interested in this matter, fails to show that these allegations against the timber trade can be substantiated.[15]

'Let the experiment continue'

William Graham is little known today, largely because of his premature death in 1932, but at the time of the debate he was a rising star in the party and had been tipped as a future party leader. He spoke now on behalf of the government as Britain's trade minister. Like Burgin, whom he praised, he was forthright in his dismissal of the evidence brought forward by the Conservatives, which he described as 'extravagant'. He insisted that a timber embargo was out of the question. An able politician, Graham was accustomed to fending off difficult questions by answering different ones. In his reply to demands for an investigation, he simply restated the position that the government of the Soviet Union had refused to admit foreign investigators. He made no reply to the suggestion made at the very beginning of the affair that government investigators be sent to Finland to talk to Russian refugees.

When Conservatives repeated their appeal to *amend* the Prison-Made Goods Act, Graham skirted the question by saying instead that the evidence had been insufficient to *satisfy* the Act. His precise words, that 'no evidence *of any kind* has been tendered' (my italics), are extraordinary, given the briefs he had received before the debate:

[We have said that] if you will produce evidence, that evidence will be carefully considered as to whether it does satisfy the position under this Act and whether action should be taken. But from that day to this no evidence of any kind has been tendered. We have remained in this atmosphere of wild and general controversy, affidavits and criticism of the Soviet Union regime, of an attack on a vast experiment, conducted to some extent in this house, and from outside in the daily press.[16]

Graham was undoubtedly well aware that the Cabinet had blocked an inquiry precisely because of the likelihood of such evidence surfacing. He then concluded with one of the most extraordinary statements ever given by a minister of the Crown in the House of Commons:

[The Soviets] are engaged in a vast and very remarkable economic experiment, and what we have always said is that they are entitled in their own way to pursue that experiment without outside interference…

I say, let the experiment continue. Let us give all the co-operation we can.[17]

CHAPTER 30

PRISONER IN THE TIMBER GULAG – THE STORY OF GEORGE KITCHIN

George Kitchin's story begins in 1921. A Finnish citizen with a British mother, he travelled to Russia in response to the economic relaxation of Lenin's New Economic Policy and set up an import business. His offices were in the Finnish Government Building in Leningrad. There, he was approached by the OGPU in an attempt to recruit him to become an informer on the activities of the Finnish Trade Delegation. He refused.

He had not been in Leningrad many years before he met the woman who was to become his wife. His fiancée was a Russian who had been arrested by the OGPU in 1922, together with her first husband, who died in prison. In 1924, now engaged to Kitchin, she was arrested again, this time as part of a sweep to arrest all those who had been known to attend social gatherings organised by Thomas Preston, the British Consul in Leningrad. Once again, the OGPU put pressure on George to spy for them, this time trying blackmail, by promising him in return for his fiancée's freedom; once again, he refused, and so incurred the enmity of the Leningrad OGPU. The Finnish consul advised him to leave the country at once, but Kitchin stayed on in order to try to secure his fiancée's release. She had been sentenced to three years in Siberia. A chance amnesty brought about her release and they were married immediately upon her return to Leningrad, whereupon she was able to obtain Finnish citizenship.

Their first child was six weeks old when George himself was arrested on 26

March 1928. When the OGPU arrived at his door that night, it appeared that they intended to arrest both George and his wife, but when the officials found out that she had a new baby and that she was actually a foreign citizen, they rang their headquarters and were told to leave her and the baby – 'for now'.

Shipped north

George was sent to a prison camp in the Northern Region and it was four years before the intercession of the Finnish government finally managed to secure his release. By then, his health was broken. Had he remained in the camps, he would undoubtedly have perished. He convalesced for a year and a half, and then spent another year preparing his notes and writing an account of his imprisonment, *Prisoner of the OGPU*. The book was published in 1935, but the decline in his health could not be halted, and he died just before its publication.

George's book is one of the most important of the early timber gulag memoirs. As an educated Anglo-Finnish businessman, he was able to write fluently in English about his experiences. He was also an acute observer who had had the good fortune to be appointed as a camp clerk. This not only helped him to survive (taking him off hard labour detail), but enabled him to gain a wider understanding of the workings of the Northern Region gulag. The nature of a centrally planned economy and OGPU demands meant that all the camps were required to send extensive reports back to Moscow. George had access to much of this data because his job was to help to compile it. He was thus able to record that in his district, at the heart of the Northern Region timber gulag, the rate of mortality among the prisoners in 1929–30 was 22 per cent per annum.[1]

In his book, George tells how he was posted to various camps in the Northern Region gulag administration centred around the upper reaches of the northern Dvina and Vichega rivers, which were the conduits for export timber, cut during the frozen winter months and then floated down-river to Archangel when the ice thawed. While he was on the headquarters staff in Kotlas*, he was appointed to join inspection teams which visited other camps in the

---

*   Kotlas was the end point on the railway that ran north-west from Viatka towards Arkhangelsk and the coast. In so isolated a region where the roads were so poor that all freight beyond there was shipped by river and its geographical location meant that it became a major gulag centre. The town held large transit camps for kulak exiles (in the Makarikha district) and convicted prisoners, where they were held before being sent on to work camps elsewhere. See the map for all the places mentioned in this chapter.

region, such as those at Ust Sysolsk (now Syktyvkar). In Ust Sysolsk, Kotlas and later in Solvychegodsk, Kitchin was an eyewitness to the conditions in which exiled kulaks were held and, at one time, he lived next to a kulak transit camp. His reports therefore describe in detail both the conditions in which political prisoners were incarcerated and in which exiled kulaks were held. He describes how kulak children 'died like flies' and those who tried to get out of the camp to find food or water were shot by guards. In his own camp he reports that there were numerous executions; on one day, in August 1930, eighty-two prisoners were shot on the orders of the national head of the gulag administration, who had just visited the camp. He also met priests who had been imprisoned as a result of the religious persecution campaign.

As part of the camp administration, he was witness to the panic which hit the camps when, after Molotov's announcement that foreign correspondents could visit the region, instructions came for prisoners to be moved en masse within three days into the interior and away from ports (which he confirmed were manned by a large number of prisoners) so that foreign visitors would not see them. In Archangel, 30,000 prisoners had been working and were loaded into over 800 railway cars for their evacuation. Some were left in open flat cars for days in sub-zero winter temperatures. Many died. Others (those in the camp lock-ups for infringing camp regulations, or those who were too sick to ship out) were simply taken into the forest and shot.

Kitchin's account provided a startling picture of the true state of affairs in the timber regions during 1930–31, just as the fate of kulaks and religious believers in the timber camps was being debated in Westminster. In the context of the denials of these conditions by Labour politicians back in Britain, his testimony is particularly powerful and damning.

Deaths in camp

Throughout his account, it is apparent that conditions in the prison and kulak camps of the Northern Region were truly appalling:

In February 1931, we were transferred to a new barracks where the temperature hung around the freezing point. At night it fell below freezing* and engineer A.

---

* Winter temperatures in the region were typically -20°C (-4°F).

once woke in the morning with a frostbitten ear. The moment we reached the barracks, we climbed into our bunks, keeping on our felt boots and overcoats and covering ourselves with every available blanket or piece of clothing.

Members of the office staff lived comparatively well, but the lot of the ordinary prisoners was quite otherwise. They were still kept in tents and barracks fit only for cattle. They were given excessive working assignments, and became worn and ill with fatigue. The reports from the timber-works were deplorable. There the rate of mortality was … high … and scurvy, typhus and other diseases were taking their toll…

The most dreadful reports continued to come from the timber regions where work had been carried on in the winter. At the end of the winter working season (April/May 1930) all prisoners who were still in fair condition were sent to Archangel to load ships, but there were not many of these. Of the total number of prisoners of the Uftug camp group* two thousand men, or about twenty-two percent of the remaining men died during the winter. More than half of the remaining men were totally disabled. The same picture confronted the administration at the Kuloy group.†

After the winter work was over, the Uftug group was liquidated, discipline slackened, and crowds of left-over invalids wandered about Solvychegodsk dressed in pitiable rags, begging alms and occasionally pilfering small food supplies. The Solvychegodsk camp hospital daily buried over twenty prisoners in common graves. The scandal finally reached such proportions that the local committee of the Communist Party reported to Moscow and insisted on immediate relief. But the camp administration paid no attention whatever to complaints. It argued that the planned objective had been accomplished, even if a certain number of prisoners had perished. 'Of what other use are criminals to the state?' asked Boksha [a prison official], 'They should be pleased to expiate their guilt towards the proletariat by giving their lives and fertilizing the fields where the seeds of Socialism are being sown'.[2]

---

*   Taking its name from the Uftyug River, a tributary of Northern Dvina, twenty-five miles north of Kotlas, the Uftug camp group consisted of eight main logging camps and numerous sub-camps stretched out over a vast area of forest. In total around 8,000 prisoners were employed in timber-cutting, hauling, and working in the sawmills.

†   The Kuloy camp group was located in the forests a hundred miles to the south-west of Kotlas.

Mass shootings

Over on the western shores of the White Sea, the casualty rate in the Solovki camps had reached such heights that the authorities had to step in. It cost money to ship prisoners north, and if too many died, productivity fell. Staff were disciplined and some were even shot. But if anyone had thought that the purge of the Solovki staff was a sign of a softening of attitude towards the 'zeks' (prisoners) on the part of the gulag administration, they were mistaken. A few months later, in the summer of 1930, Kitchin was present when the new gulag head, Lazar Kogan,* arrived for an inspection. His arrival in Ust Sysolsk was to have terrible consequences:

In August a telegram suddenly came from Kotlas stating that Comrade Kogan, chief of all the penal camps in the USSR, newly appointed by Moscow, was on his way to Ust Sysolsk accompanied by the plenipotentiary of the OGPU in the Northern area, Comrade Shiyron … At their noon-day meal the commanders discussed the question of the eighteen newly-born infants and the thirty more that were expected. The camp regulations contained no instructions fitting the case and a decision had to be made without delay. Should the infants be left with their mothers or should the mothers be sent on to remote district camps and a sort of camp crèche be organized for the care of the infants? The latter decision prevailed.

At two o'clock the high commander began inspecting the departments … Kogan stopped at the desk of one clerk and asked him the usual questions while his secretary made notes of the answers. The prisoners did not know the purpose of these notes, but as usual hoped that they would bring some change for the better. Not wishing to stand at attention before the Chekists, I had made a timely exit and had gone to the store-rooms. When I came back I was told that the names of seventeen clerks had been included in a special list. Later in the evening their fate was announced. The high commander had ordered all of them to be transferred to manual labour, since they were all serving terms on charges of counter-revolution. For some, such a change of working conditions amounted to a death sentence.

---

*   Kogan was also head of construction on the White Sea Canal from 1930–32 and, in August 1936, he was appointed Deputy People's Commissar of Forestry. Like many senior OGPU/NKVD officials, he fell in the purges, being arrested in December 1938 and shot in May 1939.

On August 8, 1930, a list of names of eighty-two prisoners was made public. The eighty-two had been ordered to be shot on various charges, such as sabotage, attempts at escape, agitation against the authorities, refusal to work, etc. The list carried a note to the effect that the order had been executed. It was signed: Kogan.

We combed the death-list. I noticed the names of some of my former friends. The amiable and amusing Petkin, who had been arrested suddenly some three weeks before Kogan's arrival, headed the list. My cell-mate from the Lefortovsky prison, Timofeyich, was among them for having twice attempted to escape from the Uftug timber-works. So was my former pupil, the Lettish [Latvian] officer Baltrusevich, who had stubbornly refused to do any kind of work ever since his arrival and until the day he was shot.[3]

At various points, Kitchin's testimony confirms details which were reported in the Western press. One of these concerns the attempts of the prisoners to alert the outside world to their plight:

At Archangel the prisoners of our camp district were employed at various tasks, but chiefly in loading timber for export. All export timber was loaded on the ships by prisoners. Reports came from Archangel concerning fabulous escapes of prisoners. Prisoners tried to communicate with the outer world by means of inscriptions on the exported timber, calling attention to the fact that it was produced by convict labour, and to their dire living conditions.[4]

The *Manchester Guardian* had reported just such a message in August 1930:

Messages scribbled on logs discharged from the Greek steamer Dorothea now at Hartlepool suggest that convict labour is employed in loading timber at Russian ports. One message interpreted reads: 'I am an orthodox Christian, and all of us believers in God. Government are trying to destroy it. We are anxiously waiting for our liberty.' Some words are illegible. A member of the crew stated that a number of priests were among the workers whose condition, he said, was pitiable.'

Deception and the Molotov evacuation

In 1931, in correspondence between the British Embassy in Moscow and the Foreign Office, Sir Esmond Ovey reported that prisoners were being moved

en masse away from the public gaze in the timber camp areas.[5] There was talk
of foreign reporters being allowed into the Northern region to see that there
was no slave labour. George Kitchin witnessed the other side of this at close
quarters and, once again, his position within the administration meant that
he knew the consequences of the rush to cover all traces of the camps: over
1,300 prisoners died.

Early in 1931 the Soviet press began printing more and more articles dealing
with the agitation in New York and London against the importation of Soviet
goods produced by penal or forced labor, particularly in the lumber industry.
The Soviet papers had never once admitted that penal labor was actually employed. The Government cared little that the employment of penal labor cast
a shadow on its reputation, but was concerned with the threat that Europe and
America might forbid the import of Soviet timber. Such an embargo would
seriously affect the foreign exchange balance, needed to pay for the machinery bought abroad for the Five-Year Plan. In the beginning of February, the
situation became acute. An embargo by the Western countries on the import
of Soviet timber and other products seemed imminent. The tension was transmitted to our camps. We could feel that important changes were impending.

In February 1931, a meeting of all prisoners was called and a camp officer
read out a resolution which had been prepared in advance:

The resolution referred to the shameful and baseless agitation against the Soviets, stated that the prisoners were satisfied with their living conditions, liked
their food, were well treated, and were eager to give all their strength to the
country so that it might successfully complete the Five-Year Plan.

The officer who had read it then addressed them all:

'Tomorrow, citizens, this paper will be handed around for your signatures.
Tonight we shall vote on it. Let anyone who opposes the resolution raise his
hand. Nobody. It is carried unanimously,' he solemnly declared. 'Has anybody
abstained from voting? Nobody again? That's fine.' With a look of importance,
as if a real vote had just been taken, [the officer] sat down and kept staring

at the assembled prisoners with a self-satisfied air. As we were told later, the meeting had been called in accordance with instructions from Moscow, but we did not know for what purpose. Similar meetings took place at all the work posts, identical resolutions were read, voted on, signed by the prisoners, and returned to Moscow, to serve as positive proof, if occasion required.

The prisoners had no idea what was going on, but a week later all became clear:

A week after the meeting had taken place the real explanation of the existing tension was given. A secret code telegram was received from the head-office in Moscow instructing us to liquidate our camp completely in three days, and to do it in such a manner that not a trace should remain. Moscow faced the probability of having to admit a foreign investigating commission and had decided to erase all evidence of the existence of penal camps.

A veritable panic ensued. The usual Bolshevik methods were employed for the liquidation. Telegrams were sent to all work posts to stop operations within twenty-four hours, to gather the prisoners at evacuation centres, to efface all external marks of the penal camps, such as barbed-wire enclosures, watch-turrets and signboards; for all officials to dress in civilian clothes, to disarm the guards, and to wait for further instructions.

In reply to these instructions, many telegrams were received stating that it was impossible to execute the orders in so short a time, that there were not enough horses to effect the evacuation, that the sick would have to be left in the forest, etc. [The commandant] answered that whoever failed to execute his orders within the stipulated time would be shot.

Pandemonium broke loose. At the Kotlas Transfer Station* the double barbed-wire enclosure was speedily removed, the shop equipment was packed. The crowded barracks were filled to overflowing by the influx of prisoners evacuated from the Uftug forest.

From all sides the forest workers were marching in groups to Solvychegodsk. They carried government equipment in addition to their own belongings. Those seriously ill were crowded on sleds, the sick who could still walk

---

*   Or 'transit camp'. The camp system was based around main transit camps, which housed the central camp, administration for the region and received prisoners before sending them on to other camps within their jurisdiction.

followed in the rear. Some of the sick died en route and were buried in the forest.

The situation at Archangel was even worse. The evacuation of the thirty thousand prisoners working there required eight hundred railway cars. None was available and the prisoners were loaded on old discarded freight and flat cars. Trains picked up groups of prisoners at the stations to which they had been forced to march from their remote outposts. While waiting for the trains, they spent several nights in the forest, hungry and freezing. Prisoners suffering from fever, scurvy or tuberculosis formed no exception, and endured the same privations. Many men died during the mad rush of the evacuation. There were also many attempts to escape, but the cordon of guards had not yet been lifted and most of the fugitives were caught.

In order to show his zeal and to merit praise by his superiors, Okunev, the commander of the Archangel camp peremptorily ordered all prisoners to leave the barracks, removed the barbed-wire enclosure, reversed the signboards and painted new names on them, calling the old penal camp buildings schools, clubs, rest-rooms, etc. His ingenious plan cost the lives of many prisoners. They spent many days in the open waiting for cars near the railway station and suffered great privations. At the end of the year, it was learned that the evacuation of Archangel and Uftug cost thirteen hundred and seventy lives.

The Kotlas Transfer Station was transfigured. The harsh-looking barbed-wire fence had disappeared, the old sign over the gates was replaced by a new one, telling the visitor that he is approaching the dormitories of 'Severoles' workers.* The new sign on the warehouses designated them as 'Warehouses of the Penug-Syktyvkar Railroad Under Construction';† to all telephone calls, the Transfer Station office responded: 'Railroad construction office talking.'

A telegram was received from Archangel stating that the evacuation had been completed on time as ordered and that no outward sign of a penal camp remained. The transformation was thorough and complete both at Kotlas and at Archangel. A commission of foreign investigators could now be freely admitted. In exactly the same manner the evacuation was carried out at the

---

*   Severoles was the Soviet timber production company, and these dormitories were presented as barracks for its employees.

†   Molotov had responded to foreign protests over the use of gulag labour in the timber trade by insisting that prisoners were only employed on construction projects that convicts in the West might also be assigned to – in this case, railway building.

Solovetsky camp, both on the islands and on the mainland. All the timber which had been cut was abandoned in the forests.

During the evacuation of the Kotlas hospital, three of the typhus patients who had recently had fresh charges of anti-Soviet agitation in the penal camps brought against them, were dragged out into the nearby forest and there Nazarov, chief of the secret intelligence department, personally shot them. They were immediately buried in a pit which was dug at the place of execution.

Several days after the evacuation the newspapers brought the report of Premier Molotov's speech. Stalin's right-hand man expressed the indignation of the Soviet government at the calumnies spread by its enemies, to the effect that the government was using penal labour in the preparation of timber in the Northern area. He categorically denied this. 'There are no prisoners employed in the timber industry of the Northern area,' said Molotov. He did not deny that penal labour was employed for other purposes, such as road construction. But even in the United States roads were built by prison gangs, so where was the argument? Molotov concluded his speech with the announcement that though the Soviet government would not admit any foreign investigating commission to its territories, it would not oppose visits to the Northern area by foreign consuls or newspaper correspondents.

Molotov did not lie. At that moment the evacuation continued and the exploitation of penal labor in the timber-works nearest the railroad line had stopped. He was very careful in his phraseology. He never once mentioned that the work at the timber-bases of the penal camps had been discontinued only a week before.

The foreign consuls knew the real condition of affairs and none of them visited our territories. Several foreign correspondents came to the Archangel region, where they were shown the camp buildings adorned with the new signboards designating them as 'schools,' 'clubs,' etc. These reporters were satisfied that all the reports about convict labor in Soviet Russia were false. They stated in their newspaper articles* that the penal camps did not even exist and that no prisoners worked in the forests. The deception was complete.

Two weeks passed. None of the prisoners were allowed in Kotlas, for there was still fear of a foreign investigation. When this danger was past, all the

---

* E.g. those by Henry Wales of the *Chicago Tribune*.

former conditions were gradually restored, the Transfer Station was again surrounded by a double fence of barbed wire and though the signs still described the buildings as ostensible boarding houses of free workers, the men behind the wire were prisoners who were daily dispatched from the Transfer Station to their new destinations in the penal camps of the Southern and Central regions of the Soviet Union.[6]

The kulak camps

As well as reporting on conditions in which political prisoners were held in the strict regime labour camps, Kitchin witnessed the appalling conditions under which the exiled kulaks ('voluntary colonists') lived and worked.

I was in Solvychegodsk when navigation opened.* Long caravans of barges went up and down the Vychegda River, some carrying winter supplies for the Komi territory and some loaded with sawn timber for export via Archangel. Many barges carried transports of 'voluntary colonists,' once well-to-do peasants who had been deprived of their land and possessions and deported from the central regions. Thousands of these unfortunates went by, men, women and endless numbers of pale, sickly children.

Already in Kotlas I had often observed these so-called 'voluntary colonists'. There they lived at the 'colonists' transfer station, which was situated on an island in the river, some six kilometres from town, and consisted of a hundred barracks designed as quarters for two hundred men each. These barracks were always overcrowded. The station generally sheltered more than forty thousand colonists with their families.† Almost daily large parties of them came and went. The colonists were strictly forbidden to go outside the barbed-wire enclosure. As the only well in camp was emptied to the bottom quite early every morning, the colonists got most of the water they needed from the river, going there twice a day, escorted by guards. It was forbidden to fetch water without an escort, but no announcement to this effect was posted. It was only after nine colonists had been killed by the sentries on watch because they had crawled under the barbed wire to obtain water to quench their thirst that the authorities

---

* I.e. when the rivers thawed in the spring.
† I.e. twenty times the number of people for whom the barracks had been designed.

decided to provide a better supply of water and to post an announcement for-
bidding anybody without escort to pass beyond the barbed wire.

When our penal camp was transferred to Ust-Vym, we found one of the
'voluntary colonists' stations of the Komi territory situated next to our barracks. It consisted of a number of large tents erected in an open field. They
adjoined each other and were surrounded by a barbed-wire fence. Guards
were constantly on watch in two turrets erected for this purpose. Within the
enclosure a multitude of men, women and children swarmed about. They were
never let out of the enclosure and all day long they moved about aimlessly
in the limited space. The women sat in groups nursing their babies, the men
talked to each other or sat about forlornly, while the boys and girls ran about
and tried to play games.

The colonists were given four hundred grams of rye bread daily and nothing else. There were no stoves, so that those who had their own supplies could
not prepare any kind of food. They subsisted on bread and water alone.

The station was under iron discipline. At seven in the morning the commander arrived, accompanied by the doctor's assistant. The women and children were driven into the tents and the men stood in line for inspection. The
commander stopped here and there in front of the lines and from time to time
we could hear his shouts and unprintable swearing. Then he would enter the
tents and instantly the air would resound with the shrieking and howling of
women and the crying of children. The doctor's assistant would carry out of
the tents the bodies of children who had died during the night, the crying
mothers would follow him to the gate where the cart was waiting. Some of
them frantically grabbed the doctor by the arms, tore their hair, fell on their
knees, begged, implored and, when they were finally dragged away by the
guards, threw themselves on the ground and gave way to heartrending sobs.

The men stood in line a little way off and did not move. The slightest resistance was considered rioting and was punished by shooting. They knew it.

After the inspection tour the children's bodies in the cart were covered with
burlap and were carted away, accompanied by the doctor's assistant, the weeping and shrieking mothers, several colonists armed with picks and shovels and
by some armed guards. They were taken to a place about half a kilometre from
the station. Quickly a hole would be dug and a little mound would appear next
to the others. There were a great number of these little mounds in the field and

from our window they looked like a natural undulation of the ground. The children died like flies.

It was strictly forbidden to go outside the barbed-wire enclosure, and sentries shot from the turrets without warning. In spite of this, many of the unfortunates were driven by hunger to brave the danger. During the night the exhausted faces of bearded peasants and the pale faces of their poor wives appeared at our windows and they would beg for a bit of food, 'in the name of Christ.' We shared what little we had. Alas, it was but a drop in the ocean.

Large parties of 'colonists' were sent to the North regularly. Loaded with their packs, they trudged along heavily, the children clinging to their mothers' skirts. It was an appalling sight. These parties had to walk hundreds of kilometres, into the very depth of the Zyryan forests, where they had to break ground and start life afresh.[7]

The toll on the political prisoners was, of course, worse. Of the 300 prisoners who came to the penal camps together with Kitchin in December 1929, he was able to discover, by examining the records in February 1932, that only 40 were still alive.[8] Kitchin was himself eventually to become one of these casualties, dying as result of the hardship that he had suffered during his imprisonment.

'Not cargo, but living people'

George Kitchin's memoir may not have been published until 1935, but in 1930–31 there were other eyewitnesses who spoke of the same things, which Kitchin's memoir serves to confirm. Foreign Office officials decided that Molotov would not have offered free access to the region unless the evidence had been removed, and decided against sending anyone to investigate. Needing copy, foreign correspondents in Moscow responded more readily to the offer. Henry Wales of the *Chicago Tribune* went north and, although his cables were censored (and in at least one case altered without his knowledge), his written reports found their way back to the Foreign Office in April.

In the Northern Department, C. H. Bateman wrote that his account was 'one of the most loathsome and horrid things I have ever read'. Hugh Dalton conceded that Wales's account of kulaks barracked in a disused church was 'very revolting', but then sought to downplay it: 'Compare the conditions in the Cairo slums, in parts of India and even in Glasgow. Let not political prejudice localise our humanitarian emotions.'[9]

One modern scholar, historian Lynne Viola, has unearthed important eye-witness evidence from a senior Bolshevik functionary, Vladimir Nikolayevich Tolmachev (1886–1937), who travelled through the Northern Region inspecting the conditions in which the deported kulak families were held. Rare for a Soviet official, he was sufficiently appalled by what he found to record his observations. These comments are taken from Viola's translations of his reports to Moscow, which are in the Soviet archives:

THE MOST EXTREME AND SHARP ISSUE IS HOUSING. People are billeted in 750 barracks, hastily assembled from logs. The crowding is unbelievable – there are places where each person has one-tenth of a square metre of living space in multi-tiered bunks (the space is smaller than a coffin). There are no floors in the barracks, the roofs are made of poles and loosely sprinkled hay and crumbled mud. As a rule, the temperature does not go above 4 degrees. [Everything] is lice-ridden. Along with the miserly feeding, and for many almost nothing, all this creates colossal [rates of] illness, and death among children...

With the advent of spring, the earth in the barracks will melt, [the roofs] will begin to leak and ALL THE POPULATION WILL STICK TOGETHER IN A MUDDY, LIVING, ROTTEN MESS...

In March and the [first] ten days of April [1930], 6,007 of the 8,000 exile children in the city of Arkhangelsk have fallen ill [with] scarlet fever, measles, flu, pneumonia, diphtheria. 587 HAVE DIED. THE GENERAL PERCENT OF ILLNESS [among] CHILDREN IS 85...

Up to now the exiles have fed themselves with their own food, but now only enough is left for a few days and IF WE DO NOT ARRANGE FOOD PROVISIONS, THEN WHOLESALE HUNGER WILL SET IN...

They treat the exiles like dangerous criminals, keeping them in the strictest isolation. This precludes the possibility for them to use their own initiative and independence, leaving us with full responsibility for servicing them. You see, they are not crates, not cargo, but living people...[10]

Tolmachev's humanity cut little ice with Moscow. The Politburo dismissed his appeals for intervention and, in November 1932, he was arrested. Released in 1935 and rearrested in March 1937, he was shot on 20 September 1937.

Another eyewitness

The mass camp clearances, carried out at such cost, had been to enable foreign correspondents to be brought in to be duped by the Soviets' deception. Guessing the true state of affairs, but unaware of how extensive the cover-up had been, the British Embassy advised London that it would not be worthwhile to send any staff to the area. W. H. Chamberlin, the *Manchester Guardian* correspondent, did go. In spite of Molotov's declaration in 1931 that foreign correspondents were free to visit the camps, the head of the prison camps at Kem (the headquarters of the Solovetsky Islands camp group) 'curtly refused' Chamberlin's application to visit them, but he managed to see something.

Foreign correspondents' reports were censored, and if smuggled out uncensored and then published, there was a real threat that the author might have his press accreditation withdrawn. So it was not until 1935 that Chamberlin, now out of Russia, could publish his own account of the trip, using extracts from his diary of March 1931:

> Although one's freedom of travel and investigation has a very definite and concrete limitation in the shape of the barbed wire which surrounds the OGPU concentration camps, it is easy by merely travelling through the country, seeing long lines of freight cars packed with prisoners and considerable numbers of men being marched off to work in Kem itself under armed guard, by talking with railroad workers and fellow passengers on trains, to find abundant confirmation of the general impression in Moscow: that Karelia has been used as a place of exile and forced labour on a gigantic scale.[11]

CHAPTER 31

THE ANTI-SLAVERY SOCIETY INVESTIGATION

The conscience of the world is outraged by this horror.
OLIVER LOCKER-LAMPSON, CONSERVATIVE MP

All this tirade about forced labour in Russia is simply a ramp in order to prejudice the marketing of Russian timber in this country.
ROBERT A. TAYLOR, LABOUR MP

Undeterred by William Graham's obduracy in the 25 March debate, opposition MPs continued to draw attention to the plight of those in the timber camps. Oliver Locker-Lampson launched his own attempt on 21 April.[1] The device he used was a Ten Minute Rule Bill, which allows one ten-minute speech from a backbencher of either side, with the possibility of a second speech from the other side, before the subject is put to a vote. Such bills are not expected to succeed, but are used to publicise an issue which particularly concerns the proposer. Locker-Lampson revisited the by now well-worn arguments for government action:

> I wish to be entirely non-party, seeing that this is not a party question at all. It rises above party questions into the realm of right and wrong. It is a question of ethics as well as of economics; it is a question of honour as well as of trade … Which party is it who professes to be the keenest against sweating? We know that hon. Members opposite are always advocating a further extension

of anti-sweating legislation. Will they remember that when they are dealing with goods which come from Russia?

We have won the fight for freedom on every front in our history – economic, political and religious. It was English voices raised in this House that sounded the death-knell of black slavery across the seas. It was 300,000 working people of the United Kingdom, 300,000 citizens in the time of Wilberforce who went without sugar for years sooner than encourage slave labour in the West Indies. They were people who would be called Socialists today.

All I ask is that the Socialists of today should raise the voice of protest against the entry of these goods into our markets.

That slavery has been proved, and it is the duty of every honest citizen to stamp it out. The conscience of the world is outraged by this horror. It is cowardly, it is un-English, it is caddish to encourage it one moment longer.

The appeal fell on deaf ears. The reply for the government was given by Robert A. Taylor, who had been one of the guests at the dinner which Dalton gave for Sir Esmond Ovey before he left for Moscow in December 1929. Taylor had also been present at the dinner given in the House of Commons in May 1927 by Labour friends of the Soviet Union for Arcos trade officials and Soviet diplomats just before their expulsion. When he died, a few months after this debate, Taylor's contribution to the Anglo-Soviet relations, which included devoting his maiden speech to their cause, was significant enough to be acknowledged by a tribute from Ivan Maisky, the Soviet Ambassador, read out at his funeral in 1934.[2] Maisky and his Moscow masters would have been delighted with the spirited defence Taylor now raised on their behalf:

> The hon. and gallant Member has used the opportunity in moving to introduce a Bill under the 10 Minutes' Rule to make a very thinly-disguised attack upon Russia. ... In India, Africa and the West Indies you will find conditions even worse than those existing among the industrial classes of Soviet Russia. If hon. Members opposite are honest, they will be anxious to deal with goods produced by forced labour whether produced in Russia or in the British Empire.

It was the argument that the Board of Trade had already dismissed. After referring to E. A. Ferguson's much-publicised letter to the *Manchester Guardian*[3] and another report which declared that the majority of the affidavits cited by the protesters were forged, Taylor was dismissive:

> All this tirade about forced labour in Russia, particularly with regard to timber, is simply a ramp in order to prejudice the marketing of Russian timber in this country. This is simply a propagandist effort in order to stir up ill-will and hostility, and to prevent the development of possible economic relations.

The Anti-Slavery Society Inquiry

The Anti-Slavery and Aborigines Protection Society remains today, as Anti-Slavery International, one of the oldest human rights organisations in the world. It was founded in 1839 and the following year convened the world's first anti-slavery convention in London. In 1890, it helped to establish the Brussels Act, which enlarged the scope of anti-slavery legislation and it campaigned strongly against slavery in the Belgian Congo. In 1920, it helped to end the indentured labour system in the British colonies, particularly the use of Indian and Chinese 'coolies', and in 1922, it successfully lobbied for the League of Nations inquiry into slavery which resulted in the 1926 Slavery Convention. It was therefore natural that the Anti-Slavery Society should take particular note of the timber affair. As Rev. John H. Harris of the Society wrote to a supporter:

> Our Committee cannot ignore these charges, because if they are established, they most certainly are a violation of the Conventions which we had been instrumental in getting past in the League of Nations, for although Russia is not a member of the League, we are apparently profiting from these conditions.[4]

On 21 January 1931, the Society announced that it had commissioned an independent inquiry into forced labour in the Russian timber export industry, in association with the Howard League for Penal Reform, another leading human rights organisation. The inquiry was to be chaired by an eminent colonial official, Sir Alan Pim, KCIE, and Edward Bateson, a former judge in the Egyptian Mixed Tribunals.* Its terms of reference were to make:

---

* Established in 1875, the Mixed Tribunals were staffed by Egyptian and foreign judges to hear civil and commercial cases between foreigners of different nationalities and between Egyptians and foreigners.

An impartial enquiry on the information available in Great Britain for the purposes of ascertaining under what labour conditions the Russian timber imported into Great Britain is felled and transported; whether they are oppressive and inhuman, and, if so, whether, if British subjects were responsible, the British government might be expected to take action as indicated in the Circular dispatch of Sir Edward Grey* (now Viscount Grey), No.10 of 1913; and in particular to ascertain what classes of labour are employed and to what extent, if any, the industry is carried on by convict of prison labour.

Over the next few months, John Harris's daughter, Miss K. E. Harris, who also worked for the Society, travelled around the country, visiting ports, interviewing timber traders, and searching out seafarers and escaped prisoners who had been in Northern Russia and could testify first-hand to conditions there.

The formality of the terms of reference did not mask the fact that the inquiry's findings were likely to have a direct bearing upon members of the British consortium formed to import Russian timber. No matter how strongly they insisted that their degree of responsibility was only tenuous, or the fact that there were no British Consuls in Archangel or Kem to make such a report to a government which had showed itself completely unwilling to intervene, a past British government had declared that British importing companies could not evade their responsibility for involvement in 'oppressive and inhuman labour conditions' abroad; those who were guilty of trading under such conditions should be exposed or prosecuted. The moral pressure under which timber importers would be if the inquiry found against them would be considerable. The trade was worth £9 million a year (approximately £530 million today). There was a lot at stake.

---

* Sir Edward Grey's dispatch had arisen as a result of a report to the Select Committee of the House of Commons on the Putumayo atrocities, the affair which Bishop Henson of Durham had taken up so publicly. The report revealed widespread slavery, murder and other atrocities committed by rubber traders against the indigenous people of the Putumayo region in Amazonia. The revelations of a damning parliamentary inquiry of the company responsible (which had some British directors) aroused national revulsion. Grey was the Foreign Secretary at the time, and his dispatch became the yardstick which defined the acceptable bounds of operation of British companies trading overseas. It formed an instruction to British consular officers abroad to note in their annual reports to the Foreign Office any details which appeared to indicate that 'labour conditions for which British subjects are responsible in any part of your district are unsatisfactory' and might require further investigation, possibly prosecution, of the companies concerned back in Britain.

It was hardly surprising that Miss Harris found it difficult to persuade those in the timber trade to talk on the record. As she reported to Sir Alan Pim:

From Friday afternoon till Sunday morning I worked at Newcastle and I must confess I was a little disappointed with the result of my efforts. I got an introduction to the firm of Dalgleish, the biggest importers in Newcastle district. I called on the son Mr Peter Dalgleish who has recently visited Russia on behalf of his firm. He said that Press reports concerning Labour conditions at the Russian ports are quite true. In fact they are worse than he has seen reported. He has in his possession photographs, slides, statements and also much information that would be of value to us. But although he is in sympathy with our enquiry, no arguments or persuasion on my part would make him give any information. He admitted quite frankly that he dared not do so, so long as his firm is engaged in importing Russian timber which is the best and cheapest that can be obtained. He told me in confidence that the entire crew of one ship had been dismissed because they protested against the Labour conditions at the Russian ports. I only report this to you to show that we have little hope of securing information from timber importers.[5]

And in a later summary, she confirmed that her experience in Newcastle had been typical:

Timber Importers and Shipbrokers: I found it extremely difficult to secure any information from these people. They were very nervous of giving any information as they considered it might damage their relations with Russia. They find the trade very profitable because the Russian timber is the cheapest and best on the market, and many of the firms have taken on contracts for large amounts of the timber.[6]

She did not fare much better in her attempts to get information from ships' crews either: 'I found it very difficult to get any information from this source. None of the crews of foreign ships would tell us anything although I tried on several occasions.'[7] Eventually, one or two provided her with useful information. She was more successful in finding Russian eyewitnesses who were prepared to talk. After diligent enquiries with local police and 'Poor Law' institutions, she tracked down a number of former Russian camp inmates who had managed to escape on timber ships. Stowaways were found in Aberdeen, North Shields, Sunderland and Hull, and arrangements were quickly made for them to be interviewed under oath.

Relations with MPs

Over the years, John Harris's work for the society, not least his involvement in the Congo campaign and Putumayo inquiry, had brought him into regular contact with members of Parliament, and Harris kept up correspondence with some of those. Carlyon Bellairs passed on copies of the affidavits which he had acquired, together with a rare written confirmation from a shipping firm in Liverpool: 'With reference to cargoes of Russian Timber ... have to inform you that, speaking with several of our Captains and Mates, we are informed by them that all timber is loaded by prisoners (mostly political) and not by voluntary labour'.[8]

Information went both ways: Harris's daughter passed copies of the stowaways' statements to Sir Arthur Steel-Maitland MP, who subsequently drew attention to the Society's forthcoming report in the Commons;[9] Harris kept Sir Austen Chamberlain, the former Conservative Foreign Secretary, advised too. When Chamberlain replied, thanking Harris for a copy of a letter, he also expressed the consternation that many of his colleagues felt about the affair:

> I confess that I am completely puzzled by the attitude which so many of the Labour Party assume in this matter of the conditions of Russian labour. The evidence accumulates that they are really indistinguishable from slavery and I cannot see what advantage the Labour Party hopes to reap by their callous indifference of them.[10]

Chamberlain added that he hoped that the Society's report would appear soon. Harris wrote to Pim and Bateson, explaining the pressure which he felt from Chamberlain and others, and suggested that they issue a preliminary statement. On 25 February, he attached one which he had already drafted for them in preparation for the next Committee meeting. It concluded:

> Our enquiry is still very far from complete. But from the affidavits which we

have taken and from the interviews which we have had with those competent to speak from personal experience, there can be no doubt that timber being brought into this country is being produced under conditions which can only be described as servile conditions, attended by great hardships and even cruelty.[11]

Neither Pim nor Bateson was prepared to be that hasty, and turned down Harris's suggestion.

The report was eventually released in typescript to interested parties in mid-May and published on 5 June 1931. It was extensive, running to 132 pages, and it completely rejected the denials of Soviet spokesmen and British apologists, confirming that Russian timber exports were widely cut and loaded by prison and forced labour.

The report

The report reviewed the evidence in three parts: (i) Soviet press reports and legal decrees, (ii) British eyewitnesses (principally seafarers), and (iii) evidence from escaped prisoners themselves. The investigators concluded that prisoners were extensively involved in timber production for export not only in Karelia (the location of the Solovetsky Islands) to the west of the White Sea, but also in the Northern Region around Archangel. The eyewitness accounts of British merchant seafarers and escaped prisoners interviewed by the panel were judged to corroborate this. The report also confirmed the widespread use of kulak labour (as well as prison labour), and that much of the so-called 'voluntary' labour was actually forced, using either kulaks or compulsorily conscripted local inhabitants. (Kitchin was to note that the kulaks were re-designated 'voluntary colonists' but the deception had not fooled the investigators.)

Among the primary Soviet documentary evidence cited by Pim and Bateson, was an article from *Trud,* the newspaper of the Soviet trade unions, dated 18 February 1931:

Foaming at the mouth, they [the imperialist countries] howl at our recent labour laws, stand up for the *kulaks, whose labour we are utilising for timber collections*. This employment of the kulaks in timber collections they represent as forced labour, not desiring to notice with what an example the leniency the Soviet power is treating its class enemies. Capitalist countries physically destroy such enemies. But the Soviet power, having conquered its class enemies and destroying the kulaks as a class, makes it possible for the kulaks as individuals to work on timber collections and to earn a living by productive labour. (My italics.)[12]

Pim and Bateson concluded that 'the essential point in this article is the candid admission that kulak labour is being largely used in timber collection'. On the subject of kulak pay, they write elsewhere in the report that, in spite of Soviet insistences to the contrary, it was 'doubtful' that they were being paid, even at a reduced rate. Other incriminating statements by leading members of the Soviet government had already been reproduced in the British press and were added to the report. One of these was an article by Karl Radek, reprinted in the Glasgow ILP newspaper *Forward* on 14 March 1931, which explicitly confirmed that the kulaks' labour was compulsory:

[Foreign critics] pick out those cases where compulsory work does exist in the USSR and generalise them, in order to represent the whole of our labour system as a system of compulsory labour. We have never concealed the fact *that we apply compulsion to the representatives of the abolished class.* We are liquidating the kulaks as a class by means of a complete collectivisation of peasant farming. This is a fact which we have never concealed. (My italics.)[13]

Documentary evidence of the use of prisoners to load ships was provided by the text of a printed notice which had been issued by a Soviet trade agency in February 1930. It showed that on 1 January 1930, SLON, the acronym for the Solovetsky prison camp group, had supplied 2,500 prisoners to load vessels in Leningrad. A further 'contract' for the supply of 400 more prisoners had been signed, and 5,000–6,000 more were to be provided that season.[14]

In the light of articles which had appeared in the Soviet press, the inquiry concluded 'that large numbers of [kulaks] had been forced to labour in the timber industry'. They believed that the total number of kulaks involved in the dekulakisation campaign 'probably considerably exceeded the estimate of five millions'.[15] Of these, they agreed that 'very large numbers were undoubtedly exiled to remote parts of the USSR', and that 'once settled there they must of necessity work in the forests for a living'. They also pointed out the immense suffering that was involved: 'Apart from the hardships involved in having to start life afresh under very difficult conditions in the northern forests, the arrangements made for their transfer appear to have been such as to have caused great suffering and *in all probability heavy mortality, more especially among the children.*' (My italics.)[16]

The inquiry's finding that prisoners from labour camps (kulaks among them) and kulaks in the lesser labour colonies were cutting timber in the forests had been the first step. The next stage had been to establish if the logs (cut by prisoners or by free labour) were then handled by convict or forced labour after they had been floated downstream to sawmills and ports and, finally, if the finished timber was then exported. On every count Pim and Bateson found this to be case.

Eyewitness evidence – escaped prisoners

Pim and Bateson devoted forty of the 132 pages of their report to an analysis of the testimonies of six escaped prisoners. A further twenty pages were taken up by statements from British Merchant Navy officers and a summary of all the eyewitness accounts, both Russian and British. In all, these contributions took up almost half of the report. The witnesses who appeared before the inquiry did so on condition of anonymity, not least to protect their surviving relatives in Russia. The report therefore refers to them as witnesses 'A' to 'E'. The archives of the society contain the transcripts of their original statements and we can now put names to them. Their statements are examined in greater detail in Appendix 4. What follows are brief extracts:

Archangel – 'witness C' (Ivan Kostalin)

Among the prisoners were many church ministers, priests of the Orthodox Church and others. The priests, however, were not allowed on board the foreign ships and they worked in the cleaning of the timber … Some of the men could not complete their tasks and they used to sometimes to fall under the weight of the logs, and then the guards would beat them, as I have myself seen several times, usually with their fists, but I have seen them strike prisoners with the butts of their rifles. If prisoners were unable to work they were sometimes put into

solitary confinement [without food], and many of them died. The general opinion of all the prisoners was that they were only there for a certain time, and that
it was not intended they should live to serve the full term of their imprisonment.

So far as I know the only labour which was not forced labour was that of
the few experts in the sorting of the wood. At the Point [camp] at which I was
working there were only two of these men. I know that they were free workers,
but I do not know what they were paid. No one else was paid anything. According to the Soviet law no person can be sent to a prison camp for less than
three years or more than ten. Sentences of more than ten years are not given,
as the maximum penalty then is that of being shot.[17]

Solovetsky Islands – witness 'F' (Ivan Kolomoetz)

The work on which we were employed was felling and stripping of trees and
cutting them into lengths to serve as pit props. Work commenced at sunrise
and ended when the task was finished or when it was too dark to work ... Logs
were conveyed to the banks of the river, and were made into rafts to be floated
down the river to Sinouka, where they were loaded onto ships.

There was one doctor, with an assistant, for the 300 people in the camp, but
the supply of medicines was very scanty – many of us suffered from internal
troubles and from scurvy. A number of men died, but I do not know how many.
Out of 25 that came with me, only 16 were alive when I left.[*] They died from
hunger and cold ... While I was there I know of three men being shot. One of
them belonged to my group ... Each of the men shot had good warm clothing:
the guard in each case sent the man off to pick berries and reported to the
commandant that the prisoner was shot attempting to escape. The group to
which the prisoner belonged had to confirm the statement of the guard. If we
had not done so we would have been shot in the same manner. The guards all
belonged to the Tcheka.

After two years in this camp I was taken ill with scurvy: I could not walk
and was therefore sent to Solovki. From the steamer at Solovki I was carried
in a buggy to the temporary hospital. There were about 30 men in hospital,
and in six days we had no medical help ... On the seventh day the doctor came

---

[*]   This amounted to a mortality rate of almost a third over about twenty months.

round and put a mark against my name and those of five other men, saying that we were to be taken to the pit (Yama) as being incurable. We all knew that being taken to Yama meant that we would be done away with and buried. I tried to explain that I was not dying, and was sure that I would recover, but the doctor would not listen to me. At about 12 o'clock on the same day one of the prisoners, whose duty it was to take the incurable cases to the pit, told me there was a parcel for me at the office ... Food, blankets and clothing ... The doctor asked if I would sell him my blanket; I said he could have it for nothing, because I was to go to the pit. The doctor was glad to get the blanket, and I also gave him a part of my food parcel. He then told me that I should be sent to the hospital in Kem and that if anybody asked me how I got there I should say that he was my cousin. That night I was put on a steamer, and taken to a hospital at Kem. I was there for two weeks, the food was good and I soon recovered.[18]

British seafarers

British seafarers who could be persuaded to give evidence told the same story. The extract that follows comes from a British second officer who made a voyage to Kem in the autumn of 1930. He kept a diary which the investigators were able to view, to confirm that his statement was corroborated by the diary entries.

Our pier was inside the barbed wire enclosure of the prison camp. We were only half a minute's walk from the barracks ... When we arrived a great deal of wood was already stacked in the camp. It came down in rafts and was taken out of the water by the prisoners. They also barked it in the camps ... This was done about 100 yards away from the pier, and the wood was cut into planks with crosscut saws ... [Prisoners] were brought down under guard every morning, and one guard remained all day on the ship ... Round the barbed wire enclosure of the camp there were elevated sentry posts, every two or three hundred yards, in which armed guards were posted. There were about two dozen barracks in the camp, and I should estimate the number of prisoners at 300 or 400. There was another large camp (much larger than ours) near the village, which was about 20 minutes' walk away. ...

Quite a number (about a dozen) [of the prisoners] could speak English and a good many had been to the United States. Several of them told my mate and myself that they were in prison because they would not turn Communists. Five or six men told us this. We could not, of course, say anything about the others, who could not speak English. Most of them looked poorly, and a good many of them had coughs, and many were dejected and looked as though they did not care what happened. Some were clean and fairly tidy, but a great many looked as if they never washed. One or two had sores, but this was not very marked. Most of them looked very frail, as though a good gust of wind would blow them off their feet. They were not allowed to take food from us, but we gave them what we could, and they used to eat it ravenously.[19]

Pim and Bateson conclude

The report found that the denials that prison labour had been used in the export timber trade were untrue. Regular Soviet and British Labour protestations that prisoners working in the Archangel region were only producing for the domestic, not export, market were firmly dismissed:

We have shown from the evidence of a reliable British witness, that a penal camp containing about 800 prisoners was located in the Dwina area in the autumn of 1930. The prisoners were employed on lumbering, which must have been for export, as the timber was floated down the Dwina ... It is most improbable that any timber produced near Archangel could be for internal consumption in Russia.[20]

Pim and Bateson determined that four types of labour were used in the Soviet export timber trade – that of local inhabitants, labour which rural Soviets were required to supply, labour which was compulsorily transferred from other industries, kulaks exiled to the north and compelled to work in the timber industry, which was the sole source of occupation, and prisoners. The report concluded: 'To sum up the evidence with regard to the conditions under which labourers were employed on loading ships ... it appears that British and other foreign vessels were loaded with timber at the ports of northern Russia in the export season of 1930 partly by Russian political prisoners'.[21]

And that, in terms of Sir Edward Grey's dispatch:

We are of the opinion that [in the case of the kulaks and prisoners], had the

British subjects been responsible and had there been a British consul in Archangel in 1930 it would have been his duty to report to his Majesty's government the existence of the conditions which we have described.[22]

They also added that, after reviewing the evidence, they believed that Edward Harby, one of the leading pro-Soviet witnesses, was lying. Harby had written to the *Manchester Guardian* on 2 January 1931, saying that he had spent nine months in the Archangel area and seen no prisoners employed in the export timber industry. His letter had been widely quoted as authoritative since then. Harby had been invited to appear to give evidence to the investigators but had refused, accusing the inquiry of being politically motivated.[*]

Government response

In the Foreign Office, Vansittart accepted the report without question, adding that there was even 'fresher and worse evidence available' which the report had not mentioned.[23] But as far as the government's response was concerned, he counselled against any acknowledgement of its contents – otherwise 'the Opposition would naturally take up the damning and revolting portions and ask us what we were going to do about them … and we should have abandoned the ground hitherto safely occupied'. Instead, he suggested that the government maintain the line that 'we consider no enquiry satisfactory in the absence and denial of full local facilities'.[24] In other words, the report was to be ignored.

This is exactly what happened. On 2 June, Carlyon Bellairs asked Henderson if the Cabinet had considered the report and what action it proposed to take. Henderson said that the Cabinet had not read it, that it would not be doing so, and that therefore the subject of a response to it did not arise. Asked to find time for its contents to be debated in the Commons, he refused.[25]

Disinformation

Tragically, Soviet disinformation resulted in one small error in the report, and it is this that was seized upon by everyone combing through the text in the hope of finding an excuse to ignore it. Just before reaching their final

---

[*]   For Harby's letter and a discussion of its authenticity, see Appendix 2.

conclusion, Pim and Bateson stated that 'local inhabitants, for whom [logging] is a customary seasonal occupation ... furnished the *bulk* of the labour required and for this class the conditions were certainly not worse than they were before the war'. (My italics.) [26] This assertion seems to be derived partly from an unsubstantiated statement by J. Yanson, the Soviet chairman of the British office of Arcos, that pay for volunteer timber fellers 'had improved since the war', coupled with a deliberate deception that had been devised by the Soviets to mask the numbers of kulaks in the north, which George Kitchin was later to expose as a Soviet ruse to deceive the West: 'The exiled "kulaks" were designated as "voluntary colonists". It [the deception] replaced the hundred thousand prisoners employed in the winter of 1930–31 with two hundred thousand 'voluntary colonists' and thus stopped foreign protests.' [27]

The mistaken inclusion of this disinformation was then picked up in the introduction, written by Lord Buckmaster, the former Liberal Lord Chancellor. The report contained 132 pages of damning evidence. Its introduction was sixty-five lines long of which ten lines (one sixth), were taken up by the following paragraph:

> That some of the labour in the timber camps is not voluntary is clearly established but the greater part of it is drawn from people accustomed to the work, who work freely and at wages and under conditions fixed after consultation with their trade unions. That these wages and conditions are such as no British workman would dream of accepting is certainly true, but it cannot be asserted that they are worse than, or even as bad as, conditions formerly existing in the Russian timber industry.

To give such prominence to the employment of local peasants minimised the plight of the 285,000 deported kulaks[28] and the tens of thousands of political prisoners held in gulag camps in the region, such as the 71,800 in Solovki in January 1931. Moreover, the suggestion that these unfortunates were paid the amounts claimed by the Soviet authorities was dismissed by the report as 'very improbable'.[29] But those who wished to find a reason to ignore the report's damning contents needed to look no further than Buckmaster's unfortunate paragraph – a few lines which were the result of highly effective Soviet disinformation.

In the Lords, it was all that Lord Parmoor needed. He is certain to have read the report carefully and must have been well aware of its overall content before he spoke for the government in the very last debate on the timber camps, prompted by a Private Member's Bill introduced by Lord Phillimore, just three weeks after the report's publication. Parmoor seized upon Buckmaster's paragraph in such a way as to imply that it was typical of the report, rather than a glaring and tragic exception. That debate and Parmoor's speech are discussed more fully in Chapter 32.

Press reaction

The report was covered widely and far more accurately in the regional press, a more weighty voice in those days than it is now. Articles appeared in the *Yorkshire Herald*, *Yorkshire Post*, *Huddersfield Daily Examiner*, *Liverpool Post*, *Western Daily Press*, and *Newcastle Evening Chronicle*, among others. The coverage was universally sympathetic to the timber camp labourers and outraged: the *Sunday Referee* called the report's findings 'appalling'; the *Brighton & Hove Gazette* declared that, 'if the conditions revealed in this report are not slavery, the word has no meaning', the *Nottingham Guardian* spoke of 'inhuman conditions'; and the *Burton Daily Mail* called it a 'scandal'.[30]

The response in the Labour press and political journals was of a different order. The *Manchester Guardian* usually downplayed Soviet excesses; only two weeks before its leader column had kept true to form:

Are there not things to be learnt from the social experiment now taking place in Russia? May it not be that when the memory of pre-war tyranny had faded a little; when the revenge motive, now understandably dominant, has died down somewhat; when the revolution is a generation old, that something fine and permanent will be found to have come from the astonishing energy and enthusiasm that have lately been manifested in Russia?

The world is not so well ordered that we can afford to ignore experiment. With our own economic chaos it ill becomes us to play the Pharisee even in regard to applied Communism.[31]

It was therefore surprising that the first part of its article on the report seemed to indicate a softening of its usual line. It described the case that prisoners were used to load timber for export as 'sufficiently proved', adding that the story told by the report 'is one which any man, Tory, Liberal or Socialist, will read with grief and indignation'. But then it unravelled, with the lamest of arguments for inaction: 'That does not empower this or any British Government to intervene. Intervention might, if successful, have the effect of worsening conditions in the timber camps.' It ended with a bizarre justification for ignoring the plight of those in the camps by adding 'is it the only brutal Government in Europe?'[32]

Olivier and Angell, the *New Statesman and Nation* **and** *The Spectator*
Sydney (Lord) Olivier was a former Cabinet minister and one of the four early leaders of the Fabian Society (itself a founder of the Labour Party, the *New Statesman* and the LSE), alongside Sidney Webb, George Bernard Shaw and Graham Wallas. John Harris appears to have known him, most likely because of Olivier's lengthy connection to the West Indies (he was a former Governor of Jamaica) and his involvement in attempts to resolve the problems posed by slavery and colonialism: Olivier had published two books on the subject (*White Capital and Coloured Labour* in 1906 and *The Anatomy of African Misery* in 1927). Harris sent him a copy of the proof of the report before it was publicly available, and might have expected a sympathetic reaction. He was mistaken. Olivier was not impressed: 'Dear Harris, Thanks for the proof of the Russian Forced Labour Report. Will you tell me why this enquiry was undertaken by the Society? On the whole it is rather a flop: [word illegible] and big headlines!'[33] It seems that an investigation of colonial slavery was acceptable, but an inquiry which discredited Soviet slavery was not.

It so happened that it was to Olivier that the *New Statesman and Nation* turned for its review of Anti-Slavery Society report. The leading socialist journal of the day, the *New Statesman and Nation* carried great weight and Olivier, with his reputation on the subject, would have been considered an authoritative reviewer. Choosing Buckmaster's paragraph as the *only* extract quoted in his review, Olivier continued with what appeared to be at least a partial justification of Soviet measures taken against the kulaks and their unfortunate families:

[The authors] report that in their opinion the conditions imposed upon Kulaks in the camps are oppressive, as many of the occupants are unsuited to the type of labour assigned to them, and their exiled state is particularly severe. The Soviet government intends that they should be severe, to punish the Kulak for having led the immoral life of a small farmer or agricultural produce dealer.

They also report that the conditions of labour for the political prisoners were for the same reasons inhumane and oppressive ... The Soviet Government intends that its penal conditions shall be deterrent.[34]

The Spectator's review was written by another eminent Labour figure. Norman Angell, a former journalist who, besides being a Labour MP, was a member of the executive committee of the League of Nations Union; he had been knighted that very year and was to be awarded the Nobel Peace Prize in 1933. From the mid-1930s, he was a prominent campaigner for international action against fascism. Earlier in his career he had described the Russian Revolution as 'an experiment which mankind truly needs'.[35] Whether or not he still held that view, his sympathies still came down, albeit somewhat grudgingly, on the side of the Soviets.

After bringing up the forestry expert J. F. Stewart's 'evidence' yet again (which the report had also completely discounted, though Angell either did not notice or chose to ignore that), the few lines he quoted from the report were again those from Buckmaster's introduction already seized upon by Parmoor and Olivier.

The bulk of Angell's review then descended into an explanation, close to a justification, of Soviet Communists – a people, he explained, who believed themselves to be at war 'as we were fifteen years ago, convinced, with what is in fact a religious passion, that never was a war fought for a higher purpose, a supreme liberation of the human race from economic bondage', beside which 'the purposes of [our] last war, strike them as almost meaningless'. Both sides in the Great War, he argued, had also had 'compulsion' (i.e. conscription, which Angell now implied was little different to the forced labour in the timber camps), and had 'conscribed men, compelled them to kill, [and] if they refused to kill usually shot them'. By comparison, Angell reasoned:

Compulsion under the Soviets does not take the form of compelling men to kill; it does take the form of compelling them to refrain from activities which the

Soviets regard as fatal to the success of that war for the new social order in which they are engaged. The kulaks (among others) are regarded as war enemies, and are treated much as some of the belligerents in war treated prisoners of war. The Soviets cultivate hate of the enemy as we deliberately, thoroughly, cultivated hate of the enemy. In one sense they give the enemy a chance, which we did not. He can cease to be an enemy by showing his readiness to join the Socialist forces.[36]

The idea that the Soviet regime was being more merciful in its treatment of the kulaks than Western nations had been to their opponents in the Great War directly echoed Kalinin's own statement, which the report had carried. Neither reviewer took into account the 30,000 kulaks who had been shot before they had even reached the camps. Angell concluded: 'It may be as wrong-headed and fallacious as you please, but we shall get nowhere by refusing to admit its sincerity ... it serves no purpose whatever to meet those convictions with intolerance or attempted coercion'. In other words, leave the prisoners alone and do nothing to stop the trade; instead, try to understand the Soviets' point of view. Being 'sincere' somehow excused their excesses.

A few weeks later, a sarcastic editorial by Kingsley Martin in the *New Statesman and Nation* showed that even though the Labour press acknowledged the now undeniable reports coming from Russia, it would not condemn them, nor express any sympathy towards the victims:

Mr Winston Churchill, the notorious British agitator (we adopt the phraseology of the *Morning Post* when describing M. Bukharin and other distinguished Russians now in this country) has now decided that disarmament is impossible, because of the menace of Russia. He can see in Russia nothing but a menace ... [He] hates youth and its idealism ...

We have never defended, nor shall we defend, cruelty in Russia or elsewhere, and we believe that, even from its own point of view, the Russian Government has often been quite unnecessarily repressive. That, one may notice, is the view of Stalin ... The actual conflict now proceeding in the villages of Russia does, of course, involve great hardship ... The change in Russia does not ... involve a half of the long drawn-out suffering of our own Industrial Revolution, when whole generations of men, women and children were ruthlessly sacrificed for the sake of the new profits. The laments of the older peasantry read like the heartrending complaints of our own hand-loom weavers, when they too were deprived of their old method of livelihood by more efficient mechanical means.

Why then should we not welcome this attempt to break the ice of ages? We do not hold the same methods are necessary or desirable here, and there is plenty of room for criticising the Soviet Government. There have been and still are excesses. But we see in Russia the one country in the world which is doing great things, which is tackling, in the interests of the many, the problem of economic organisation which we have so far failed to tackle. It seems an opportunity for learning something, not indulging in Churchillian bombast.[37]

Sydney Olivier, Kingsley Martin and Norman Angell could hardly be described as far-left extremists, so close to Moscow that, like the CPGB, they slavishly followed the line dictated by the Comintern. They were eminent, highly respected figures from the heart of the Labour Party. But they all dishonestly ignored the central conclusion of the report, which was that Britain was trading, in enormous quantities, in products manufactured or loaded by convict and forced labour, something which was *already* proscribed under international convention and banned under the spirit, if not the letter, of existing British law.

If that point had been proved, as the investigators insisted it now had been, those reviewing the report in the papers would have had no option, morally, but to agree with its condemnation and to call for the trade to cease. It is hard to imagine the same men urging that African slaves should be left in their fetters lest disturbing the status quo make their lives more miserable, or in some way explaining that their chains were deserved because they were heathen. But Archangel and Kem were not the Amazon or the Congo. And, crucially, it was neither the capitalist Peruvian Amazon Company, nor the Belgian monarch's African enterprise that was under scrutiny, but the conduct of the Socialist Soviet government, towards whom so many in the British Labour movement at that time had offered expressions of support and solidarity. That loyalty seemed too strong to be put aside.

CHAPTER 32

THE LAST ACT: LORD PHILLIMORE'S BILL (MAY–JULY 1931)

On 23 June 1931, Alfred Gough had a heart attack while on the platform in a public meeting, still campaigning on behalf of those in the Soviet prison camps, as he had been tirelessly doing for the previous year and a half. It was his last act in the campaign to which he had given so much. He never recovered and died on 8 October. Others, however, remained to carry on the fight.

As campaigners frequently reminded the government, legislation already existed to ban the import of goods produced by prison labour – the Foreign Prison-Made Goods Act of 1897. From the beginning, the government had put up a number of reasons why the act could not be used (including the suggestion that the gulag camps could not be properly defined as 'prisons'[1]), and all Conservative offers of cooperation to help amend that detail were refused. William Graham repeated that refusal in the Commons on 7 July 1931.[2] Coming just three weeks before the summer recess during which the government collapsed, that refusal became Labour's last word on the matter in the Commons. Soon after that, the very last parliamentary skirmishes on the subject took place in the House of Lords when Lord Phillimore launched his own brief private bill to close the loopholes in the Foreign Prison-Made Goods Act.

Throughout the affair, the government's response to those who appealed for it to use the provisions of the act was that it could not be used to halt the import of Russian timber because its terms were too imprecise. It gave three specific reasons why it was impossible to apply or amend it:

1. The existing act banned the products of 'prison' labour but not 'forced' labour. It would be too hard to determine into which category Russian timber exports fell.
2. Timber camps were not 'prisons' and were therefore not covered by the existing act.
3. A parcel or cargo of timber could not be banned unless it was proven to be *wholly* produced by prison labour.

Lord Phillimore's Bill, the Prevention of Imports of Products of Convict or Forced Labour,[3] was a succinct measure, just under forty lines long, which answered every one of these objections.

'Convict labour', 'forced labour' and the definition of 'prisons'

The bill provided, first, a clear definition of convict labour, as distinct from forced labour, which was drawn wide enough to encompass the Russian labour camps and colonies:

> The expression 'convict labour' means all work or service exacted from any person as a consequence of a conviction before a court of law, or other judicial tribunal, whether the work or service has been performed within or without any prison, penal settlement, people workshop, or penal camp.

When it came to 'forced labour', Phillimore turned to a definition which the government itself had already accepted when Labour had ratified the International Labour Organisation's Forced Labour Convention in 1930: 'The expression "forced labour" means all work or service exacted from any person under the menace of any penalty for its non-performance and for which the said person has not offered himself voluntarily'.

Phillimore's astute use of the ILO's definition placed the government in an embarrassing position. The ILO had been created in 1919, as part of the Treaty of Versailles, to reflect the belief that universal and lasting peace could only be accomplished if it was based upon social justice. Its principles were reinforced by the commitment in article 23a of the League of Nations to 'endeavour to secure and maintain fair and humane conditions of labour for men, women and children, both in their own countries and in all countries to which their commercial and industrial relations extend'.

The British government had ratified the Covenant of the League of Nations, and so article 23a was important in that it specifically addressed the very issue campaigners raised. The government had thus far resisted all appeals to act in accordance with it. Six months previously, in January, when Carlyon Bellairs had pressed them to do so, George Gillett, for the government, had replied that 'His Majesty's Government have come to the conclusion that no useful purpose would be served by referring the matter to the League'.[4] Gough, as chairman of the CPM, had written to Henderson in May 1931, urging the government to oppose the admission of Soviet observers to the League of Nations:

> The Movement urges that before fellowship of this kind can be practised the USSR should be required:
> 1. To release the countless ministers of religion and others who are suffering for religious belief
> 2. [To] cease to discriminate against religious believers
> 3. [To] grant freedom to believers to worship
> 4. [To] restore the right of religious propaganda and church organisation
> 5. [To] cease vexing believers by closing their churches or subjecting these places of worship to crushing taxation
>
> The Christian Protest Movement is further of the opinion that no civilised Government can have relations with the USSR [while it] persists in its cruel enslavement of vast numbers of its people.

While Henderson had replied that he did not 'feel able to endorse or present' Gough's appeal to the League,[5] the fact that the British Labour government had ratified the Forced Labour Convention of 1930, as we have seen, was significant. As British officials had told Margaret Bondfield, MacDonald's new Minister of Labour, soon after she took office, the discussion at the ILO over the Forced Labour Convention 'showed that there was complete agreement on the fundamental principle that forced labour is repugnant to modern public

opinion'.[6] The convention imposed on each member who ratified it an un-
dertaking to suppress the use of forced or compulsory labour in all its forms
within the shortest period. Now, in July 1931, Phillimore's bill proposed to do
just that. The government could hardly oppose it without seeming to renege
on all these obligations.

Onus of proof and empire trade

To respond to the charge that it was impossible to know which part of a load
of timber had been produced by convict labour, the new bill would require
customs only to have a suspicion that *part* of a parcel had been produced
by forced labour. The onus would now be on importers, not anti-slavery
campaigners or protesters, to prove their case. It was a simple alteration in
approach which had already been adopted by United States customs.

The Board of Trade had made it clear in its original memorandum on 5
January 1931 that Labour's oft-repeated defence of the Russian timber trade,
that a ban would adversely harm empire trade too, had little ground in fact.[7]
The other side of the argument, also put forward, was that there may still have
been essential imports which the country needed, but which at that time were
only available from countries which used forced labour to produce them, and
that a ban might block those too.

Phillimore took the latter concern into account and cleverly added a clause
exempting any goods (by implication those produced by forced labour) which
could *not* be produced in the empire and dominions. In other words, if those
same goods could be found in the empire, produced without forced labour,
their import from other nations would be banned. If there was no free-labour
alternative available in the empire, they would then be permitted for import
from elsewhere.

The Foreign Office scrambled to find a trade argument to oppose the Bill
in the debate set for the Lords on 24 June. Seymour, in a department minute
on 13 June, appeared to be casting the net wide to find reasons to defend the
continuance of the Russian imports.

As regards the Bill itself, it may be observed that [the clause banning the
products of forced labour] would apparently cover every country in which
forced labour of any kind exists. In view of the existence of indentured labour

of various kinds in so many countries, to say nothing of domestic slavery, it is probably that the list of countries contemplated in Clause 3 (2) would cover most of Africa, the Arab States, and probably parts, at any rate of Dutch East Indies and other colonial empires.[8]

Seymour's scaremongering about 'indentured labour' was groundless. As one modern authority has observed, by 1929, 'the overseas indentured labour trade involving the British Empire was over and there was little such labour trade elsewhere'.[9] As for the Board of Trade's insistence that the likely impact on empire trade would be negligible, Dalton's solution was simple: 'The B of T brief is, at certain points, in conflict with Mr Seymour's observations. It should be amended.'

Dalton saw the merit of using Seymour's arguments, and added: 'The marked passage in Mr Seymour's Minute is important. It should be embodied prominently in the brief so that the Govt statement should not be concentrated exclusively on Russian conditions.' Opposing the Bill on the grounds that it was technically flawed would present the government as reasonable and objective, allowing it still to express its regret at being unable to intervene, rather than as hard-hearted and deaf to the cries of those suffering in the Russian camps.

In the debate, Parmoor was on classic form. Opening with a condescending reference to his time in the House of Lords alongside Lord Phillimore's father, to put the son firmly in his place, he emphasised how strong was his abhorrence of slave labour and forced labour and how, in his view, the two 'could not really be differentiated'. As his speech progressed, it became clear that, also true to form, such an apparent concession meant nothing. He skirted briefly around the Anti-Slavery Society Report, which he once again misrepresented, dwelling on Buckmaster's unfortunately erroneous comment in its introduction, to reach a conclusion diametrically opposed to the report's own, before accepting it 'entirely'. The government, he insisted, believed that the bill's impact on wider trade meant that it was technically flawed, and would not give its 'assistance and blessing' to a measure which 'quite obviously' would not carry out the purpose that was intended.

Phillimore kept his sense of humour and made it plain that he saw through Parmoor's strategy. After saying how 'greatly honoured' he was that Parmoor had ventured to pay 'so much attention' to his 'few remarks', he suggested that Parmoor had 'shut his eyes when he reached out for the bucket' to cast sand 'into the machinery' by using the empire trade argument:

> How can [he] bring up that objection when he knows perfectly well that his own Government has just agreed that all forced labour in all our mandated territories and non-self-governing Colonies, and so on, for which we are responsible should be immediately and forthwith suppressed or, at any rate, suppressed in the shortest possible time? How can that be a valid objection?[10]

But, as Phillimore knew, the government was way beyond persuasion by logic.

Lord Ponsonby spoke next for the government and was also on his usual form, giving enough ground to defuse the accusation of heartlessness ('We are absolutely in sympathy with the underlying principle of this Bill ... we should like to see forced labour and convict labour abolished'), even acknowledging that 'there is no question that forced labour and convict labour exist in the timber trade in Russia', before rallying, once again, to the Soviets' defence:

> On the other hand, we have been informed by the Soviet Government that, so far as the export of timber is concerned, no convict labour or forced labour is used. Say that this is not true, that they are not speaking the truth. After all, it is a perfectly credible statement.

Ponsonby's statement, as was obvious to all, had no credibility whatsoever. After months of public debate, extensive press coverage, sworn affidavits from escaped prisoners, civil servants' briefs, conclusions in the Cabinet, diplomatic dispatches, and a detailed judge-led investigation by the Anti-Slavery Society, all of which emphatically confirmed the widespread use of prisoners of all types (convict or forced, kulaks, priests or other categories of political prisoners) in the Russian timber export trade, the truth was beyond any doubt. Ponsonby was either lying or deluded.

The debate was reported the day after in the *Manchester Guardian*, which showed that the paper, too, was keeping true to its usual form, insisting that

Phillimore's bill 'arises from the attempt to drape an ethical cloak round a purely interested motive. The Bill is just one more case of [trade] Protection masquerading as virtue.'[11] As Eden had said, the real problem was that the Labour movement as a whole refused to admit what was blindingly obvious to everyone else.

Lord Parmoor told the House that the government would not support the bill if it was passed and was sent to the Commons. The Lords passed it without further debate on 15 July. It was sent to the Commons the next day, where it was allowed to die. Two weeks later, Parliament broke for the summer recess. By the time the recess was over, the Labour government had fallen and a national coalition government had taken its place.

CHAPTER 33

THE BISHOP'S NEMESIS: THE FALL OF THE LABOUR GOVERNMENT (JULY–OCTOBER 1931)

There is a greater question – the moral disgrace involved in our indifference to these horrors, and in being in any degree associated by the Government of this country with some kind of apology for them. That is too terrible for any self-respecting man to contemplate.

I believe that there is a Nemesis upon the kind of moral indifference to which we are tending at this moment.

HERBERT HENSLEY HENSON, BISHOP OF DURHAM, FEBRUARY 1931[1]

In the debate in February 1931, the Bishop of Durham had warned the government that there was 'a Nemesis upon the kind of moral indifference' which it was exercising. His words were to prove strangely prophetic.

On 15 July, the same day on which the House of Lords passed Phillimore's bill, a run on gold began. The Bank of England lost £1.9 million in gold on 15 July, and by the end of the month the losses totalled a staggering £34 million (£2.1 billion today). Ramsay MacDonald returned early from his holiday and spent the next fortnight with a Cabinet committee trying to find a way through the mounting crisis. When he and Snowden, the Chancellor, proposed a budget of cuts, the TUC and half the Cabinet refused to support them. With the encouragement of the King, MacDonald then announced the end of the Labour government and the establishment, in its place, of a National

Government, drawing upon individual members from other parties with the specific aim of forming a coalition for the duration of, and to respond to, the financial crisis.

The Labour Party national executive promptly expelled MacDonald, Snowden, J. H. Thomas, Lord Sankey and the few other Labour MPs who joined him. MacDonald would thereafter go down in Labour history as a 'traitor', almost universally demonised. Clement Attlee, writing over twenty years later with a bitterness that many still shared, described it as 'the greatest betrayal in the political history of this country'.[2] Deserted by the 265 dissenting Labour MPs, a new coalition under MacDonald was formed with the Conservatives, the Liberals and a handful of former Labour MPs. Had MacDonald had the support of all parties, the National Government might have been able to continue without a further election, but he decided under the circumstances to go to the country and seek a fresh mandate for his leadership and the new coalition.

The 1931 General Election

As it prepared for the October General Election, the Labour Party not only came out against their former Prime Minister and Chancellor; its manifesto proposed a socialist programme that was more radical than anything to date. It was hard not to notice the similarity between its pronouncements now and those that were more commonly heard coming from Moscow:

> The Capitalist system has broken down ... The Labour Government was sacrificed to the clamour of Bankers and Financiers. Because it placed the needs of the workers before the demands of the rich, a so-called 'National' Government was installed in its place to wrest from Parliament the authority to satisfy them. [It had achieved what it had] under the intolerable restrictions of its minority position in the House of Commons, frustrated by political intrigues and the class-conscious hostility of the House of Lords and undermined by the organised pressure of business interests.[3]

In the face of the 'impossible task of rebuilding Capitalism', Labour proposed a different solution, one with deliberate echoes of the Soviets' own Five-Year Plan, which had appealed to so many Labour MPs – the planned economy:

The Labour Party ... reaffirms its conviction that Socialism provides the only solution for the evils resulting from unregulated competition and the domination of vested interests. It presses for the extension of public-owned industries and services operated solely in the interests of the people. It works for the substitution of co-ordinated planning for the anarchy of individualistic enterprise.

The Labour Party has no confidence in any attempt to bolster up a bankrupt Capitalism by a system of tariffs. ... [It] urges a better way ... the definite planning of industry and trade so as to produce the highest standard of life for the Nation.

'Socialist reconstruction', another Soviet catchphrase, was thrown in too:

The Labour Party recognises that the present situation calls for bold and rapid actions. The decay of capitalist civilisation brooks no delay. Measures of Socialist reconstruction must be vigorously pressed forward. That is the task to which Labour will lay its hand.

Proposals were then put forward for mass nationalisation:

As a first step, it proposes to reorganise the most important basic industries – Power, Transport, Iron and Steel – as public services owned and controlled in the national interest ... [Regarding the coal industry,] Labour in power will proceed at the first opportunity to the unification of the industry under public ownership and control.

The banking system would follow and even agricultural land would be taken into state ownership:

The Labour Government has already made a real beginning toward the scientific re-organisation of agriculture. The Labour Party will seek to press forward that development. It holds that, for this purpose, the land must be publicly owned and controlled, and much more fully utilised for food production and the provision of employment under good conditions.

It was not quite the Soviet total collectivisation, but a definite step in that direction. A number of people saw the parallels. Philip Snowden, Chancellor of the Exchequer in two Labour Cabinets, who had now been expelled from the Labour Party for taking the same post in the new National Government, observed, in a comment which has earned him a place alongside MacDonald in Labour demonology, that the proposals were 'Bolshevism run mad':

> I hope you have read the election programme of the Labour Party. It is the most fantastic and impracticable programme ever put before the electors. All the derelict industries are to be taken over by the State, and the taxpayer is to shoulder the losses. The banks and financial houses are to be placed under national ownership and control, which means, I suppose, that they are to be run by a joint committee of the Labour Party and the Trades Union Council. Your investments are to be ordered by some board, and your foreign investments are to be mobilised to finance this madcap policy. This is not Socialism. It is Bolshevism run mad. I have been an advocate of sane and evolutionary Socialism for 40 years, but I have always attacked such a revolutionary policy as set out in this manifesto.[4]

The electorate agreed. The result of the October 1931 general election was the biggest landslide in British electoral history, with the national government winning 556 seats and achieving a majority of 500. No party was ever before or afterwards so crushingly defeated at the polls. Labour was not to return to power for fourteen years. When Lloyd George, the Liberal leader who had supported the Labour administration, tried to take his party out of the National Government, his party deserted him, leaving him too, like the few remaining Labour MPs in Westminster, in a political backwater.

The Bishop's 'nemesis' had come.

POSTSCRIPT

The Foreign Office and Russian timber 1931–34

It might be supposed that, with a more sympathetic government in place, a ban on Soviet timber imports would have been shortly forthcoming. Soon after the new parliament began, the Duchess of Atholl, a vocal and leading campaigner on behalf of the persecuted in Russia, who had stepped into the late Prebendary Gough's shoes as joint president of the Christian Protest Movement after his death, urged the new government to intervene:

> Canada, Rumania, Jugoslavia and Bulgaria have practically excluded Soviet goods; but they are not big purchasers and perhaps their embargo makes little difference. Belgium, however, is a bigger purchaser, and she has a system by which she imports only certain Soviet products under licence. Because we are the biggest purchaser of Soviet exports, a tremendous responsibility rests upon us in this matter, and if, after mature deliberation, the Government felt that this was a step that they were ready to take, I believe that other large purchasers of Soviet imports would inevitably be obliged to follow our example.[5]

In early December 1931, Sir Victor Warrender, a government whip, contacted Anthony Eden, who now held the same position that Hugh Dalton had in the previous government – Under-Secretary of State at the Foreign Office. Warrender wanted to know if there would be an objection to the reintroduction of Lord Phillimore's Bill as a Private Member's Bill.

Eden referred the matter to Horace Seymour at the Northern Department. Once again, Foreign Office officials dug in their heels. Seymour opposed it:

> I doubt we should be justified in trying to exert any influence to prevent this bill being introduced as a private bill. The main object would presumably be to give an opportunity for attacks on Russia … It is hardly the moment now to introduce further complications in trade. While it therefore could be awkward for the F.O. to appear to be discouraging the introduction of a bill to deal with slave labour etc, we ought I think to do nothing to encourage its introduction. Debates consisting entirely of adverse comments on foreign countries are of course always awkward.

> The memorandum ended with a final comment added by Eden's secretary:

> Mr Eden will inform Sir V. Warrender that we don't like it but if the board of trade wanted it we would not oppose. 10/12[6]

By October, the Russian northern ports had frozen over again, and trade ceased until the following June. By early 1932, massive transfers of prisoners had taken place to provide a workforce of 100,000 for building the new White Sea Canal which had no connection with Soviet foreign affairs. Soviet cover-ups made it harder to prove that export timber was being cut by slave labour. In October 1932, the new Ottawa Agreement compelled the British government not only to give trade preference to the Commonwealth, but also to 'take all the necessary steps to see that no country shall frustrate that effort by the dumping of sweated goods'.[7] The British government accordingly gave the Soviets the six months' notice of its severance, which was required under the terms of the Anglo-Russian Trade Agreement. When the step was announced in the Commons on behalf of the National Government by former Labour minister J. H. Thomas, it was vigorously opposed by Lansbury and future Labour leader Clement Attlee.

The notice was due to come into effect on 17 April 1933 but, on 11 March 1933, six foreign engineers, two of them British, employed by the British firm of Metropolitan-Vickers on a contract for the Soviets to build up the country's electrical generating industry, were arrested by the OGPU. They were charged with conspiracy to destroy the electrical generating capacity of Russian power stations. The charges were fabricated and a ruse by the Soviets to cover their shortage of foreign currency (a large bill was due to be paid to the engineering firm) and to distract the foreign press correspondents from the famine that was killing millions of people in Ukraine and Southern Russia.[8]

The Conservatives in the new government had none of the tolerance of their Labour predecessor towards such Soviet tricks, nor would they stand idly by while British citizens were threatened with the death penalty. On 5 April 1933, all Russian imports, including timber, were banned.

PART V

FELLOW TRAVELLERS

How deeply the Left craved to give the benefit of all the doubts to Moscow! No one who did not live through that period can appreciate how overwhelming that craving was.
MICHAEL FOOT[1]

Freedom is, in reality, rigidly subordinated to the State purpose. So long as the people submit to be disciplined and regimented in the name of Socialism, or any other name, it is not for us to interfere, only to watch this amazing triumph of human endurance.
MANCHESTER GUARDIAN, 24 FEBRUARY 1931

There are no warders, no police, there are no prison bars, there are no wire entanglements. Why then do the prisoners stay there? For the quite simple reason that they have assured work at trade union rates of pay in a community which they regulate themselves.

I defy anyone who was not let into the secret to know from the look of them that the inhabitants of Bolshevo [labour correction colony near Moscow] were old criminals.

The experiment has become an almost incredible success, and when their prison terms are over many of the inhabitants stay on in the colony as free workers. It must not be supposed that this experiment is an isolated effort. There are other colonies run on similar lines in other parts of Soviet Russia. This [is a] grand method of human regeneration.
SIR CHARLES TREVELYAN MP, PRESIDENT OF THE BOARD OF EDUCATION, 1924, 1929–31[2]

CHAPTER 34

DEFEAT

The scale of the disaster of 1931 was profound. 'We are deluding our-selves if we minimise the catastrophic character of the defeat and its significance to the cause of Socialism all over the world', Fenner Brockway, the ILP chairman, told its post-election conference in the spring of 1932. As the ILP and Labour Party tried to come to terms with what had happened, impatience led to factionalism. The conference then heard a series of calls for disaffiliation from the Labour Party. Patience for gradual change, the policy of the mainstream of the Labour Party, was wearing thin. That summer it ran out, and the ILP officially disaffiliated from the Labour Party.

Brockway's own speech to the spring conference was a direct call for revolution, though it was left to listeners to surmise the extent to which that 'revolution' would be peaceful or violent. What was said made clear that all constraints were being abandoned:

> It is clear that Socialists must revolutionise their policy to face the new situa-tion ... Whilst the Labour Party regarded Socialism as an ideal to be reached generations hence, the ILP put forward a programme of planned advance within one generation. That was appropriate five years ago. But the present economic situation demands, not a series of measures over a period of years, but an entire rebuilding of the whole economic system to save it from chaos.

That meant taking power:

> In other words, it means that we must concentrate upon securing and retaining

such power that we will be able to carry through the decisive change from Capitalism to Socialism without fear of effective interruption or obstruction. *Our policy must become revolutionary instead of reformist.* (My italics.)[1]

Brockway was convinced that, once the capitalist press was no longer able to hide from the British working class that there was no unemployment in Russia, it would have 'an explosive effect' and they would rise up 'to build a new economic system as Russia is doing'.* This and other developments would then 'make for a revolutionary situation'. It was anticipated that Parliament would be obstructive, but at that point 'organized action by the working class in the country would almost certainly be necessary to support the political action of their representatives in Parliament'. In other words, there would be a general strike to bring down the government and clear the way for socialists to take over. Then, Brockway explained, in a section of his speech entitled 'The programme of the Revolution', an extra-parliamentary body, a 'National Authority', would take over:

> The key resources of economic power, including banking, transport, mining, and electrical generation, and the land, not in a series of measures over a period of time, but in one comprehensive scheme of reorganisation which would probably extend to the steel industry, the textile industries and, indeed, to the general economic the life of the nation.

The Labour movement had long been committed to wide-ranging 'expropriation'. The ILP was prepared to wait no longer.

The Labour Party

Arthur Henderson had led the Labour Party following MacDonald's expulsion, but two and a half years spent holding one of the great offices of state, after a lifetime at the helm of a burgeoning party, had left him with little enthusiasm for leading a beaten group of MPs that now had a mere 10 per

---

* When Lord Marley repeated the familiar claim about there being no unemployment in Russia, it drew a deserved retort from Snowden, who by then had been expelled from the Labour Party: 'The noble Lord said that there are no unemployed in Russia. I do not think he would find many unemployed in Dartmoor gaol. Russia is under a system of industrial conscription ... May God save England from such a Socialism as they have in Russia to-day!' Hansard, HL Deb, 22 June 1932, vol. 85, col. 347.

cent of the seats at Westminster. He resigned the following year in favour of George Lansbury. He was awarded the Nobel Peace Prize in 1934.

Lansbury's enthusiasm for Soviet Communism as the world's beacon of hope remained undiminished. In 1933, the year after he became party leader, he continued to write of Soviet Communism as 'a wonderful experiment', and insisted that the continued allegations of widespread Russian slave labour were a 'gross distortion' of the facts, adding: 'The colossal task set themselves by the Russian Socialists is one which should be supported by all lovers of the race. ... We are not called upon to judge or accept all the means they adopt to attain their ends.'[2]

The reality was very different. In Russia that year, 100,000 gulag inmates, many transferred from the timber camps, were completing the construction of the Belomor Canal, connecting the White Sea with the Baltic. Ten per cent of them perished. When the Soviet authorities produced a commemorative book praising their own enlightened and compassionate penal policy, which had led to the reformation of so many criminals through their work on the canal, John Strachey's sister, Amabel Williams-Ellis, wife of the architect of Portmeirion, Clough Williams-Ellis,[3] wrote a glowing introduction to its English translation.[4]

Lansbury offered a seat in his shadow Cabinet to James Maxton, the former chairman of the ILP but, given the ILP's growing impatience with Labour, Maxton unsurprisingly turned it down. Lansbury was no doubt well aware of Maxton's views on Soviet Communism, which were clearly no bar to his inclusion in Lansbury's Cabinet. That same year, in 1932, Maxton had published a biography of Lenin which showed that his enthusiasm for the 'experiment' was undimmed. 'Nowhere', the book concluded, 'is to be found in any single man the peculiar combination of devotion, courage, wisdom, skill and human understanding except in the man Lenin'.[5] The year after that, he made his loyalty to Marxism still clearer: 'The only teaching which I know which gets anywhere near to providing intelligent explanations and intelligent solutions of the troubles of the world is the Marxist teaching, which includes within it the destruction of the idea of a supernatural God'.[6]

One person who did accept a post in Lansbury's shadow Cabinet was Stafford Cripps, Lord Parmoor's son, who had been Solicitor General under MacDonald. The next year, in April 1933, in a debate in the House of Commons on the plight of the British Metropolitan-Vickers engineers, Cripps would hear no ill of Moscow's possible verdict: 'If the Russian system is a system of justice, as I accept, and if they have a crime the penalty of which is death, then the person who is guilty of that crime must be put to death.'[7]

Four years later, Stalin was to extend the death penalty to children as young as twelve years old.

The wider party was no less enthusiastic in its continued support for the Soviet Union and the 1933 Labour Party conference passed yet another motion confirming that position:

> This conference condemns all efforts to discredit the practice of Socialism in Russia and instructs the National Executive to establish such cordial relations with the Socialist rulers of Russia as ought to characterise two bodies professing a similar economic and social objective under different conditions, to encourage a regular interchange of ideas and to consolidate the basis of future understanding.[8]

Reality dawns slowly

Cripps may really have believed what he had said about the justice of the Soviet death penalty in 1933 but, the following year, his own party found itself hesitating over that conviction. On 1 December 1934 Sergei Kirov, the Communist Party leader in Leningrad, was assassinated, probably on Stalin's orders. A conspiracy to overthrow the state was announced and mass arrests followed, many of them of party members. A dozen people, named as the immediate conspirators, were shot, some without trial; many more were purged over the following weeks and months.

British socialists were horrified. Fellow socialists were once again being arrested and shot without trial in Russia as had been the case in the '20s. In the period 1929–31, there had been silence when the victims were religious believers and kulaks. Indeed, in September 1931, Ernest Bevin, in a reference to Prebendary Gough's campaign, had contemptuously dismissed 'the hiring of priests and parsons to denounce Russia' as 'unctuous hypocrisy'.[9] Now there was an outcry. On 21 December 1934, the General Council of the TUC and the National Executive Committee of the Labour Party issued a joint declaration:

> The General Council of the Trades Union Congress and the National Executive Committee of the Labour Party desire to express their abhorrence at the recent assassination of M. Kirov and extend their sincere sympathy to the

Soviet government and the people of Russia and in the loss by violence of one of their most active leaders.

While fully appreciating the sense of loss felt throughout the USSR and the outraged feeling provoked by this criminal act, the General Council and the National Executive are also profoundly shocked and alarmed by the reprisals which followed in the form of summary executions. They are firmly of the opinion that all persons under arrest or who may be arrested should be afforded full facilities for a proper legal defence in a public trial.[10]

The total number arrested in Leningrad represented a paltry 1 per cent of the 30,000 kulaks who had been rounded up and shot, also without trial, in 1930.

A Labour delegation went to see Maisky, the Soviet ambassador, to express their unease. Maisky expressed regret that their statement had been published 'without first ascertaining the facts', which he then proceeded to elaborate. The truth was that those who had been shot *had* been tried and found guilty of carrying out major terroristic acts; they had openly declared themselves in court to be enemies of the Soviet Union and had admitted the crimes for which they had been charged. Many had come from abroad and were found in possession of bombs and other weaponry and, Maisky insisted, it was actually European governments who were really to blame for previously harbouring the enemies of the Soviet Union who carried out these attacks.[11]

Over the next few years, the purges continued, eliminating many of Stalin's key rivals. In staged show trials, one leading Bolshevik after another confessed their guilt as plotters to assassinate Stalin and overthrow the Soviet government. Many were shot. At least one (Grigori Sokolnikov, Maisky's predecessor as ambassador) who was only imprisoned, was later murdered by fellow inmates on orders from above.

British pro-Soviets were deeply conflicted: they defended or excused the purges and trials or blamed them on hostile foreign governments in equal measure. This editorial by Kingsley Martin in the *New Statesman and Nation* in 1936 is typical:

The truth about the plot for which Zinoviev, Kamenev, and the others were executed, we do not know. We are unconvinced [but] Mr Pritt, K.C.*, who

---

* Pritt was a Labour MP, one of the greatest British Soviet enthusiasts in the Labour Party – for which, it is fair to add, he was not always popular within his own party.

should be a good judge of evidence, was present at the proceedings and cabled that the trial was fair. Very likely there was a plot. Even assuming the whole story of the plot, such a general purge means much individual injustice. Every effort is, of course, being made to exploit this proof of difficulty and violence in Soviet Russia. It is grist to the mill of Conservatives, who hate Socialism.

Let us see this matter in perspective. A social revolution is accompanied both by violence and by idealism. Its success must be judged primarily by the permanent achievement of its economic aims ... It is bad tactics as well as bad morals [to adopt] a pretence that nothing can be amiss in Soviet Russia. The right reply is honestly to admit that there is a great deal amiss, and that political liberty has a long battle to fight before it becomes a reality in Soviet Russia.

But that makes no difference to the essential fact that Russia is a Socialist country with an overwhelming desire for peace. *The Russian Revolution is in any case the greatest achievement of this generation.* It always takes a totally disproportionate amount of steam to accomplish an obviously necessary social change.

The essential economic change of our generation has been carried out in Russia and in Russia only, and the power of the GPU and the excessive and increasing control of the Soviet bureaucracy, historically speaking, of secondary importance ... Russia is necessarily an ally, even though at times a singularly awkward ally. Much that is disappointing in Russia today is due to the fear of invasion and the vast military preparations that follow from such a fear. (My italics.)[12]

At the height of the purges in 1937, when hundreds of thousands were being shot, it became impossible to plead ignorance of the slaughter, even if its precise scale was not fully known; some British Communists, trapped in Russia, were among the victims.[13] Even then, Kingsley Martin still could not bring himself to turn his back on Soviet Communism:

All governments tend to justify the suppression of their opponents; dictatorial governments grow more ruthless and more unjust because they are not subject to criticism. It is not the part of the friends of the USSR to refrain from asking awkward questions about the methods it uses for the suppression (necessary or not in itself) of those it regards as dangerous. One is glad in a world which is so busy denying the rights of man to find the Soviet Union committing itself so definitely to their extension (in the introduction of the 1936 Soviet Constitution).

The only honest attitude for a Socialist is to give general, but critical, support to the one country in the world which has adopted a planned socialist economy.[14]

Approximately 2.8 million prisoners died in gulag camps.[15] More than 800,000 more were shot before they got there, many of them in 1937, the year in which Martin wrote these words (unlike the Germans, who used their camps for extermination, the Soviets usually shot those they intended to kill before they got to the camps). The reputation of any editor of a political journal who apologised for and excused the Nazis in the 1930s, or the journal they were written in, would still be tarnished today. The *Daily Mail* is regularly scorned for its initial support in 1934 for Mosley's Blackshirts, which it disavowed a year later. Kingsley Martin and the *New Statesman*, which defended Stalin for many years longer than that, have suffered no such stain on their reputation.

In 1937, long before he was Labour leader, Michael Foot was a journalist for *Tribune*, the newspaper which was the main legacy of the short-lived Unity Campaign (see p. 512). Writing twenty years later, he had this to say of the studied ignorance of the British left at that time:

> All papers have their Achilles heels, their blind spots, or what, less charitably, may be called their streaks of cowardice. Ours was the Russian trials. We said nothing or next to nothing on the subject. Our excuse was that we were engaged in a unity campaign on the supreme issue of the international crisis. Let us hope that we have learnt the moral which might be put in a maxim to be inscribed above every editorial chair: 'Never funk the truly awkward issues; they are the very ones your readers most want to hear about. And if by any chance they don't, to hell with them!'[16]

Tribune journalists were not the only ones who preferred silence. Clement Attlee, who had become leader of the Labour Party in 1935, was in Moscow in August 1936. While he was there, the British communist Robin Page Arnot managed to gain him entrance to the trial of Kamenev and Zinoviev.[17] The two former Bolshevik leaders were accused, alongside Trotsky, of allying with the Gestapo to assassinate Stalin and Kirov. The charges were fantastic (even Beatrice Webb suspected that the defendants had been tortured to confess[18]) and the trial, like many, was a set-up, engineered by Stalin to wipe out all possible rivals. But just over a year later, Attlee still proposed this toast at a grand dinner held to commemorate the twentieth anniversary of the Revolution:

> The remarkable thing is that the Russian Revolution should have endured. It is a miracle. Out of the chaos the Russians are building a new society based upon social justice. Enemies of the Soviet Union dislike it not because they are afraid it will attack them, not because it is 'godless', but because they are afraid lest a State should go forward based upon the principle of social justice.

Seconding his toast, H. H. Elvin, Chairman of the TUC General Council added: 'The Soviet Republics have done a marvellous work. They have passed from the stage of experiment to the stage of achievement.'[19]

In the end, however, it became too much for the ILP leadership. As their eventual statement, published in *The Times* in March 1938, makes clear, it was a deeply traumatic capitulation:

> ILP members appeal to Stalin: 'End This Regime of Blood'
>
> The following communication to Mr Stalin from Mr Maxton MP, Mr Buchanan MP, Mr McGovern MP, Mr Stephen MP, of the ILP Parliamentary Group, and Mr F. Brockway, general secretary of the ILP, was delivered yesterday to M. Maisky, the Soviet ambassador in London:
>
> We were among the first of the British workers in 1917 to hail the victory of the Russian workers and peasants over the Tsar, the landlords, and capitalists. In the Russian Revolution we found the inspiration for the working-class movement of our country and of all lands. With pride we watched the Russian people lay the foundation, despite the severest obstacles, of a new Socialist society. We did everything possible to advance the solidarity of [the] working class with the Russian masses in their progress toward a society free from exploitation and oppression.
>
> But recent developments in the USSR have shocked us. Because of our faith in Soviet Russia and the support which we had given it, we are compelled now to voice our protest. The workers of Britain can never be convinced that the majority of the Bolshevik leaders, the most intimate associates and co-workers of Lenin, men who gave their all to the cause of the workers, have become, as if overnight, champions of capitalism, spies and agents of the Imperialist Powers, and tools of Fascist reaction ... If the charges were true we would

be compelled to conclude that there was something inherently wrong in the Russian Revolution to attract such degenerate types to the top of the ladder of leadership. That explanation we unreservedly reject.

The very nature of the 'confessions', the manner and technique of the trials, their preparation, the inconceivable character of the alleged crimes, not only failed to convince – they have the opposite effect … This is not working-class justice. It is barbarous injustice. It is an insult and injury to all international working-class ideals and interests.

We cannot believe that you realise how much harm, how much incalculable and irreparable damage you are inflicting through this ruthless terror upon the cause of the entire international working class and the ideals of Socialism. The most bitter foes of the Soviet system could never have done as much to shake the faith of the class-conscious workers and to ensure doubt and demoralisation in their ranks.

We cannot condemn with sufficient vigour methods and policies which are dangerously undermining the moral influence in political prestige of the Russian Revolution among the workers of the world.

In the name of international working class solidarity, in the name of the cause of Socialism, on behalf of the very ideals which inspired the Russian workers to their victorious Revolution, we call upon you to end this regime of blood against the trusted associates of Lenin, against those who but yesterday were your worthy comrades, your own confidants and colleagues, against scores of thousands of workers, four years members of the Communist Party, now suffering in dark dungeons.[20]

It was far too late for international pressure to achieve anything. All of those who, in the early days, might have been able to rein Stalin in were now dead. Disastrous miscalculation and inept interference by Moscow had already split the German opposition and enabled Hitler's rise to power.* War was eighteen months away. Much as Churchill was to dislike it, everything then had to be done to attract and then keep the Russians on board.

---

* At times, the Comintern seemed to be more hostile to non-communist socialist parties in Europe than their Conservative opponents. British Labour leaders were frequently dubbed as 'traitors' for refusing to endorse some reckless strike or other. Similarly, in the early 1930s, Stalin instructed the German Communist Party (KPD) to have nothing to do with the Social Democrats (SPD) in their elections. In March 1933, Hitler gained only 196 seats in the Reichstag elections, against the SPD's 121 seats and the KPD's 100, a combined potential majority of 221. But the KPD branded the SPD 'social fascists', and all chance of creating a united opposition to Hitler was lost. Three weeks later, Hitler suspended the Reichstag and took dictatorial power.

CHAPTER 35

LABOUR AND THE METROPOLITAN-VICKERS TRIAL (1933)

In March 1933, a number of British engineers working in Russia for the firm of Metropolitan-Vickers were arrested on charges of wrecking and espionage. The charges were fabricated and had been prompted by the Russians' acute shortage of foreign currency (the next instalments of payment from the Russian government to Metro-Vickers were about to be due) and their need to deflect attention from the famine in Ukraine, which was claiming millions of lives. The case is significant because it provides an insight into Labour's continuing attitude to events in Russia. When the British government protested the arrests, Labour, now in opposition, vigorously defended the Soviets and insisted that Moscow's perspective on the men's actions was credible.

By February 1933, Stalin was facing problems on a number of fronts. Each day, approximately 7,000 people were dying of famine in Ukraine.[1] Repression had not quelled unrest in the famine regions, and there was dissent in the cities. It appeared that the vital spring sowing would be held up by inadequate supplies of seed, and by manpower shortages caused by the famine as well as by the inefficiencies which had resulted from the mass deportations of the kulaks. In response, grain requisitions in the Ukraine, which had been running at a punitive rate, were suspended on 15 March.[2] The following month, grain was released from Red Army stockpiles; by May, the famine was beginning to ease. In spite of the desperate need in the starving villages, the Soviets were still exporting grain to earn the foreign currency needed to pay for the industrialisation which was part of the Five-Year Plan. In the years 1932 and 1933, when the famine was at its height, the government exported 3.5 million tons of grain – almost a sixth of a ton for each famine death.[3]

News of the famine had already filtered out to the West, but it was not yet well known. The Soviets were aware that if it hit the international press and was taken up by opponents of the Soviet Union abroad, grain exports would be jeopardised. The 1930 boycott of Russian timber by a number of Western nations showed that this was no groundless fear. The foreign press corps needed to be contained, while at the same time internal criticism within the Soviet Union needed to be deflected.

The kulaks had already been named as the instigators of wrecking in the fields and farms, but the dekulakisation campaign of 1929–31 had been fought to 'smash the kulaks as a class'; they could not now be held up as the sole cause of the trouble without it appearing as though the government had failed in its task to 'liquidate' them. More scapegoats were needed. So vets were shot for secretly engineering livestock mortality; meteorologists were arrested for falsifying weather forecasts in order to damage crops; in Ukraine, there was a mass purge of governmental and academic institutions, as well as newspapers; the Ukrainian Chamber of Weights and Measures was held responsible for deliberately sabotaging the measurement of the harvest. Stanislav Kosior,* the Ukrainian party general secretary, declared that there were 'whole counter-revolutionary nests' everywhere.†

Casting around for more people to blame, agricultural specialists were an obvious target. The director, deputy director and a number of other senior staff of the Ukrainian Agricultural Academy were arrested. Most of them

---

* Kosior, considered by many today to be one of Stalin's chief enforcers during the famine, did not survive the Great Terror of 1937–38. He was arrested in 1938 and, broken under torture, confessed to being a Polish spy. Kosior, his wife, and two brothers were shot. At least one other relative was sent to the camps.

† The suppression of the truth about the famine was not to end in 1933–34. Historian Robert Conquest relates how, in 1937, the census-takers were scapegoated too: 'The preliminary results (of the January 1937 census) seem to have been before the authorities on about 10 February 1937. The census was then suppressed. The Head of the Census Board, O. A. Kvitkin, was arrested on 25 March. It turned out that "the glorious Soviet intelligence headed by the Stalinist Peoples' Commissar N. I. Yezhov" had "crushed the serpent's nest of traitors in the apparatus of Soviet statistics". The traitors had "set themselves the task of distorting the actual numbers of the population", or (as *Pravda* put it later) "had exerted themselves to diminish the numbers of the population of the USSR", a rather unfair taunt, since it was, of course, not they who had done the diminishing.' Conquest, *Harvest of Sorrow*, p. 299.

perished in the camps.[4] In Moscow, the OGPU arrested seventy employees of the Commissariat of Agriculture of the USSR, including a vice-commissar. They were convicted of 'agricultural sabotage' – a charge which included not only arson but 'the deliberate propagation of weeds with a view to lowering crop yields'. Thirty-five were shot; the remainder were sentenced to between eight and ten years' imprisonment.

The press announcement of the Moscow agriculturalists' executions was made on the morning of 12 March; on the same day, the OGPU launched an investigation of both Russian and foreign employees of the Metropolitan-Vickers engineering company, which was working on contract for the Soviet government installing generating equipment. Within days, they were charged with conspiracy to destroy the generating capacity of Russian power stations. One possible interpretation of the timing of these two events is that they were connected – that the same OGPU investigative team moved from the Commissariat of Agriculture case straight on to the Metro-Vickers one. If this was indeed the case, it is likely that the two were part of the same disinformation campaign planned by the Moscow OGPU: first targeting the domestic audience with the arrest of the agriculturalists, and then, with that of the engineers, aiming to deflect international attention from the famine by provoking a crisis which would absorb all the energy and attention of the foreign press corps – and which might in the process provide the Soviet government with an excuse to default on all or part of its payments to the company.[5]

At 9.30 p.m. on Saturday 11 March 1933, twenty OGPU agents descended upon the home of British Metropolitan-Vickers engineers Allan Monkhouse and Leslie Thornton in a compound just outside Moscow. Thornton was Metropolitan-Vickers chief engineer in Russia and Monkhouse, who had lived in Russia for nine years, was the firm's representative in the country. After a search which lasted until after 2 a.m. the following day, the two were arrested and taken to the Lubyanka. Early the next morning, a second raid resulted in the arrest of two more British engineers, John Cushny, and William MacDonald. Shortly afterwards, the police picked up Albert Gregory, and Charles Nordwall, also engineers for the firm. The OGPU quickly identified Thornton and MacDonald as the two defendants most susceptible to sign a confession under pressure. Thornton lived in a fairly comfortable compound a dozen miles outside Moscow with his mistress, Anna Kutusova, who was also the Russian secretary of the company. He had a wife in England and would not have wanted his affair to become public knowledge.

Some weeks earlier, the firm's Russian chauffeurs had been questioned, and they warned the British managers that they were being investigated. Then Kutusova disappeared. When she surfaced, twenty-four hours later, beaten, it turned out that she had been held by the OGPU. After the engineers' arrest she was brought into the same room as Thornton and, as they sat back to back, mechanically repeated a long list of the acts of sabotage and espionage which she had committed at Thornton's instigation. Similar written confessions from Russian engineers employed by the firm were read out to him. Thornton denied everything. Then the interrogator said that if he was right, then Kutusova was lying and she would be shot. He signed the confession they put in front of him.

MacDonald's entrapment was described in some notes on the affair written by A. T. Cholerton, the *Daily Telegraph* correspondent who had become a close of friend of Malcolm Muggeridge:

MacDonald, 28, a club-foot, sick childhood, never went to school much or played with other the boys, a burden on a poor family who let him feel it but mother's darling, somehow became a competent engineer … He was only earning a few pounds a week (in Manchester) but sent with a good salary on an erection job in Siberia (Novosibirsk, if I remember rightly) where with his own special supplies of food and drink he was a rich man right in the midst of a starving population.

But he was miserable, very lonely. He stayed in the engineers' hostel and the kindly middle-aged woman who ran it looked after him when he was ill. He needed [a] mother and persuaded her to join him on other assignments as his housekeeper…

This pale-eyed neurotic was red meat for the OGPU interrogators. They brought in his Siberian foster mother. She didn't look as if she had been knocked about but she was filthy (doubtless coming from one of those common cells in the old Butirki Tsarist remand prison made to hold a dozen but crammed with 50). The silly fellow betrayed his affection for her. Could she have a food parcel? Some soap? This was luck indeed in a land where families often fall apart on arrest and the devil take the hindmost.

So they casually informed him that one of his housekeeper's sons was already in jail, the other would now be arrested and they were not quite certain what would become of them. They treated him almost throughout with a genial condescension as a poor fish who was caught up in a grand international spy conspiracy, and in general as a sort of menial. Of course there would be no trial. It was just for their files. He would soon be released of course but wouldn't he like to get himself clear at once by making a statement? Then suddenly: 'Sit down! Take this down!' And then they brought him and read him a statement of Thornton's, signed or not. He thought: 'Thornton was an old Russian hand and important. He knows how to play his way out of this'...[6]

Sir Esmond Ovey had previously, much to the frustration of some of his junior colleagues, refused to hear any ill of the Soviets, but by now he had reversed the good opinion he had held of them in the days of Ramsay Mac-Donald's Labour administration. The change had not gone unnoticed by the expatriate community.[*] On hearing of the arrests, his assessment of the plight of the engineers was uncompromising:

> While obviously His Majesty's Government in the United Kingdom cannot deny the right of any sovereign Government to arrest suspected criminals, a right which they reserve to themselves, *conditions under the present reign of terror in this country are without parallel in Great Britain*. It is inconceivable that the Soviet Government can produce credible evidence of any criminal malpractice on the part of the company. (My italics.)[7]

The situation was serious. The OGPU had just been given special powers to investigate cases of 'sabotage, arson, explosion, damage to machine plant of State undertakings', and charged with 'applying all measures of repression' which were to be 'exercised with especial severity in regard to employees of State institutions and undertakings convicted of such offences'.[8] The engineers were accused of sabotage, the same charge that had just led to the

---

[*]   Reader Bullard was one to remark on it: 'The Ambassador is a changed man. The ordinary observer would say that he was pro-Bolshevik [until recently]. But he has changed. Only a month ago ... he was trying to persuade me that the Soviet officials were about as honest as those in the United Kingdom, and now he is cursing them.' Bullard, diary, 16 November 1932.

thirty-five agriculturalists being shot without trial ('all measures of repression' included the death penalty). They were under contract to the Russian government and could technically be classified as employees of the state. The risk to them was very real.

The engineers were put through the mill. Monkhouse was arrested at 2.15 a.m. after a five-hour search of his house. He cannot have got to his cell until 3.15 a.m. at the earliest (all prisoners arriving in the Lubyanka were processed at some length before being taken to their cells). The interrogators started on him at 8 a.m. and continued without a break for nineteen hours. At 7.30 p.m. the next night he was again taken from his cell and questioned for a further seventeen hours. By then, the OGPU had decided to concentrate on Thornton and MacDonald, and Monkhouse was released on bail. The *Daily Herald* interpreted Monkhouse's release as an 'unexpectedly conciliatory' gesture.[9] It was not. The OGPU had simply worked out by then which of the engineers would prove the easiest victims.

When Ovey's staff were eventually allowed to see the other engineers, it appeared that they too had been similarly treated: 'While the prisoners seemed generally in good health, the drawn expressions of Messrs Thornton and Cushny gave me [the] definite impression of their having been "put through it". They were all obviously terrified of speaking and confined themselves to [the] minimum of replies.'[10] The embassy officials were not allowed to talk to them about their case, ask how they were being treated, or even mention that other Metro-Vickers staff had been arrested. It seemed that Thornton was on the verge of a breakdown.[11]

In an earlier 1928 show trial (of engineers at the Shakhty mine near Rostov-on-Don, also accused of sabotage) two members of the defending team had themselves been sent to the camps (Bullard thought that 'they were lucky not to have been shot'[12]). Fearing that similar pressure might be brought to bear on the state-appointed defending lawyers, the British government had asked to be allowed to add their own defence lawyer as part of the legal team. The request was refused. Litvinov, in return, went out of his way to be offensive:

The Soviet Foreign Commissar … began by being very rude to the Ambassador and insisting that they could do just as they pleased with British subjects.

... In his last interview with the ambassador, Litvinov ... surpassed even his ordinary rudeness. He said that our methods might do in Mexico, but they couldn't be employed in Russia.* Moreover Litvinov had this published in the Soviet press at once.[13]

When Ovey was recalled to London for consultations, the Soviets refused to give him permission to return Moscow. Given this refusal, Litvinov's rudeness, and the suspicion that the Soviets had brought the case in order to get out of settling the £1.5 million (£97 million today) due to Metro-Vickers, it looked highly unlikely that the Russians were going to back down voluntarily.[14] The Conservative-dominated National government had one major weapon – trade. In October 1932, the British had given notice (as required by the Ottawa Agreement which they had signed on empire trade) that they intended to end the current Anglo-Soviet Trade Agreement and negotiate a replacement. The six months' notice was due to expire on 17 April, five days after the Metro-Vickers trial was set to begin. A full trade embargo beginning then was the obvious next move.

Parliament

The debate on the Russian Goods (Import Prohibition) Bill on 5 April 1933 was seven and a half hours long, and revealed how deep the Labour Party's delusion about Soviet Russia still was. The two leading speakers were Sir John Simon, the Foreign Secretary, who spoke for the government, and Sir Stafford Cripps for the opposition. Each took an hour to set out his case. Simon presented the facts as the government saw them, his fear for the lives of the engineers, and why a trade embargo was the appropriate next step to secure their release.

Stafford Cripps had been Solicitor General in the previous Labour government. As one of the few Labour Cabinet ministers to survive the October 1931 election, he had been a possible candidate for the leadership, which had gone instead to George Lansbury, who also spoke in the debate. His speech displayed a complete inability to believe the Soviets capable of any malicious intent.

---

* This was a personal insult to the ambassador, whose last post was Mexico.

Cripps's hour-long speech consisted of just a few points. Ignoring Simon's significant mention of the alarming precedent set by the shooting of the agriculturalists, Cripps insisted that there was no evidence of the British engineers' innocence; that the process of Soviet justice was fair and should be allowed to take its course; and that, because it was fair, the government had 'no right to demand that a British subject, arrested in the due course of justice in Russia, should be liberated before the trial'.

Cripps was so convinced of the Soviets' goodwill and impartiality that he found it inconceivable that they could have fabricated the charges against the engineers, which was the conclusion reached by the vast majority of the diplomatic community in Moscow and by the British government: 'I think it is impossible for anybody to say, as regards any individual, that under no circumstances could he possibly be guilty before he knows the charge.' Cripps did not go quite as far as some of his Labour colleagues in and outside the House of Commons; they were quite prepared to believe that British intelligence were running an operation to bring down the Soviet Communist regime and that the Soviets had uncovered it.

If anyone was to blame in this, Cripps suggested, it was ambassador Ovey. Ovey had made things worse. He had been 'hasty' to talk about 'the trumping up of frivolous and fantastic accusations against a friendly and reputable British company' when he knew nothing of the true state of affairs. In Cripps's view this had only inflamed the situation and Ovey would never have dared make such accusations against another country – America, for example. His conclusion was that Ovey was motivated by anti-Soviet prejudice and hostility.

As for the engineers themselves, if people did not like the way the Soviet legal system worked, they had one option – not to go there in the first place: 'It is the known method of Russia, and people who go to Russia know that if they are accused that is the way in which proceedings will be conducted. The remedy, of course, if you do not like it, is to stay out of Russia.'

But Cripps overstepped the mark when he added that 'the House will remember that the Ambassador had stated that they had all been treated extremely well'. It was a complete misrepresentation of Ovey's actual words. Conservative MP John Hills would not let him get away it: Cripps referred frequently in his speech to the White Paper published by the government prior to the debate, containing copies of all Ovey's dispatches;[15] the ambassador's words (quoted by Hills) had been that 'while the prisoners seemed generally in good health, the drawn expressions of Messrs Thornton and Cushny gave [the] definite impression of their having been "put through it" [and that] they were all obviously terrified of speaking and confined themselves to [the] minimum of replies.' There was no possible way that this statement, and the fact that the prisoners had been subjected to prolonged interrogation and sleep deprivation, could be construed as their having been treated 'extremely well'. And, Hills continued, Cripps had just heard Sir John Simon remind the House that thirty-five Russians had been shot for similar sabotage offences: 'If they would shoot Russians, they would shoot Englishmen ... We know what they did to Russians. They shot them without trial.' This was not a mere matter of legal debate. British lives were at risk.

One of the pillars of Cripps's argument had been that the British government had no right to intervene unless, on its conclusion, the trial proved to be unfair in some way; that they should wait and see how it turned out. What, Hills asked, would they do if the trial was unjust, the engineers were found guilty and then shot straight after the verdict – for offences that, even if they were guilty, did not carry the death penalty in Britain? It would be too late. Cripps replied that this could not happen because the Russian legal system was fair and a just verdict would be returned. There was nothing to fear.

Hills pressed Cripps further. Did he really believe that Russian justice was fair and impartial? Cripps's reply made it clear quite how untroubled he was:

> If the Russian system is a system of justice, as I accept, and if they have a crime the penalty of which is death, then the person who is guilty of that crime must be put to death, just as a Russian in this country, if he has done a murder, will be hanged. The course of justice will be carried out, unless the prerogative of mercy is exercised.[16]

Cripps's spirited defence of the Soviet legal system did not go unnoticed in Moscow. During the trial itself, the beleaguered British engineers heard the Soviet prosecutor Vyshinsky use Cripps's remarks as a vindication of the integrity of the trial process to which they were being subjected.[17]

While Cripps's assessment of Soviet justice was based on optimism and naïveté, Colin Patrick, the Conservative MP for Tavistock, had first-hand experience of it and was far better qualified to speak on the matter. He had been first secretary in the Moscow embassy for six months, before resigning in June 1930. It is not hard to speculate that he would have found it difficult to work under Ovey at a time when the ambassador's sympathy for the Bolsheviks had been quite pronounced, for Patrick's opposing view had been no secret in the embassy. He had been described as 'a bit of a diehard' by Ovey's chargé d'affaires, Col. Mitford, in a conversation with Hugh Dalton, when Mitford had passed through London in March 1930.[18]

Patrick had sat through a so-called 'wrecking trial', that is, where the accused is charged with sabotage. He had researched and drawn up the first memorandum on religious persecution. He could not let Cripps's comments pass unchallenged. His understanding of the Soviet investigative and court process was acute, and his speech contained a definitive description, which bears repeating. Patrick's first point showed that the verdict and severity of sentence depended on one's class, not on the facts of the alleged crime.

If I heard [Cripps] aright, he said, in answer to a question, that he accepted the Soviet system of justice, or that he accepted it as a system of justice. [But] I am convinced – and I wish to put it to the House with all earnestness – that we cannot accept the Soviet system as a system of justice at all in our sense of the word. It is not a question of degree; it is a question of kind.

Our conception of justice is absolutely contrary to the Soviet conception. Our ideas of law in this country, and, indeed, in Western Europe, is that it is based upon a general and universal standard and is, or should be, applicable to all men, at all times, alike. Go to Soviet Russia, and you will find precisely the opposite idea in force.

The Marxian idea of justice and law is not that it applies to all men alike, but that it is a matter of class. Take the same crime committed by two different people. If a member of the bourgeoisie steals a watch, it may be a crime of the first order. For the same offence, precisely for stealing the same watch at the same place, it may be a completely venal offence on the part of a proletarian. The whole idea of justice, in fact, is on the basis of class.

'This Court is the organ of the Proletariat.' ... is one of Lenin's classic remarks; Those words mean precisely what they say. The Court is the organ of the class war, and exists for that main purpose...

The Kremlin very naturally feels that a diversion of some kind is necessary and they have raised the old cry 'The Fatherland is in Danger' from foreign machinations, and this trial, so called, which we are about to witness, in my opinion is nothing more or less than the modern Communist version of that ancient cry.

If that is the Class basis, and the circumstances in which the trial is to be carried out, justice is impossible.

Having correctly outlined the direction which a typical Soviet trial would take, Patrick turned to the wider picture of life in a country ruled by what he described as the twin pillars of 'propaganda' and 'terror'.

[It is] decided in advance what type of evidence is required, and the usual course has been to arrest the appropriate number of people and put them into prison ... The arrests are usually made in the early hours of the morning. The arrested man disappears, and very often his family hears nothing of his where-abouts for weeks or months. At the end of that time, possibly, his family may receive a curt message that he has been shot a fortnight or so before. In other cases they may hear nothing. Their relative is lost to them, without any news at any time.

Having obtained the necessary number of prisoners, and determined on the plan of action, the next step is to get the evidence, and it is done by selecting one or two, who must be called the lucky ones. They are subjected to long cross-examination, and when the prisoner is in the right frame of mind they say to him: 'In exchange for your signature to this confession, we will prom-ise you a light sentence. In default of that signature, your sentence will be death.' The prisoner knows that that is not an idle threat. Therefore, he has no alternative, and he signs a confession implicating himself, very often in most fantastic charges, and, what is more painful, from our point of view, he almost inevitably implicates a great number of his comrades.

It is difficult to convey how fantastic and absurd these long series of trials and convictions have been. The same motive runs through all of them. The charge has practically always been one of sabotage or, in the more modern form of the word in Russia, 'wrecking.' In most cases the accused have been selected from among the remnants of the pre-War bourgeoisie. Without being cynical or attempting to be humorous on the subject, I might add that the supply of the bourgeoisie seems to be running short and that the Proletariat is becoming increasingly involved. The charge is almost always one of wrecking or sabotage. One has to be on the spot to realise how utterly unreal that charge may be.

In all these numerous trials I am convinced that there has very seldom been a single conviction that has really been based on reality.

It was a perfect picture of a police state. Patrick's conclusion was simple:

[If Labour] Members opposite could really appreciate what lies behind this so-called trial, they would be filled with as much horror of the system as I am. That system is not justice but the most repulsive compound of which I can think – it is a compound of blood and slime.[19]

This was the reality of life under Soviet oppression, correctly represented by Patrick to members of the House of Commons, But it was a reality which the British left, clinging to the fiction of the Soviet regime's fundamental benevolence and integrity, simply refused to accept. James Maxton of the ILP, who replied to Patrick, illustrated this well. He dismissed what Patrick had said, and accused him and the rest of his Conservative colleagues of class-motivated delusion:

The hon. Member for Tavistock [Mr. Patrick] has given a very clear indication of how his prejudices guide him in looking at Soviet Russia … I rather fancied from the hon. Member's speech that he was not completely conscious of the amount of prejudice that was displaying itself in his utterances.

I stand here as one who has been very anxious, and is anxious now, that the great experiment of the Russian people should work out to a complete success, but I cannot but feel that the spirit of the House, as displayed in recent weeks, has been very largely actuated by the fact that in the House there is a large number of people who are very anxious that the Russian experiment should fail.[20]

Maxton's only concession to the truth in Patrick's speech, which had detailed the way in which the OGPU picked suspects at random, forced them to make false confessions and then fixed the trial verdicts, was a reluctant admission that Monkhouse's 'nineteen hours' of cross examination' (it had actually been thirty-six hours) 'was not fair', but he then qualified that admission by a *tu quoque*: 'But I know that it is done in the United States [and] in France – though perhaps not to that extent,' he added grudgingly. He then accused the British government of treating Indian prisoners unfairly and concluded:

> Before you can stand on this high pedestal of virtue in the eyes of the world you have to have a clean record yourselves. The Russian Government have gone as far as they can reasonably expect any sovereign State in the world to go; and *you have the assurance that they will be subjected to a fair and square trial*. (My italics.)[21]

Aneurin Bevan

Aneurin Bevan, next to speak, shared the faith of his Labour colleagues in the absolute integrity of Soviet justice and also took the line that, if the engineers did not like the Russian system, they should not have gone there in the first place:

> [Should] every Englishman in a foreign country … always be considered inno-cent of any charge against him, without trial? … You could not get any decent Englishman in Great Britain to agree that an Englishman abroad should be released without trial. … The Russians have said that they will have an open trial … The men are on bail. Are we then going to … demand the release of these men without trial?
>
> Such an individual has no right to complain of the operation of the laws of a foreign State upon himself if they are executed impartially and in the same manner in which they would operate among native subjects. The fundamen-tal principle is this: an Englishman going into a foreign country accepts the authority of its legislation, abdicates for a time the benefits of British jurispru-dence, and subjects himself to all the consequent inconveniences.[22]

When another speaker interjected that the crucial difference between the two countries was that sabotage in Russia was a capital crime, Bevan merely replied that 'there is a different social system in Russia. There are different laws. Men who go there know what the laws are, and they accept all the risks.'

Bevan continued his apologia for the Soviet system with an excursion into conspiracy theory which showed that the Soviet leadership in Moscow were not the only ones inclined to paranoia:

> What we are discussing is the beginning of a most serious chain of events in Europe … I do not believe the Foreign Secretary, when he tells the House that the purpose … is to seek justice for these Englishmen. I believe its purpose is wider and more sinister … The suggestion is made that these powers [to impose a trade embargo] are being sought to protect these men. They are not sought for any such purpose at all. They are being sought to sacrifice these men in Russia in the service of a conspiracy which will emerge in the course of the next few months.
>
> The Foreign Secretary will go down to history as the most sinister of persons who ever occupied that office … the main architect of the troubles which will come in the future will be the Foreign Secretary and his chauvinistic and jingoistic followers in the House of Commons who for years have sought an opportunity of declaring war against the one nation, which, despite all the difficulties, is still showing that it is possible to have a world order in which people can live with more security than we have here.
>
> The dictatorship which has existed [in Russia] would have been relaxed had it not been for opposition from without. When you have a classless society you can abolish dictatorships, because it will not then be necessary to rest privilege upon the shoulders of an oppressed people.[23]

In other words, any deficiencies in Russia were solely the fault of the West. It was a refrain that had been repeated many times over the years whenever unanswerable accusations of cruelty had been made against the Soviets.

Bevan was known for his intemperate outbursts and fiery temper but his speech also contained elements that were both chilling and threatening:

> Any impartial examination of the British courts will show that even now, when the capitalist class of Great Britain can afford the luxury of apparent impartiality, there is evidence of bias in the courts and when we start to challenge your

position and when your property is in peril your judicial impartiality will go as it has in the past, as it has in Germany, as it has all over the world. The reason why you are so kind and benevolent at the moment is that we do not threaten you. Political toleration is a by-product of the complacency of the ruling class. When that complacency is disturbed there never was a more bloody-minded set of thugs than the British ruling class.

You are daring to suggest that as the present Russia has now been established for 12 or 15 years there is no reason at all for class legislation in Russia. Our newspapers speak with an abandon, with a virulence, about Russian affairs such as they would not dare to use about any other country, and day by day there is anti-Russian propaganda in this House. We do not use such language of any other country. [An HON. MEMBER: 'They do not deserve it!'] Exactly, that is your class prejudice.

Believe me, if I had the power you would not have a good many of the things you think you deserve now; and I am perfectly satisfied, as I said just now, that *when you are sufficiently frightened of us* there are many things that you will not accord to me. (My italics.)[24]

The debate included many more contributions of a similar nature. David Kirkwood freely admitted that, when he had worked for a Scottish engineering firm before entering Parliament, the Soviet inspector examining machinery to be sent to Russia had told him that if any faults were discovered he would be shot – but Kirkwood *still* exonerated the Soviets, and concluded: 'I believe that Russia will win through, and that most States all over the world will become Socialist States as a result.'[25]

George Lansbury's position was typically contradictory, one moment insisting that the Moscow leadership was fundamentally benign and should be trusted to be fair ('Let the Government withdraw, and let them start all over again. The men are out on bail, they are guaranteed a trial, they are allowed to have a solicitor') and, the next, condemning the excesses of their leadership ('we do not agree with the dictatorship methods of Mussolini, Hitler or Stalin'). Such a statement about Stalin was admirable, but Lansbury reverted to his usual form a few months later, writing that it was a 'lie' and a 'gross distortion of facts' to 'describe the Russian workers as a nation of slaves held in subjection by brute force', adding that what was happening in Russia was 'a wonderful experiment' and that 'we are not called upon to judge or accept all the means they adopt to attain their ends'.[26]

Lansbury was Leader of the Opposition, but his solution was hopelessly out of touch with the reality of dealing with a deeply amoral regime in Moscow. In the hard business of confronting repressive totalitarian government regimes, 'do unto others as you would have them do unto you' is useless as foreign policy.

As in so many debates, it was not difficult to highlight the inconsistency of Labour's position. Given their previous protests against the persecution of non-Bolshevik socialists in the 1920s, the incongruity of their current lack of concern over the agriculturalists' fate was striking. Conservative Oliver Locker-Lampson, having first dismissed the logical fallacy of Labour's counter-accusation that their own members had been on the receiving end of British police brutality in the past ('I do not care whether that has ever happened in England. It never ought to happen in England or anywhere else in the world'), then spoke up on behalf of the executed Russians:

A body of 35 Russians, for so-called crimes, were condemned to death in Russia and automatically executed. They were condemned to death for crimes for which no man in England would be executed. Why do not Members of the Labour party stand up for them? I remember a Trades Union Congress which unanimously carried a resolution of protest against the execution of a working man in Russia who had committed nothing but a political crime. I invite the Labour party to protest against this judicial murder in Russia, and to assist the Government in proving that it is justice and fair play that we want.[27]

• • •

The trial ran from 12 to 18 April. As was common, it was based upon the confessions which all the accused had signed. On the second day, William MacDonald tried to change his plea to 'not guilty', and withdrew his confession on the grounds that it had been signed under duress. The judge adjourned the court. Twenty minutes later the court reassembled. Bullard reported that 'Macdonald was brought in by the guards looking like death, and answered

"Yes" to every question put to him about his wrecking activities and so on. Cave [another embassy employee] said it was a dreadful sight.'[28]

The pressure on the men was immense. As Bullard wrote:

> I felt a little sad yesterday on reading about the evidence given by Macdonald against himself and some of his colleagues at the trial, for though I knew that the evidence was false at least as against the others, it was saddening to think that any pressure could make a man perjure himself so grossly ... I try not to despise Russians who will confess anything when in the power of the OGPU, because I don't know how long I should hold out *if I were a Russian.* Without ever knowing what one is charged with one's wife and children can be sent away, or one can be sent to the North to cut wood and live on bread and kasha for ten or twenty years. I don't see how the case will end, and yet I feel that so gross a fraud cannot in the long run succeed.[29]

In prosecutor Vyshinsky's closing speech, he urged the court to impose severe punishment upon the accused, even if that meant the death penalty. He urged the judges not to 'hesitate ... if you find it necessary to pronounce the sentence of the supreme measure of social defence upon one of the accused ... You, of course, will pronounce it, and your hand will not tremble when you sign it'. His remark to Thornton – 'Perhaps you will be used as manure for our Socialist fields somewhere'[30] – was unsurprisingly omitted from the published British transcript of the trial.

In spite of Vyshinsky's threat, the British government's pressure paid off.[31] Bullard noted in his diary that 'a high-up official in the OGPU said to an Englishwoman who has been many years in Russia: "Your country is very powerful. You've won." Nothing about the guilt or innocence of the accused, but merely an assumption that the whole affair was a trial of strength between the two governments.' Thornton's corpse was therefore not consigned to 'Socialist fields'. He and MacDonald were sentenced to three and two years' imprisonment, the minimum which the Soviets could have imposed without losing face. The three other British engineers were expelled and the fourth was acquitted. The Russian staff fared worse, ten of them receiving prison sentences, some up to ten years. Anna Kutusova got eighteen months. Though it is likely that she was released at the end of her sentence, the fate of this group of 'wreckers' in the purges of 1937–38 would have been in the balance. Rearrest without trial for earlier offences became common at that stage, even if the convicted person had served a full prison term. By then the NKVD, the OGPU's successor, was given quotas of death sentences to fill; it is probable that many of them perished.

The decision to imprison only MacDonald and Thornton was a clever one. The fact that Thornton had a Russian mistress, something he would have wished to keep secret from his wife back in Britain, and that MacDonald was so attached to his housekeeper served to ensure the men's long-term silence. It may even have saved them; Bullard initially thought that MacDonald, at least, was in very great danger: 'I feel that he will never be allowed to leave Soviet Russia alive, for fear he should tell the truth.'[32] When, after a token period of two months, the Soviets released them, many in the West hoped that the men would provide an insight into the case and an explanation for their guilty pleas. Little detail was forthcoming. Soviet friends in Britain took their guilty pleas at face value.

On 26 April, Lord Ponsonby, the Labour leader in the House of Lords, accused the government of 'violent action … pure melodrama … the diplomacy of Ruritania … of a penny novelette'. The government's action 'was the most blundering move conceivable. I venture to say if they had waited forty-eight hours [before imposing the embargo] Mr Thornton and Mr Macdonald would have been in London today.'[33] As far as Labour was concerned, the government had engineered the crisis to provoke a permanent breach with Moscow.

Reader Bullard would have described Ponsonby's optimism as naive in the extreme. He had written in his diary a few weeks earlier:

The [Manchester] Guardian's line is that Russia is an independent country and can therefore do as she likes, but, as I think I have said before, not even Russia really acts on that assumption. If HMG had not protested it is probable that all [the] men would have been condemned in secret to years of imprisonment. As it is, although there is to be a trial, the trial is to be public, [most] are out on bail, the assistant judges are men of science instead of fanatics from some factory, and the eyes of the world are on the trial. It is bad enough as it is, for who knows what 'confessions' have not been extracted from men half mad with want of sleep and ceaseless questioning. And who knows what the

Russians have not been forced to say. No one can do anything for them, poor creatures. Several of them are women who were employed in the Moscow office of Metro-Vickers.[34]

Replying to Ponsonby, Lord Hailsham, for the government, expressed the resigned incredulity that many on his side of the House felt over Labour's persistent refusal to accept any criticism of the Soviet regime:

The Foreign Secretary stated that, after having seen these four men, he was absolutely satisfied of their innocence and of the innocence of the other two, and that the four men themselves were absolutely confident of the innocence of their two colleagues. The noble Lord [Ponsonby] complained that when the arrest took place we lost no time in assuring the Soviet Government that we were confident of their innocence. It is difficult for me to understand the mentality of a serious politician who apparently thinks that when one of our fellow-subjects is charged with acting as a spy on behalf of the British Government in a foreign country, and when we, the Government, know that he is innocent of that charge, it is wrong of us to tell the foreign Government that they are making a mistake and that there is absolutely no ground for their suspicion.[35]

Hailsham also flatly denied Labour accusations that the government had any ulterior motive in acting as they had done: 'The embargo can be removed, and will be removed, as soon as Mr. Thornton and Mr. Macdonald return safe to Great Britain.' It was. The government withdrew the embargo when Macdonald and Thornton were released.[36]

Sidney and Beatrice Webb with George Bernard Shaw, June 1930.
© National Portrait Gallery, London.

CHAPTER 36

FABIANS (I) – SIDNEY AND BEATRICE WEBB

Have there ever been five more respectable, cultivated and mutually devoted, and be it added, successful couples – the ultra-essence of British bourgeois morality, comfort and enlightenment – than the Peases, Shaws, Wallases, Oliviers, and Webbs, who founded and carried on the Fabian Society during the half century from 1883 onwards?

And it must be added that they all made the best of both worlds. Two became Cabinet Ministers and peers, one the most famous and largest income earning litterateur of his generation, and another a revered philosophic writer and lecturer in the UK and the USA.

BEATRICE WEBB, DIARY, 16 JULY 1935

The Fabian Society began as a group of London-centred political intellectuals and theorists. Founded in 1884, it is today the oldest Socialist society in Britain. It has been variously described as 'a deep reservoir of talent for the emerging Socialist movement' and 'one of the most famous and successful agents of social reform in our history.'[1] When the Labour Representation Committee was formed in 1899 it linked the trade unions, the ILP and the Fabian Society. The Society was therefore one of the three founding pillars on which the Labour Party was built.

What later developed into a think tank for the modern Labour Party was dominated in the early years by George Bernard Shaw, Graham Wallas, Sydney Olivier, and Sidney Webb, joined, after their marriage in 1892, by Beatrice Webb. The four men were co-authors of the original *Fabian Essays* in 1889. Among the more notable of the second generation of Fabians were Harold Laski and G. D. H. Cole, two of the most eminent Labour theoreticians of the 1930s and 1940s. The 1929 Labour government numbered forty-nine Fabian Society members among its 288 MPs.

When a substantial legacy was bequeathed to the Fabian Society, the Webbs and Shaw used it to found the London School of Economics; they appointed fellow Fabians Wallas and Laski professors of political science from 1914 to 1950. The link between the Fabians, Labour and 'anti-Godism' was cemented by Wallas's and Laski's consecutive tenures as president of the Rationalist Press Association (now the Rationalist Association), which was an influential body in the cause of militant atheism.* Between them, these seven individuals were some of the most influential figures in the first forty years of the Labour Party.

The Webbs

The Webbs' leading role in the Labour movement since the end of the nineteenth century had given them hallowed status within the party. 'The modern Labour Party was born at its Nottingham conference in January, 1918. Sidney Webb ... was the architect of its constitution and the framer of its first political programme', wrote Margaret Cole, secretary of the Fabian Society and wife of G. D. H. Cole, who was its post-war chairman and president. Indeed, she insisted,

> The very existence of the Labour Party, with its foundation of trade unionism, owes much to the work of the Webbs [and] the London School of Economics ... which is training in economic and social problems literally thousands of young men and women who are now filling responsible posts ... owes its entire existence to the farsighted use made of the Webbs the legacy left the Fabian Society.[2]

Sidney Webb was a member of the 1924 and 1929–31 Cabinets. His policy statement, 'Labour and the New Social Order', was adopted by the party in

---

*   'Atheism' is non-belief in God. It is an inadequate term to use for those who progress beyond passive non-belief to vigorous opposition to religion. It is in this sense that the description 'militant atheist' is used.

1918 as its constitution and remained the basis of Labour Party policy for the next thirty years.[3] Margaret Cole described Beatrice as 'the greatest woman I have ever known'.[4] After their marriage, the Webbs became leading social theorists with an extensive and influential literary output. As founders of the London School of Economics they played an important part in its senior academic appointments, including that, already mentioned, of Harold Laski, the professor of political science and Soviet enthusiast. They, like Laski, were to influence the next generation as it formed its own political worldview.

Initially hostile to the Revolution, the Webbs were gradually won over to Soviet Communism; Lenin's insistence that the Russian translation of Sidney's *History of Trades Unionism* should be compulsory reading in the USSR helped. By the early 1930s, befriended by the Soviet ambassador Grigori Sokolnikov, who passed reading matter from the Soviet Union on to them, the Webbs became Soviet Communism's most ardent and public British enthusiasts. Beatrice likened their conversion to a romantic infatuation. Others close to the couple, on whom Beatrice's comparisons of the Soviet Communist Party to a Catholic monastic sect were not lost, saw it as a religious conversion late in life by two dedicated atheists who had not previously encountered an object for their spiritual thirst. This was certainly the impression given by Beatrice's diary:

> The salient and distinctive feature of Soviet Russia is, however, the establishment of Spiritual Power over and above the ostensible government, dominating all other elements, central and local ... This Spiritual Power knows no boundaries; it claims, like the Roman Church, to be a world-power and opens its arms to all peoples who subscribe to its creed and accept its discipline. Almost without intention, on the part of its founders, the Communist Party has taken on the characteristic features of a religious order; it has its Holy Writ, its prophets and its canonised saints; it has its Pope, yesterday Lenin and today Stalin; it has its code of conduct and its discipline; and it has its creeds and its Inquisition.[5]

Whether it was infatuation or conversion, in their new enthusiasm, emotion overruled logic. Of their new love they would believe no ill. Once soundly converted, challenges to the Webbs' new faith were too threatening to examine objectively. Philip Snowden, the Chancellor of the Exchequer, and his

wife came to visit in August 1931, a few days after Shaw's talk on Russia at
the Fabian summer school. Snowden was unimpressed by Shaw and the two
couples argued:

> The Snowdens, who lunched here yesterday, were full of GBS's speech … 'It
> was a wickedly mischievous speech,' Philip muttered, whereupon they and
> we had a hot dispute over Sovietism, and they denouncing it as a cruel slave
> state and we upholding it as a beneficial experiment in organising production
> and consumption for the common good. It was significant of our completely
> different outlook on life.[6]

The Webbs and the Snowdens were not to meet again before Snowden was
expelled from the Labour Party.

'Soviet Communism – a new civilisation?'

In 1932 the Webbs sailed for Leningrad and spent the next couple of months
travelling around the USSR, accompanied by guides provided for them by
the authorities. They returned enraptured. So enormous was their reputation
in Labour circles that when they published *Soviet Communism: A New Civilisation?* in 1935, it was widely read and accepted as the definitive picture of
Soviet Communism.[7] In fact, the book was a combination of fiction, denial,
dissemblance, and half-truths. It presented a glowing portrait of Stalin,
whitewashed the kulak deportations, and denied outright the 1932–33 famine
which caused the deaths of millions.

The Soviets' London ambassadors Ivan Maisky and his predecessor Grigori Sokolnikov had carefully cultivated a friendship with the Webbs and encouraged them to visit the Soviet Union to gather material for the book. There,
they were feted, flattered and duped. As they were writing the manuscript, the
Webbs sent sections of text through to Maisky for comment. The manuscript
pages were duly altered to conform with the Soviet line and returned, together with suggestions of more material to include in future chapters. This input
was confirmed by a Soviet defector in evidence given to a United States'
Senate committee in 1952. The defector, Ivan Nyman, had been an official in
the Soviet Foreign Office at the time, and testified, under the assumed name
Igor Bogolepov, regarding his first hand-experience:

The materials for this book actually were given by the Soviet Foreign Office. (Senator Ferguson, questioning: 'Given to the Webbs?')

Yes. They had only to remake a little bit for English text, a little bit criticizing, but in its general trend the bulk of the material was prepared for them in the Soviet Foreign Office ... I participated myself in part of this work.[8]

Born in 1904, Nyman had joined the Soviet Foreign Commissariat in 1923. After returning from a tour of duty in Spain in 1937, he was arrested but was unusually fortunate to escape execution or lengthy imprisonment. He was released the following year. In 1941, now a colonel in the Red Army, he deserted to join the army of General Vlasov, fighting against Stalin on the German side. Captured by the Americans, he managed to persuade them to allow him to defect; to have been sent back to Russia would have meant certain death, probably torture too. His experience in the Soviet Foreign Office no doubt made him a valuable source for American intelligence services, who debriefed him extensively.

Left-wing attempts to discredit Nyman have highlighted his role in the German-supported anti-Soviet army led by Vlasov, but it is simplistic to make such generalisations about Russians who joined Vlasov against Stalin in the years immediately following the Great Terror. Regardless of what may be said about Nyman himself, in this particular instance he must have been telling the truth to the Senate committee, since Beatrice Webb herself recorded, in a diary entry at the time of the book launch, that Ivan Maisky, among others, had helped with the text: 'December 20, 1935. Celebrated the publication of our book. Lunch at the London School of Economics (Maiskys, Hogbens, Shaws, Laskis, Lloyds, Turins, Beveridge, Professor Blackett and Levy) *represented those who had read and corrected proofs*'. (My italics.)[9]

It is highly unlikely that Maisky would have corrected the proofs himself; a task as sensitive as that would have been referred back to Moscow. If Nyman/Bogolepov had not done the editing, someone else certainly had. Nyman's account is therefore quite plausible – especially as the text of the book so faithfully reflects the Soviet propaganda line on a number of controversial issues. It should be remembered, too, that this was not the first time that key British opinion formers had naively relied upon Soviet sources to report on controversial matters. In 1930, ambassador Ovey had delayed his report to the Labour Cabinet on religious persecution until he could obtain the help of an 'expert' offered by Foreign Minister Litvinov.

On the evening of the same day as the LSE lunch, ambassador Maisky hosted a dinner in honour of the Webbs at the Soviet Embassy. Stafford Cripps, Kingsley Martin (editor of the *New Statesman*, which had been founded by the Webbs), Lord and Lady Marley and George Bernard Shaw and his wife were among the forty guests. Among those present whom Beatrice identified as Soviet sympathisers were Victor Gollancz, the publisher, and David Low, the *Evening Standard* cartoonist. She described the British guests as 'proletarian ... in sympathy (if) not in class with eminent Fabians as the central figures'.[10]

Soviet Communism remained in print for over ten years, with six new editions between 1935 and 1944. It was by far their best-selling work. In the first year it sold 20,000 copies in Great Britain; sales in America reached 5,000 copies in the first six months. Around the world, copies of the book turned up in Japan, Australia, South Africa, New Zealand and India.[11] Trade unions commissioned special editions.[12] It became, in an age when books were the main source of information, and when newspaper articles were quickly lost and forgotten, the standard reference work on the Soviet Union. Future comment on the famine, attempts to counter the rewriting of its history, and criticism of Soviet collectivisation (both in the 1930s and later, in the Baltic States*): all were answered by those on the British left with reference to the Webbs' book. Two of the six early editions were published during the war, when it was recommended as a source book on the USSR by the British government's Ministry of Information, possibly because the Soviet desk at the ministry was by then run by a Russian agent, Hans Peter Smolka.†

---

* In the Baltic States in 1949, in order to subdue the three conquered nations, the Soviets repeated the forced collectivisation of the Ukraine of 1929–31. Over 90,000 Balts were deported to labour camps and colonies in the Soviet Union.

† Smolka, who had been a friend of Kim Philby in Vienna in 1934 when Philby became a communist, came to the UK and anglicised his name to Peter Smollett. He achieved the rare distinction for a Soviet agent of being awarded an OBE for his work for the British. At the Ministry of Internal Affairs Soviet Desk, responsible for pro-Soviet propaganda for the war effort, his achievements included dissuading a number of publishers (including Gollancz) from taking Orwell's *Animal Farm* because of its implied criticism of an ally. Fearing discovery, he fled to Vienna after the war, where he managed to aid the Soviet cause one last time by persuading the film director Carol Reed, for whom he worked as a local fixer, to remove the anti-Soviet element from the shooting script of *The Third Man*.

In *The Truth about Soviet Russia*, an extract from *Soviet Communism* published in 1942, with a new preface by George Bernard Shaw, the Webbs repeated their insistence that Stalin was 'not a dictator'[13] and that the USSR was 'the most inclusive and equalised democracy in the world'.[14] That such a statement was complete fiction is borne out by contemporary events: the brutal Soviet treatment of their own soldiers, in particular those who had escaped German capture or encirclement. As many as 994,000 were declared guilty of treason, espionage or deliberately engineering their own capture. Of these, 157,000 were shot.[15] Many of the others were sent to the camps.

Over the decades since the war, the book has become an embarrassment to the Labour Party, which has tried to distance itself from it and downplay its contemporary impact. In 1961, Margaret Cole herself took this line in her book *The Story of Fabian Socialism*:

> Some may wonder about the influence of *Soviet Communism* itself on Labour thought; my own impression is that the enormous political guide-book, for all its sheer size and weight and the fame of its authors, had, in fact, remarkably little.[16]

Margaret's husband (of whom more below) remained loyal to the Soviet Union until the invasion of Hungary in 1956. Her statement is probably more a product of that disillusionment, shared by many left-wing intellectuals, and of her embarrassment, rather than an accurate reflection of the situation twenty years earlier.

The actual contemporary view appears to have been very different. Kingsley Martin, writing in the *New Statesman and Nation*, reviewing a seventy-page postscript which was added to an updated version of *Soviet Communism* in 1937, still referred to it as 'vast and brilliant' and praised its authors for 'no loss of vigour, care or ingenuity' in the new edition.[17] Harold Laski, writing in the same paper the following year, in celebration of Beatrice's eightieth birthday, was equally effusive: 'Even those who dissent from its conclusions admit that their work on Soviet Communism is one of those rare books which at once attains the status of a classic.'[18] Conveniently, Margaret Cole's memory in 1961 of her own previous enthusiasm seems to have waned too. In the same 1938 edition of the *New Statesman and Nation* she was in no doubt as to the book's significance:

What has lifted [the Webbs] far out of the class of merely first-rate organisers is the touch of genius, of political imagination which has enabled them to see, and to catch hold of, the new and fruitful idea … Five years ago they saw, with the clarity of new vision, what was coming to birth in Soviet Russia. And anyone who knows them, I imagine, will agree that at 80 years old Mrs Webb shows more eagerness to understand and to welcome the new developments than most people half her age. There will not, I fear, be another book like *Soviet Communism*.

Nine years later, in 1946, she was still convinced of its brilliance:

[The book] was immediately a resounding and continuous success. By 1937, two years after publication, it had already sold nearly 40,000 copies, many of them to working-class people, Trade Unionists, and Co-operators – the audience which she was delighted to secure; and it continued to sell, in revised editions, until the remaining copies, together, alas, with all the sheets and stock of the Webbs' other big books, were destroyed at the publishers' offices during the City fire-blitz.[19]

The reputation of the book was enduring too. In 1947, one year after his tenure as chairman of the Labour Party, Harold Laski gave the Webb Memorial Lecture at the London School of Economics. It was a grand affair, graced by the presence of Prime Minister Clement Attlee. For his subject, Laski chose 'The Webbs and Soviet Communism', once again paying effusive tribute to their 1935 book. The Fabian Society even published the lecture as a pamphlet. Probably the most authoritative assessment of the impact of *Soviet Communism* comes from Neal Wood. He is in no doubt of its influence. His *Communism and British Intellectuals* (1959) describes the Webbs' book as 'one of the most widely read and influential works in Britain'.[20]

Modern critics of the book usually restrict themselves to one or two remarks and a couple of extracts, but a few quotations cannot adequately illustrate the full extent to which the book represents the intellectual degeneration of the pro-Soviet left of the inter-war period. A more detailed examination must be done for the record.

The Webbs, the deportations, and the famine

Soviet Communism takes many liberties with history. One of the most blatant examples is its re-telling of the Ukrainian famine. The famine swept through Ukraine and southern Russia in 1932–34 in the wake of dekulakisation and collectivisation, exacerbated by drought, and caused between five and seven million deaths.[21] Today there remains much evidence that it was deliberately exploited by Stalin to neutralise the countryside as a base for future counter-revolution and that many of the millions who died were, in effect, victims of a political genocide.

In their book, the Webbs assured their readers that actually there had been *no* famine. They admitted that there had been food shortages, but downplayed them and used careful paraphrase to minimise its significance: 'starvation' became 'defective nutrition'; 'famine', the 'total absence of foodstuffs'. Though people were reduced to chewing bark and grass, and even cannibalism, the Webbs insisted that instead of 'starving', the hungry were 'unprovided with a sufficient store of cereal food, and specially short of fats':[22]

> Soviet officials on the spot, in one district after another, inform the present writers that, whilst there was shortage and hunger, there was, at no time, a total lack of bread, though its quality was impaired by using other ingredients than wheaten flour; and that any increase in the death-rate, due to diseases and accompanying defective nutrition, occurred only in a relatively small number of villages.[23]

Having initially denied that there *had* been famine, they then half-admitted it, but sought to explain it away. Under the Webbs' pen, famine was transformed into politically motivated mass sabotage coupled with self-inflicted suicide-by-apathy, a deliberate refusal by the kulaks, even at the cost of the lives of their own family members, to sow or thresh their crops or weed their fields:

> Whole groups of peasants, under hostile influences, got into such a state of apathy and despair that they ceased to care about whether their fields were tilled or not, or what would happen to them in the winter if they produced no crop at all. Whole villages sullenly abstained from sowing or harvesting on all but a minute fraction of their fields, so that, when the year ended, they had no stock of seed, and in many cases actually no grain on which to live ...

Individual peasants made a practice, out of spite, of surreptitiously 'barbering' the ripening wheat; that is, rubbing out the grain from the ear, or even cutting off the whole ear, and carrying off for individual hoarding this shameless theft of community property.[24]

Conveniently reversing the actual course of events (the famine followed the dekulakisation) the deportation of the kulaks to the northern and Siberian forests, which amounted to ethnic cleansing by class, was transformed into a benevolent gesture of the authorities aiming to save lives by providing people with a means of earning a living:

> The most guilty of the sabotagers, often ex-kulaks, were expelled ... and in some of the worst cases the inhabitants of whole villages, if only in order to save them from starvation, and were summarily removed from the land that they had neglected or refused to cultivate, and deported elsewhere, to find labouring work of any sort for bare maintenance.[25]

While they acknowledged that the deportations had caused hardship, to blame the Soviet authorities, the Webbs insisted, was 'irresponsible criticism':

> There seems nothing unreasonable or inequitable in the view that, wherever the land is entrusted to a peasant class by the community, it is on the paramount condition that they should produce, up to their ability, the foodstuffs required for the maintenance of the community. Any organised refusal to cultivate must inevitably be met by expropriation.[26]

That 'entrusting' of the land to peasants by the 'community' (state) was in reality the seizure by force of all that they possessed and its amalgamation into vast state-owned farms. Now condemned to work as virtual slaves, the Webbs blame them for not taking care of the land for the new owners. As for the 'great hardship' caused, about which the authors did not utter a word of condemnation, there was an excuse – the building a new state:

> It is not denied that in these summary removals, as in those of the individ- ual kulaks who had refused to conform to the government's requirements,

great hardship was inflicted on a large number of women and children, as well as on the men. Without such cost in suffering, it is argued, the rapid reorganisation of peasant agriculture, which seemed the only practicable means of solving the problem of a national food supply, could not have been effected.[27]

But once they got there, the Webbs assured their readers, the kulak camps were no more than the Soviet equivalent of the British workhouse:

> The Soviet Government had no workhouses available and no time to build them. Its device was forcibly to remove the peasants who were found to be without food from the villages which they were demoralising to places at a distance where they could be put to work at the making of railways, roads or canals, at the cutting of timber, or at prospecting or mining for mineral ores – all tasks of discomfort and occasionally of hardship, by which they were enabled to earn the bare subsistence wage of relief work. It was a rough and ready expedient of 'famine relief', which undoubtedly caused much suffering to innocent victims. But candid students of the circumstances may not unwarrantably come to the conclusion that, when the crisis of possible starvation arrived, as the result largely of deliberate sabotage, the Soviet Government could hardly have acted otherwise than it did.[28]

In fact, as has already been shown, even some Soviet officials were appalled by the conditions in the camps.

The famine is still commemorated in Ukraine, in the same way that the Holocaust is remembered in Israel. The Webbs' preposterous alternative narrative of an event which killed a similar number of people is little different from Holocaust-denial.

Experts dismissed

Anyone who offered facts to contradict the Webbs' position on any matter to do with the Soviet Union received one of a similar set of responses: they were dismissed as 'prejudiced' or hostile to Soviet Communism or as being too simplistic; or their observations were discounted because they 'seldom had any opportunity of going to the suffering districts' – though neither had the Webbs, whose sole source of information was the Soviet Foreign Ministry. Evidence which seemed unassailable was dealt with more subtly: after a superficial, apparently objective, examination, it was bluntly and confidently dismissed:

> We note that Mr W. H. Chamberlin* ... continues to assert that there was a terrible famine in 1932–1933, 'one of the greatest human catastrophes since the world-war,' which caused, from disease and starvation, some four or five million deaths beyond the normal mortality.
>
> After carefully weighing Mr Chamberlin's various assertions we can find no evidence of there having been any 'natural' or 'climactic' famine in 1931–1934. There is abundant testimony from many sources that the shortage of the crop was, for the most part, 'man-made' ... in 1932 there was a widespread refusal to sow, neglect to weed, and failure to reap ... This 'man-made' shortage it was that Mr Chamberlin calls a famine.
>
> We find, in the statements of Mr Chamberlin and other believers in the famine, nothing that can be called statistical evidence of widespread abnormal mortality; though it may be inferred that hardships in particular villages must have led, here and there, to some rise in the local death rate.[29]

Metropolitan-Vickers

In their book the Webbs also severely criticised the National Government's conduct during the Metro-Vickers affair two years earlier. It put into print an analysis which, because of the popularity of *Soviet Communism,* was referred to, and considered definitive, by British socialists for the next twelve years. Their account was permeated by a sense of outrage at the unfairness, not of the treatment of the innocent engineers, but at the treatment of the Soviet government by a hostile, prejudiced, British administration:

> The British Ambassador manifested at the outset a resentment, for which there was no diplomatic justification, at British engineers being even suspected of any criminal offence, let alone being prosecuted! He peremptorily demanded the immediate discharge without trial. What made matters more difficult was

---

*   A journalist for the *Manchester Guardian* and *Christian Science Monitor.*

the very undiplomatic action of the British Government in publicly threatening to impose an embargo on all imports from the USSR, should any one or
more of the British defendants be found guilty and sentenced by the Supreme
Court of the USSR.[30]

It appeared that the Webbs really believed that the engineers were guilty, their
confessions true, and that the OGPU investigation and subsequent trial had
been conducted with absolute propriety:

> The Supreme Court found evidence of guilt, *supported as it was by manifold*
> *confessions*, convincing in 16 out of the 17 cases ... one was acquitted ... three
> others sentenced only to immediate expulsion, whilst the other two, who had
> elaborately confessed their and their own comrades guilt, were condemned
> respectively to two and three years' imprisonment. The British Government,
> without even waiting to consider the verbatim stenographic reports of the evi-
> dence that were so promptly published, imposed the embargo which had been
> so precipitously threatened, and by which – followed as it was by counter-em-
> bargo on the other side and practically all trade between the two countries was
> stopped. The pecuniary loss thus caused to individual British manufacturers
> and shipowners at least compatible with the inconvenience inflicted on the
> Soviet Government. This irrational outcome of regular judicial proceedings,
> taken in *a proper form* before the highest tribunal of an independent sovereign
> state, was endured for over two months. (My italics.)[31]

It appeared that, in print at least, the Webbs' delusion about Soviet Russia was
total. It seemed that nothing could deflect them from their conviction that it
was a nation founded upon principles of justice and integrity.

Repression and executions

The Webbs could hardly deny the Red Terror, the mass killings which the
Bolsheviks initiated, and then encouraged in the wider population during the
first years of the Revolution. They still found reasons to excuse it:

> The Communist Party, however one may criticise it, does embody an idea and
> can be relied on to stand by its idea. [After the Revolution] it restored order

– after a frightful lot of shooting – in the great towns. For a time everybody carrying arms without authority was shot. The action was clumsy and brutal but it was effective. To retain its power the Communist Government organised Extraordinary Commissions [the *Cheka*] with practically unlimited powers, and crushed out all opposition by a Red Terror. Much that the Red Terror did was cruel and frightful ... *but if it was fanatical it was honest. Apart from individual atrocities, they did on the whole kill for a reason and to an end. Its bloodshed was not like the silly aimless butcheries of the* [White Russian] *Denikin regime* ... [Today] the streets of the Russian towns are as safe as any streets in Europe. (My italics.)[32]

As before, regarding the famine, any further criticism was dismissed as biased:

With regard to any particular incident, the evidential value of the greater part of the mass of lurid literature on the subject is of the slightest. Very naturally, these volumes betray intense bias. They are full of 'hearsay evidence', and of unsupported allegations and letters, wholly unverifiable. No archives have been published, and no such publication is ever likely.[33]

When the Webbs turned to the tricky subject of executions, they downplayed the problem too, just as Beatrice's nephew Stafford Cripps had done. 'For a population exceeding 160 millions [the] number of executions does not compare badly with the statistics of various other countries deeming themselves civilised,' they insisted.[34] The Webbs' assertion was a fantasy; the actual figures tell a very different story.

The number of executions in Britain in 1900–31 totalled 447, an average of thirteen per year. The British population in 1931 was 46 million. With a Soviet population of 160 million, the pro rata number of Soviet executions should therefore have been forty-five per year. In 1930 alone, the NKVD's own statistics record 20,201 executions. This means that the number of executions that year, the first year of the kulak deportations, were actually *500 times* above the norm in 'civilised' countries. Over the eight years 1930–38, the NKVD's official figures for executions for counter-revolutionary crimes are:[35]

1930	20,201
1931	10,651
1932	2,728
1933–36	6,557 (average per year 1,600)
1937	353,074
1938	328,618

It has been estimated that about 30,000 kulaks were shot in 1929–30, and it is not clear how many of those are part of the statistics quoted above. Different NKVD figures suggest that 98,000 died in all camps and prisons in 1930–33, but it is not possible to tell how many of these deaths were executions. It is also unclear if these figures include kulaks in their labour 'colonies' and settlements or only cover the inmates of hard labour camps. Other estimates, also derived from NKVD figures, show that of the 1,804,000 men, women and children deported under the anti-kulak measures in 1930–31, only 1,317,000 remained in camps in 1932; a shortfall of 487,000. Modern researchers estimate that of these kulaks, 50 per cent (243,500) escaped and 50 per cent perished.[36]

If you lie boldly enough, you will be believed. The Webbs believed their Soviet friends when they supplied them with statistics. The text written by the couple using these numbers bore no resemblance to reality.

These figures in the table above cover executions for counter-revolutionary crimes only – not those punishing ordinary criminal acts. In 1932, a new Soviet law, dubbed the 'law of three spikelets', extended the definition of theft to include the taking of as little as a few ears of corn. The Webbs, following the Soviet line, described the desperation of those whose hunger drove them to glean directly from the fields as criminal acts: the painstaking ear-by-ear destruction of crops on orders from White Russian émigrés abroad, the 'shameless theft of community property'.[37] The repressive measures of which the 'spikelets' law formed a part resulted in gulag sentences, typically of five to ten years, for more than 190,000 people. A further 11,000 were shot.[38]

Even among the Webbs' political contemporaries, occasional voices of dissent were raised by those who refused to accept that the sacrifices were justified. Dorothy Warriner, writing in the *New Fabian Research Bureau Quarterly*, was one of the few who did, albeit cautiously:

When it was decided to socialise agriculture the resistance [of the more well-to-do peasants] had to be crushed: they have now been successfully liquidated, i.e. killed, or sent to Siberia. Here it is not necessary to comment on the Webbs' plea that these methods were necessary because the Russian peasant was so extraordinarily primitive that he could not see the advantage of collectivisation.[39]

Ignorance

When all else failed, the Webbs' final defence was to plead ignorance. Difficult facts were sidestepped with the rejoinder that no one could know the real truth. The extent of the crop failures (qualified as 'partial') was 'impossible to ascertain with any assurance', something which 'we cannot pretend to estimate'.[40] Weather damage in the fields was supplemented by the deliberate wrecking of the crops, but it was 'to a degree that we find no means of estimating' and, about the scale of the famine, there was 'nothing that can be called statistical evidence'.[41] As for the deportations, the Webbs reluctantly admitted that they affected hundreds of thousands of families (Stalin had publicly acknowledged this, so it could hardly be denied) but prefaced this admission by multiple assertions that the real truth could not be known. These are all from just two pages of the book:

We can form no estimate of the number of cases in which practically the whole property of these families was confiscated ... we can form no idea as to how many of them could accurately be described as kulaks, or persons guilty of economic oppression of their less successful neighbours ...we do not know to what extent or by what means their cases were investigated before they were forcibly ejected from their homes. We have been unable to learn how many of these peasants were removed to prison, or (as is specifically alleged) deported to the lumber camps in the northern forest areas, or employed on public works of railway or canal construction ... Nor is there any account known to us of the conditions under which these hundreds of thousands of men, women and children have had to live in this process of arbitrary removal and resettlement, nor any estimate of the mortality involved in their displacement.[42]

Doubts

Notwithstanding the confidence expressed in the book, Beatrice, more than

Sidney, experienced moments of doubt which, as a woman whose reputation rested upon her brilliance as one of Britain's leading objective social researchers, she had to fight hard to suppress. From time to time this surfaces in her diary.

Some of her doubts were provoked in 1933 by the reports of her nephew, Malcolm Muggeridge, on the Ukrainian famine. Muggeridge had gone to Moscow as acting correspondent for the *Manchester Guardian*. With impeccable Socialist credentials, the son of a Labour MP, nephew of a cabinet minister, and an occasional writer for a left-wing newspaper, he started out as moderately sympathetic towards Soviet Communism. His perspective quickly changed.[43] W. P. Crozier, then editor of the *Manchester Guardian*, told him that they would not print some of his most critical observations 'as they would then be in bad company – i.e. with the out-and-out opponents of Soviet Russia'.[44] In the end, Muggeridge told another journalist, his articles on the famine were 'villainously cut'.[45] When a Ukrainian émigré organisation asked the paper for permission to reprint his famine articles, Crozier refused, even though he had already heavily edited them. The Ukrainians approached Muggeridge directly and he wrote a pamphlet for them instead.[46]

Two years earlier, Beatrice had had nothing but praise for him, calling him: 'the most intellectually stimulating and pleasant mannered of all my "in-laws" … What is attractive about him … is the total absence of intellectual arrogance'.[47] But when his opinion of her beloved Soviet Union changed so did her feelings towards him. In her diary, she wrote of his 'curiously hysterical denunciations of the USSR' and of his 'arrogantly expressed' reports.[48] A few months later, she described him as 'rabidly abusive' of Russia.[49] 'There is a well of hatred in Malcolm's nature,' she wrote, 'and his experiences in the USSR have released and canalised it.'[50] As Muggeridge's reports on what he had found in Russia made him a pariah in Labour circles, Beatrice was in no doubt that he had only himself to blame: 'Why did he imagine he would like Soviet Russia? All its bad features were well known … He ought to have smelled a rat and, if he wanted to remain in the Labour world, carefully avoided discovering its stinking body.'[51] Beatrice seems to have been oblivious to the moral implications of what she writes here – that Muggeridge should have 'smelled a rat' and turned his back upon the truth to save his own career and popularity (he had resigned from the *Manchester Guardian* and was having difficulty earning a living). Or perhaps this was the only way in which she could deal with her own predicament, to remain blind to the dissonance between her Soviet fantasy and its reality.

She did not speak to him again until a chance meeting in 1937. To her, he was now a 'queer thin little figure, colourless face and hair, neurotically active eyes and continuously moving mouth, with his ingratiating manner'.[52] He 'half repelled, half attracted' her. She even wondered if he was 'a bit mad'.[53]

This is not to say that she did not hear the criticisms that he made. Each sudden squall shook her sails before the boat was righted once again. She acknowledged that there was '*some* fire behind the smoke of Malcolm's clearly malicious but sincerely felt denunciation of Soviet Communism', and that there was 'no evidence to the contrary' that the starvation would not become 'catastrophic' the following year.[54] But Sidney was there to console and reaffirm her faith even in hard times:

> Another account of famine in Russia in the Manchester Guardian, which certainly bears out Malcolm's reports. A melancholy atmosphere in which to write a book on Soviet Communism, especially when one of the partners is failing in strength and capacity. Sidney is not daunted. The thought that there may be famine in some districts of the USSR does not disturb his faith in the eventual triumph of the Soviet economic principle ... Fortunately for the USSR the attention of the capitalist countries is today concentrated on the Mad Dog of Europe – Hitler's Germany.[55]

The dissonance did not go away. Although both Webbs publicly rejected or excused every criticism of the USSR in *Soviet Communism*, facts kept intruding upon the fantasy. On her return from Russia in 1932, Beatrice privately admitted them: 'There is of course in our vision of Russia a dark side ... the repression of free thought and free expression ... the occasional physical terrorism, the trap door disappearance of unwanted personalities ... the putting out of office and power of upright but indiscreet citizens'.[56]

Those doubts remained. In her diary entry of 25 November 1936, the first anniversary of the book's publication, Beatrice candidly acknowledged this as she would never have done in public:

What do we think of our child today? So far as the material and constitutional progress of the USSR is concerned our presentation has been more than justified … But there remains as the big blot on the picture – the terror, suspicions, suppression of free opinion, the arrests, prosecutions, death penalties, characteristic of an unfinished revolution. Those amazing confessions, which would not be considered as evidence in an English court, how are they obtained? And the sycophantic adulation of Stalin – also unpleasant to British ears … The USSR is still mediaeval in its savage pursuit of the heretic.[57]

And yet, with Sidney's help, she was able to steady her nerve. Five years on, in *The Truth about Soviet Russia* (1941), the Webbs still found themselves able to assert with confidence that the USSR was 'the most inclusive and equalised democracy in the world'.[58] As the war on the Eastern Front turned in the Soviets' favour, Beatrice felt that their faith had been justified: 'We have lived the life we liked and done the work we intended to do; and we have been proved to be right about Soviet Communism: a new civilisation. What more can we want than a peaceful and painless ending of personal consciousness?'[59] Five weeks later, on 30 April 1943, Beatrice died. The faith which she had chosen had comforted her until the end. Sidney's death followed four years later.

History has been kind to the Webbs. When their ashes were interred in Westminster Abbey, the resting place of the nation's greatest statesmen, artists, generals and monarchs, Prime Minister Clement Attlee's tribute could not have been more effusive: 'Millions are living fuller and freer lives today because of the work of Sidney and Beatrice Webb'.[60]

CHAPTER 37

FABIANS (II): GEORGE BERNARD SHAW

The influence of Bernard Shaw on the growth and activity of the Fabian Society and on the Labour and Socialist movement generally can hardly be overestimated.
THE BOOK OF THE LABOUR PARTY, 1925[1]

The last of the giants, but perhaps the first of the truly civilized.
J. B. PRIESTLEY, NOVEMBER 1950[2]

When George Bernard Shaw died, on 2 November 1950, tributes came from statesmen, artists and intellectuals around the world: President Truman spoke of his 'genius'; the lights on Broadway were dimmed; to Jawaharlal Nehru, the Indian Prime Minister, the world had lost 'one of the greatest figures of the age', a man of 'deep wisdom'. *The Times* paid tribute to his greatness:

> In the early years of the century Shaw could justly claim that he was covering the mind of a whole generation. Later he sought no less strenuously, with dialectic no less brilliant, to communicate his own passion for social justice and to insist that every man is morally responsible for his own deeds, which are irrevocable, and that his life depends on his usefulness.[3]

From the world of the arts, the tributes were no less fulsome. 'Now that we have lost Shaw, the world seems a smaller and drearier place. He was not only the last of the giants, but perhaps the first of the truly civilized men', wrote J. B. Priestley. Fellow Irishman and playwright Sean O'Casey was equally convinced of Shaw's stature:

> Shaw is one of those mentioned by Yeats who will be remembered forever; remembered for his rare and surprising gifts and for the gallant way he used them. In time these will blend together, and Shaw will shine forth in the cathedral of man's mind a sage standing in God's holy fire as in the gold mosaic of a wall.[4]

Labour Prime Minister Attlee praised him as a 'social revolutionary and prophet', one of the most remarkable men of the age, and he highlighted Shaw's outstanding place in the British Labour movement.

> Death has taken away in the fullness of years one of the most remarkable personalities of our time. Bernard Shaw excelled in many fields. As a critic, dramatist, man of letters, humourist, social revolutionary and prophet, he was our greatest entertainer and teacher. His influence on the men and women of the generations which came to maturity during the last 60 years was immense. No man did more to stimulate thought and to break through the conventional outlook on life of the Victorian era. We Socialists who knew him as a fellow worker revered him for the many years of devoted service and effective support by word and pen which he gave to our movement.[5]

Shaw arrived in London from Dublin in 1876, at the age of 20. For the next fifty years his contribution to socialist politics had almost as much impact as the literary output for which he is better known today. He joined the Fabian Society in 1884, the same year as his friend Sidney Webb. In 1889, he co-edited the society's landmark *Fabian Essays in Socialism*, as one of the foremost works of British socialist literature. The book included contributions by Shaw himself, Webb, Sydney Olivier, and Graham Wallas. He was highly active in politics, campaigning widely for Socialist candidates, and he played a part in the foundation of the Independent Labour Party in 1893.

Shaw's direct involvement in electoral politics was brief. He was elected as a local councillor for St Pancras in 1897, but lost the seat in 1903. He did not stand again in any national or local election, but he energetically involved himself in many other aspects of political life. He was a powerful and effective public speaker and, as such, influenced a whole generation of socialists. One of these, who testified to his powers as an orator, was the young Fenner Brockway. The future chairman of the ILP recorded his early impressions in his memoirs:

> One evening Bernard Shaw came. I was a Shaw worshipper, and was thrilled by this opportunity of meeting him at close quarters ... I can still see Shaw as he stood on the shallow platform at the end of the hall – crowded to suffocation, of course – tall, slight, straight-backed, arms folded across his chest, throwing out his stream of challenging sentences with the confidence of a God ... [we] were entranced.[6] ... I think he influenced my thought, indeed my life, more than anyone when I was young.[7]

Shaw was on holiday with the Webbs and Wallas when the news arrived of a substantial bequest to the Fabian Society for the promotion of Socialism. The decision was made to devote half of the money to setting up an educational institution: so the London School of Economics was founded. Many key intellectual figures of the left were to pass through its doors, either as staff or students, over the following decades. One of these was Kingsley Martin, who had been a lecturer at the LSE before he became editor of the *New Statesman*, which was set up in 1913 by the Webbs, with the support of Shaw and other Fabians. Martin, too, remembered hearing Shaw speak at a meeting just after the end of the First World War:

> He made an indelible impression on me at this first meeting. I cannot recall what he spoke about. It mattered little. It was George Bernard Shaw you remembered; his physical magnificence, splendid bearing, superb elocution, unexpected Irish brogue, and continuous wit were the chief memories of his speech. He would give his nose a thoughtful twitch between his thumb and finger while the audience laughed. He was one of the best speakers I ever heard. Speaking for Labour candidates at elections, it was said he would fill every hall and [draw in] scores of votes.[8]

By the mid-1920s, Shaw's reputation in the Labour Party was enormous. In *The Book of the Labour Party – its History and Growth Policy and Leaders*, the three-volume semi-official history of the party written to coincide with its historic first term in 1924, but eventually published a year later, after the government had fallen, Shaw's prominent role in the Labour movement was acknowledged:

> The influence of Bernard Shaw on the growth and activity of the Fabian Society and on the Labour and Socialist movement generally can hardly be overestimated. But his power as a propagandist, both with pen and tongue, was only acquired by the exercise of the infinite capacity for taking pains which is said to be the sign of a genius. His gifts as a speaker were cultivated by him with an intensity rarely equalled by protagonists of any cause.
>
> During the early years of the Fabian Society he spoke night after night, Sunday after Sunday, at meetings large and small, in halls or in the open air, until he became, and remains, the one public figure who can, not only in London, but in all large centres of population, always draw a great audience of people willing to pay for the pleasure of hearing him speak. A lecture by Bernard Shaw will always attract a big assembly made up of individuals of all classes in the community who have some elements of intellectual life and intellectual curiosity … through [his] experiences in many and widely different spheres he obtained the knowledge of human nature – especially from the social point of view – which flashes out so brilliantly in his dramas and in his political and economic writings.[9]

Shaw's reputation remains high today, both generally (he is the only person to have won both a Nobel Prize and an Oscar) and among the British left. The 2001 *Dictionary of Labour Biography* says of Shaw that

> 'from the late 1890s through to the end of the 1920s he was possibly the most nationally famous and influential of Socialist propagandists … If intellectuals in the inter-war period typically were (or thought to be) socialist, Shaw was as much the cause as either Methodism or Marx…'[10]

In 2006, on the 150th anniversary of his birth, Tony Blair unveiled a window in Shaw's honour in the LSE. In his speech, he said:

> A lot of the values that the Fabians and George Bernard Shaw stood for would

be very recognisable, at least I hope they would, in today's Labour party. One of the things I think they were best at was being utterly iconoclastic about the traditional thinking that governed our country and indeed constantly, whenever a piece of conventional wisdom came out, they questioned that conventional wisdom in its fundamentals, and did so with remarkable success.[11]

The accompanying BBC report described Shaw as 'one of the most influential, and creative, minds ever to come out of the British Isles'.[12]

The other Shaw – political eugenicist

According to one modern commentator, 'by the 1930s [Shaw] was preaching the case for a kind of benevolent autocracy of a Socialist elite'.[13] In fact, the reality behind the myth was very different. Shaw had a darker side which is little-known or mentioned today, a brutal and cruel streak to which the written record abundantly attests. In July 1935, as Beatrice and Sidney Webb, close friends of Shaw's, were finishing the text of *Soviet Communism*, Beatrice wrote of her concerns about him:

> This strange admiration for the person who *imposes* his will on others, however ignorant and ugly and even cruel that will may be, is an obsession which has been growing on GBS for the last years of his life. And yet he himself is so kindly and tolerant toward others ... As a young social reformer, he hated cruelty and oppression and pleaded for freedom ... Today he idealises the dictator, whether he be a Mussolini, a Hitler or Stalin* ... What he really admires in Soviet Communism is the forceful activities of the Communist Party.[14]

Beatrice was correct in her reflections about Shaw, but wrong in absolving him of the same sentiments in earlier years. Shaw had first called for the development of gas chambers in 1910; for three decades he advocated the extermination of all those who were unable or unwilling to make a useful economic or social contribution to a socialist state, people he described as

---

*   It is worth noting that here, in the privacy of her diary, Beatrice calls Stalin a 'dictator', something that, in print, she and Sidney both consistently and vehemently denied (e.g. *Soviet Communism*, p. 431; *The Truth about Soviet Russia*, p.14).

'not fit to live', a philosophy of political eugenics far removed from any concept of 'benevolent autocracy':

> The moment we face it frankly, we are driven to the conclusion that the com-
> munity has a right to put a price on the right to live in it. If people are not fit
> to live, kill them in a decent way ... [It is] the only solution that will create a
> sense of full social responsibility in the modern populations.[15]

Given Shaw's public image today, fostered by the enduring popularity of *My Fair
Lady* and the fact that generations of English literature students will have studied at least one of his plays, it is almost impossible to believe that he so openly
expressed such anti-libertarian and murderous sentiments. But the evidence is
clear in print. It is so incomprehensible that one's first reaction is to dismiss it
as macabre humour or hyperbole. Beatrice Webb, who knew him well, did not.
Closer examination of what he actually wrote does not permit us to do so, either.

'The Dictatorship of the Proletariat' (1921)

In 1921 Shaw published a lengthy article in *Labour Monthly* entitled 'The
Dictatorship of the Proletariat'.[16] In it, Shaw proposed that the leaders of a
socialist revolution, be they Russian 'Bolsheviks' or British 'Labour Leaders'
(it is clear in the article that he is hypothesising about a British scenario),
would have to so completely overturn public perceptions of right and wrong
that, in the place of existing Judaeo-Christian morality, a new 'Socialist morality' would arise – one which would support state repression and extermination. Once this transformation in the collective mindset had come about,
certain other essential components of the revolution could then take place. He
outlined them as follows:

1. Conditions would be laid down in a new constitution whereby citizens
   would be permitted to live freely in the new Socialist state but penalised
   if they infringed them.
2. The state would define new classes of crimes which would be subject to
   the death penalty.
3. These new crimes would be counter-revolutionary acts which society
   had previously tolerated or even praised.

4. The exercise of 'rights which have for centuries been regarded as the most sacred guarantees of popular liberty', previously accepted rights, such as those of public assembly and free speech, would be forbidden. Public demonstrations would be fired upon.

5. Those who evaded their 'debt to the community' would be treated as 'social parasites' and penalised accordingly.

6. Compulsory labour (i.e. labour camps) would be an essential component of the new Socialist state.

7. The numbers dispatched to the camps might be considerable and their labour would be forced labour with minimal or no pay.

8. Resisters (i.e. counter-revolutionaries) would be punished by sentence to labour camps or execution. (In Shaw's language, 'compulsory social service ... on pain of death' would render 'resistance injurious').

9. The transition from capitalism to Socialism in Britain could not be achieved without these extreme measures and mass propaganda.

10. These measures were so radical that they would be resisted by the press and the Civil Service and the opposition parties in Parliament.

11. Accordingly, the success of socialist revolution could not be ensured without the suppression of the press, the judiciary and Civil Service and the suspension of Parliament.

12. Socialism was unlikely to be successfully introduced in Britain without bloodshed – though, he charitably added, avoiding bloodshed was still to be desired.

That it would not be easy for those called upon to kill their fellow human beings for these new 'crimes' Shaw freely admitted. It would require 'iron nerve'. Perversely, he ascribed nobility to those who were to carry out these new state-sanctioned executions (a theme to which he was to return in his preface to *On the Rocks* in 1934). Beatrice Webb had remarked on Shaw's admiration for Hitler, and the parallels are hard to avoid; Himmler expressed the same admiration for his own troops' iron resolution in killing Jews.[17] These twelve statements, which provide a summary of Shaw's twenty-page article, are so far-fetched that it seems difficult to believe that they were really what he intended to write. An extended examination of extracts from the original text, however, inevitably leads to precisely the same conclusions:

The Task of Advocates of a changeover to Socialism, whether they call themselves Labour Leaders, Socialists, Communists, Bolsheviks, or what not, is to
create a Socialist conscience … And when this task is accomplished, there is
still the very arduous one of devising a new constitution to carry out the new
ethic of the new conscience …

What, exactly, does making a new constitution mean? *It means altering the
conditions on which men are permitted to live in society**. When that alteration
reverses the relation between the governing classes and the government, it
is a revolution. Its advocates must therefore, if they succeed, undertake the
government of the country under the new conditions, or make way for men
who will and can.

*The new rulers will then be faced with a responsibility from which all
humane men recoil with intense repugnance and dread. Not only must they,
like all rulers, order the killing of their fellow creatures on certain provocations; but they must determine afresh what those provocations are to be.*
(My italics.)

And, Shaw believed, the preparation of the next generation who will enforce
this new moral order must begin early:

Further, they have to see that in every school a morality shall be inculcated
which will reconcile the consciences of their executive officers to the carrying
out of such grim orders.

That is why reformers cling so desperately to gradual modifications of existing systems rather than face revolutionary changes. It is quite easy to sign
a death warrant or order the troops to fire on the mob as part of an old-estab-
lished routine as to which there is no controversy, and for which the doomster
has no personal responsibility. *But to take a man and kill him for something a
man has never been killed for before: nay, for which he has been honoured and
idolised before, or to fire on a body of men for exercising rights which have
for centuries been regarded as the most sacred guarantees of popular liberty:
that is a new departure that calls for iron nerve and fanatical conviction. As*

---

*   In the context of the next paragraph, it becomes clear that Shaw's use of the word 'live' in 'per-
     mitted to live in society' is not part of a relative clause modifying 'conditions', but is used in the
     existential sense ('live or die').

a matter of fact it cannot become a permanently established and unquestioned part of public order unless and until the conscience of the people has been so changed that the conduct they formerly admired seems criminal, and the rights they formerly exercised seem monstrous. (My italics.)

In short, Shaw proposed that the moral principles which have undergirded Western civilisation for centuries were to be turned on their heads. His next proposal, made concrete in the labour camps of Communist Russia, China, and Cambodia, is so shocking that at first the reader thinks that it must be sarcasm. It is not. It might be added that in this overturning of Judaeo-Christian morality, his bizarre appeal for support from the writings of the Apostle Paul is most illogical:

There are several points at which Socialism involves this revolutionary change in our constitution; but I need only deal with the fundamental one which would carry all the rest with it. That one is the ruthless extirpation of parasitic idleness. *Compulsory labour, with death as the final penalty (as curtly stipulated by St Paul) is the keystone of Socialism…*

A Socialist State would make a million now work without the slightest regard to his money exactly as late war tribunals made him fight. To clear our minds on this point, we must get down to the common morality of Socialism, which, like all common morality is founded on a religion…

The Socialist morality on the subject is quite simple. It regards the man who evades his debt to the community, which is really his debt to Nature, as a sneak thief to be disfranchised, disowned, disbanded, unfrocked, cashiered, struck off the registers … Every child in a Socialist State would be taught from its earliest understanding to feel a far deeper horror of a social parasite than anyone can now pretend to feel for the outcasts of the Capitalist system.

There would be no concealment of the fact that the parasite inflicts on the community exactly the same injury as the burglar and pickpocket, and that only in a community where the laws were made by parasites for parasites would any form of parasitism be privileged …

Superficial thinkers easily persuade themselves that [capitalism] will finally progress into Socialism; but it could never do so without making a complete *volte face*. Slavery is always improving itself as a system.

With compulsory social service [forced labour] imposed on everyone, the resistance to the other measures involved with Socialism would not only become pointless but injurious to the resisters ...

Such a change as this, however little its full scope may be understood at first, is far too revolutionary to make itself effective by a simple majority of votes in a Parliamentary division under normal circumstances. The civil service would not administer it in good faith; the tribunals would not enforce it; the citizens would not obey it in the present state of public conscience. The press would strain all its powers of comminatory rhetoric to make it infamous ... Several years of explicit propaganda will be necessary to create even a nuclear social conscience in its favour ... (My italics.)

Only four years after the Revolution, when the civilised world was still horror-struck by the bloodletting of the Red Terror, Shaw unbelievably follows this by praising Bolshevik repression in Russia:

Communists ... no sooner took the country in hand than they were led in the irresistible logic of facts and of real responsibility, to compulsory social service on pain of death as the first condition not merely of Communism, but a bare survival. They shot men not only for shirking and slacking, but for drinking at their work ...

Capitalism is much stronger in the West than in Russia ... [and so] we may have [to have] the Dictatorship of the Proletariat in the sense in which the phrase is being used by the Russian Communist statesman. To them dictatorship means overriding democracy ... [The government] may even treat the majority as rebels. The British Democrat is scandalised by this ... The British Democrat, dazed, asks whether it is cricket to exclude the Opposition from the governing bodies. The Russian Statesmen reply that they are fighting a class war, and that during the war an Opposition is the enemy...

If ... the class struggle ... is brought to a head in England let no one imagine that either side will have any more regard for democracy than the Russian Communists, the Irish Republican Army, the British occupation of Egypt, Dublin Castle, or any government in time of war...

When the so-called class war comes to blows in England (and I'm afraid our proprietary Whites will not give in without a fight even if the Labour Party

in Parliament comes in 600 strong) the Whites and the Reds will argue in
exactly the same way...

I should very much like to see Communism tried a while ... At any rate, it
can hardly produce worse results than Capitalism.

I make no apology for such extensive quotation. Without such extensive quotation, it is impossible to comprehend the enormity and the ruthlessness of
Shaw's vision, laid out clearly at precisely the time when he was a Labour
hero to thousands of young socialist admirers. This is a Socialism which
dismisses any form of 'gradualism' – the doctrine commonly held to be the
Labour Party's peaceful alternative to the brutal route to Socialism taken by
the Soviets in the inter-war years. Shaw's Socialism, for which this article is a
manifesto, endorses compulsory labour, the execution of political opponents
and the suppression of parliamentary democracy. Half a century later, communist critics of his fellow Nobel Literature laureate, Alexander Solzhenitsyn, hotly contested Solzhenitsyn's insistence the gulag was an inescapable
consequence of Socialism, rather than its accidental by-product. Shaw and
Solzhenitsyn are in complete agreement.

'A well-kept garden must be weeded' (1931)

In the summer of 1931, Shaw went to Moscow. There, in front of the world's
press, he was feted by the Soviets. On his return, he declared that Soviet
Communism and Fabian Socialism were one and the same:

What was it that saved Russia from ruin after 1917? – her adoption of British
Communism, made constitutional and practicable by myself, Sidney Webb,
and our fellow Fabians ... I have been preaching Socialism all my political life
and here at last is a country which has established Socialism, definitely made
Socialism the basis of its whole political system. ... The Socialism which has
established itself and is being worked out in Russia is a Fabian Socialism.[18]

To a critic one obvious inconsistency between Shaw's Fabian ideal and Russian reality might have been the tens of thousands of kulak executions which
had taken place over the previous eighteen months. But a few months later,
Shaw was not reticent about claiming a connection there too. In October

1931, he made a radio broadcast to the United States, based upon his experiences in Russia. People sometimes mask what they cannot say outright by using humour, and Shaw's talk was humorous. It was also mischievous and insulting (his remarks about America and Americans caused outrage); but, given the other examples of his thinking that we have seen, and in light of Beatrice's comments about him recorded not long afterwards, it is impossible to dismiss the broadcast as merely a poor joke:

> The first thing that would occur to a real hundred percent American in Russia is that with its huge natural wealth it must be a splendid country to make money in … [so] why let all the profit be wasted on the Government when a capable man can organize business for himself and put the profit in his own pocket? … If you take that line in Russia you will soon get rich. But when this fact comes under the notice of the income tax authorities, they will ask the Gay Pay Oo [OGPU], the celebrated secret police which acts as an Inquisition, to enquire into your methods.
>
> An agent will tap you on the shoulder and conduct you to the offices of that famous force. There you will be invited to explain your commercial proceedings and your views of life in general … You will not be reproached, nor bullied, nor argued with, nor inconvenienced in any way. All that will happen to you is that when you have made yourself quite clear, you will suddenly find yourself in the next world, if there be a next world. If not, you will simply have ceased to exist; and your relatives will be politely informed that they need have no anxiety about you, as you are not coming home any more.
>
> The Russian putty has been shaped to believe that idiots are better dead … Your views will satisfy the Russians that you are an idiot; and in mercy to yourself and society they will just liquidate you, as they call it, without causing you a moment's unpleasantness.
>
> In this they are merely carrying out a proposal made by me many years ago. I urged that every person who owes his life to civilised society, and who has enjoyed since his childhood all its very costly protections and advantages, should appear at reasonable intervals before a properly qualified jury to justify his existence, which should be *summarily and painlessly terminated if he fails to justify it*, and is either a positive nuisance or more trouble than he is worth. Nothing less will make people really responsible citizens.

A great part of the secret of the success of Russian Communism is that every Russian knows that unless he makes his life a paying proposition for his country then he will probably lose it.

I am proud to have been the first to advocate this most necessary reform. A well-kept garden must be weeded. (My italics.)[19]

'To kill them is quite reasonable and very necessary' (1933)

In 1933, in the preface of *On the Rocks*, Shaw once again went on record applauding the execution (as long as it were done by a Communist state) of those he considered to be 'social parasites'. Then, just four years before the Soviet secret police shot over 700,000 of their countrymen, he praised them for their work as state executioners:

[There are] untameable persons who are constitutionally unable to restrain their violent or acquisitive impulses, and have no compunction about sacrificing others to their own immediate convenience. To punish such persons is ridiculous ... But to kill them is quite reasonable and very necessary.

Every normal human group contains not only a percentage of saints but also a percentage of irreclaimable scoundrels and good-for-noughts who will wreck any community unless they are expensively restrained or cheaply exterminated ... The essential justification for extermination ... is always incorrigible social incompatibility and nothing else.

My Essay on Prisons ... disposes with the dogma of the unconditional sacredness of human life ... but it covers only a corner of a field opened up by modern powers of extermination. In Germany it is suggested that the Nordic race should exterminate the Latin race ... The extermination of whole races and classes has been not only advocated but actually attempted ... The extermination of the peasant is in active progress in Russia ...

Extermination must be put on a scientific basis if it is ever to be carried out humanely and apologetically as well as thoroughly. That killing is a necessity is beyond question by any thoughtful person ... Killing can be cruelly or kindly done; and the deliberate choice of cruel ways, and their organization as popular pleasures, is sinful; but the sin is in the cruelty and the enjoyment of it, not in the killing...

In the long run the power to exterminate is too grave to be left in any hands but those of a thoroughly Communist Government responsible to the whole community...

The only country which has yet awakened to this extension of social responsibility is Russia ... the Russians were forced to set up an Inquisition or Star Chamber, called at first the Cheka and now the Gay Pay Oo, to ... 'liquidate' persons who could not answer them satisfactorily. The security against the abuse of this power of life and death was that the Cheka had no interest in liquidating anybody who could be made publicly useful, all its interests being in the opposite direction.[20]

So alien are these remarks that even Shaw's modern enthusiasts do not know how to react to them. Michael Holroyd's three-volume biography of Shaw passes them over in just nine lines.[21] Although he records the opinion of two critics who call the preface 'crazed and insidious' and 'peculiarly bloodthirsty', Holroyd gives no sense of the contents themselves. Perhaps he wishes to believe that the preface is an aberration.

If anything, what is so remarkable about these comments is that they show that Shaw's views remained consistent. From his 1921 essay through to the 1931 broadcast and this piece in 1933, he maintains the unquestioned necessity of political execution in a socialist state, the ennobling of Soviet mass murder and its executioners, the OGPU, his contempt for the targets of their repression, variously expressed as 'social parasites' (1921), capitalists (1931) and the socially incompatible (1933).

'The lethal chamber' (1910, 1934)

Shaw returned more than once to the concept of mass extermination, urging scientists to develop the technology to make it 'painless' and 'humane'. In 1910, in a speech in which he advocated 'going further in the direction of political revolution than the most extreme Socialist at present advocates in public', he continued:

We should find ourselves committed to killing a great many people whom we now leave living, and leave living a great many people whom we at present kill ... A part of eugenic politics would finally land us in an extensive use of the lethal chamber. A great many people would have to be put out of existence simply because it wastes other people's time to look after them.[22]

In 1922, in his preface to the Webbs' *English Local Government*, Shaw once again wrote of the 'lethal chamber', concluding that 'the moment we face it frankly we are driven to the conclusion that the community has a right to put a price on the right to live in it'[23] and he elaborated on the kinds of people (including the wealthy who did not need to work) who would be dispatched by it:

> We have whole classes of persons who waste, squander and luxuriate in the hard-earned income of the nation without even a pretence of social service or contribution of any kind; and instead of sternly calling on them to justify their existence or go on the scrap heap, we encourage and honour them, and indeed conduct the whole business of the country as if its object were to produce and pamper them.

A few lines above, he had already made it clear that his understanding of the 'scrap heap' was terminal, for he looked forward to a time when 'we shall drop our moral airs [and] persons who give more trouble than they are worth will run the risk of being apologetically, sympathetically, painlessly, but effectually returned to the dust from which they sprung'.[24]

Twenty-four years later, he was still pursuing the same theme: 'I appeal to the chemists to discover a humane gas that will kill instantly and painlessly. Deadly by all means, but humane not cruel.'[25] Shaw's views are remarkable for their consistency over more than two decades. The *National* Socialists, sharing Shaw's view that those who were unfit for life in a utopian society should be disposed of, were to be the first to realise Shaw's goal, though Zyklon-B was in fact far from 'painless'.

Confiscating the children of religious believers

Shaw was not reticent about expressing views on other aspects of social control in a future socialist state. One of these was his endorsement of the suppression of religion. His *Intelligent Woman's Guide to Socialism and Capitalism* (1928) has already been mentioned briefly. It was unmistakably hostile to religious upbringing:

A fully developed Socialist State will [not] either impress [Christian] beliefs on children *or permit any private person to do so* until the child has reached what is called in another connection the age of consent.

To put it quite frankly and flatly, the Socialist State, as far as I can guess, will teach the child the multiplication table, but will not only not teach it the Church Catechism, but if the State teachers find that the child's parents have been teaching it the Catechism otherwise than as a curious historical document, the parents will be warned that if they persist *the child will be taken out of their hands and handed over to the Lord Chancellor*.

Further, a Socialist State ... will not allow the Bible to be introduced in schools otherwise than as a collection of old chronicles, poems, oracles, and political fulminations, on the same footing as the travels of Marco Polo ... The doctrine that our life in this world is only a brief preliminary episode in preparation for an all-important life to come ... will be prosecuted as seditious and blasphemous. (My italics.)[26]

The idea of banning the religious education of children and abducting the children of believers and placing them in state orphanages seems to have raised no eyebrows among the British left. Quite the reverse: the journalist H. N. Brailsford had nothing but praise for the book, even calling it 'humane':

The appearance of a big book on Socialism, at which Bernard Shaw has worked for several years, is an event in the history of our time ... [Shaw] has written a classical statement of the case of equality, so persuasive, so humane, so triumphantly reasonable that it must count among the forces that are destined to crown this splendid veteran a victor.[27]

On Russia, even as others began to weaken, Shaw remained constant. When the ILP, outraged by the third of the great Moscow show trials, sent their letter of protest, Shaw gave a written interview to a journalist. Her first question concerned the ILP protest:

As you are aware, the leaders of the I.L.P. Messrs. Maxton, Buchanan, McGovern, Stephen and Fenner Brockway addressed a letter to M. Stalin in which it was stated either that the charges were untrue or the Russian Revolution has attracted degenerate types at the top of the ladder of leadership. In your opinion has the Russian Revolution attracted degenerate types?

Shaw's reply was unambiguous:

On the contrary it has attracted superior types all the world over to an extraordinary extent where ever it has been understood. But the top of the ladder is a very trying place for old revolutionists who have had no administrative experience, who have had no financial experience, who had been trained as penniless hunted fugitives with Karl Marx on the brain and not as statesmen. They often have to be pushed off the ladder with a rope around their neck.[28]

Did it matter?

This chapter began with a review of the awe in which Shaw was held by British socialists in the years between the wars, an admiration reflected in the fulsome obituaries published after his death and tributes made even in this century. His influence was profound. The respect in which he was held gave his utterances a power that few of his generation carried. When he insisted that allegations about Russia were all lies,[29] and denied Soviet religious persecution,[30] the forced labour of the gulag,[31] and the Ukrainian famine,[32] he helped the Russian government in their efforts to resist foreign pressure to temper their repression; he also disempowered the voice of British humanitarians who were campaigning to relieve the distress of the millions who were suffering under the Soviet regime.

Beyond the strength of his own voice in support of Moscow, Shaw's promotion of Soviet Communism and his association of it with Fabian Socialism drew many to the Soviets' cause. He was a strong influence in converting the Webbs to Soviet Communism, which they then went on themselves to promote so effectively.[33] The fact that it took so many on the left so long to wake up to the evil of what was happening in Russia is at least in part the responsibility of men like Shaw.

It seems clear that Shaw held views on the necessity of state repression and terror which were extreme and inhumane and bordered on the deranged. It would be quite wrong to ascribe them to the rest of the Labour Party in general. But they were clearly repeated over many decades. No one seems to have challenged him. No one on the left stood up to him. The editors of *Labour Monthly* did not refrain from publishing his views in 1921; Brailsford did not challenge him in 1927 when he recommended the confiscation of Christian children; the BBC allowed him to commend Soviet mass murder in 1933.

This raises a further question. One of the unanswered questions about Labour's 'gradualism' (the concept that, in Britain, socialist revolution could be introduced by gradual, parliamentary, means rather than by sudden violent revolution) was: what would happen if it was resisted, as seemed likely? Would violence and repression be necessary? MacDonald, Snowden, Henderson and many others would surely have balked at taking that course (though they did not condemn the Bolsheviks for having done so) but what of others on the left? Revolutions start slowly, but as they gather momentum they spin out of control. Shaw's was not the only voice which spoke in these harsh terms. Would Shaw have supported British labour camps and political executions by British secret police if they had started? Unless he was a hypocrite, it seems impossible to believe, from his writings quoted here, that he would have objected. It is more likely that his would have been a powerful voice in favour of neutralising dissenters in Labour ranks who were uncomfortable with violence.

There is another deeply discomforting inconsistency in Shaw's behaviour which cannot be ignored. Between 1930 and 1933 he made numerous and influential public statements refuting the British protesters' claims about executions, labour camps and widespread repression in Russia – while simultaneously writing about the need to execute social parasites, praising the Soviet secret police for its 'weeding of the garden' and having, ten years earlier, set out a programme which included 'compulsory social service' 'on pain of death' in order to render 'resistance injurious' – in other words, labour camps. If he was not deceiving himself about the goings-on in Russia (which he may well have been), the only other option is that he was brazenly lying.

P. G. Wodehouse's unwise agreement to broadcast a mildly comic reflection on life in an internment camp on German radio while being held by the Germans during the Second World War resulted in his being shunned for years afterwards. Shaw openly advocated policies of mass extermination that were very close to those embraced by the Nazi regime – and yet his reputation seems unassailable.

Given Shaw's hugely influential status in his day as one of the most famous men in England, whose political speeches drew crowds of admirers, these deeply disturbing utterances, made over twenty-five years, cannot be dismissed as the rants of an insignificant madman. If Shaw's sentiments had been expressed by a member of any party on the right, there would surely have been calls for the speaker's expulsion from the party and, today, possibly even prosecution. What Shaw's writings and other chapters in Part V show, is that Labour was prepared to extend considerable indulgence towards its members' utterances on Russia, no matter how extreme.

CHAPTER 38

SHAW, THE WEBBS
AND THE FATE OF
FREDA UTLEY'S HUSBAND

Freda Utley was a woman with impeccable Socialist credentials. Her father had been secretary of the Fabian Society and was a good friend of Shaw's. Her parents had been introduced by Edward Aveling, Marx's son-in-law. At university, she soon became politically active. She joined the ILP and writes in her memoirs that she became 'well acquainted with Fenner Brockway, Jimmy Maxton and other dedicated Socialists'.[1] In a debate in 1923, she defended the Soviet Union alongside H. N. Brailsford. She travelled with A. J. Cook, the miners' leader, speaking at the same meetings. She nannied Bertrand Russell's children and knew Harold Laski, finding him, in contrast to his wider reputation for vanity, to be kind and helpful to her in her career. In 1926, possibly aided by her acquaintance with Laski, she was awarded a fellowship at the London School of Economics. She became chairman of the London University Labour Party and then, in 1927, vice-president of the University Labour Federation, which comprised the Labour and Socialist clubs of all British universities. In that capacity, she visited Russia and, on her return, joined the CPGB. In the 1920s, she writes, 'the distinction between a Socialist and a Communist was not clearly demarcated'.[2] Those who knew her expected her to become a leading economic historian.

In 1926, Freda met the man who was to become her husband, Arkadi Berdichevsky. Berdichevsky, a senior manager at the Soviet Trade Delegation in London, had worked for Arcos since 1920, and was expelled with the others after the Arcos raid in 1927. Though already married with a son, he divorced his wife and married Freda, who had moved to Moscow to be with him, in 1928. Together, they travelled on missions for the Comintern to Siberia, China and Japan. The turning point for the couple came when Arkadi was sent on an assignment to famine-hit Ukraine in April 1932:

> He came back white and miserable and shaken. Down there he had seen the starving and dead in the streets. At each railway station en route there had been hundreds and hundreds of starving wretches, emaciated women with dying babies at their milkless breasts, children with the swollen stomachs of the starving, all begging, begging for bread. In the station waiting rooms he had seen hundreds of peasant families herded together waiting for transportation to concentration camps. Children dying of starvation and typhus, scarecrows of men and women pushed and kicked by the OGPU guards. It sickened even those who are hardened to the sight of suffering in the Far East.[3]

Disillusionment quickly set in and, with it, increasing isolation and fear. Freda's experience of Russia had now become a 'storm of terror, hate, regimented sadism, hunger, cold and wretchedness and the nauseating cant and hypocrisy of Soviet life'. But she had to be extremely careful whom she talked to, even among the groups of British socialist visitors, many of whom she already knew:

> Foreign visitors, carefully shepherded by Intourist and given huge meals in the hotels of the starving land, went home to deny the rumours of famine. I well remember the delegation from England in 1932 which included Mrs G. D. H. Cole and various professors from London University.* One of them, a lecturer

---

* The delegation was from the New Fabian Research Bureau, founded in 1930 to follow the tradition of the first Fabians in conducting detailed 'impartial' research on social topics. The NFRB team sent to investigate the Soviet Union published *Twelve Studies in Soviet Russia* (1933) on its return. The book included contributions by G. D. H. and Margaret Cole, F. Pethick Lawrence, Hugh Dalton, G. R. and Naomi Mitchison and Raymond Postgate and an introduction by G. D. H. Cole and Clement Attlee. The contributions by John Morgan on 'Soviet agriculture', and D. N. Pritt on the 'Russian legal system' were particularly questionable. Pritt insisted that Russian prisons were so humane the prisoners didn't want to leave. Naomi Mitchison's chapter, 'Archaeology and the intellectual worker', met with particular scorn from Bullard, who had met many of the NFRB team, and read *Twelve Studies* afterwards. With first-hand knowledge of the real plight of intellectuals in the Soviet Union, his picture was very different from the glowing account she published.

at the London School of Economics, told me as we ate a wonderful meal at the New Moscow hotel (at his expense) that it was all nonsense about the famine, for at Kiev he had been given caviar, butter, eggs and coffee for breakfast! I had to let him talk, for I knew if I told them the truth and he repeated it, my husband would be sent to prison.[4]

In 1934, she gave birth to a son, Jon, but his father was not to see the child for long. In 1936, Arkadi was arrested. Freda never saw him again. Ten days later, she fled Russia, taking her son, fearing that if she was arrested he would have been taken to an orphanage. Arkadi was sentenced to five years in prison. Freda afterwards feared that it was Margaret Cole's indiscretion that had contributed to Arkadi's arrest:

> On my return to England in 1936 I learned that she had betrayed the confidence that I had reposed in her during her visit to Moscow not long before when I had told her in strict secrecy my real views. She had, I heard, been going around telling people that 'Freda was very soured on Russia' – her terms for my profound disillusionment. This was surely not because she was malicious or wished to jeopardise my husband's life, but simply because she had remained as ignorant or innocent as I had once been. She simply had not believed me when I told her in Moscow how dangerous it is to speak the truth under a Communist dictatorship.[5]

In truth, as a member of the Comintern, Berdichevsky's days (and Freda's) would already have been numbered. The contact that so many Comintern officials had had with foreign countries rendered them suspect, and in the paranoid climate of the Great Terror, many of those who had Comintern connections were purged as spies. Freda had managed to use her English surname and British passport to escape and return to England. Other foreign Communists who had taken Soviet citizenship were not so fortunate and, over the next two years, many were unable to leave the country and perished.

Back in England, Freda set about gathering support for a letter of appeal to have Arkadi released from the camps. In this she was helped by Bertrand Russell and his wife, Patricia, who took on her cause. With the Russells' help, a carefully drafted four-page letter of appeal was written, and Bertrand used his network of friends to try to obtain a selection of impressive co-signatories. Freda herself, already known to many senior figures on the left, naturally used her contacts too. In time, Harold Laski, Kingsley Martin, the editor of the *New Statesman and Nation* and C. M. Lloyd, the paper's foreign editor and a former mentor of Freda's, all added their names.

It was not to prove so easy with Sidney and Beatrice Webb, who, like Shaw, were good friends of Russell's. By now, three years after the publication of *Soviet Communism*, they were Britain's most famous Soviet enthusiasts; their signatures would have carried great weight, even though it is highly unlikely that the Soviets would have paid any attention to the appeal, whoever had signed it. Beatrice refused to sign. Russell hinted that if she didn't change her mind he would never speak to her again. She finally consented, but in the end their contribution was so grudging as to be of little use. They refused to sign the main letter of appeal and instead added a separate note of their own:

> We both of us know Freda Utley and her writings. We warmly commend the accompanying memorial, with which we agree, to the kindly consideration of the authorities. We have not the advantage of knowing Miss Utley's husband, and it is for this reason that we signed this separate note.[6]

It was the same as saying that they believed it was quite possible that Arkadi was a spy, but that nonetheless they appealed for clemency on his behalf.

Shaw's response was even more inexcusable, and led to a breach in his relationship with the Russells. Bertrand took Freda to lunch with Shaw and his wife Charlotte. Believing that she was among sympathetic listeners, Freda was unguarded in her criticism of the Soviet regime. Charlotte wrote to Russell that they wanted to help but 'it is difficult, as she is so strongly prejudiced against what we are sympathetic to: the USSR'.[7] Shaw refused to sign the letter. Russell continued to put pressure on him and in the end he reluctantly sent a draft of a separate letter to the Soviet government, no less grudging than the Webbs':

> I don't know Mr Berdichevsky personally nor have I any knowledge of the reasons for his seclusion, but unless they are very grave I venture to suggest that he may be doing more harm to the reputation of the Soviet in the Arctic

Circle than he could possibly do in England where he would have no claim on public attention or sympathy. G. B. S. 30 June 1937.[8]

In the letter, Shaw also said that he was aware that Freda was 'using every means' in her power 'to bring pressure of public opinion to bear out on the Russian government'. She had actually been doing the opposite, knowing that if the Soviet authorities felt they were being backed into a corner and might lose face if they gave in, they would become even more obstinate. The letter could not be sent while those comments remained in it. Instead of being of only limited help it would become positively harmful. Freda wrote to Charlotte, begging her to use her influence to get Shaw to change the text. Shaw misinterpreted her letter as a decision now to keep quiet instead of creating a public outcry (which she had never done in the first place) and he replied with words of scant comfort:

Now that you have resolved to withdraw, do so completely. Burn all the letters [of support received from other notable Socialists] and take comfort in the fact that five years will not last forever; that imprisonment under the Soviet is not as bad as it is here in the West; and that when I was in Russia and enquired about certain engineers who had been sentenced to 10 years for sabotage, I learned that they were at large and in high favour after serving two years of their sentence.[9]

Shaw could not have been more wrong. Arkadi had been sent to Vorkuta in the far north, one of the harshest camps in the gulag, infamous for the severity of its regime. There he was shot on 30 March 1938.

For the Russells, Shaw's response was the final straw. Patricia Russell wrote to him on 12 July 1937:

I thought when I met you that you were kind. Now I realise that it is only Mrs Shaw who was kind, and that you, as I had often been told, are frivolous and cruel. And if you really believe what you say about Soviet justice you must also be rather stupid. My husband asks me to say that he concurs in what I write.[10]

Shaw finally gave in, reluctantly, and not without a final barbed comment that he suspected that 'Mr Berdichevsky's exile [to Britain] may be less stormy than his home life'. Freda did not discover Arkadi's fate until 1956, almost twenty years later, and it was only after the fall of Communism that her son was able to establish the details of his sentence and death. According to Soviet archives, his father had been shot for leading a prison hunger strike. With so many trumped up charges used as an excuse for politically motivated executions, the truth of even that remains uncertain.

Raisa Krynine

The sad case of Freda Utley's husband was not the only example of Shaw's callous refusal to support humanitarian appeals made on behalf of individuals suffering unjust persecution in Soviet Russia. In the summer of 1931, accompanied by Lady Astor, he made a highly publicised visit to Moscow. While there, both received telegrams from Dimitri Krynine, a Russian expatriate who was now a professor at Yale University, on behalf of his wife Raisa. Dimitri had worked abroad for numerous American companies and had finally settled in America, where their son Paul had joined him. In spite of numerous appeals, over many years, accompanied by Dimitri's offers of money and even the offer of the donation of his technical library to the Russian state, Raisa had been refused permission to leave Russia to join him. Nancy Astor took the matter to heart and, in a dramatic gesture, went down on one knee before Litvinov (and the accompanying foreign press) at a garden party in Moscow, to plead for Raisa's release.[11]

Shaw would have nothing to do with it. As Michael Holroyd, Shaw's biographer remarks, 'It is not easy to sympathise with such unresponsiveness, especially when set against Astor's courage and persistence.' Holroyd tries to explain this away – unconvincingly, given what we know of Freda Utley's story: 'In the years following the war GBS had increasingly detached himself from such appeals, feeling that he would otherwise be overwhelmed.'[12] Perhaps for Holroyd, as for others, it is still too hard to accept that the Oscar-winning Nobel laureate and literary giant could also be, as Patricia Russell had written, both frivolous and cruel.

Raisa was forced to make an immediate statement that she had not been in any way singled out as an object of particular persecution and had no complaint to make of her treatment. Several months later, when foreign journalists attempted to talk to her again, they found that she was no longer living in her apartment. Neighbours said that some men had come in the middle of the night to her flat and she had left with them and not returned. Two years later it became known that she had been sent to the camps.[13] She died there some time in the 1940s, a period in which wartime privations and food shortages saw the death rate rise in some gulag camps to a peak of 20 per cent a year.

On his return from Russia in 1931, Shaw had nothing but good to say of life under Soviet Communism: 'I should advise a young man to go to Russia and settle there,' he foolishly proclaimed.[14] A number took his advice and of those many were bitterly to regret having done so.

CHAPTER 39

'GUARDS OF THE REVOLUTION': THE NEXT GENERATION: CRIPPS, COLE AND LASKI

The Fabian Society is the oldest and the most continuous and effective British centre of socialist thought and propaganda. Today it is from among its members that Soviet Communism finds its most effective exponents and defenders: Shaw and Webb, Laski and Cole. We have all been very comfortable and even honoured in the old civilisation of profit-making capitalism: we welcome and are welcomed to the new civilisation of revolutionary Communism.

BEATRICE WEBB, JULY 1935[1]

The English intelligentsia ... have ... become infected with the inherently mechanistic Marxist notion that if you make the necessary technical advance the moral advance will follow of itself. I have never accepted this...

The thing that frightens me about the modern intelligentsia is their inability to see that human society must be based on common decency, whatever the political and economic reforms may be ... Dickens, without the slightest understanding of Socialism, etc., would have seen at a glance that there is something wrong with a regime that needs a pyramid of corpses every few years ... All people who are morally sound have known since about 1931 that the Russian regime stinks.

GEORGE ORWELL, 1941[2]

George Bernard Shaw, Beatrice and Sidney Webb were all born in the 1850s. As they grew older, a new generation of Fabians arose, under their patronage. Among these were three significant men who would carry the torch of socialist revolution through the 1930s – Stafford Cripps, G. D. H. Cole, and Harold Laski.

Sir Stafford Cripps (1889–1952), had been Solicitor General in MacDonald's Cabinet and was a member of Lansbury's shadow Cabinet from 1931. He was from an eminent Labour family. His father, Charles Cripps, Lord Parmoor (1852–1941), served in both the 1924 and 1929 Labour governments, latterly as Leader of the House of Lords. Through his mother, Cripps was nephew to Beatrice Webb and cousin to Malcolm Muggeridge, whose father, ILP member H. T. Muggeridge, was an MP and had been an early member of the Fabian Society executive. Cripps was subsequently appointed ambassador to Moscow (1940–42), Lord Privy Seal (1942), president of the Board of Trade (1945), Minister for Economic Affairs (1947) and finally Chancellor of the Exchequer (1947–50).

G. D. H. (George Douglas Howard) Cole (1889–1959), is credited with being 'one of the most influential socialist intellectuals to influence the Labour Party for much of the twentieth century, shaping the party's thinking through various stages of its evolution'.[3] Cole had been an Oxford academic in the 1920s and had written widely for the Labour press. Although ill health prevented his entry into Parliament in 1930, he still 'devoted his remarkable gifts of intellect and character to the Labour cause'.[4] He was chairman of the Fabian Society in 1939–46 and 1948–50 and its president from 1952–59. In 1944 he became Chichele Professor of Social and Political Theory at All Souls College, Oxford. At Oxford, the famous 'Cole Group' comprised students from almost every college and was, in the words of one member (future Prime Minister Harold Wilson), 'undoubtedly Oxford's biggest contribution to the education and inspiration of successive generations of Oxford-trained Socialists'.[5] Cole's numerous public appointments included membership of the Central Council For Broadcast Adult Education (1929), Ramsay MacDonald's Economic Advisory Council (1930), the Social Reconstruction Survey (1941) of which he was chairman, and the Public Schools Committee (1942).

Harold Laski (1893–1950) joined the LSE in 1921 as a lecturer, becoming professor of political science in 1926, a post he held until his death. He joined the Fabian Society in 1921 and was its chairman from 1946 to 1948. He was on the Labour Party NEC 1937–49 and was president of the atheist campaigning Rationalist Press Association in 1930. He was chairman of the Labour annual conference in 1945–46. In the first Labour majority government of 1945, 67 MPs were former students of his.

Laski's impact extended far beyond the British Isles. In the late 1970s, the Labour Prime Minister James Callaghan wrote that wherever he went in the world he was 'bound to meet a distinguished academic, administrator, or politician who would boast that he had been taught by Laski'. Through his Indian students at the LSE, his influence upon the political life of India was particularly strong. One Indian Prime Minister is said to have remarked that 'there is a vacant chair at every cabinet meeting in India reserved for the ghost of Professor Harold Laski'.[6] Indeed, Laski's reputation looms so large over the 1930s and '40s that historian Max Beloff has dubbed the period 'the Age of Laski'.[7]

As the 1930s progressed, it was Cripps, Cole and Laski, all eminent figures in the Labour Party, two of whom were among Labour's foremost twentieth century political theorists, who became increasingly prominent as the party's most articulate advocates of Soviet-inspired radical Socialism.

The left moves further left

The crisis of 1931 had thrown the Labour movement into disarray. Disaffection with the Labour Party's 'gradualism' had radicalised the ILP still further and, the following year, it disaffiliated from the Labour Party, which it had played a large part in founding. As Maxton and Brockway led the ILP into the political wilderness (from which it would never return) some members refused to endorse the split; in September 1932, a new Labour organisation, the Socialist League, was formed with the intention that it would take the place of the ILP, being affiliated to the Labour Party. Cripps, Cole and Laski were among its founders. Others who joined included Clement Attlee, H. N. Brailsford and Frank Wise.[8] (Wise's loyalty to Russia remained undiminished: Beatrice Webb even warned one visitor, Rhea Clyman, to be careful with him, as it was likely that he would report any indiscreet comments to his Soviet masters[9]). Among its younger members were future Labour leader Michael Foot and Barbara Betts (later Barbara Castle).

At the Labour Party conference in January 1932, Cripps had urged that
'Socialism could no longer be put forward to the distant future'. Russia had
taught British socialists that 'however Utopian it might be to imagine a state
in which they have equality, at least it was a matter that could be put to
practical experiment … a crumbling building had to be demolished and a fine
and better one put in its place … Socialism *would* replace capitalism' (my
italics).[10] Just a month after the launch of the Socialist League, Harold Laski
was as emphatic as ever that Russia provided a model for others to follow:
'Russia is the effective centre of creativeness in the world which otherwise
does not seem to know how to turn its feet from the abyss.'[11]

Cripps called for the establishment of a new socialist leadership, to 'create
guards of the revolution and create them now for when the revolution comes
it will be too late'.[12] The urgency which he expressed in 1932 energised him
and other Socialist League members to develop a more concrete strategy for
a new government swiftly to establish a truly socialist state in Britain. This
resulted in two notable 1933 publications: *Problems of a Socialist Government* by Cripps, Cole, Wise, Brailsford and others, and *The Intelligent Man's
Review of Europe To-Day* by Cole and his wife Margaret. *Problems of a Socialist Government* began as a collection of pamphlets containing the texts
of keynote speeches delivered by Socialist League members. Even before
they were combined in one volume they had caused controversy, and Cole
and Cripps were forced to tone down some of the language, though their
other writings make clear that this moderation was for pragmatic rather than
heartfelt reasons.* Both books explored the issues presented by the abandonment of gradualism, the problems raised by an obstructive Parliament,
and the degree of compulsion that would be required for the establishment
of Socialism. 'We shall have at the outset to establish a system that can be
relied upon to work quickly and dictatorially [and] we cannot … put limits to
the degree of dictatorial power which, under the stress of the emergency, our
Socialist Government may have to assume,' Cole wrote.† Cripps's proposals

---

*   The quotations here are from *The Times* review of the book which compared to the original transcripts of the speeches, previously published by the Socialist League, with their final versions as
published in *Problems of a Socialist Government. The Times*, 29 August 1933.

†   The book version of the text omits 'and dictatorially', and replaces 'dictatorial' with 'administrative'. The difference is only one of presentation – in Soviet Russia those sentenced to the camps
without trial were said to be sentenced 'administratively'.

for pushing through socialist revolution in the face of what he described as 'the present form of Parliamentary dictatorship' sounded little different from those of the Bolsheviks in 1917:

> Unless some adequate democratic machinery can be devised, Socialists will be left with but two alternatives. Either to seize a dictatorship or else to abandon power and hand it back to the Capitalists. I can regard neither of these with equanimity, as I am convinced that both would mean dictatorship. Obviously a dictatorship of the Left based upon a majority in favour of Socialism would be the better of two bad alternatives.[13]

Cole agreed: 'It will be best, as soon as Parliament has conferred on the Government the necessary emergency powers, for it to meet as seldom as possible, leaving the Socialists to carry on ... with the minimum of day-to-day interference'.[14]

Frank Wise's contribution to *Problems of a Socialist Government* was equally radical: to take 'control of [both] finance and the financiers', transferring not only banking, but the leading industries and services of the countries to communal ownership in such a way that the measures could not be reversed by an anti-socialist government in the future: 'We must make such an omelette that it is impossible for the eggs to get back into their shells.'[15] But it was in *The Intelligent Man's Review of Europe To-Day* that Cole's exploration of the implications of the socialist model for Britain developed an even more disconcerting theme:

> Socialism ... must create for itself a [new] political instrument [model of government] ... actively in opposition to capitalist notions of property and individual rights. In seeking for a basis for this new instrument of socialisation Communists repudiate not only the capitalist conception of the rights of property but also the capitalist conception of individual liberty.[16]

Disturbing though it was, the abandonment of 'the capitalist conception of individual liberty' was an idea that was not new in Labour circles; Shaw had raised it in his 1921 article. Was Cole now perturbed by its application in Soviet Russia, particularly by the suffering that had been caused? Not at all:

Critics of Russian institutions in capitalist countries are apt to dwell very greatly on the alleged suppression of liberty in Russia to-day, and to base their arguments on the disappearance of the characteristic liberties associated in their minds with the liberal-parliamentary State.

But though the Soviet system in its present working *does undoubtedly restrict individual liberty very seriously* in certain directions, above all in the expression of political views hostile to the system itself, it has resulted in other directions in an enormous extension of the liberties of the great mass of the Russian people. Observers who come back from Russia, unless they are too prejudiced to notice what they see, practically all report that there exists among the Russian people of to-day, in non-political matters, a sense of freedom and of self-expression quite unknown among the mass of the people in any capitalist country. (My italics.)[17]

And anyone who thought otherwise, Cole was saying, was simply 'prejudiced'. Socialism, as an end, was so desirable that it justified almost any means used to achieve it. Cole showed himself to be aware of the specifics of the suppression of liberty in Russia too:

[Those Russians] debarred from civil rights consist of persons employing hired labour for profit (*this includes kulaki*), or living on unearned income; *monks and priests*, imbeciles, and former agents of the Tsarist regime ... It is commonly estimated that about 8 millions of the population fall into one or other of these classes. Deprivation of civil rights means, in effect, *much more* than disfranchisement; it also involves loss of Trade Union membership, *ration cards*, and other essentials. (My italics.)[18]

Two years earlier, a Soviet official had openly admitted to Sir Esmond Ovey that, with too little food to go round, the refusal to give the regime's opponents ration cards would inevitably result in the death of some. Now, at the height of the Ukrainian famine, Cole was commending the principle.

The storm created by *Problems of a Socialist Government* was such that the Labour NEC was forced to respond. As Lansbury, the party leader, told the annual conference the following autumn:

Toward the end of 1933 and the beginning of 1934 considerable misrepresentation appeared in the Press and was uttered on the public platform concerning the party's attitude toward Dictatorship. Attempts were made to demonstrate that the Party had renounced its democratic principles. In order to reassure the rank and file of the Movement and to make the Party's position quite clear to the electorate generally the following pronouncement was issued by the National Executive Committee on 4 January:

'The attitude of the Labour Party toward Dictatorship has recently been subject to grave misrepresentation by supporters of the National Government. The Labour Party, as has repeatedly been made plain in its official decorations, stands for Parliamentary Democracy. It is firmly opposed to Individual or Group Dictatorship, whether from the Right or from the Left.'[19]

But could Lansbury, who had once admitted that he looked forward to the time 'when the workers have social revolution [and] we will not have a king or queen',[20] *really* disassociate the Labour Party as a whole from ideas which so many leading Fabians, ILP members and party political theorists had endorsed for so many years, regardless of the precise words used to describe them? By the time of their expulsion, MacDonald and Snowden had stood firmly for peaceful gradualism (no matter how improbable its success might have been), but they were gone, thrown out of the party, which the departing Snowden had accused of 'Bolshevism'. Was Lansbury simply too naive and too blinded by his own enthusiasm for Soviet Communism to see its reality?

The same year, 1933, Lansbury wrote condemning 'the many cruel and unjust statements made by interested persons against the Government of that great country [Russia]' and praising W. P. Coates's new book, *More Anti-Soviet Lies Nailed*, which 'has once again given the lie to those who choose to describe the Russian workers as a nation of slaves held in subjection by brute force':

The colossal task set themselves by the Russian Socialists is one which should be supported by all lovers of the race ... *We are not called upon to judge or accept all the means they adopt to attain their ends* ... Time is on the side of Socialism and the more the facts of life and work in Russia are known, the greater will be the demand which will rise from the peoples of all lands that

each and all of us in our own way and by our own methods will win our way
to Socialism. (My italics.)[21]

Lansbury simply chose not to see what others saw, or else discounted it when
he saw it.

Harold Laski, as professor of political science at the LSE, could reasonably be described in this period as Labour's leading political theorist. He
had already dismissed objections to the compulsory expropriation of private
property in Russia ('I cannot see anything worse in Russian confiscation of
private property than in the Allied confiscation of German property during the
war'[22]); in Laski's own 1933 publication, *Democracy in Crisis*, he speculated
that civil war might break out as capitalists tried to resist Labour reforms. If
that happened, the government would need 'to take vast powers' and 'suspend
the classic formulae of opposition'.[23] As he had written the previous year in the
New Statesman and Nation, 'the necessity and value of delegated legislation
and its extension is inevitable if the process of socialisation is not to be wrecked
by the normal methods of obstruction which existing parliamentary procedure
sanctions'.[24] At times, his proposals expressed in even more extreme terms:
'Socialist measures, in a word, are not obtainable by constitutional means ... if
Socialists wish to secure a State built with the principles of their faith, they can
only do it by revolutionary means.'[25] Whatever Lansbury said, it would be hard
to find another word to describe all this other than a 'Socialist dictatorship'.

Precisely *how* those who saw what was happening in Russia in the first half
of the 1930s chose to interpret them is a complicated question. One response
was denial. Another was adopted by Cripps in his Commons intervention in
April 1933 when he insisted that execution in Russia was always fair because
the Soviet legal system was a 'system of justice'.[26] All must be well because the
Soviet state was founded on integrity. Laski took a different course – to admit
the excesses but to dismiss them as of less consequence than the gains achieved.

In 1935, Laski was commissioned by the *Manchester Guardian* to write a
review of the Webbs' *Soviet Communism*. The review, which would have been
widely read, was notable because it tied together a number points, combining
them in the reader's mind in such a way that Soviet excesses were made to
appear acceptable, outweighed by the benefits of Communism. Laski's conclusions were clearly stated: the book was a landmark publication, 'scores'

of Russians, including kulaks, certainly had been summarily shot without trial or just cause, but the 'Communist achievement' in Russia was of epoch-making 'magnificence', and the benefits for Russia would not have been attainable without 'the price that has been paid', even though those crimes committed by the state in another nation would not have gone unpunished:

> All in all there is no book on the Russian system which remotely compares with it in either insight or intellectual calibre. It ought to mark an epoch in Western understanding of its vital theme. [It exhibits] a freshness and vigour which it is impossible to over praise.
>
> [The Webbs do not] deal adequately with the problem of the liquidation of the kulaks. Granted the end, the means no doubt followed, but, also, granted Hitler's premises, it is not difficult to justify his treatment of the Jews. So with the Kirov trial.* When all that can be said has been said the fact still remains that scores of people were shot without one jot of evidence being produced to connect them with the assassination which involved their death. Granted that many of them were involved in conspiracies against the Soviet Union, one is still left with the sense that there was more indignant revenge than careful justice in what occurred...
>
> But when all this is said, what remains is the unshakable conviction that Soviet Communism has opened a new epoch in the history of the world. It has redefined the canons of human behaviour as surely and as impressively as the Reformation or the French Revolution. Like each of these great movements, it has done so in the name of a doctrine which it seeks to prove in the event. It has its trials, its hesitations, its set-backs; but, all in all, *it sweeps forward with a magnificence which can escape no eye prepared to view it with any measure of objectivity*. The price paid, as Mr. and Mrs. Webb do not seek to conceal, has been immense. But it is also true that young Russia today has won immense benefits not otherwise attainable from the fact that the price has been paid. (My italics.)[27]

The 1935 general election saw the beginning of a recovery in Labour's fortunes. Its parliamentary representation increased to 154. Over the decade from 1928 to 1937, the party's membership doubled.[28] The mid-1930s also

---

* Sergei Kirov was a leading Bolshevik who was assassinated in 1934. Stalin used his killing as an excuse to launch widespread purges and in a show trial in 1936 some of his main rivals were found guilty of the murder and shot.

saw the growth of the role of the General Council of the TUC in the Labour leadership, particularly in the persons of Ernest Bevin, the general secretary of the Transport and General Workers' Union, and Walter Citrine, the TUC General Secretary. Citrine visited Russia in 1936 (his second visit, the first having been in 1925), and he was 'profoundly disturbed by the curtailment of personal liberty and the complete suppression of independent political criticism'. While acknowledging the regime's achievements, he could not discount that they had come 'at a great cost in human suffering'.[29] Unlike Laski, Citrine did *not* consider that the end justified the means.

Both Bevin and Citrine shared the majority of the Labour Party's deep hostility to the CPGB, which on Moscow's orders had striven for years to affiliate with Labour in order to subvert it from within ('entryism'), moves which had been consistently and firmly rebuffed. In this context, a clash between the leadership of the Labour Party and the contingent seeking closer unity with the CPGB, represented by the Socialist League and its leader Stafford Cripps, looked increasingly likely. It came with the League's establishment of the Unity Campaign in 1937.

The Unity Campaign

The Unity Campaign was a short-lived attempt to unite the CPGB, the ILP and the 'left' of the Labour Party, represented by the Socialist League, in a movement for the 'unity of all sections of the working-class movement in the struggle against Fascism, Reaction and War, and against the National Government'.[30] The campaign's 1937 manifesto was signed by William Mellor, Stafford Cripps, G. R. Mitchison (the husband of writer Naomi Mitchison) for the Socialist League, James Maxton, F. W. Jowett, Fenner Brockway for the ILP, and CPGB members Harry Pollitt, William Gallacher, and Clemens Palme Dutt, who was married to George Lansbury's daughter Violet.* Other

---

*   Violet Lansbury (1900-1972) was a secretary at the Russian Trade Delegation, London, 1920-1925. She was active in espionage for the Soviets c.1921-1925 and emigrated to the USSR in 1925, travelling abroad (e.g. to India in 1932 and 1934) as a Comintern 'courier' (spy). In Moscow she married Igor Reussner, an agricultural specialist. Reussner's brother Lev was arrested in Sept 1937 and shot in 1941; Igor appears to have survived. Possibly prompted by that arrest, Violet returned to the UK in 1938 leaving her husband and their two children behind. The youngest was aged no more than five. She married again in 1938 to Clemens Dutt, an active senior member of the CPGB since the early 1920s, a man who was well known to the British security services for his pro-Soviet activities. Violet worked as a journalist for the *Daily Worker* in the 1940s and, together with Dutt, they became prolific translators of Soviet publications.

leading figures involved in the campaign included Harold Laski, George Strauss, Aneurin Bevan, H. R. Brailsford, John Strachey, and Tom Mann. The name of Frank Wise, the first chairman of the Socialist League, does not appear on the list; he had died in 1933.

In the light of the ILP's increasing unease over the show trials in Russia, unity was fragile from the start. Maxton was reluctantly persuaded by Cripps to agree to a clause in the launch manifesto which described the Soviet Union as both free and peace-loving. Maxton wrote to Cripps to express his concern at the clause but, in his own launch speech, Cripps expressed no such reservations: 'Russia, alone among the countries of Europe, has shown herself a champion of working-class power, and has done what she can in a world over-ridden by capitalism and imperialism to stem the tide of fascist aggression.'[31]

In Spain meanwhile, the CPGB- and Moscow-backed Communists were shooting at their nominally republican allies, the ILP-backed POUM (Workers' Party of Marxist Unification). When the Labour Party conference threatened to disaffiliate the Socialist League and rejected unity with the Communists, Cripps's place on the powerful Policy Sub-Committee of the Labour National Executive was no protection. He was forced either to dissolve the League or to face expulsion, the latter a fate he was unable to avoid two years later when, in January 1939, a similar project (the 'popular front') led to the National Conference's overwhelming vote to expel him.[32] George Strauss, his fellow backer at *Tribune* (the magazine founded by the Socialist League in 1937), who had previously declared conditions in Russian prisons 'very much more favourable than in our English prisons',[33] was among those who were expelled alongside him.

The war years and beyond

When in 1938 the ILP issued its appeal to Stalin to 'end this regime of blood', it would not mark the end of the road for all of Soviet Communism's British Labour enthusiasts. G. D. H. Cole's most unambiguous endorsement of Soviet repression was still to come in 1942. He even looked forward to a day when Britain might be subject to Soviet-enforced terror, ruled by Stalin:

I have never allowed my dislike of much that Stalin has done to blind me to the fact that the USSR remains fundamentally Socialist, or that the Soviet form of revolution and of government may be the only one that is capable of sweeping clean the stables of Eastern and Southern Europe, or of solving the basic economic problems of the unhappy peasants of these impoverished states.

I would much sooner see the Soviet Union, even with its policy unchanged, dominant over *all* [*sic* – Cole's italics] Europe, including Great Britain, than see an attempt to restore the previous-war states to their futile and uncreative independence and their petty economic nationalism under capitalist domination. *Much better be ruled by Stalin than by the restrictive and monopolistic cliques which dominate Western capitalism.* Nay more: much better be ruled by Stalin than by a pack of half-hearted and half-witted Social Democrats who do still believe in the 'independence' of their separate, obsolete national states. For it would be much better to live within a system, *however barbaric in some of its features*, that has within it some creative force making for the liberation of mankind from class-oppression and primary poverty than to be thrust back under the dead hand of a decaying capitalism utterly incapable of fresh, creative effort.

I value intensely the particular kinds of personal and group freedom which have won considerable scope under the parliamentary capitalism of Western Europe ... I am keenly aware that Russian Communism, mainly because of the conditions under which it has grown up, *sets little store by these kinds of freedom* (though it sets much store by others which in the eye of history may well seem of even greater account) [but] I am fully convinced that *what matters most is to eradicate the class system, even if the particular liberties by which I personally set most store suffer severe damage in the process.* (My italics, except where indicated.)[34]

Labour historians are nonplussed when confronted with such remarks. One has excused Cole by saying that he wrote at a time when many Labourites were highly impressed by the heroism of the Red Army and that he was merely 'making a rhetorical point – albeit a rather astonishing one – rather than hoping that such an eventuality would come about'.[35] But there had been no Red Army heroism in 1937 when Cole reaffirmed his loyalty to Soviet Communism, fully accepting the cost:

Nor am I one of those who, when everything in the new and struggling Socialist community does not go as they would like, turn their backs on the struggle and proclaim the Revolution is being betrayed ... Alas, men cannot make a new civilisation without growing pains, or liquidate an ancient tyranny without suffering.[36]

In fact, in Peter Shore's 1956 tribute to Cole in the *New Statesman*, Shore, who added a similar endorsement of Soviet Communism even with its 'repulsive features', showed that his contemporaries knew that Cole's extremism was not 'rhetorical' – he admired Mao as well as Stalin:

What, then, should be our attitude to Communism? It must begin with the recognition that Communism has proved to be the most speedy, effective, and in some ways attractive instrument yet devised for transforming primitive into modern societies ... Furthermore [even] when its repulsive features are weighed Communism remains an infinitely superior system of social organization to the feudalism which, with minor exceptions, it has so far replaced. Professor Cole speaks for most of us when he says he is 'on the side' of the Russian Revolution, the Chinese Revolution and the Viet Minh.[37]

Laski post-war

Laski continued to make contentious statements supporting the Soviet Union, but he was increasingly positioning himself as a maverick outside the Labour mainstream. Perhaps he had not changed so much as Labour had passed him by. Nonetheless, he remained a significant figure. In 1945, Laski clashed with Prime Minister Attlee over interviews in which he appeared to pre-empt aspects of Labour's foreign policy: 'Attlee informed him that he had no right to speak for the government and that "a period of silence on your part would be welcome"'.[38] In Laski's 1946 chairman's speech at the Labour Party conference, however, he paid no attention. After announcing that Labour would promote the 'fullest understanding' of Russia at the United Nations, he urged the Soviets to remember how, in its early days, the British Labour movement, through the Councils of Action in 1920, had 'broken the effort of Winston Churchill to destroy the Bolshevik Revolution'. Labour had only been a small party then, but now Labour was 'the greatest working-class party in Western Europe' and it would 'lend support directly or indirectly, to any government which sought to threaten Russian security.' Furthermore, he continued:

I say to the rulers of the new Russia that the achievements of their revolution are one of the pillars of our own strength and we shall help them to guard those achievements as part of the conditions of our own safety as a movement seeking to build a socialist commonwealth in Britain ... Governments like the Russian, and our own, are the surest hope of peace where they find the road to the same ends and combine their strength to fight whatever dangers they may encounter on the way.[39]

He finished by offering the support of Labour to the Russian government to ensure that 'the "hooded men" of counter-revolution' around the world would not revive.

The following year, Laski delivered the prestigious Webb Memorial Lecture at the London School of Economics (in the presence of Prime Minister Attlee as honoured guest). His subject once again was the Webb's *Soviet Communism*, and his mantra unchanged:

The Russian Revolution is the greatest, and the most beneficent event in modern history since the French Revolution, and that it has opened more avenues of creative fulfilment to more people than even its remarkable predecessor.

What there has been in it of ugliness and of evil is, no doubt, so dramatic and impressive that, when we are not in broad agreement with its principles, these appear in the foreground of discussion. But I think that Mr and Mrs Webb are right in asking us to remember the remorseless accumulation both of pain and of frustration in the history of past civilisations, which have not even attempted to make what is available of goodness in living to any but a small fragment of their citizens ... Further, it is important for us to bear in mind that much that has been seen in all its harshness and crudity in Russia, has been largely concealed from us in Western countries because the Industrial Revolution here has been spread over a century and a half, while in Russia its impact was compressed within 30 years.

They are, I am sure, right in insisting that neither Lenin nor Stalin ever played the part of a dictator ... I accept, without question, the high and benevolent purposes of the Russian Communist Party. I understand the reasons which persuade its leaders still to insist on the maintenance of controls which operated to exclude the democratic idea of freedom from the life of the Russian citizen...[40]

By the time this speech was given, Stalin, who, Laski claimed, had never 'played the part of a dictator' had killed at least as many people as the number of Jews that had perished in the Nazi concentration camps.

The centenary *Communist Manifesto*

1948 marked the centenary of the publication of Marx's *Communist Manifesto* and the Labour Party turned to Laski to edit a new edition, another indication of his enduring place in the party, notwithstanding his clashes with Attlee. Laski contributed a ninety-page essay on Marx which took up almost two-thirds of the book. *Communist Manifesto, Socialist Landmark: A New Appreciation Written for the Labour Party* shows how highly the Labour Party esteemed Marx and the *Communist Manifesto*, as even the dust jacket makes clear: 'The Labour Party regards this statement of Marx and Engels as one of the great historical documents in socialist history, which has had an immense influence on Socialism as it is expressed in so many countries of the world.' The party's debt to Marx in its legislative programme was also explicitly acknowledged in the anonymous 'Foreword by the Labour Party' which opens the book. These words may not have been penned by Laski himself, but as the overall editor of the volume, it is unlikely that they would have been included without meeting with both his and the National Executive's approval:

> In presenting this centenary volume the Labour Party acknowledges its indebtedness to Marx and Engels as two of the men who have been the inspiration of the whole working-class movement. The authors' detailed programme is of great interest to us. Abolition of private property in land has long been a demand of the Labour movement. A heavy progressive income tax is being enforced by the present Labour government as a means of achieving social justice. We have gone far toward the abolition of the right of inheritance by our heavy death duties…[41]
>
> Who, remembering that these were the demands of the Manifesto, can doubt our common inspiration?

Laski's signed contribution (assuming that the anonymous dust jacket copy and the foreword may have been his as well) was of the same tone, declaring that 'few documents in the history of mankind have stood up so remarkably to the test of verification by the future'.[42]

'Violence' and the Newark libel trial

Laski never properly clarified his position over the place of violence in socialist revolution – perhaps because it was an impossible task. It was this ambivalence which was to land him in his most distressing difficulty. In 1946, he launched a libel action against a regional newspaper, the *Newark Advertiser*, for reporting that he had advocated violent revolution in an electioneering speech in 1945. The newspaper wrote that Laski had said in a speech that 'if Labour could not obtain what it needed by general consent, "we shall have to use violence even if it means revolution"'.

Laski insisted that he did not advocate *violent* revolution and that he merely believed that it was not unlikely if the ruling classes refused to accept its more peaceful variant. But in court, when asked the question: 'Do you believe that if political ends cannot be achieved without physical violence such violence is justified?' he prevaricated: 'Violence may be inevitable because the burden is intolerable' was not a direct answer. Other questions produced similar responses. Asked if he meant that capitalists 'must consent to their own elimination', Laski replied they must consent to their own loss of power, and added that it was historically unlikely that they would do so. 'It is open to the people of this country to begin revolution by general consent or face the danger of revolution by violence if they did not'.[43]

In his *Democracy in Crisis* (1933), Laski had speculated that civil war might break out as capitalists tried to resist Labour reforms. If that happened, the government would need 'to take vast powers' and 'suspend the classic formulae of normal opposition'.[44] When the newspaper's barrister read extracts from the book out loud the court, Laski was forced to agree that his argument had been that the conditions that created capitalist resistance might make the use of force to destroy those conditions inevitable; and that, if Labour government was obstructed in its plans to see through its programme, it would resort to a Defence of the Realm Act – in other words, it would introduce martial law. The finer points of his argument were lost on the jury. The judgement went against him and he was forced to drop similar actions against the *Daily Express* and the *Evening Standard*. The judge ruled that his remarks, though not treason, amounted to sedition and a breach of the peace. It was a humiliating defeat from which he did not really recover.

The jury's decision may or may not have been right, but it is hard to resist the conclusion that Laski brought at least part of his problems upon himself. In spite of his protestations, Laski's comments in the centenary edition of the *Communist Manifesto*, written the following year, still seem not to absolve him completely of the charges:

> [Marx and Engels] recognised that at certain periods of history changes are necessary, and if … they are resisted they will impose themselves by violence … Violent revolution may bring with it good in its train. The usurpation of the power of a possessing class is, at such vital times, the source of well-being in society.[45]

R. H. Tawney

No account of these years would be complete without a brief mention, alongside Laski and Cole, of the third notable Labour political theorist of the first half of the twentieth century: R. H. Tawney (1880–1962). As eminent as the other two in Labour history, he nevertheless stands apart from them in their admiration for Marx and Soviet Communism and acts as proof that sympathy with Communist Russia was not an inevitable consequence of being a serious thinker of the period with socialist tendencies. Whereas many British inter-war socialists had their eyes fixed, like Hugh Dalton's, 'on Russia as the exemplar',[46] Tawney's Russian trip in 1931 had confirmed him in the opposite view. He had seen the trainloads of deported kulaks, he had been 'appalled at the lack of freedom' and 'aghast to find pure class war being taught as history',[47] a particular affront to the man who held the position of professor of economic history at the LSE. In 1949, his antipathy remained as strong as ever, declaring himself 'not an admirer of Communist doctrine, much of which, as expounded by the faithful, appears to me not only morally repulsive but of an intellectual naïveté almost passing belief'.[48]

Tawney's Socialism was driven not by Marx, but by his profound Christian faith. In the words of his biographer, 'he judged policy not by its utility and outcome, but by its moral intentions [and] rejected as morally unworthy versions of Socialism which simply sought to materially enrich workers and their families'.[49] His philosophical foundations led him to reject as false the conviction of many intellectual socialists that a change in the machinery of government was enough in itself to change the nature of human beings.

These conclusions led also to a parting of ways on foreign policy with Cripps, Cole and Laski. Decrying Russia's 'despotic government' and 'police collectivism',[50] and British Communists' 'drawing room cult of violence',[51] he supported Attlee's and Bevin's alliance with America against Soviet Communism. He was not a pacifist either: he had volunteered to fight in the Great War, believing it to be a just cause. His perspective on international peace, the movement for which the USSR had sought to co-opt for its own advantage, was far more nuanced than that of many of his contemporaries: 'I differ from my fellow socialists', he declared; 'I do not believe that capitalism is the sole cause of wars.'[52]

All this serves to distance Tawney from the dominant stream of pro-Soviet intellectual Socialists with which this book is concerned. Tawney remains an intriguing figure who stands apart, on Marx and Soviet Communism, from many others claimed by Christian socialists today.[53] He was a socialist whose moral compass was directed by a different faith, drawing different conclusions, to that of many of his contemporaries – for both Marxism and Christianity ultimately required of their followers that they place their faith in an as yet unrealised utopia.

CHAPTER 40

REALISM: ATTLEE AND BEVIN

For all Laski's protestations and Cole's continuing support for Stalin, the nigh on universal enthusiasm of early 1930s Labour for the Soviet experiment had waned by the end of the decade. Although quite a number of Labour voices continued to join those of British Communists in support of Russia in the post-war years, they no longer held centre stage, especially after the Soviet invasion of Hungary in 1956.

Labour's post-war Anglo-Soviet policy was driven by the partnership of Prime Minister Clement Attlee and his Foreign Secretary, Ernest Bevin, who had faced down Cripps in 1937. Attlee was no longer under any misapprehension about the danger of Soviet subversion from within and, according to Christopher Andrew, historian of the intelligence services, 'Attlee, at his own request, had more one-to-one meetings with the DG [Director General] of MI5 than any other twentieth-century Prime Minister (probably more than all the other British Prime Ministers combined)'. Andrew adds that Attlee had instructed MI5 to inform him personally whenever it had 'positive information that a Member of Parliament was a member of a subversive organisation'.[1] It was a stark contrast with Ramsay MacDonald's dismissive 1924 cancellation of the Home Office monthly intelligence reports to Cabinet on British revolutionary organisations.

Ernest Bevin, whose competence during the war years had earned Churchill's respect, proved to be a remarkable minister. In the Foreign Office, his officials responded to him with 'respect and a good deal of affection, [and] as Bevin came to appreciate his officials' ability and professionalism, they in turn came to appreciate his intelligence, political skill, and integrity'.[2] Under

Bevin's direction, Britain's stance towards Russia acquired a robustness that pre-war Labour would never have countenanced. Three remarkable Cabinet papers by Bevin encapsulate that transformation: *Extinction of Human Rights in Eastern Europe* (24 November 1947), *Review of Soviet Policy* (5 January 1948), and *The Threat to Western Civilisation* (3 March 1948).[3] The year after the last of these, Bevin added to the strength of the Foreign Office's Russia contingent by appointing Sir William Strang as his Permanent Under-Secretary of State, the role that Vansittart had played for Henderson in 1930. Strang had been Sir Esmond Ovey's number two in the Moscow embassy in the early 1930s and had seen at close quarters the Soviet system in all its ruthless brutality. In contrast to Ovey's more naive perspective, Strang knew from experience that the Soviets were by nature duplicitous – that their word could not be trusted and that their signature on treaties was often worthless.

Extinction of Human Rights

Extinction of Human Rights in Eastern Europe begins with the words: 'Totalitarian regimes now rule over the whole of Eastern Europe except Finland, Greece and Turkey. They rule over or threaten important parts of Central Europe', and then asks the question: 'What should be our attitude to the rapid extinction of human rights and the fundamental freedoms in this area?' Bevin's answer was resistance: 'I recommend that we should continue, in regard to Eastern Europe as elsewhere, to maintain our stand against totalitarianism in all its manifestations and particularly the suppression of human rights and fundamental freedoms'.[4]

Back in 1930, confronted with the Soviet Union's 'suppression of human rights and fundamental freedoms', in the form of the persecution by imprisonment, execution or discrimination of religious believers, Ramsay MacDonald's Cabinet had memorably hidden behind the excuse that it could not 'interfere in the internal affairs of a foreign state'.[5] It was a position supported by backbench Labour MPs in the Commons.[6] Lord Parmoor had sought to silence opposition protests with the warning that they might harm those in Russia on behalf of whom protest was made.[7] In 1934, his successor, Lord Ponsonby, continued to insist that Russia's internal affairs should not be discussed in Parliament.[8] Now, thirteen years later, a Labour Foreign Secretary emphatically contradicted them all. Bevin insisted that the government could not take any line on human rights in Eastern Europe which differed from the one which it took elsewhere in the world: experience now showed that, far from helping its victims, refusing to confront Soviet repression brought them no relief.*[9] It was all that the protesters had ever wanted in 1931.

Written the following year, *Review of Soviet Policy* contained the disturbing revelation that, far from closing down all the Nazi concentration camps in its sector, the Soviets had resurrected some, notably Sachsenhausen and Buchenwald, and were using them for their own purposes. Over 250,000 German civilians had been processed there and sent on to gulag camps in Russia. German prisoners of war, released from Western captivity and returned to their homeland, were being immediately rearrested and deported en masse as Soviet slave labour – 'trainloads of prisoners, still wearing British battledress issued to them in this country, have been seen on their way to labour camps in the East'.[10] Bevin estimated their number at that point to be around 275,000.

Brailsford, the Webbs, Laski and others had acknowledged the existence of the gulag before the war but, after protesting about the repression of Russian socialists in the mid-1920s, had stayed mostly silent or had attempted to justify the camps' existence. In the late 1940s and early 1950s, Bevin had no intention of doing the same. In July 1949, the Foreign Office sent copies of the Soviet Forced Labour Code with its delegation to the United Nations Economic and Social Council in Geneva. The Code clearly revealed the widespread use of forced labour in the gulag system and the subject was reported widely (and with sympathy for the prisoners) throughout the British press. Even the formerly pro-Soviet *Daily Herald* headlined its report on the subject 'Soviet slave camp code shown to the world'.[11]

The defence of Western civilisation

In his papers, Bevin was equally forthright about the situation now facing European governments:

The Soviet government have ruthlessly consolidated their position within their orbit and in Eastern Europe. They have made a mockery of their many pledges

---

* The extract from Bevin's memorandum which refers to this is reproduced in the next chapter.

about free elections etc. in the Yalta and Potsdam Agreements ... All opposition organisations within the Soviet orbit have been or are being liquidated ... The pattern of Communist policy in the Soviet orbit of Eastern Europe is now plainly visible ... In [the] bloc of Communist-administered territory ... human rights and freedoms no longer exist. ...

Ever since the European recovery programme was devised, the Soviet government have been carrying on a war of nerves behind it, resolutely using the Communist party to achieve dictatorship. It is their intention to endeavour to expand their activities to cover the whole of Europe at the earliest possible date ... Events have moved quickly and aggressively ... It has really become a matter of the defence of Western civilisation, or everyone will be swamped by the Soviet method of infiltration.[12]

Bevin noted that the Soviets had made attempts to establish Communist influence, even to take government, in Italy and France. Even though they had failed so far, he believed that they would not stop trying: 'The immediate Soviet object is to dominate Italy, Austria, Greece, France, and French North Africa.'[13] In the empire, he warned, 'we must beware of the far-reaching effects of colonial propaganda even where it is disguised as support for nationalist aspirations ... Soviet policy is actively hostile to British interests everywhere ... A concerted and co-ordinated attempt is being made to spread hatred against us throughout the world.'[14]

Much had changed in thirty years. Now, a Labour Foreign Secretary was alerting his colleagues to the threat from Soviet Russia in terms that were virtually identical to those expressed by Lord Curzon, his Conservative predecessor, in the early 1920s.

The 'special relationship' with America

After years of fighting off Communist subversion within the unions, Bevin understood the Communist mindset in a way that his Conservative counterparts could not. That experience led him to conclude the Soviets would only take military action where they saw weakness and believed there to be a likelihood of victory. Western unity was therefore the strongest defence and, at an international level, the highest priority.[15] Bevin's consequent support for close partnership with the United States and for a strong British defence policy brought him into conflict with the left of the Labour Party which, even as it became ambivalent towards the policy of the Soviet Union, remained ideologically hostile to America and sympathetic to Communist ideals. It was a hostility that the Soviets were only too keen to exploit, but the story of their influence within the British anti-nuclear Campaign for Nuclear Disarmament, and other parts of the world peace movement, is not for this book.

• • •

Around the world, the delusion continued. While Solzhenitsyn records that Stalin's death in March 1953 brought a moment of hope and joy to those in the camps, the event triggered an outpouring of grief not only within the Soviet Union but among its thousands of friends abroad. One of those so moved was Paul Robeson, the American bass singer best remembered today for his rendering of 'Ol' Man River' in the movie *Show Boat*, but at the time well known as a social activist in addition to his fame as a performer. Robeson, who had been awarded the Stalin Peace Prize the previous year, penned his own tribute to Stalin, under the title 'To you beloved comrade'.[16] He began with his memory of seeing Stalin arrive at a theatrical performance in 1937:

Suddenly everyone stood – began to applaud – to cheer – and to smile. The children waved.

In a box to the right – smiling and applauding the audience – as well as the artists on the stage – stood the great Stalin.

I remember the tears began to quietly flow and I too smiled and waved. Here was clearly a man who seemed to embrace all. So kindly – I can never forget that warm feeling of kindliness and also a feeling of sureness. Here was one who was wise and good – the world and especially the socialist world was fortunate indeed to have his daily guidance.

Today in Korea – in Southeast Asia – in Latin America and the West Indies, in the Middle East – in Africa, one sees tens of millions of long oppressed colonial peoples surging toward freedom. So much of this progress stems from the magnificent leadership, theoretical and practical, given by their friend Joseph Stalin.

They have sung – sing now and will sing his praise – in song and story. Slava – slava – slava – Stalin, Glory to Stalin. Forever will his name be honored and beloved in all lands.

In all spheres of modern life the influence of Stalin reaches wide and deep. From his last simply written but vastly discerning and comprehensive document, back through the years, his contributions to the science of our world society remain invaluable. One reverently speaks of Marx, Engels, Lenin and Stalin – the shapers of humanity's richest present and future.

Yes, through his deep humanity, by his wise understanding, he leaves us a rich and monumental heritage. Most importantly – he has charted the direction of our present and future struggles. He has pointed the way to peace – to friendly co-existence – to the exchange of mutual scientific and cultural contributions – to the end of war and destruction. How consistently, how patiently, he labored for peace and ever increasing abundance, with what deep kindliness and wisdom. He leaves tens of millions all over the earth bowed in heart-aching grief.

Inspired by his noble example, let us lift our heads slowly but proudly high and march forward in the fight for peace – for a rich and rewarding life for all.

CONCLUSION

The record against Labour on Soviet Communism, as it has been presented in this book, is so damning that every argument which can be put forward in the party's defence deserves close scrutiny.

Only extremists?

Do the views put forward in these pages only represent those of a fringe minority in the party? Can we dismiss them as the opinions of a few that were unrepresentative of the wider Party and Labour movement?

Given the statistics, it is hard to do so. The pro-Soviet positions of the Fabian Society (as expressed by the Webbs, Shaw, Olivier, Laski and Cole) and of the ILP have already been made clear and do not need repeating. They were extreme. Both were strongly represented in Labour ranks and far from an insignificant minority. The 1929 Labour government numbered 49 Fabian Society members among its 288 MPs. Half of the 1929 intake (142 of the 288) belonged to the ILP, as did two-thirds of the 1923 intake (100 of 156). That is no small number.

What of the moderate voices? If there were any, we should be able to find them in Hansard speaking up on behalf of the non-socialist victims of Soviet Communism, or to see that there were significant Labour abstentions on key votes on Russia, not least because the Labour parliamentary party rules permitted abstentions on matters of conscience. There are none.

The trade unions form the third main component of the Labour movement. Certainly, the TUC relationship with Moscow was far from smooth on occasions but, even so, TUC presidents and individual union leaders voiced some of the most strident support for Russia and most emphatic denials of the 1929–31 repressions.[1]

Would protests have made any difference?

There is an argument that, even if the Labour movement had admitted to itself (as some individuals clearly did) that the Soviet Union was not a socialist utopia in the making, there was no point in protesting because it would have achieved little.

The historical record stands against that. Conservatives and churchmen spoke up vigorously in 1923 after the arrest of Patriarch Tikhon and when his life was threatened. In the light of the international pressure over the affairs, the regime was forced to back down.[2] And while the death of Monsignor Budkevich was not prevented, Archbishop Jan Cieplak's life had also been saved by the strength of protests from abroad.

Twenty thousand children died in the Northern Region camps in 1930 and 1931 alone, all as a result of malnutrition and disease arising from the harsh climate and the appalling conditions in the camps. There was already a groundswell of international revulsion against the timber trade and a number of nations had suspended imports of Soviet timber. Britain, Moscow's biggest customer, did not. A ban would have bolstered the international campaign, and if the world's trading nations had together refused to buy gulag timber, the camps would have had to close. In the absence of any other exports which could pay for their food and guards, the authorities would have had no choice but to ship them further south or, even, to send them home. To suggest that protests would not have had much effect on the long-term mortality in the famine, gulag or Great Terror of 1937–38 is a false argument. No one knew in 1930 what was going to happen in 1937.

Did they really know what was going on?

Is it unfair to blame Labour for its callousness towards a state of affairs which we have only found out about decades later? Or was enough known at the time? Are we unfairly judging on the basis of hindsight? This was Tony Benn's argument in a tribute he wrote to British Communists in 2001:

It is true that the British [Communist] party made a mistake when it opposed the British declaration of war against Germany and only changed its policy when Hitler invaded Russia in 1941. But the charge that it uncritically support-ed all the excesses during the Stalinist period ignores the fact that those ex-cesses were not widely known, even in the Soviet Union, until Khrushchev's famous speech which disclosed them.[3]

This is completely untrue. The excesses were widely known; they were simply not accepted by many on the left. Over a million people had joined in prayers for the persecuted in 1930. Fifty thousand had attended a special service in St Peter's Square. That hardly qualifies as 'not widely known'. And Tony Benn's father, William Wedgwood Benn, must have been well aware of what was going on twenty-five years before Khrushchev's 1956 speech: he was Secretary of State for India in Ramsay MacDonald's Cabinet when it agreed not to return Russian stowaways because they were likely to be shot; he was present when it was decided in secret to refuse to hold an inquiry into the camps because it believed that such an investigation would confirm that human rights abuses were so widespread that trade would have to be halted. Moreover, the Foreign Office during this time received multiple reports which confirmed the deportation and incarceration of hundreds of thousands of kulaks, widespread religious persecution and the shooting of at least 30,000 innocent peasants. Reports of Soviet oppression and brutality were frequent throughout the years from 1917 to 1929 and, where they related to the mass imprisonment and execution of non-Bolshevik socialists, were accepted as authentic by the British left. Some socialist journalists even praised the kulak expulsions. All this has already been examined earlier in this book.

Are we judging by modern norms, not contemporary ones?
If the argument that the evidence *was* known stands, are we judging by human rights standards that have become only accepted in the second half of the twentieth century, but did not apply at the time?

This defence is inadequate too. The cruel exploitation of the Putumayo Indians by European rubber traders had led to Sir Edward Grey's diplomatic instruction in 1913 that British consuls had to report on any British compa-nies whose foreign workers were employed in conditions that were oppres-sive and inhumane; employers found guilty were liable to prosecution back in Britain. Before that, the horrors of the Congo rubber trade had stirred the nation and led to massive national protests. The man who had publicised the Congo scandal, Edmund Morel, became a Labour MP. There was already a well-developed public understanding that these things were morally repugnant and should be stopped.

International legislation was clear too. In 1924, article 23a of the Covenant of the League of Nations committed the British government to 'endeavour to secure and maintain fair and humane conditions of labour for men, women, and children, both in their own countries and in all countries to which their commercial and industrial relations extend'. The British government had ratified the Slavery Convention (1926) and the Forced Labour Convention (1930). Closer to home, the Foreign Prison-Made Goods Act was passed in 1897 and in 1926 Labour's own Sweated Goods Committee called for imports of goods produced by 'sweated' labour abroad to be banned. Mac-Donald repeated that call in the Labour Party conference two years later. The spirit behind all of these was consistent with enacting a ban on gulag timber.

The concept of 'crimes against humanity' is not a later invention, either, even though the term acquired greater use after the Universal Declaration of Human Rights in 1948. It originated at The Hague Convention in 1899 and was included in a declaration signed by the Allies in 1915 when they charged Turkey with committing a 'crime against humanity' in its massacre of the Armenians.[4]

Did the unemployment crisis excuse Labour?

One leading Labour historian and writer on Anglo-Soviet relations describes the MacDonald government's approach as one of 'pragmatism and principle'.[5] If the pragmatism was justified by the circumstances (whether or not it was 'principled'), do the figures bear that out? Again, the answer is 'no'. It is quite true that the country was in the middle of a severe financial crisis and that there was tremendous hardship from unemployment, but trade relations with Russia were not helping the economy. According to the Board of Trade, imports from Russia in 1930 were worth £34,200,000; by contrast, British exports to Russia were only worth £6,800,000, a ratio of more than five to one. The amount of credit extended to the Soviet government by the British during those years was almost double the amount extended to the rest of the world combined.[6]

Furthermore, Russian 'dumping' of artificially cheap exports on the British market (the Soviets did not pay their prisoners and rates on collective farms were paltry) put many British firms out of business and forced farmers to leave their crops unharvested. At a time of high unemployment, Britons lost their jobs because of Russian imports. Complaints about unfair Soviet trade practices by the Tories were dismissed by Labour as driven solely by anti-Soviet prejudice.

As for 'principle', the examples in this text which show how often Labour abandoned it are numerous. Principle was abandoned when Labour first said that the gulag camps could not be defined as prisons and then refused to alter the Foreign Prison-Made Goods Act to include them. The Sweated Goods Committee report had committed Labour to ban the very type of trade 'on moral grounds' that it refused to four years later. It could be said that Labour spokesmen lied to both Houses of Parliament on a number of occasions. William Graham told the Commons that no evidence had been produced to back protesters' claims, even though his own civil servants had briefed him to say that there was such evidence, and the Cabinet was so sure that this was the case that they blocked an inquiry.

Graham's declaration that the Soviets' 'very remarkable economic experiment' (which in the context of the debate that day included the deportations and the gulag) deserved to be allowed to continue without outside interference, and would be supported by the Labour government, was morally indefensible. Looking beyond the 1929–31 government to the 'giants' of the inter-war Labour movement, the Webbs' deluded *Soviet Communism* and George Bernard Shaw's terrifying ramblings are similarly inexcusable.

There are hints that some individuals wrestled with the policy to which the government had committed itself and with some of the wilder sentiment that had been expressed over the preceding decade. It would not be appropriate to omit to mention these. Lord Sankey, the Labour Lord Chancellor, privately expressed his unease to Bishop Henson after Henson spoke on the subject in the Lords. An anonymous member of the Cabinet asked whether or not the Prison-Made Goods Act could be made to cover the camps; he or she was overruled. Philip Snowden described Labour's 1931 election manifesto as 'Bolshevism gone mad', but by then he had already been thrown out of the party, as were Sankey and J. H. Thomas, who consistently had tried to put a brake on union extremism. Henderson also clearly agonised over the Russia question, much to Hugh Dalton's irritation.

Dalton expressed no such hesitation. When the Foreign Office received a report on the conditions in the kulak camps, described by one civil servant as 'loathsome and horrid', he wrote, 'Compare the conditions in the Cairo slums, in parts of India and even in Glasgow. Let not political prejudice localise our humanitarian emotions.'[7] The tragedy is that this is *exactly* what so many Labour figures, Dalton included, actually did.

Bevin's verdict

In the end, the inter-war Labour movement stands condemned not by Conservatives or churchmen but by one of their own number. The most persuasive denial of all Labour's arguments for inaction came from Ernest Bevin, Attlee's post-war Foreign Secretary. In memoranda to the Cabinet, Bevin rebutted all the excuses that had previously been put forward:

> It is sometimes suggested that for the sake of good day-to-day relations with these totalitarian regimes we should overlook their internal practices, acting on the theory that they are no concern of ours and that by expressing our repugnance of them we do not stem the tide of totalitarianism, but rather make matters worse. There are, I believe very strong reasons against taking such a course and it is certainly not true that by refraining from criticising the Soviet or Yugoslav internal regimes we have achieved good relations or made internal conditions less severe ...
>
> We cannot ... take a line on human rights in regard to Eastern Europe contradictory to the line we take at the United Nations and apply to the rest of the world. Our belief in the human rights and in the liberties of Western democracy is part of our way of life, which must be the basis of all our publicity. This belief represents in foreign countries more than anything else what we stand for in the world.[8]

Labour's failure: a wider perspective

The Labour government of 1929–31 led one of the most powerful nations on the planet – at that time still an imperial power which ruled over a fifth of the world's population. Millions of people looked to it for leadership and protection. It had a voice and influence among other nations. This was a heavy responsibility and called for mature statesmanship. It had a moral obligation to govern well and with integrity. In its abandonment of the hundreds of thousands of men, women and children suffering under Soviet oppression, it failed.

It failed, too, in the credibility which it gave to Marxism and the political culture that it allowed to flourish in Britain by doing so. Those with little knowledge of Marxism believe it to be benign and about those who have sharing with those who have not. Ten years ago, a BBC poll voted Marx the greatest philosopher of all time.[9] His popularity in the newly left-leaning Labour Party is growing. It seems that, as memories of the Soviet Union fade, Marx is being rehabilitated.

But Marxism has dark elements within it. It promotes the supremacy of one class, the proletariat, and the irredeemability of other classes, in exactly the same way that Nazism (National Socialism) taught the supremacy of the Aryan race over others, especially over the Jews. Marxism declares that the destiny of the working class is to rule over the other classes, that it is its unquestioned right. Marx and his Leninist followers in Russia believed that class war was not only inevitable but that it was the duty of the proletariat to embrace and, even, to provoke it. And Marx made it clear that violence and terror were inevitable if the proletarian revolution was to be successful.

By endorsing Marx and vesting his theories with moral authority, the Labour movement gave class prejudice a veneer of ethical justification. That attitude, and the resentment it nurtured, became engrained over decades in a movement which sprang out of an honourable impulse to defend those whom society had neglected or abandoned. While the Church, so hated by the Soviets, preached the brotherhood of all humanity regardless of race or class, Socialism preached the supremacy of one class only. Of course, not all British socialists would have verbalised that sentiment, but it remained a pervasive part of the Labour's inter-war culture – as it does in almost every hard left splinter group today.

A second strand of concern also emerges from Marx's Socialism – the negation of individual human rights in pursuit of a grand plan for social reconstruction. It is what the Bolshevik functionary Tolmachev was criticising when he wrote despairingly of the kulaks' plight, that 'they are not crates, they are not cargo, but living people'. It appears in H. N. Brailsford's writing when he applauds the Bolsheviks' 'rashness and severity' as 'the excess of a great quality'. It appears closer to home when G. D. H. Cole justifies the suspension of the 'capitalist conception of individual liberty' for the greater socialist good, and in Stafford Cripps's contemplation of the suspension of Parliament and its replacement by a 'dictatorship of the proletariat'. It was a tendency to inhumanity that Labour theorists were not always able to overcome.

How?

It has to be asked how the Labour movement could so blindly have adopted such a philosophy, have convinced itself that it was being realised in Communist Russia, and then so resolutely closed their eyes to 'see no evil' whenever unpalatable facts about the utopia emerged.

Much is still said about Labour's roots lying 'more in Methodism than in Marx'. It is true that the religious impulse was very strong in Labour in the 1920s, but that religion was not Christianity; it was a secular one, Marxism – one which, although it would despise such a description, required just as much faith in the operation of supernatural mechanisms outside the control of man as its Judaeo-Christian equivalent.

In reality, the party had abandoned any roots it once had in Protestantism by the end of the first decade of the twentieth century.* The theology of Marx drove the movement far more directly than that of the Bible. Hardie's illiterate faith and Lansbury's smorgasbord semi-Christianity were suborned to messianic Marxism. No devout nineteenth-century Methodist or participant in the revival that swept Wales in 1904–05 would have said, as Hardie did, that Marxism, rather than Christianity, was 'the greatest revolutionary ideal that has ever fired the imagination, or enthused the heart of mankind'. Lansbury insisted that it was in Russia that Socialists (not Christians) were building 'the New Jerusalem'. It was Beatrice Webb, a lifelong atheist, who openly likened Soviet Communism to a 'Spiritual Power' and its Russian adherents to a religious order with 'its Holy Writ, its prophets and its canonised saints ... its Pope, yesterday Lenin and today Stalin ... and its Inquisition'.[10]

---

*   Even those are disputed, as the main text explains.

There are reasons for which British socialists embraced their faith in Marx with all the devout single-mindedness of the convert, the first being the devastation of the Great War, the like of which had never been known before. European Christianity had failed to keep the peace and seemed to be bankrupt.[11] Marxian Socialism gave life meaning, gave them a sense that they were part of something bigger, something that was noble, gave them a cause to fight for. It explained the war, too, as the fruit of capitalism. The mechanisms of Marx were a grid for understanding the world and, as such, were as much a religion as Christianity. They were immensely attractive.*

But a reason is not an excuse. Converts must not discard all objectivity when they embrace a new faith. Otherwise, they behave like members of a cult. Sadly, many in Labour's ranks did just that.

The centenary of the Revolution

This year is the centenary of the 1917 Bolshevik Revolution. Time dulls our perception of history and it is probable that there will be interpretations of the Revolution put forward which downplay its horrors and suggest that there were redeeming features which somehow mean that on balance it was a good thing.

I hope that this book will contribute to setting the record straight. The Revolution was a hideous and unnecessary event. There had already been a revolution earlier in 1917. Russia was on the road to becoming a more just state, albeit a very rocky one. The Bolshevik Revolution was a coup d'état by a small group of ruthless terrorists. Its poisonous legacy festered for over seventy years, spawning immeasurable further suffering around the world.

For reasons already mentioned, it is impossible to redeem Marx. The enthusiasts who try to redeem the 'great experiment' of Soviet Communism blame Stalin for corrupting Lenin's pure ideals. They praise Lenin and admire Trotsky. This is pure sophistry; Lenin, Marx's pupil, was a ruthless and cruel revolutionary who bears ultimate responsibility for the deaths of millions. The gulag was established under Lenin; Stalin merely continued in

---

* Two other interesting phenomena that appear in British society in the 1920s also spring from the national trauma and the search for meaning behind a slaughter which touched almost every family: a surge of interest in spiritualism and, among the upper classes, rampant hedonism. Lord Ponsonby's daughter Elizabeth was one of the 'bright young things' of the 1920s. Living from party to party, she drank herself to death at the age of forty.

his footsteps. Yes, Stalin may have been a psychopath, but so were many of the other early Bolshevik leaders. How else could they have supported Lenin in so terrible a project? They had to be bordering on psychopathy themselves or they would have gone mad or fled in horror from the suffering for which they were collectively responsible. As Commissar of War until 1925, Trotsky does not escape with his reputation any less sullied than the others either.

Solzhenitsyn saw this clearly. Sadly, today history is being rewritten in his homeland, and statues to Stalin, removed after the Khrushchev revelations, are being restored.

In the longer term

Most of the remaining conclusions which we can draw from all this will by now be obvious. One which has not yet been mentioned is the warning that springs from these events. Any group of people in a party or movement can persuade themselves of some truth merely by the fact that they all think it true even when those outside the group tell them it is not. Majority decisions are not always right just because they are decided by a majority. One needs only to consider the adulation of the German people towards Hitler in the early 1930s to see where that can lead.

.   .   .

All those involved in this affair are now dead. Its perpetrators, its victims and those in Britain who stood to one side, some out of mistaken but good motives, but others out of less comfortable ones. Suffering leaves an inheritance which passes down the generations. Even now, there are citizens of the former Soviet Union and its satellite states who struggle with the emotional legacy of those days: grandparents who were in the camps themselves or saw their own parents taken from them; their children, now adult, brought up in homes blighted by the psychological scars which their own parents carried, now struggling in their own lives. These people may be in a minority, but their experience is not fanciful or exaggerated.

Perhaps the time has come to consider an apology – though of course I am not so naive as to think that is likely to happen. An apology by whom, to whom? By the British government or, more appropriately, by the Labour

Party; to the people of Ukraine mostly, but also to those of Belarus and Russia, the descendants of the kulaks and of the spiritual leaders and ordinary believers who lost their liberty, their homes, and, in many cases, their lives.

Would an apology make any difference? Maybe that, too, is the wrong question. Perhaps, as Bevin said in his day, it should be done because it is the right thing to do. In the 1930s, Britain did nothing because it put other considerations in the way, considerations which, for the government, took precedence over right and wrong. A more recent Labour Foreign Secretary, Robin Cook, famously committed his party to an 'ethical foreign policy'; an apology would be consistent with that principle.

It is my hope that the publication of the story of these events can go some way to restoring the balance that such a hypothetical apology would achieve, bringing that which was hidden into the light. If you have read thus far, thank you.

POSTSCRIPT

The battle for the Labour Party between those on the radical left (identifying themselves variously as Marxist, Marxist-Leninist, Trotskyite, or Stalinist) and those on the more moderate end of the Labour spectrum has continued intermittently since the Second World War. Under Neil Kinnock and Tony Blair, the moderates seemed to be in the ascendant and it looked as though the re-invention by Blair and his inner circle of the party as 'New Labour' was set to stay for good. The complaint by a number of Labour MPs and members who objected to these reforms was that the Labour Party had abandoned Socialism. On the basis of the Socialism described in this book, they were completely correct. In pre-war terms, Tony Blair was not a socialist.

The 2015 British general election and subsequent events produced an extraordinary development in the election of Jeremy Corbyn as leader of the Labour Party. In many ways, the party was revisiting 1931–32. Then, too, there was disillusionment after a lost election, and, before that, a campaign of character assassination against the former charismatic leader who had won the party successive elections (MacDonald had defined the party of the 1920s in the same way that Blair defined New Labour). In both cases the party shifted to the left in the wake of the leader's departure.

But there is one important difference between 2015 and 1932. Although Lenin had instructed British Communists to infiltrate Labour to subvert it from within, the party recognised each attempt and resisted it. Since the early 1920s, the party leadership had resolutely refused all the attempts by the CPGB to affiliate with the Labour Party; in 1937, when Stafford Cripps got too close to the CPGB in his Unity Campaign, he was forced to withdraw.

'Entryism' was rejected wherever it appeared. Again, in the 1980s, when the Trotskyite group Militant Tendency attempted to take over the party, it was firmly rebuffed and its members were expelled.

Not so in 2015, when the Labour Party changed its membership rules and accidentally made entryism a party policy. No one in the party leadership realised the mistake until it was too late. That they did not see it coming bears out the maxim that politicians have eyes only for the short term while historians see the present in the context of the past. The radical left, however, know their history. They still argue hotly over subjects as esoteric as Khrushchev's post-Stalin reforms and Trotsky's critique of Stalinism. Only time will reveal the extent to which this coup, finally successful almost a century after it was first contemplated, was accidental or planned.

Now, the British Labour Party has a shadow Chancellor who has described Marx, Lenin and Trotsky as the 'most significant' influences on his thought.[1] After a failed attempt in the summer of 2016 to oust Jeremy Corbyn, the party's radical leadership has only strengthened its control. The compulsory reselection of MPs, a direct threat to all those unwilling to embrace this new direction, is being openly suggested. The long-term future may be uncertain, but one thing seems clear: Labour is now returning to familiar territory – Marxian Socialism.

February 2017

APPENDICES

THE FATE OF THE USSR'S BRITISH TRADE OFFICIALS AND DIPLOMATS

As representatives of the world's first socialist republic, Soviet ambassadors and senior officials serving in Britain were held in high regard by British socialists and a number were on friendly terms with Labour leaders. Soviet ambassadors were welcomed at the Webbs' weekend house parties. When the Arcos raid took place in 1927, the first response of the Soviet chargé d'affaires was to rush to see Arthur Henderson and after the officials' expulsions were announced, a dinner in their honour was held by Labour members and trade union leaders in the House of Commons.

The tragic irony is that, with rare exceptions, almost every Soviet official feted by British socialists perished at the hands of the regime that Labour so admired. Of the six leaders of the Soviet diplomatic mission to Britain between the wars, only one, Leonid Krasin, escaped the purges altogether, dying of natural causes in London before they began. Had he lived that long, he would undoubtedly have shared their fate. Of the other five, four perished and the fifth, Ivan Maisky, survived only because his imprisonment was cut short by Stalin's death. Many other Soviet trade officials and diplomats who served in Britain were shot too.[1]

Senior Soviet diplomats

The following led the Soviet diplomatic mission to Britain, first as leaders of the Soviet Trade Delegation, then as chargés d'affaires, and finally as Soviet ambassadors:

Krasin, Leonid Borisovich (1870–1926), Soviet Trade Delegation leader (1920–23). *Died in London 1926.*

With the exception of a brief two-month interlude when the role passed to Lev Kamenev (see below), Leonid Krasin led the Soviet Trade Delegation from its arrival in May 1920 until 1923. He was succeeded by Christian Rakovsky and took over from him again at the end of September 1926, but died two months later on 24 November. Six thousand British Soviet supporters attended his funeral.

Kamenev, Lev Borisovich (1883–1936), Acting Trade Delegation leader (1920). *Shot 1936.*

Kamenev, Trotsky's brother-in-law, was head of the Soviet Trade Delegation briefly from August to September 1920 before evidence from intercepted telegrams confirmed what Lloyd George claimed was 'irrefutable' evidence of Kamenev's 'gross breach of faith' and he was refused permission to return to the UK. Kamenev fell victim of one of the most famous Moscow Show Trials. His wife, two sons, his brother and his sister-in-law were all killed as well.

Rakovsky, Christian (1873–1941), Soviet Trade Delegation leader (1923–24), Soviet chargé d'affaires (1924–25). *Imprisoned 1936, shot 1941.*

Originally from Bulgaria, Christian Rakovsky led the Trade Delegation until, as one of his first acts on taking office in 1924, Ramsay MacDonald granted legal recognition to the Soviet government. Rakovsky then became Soviet chargé d'affaires until November 1925. Found guilty of spying for the British and Japanese in the Bukharin Show Trial in 1938, he was one of the few who escaped immediate death, being sentenced instead to twenty-five years' imprisonment. When the Nazis invaded Russia in 1941, the NKVD carried out a number of mass executions to prevent their prisoners falling into German hands. On 11 September 1941, on Stalin's orders, Rakovsky and 150 other important inmates of Oryol prison were shot in the Medvedev Forest Massacre.

Rosengoltz, Arkady Pavlovich (1889–1938), Soviet chargé d'affaires (1926–1927). *Shot 1938.*

Arkady Rosengoltz was Soviet chargé d'affaires in London from 1926 until the expulsions that followed the Arcos raid in 1927. He was arrested in October 1937 and, in the same trial as Bukharin and Rakovsky, found guilty of spying for the German High Command and for British Intelligence. He was shot on 15 March 1938.

Sokolnikov, Grigori Yakovlevich (1888–1939), Soviet ambassador (December 1929–32). *Imprisoned 1937, killed in prison 1939.*

Born Girsh Yankelevich Brilliant, son of a Jewish railway doctor, Sokolnikov had already served a term in prison for his Bolshevik activities before the Revolution. He held the post of Commissar of Finance before his appointment as Soviet ambassador in Britain in 1929. Imprisoned in 1937, he was killed on 21 May 1939 by other convicts. Investigation after Stalin's death established that murder had been carried out on the orders of the NKVD. His wife, Galina, survived a twenty-year sentence in the camps and was released in the 1950s.

Maisky, Ivan Mikhailovich (1884–1975), Soviet ambassador (1932–43). *Imprisoned 1953, released on Stalin's death 1955.*

Ivan Maisky left his post in London to take up a position as Soviet Deputy Foreign Minister. In 1953, Stalin took the first steps to begin new purges of the old guard at the Foreign Ministry and of leading Jews. Maisky was arrested and sentenced to six years' imprisonment. Stalin died in March that same year. Maisky was eventually released in 1955.

Other Soviet trade officials and diplomats

Bogomolov, Dmitri Vasilievich (1890–1937), first secretary, Soviet Embassy (1931?–32?). *Shot 1937.*

Bogomolov's official position was first secretary to the ambassador, Grigori Sokolnikov, but Hugh Dalton suspected that he was more than that: 'Sokolnikov and Bogomolov to lunch at the flat with Pethick, Matters, and John Morgan. We had invited Sokolnikov and wife and they had accepted. We had not invited Bogomolov. But that morning in the office, the Soviet Embassy rang up and asked for my private telephone number. Then they rang the flat and someone told R. that "Mme Sokolnikov has caught a chill ... and can't come to lunch, but Bogomolov can come." It appears that Sokolnikov isn't allowed to go anywhere without Bogomolov, who is appointed to spy on him.'[2]

Klishko, Nikolai Klementevich (1880–1937), Soviet intelligence head of station (cover: assistant to the Trade Delegation) (1920–23). *Shot 1937.*

Klishko was in reality the first Soviet intelligence resident (head of station) in London, though he posed as the secretary to the delegation; his nominal boss, Leonid Krasin, was actually his subordinate.[3] For three years he directed Soviet intelligence operations in Britain. Born in Vilnius in 1880, Klishko had lived in London as an exile from 1907 to 1918, marrying an Englishwoman, Phyllis Frood.[4] Klishko was interned in August 1918 and subsequently deported, before returning to London in May 1920.[5] He was Soviet consul in Peking (1924–1928), before working in Berlin and eventually returning to Moscow in 1932. He was arrested on 2 September 1937 on charges of involvement in an anti-Soviet terrorist organisation, and shot on 9 October 1937. His wife appears to have survived him as she is reported to have been back in the UK in the 1970s.

Khinchuk, Lev (1869–1944), Soviet Trade Delegation chairman (1927). *Imprisoned 1937, died in camp 1944.*

Other Soviet witnesses

In March 1931, four days before the Commons debate on Russian timber imports, the pro-Soviet British trade journal, *The British Russian Gazette*, published a 46-page booklet, *Forced Labour in Russia: Facts and Documents.*[6] The arguments of the booklet were supported by quotations from six leading Soviet officials. Five of these were all shot in 1938:

Karl Danishevsky (1884–1938), president of USSR Timber Export Corporation ('Exportles'); Abram L. Gorski-Ekelchik (1889–1938) ('A. L. Gorsky'), forestry commissar; A.P. Smirnov (1877–1938), commissar of agriculture; Edvard O. V. Gylling (1881–1938) ('Mr Gulling'), chairman of the Council of People's Commissars of the Karelian Republic and Yakov Davidovich Yanson (1886–1938) ('J. D. Yanson'), chairman of Arcos.

THE *MANCHESTER GUARDIAN'S* FLAWED WITNESSES

As the arguments over the existence of human rights abuses in the Russian timber camps continued throughout 1931, three pieces of evidence, letters by Edward Harby, E. A. Ferguson and J. F. Stewart, were consistently referred to by Labour supporters and timber traders as proof that the protesters' claims were fictitious. The letters were first published in the *Manchester Guardian* and Tom Shaw, the Minister of War, addressing a meeting in March 1930, would have been referring to these when he told his listeners that: 'We have no right to interfere in the internal affairs of any other country ... Those of you who read the *Manchester Guardian* will have already found what a campaign of lying – it is no use mincing words – has been conducted.'[1] H. N. Brailsford, writing in *New Leader* a month before, was in agreement: 'The Manchester Guardian has devoted much space to the dissection of these atrocities, and has effectively disposed of most of them. It is evident that Prebendary Gough has been misled by unscrupulous translators.'[2]

So definitive were these witnesses believed to be that their assertions formed the core of Labour's defence of its policy of inaction in the only Commons debate on the timber camps held on 26 March 1931. Hugh Dalton had given instructions that the briefing notes for William Graham, the minister defending the government, should be altered to be consistent with their evidence. George Strauss MP, opening the debate for the government, referred to all three. Leslie Burgin, the only speaker for the Liberals, supporting the government, quotes Stewart's testimony at length.

Closer examination reveals that all three were deeply flawed – in at least one case, possibly two, as an act of deliberate deception. So foundational did they become that it is necessary to examine them at greater length.

Edward Harby

Edward Harby wrote to the *Manchester Guardian* on 2 January 1931, claiming to have 'just returned' from nine months' stay in and around Archangel. During that time, he said he had visited 'every sawmill' and attended the loading of over 100 cargoes. Writing in response to Sir Edward Hilton Young's affidavits, which were then being referred to in *The Times* (see Chapter 25), Harby declared that Hilton Young's affidavits 'in no way resemble the state of affairs observed by me whilst working in the region'. Nowhere, he continued, was he able to find evidence of prisoners being engaged in timber work, and added: 'I actually visited both a prison and a prison camp. In neither of these were the prisoners engaged in producing goods for export'. It seemed cast-iron proof the campaigners were in the wrong.

Those in Russia, including the Norwegian consul at Archangel, were not convinced, as Reader Bullard recorded in his diary:

> The Consul told me that Harby, the man who wrote to Manchester Guardian and said he was nine months there & saw no forced labour, may be right in saying he didn't *see* it, but he must have known it was there. Often no guards, but the men are under collective responsibility. If one escapes all are for it.[3]

When Sir Alan Pim and Edward Bateson set up their inquiry for the Anti-Slavery Society (see Chapter 31), it was obvious that they should interview so well-known and outspoken a witness. They wrote to him and invited him to give them evidence. He refused:

> It is not necessary to have had, like myself, an opportunity to see conditions on the spot, to perceive the nature of this campaign. I fail to see therefore what justification there is for an impartial body to institute an enquiry on such a basis, and I cannot consider an enquiry thus instituted as in any way justified by facts. This is the reason why I do not feel able to accept your invitation to produce evidence at your enquiry, although, of course, I have no objection to your using either this letter or other letters from myself that have appeared in the press.[4]

In their report, Pim and Bateson concluded that his evidence did not stack up. They said so, directly, in the report itself: 'These facts cannot, therefore be reconciled with the statement published in the Manchester Guardian of 2 January 1931 and quoted in the House of Commons on last 25 March, which Mr Harby invited us to use'.[5] So public a rebuke did not stop Harby and, when the Anti-Slavery Society report was published, he took up his pen again to write to *The Spectator* to criticise it. Rev. Harris from the Society wrote back to the paper and firmly dismissed Harby's protestations.[6] *The Tablet* went even further than the Anti-Slavery Society: it suspected that 'Harby' did not actually exist and that the letter was a forgery by Soviet sympathisers.[7]

Dr E. A. Ferguson

Dr E. A. Ferguson's letter was published in the *Manchester Guardian* on 11 February 1931. He laid claim to authenticity by virtue of his position as a 'former Medical Inspector of Lumber Camps in Northern Canada'. Although his opinion was quoted widely, he only wrote to criticise *one* escaped prisoner's affidavit, claiming that it was written by someone who knew nothing of lumbering or lumber camps chiefly because of the number of trees which the writer of the affidavit said needed to be cut per day (thirty-five) was the equivalent of an acre of timber and therefore impossible.

It was one detail capable of having been mistranslated or misunderstood, but it did not prevent him from concluding that 'the whole affidavit appears to have been written by someone who knows nothing of lumbering or lumber camps', a remark which was widely reported as expert corroboration. It was hardly conclusive. The quotas reported by escaped prisoners were variously described as being set per man or per work gang, and translators did not always distinguish between 'trees' and 'logs' – the usually two-metre sections into which the felled trunks had to be cut. Furthermore, Ferguson based his assumption on his knowledge of Canadian, not Karelian forests, where he had never been. He was not a forestry specialist either; he was a medical doctor.

In fact, an affidavit written by an escaped professional forester had already given detailed technical information on forestry practices in Karelia which discredited Ferguson's assertion.[8] The escapee said that north of Kem only large trees were cut (about fifteen to twenty-five per hectare, and to the south much smaller trees were cut (up to 250 trees per hectare). The basis of Ferguson's 'expert' opinion was therefore wrong.

'I hold no brief for the Soviet Government,' Dr Ferguson had written in his letter, a remark which was repeated as proof of his objectivity by Labour MP R. A. Taylor, speaking for the government in the Ten Minute Rule debate on 21 April.[9] While this was technically true, Ferguson had already been shown to be related by marriage to an MP who was a great admirer of the Soviet experiment – Labour MP Alex 'Lex' Haycock. 'I rejoice that the Bolsheviks were successful … it is a good thing for the world that the Soviet Government are there', Haycock had declared when diplomatic relations were re-established in 1929,[10] and he was a bitter critic of the 'Riga lie factories' which had been such a valuable source of information about what was happening inside Russia.[11]

Ferguson's objectivity would probably have gone unquestioned had Haycock not lost his temper at the end of the 25 March 1931 debate, in an outburst during which he even suggested that Churchill should have been impeached and hanged for his part in the Allied intervention in Archangel after the Revolution. With the retort that those spreading stories about the timber camps were 'not even artistic liars', and bent on 'stirring up the fires of hatred' and starting another war, he added 'the name of Dr Ferguson has been mentioned during this Debate. He is my brother-in-law, and I'm going to encourage him to write more letters of the same kind.'

J. F. Stewart

J. F. Stewart was a forestry specialist from the University of Edinburgh, and neither side disputed the quality of his evidence or his impartiality. His opinion had also been printed in the *Manchester Guardian*, on 10 February 1931. He said that he had found no evidence of forced or prison labour during a very extensive tour of the Northern Region forests. As has already been noted (in Chapter 27), his evidence fell down on one crucial detail – that he visited the region a year before the kulak deportations began. Furthermore, Stewart had only visited the Northern Region and had not been to neighbouring Karelia, where he might have seen that the longer established Solovki labour camp group was already making extensive use of prisoners in timber felling. Even after these discrepancies had been revealed, Stewart's statement continued to be repeated extensively both in Parliament and by timber trade leaders to prove that there was no prison or forced labour in the Russian timber industry.

Those who used Stewart's statement also ignored the fact that it contained sufficient expert evidence to imply that widespread mortality among exiled kulaks working in timber camps was highly probable. Stewart had made clear that untrained townspeople would *die* in the forests and that it was highly likely that, if there were to be massive emigration, it would be accompanied by starvation. That detail was consistently ignored, although his meaning could not have been clearer:

> Lumbering is one of the roughest occupations in the world at the best of times, and no weakling can stand up to it. Nor can anyone stand the life if pitched into it without any preparation. It is particularly rough and hard in North Russia … If the government sent up many extra mouths they would find it next to impossible to feed them … The work itself is not unduly trying to a healthy man who is used to it, but it can be deadly to the townsmen or one who has not been brought up to it.[12]

Stewart's grim predictions were overlooked, as was the date of his account. The Timber Trade Federation, in its brief to William Graham before the crucial 25 March 1931 debate, laid great store by it as 'reliable and independent evidence' and Hugh Dalton insisted it be inserted in Graham's Foreign Office brief before the debate. Dalton had either not seen, had forgotten or had chosen to ignore a remark in a letter which Stewart had written on 6 January 1931, when he offered his services to the Prime Minister to carry out an inquiry into conditions in the camps, a copy of which had been sent to the Foreign Office. 'All of the horrors which have been published may be perfectly true. From my observation there is no cruelty that any Russian, no matter of what party, would not perpetrate to gain his ends.'[13]

The fact that all three statements had appeared in the *Manchester Guardian* (irresponsible as that publication may have been) gave them weight. Moreover, the newspaper was consistently sceptical of the motives of those campaigning on behalf of prisoners in the timber gulag. It chose to publish material which supported its own position: that the underlying basis of the anti-slavery campaign was prejudice against Socialism rather than humanitarian concern. The *Guardian*'s support for the Soviet experiment was firm, as it made quite clear in an editorial on 24 February 1931, published in the midst of the slave labour affair: 'Freedom is, in reality, rigidly subordinated to the State purpose. So long as the people submit to be disciplined and regimented in the name of Socialism, or any other name, it is not for us to interfere, only to watch this amazing triumph of human endurance.'

APPENDIX 3

THE ANGLO-RUSSIAN PARLIAMENTARY COMMITTEE, 1924–*c*.1961

From 1919 until the early 1960s, the Anglo-Russian Parliamentary Committee (the 'Hands Off Russia' organisation until it changed its name in 1924) was run by its modestly titled 'secretary', William Peyton Coates (otherwise 'W. P.' or 'Pat') and his wife Zelda. Coates was a founder member of the CPGB, national organiser of its forerunner the British Socialist Party, and had been 'lent' by them to the 'Hands Off Russia' Committee. Zelda's brother-in-law was the same Theodore Rothstein who was the clandestine Bolshevik representative in London until he was refused re-entry into Britain in August 1920. Rothstein acted as the Bolshevik paymaster in Britain, and intelligence reports show that 'Hands Off Russia' received at least £1,000 from him in 1919 and that at one point he was paying Pat Coates's salary.[1] There is no evidence, one way or another, regarding the source of ARPC funding.

From the 1920s to the 1950s, the ARPC worked tirelessly as Britain's home-grown Soviet propaganda outlet. The important difference between the ARPC and the official Soviet press office in London was that all its writers and members were British. The ARPC's literary output, mostly written by Pat Coates, but sometimes co-authored with his wife, was extensive. It published over fifty political books and pamphlets and distributed a regular *News Bulletin*, which carried transcripts of Soviet leaders' speeches, glowing descriptions of life in the Soviet Union, and Soviet trade and industrial statistics to MPs and news outlets. Whatever the USSR was being accused of – religious persecution, trade dumping, slave labour or the imprisonment of the Metro-Vickers engineers – the ARPC countered with volumes of statistics and denials which bolstered the Soviet point of view. The tone of ARPC publications never faltered, always faithfully reproducing the Moscow line, no matter how far-fetched. Most of those who contributed prefaces, introductions or texts of their own, were sufficiently pro-Soviet not to question the statements they endorsed. Of the rest, only naïveté can excuse them of being unaware that they were being used.

That the ARPC has been largely neglected by historians is a tribute to its success as a front organisation. Examination of the organisation's output reveals a consistent pattern of distortion, disinformation and even outright fabrication. It is important to note that those on the committee were not ordinary members of the public, but leading political figures who would have known what weight their endorsement carried. Without doubt, this calls their judgement into question.

One of the more interesting examples of the Anglo-Russian Parliamentary Committee's disinformation, a classic Soviet forgery, was published in its *News Bulletin* on 19 March 1931, at the height of the slave labour affair. For two months, the press had featured a succession of sworn affidavits from prisoners who had escaped the timber gulag, either by fleeing across the border to Finland or by stowing away in foreign ships. These affidavits were the strongest evidence that the protesters' claims were true. The story run by the ARPC *News Bulletin* appeared to show that members of the anti-Soviet community of White Russian émigrés were warning that these statements were forged. In fact, that story was itself a forgery, one which was then prominently repeated elsewhere to discredit the campaign on behalf of the imprisoned kulaks. This is the *Bulletin*'s report:

Fictitious Affidavits – a 'White' Admission

As we have shown, the affidavits purporting to describe conditions in the Soviet labour camps have piled on absurdity upon absurdity without a protest from their purveyors in this country. Emboldened by the ease and greed with which the most ridiculous anti-Soviet stories have been swallowed by the diehards the authors have now gone to such lengths that even the Editor of that bitterly anti-Soviet 'White' publication, the Anglo-Russian News, has jibbed. In the issue of that sheet, No. 297, March 14, 1931, we read:-

'Soviet Slavery Affidavits – a Warning

'Offers of affidavits and sworn declarations from escaped Soviet prisoners are reaching this country from Finland, Poland and other countries. The majority of these affidavits are fictitious and British politicians and businessmen are warned against purchasing these "documents." The Editor of this Service has recently examined a number of these declarations and he has found them unreliable and misleading.'...

And yet this is the sort of evidence upon which a Government with which we are in normal diplomatic relations has been attacked day in, day out.

What is most curious about this is that it was not beyond the White Russian émigré community to fabricate material to *discredit* the Soviet regime (White Russians are still suspected of having had a hand in the Zinoviev letter, if indeed it was a forgery) but it is inconceivable that, even if a White Russian organisation had genuine evidence of falsehood in the campaign on behalf of those held in the prison camps, such an organisation would make it public.

What of the apparently authentic reference to 'No 297' of *Anglo-Russian News* of March 14, 1931, a supposedly White Russian publication which had already been in existence for 297 editions? That appears to be false too. Assuming that the *Anglo-Russian News* was at least a weekly publication (there is hardly likely to have been enough material, or available funds, for a daily bulletin), the existence of a 297th edition would imply that it had been in print for almost six years, eleven if it were a fortnightly publication, or twenty-four years if monthly. With such an extensive publication history, such a title would be known. And yet no trace of the title *Anglo-Russian News* can be found in the library catalogues of the leading collections of Russian material in the UK.[2] Neither is the title mentioned in the most extensive contemporary Soviet bibliography.[3] The most likely explanation is that the whole story was Coates's own invention to counter the highly damaging effect of eyewitness accounts of the camps which were being published in the West.

The success of the regular *News Bulletin* was not only that it managed to keep British Soviet enthusiasts firm in the face of adverse news. It also gave ammunition to those who might not have believed its contents but found it convenient to use them to deflect criticism of the government. One example which has already been mentioned is Lord Parmoor's response to Archbishop Lang's first speech on religious persecution in Russia in the House of Lords on 13 February 1930. Lang's speech was measured, sombre and, given his position, it was incumbent upon the House to take his words seriously but the government had no intention of accepting his verdict on the dire state of human rights in Russia. Parmoor used a passage in an ARPC *News Bulletin* to cast just enough doubt upon the veracity of Lang's assertions to justify the government's inaction. [4]

The ARPC's *News Bulletin* was supplemented by a series of more detailed pamphlets and books. To add credibility to these, Coates called upon his influential committee members for further endorsement. George Lansbury was one. In 1933 (while he was leader of the Labour Party), Lansbury wrote the preface for Coates's *More Anti-Soviet Lies Nailed*, published to refute allegations of religious persecution and slave labour. Parts from this preface have already been mentioned, but it merits fuller reproduction:

Preface by Rt Hon George Lansbury, MP, Leader of the Labour Party

My friend and comrade Pat Coates has on many occasions rendered valuable service to the cause of peace between Russia and Britain by clearly refuting the many cruel and unjust statements made by interested persons against the Government of that great country. *In this book he has once again given the lie to those who choose to describe the Russian workers as a nation of slaves held in subjection by brute force.* My friend gives chapter and verse for his case against those who so grossly distort the facts ...

It is said that facts are stubborn things, and so they are, and the fact is that in Russia a Government rules which was established in 1917 to take over the rich natural resources of that great country and develop them for and on the behalf of the Russian nation. *This is a wonderful experiment*, one which only people with faith, courage and industry could undertake ...

The colossal task set themselves by the Russian Socialists is one which should be supported by all lovers of the race: the aim at establishing a social order within which they will ultimately be a nation banded together in the bonds of economic security and equality. That day is not yet, but is the goal they seek to obtain. *We are not called upon to judge or accept all the means they adopt to attain their ends ...*

[The USSR] is an economic fact. Her people are pulsating with a new life, her young people dream dreams by night and strive might and main to make them real, and who shall dare to say them nay ... Time is on the side of Socialism and the more the facts of life and work in Russia are known, the greater will be the demand which will rise from the peoples of all lands that each and all of us in our own way and by our own methods will win our way to Socialism which means peace, progress and brotherhood. (My italics.)[5]

In his foreword, Coates added:

About three years ago (in May, 1930), we issued a brochure entitled 'Anti-Soviet Lies Nailed.' Since then the constant stream of misrepresentations and distortions in our Tory Press has not only not ceased, but from time to time it has become more and more virulent and shameless. This has been particularly the case when ever for one reason or another relations between Great Britain and the USSR had become more than usually strained. The denunciation of the Anglo-Soviet Commercial Agreement and later the arrest and trial of six British engineers have been two such occasions.[6]

Airbrushing 'non-persons'

One final and interesting example of the Anglo-Russian Parliamentary Committee's dissembling comes from the Coates' major work, *A History of Anglo-Soviet Relations*, published in 1943. At over 800 pages, and only covering the years 1917 to 1942, it seems to be one of the most detailed and comprehensive books on the subject. As such, it is an attractive source of material for students of the period. It must, however, be read with great caution, as no information it contains can be believed without exhaustive checking in other sources.

One example illustrates this clearly. When someone fell victim to the purges in the Soviet Union, all public mention of them ceased. Their faces were erased from photographs, their portraits taken down, and their books and articles taken out of circulation. They became 'non-persons'. An accidental reference to them in print brought the risk of sharing their fate.

For the Coates, this presented a problem. By 1942, as detailed in Appendix 1, four of the six inter-war leaders of the Soviet diplomatic mission to Britain

had been found guilty of anti-Soviet conspiracy or espionage. The former diplomats had all become 'non-persons' but it was hardly possible to ignore them
in a book about a subject in which they figured so prominently. Even so, the
authors went through some extraordinary contortions to do so. First, to provide points of comparison, Leonid Krasin never fell from favour in Moscow;
he is mentioned forty-one times in the book. Ivan Maisky was in Britain at the
time the book was written and was only arrested in 1953. He was still in favour
when the book was written and so merited forty-four entries in the index and
his wife is mentioned more than all the disgraced diplomats put together. This
is how the book treats the ones who had been purged:

Lev Kamenev, was, with Zinoviev and Trotsky, one the three great public
enemies of the early Stalin era. Although he led the Soviet Trade Delegation
over the summer of 1920 and was famously expelled by the British government, the book makes *no mention* of him.

Christian Rakovsky is mentioned *just once* in the Coates' book, at a point
where to continue to refer to him as the chargé d'affaires would have been
too confusing. His name does not appear in the otherwise voluminous index.

Arkady Rosengoltz is *not mentioned by name* in the book and is referred to
only as the 'Soviet Charge [*sic*] d'Affaires'. In the two pages which cover his
final departure, Coates twice refers to him as 'the Charge d'Affaires and his wife'
but names 'M. and Mme Maisky' (Maisky was Rosengoltz's deputy at the time).

Grigory Sokolnikov was the first Soviet ambassador to Britain; it was impossible to avoid mentioning him altogether, but the Coates did their best: he
is named *just once* in the text. Sokolnikov appears by name only three times
in the index and two of these refer to pages where he is only mentioned as
'the Ambassador', and not by name.

Surprisingly, the Coates' distortions have gone unnoticed by some modern
Labour historians who have then made assertions based upon the Coates'
propaganda, of which the following is one example:

After 1924 an 'Anglo-Russian Parliamentary Committee' run by William and
Zelda Coates made a full-time career of exposing 'Tory lies' about Russia,
to which prominent and respected members of the British labour movement
gave their support on occasion … The *Daily Mail's* 'fairy tales' were regularly
exposed by the Coates' Weekly Bulletin showing misquotes as normal and

accusing the diehard press of 'specialising in highly spiced but wholly unreliable news from their Riga correspondents'.[7]

As we have seen, in reality it is statements such as the Coates' which were the real 'fairy tales'. For the most part, the 'Tory lies' were based entirely on fact.

Eminent members

One of the ARPC's most successful ruses to mask its Moscow links was in its recruitment of a group of eminent Labour figures to sit on its committee or to contribute to its pamphlets, bulletins and books. As they were all Soviet enthusiasts, they could be relied upon to support rather than challenge the distortions and inventions that were common in William Coates's publications. These were the committee members:

- A. A. Purcell, MP (chairman), chairman of the TUC; president of the International Federation of Trade Unions
- John Bromley, MP, general secretary of the Associated Society of Locomotive Engineers and Firemen; General Council of the TUC
- Duncan Carmichael, secretary of the London Trades Council
- W. M. Citrine, General Secretary, General Council of the TUC
- W. N. Ewer, foreign editor of the *Daily Herald*
- Alex Gossip, general secretary of the National Amalgamated Furnishing Trades Association
- A. W. Haycock, MP, Independent Labour Party
- George Hicks, MP, secretary of the Amalgamated Union of Building Trade Workers; General Council of the TUC
- George Lansbury, MP, Executive Committee of the Labour Party
- W. Lawther, MP Miners' Federation of Great Britain, Executive Committee of the Labour Party
- W. Mackinder, MP, National Union of Distributive and Allied Workers
- Neil Maclean, MP, Executive Council of the Workers' Union
- James Maxton, MP, chairman of the Independent Labour Party
- J. E. Mills, MP, Amalgamated Engineering Union
- E. D. Morel, MP, editor of *Foreign Affairs* magazine; secretary of the Union of Democratic Control

- John Scurr, MP, editor of the *Socialist Review*
- A. B. Swales, Amalgamated Engineering Union; General Council of the TUC
- Ben Tillett, MP, Transport and General Workers' Union; General Council of the TUC
- Ben Turner, MP, president of the National Union of Textile Workers; General Council of the TUC
- R. C. Wallhead, MP, treasurer of Socialist and Labour International
- Robert Williams, president of the International Transport Workers' Federation; Executive Committee of the Labour Party[8]

Turner and Lansbury were Cabinet Ministers in 1924 and 1929–31; Lansbury was Labour Party leader in 1932–35, and Labour chairman in 1927–28; James Maxton was Independent Labour Party chairman in 1926–31 and 1934–39; Robert Williams was Labour Party chairman in 1925–26. Purcell, Turner, Tillett, Bromley, Swales, and Hicks were all TUC presidents; and Citrine, whose views on Russia became more hostile by the mid-1930s, was the TUC General Secretary.

In addition to works to which committee members contributed, ARPC publications carried the endorsement of forewords and prefaces written, among others, by A. V. Alexander, H. N. Brailsford, F. Bramley, G. D. H. Cole, Arthur Greenwood, A. Henderson, R. T. Miller, Arthur Ponsonby, D. N. Pritt, R. C. Trevelyan, A. G. Walkden and Ellen Wilkinson. Many of these individuals already figure in the main text of this book and require no further description. Of the others, A. V. Alexander, MP (eventually Earl Alexander of Hillsborough) was First Lord of the Admiralty in MacDonald's 1929–31 Cabinet, Fred Bramley was General Secretary of the TUC (1923–24) and Arthur Greenwood was Minister of Health in 1929–31 and deputy leader of the Labour Party in 1935–54.

STOWAWAYS AND SAILORS: WITNESSES TO THE ANTI-SLAVERY SOCIETY INQUIRY, 1931

Sir Alan Pim and Edward Bateson devoted 40 of the 132 pages of their report to the testimony of six escaped prisoners.[1] A further 20 pages were taken up with statements by British Merchant Navy officers and an analysis of the eyewitness accounts. In all, these contributions took up almost half of the report.

In the main text of this book it has not been possible to quote from these statements at any length or to recount the stories of those who told them. Furthermore, the original transcripts of the witness statements included details of the experience of prisoners in the timber gulag which Pim and Bateson had to leave out because they were not relevant to the specific question their inquiry had been commissioned to investigate – whether or not timber destined for the United Kingdom had been cut or loaded onto ships by prisoners.

The witnesses who appeared before the Anti-Slavery Society inquiry did so on condition of anonymity, not least to protect their surviving relatives in Russia. In the Report they were therefore denoted merely as witnesses 'A' to 'E', but their original statements, preserved in the Anti-Slavery Society archives, enable us to put names to them and tell more of their stories. Testimony from two British merchant seafarers follows.

Stowaways

Alexander Scheluchin ('Witness A')

Alexander Scheluchin was thirty-one years old, the son of a farmer from the Caucasus who owned 1,000 acres, mostly vineyards. Their land was seized in 1920. He served in the White Army, was captured and was offered the opportunity of joining the Red Army, which he refused. Prisoners who refused were normally killed, but the commander of his prison camp was from the same village and released him. With no land remaining but some money he had saved, Scheluchin bought a windmill. As a former White Army soldier, he had to report to the authorities every week. He was arrested in January 1928 because he could not supply the punitive grain quota demanded. He was sentenced to a year's imprisonment in a town nearby, together with fifty others from the same village, all imprisoned for the same reason. He spent six months in prison but was released early because manpower shortages on the land meant that extra labourers were needed. He was arrested again, along with 230 other men, in June 1929 for organising a revolt against the government (he was a member of a Cossack organisation, one of many groupings which was viewed with suspicion by the Soviet authorities). There was no trial; sixty-seven of them were shot and the rest sent to prison camps at Archangel.

Scheluchin and Ivan Kostalin ('Witness C') were sent to work on the Penuga to Ust Sysolsk railway line near Kotlas. He arrived in November 1929 and remained until April 1930; Kostalin arrived in February 1930 and worked until the end of May 1930. Although it was winter when they arrived, they had to live in tents until barracks could be built. They estimated that between 25,000 and 35,000 prisoners were employed at various places along the proposed railway line.

In his testimony, Scheluchin stated that there were epidemics, and that the cold was so intense that many died from it. Those very badly in need of clothes were given some, but they were insufficient in the cold weather. No blankets were supplied and a number of people froze to death. No medical attention was provided and approximately three to five prisoners died each day, mostly from the cold. Some of the prisoners tried to run away, but they were nearly always caught because the snow was very deep and they could easily be tracked. Once caught, they were shot.

Speaking about conditions in the Archangel camps, Scheluchin said that the daily ration of bread was 800g, but because there was a shortage, prisoners often received less, and that the ration varied according to the extent to which they fulfilled their daily quota. A typical quota that he (or his gang) might be given was to carry 170 logs, each weighing about 80 lbs, for a distance of 500 feet. He said that he could not carry more than 70 to 80 logs per day, and never got more than half the ration.

Every day the people got weaker through lack of food, and many died. Several died each day, and men who got very weak were taken away, but where they were taken I do not know … the prisoners were under guard, and loaded timber onto American, British, Chinese and Norwegian ships.

The loading was done at Archangel entirely by forced labour; no one was paid. Most of the workers were political prisoners, largely kulaks, and there were also a number of priests, but they were not allowed to work on the ships … Women and children were in special camps, and I have seen them in the towns of Viatka and Vologda, and in these two towns they were living in the churches, which were quite full up with the women and children of political prisoners … Whilst I was still in prison I had a letter from my wife, and she said that most of the wives and children of the political prisoners and kulaks were sent away, but that she herself had not yet been sent. I do not know if she escaped nor where she is now.

Hermann Kindsvater ('Witness B')
Hermann Kindsvater was thirty-two years old, the son of a Volga German* farmer who planted and owned 2,000 acres. A White Army soldier, he was taken prisoner but later released. The family's land was seized, though each member was allowed to continue farming about fifteen acres. With the advent of the Five-Year Plan in 1927, the family was taxed according to the amount of land they cultivated, so they reduced the area they were actively farming.

---

* Volga Germans had arrived in the second half of the eighteenth century at the invitation of empress Catherine II, herself a native German, to settle in the Volga region. They had kept their own language, customs, and religion. In August 1941, fearing their collaboration with the Germans, Stalin deported them en masse (about 440,000 men, women and children) to Kazakhstan. Lacking food and shelter, many died (especially the old and the children). Some estimates put the fatalities as high as forty per cent.

Kindsvater, his father and brother were arrested in January 1930 as kulaks, and accused of counter-revolutionary activity. They were sentenced without trial – Kindsvater to five years' imprisonment and his father to three. While in prison awaiting his sentence, he was told that his brother had gone mad and died; Kindsvater suspected that he had been shot.

He eventually met Alexander Scheluchin ('Witness A') and Ivan Kostalin ('Witness C'). He confirmed that at sub-camp 21* in Archangel, his quota was 180 logs per day. There were very few women in the camps; of those few, most were nuns. One woman, a Volga German, had been sentenced to ten years. So far as he heard, no one working on the loading at Archangel received payment. When he was imprisoned, his wife managed to go to her sister, and so 'escaped being sent away to the north, where the wives and children of many political prisoners were sent'.

Ivan Kostalin ('Witness C')

Forty-three years old, Kostalin was the son of a Crimean peasant who rented a hundred acres, growing grain and sheep farming. He joined the White Army and, after its collapse, found work in a bakery. He started his own business, but from the end of 1923 punitive taxation on small merchants made it harder and harder to survive. He was arrested in May 1929 for 'counter-revolution-ary sympathies' (because he had originally been in the White Army). After spending seven months in prison without trial, he was informed that he had been sentenced to ten years' imprisonment, with three years' subsequent exile, and a further five-year suspension of his civil rights. In February 1930, he was sent to Kotlas (where George Kitchin was also imprisoned).

Kostalin stated that the camps had armed guards. Those who worked without complaint were more or less let alone, even if they did not accomplish their tasks, but those who expressed an opinion that their work was too hard, or made any other complaint, were liable to be taken into the forest by the guards and shot. Their disappearance was then explained by saying that they had tried to escape.

---

* The original British text uses the word 'point' to translate the Russian *lagernyi punkt* (лагерный пункт, 'camp point') or *lagpunkt* (лагпункт), which was used to denote a sub-division of a main camp (*lagernoe otdelenie*). A *lagernyi punkt* was usually set up at a location where a specific task needed to be performed, and the number of inmates held there would be smaller than that in a *lagernoe otdelenie*. To clarify the sense of the testimony, the word 'sub-camp' is used here in place of 'point' in the original. The rest of the text is reproduced as it is in the original report.

I did not myself see any men taken away and shot, but I know of a group of men, more discontented than others, who were sent to a lonely place to cut trees and were reported to have been all shot. At any rate they did not return ... Men who managed to do their work fairly well were not given punishments, but some were put into solitary confinement, and some were even beaten, though I have not actually seen this done. The men were very much afraid of solitary confinement, because all their warm clothing was taken away, and they were kept there for two or three days without food. Several men who were with me and spoke about the treatment they were getting, were sent to solitary confinement and were treated very badly.

There were not many deaths at the camp where I was working, about three a week. In Penuga, where the weaker men were sent, the conditions were very bad.

At the end of three months a good many steamers had arrived at Archangel for wood, and all the more able men were collected from the camps along the railway and sent to load the ships. They were sent from all the northern prison camps, and 550 men were taken from the camp where I was working and were sent by rail to Archangel.

Kostalin was in Archangel for six weeks before he managed to escape.

When we got to the railway station at Archangel we were put on a barge and taken to sub-camp No.2, which was the general distribution centre for prisoners. There were all together about 45 sub-camps, and at some of these camps, including No.2, there were saw-mills. As regards the total number of prisoners in Archangel all I know is that, when we were taken on the barge to [sub-camp] No.2, one of the prisoners was speaking to the captain, and he told them that where [sic] were 100 ships loading wood in Archangel. At [sub-camp] No.2 they had 1,600 prisoners and could only load two boats, so from that rough estimate could be made the number of men required at all the [sub-camps] ... From [sub-camp] No.2 I was sent to [sub-camp] No. 21, which consisted of four barges fastened to an island ... all round this island, where the barges were anchored, sentries were posted on high points, and they were given full power to shoot anybody who they considered was behaving in a suspicious manner or trying to escape. The shift had to work a full 12 hours without a break. No holidays were allowed, except the first of May ... We worked day and night in two shifts, but it was always daylight in Archangel at that season.

Kostalin's evidence on the presence of clergy in the camps and the extent of forced labour in the handling of timber cargoes has already been reproduced in Chapter 31.

Grigori Tereshin ('Witness D')

Aged forty-eight, Tereshin was from the Leningrad region, the son of a peasant farmer who owned ten acres and rented another thirteen. As a local official, he did not serve in the Great War and remained in Petrograd at the time of the first 1917 revolution (February 1917). When the Civil War began, he fled from Petrograd to a neighbouring country, where he lived until 1923. Hearing that a Bolshevik ambassador encouraged expatriates to return and assured them that they would be safe, he went back to Petrograd in December 1923. There, he was interrogated by the *Cheka*, and allowed to return to his village, but warned privately by someone at the *Cheka* headquarters that he needed to be careful because he was now a marked man.

Soon after he got back to his village, the local Bolsheviks tried to arrest him, but they were persuaded to leave him alone when he produced his papers from the Petrograd *Cheka*. Fearing that it would only be a matter of time before he was arrested, he sold up and took his family south to the Volga German region. After his arrival there in 1925, the Bolsheviks started arresting peasants in the region and seizing their land. In 1927, they began to persecute former officials and so Tereshin left his family in the south to return to Petrograd. However, the situation in Petrograd was too dangerous, and in 1928 he went back to his family in the Volga region. He was finally arrested there in March 1930. He was sentenced without trial to five years' imprisonment and, in May 1930, was sent to Archangel. Tereshin's testimony included the following statement:

Two or three dead were taken into the bushes every day. A priest working in my gang died, and when the other priest in this gang wanted to hold a Christian Orthodox burial service permission was denied. I helped in loading seven ships. I was on a night shift. About the 14th of July there were no ships, and a rumour went round that the British government had called their ships back. We were very pleased, as we thought there might be a war and that we should be released. Then all of a sudden 10 ships arrived for loading. Then all the prisoners, ex-officers and others, began to abuse the British, saying they were fat-bellied and grew fat on cheap timber from Russia. Into each boat we would drop notes in different languages praying for help, and messages were written on timber.

Grigori Skripka ('Witness E')

Aged twenty-six, from Ukraine, Skripka was the son of an officer in the White Army. His family owned 150 acres, four-fifths of which was confiscated in 1921. His brother was away from the village, studying at a commercial college, hiding his identity because people of his class were not allowed to receive higher education. Skripka continued working their land until 1929. His brother had just returned when the OGPU arrived, tipped off by the head of the village, and Skripka, his brother and mother were arrested. Skripka was married with a daughter. His sister lived with them. On his arrest, all their property and possessions, even personal clothing, were confiscated. After one month in prison, his mother was released. In April 1930, his brother escaped, whereupon the authorities arrested his mother again in reprisal. Skripka was sentenced without trial to ten years' imprisonment for anti-Bolshevik agitation. His mother was sentenced to five years.

In May 1930, he was sent in a convoy of 170 prisoners to a second prison in Ukraine, and at the end of the month was sent to Archangel. His mother arrived in Archangel in a separate transport convoy. Skripka was also sent to sub-camp No. 21 in Archangel, and from there to sub-camp No.5, where there were 8,000 prisoners. Here, in two shifts of twelve hours each, the prisoners stripped the bark from pit props and stacked them.

Skripka stole a rowing boat and attempted to escape from sub-camp No.5. He was recaptured and sent to a 'punishment barge', one of four, each of which contained 150 prisoners. He was told that the next time he tried to escape he would be shot. Escape attempts were numerous and on one occasion he saw four men shot out of a group of fifteen who tried to escape from the punishment barge. After a subsequent unsuccessful escape attempt he was beaten with rifle butts and denied food for two days. Yet a third escape attempt ended in failure, and he was then told that he would now be 'taken to Archangel prison', which he understood to mean that he was to be shot. He was therefore determined to escape again and managed to succeed in stowing away on board a foreign ship.

Ivan Kolomoetz ('Witness F')

Kolomoetz was aged twenty-five and was from Ukraine. He was the son of a smallholding farmer who owned thirteen acres and rented 120. He did not join either army in the Civil War. In 1919, the family's rented land and six of their eight horses were confiscated. Kolomoetz was arrested in 1926 by the *Cheka*, along with five other men from his village, because someone had attacked the chairman of the local soviet. At his trial, he denied the charges and was sentenced to two years in solitary confinement, confiscation of all his property and deprivation of his civil rights. This was reduced on appeal to ordinary imprisonment (without solitary confinement) for two years. After eighteen months in a prison camp in Ukraine he was released and returned home. He was re-arrested in 1928 for counter-revolutionary agitation and after five months was sent without trial to Kem on the White Sea, part of the Solovki camp group. Kolomoetz was sent from Kem to a camp at Letnia Rechka, where about 300 prisoners were living in old barracks. The new arrivals slept in tents until they could build barracks for themselves. They had no blankets and slept on boards.

Kolomoetz's account of how he narrowly escaped being shot when his deteriorating health prevented him from being able to work is recounted in Chapter 31. After his recovery, he was sent to a camp in Sinouka, where about 3,000 men lived in tents. Their work was to sort timber which had been floated down to them in rafts, and to prepare logs for loading on foreign ships which arrived in the port. He was then assigned to loading a Norwegian vessel, and given special new clothes to do so, so that the Norwegian sailors would not be aware of the conditions in which they were being held. Two days later, a Swedish ship arrived and, at one point, the captain invited the prisoners and their guards on board for a glass of vodka. 'I did not take any vodka but went round the ship looking for a place to hide. A sailor saw me and calling out "Russ, Russ", pointed down to the stokehole.'

Kolomoetz succeeded in concealing himself with the help of the sailor and so he made his escape, arriving in England at the end of August 1930.

British witnesses

Reference has already been made to the eyewitness account offered by a British second officer whose ship docked at Kem in 1930. The inquiry investigators also heard from other British witnesses, including these two:

1. A. S. Mills, wireless operator on a British merchant ship loading timber in Archangel:

The penalty for anyone caught stowing away on a ship is death. I saw a boy who was caught on a ship lying alongside mine, murdered in the most cold-blooded manner possible. He was first flogged with long sticks while he was almost naked, and then, while he was on his knees crying, two guards, one of them smoking a cigarette, unslung their rifles and in the most nonchalant manner possible shot him dead.

In a sister ship of ours, on one occasion, the dead bodies of four Russians were found among the timber soon after leaving Archangel. They were stowaways who had been discovered by the guards before the ship left Archangel. The guards had shot them in the place where they had found them without mentioning a word about the matter to the captain of the ship...

When my ship was being loaded by a batch of prisoners on one occasion, I recognised one of them, an old man. I had met him at another port. Seeing me, the old man slackened off work for a moment. He was immediately subjected to a brutal beating with the butt end of the rifle of one of the guards. He collapsed on the ground. The guard was about to push his bayonet through him when the other prisoners lifted him to his feet.[2]

2. Gordon Whitefield, chief steward of the SS *Grelisle*, 12 March 1931 (extracts from the statement given to Travers Buxton of the Anti-Slavery Society).[3]

Chief Steward Whitefield was in Arkhangelsk ('Archangel') over the summer of 1930, before the international furore over conditions in the camps broke. The free access he and his fellow crew members had to the punishment barrack and his candid conversation with the Camp 15 Commandant, etc. would not have been possible six months later when the international campaign in protest against conditions in the camps had gathered momentum ...

I, Gordon Dickson Whitefield, of 22, Galston Street, Adamsdown, Cardiff, in the County of Glamorganshire, do solemnly and sincerely declare as follows:-

1. My age is 36 years. I have been Chief Steward on a number of ships exporting coal from South Wales and bringing timber from Russia. In connection with these voyages I have visited Kem, Archangel and Vladivostok for the loading of timber...

15. The voyage on which I saw the most was on the S. S. 'Grelisle' leaving Cardiff on the 10th of June 1930 for Archangel Lightships and arriving in Barry 15th of September 1930. At that time we were exactly a month in No.10 Camp in Archangel, loading pulpwood for the United States of America. I have a diary at home, kept regularly for each voyage, written up every evening.

16. The pulpwood at Archangel all goes down by train on a little line running along the jetty. It is dumped out of the railway tracks and loaded on to small trucks, and then pulled down to where it is loaded into the ships' slings.

17. All the labourers employed were political prisoners, not only those working on shore, but also those loading on the ships. The shifts were very different from those in Kem; one shift commenced at 7 o'clock in the morning and ended at 6 in the evening; the second commenced at 6.30 in the evening and ended at 7 in the morning. There was one hour's interval in the middle for a meal.

18. The ration was the same as in Kem, with the addition that at the end of the shift they got a small amount of fish soup. The prisoners lived in huts on the other side of the railway. The huts were in a circle; there were no barbed wire enclosures, but there were elevated sentry posts. There were three huts for women. The women were employed on ordinary camp tasks of washing etc., and they were also employed in the sawmills. They also acted as servants to the families of the warders. The guards were, as at Kem, soldiers of the Red Army, and the foremen were members of the secret police.

19. The general treatment of the prisoners was the same as at Kem, except that they wore their own clothes and there was no uniform. A Norwegian called Captain Bieza was the Commander of the Camp. We entertained

him on board and he told me that there were 50 or 60 priests in the Arch-angel camp out of the 16,000 prisoners in that camp. He said that the prisoners were of every class, including old Army and Navy Officers, Cossacks and peasants of all types…

20. The conditions at all the Camps were much the same. I did not visit any logging camps. We went over to the sawmills, in which all the work was done by women. The prisoners employed were all women and the guards also were women. There were no men in the sawmills. The same Com-mander of the Camp told us that the women were of all types, including both political prisoners and ordinary convicts.

21. I saw a good deal of brutality in the treatment of the men, who were kicked and knocked about by the soldiers of the Red Guard. I also saw women being ill-treated in the same way by the guards. I believe that the conditions in this Camp were harder than in any other Camp.

22. One evening at about eight o'clock we were all sent on board the ships from the International Club. Next morning we heard firing at about 6.30 [a.m.]. On the same day posters were put up all round the encampment and Captain Bieza told us that the posters were to report that one hundred men had tried to escape the evening before during the change of shifts, but had been captured, that 99 had been shot and one was being sent to Moscow. I did not hear of any other people being shot.

23. The prisoners were in a terrible condition, as I saw from my visits to the Camps and to the huts. Captain Bieza told us that some 10 to 20 people died each day. I believe that he spoke the truth from what we saw our-selves. There was only one Doctor for the whole of the Camp, and he used to come on board the ships to get his meals. There was no hospital at all, not even for the women. People who fell ill were left in the huts to live or die as they could. The doctor once asked me for some aspirins and he told me that he could not get any medicines, as all the medicines were kept for the use of the civilian population…

24. The political prisoners were given twenty kopeks per day as wages, in the form of camp money. This could only be spent in the Government shop in the Camp, and the only thing which they could get in that shop was cigarettes. So far as I know, the prisoners were not allowed to keep any other money of their own in addition to the twenty kopeks per day.

25. As in Kemm [*sic*], we all had Communist passes and among other places we went round a punishment barrack in which there were at that time ten men with chains on their hands and legs. They were sitting on a bench and the chains fastened their hands to their ankles so they could not move. I do not know what they were punished for, nor how long they remained in that position. We also saw a number of women in fetters of a different kind, their arms and legs being chained separately. There was a hut full of women chained in this way, and there were probably about one hundred of them.

26. When we were at Archangel, 99 British ships were loading timber, 45 being from Cardiff alone. There are hundreds in Cardiff who have seen the things of which I am now speaking. A surprising number of prisoners spoke English, and we were told by them that the women were grossly maltreated by the Red Guards. We saw some instances of maltreatment of a brutal kind.

27. So far as I could learn, any prisoner who attempted to escape was shot. I should be surprised to hear that any man made three attempts and only succeeded on the fourth attempt.

28. The other two voyages I did were to Vladivostok and Novorozisk on the Black Sea. The voyage to Vladivostok was for loading timber, and the conditions there were much the same as in Archangel. The people who loaded the timber were all prisoners and mainly Mongolian Chinese…*

32. The prisoners everywhere had a haggard and a half-starved look. I do not know how far the prisoners had had any trial. I was told by a Priest there that he had no idea why he was sentenced, although he had been there seven years. He said most of the prisoners had no idea why they were sentenced. A case which we saw personally was that of the Manager of the Government Bank in Archangel, whom we saw brought in chains to Archangel Camp. Both the Camp Commandant and the Soviet Control Officer told me that they did not know why the Bank Manager had been arrested. His wife had tried to protect him and was shot. When we heard of it we all went over to Archangel and saw the dead body of the wife. Four days afterwards we saw the dead body of their child, next to the International

---

* Paragraphs 29–31 relate to Novorossiysk and Vladivostok and are omitted.

Club. A whole crowd saw the body. We were told by the Control Officer that the child had been sealed up in a drawer and suffocated. I only know this from what he told me, but I do not know that the Bank Manager was still in the Archangel Camp when we left.

APPENDIX 5

MEMORANDUM FROM THE RUSSIAN NATIONAL COMMITTEE, PARIS, (JULY 1927)[1]

The Russian National Committee was established in Paris after the Revolution by Russian exiles committed to continuing the struggle against Bolshevism from abroad.

The Russian National Committee consider it their duty to broadcast to the whole world the real sentiments of the Russian people now become slaves. They draw the attention of all free nations that profess the Christian faith to the terror now reigning in Russia, and the cruelties committed by the Third International; and they once more reiterate their appeal: Europe must be expunged of the disgrace which weighs her down; you must cease holding out your hands to those who belong to that band of wicked criminals calling themselves the Soviet Government...

Signed

Pres: A. Kartasheff, VPs: V. L. Boutzeff, Michael Fedoroff, M. Kindaikoff, E. Kovalevsky, Peter Struve, Gen Sec: B. Kateneff

TO THE WRITERS OF THE WORLD

We appeal to you writers of the world.

How is it that, with all your insight into the human soul, and the spirit of epochs and nations, you take no heed of us Russians, who are doomed to gnaw at the prison bonds which restrain free speech? You, who had been brought up on the works of the great masters, some of whom were of our race, why do you say nothing when in a great country the ripe fruit as well as the buds of a great literature are being crushed underfoot[?] …

We know you cannot help either us or our people, except by giving your sympathy and moral support to the principles of and workers for Freedom, and by expressing a moral condemnation of the most cruel tyranny that has ever existed. We do not expect anything more, but all the more passionately do we want you to do that which is possible: do your utmost everywhere, and at all seasons, to unmask before the consciousness of the whole world the artful hypocrisy of the terrible Communist power in Russia. We are powerless to do so. Our sole weapon – the pen – has been wrested from our hands; the air by which we breathe – literature – has been taken from us; we are fettered.

It is not only for us that your voices must be raised. Think of yourselves. With diabolical energy, the full scope of which we alone are able to realise, your own nations are being pushed on to the same path of blood and horror to which our people, in a fatal moment of their history, worn out by war and of the policy of pre-Revolutionary Government was driven to years ago. We have trodden this path to the Golgotha of the nations, and we warn you.[*]

We are perishing! The coming dawn of liberation is not yet in sight. Many of us are no longer capable of passing on to posterity the terrible experiences we have been through.

Learn the truth about us, write of it, you who are free, that the eyes of this present generation and those that are to come may be opened. Do this – and it will be easier for us to die.

If our voice beyond the grave is heard by you, we bid you listen, read and ponder what we say. You will then follow the line laid down by our great author – L. N. Tolstoy – who in his own time cried out to the world: 'I cannot be silent.'

---

[*]   The final section of the memorandum (from 'We are perishing' to 'I cannot be silent') was reprinted as 'Letter from a group of Russian writers' on the opening page of *The Russian Crucifixion* by F. A. Mackenzie. The book was sent to Labour Foreign Secretary Arthur Henderson in March 1930 by S. M. Dawkins of the Christian Protest Movement. Henderson's secretary replied on 1 April 1930 acknowledging receipt of it.

'PERSECUTION OF RELIGION IN RUSSIA MUST CEASE' (JANUARY 1930)[1]

Dear Sir or Madam,

It must be known to you that the Soviet government of Russia has in the forefront of its definite policy the destruction, root and branch, of all religions within the territories under its control and that priests and laymen of the Christian churches are being persecuted and in many cases tortured and killed on the sole ground of their religious belief and their desire to practice in worship and the teaching of their children the religion they believe.

Can we, if we have any belief in God or any respect for the worth and dignity of humanity, hold our peace while these outrages on religious liberty and life are going on?

We are not moved to this protest by the suggestion of the sufferers – whose sufferings would only be increased were their persecutors to be able to blame them for what we are doing. We have no occasion to imperil them by asking them for information. All that we need to know – all that the civilised world needs to know that it may be moved to a united protestation of sympathy for the victims and repulsion for their sufferings – can be otherwise and better obtained.

But, do we, it will be asked, hope to do any good? Will our protest be anything but an impotent relief of emotion? We cannot doubt, if it be the expression of an awakened conscience and a revived moral and spiritual courage, that it will be much more than this; it will release energies that have been feeble in the Western nations, and by releasing them, do something not only for Russia but for humanity everywhere.

To refrain from protest – to keep silence – is shameful, morally and spiritually degrading, and dangerous. Nor would closed lips and stifled consciences alleviate the lot of the persecuted; for such a silence would only be attributed – and rightly – to fear or greed or blindness; it would have no protective or mitigating influence.

Therefore let us speak out – not as politicians or as prophets of war but as men and women who believe in God and in the immeasurably superior power of good – when faithfully served over that of evil; and let us speak as men and women who claim that the human soul in Russia, as in other lands, belongs not to the state but to God.

We therefore ask every believer in God, and every lover of liberty, who reads this appeal to show by voice and written word, by mass attendances at meetings and especially by letter to the press that he has faith in the objects of what we believe is going to be one of the greatest movements of our time.

Signed,

Glasgow, President,

A. W. Gough, President of the Council and of the Executive Committee,

J. Knowles, chairman of the Executive and Finance Committee, Sydney M. Dawkins, General Secretary

Joint Presidents:

The Rt Hon the Earl of Glasgow DSO, The Rt Hon Viscount Brentford PC

Vice Presidents:

The Most Reverend Archbishop of Armagh, The Rt Rev Lord Bishop of London, The Rt Rev the Bishop of Gloucester, The Rt Rev the Bishop of Chelmsford, The Rt Hon Earl Winterton, The Rt Hon Lord St John of Bletsoe, The Rt Hon Lord Clifford of Chudleigh, The Rt Hon Lord Charnwood, The Rt Hon Lord Cushenden, The Rt Hon Lord Ebbisham, Bishop A. E. Knox, The Very Rev Dr J. H. Hertz (Chief Rabbi), The Reverend Sydney M. Berry DD, Douglas Brown DD, Archibald Fleming DD, J. D. James DD, D. J. Maclagan DD, Dinsdale T. Young DD

FALSE ATROCITY STORIES: AN APPEAL ON THE 'CAMPAIGN AGAINST RUSSIA' (MARCH 1930)[1]

A statement on the 'campaign against Russia' on the ground of religious persecution was issued yesterday by Mr George Hicks on behalf of 12 signatories, the other 11 being Mr George Bernard Shaw, Miss Ellen Wilkinson, MP, Mr A. E. B. Swales, Mr A. J. Cook, Mr C. T. Cramp, Mr Ben Tillett, MP, Mr W. H. Hutchinson, Mr William T. Good, Dr Norman Leys, Mr John Bromley, MP, and Mr James Maxton MP. It reads as follows:-

'We have witnessed during the last few weeks a fierce campaign on the part of the capitalist press, with one or two honourable exceptions, against Soviet Russia, with whom the Labour Government has just resumed normal diplomatic relations. We note with satisfaction that the Labour Government has not been deceived by the Tory allegations of religious persecution, and has refused to be intimidated.

'The statements of the Metropolitan and Bishops of the Russian Orthodox Church, the authenticity of which are not questioned by anyone, with the exception of Lord Birkenhead, are some of the many irrefutable proofs that the campaign of the press is not based on facts but upon malicious inventions.

'In this connection, the recent dispatch of the Moscow correspondent of the 'Daily Herald' is very illuminating. It states that according to official figures there are at present in Soviet Russia no less than 46,500[2] churches open for the free use of worshippers, and that tens of millions of Soviet citizens are freely exercising their right to worship. Thus reports of alleged religious persecution in Soviet Russia are effectively repudiated.

'We are most strenuously opposed to any kind of religious persecution, wherever such is taking place, but at the same time we are bound to express protest when we realise that the religious feelings of the British people are being cynically exploited in the interests of a class whose hostility to the Russian Government is of precisely the same character as their hostility to the majority of the British people.

'We trust British public opinion to resist most emphatically any attempts to injure the development of friendly relations between these two great countries by means of false atrocity stories and malicious inventions.'

'SOCIAL CONDITIONS IN RUSSIA' (MARCH 1933)

To the Editor of the *Manchester Guardian*,

Sir – Increasing unemployment and the failure of private capital to cope with it throughout the rest of the world is causing persons of all classes and parties to watch with increasing interest the progress of the Soviet Union.

And yet this is precisely the moment that has been chosen to redouble the intensity of the blind and reckless campaign to discredit it. No lie is too fantastic, no slander is too stale, no intervention too absurdly contrary to what is now common knowledge for employment by the more reckless elements of the British press. A manifest lunatic assassinated the President of the French republic. He must be a Bolshevik. A child of Colonel Lindbergh is kidnapped and murdered; certain of our newspapers are not ashamed to mock its parents' distress with the same senseless cry. It is ascertained that the Russians have to work daily for their living under the Five-Year Plan and immediately a British Duchess* leads the protest against Bolshevik slavery.

Particularly offensive and ridiculous is the revival of the old attempts to represent the condition of Russian workers as one of slavery and star-vation, the Five-Year Plan as a failure, the new enterprises as bankrupt and the Communist regime as tottering to its fall. Although such inflammatory irresponsibility is easily laughed at, we must not forget that there are many people not sufficiently well informed politically to be proof against it, and

---

* Katharine Stewart-Murray, the Duchess of Atholl MP was a leading campaigner on behalf of those suffering persecution in the Soviet Union. The case presented in her book *Conscription of a People* (London: Philip Allan, London, 1931) was both detailed and well documented.

that there are diehards among our diplomats who still dream of starting a counter-revolutionary war anywhere and anyhow, if only they can stampede public opinion into the necessary panic through the press. The seriousness of the situation is emphasized by the British Government's termination of the trade agreement with the USSR and the provocative questions and answers in the House of Commons.

We the undersigned are recent visitors to the USSR. Some of us travelled throughout the greater part of its civilized territory. We desire to record that we saw nowhere evidence of such economic slavery, privation, unemployment and cynical despair of betterment as are accepted as inevitable and ignored by the press as having 'no news value' in our own countries. Everywhere we saw [a] hopeful and enthusiastic working-class, self-respecting, free up to the limits imposed on them by nature and a terrible inheritance from tyranny and incompetence of their former rulers, developing public works, increasing health services, extending education, achieving the economic independence of woman and the security of the child and in spite of many grievous difficulties and mistakes which all social experiments involve at first (and which they have never concealed nor denied) setting an example of industry and conduct which would greatly enrich us if our systems supplied our workers with any incentive to follow it.

We would regard it as a calamity if the present lie campaign were to be allowed to make headway without contradiction and to damage the relationship between our country and the USSR. Accordingly we urge all men and women of goodwill to take every opportunity of informing themselves of the real facts of the situation and to support the movements which demand peace, trade and closer friendship with an understanding of the greater Workers Republic of Russia.

Yours etc.

George Bernard Shaw, Helen C. Bentwich, Margaret I. Cole, J. G. Crowther, Louis Golding, Somerville Hastings (MP), J. L. Hodgson, Beatrice L. King, C. Mansell-Mouillin, Edith Ruth Mansell-Mouillin, Rudolph Messel, R. W. Postgate, D. N. Pritt, J. Reeves, Amabel Williams-Ellis, Clough Williams-Ellis, E. F. Wise (MP), (Rev) James Barr (MP), Haydon Lewis, Albert Boyce
33, Ormond Yard, London

MALCOLM MUGGERIDGE TO JAMES MAXTON MP (LETTER OF 8 APRIL 1933)[1]

The journalist Malcolm Muggeridge wrote this letter to James Maxton in April 1933, shortly after he had resigned from the Manchester Guardian *after disagreements with its editor over the paper's editing of his reports from Moscow on the Ukraine famine. Maxton was one of those who had spoken up in defence of the Soviets in the debate in the House of Commons that followed the arrest of the British Metropolitan-Vickers engineers working in Russia.*

Dear Mr. Maxton,

I have just returned from Moscow where, for the last six months, I have been acting as correspondent for the 'Manchester Guardian'. Just before I left, a man came to my room in rather peculiar circumstances and asked me to write to you for him. I promised to do this, and herewith discharge my promise. This man had read in 'Izvestiya' some remark of yours in the House of Commons about Soviet justice. I am not sure of the exact nature of the remark but as the man understood it from the 'Izvestiya' report it implied that, in your opinion, people arrested by the Soviet Government could rely on getting as fair a deal as those arrested by any other government. 'I want you to tell this man Maxton', he said, 'about what happened to my brother then he'll have a better idea of Soviet justice'. You should understand that by coming into my room in this way the man took a big risk. I pointed this out to him. He said he knew about the risk but that he had taken it deliberately because he was determined at all costs that you should know about his brother, of whom incidentally he had been very fond. He told me about his brother in great detail. I shall repeat to you the general facts of the case.

The brother was a lawyer, and, in the early days of the revolution had been a member of one of those mushroom constitutional governments that were set up in the Ukraine. After the Bolsheviks took power he worked as a lawyer in various Soviet institutions, not trying to hide the fact that he had been a Moderate; and was given some fairly important jobs which, as far as I could gather, he discharged creditably. While working in the North Caucasus he was called up before the GPU and cross examined, but not arrested. However, he realised that trouble was brewing, and came to Moscow. In 1930, a GPU party raided his wife's room. He was not there; had, in fact, divorced. The GPU officer asked where he was. The wife said she didn't know. Then the GPU officer threatened to arrest his daughter, aged 15, and to hold her in prison unless the wife would disclose where he was. They took the daughter off in a motorcar. She broke down and said she'd take them to where her father was – in a datcha on the outskirts of Moscow. This she did. The GPU party sent the daughter into her father with instructions to bring him out on some pretext. When he came out they arrested him and took him away. The family heard nothing for months after that. They spent hours and hours trying to get information as to his whereabouts, and were able to send parcels of food through the Red Cross. After a while these parcels began to come back and, after repeated enquiries, they were told that he had been shot for having tried, but not succeeded, to bring about a foreign intervention in the Soviet Union.

The man told me his story not passionately but with a curious kind of intensity as though he had been long brooding on it. His lips were dry, and every now and then he licked them. The fact that he was starving – white gums, hollow cheeks, etc. – added to the strangeness of the effect, though I had, by that time, got used to seeing and talking with starving people. 'It was', he finished up, 'my only brother, and I loved him'.

I do not expect you to believe me when I say that I could, from my own experience in Russia, give you hundreds of instances of the kind of thing described by this man, only often much crueller, more unjustified. I certainly do not expect you to believe me when I say there is no such thing as justice

in Soviet Russia; that the word has lost its meaning; that, apart from ex-bour-
geois and intellectuals, the workers and peasants themselves live in a state of
perpetual terror of the Government and its agents the GPU. You may even
think the man's story itself is exaggerated by him and by me to discredit the
Soviet Government. But anyway, I told the man I'd tell you the story, and I
have. I have deliberately withheld his name for obvious reasons but he gave
me his name.

Yours,
Malcolm Muggeridge

COUNTESS TOLSTOY'S APPEAL (JANUARY 1933)[1]

Countess Alexandra Lvovna Tolstaya (1884–1979) was the novelist's twelfth child. After being imprisoned by the Bolsheviks in 1920 and arrested four further times, she managed to leave the Soviet Union in 1929. She eventually established a foundation in the United States which sponsored the emigration of over 30,000 refugees, many of whom had fled Russia and neighbouring Soviet-occupied countries. In 1933 she published this public appeal.

When in the year 1908 my father Leo Tolstoy read about the proposed execution of twenty revolutionaries by the Czar's Government, his immediate reaction was to write his famous article 'I Cannot Be Silent'. And the Russian people took up his outcry in a common protest against murder!

Now in the year 1933 when in the Northern Caucasus a terrible slaughter is going on,* when thousands of people are shot and exiled daily and my father is not here to protest, I feel it is my duty to raise my weak voice against this wholesale murder.

For twelve years I have worked in Soviet Russia, for twelve years I have tried to serve the people in the spirit of my father's teaching. The terror was progressing under my very eyes. But the world was silent. Millions were exiled, died in prisons or in labour camps in the North of Russia, thousands were executed.

The Bolsheviks began by persecuting class enemies, religious people, old

---

* The 'Ukrainian' famine in fact affected a far wider area than that of present-day Ukraine alone. The North Caucasus is the neighbouring region, but it is to the famine as a whole that she is referring.

priests, scientists, professors. Now the time has come for the working classes, the peasants. And yet the world is silent.

For fifteen years the Russian people have suffered famine and slavery. The Bolshevik government was robbing people of their bread and their food and sending it abroad to obtain currency not only for buying machinery, but for their worldwide campaign of propaganda. But if the peasants protest, if they hide the bread for their own families, if they refuse to till the soil, they are punished, sometimes shot.

The Russian people cannot suffer it any longer. Here and there results are startling. Confronted by death, crowds of famished peasants flee from the Ukraine – a country which formerly was the granary of the world.

How does the Soviet Government respond to this?

It issues decrees, banishing one third of the Moscow population from the city, and subdues the revolting peasants and workers by bullets and gas. Since the times of Ivan the Terrible Russia has not seen such terror! Now when the population of Kuban* has risen in protest, the Soviet Government is taking the most terrible revenge. Whole families are executed and 45,000 people – women and children – are driven out of their homes and sent by Stalin's order to Siberia to labour camps to meet their certain death.

Is it possible that the world will still be Silent?

Is it possible that governments will continue to make trade pacts with the Bolshevist murderers, strengthening the Soviet Government and undermining their own countries?

Will the League of Nations go on discussing questions of peace and disarmament with the representatives of a government whose chief method of work is terror?

Will such idealists as Romain Rolland, who has so subtly grasped the soul of the greatest pacifists of our time, Gandhi and Tolstoy – or writers like Henri Barbusse, Bernard Shaw, and others, continue to sing the praises of the 'socialist paradise'? Don't they really understand that by associating themselves with the Soviets, they are making themselves responsible for their activity, and spreading the contagion of Bolshevism, which threatens the world with ruin?

---

* The Kuban region formed the western part of the North Caucasus. Peasant unrest there, provoked by the food shortages, was savagely repressed.

Is it possible, that there are still people who believe that the cruel dictatorship of a small group, whose aim is to destroy the world's culture and religion and morals, is Socialism?

Who is going to proclaim 'I cannot be Silent'!?

Where are you preachers of love, truth, and brotherhood?

Where are Christians, true socialists, pacifists, writers, social workers?

Why are you silent? Do you need proofs, testimonies of witnesses, figures or statistics? Don't you hear the shouts for help? Or perhaps you still believe that human happiness may be obtained by murder, violence and slavery?

This is not addressed to those whose sympathies for the Bolsheviks had been bought with money, robbed from the Russian people. I am addressing all those who still believe in a brotherhood of man; religious people, socialists, writers, social workers, mothers and wives, open your eyes.

United in a common protest against the tortures of 160 millions of defenceless Russian people.

Alexandra L. Tolstoy

INTERVIEW WITH DR NICHOLAS ARSENIEV AND HIS SISTER (MAY 1934)

O*n 17 April 1934, Dr Nicholas Arseniev, who was on a lecturing tour in Britain, wrote to Archbishop Lang, explaining that his sister had been 'ransomed out of Solovetski' and offering that they both meet Lang to inform him of the current situation inside Russia. What follows is a handwritten memorandum by Archbishop Lang, dated 1 May, 1934.*[1]

I saw Dr Arseniev, now Professor at Königsberg, and his sister at Lambeth on May 1, 1934. For the last fifteen years she has been more or less continuously imprisoned or under suspicion or in the labour camps.

She gave me a full account of her experiences.

1) December 1919 suspected like her brother, because of her relations among diplomats. Sent by the Secret Service for nine months' imprisonment – five months in a cell; four months in a better cell; on a charge of counter-revolution. Her father, mother and brothers were also imprisoned. Her brother [Dr Arseniev] subsequently escaped to the frontier, and has since been ceaseless in his efforts to procure the release of his sister. The others have been released before now.

2) November 1922 to January 1924. She was sent to the inner prison at Moscow on the same charge as a foreign spy. The conditions were very bad. The walls between the different cells were so slight that the prisoners

were kept almost wholly in silence.[*] Sometimes she was sent to labour camps. She went on hunger strike as a protest against the bad treatment and was therefore released as useless.

3) Again in May to September 1924 – she was taken to Petrograd but obviously and afterwards confessedly in mistake for someone else.

4) November 1924 to June 1926 kept under observation at the Stovolsky [Solovetsky] Monastery on the White Sea. Here she fell ill and was liberated and kept in exile in Archangel till June 1931. It was true that this is the way in which investigation is prevented.[†] Word came that an English deputation was coming to inspect conditions of prison life and steps for dealing with famine in the country districts. Accordingly she and her fellow prisoners were removed to cattle trucks which were carefully covered over with only an aperture in the roof. About 40 in each truck, sent wandering about the railways for three or four weeks; not allowed to go out, in circumstances of great dirt and discomfort. The tracks were labelled 'Corn, Wheatflour, etc'. Result – visitors were shown that there was no one in the prisons, and these tracks showed how supplies were taken to famine districts.[‡]

5) In 1931 she was again arrested and imprisoned for three months, this time for merely helping the clergy which meant taking them food and occasionally a little money. It was at this time that she saw Archbishop Antonios of Archangel and they were arrested the same day and she was familiar with all the circumstances that led to his death. An account of this appears in The Living Church of March 17, 1934, a copy of which Dr Arseniev gave me.

---

[*] Soviet jailers made every effort to ensure prisoners were kept isolated and ignorant of the identity of those they were incarcerated with. If two inmates passed in a corridor, their guards would turn one towards the wall until the other had gone by. Although frequent cell overcrowding meant that some interaction was inevitable, all communication between different cells was forbidden. In this instance, as the cell walls were so thin, the prisoners were ordered to stay silent. Those who broke such rules would be severely punished.

[†] Lang is referring to the removal of prisoners from camps to deceive international investigators – who actually never came – into believing that the timber trade was carried out by free labour.

[‡] In fact, fearing a whitewash, no international investigators came. Stranded in unheated railway wagons, some without roofs, for many nights in February in conditions well below freezing, many prisoners died.

He said that conditions were now almost worse than ever because there was a wholesale exile and imprisonment of villagers who were alleged to be indifferent to the collective system of Soviet farms.

He is giving lectures in different parts of England on invitation but more or less privately. He fears the consequences of too much publicity.

C[osmo] C[antuar]

NOTES

Preface

1 The three leading writers on this period of Labour foreign policy devote no more than a few paragraphs to the whole affair. Jonathan Davis in 'Labour and the Kremlin', in John Shepherd, Jonathan Davis and Chris Wrigley, (eds), *The Second Labour Government 1929–1931: a reappraisal*, (Manchester: Manchester University Press, 2011), pp. 150–69 gives four paragraphs to the persecution affair, but makes no mention of the timber camps; Andrew Williams in *Labour and Russia: The Attitude of the Labour Party and the USSR*, 1924–34, (Manchester: Manchester University Press, 1989) also gives four paragraphs to the persecution affair, dismissing the timber camps in twenty-nine lines. Williams's book, which is referenced as a source by Davis, contains some startling inaccuracies – such as referring a number of times to 'PQs' (the acronym for parliamentary questions) as 'propaganda questions'. He also asserts that 'the notion of "fellow travelling" in the Party [in this period] is nonsense.' David Carlton in *MacDonald Versus Henderson*, Macmillan 1970 devotes just thirty-four lines to both. He dismissed the protesters' claims as dubious and insists that the newspaper reports attesting to the existence of the camps and persecution were unreliable.

2 For more detail, see Richard Pipes, 'Lenin's Gulag', *International Journal of Political Science and Development*, 2:6 (2014), 140–6.

3 <http://www.bankofengland.co.uk/education/Pages/resources/inflationtools/calculator/default.aspx>

Part 1

1 Hansard, HC Deb, 5 November 1919, vol. 120, col. 1633.

2 For the full text of this appeal, see Appendix [0000].

Chapter 1

1 *Beatrice Webb's Typescript diary*, 11 November 1918 (p. 170), *LSE Digital Library* [online] (n.d.) <http://digital.library.lse.ac.uk/objects/lse:vat325giy/read/single#page/170/mode/2up> accessed 22 January 2017.

2 TNA, CAB 23 (WC539), 3 March 1919.

3 N. Valeryev, 'It's Impossible to Forget (the Story of Aleksandr Dmitrievich Chernykh)', *Dvinskaya Pravda* (15 December 1992) <http://www.kotlas.org/kotlas/history/sleigh-driver.php>, accessed 9 November 2016.

4 GULAG is the Russian acronym for Glavnoe Upravlenie Ispravitel'no-Trudovyh Lagerej i kolonij (Главное Управление Исправительно-Трудовых Лагерей и колоний), meaning 'Chief Administration of Corrective Labour Camps and Colonies'.

5 S. A. Pavlyuchenkov, *Kestyanskii Brest* [The Peasants' Brest] (Moscow: Russkoe knizgoizd, 1996), pp. 25–6.

6 'As long as we fail to treat speculators the way they deserve – with a bullet in the head – we will not get anywhere at all'. V. I. Lenin, *Polnoe Sobranie Sochinenii* [Complete Collected Works] 55 vols (Moscow: Gos. Izd-vo polit. Lit-ry, 1958–66), vol. 35, p. 311.

7 Ibid., vol. 50, p. 143.

8 Stéphane Courtois et al., *The Black Book of Communism: Crimes, Terror, Repression* (trans. Jonathan Murphy and Mark Kramer) (Cambridge, Mass.: Harvard University Press, 1999), p. 73.

9 Richard Pipes, 'Lenin's Gulag', p. 142.

10 P. M. Losev and G. I. Ragulin, *Sbornik normativnykh aktov po sovetskomu ispravitel' no-trudovomu pravu (1917–1959)* [A Collection of Normative Acts on the Soviet Corrective Labor Law, 1917–1959] (Moscow: Gosyurizdat, 1959), p. 33.

11 Courtois et al., *The Black Book of Communism*, p. 118.

12 Iu. V. Doikov cited in Richard Pipes, 'Lenin's Gulag', p. 143.

13 *The Times*, 13 January 1919.

14 For a more detailed description, see Anthony Read, *The World On Fire* (London: Pimlico, 2009), pp. 87–8.

15 TNA, CAB 23 (WC533).

16 *The Times*, 20 January 1919.

17 *The Times*, 24 March 1919.

18 *The Times*, 28 June 1919.

19 Ibid.

20 Herbert Tracey, *The Book of the Labour Party*, 3 vols (London: Caxton, 1925), vol. 3, p. 316.

21 Andrew Davies, *To Build a New Jerusalem: The Labour Movement from the 1880s to the 1990s* (London: Michael Joseph, 1992), p. 117.

22 Harold Laski, 'Introduction', in George Lansbury, *My Life* (London: Constable, 1928).

23 *The Times*, 20 March 1920.

24 George Lansbury, *What I Saw in Russia* (London: Parsons, 1920), p. xiv.

25 Ibid.

26 TNA, CAB 23 (WC539), 3 March 1919.

27 TNA, CAB 24-110, CP 1730, 20 July 1920. Memorandum by Winston Churchill on the Declaration from the Second Congress of the Third International.

28 TNA, CAB 24-127, CP 3247, 'Undated' (late August 1921). *Draft Note to the Russian Soviet Government*. The date of Lenin's speech is given in the paper as 28 June 1921, but this was later corrected to 8 July in CP 3442, thanks to details obtained from a Russian radio broadcast. The protest note was delivered 7 September 1921.

29 Ibid., quoting Stalin at the Central Committee of the Third International on 1 June 1921.

30 TNA, CAB 24-129, CP 3448, September 1921. Home Office Directorate of Intelligence Monthly Review of Revolutionary Movements in the British Dominions Overseas and Foreign Countries (MRRM), no. 35. Speech to the Third Congress of the Third International (June-July 1921).

31 *The Times*, 3 April 1922.

32 *Churchill Papers* Companion Volume IV, Pt 2, p.1053 cited in Roy Jenkins, *Churchill*, (London: Macmillan London 2001), p. 368.

33 Christopher Andrew, *The Defence of the Realm: The Authorised History of MI5* (London: Penguin, 2010), p. 145.

34 Andrew Thorpe, *The British Communist Party and Moscow, 1920–43* (Manchester: Manchester University Press, 2000), p. 43.

35 TNA, KV 2/1410-1416 contain the intelligence files on Klishko.

36 *The Times*, 1 October 1920.

37 Andrew Williams, *Trading with the Bolsheviks: The Politics of East-West Trade, 1920–1939* (Manchester: Manchester University Press, 1989), p. 67.

38 Noel Thompson, 'Wise, Edward Frank (1885–1933)', *Oxford Dictionary of National Biography* (Oxford: Oxford University Press, 2004). [online edn] (May 2008) <http://www.oxforddnb.com/view/article/38704>, accessed 19 January 2017.

39 'Constitution and Rules, as Amended at the Annual Conference, 1918', *Report of the Annual Conference, Leicester, April 1918* (London: Independent Labour Party, 1918), p. 93.

40 *Report of the Annual Conference, Leicester, April 1918* (London: Independent Labour Party, 1918), p. 58.

41 *Report of the Annual Conference, Huddersfield, April 1919* (London: Independent Labour Party, 1919), p. 10.

42 TNA, CAB 23, 62(20), 18 November 1920.

43 TNA, CAB 24-106, CP 1309, 11 May 1920. *Resumption of Trade with Russia* (Winston Churchill on the memorandum submitted by Mr Wise from the San Remo conference, with extracts from Wise).

44 Ibid.

45 TNA, CAB 24-106, CP 1326, 12 May 1920. *Recent Tendencies in Soviet Russia* (Foreign Office).

46 '1919–1922 – Famine in Soviet Russia' [Global Security.org] (n.d.) <http://www.globalsecurity. org/military/world/russia/famine-1919.htm>, accessed 11 February 2016.

47 TNA, CAB 24-106, CP 1349, 27 May 1920. *Conclusions of the Inter-Departmental Russian Trade Committee.*

48 TNA, CAB 24-106, CP 1369, 29 May 1920. *Resumption of Trade with Russia.* Memorandum by the Secretary of State for War, Winston Churchill.

49 TNA, CAB 23-22 (CM), 8 September 1920.

50 TNA, CAB 24-111, CP 1885, 23 September 1920. Report on Revolutionary Organisations in the United Kingdom (RROUK), no. 73.

51 *The Times*, 16 May 1923.

52 TNA, CAB 24-111, CP 1885, 23 September 1920.

53 The members of the Anglo-Russian Parliamentary Committee were: A. A. Purcell MP, John Bromley MP, Duncan Carmichael, W. M. Citrine, W. N. Ewer, Alex Gossip, A. W. Haycock MP, George Hicks, MP, George Lansbury MP, W. Lawther, MP, W. Mackinder MP, Neil Maclean MP, James Maxton MP, J. E. Mills MP, E. D. Morel MP, John Scurr MP, A. B. Swales, Ben Tillett MP, Ben Turner MP, R. C. Wallhead MP, and Robert Williams. Of these, Ben Turner and George Lansbury were Cabinet members in 1924 and 1929–31; Lansbury was party leader in 1932–35 and Labour chairman in 1927–28; Robert Williams was Labour chairman in 1925–26; Purcell, Turner, Tillett, Bromley, Swales and Hicks were all TUC presidents; Citrine was TUC General Secretary. See W. P. and Zelda Coates, *History of Anglo-Soviet Relations* (London: Lawrence and Wishart, 1943), p. 152; Lambeth Palace Library (LPL) *The Papers of Cosmo Gordon Lang*, vol. 74, p. 29.

54 Further details of the ARPC and its committee are given in Appendix 3.

55 E.g. George Strauss, who declared that conditions in Russian prisons were 'very much more favourable than in our English prisons'. (Hansard, HC Deb, 25 March 1931, vol. 250, col. 432); George Lansbury, writing about his return visit to Russia in 1926: 'We discovered that prisons were simply workshops and factories, those residing in them being paid wages and giving freedom to buy food and other necessities, and to move freely about the prisons.' (*My Life*, p. 257); Sir Charles Trevelyan, Minister of Education in the 1924 and 1929-31 Labour Governments: [In Bolshevo prison, near Moscow] 'There are no warders, no police, there are no prison bars, there are no wire entanglements ... Why then do the prisoners stay there? For the quite simple reason that they have assured work at trade union rates of pay in a community which they regulate themselves ... The experiment has become an almost incredible success, and when their prison terms are over many of the inhabitants stay on in the colony as free workers. It must not be supposed that this experiment is an isolated effort... There are other colonies run on similar lines in other parts of Soviet Russia... This [is a] grand method of human regeneration.' (*Soviet Russia, A Description for British Workers* (London: Gollancz, 1935) p. 38) ; Sidney and Beatrice Webb: [So popular is Bolshevo] 'that many prisoners refuse to leave when their sentences expire.' (*Soviet Communism,* p. 588); the British T.U.C.: 'The ordinary criminal is detained in prison not for the purpose of punishment but with a view to educating him to become a useful citizen and worker. This is perhaps one of the most remarkable changes in Russia, and is apparently working with the most excellent results. The atmosphere of a Russian prison is now more that of a workshop of free workers than that of a house of detention or a jail.' (*The Official Report of the British Trades Union Delegation to Russia in November and December, 1924* (London: Trades Union General Council, 1925), p. 132).

56 See United States Information Agency, *Soviet Active Measures in the 'Post-Cold War' Era 1988–1991: A Report Prepared at the Request of the United States House of Representatives Committee on Appropriations by the United States Information Agency* (Washington: United States Information Agency, 1992).

57 'On the day it made its appearance the Soviet state inscribed the world "Peace" on its banner and made the struggle for peace the objective and highest principle of its foreign policy. When the new communist social system has triumphed worldwide and a classless society established, peace, the dream of the greatest minds throughout the ages, will be the natural situation ... Peace can only be guaranteed through the ultimate triumph of Communism worldwide.' F. Petrenko and V. Popov, *Soviet Foreign Policy: Objectives and Principles* (Moscow: Progress Publishers, 1985), p. 155.

Chapter 2

1　TNA, CAB 24-107, CP 1694, 26 July 1920, 'Memorandum by the President, Board of Education on a conversation with Mr Bertrand Russell'.
2　*The Times*, 9 June 1920.
3　*Daily Herald*, 20 May 1920.
4　*The Times*, 9 June 1920.
5　TNA, CAB 129-25, CP 72, 3 March 1948. *The Threat to Western Civilisation.* Memorandum by the Secretary of State for Foreign Affairs, Ernest Bevin.
6　*The Times*, 5 June 1920. The excerpt is from a letter from the International Federation of Trade Unions. Bevin stated that it was a legitimate appeal and urged the British Labour movement to support it.
7　*British Labour Delegation to Russia 1920: Report* (London: Trades Union Congress & The Labour Party, 1920).
8　*Daily Herald*, 14 July 1920. Cited in *Report of the Special Conference on Labour and the Russo-Polish War, Friday 13 Aug. 1920* (London: Council of Action, 1920).
9　Andrew Thorpe, *The British Communist Party and Moscow*, p. 44 (n. 38).
10　*The Times*, 10 August 1920.
11　Ibid.
12　*The Times*, 6 August 1920.
13　*The Times*, 14 August 1920.
14　Ibid.
15　TNA, CAB 23, 51(20), 15 September 1920. Appendix I.
16　TNA, CAB 24-111, CP 1848, 9 September 1920. RROUK no. 71. The instruction was issued on 17 August 1920.
17　The Council of Action logged twenty-seven different reports of shipments of arms, ammunition and military equipment. 'Report of the Council of Action, August to October, 1920, typescript, 18 October 1920. http://wit.lib.warwick.ac.uk/cdm/landingpage/collection/russian accessed 8 March 2016.
18　*The Times*, 11 August 1920.
19　*The Times*, 14 August 1920.
20　*The Times*, 16 August 1920.
21　TNA, CAB 24-111, CP 1862, 16 September 1920. RROUK no. 72.
22　TNA, CAB 24-111, CP 1848, 9 September 1920. RROUK no. 71.
23　Ibid.
24　TNA, CAB 24-111, CP 1862, 16 September 1920. RROUK no. 72.
25　TNA, CAB 24-111, CP 1830, 2 September 1920. RROUK no. 70. Speech at Manchester, 29 August 1920.
26　V. I. Lenin, 'Speech Delivered at a Congress of Leather Industry Workers, October 2 1920' (trans. J. Katzer), *Marxists Internet Archive* [online archive] (2002) <https://www.marxists.org/archive/lenin/works/1920/oct/02b.htm>, accessed 7 October 2016.
27　*The Times*, 18 August 1920.
28　*The Times*, 23 August 1920.
29　'The Daily Herald. Bolshevist Help Sought. Promise of Paper and Subsidy. Lansbury's Orders from Moscow', *The Times*, 19 August 1920. One of the cables leaked to the paper ran: 'Chicherin to Litvinov February 23, 1920: [Lansbury] wishes to pay us a small sum as commission for the credit we are opening for him for purchasing paper in Sweden or Finland'.
30　TNA, CAB 24-111, CP 1897, 16 September 1920. *Krassin and Klishko.* Memorandum by the Secretary of State for Foreign Affairs.
31　*The Times*, 19 August 1920.
32　TNA, CAB 24-111, CP 1897. *Krassin and Klishko.* Text of cable 'from Klishko, London, to Tchicherin, Moscow', 14 July 1920.
33　TNA, CAB 24-111, CP 1848, 9 September 1920. RROUK no. 71. The report says that around 20 August 1920, Meynell received £40,000, which was then invested in government Exchequer bonds.
34　TNA, CAB 24-111, CP 1897. *Krassin and Klishko*, p. 2.
35　Ibid. Text of cable 'from Klishko, London, to Tchicherin, Moscow', 23 July 1920.

36 'The "Daily Herald" is now Lenin's subsidized organ. A number of Chinese Consolidated Gold Bonds 1913 are now being sold by Krassin's delegation and the proceeds are to be handed over to Lansbury after deducting the money that has been lent to him.' TNA, CAB 24-11, CP 1743, 5 August 1920. RROUK no. 66.

37 *The Times*, 19 August 1920. Text of cable from Litvinov in Copenhagen to Chicherin in Moscow: 'I have given instructions that the Chinese bonds which are there [in London] to be handed over to the Herald'. See also TNA, CAB 24-110, CP 1706, 29 July 1920. RROUK no. 65.

38 'Scotland Yard From Within', *The Times*, 8 December 1921. This was the serialisation of the memoirs of Sir Basil Thomson (1861–1939), assistant commissioner at Scotland Yard and Director of Intelligence at the Home Office.

39 TNA, CAB 24-114, CP 2067, 4 November 1920. RROUK no. 79. 'Almost £2m of gems had been sold by the Russians on the London market, deflating the diamond price from £35 to £18 a carat'.

40 'Among the staff there were moments of panic. Last week a rumour was started in Fleet Street that Francis Meynell was "wanted for high treason" and he fled through the country in a motorcar "like a hunted man". It required a member of the Editorial staff to reassure him.' TNA, CAB 24-111, CP 1885, 23 September 1920. RROUK no. 73.

41 *The Times*, 15 September 1920.

42 *The Times*, 15 September 1920.

43 TNA, CAB 24-111, CP 1885, 23 September 1920. RROUK no. 73.

44 TNA, CAB 23, 51(20), 15 September 1920. Appendix I.

45 *The Times*, 16 September 1920.

46 TNA, CAB 24-111, CP 1830, 2 September 1920. RROUK no. 70.

47 TNA, CAB 24-111, CP 1897, 16 September 1920. *Krassin and Klishko*. 'From Tchicherin, Moscow, to Krassin, London', 1 July 1920.

48 Ibid. 'From Tchicherin, Moscow to Krassin, London', 15 August 1920.

49 Ibid. 'From Kamenev, London to Litvinov, Copenhagen', 25 August 1920.

50 'Editorial', *The Socialist Review* (October–December, 1920).

51 TNA, CAB 24-111, CP 1830, 2 September 1920. RROUK no. 70.

52 TNA, CAB 24-111, CP 1897, 16 September 1920. *Krassin and Klishko*. 'From Tchicherin, Moscow, to Krassin, London', 9 September 1920.

53 *The Times*, 18 August 1920: 'In Bradford it is reported that the local Council of Action consists of representatives of the Bradford Trades and Labour Council, the Bradford Labour Party and Independent Labour Party, and the "Hands Off Russia" Committee'.

54 *The Times*, 26 August 1920.

55 TNA, CAB 24-97, CP 544, 2 February 1920. *Revolutionaries and the Need for Legislation*, Special Report no. 14, Directorate of Intelligence (Home Office).

56 TNA, CAB 24-129, CP 3410, 15 October 1921. *Foreign Support of Communist Agitators in the United Kingdom: Memorandum circulated by the Home Secretary*.

57 TNA, CAB 24-99, CP 791, 4 March 1920. RROUK no. 24.

58 Ibid.

59 TNA, CAB 24-97, CP 544, 2 February 1920. *Revolutionaries and the Need for Legislation*, Special Report no. 14, Directorate of Intelligence (Home Office).

60 Keith Neild, 'Rothstein, Theodore', *Dictionary of Labour Biography*, ed. Joyce M. Bellamy, John Saville et al., 13 vols, (London: MacMillan, 1972–2010), vol. 7, p. 200-9.

61 Andrew Thorpe, *The British Communist Party and Moscow*, p. 44 (n. 38).

Chapter 3

1 TNA, CAB 24-114, CP 2067, 4 November 1920. RROUK no. 79.

2 TNA, CAB 23-22, (CM), 2 September 1920.

3 TNA, CAB 23-22, (CM), 8 September 8, 1920.

4 TNA, CAB 24-111, CP 1897, 16 September 1920.

5 TNA, CAB 24-111, CP 1898, 21 September 1920.

6 TNA, CAB 24-112, CP 1909, 30 September 1920.

7 TNA, CAB 24-112, CP 1917, 27 September 1920.

8 TNA, CAB 24-112, CP 1950, 5 October 1920.

9 TNA, CAB 24-112, CP 1944, 6 October 1920.

10 TNA, CAB 24-111, CP 1880, 24 September 1920. *Negotiations for the Resumption of Trade with Russia*. A note by the Cabinet Secretary, M. P. A. Hankey.

11 TNA, CAB 24-111, CP 1899, 27 September 1920. *Trade with Soviet Russia*: Admiralty Memorandum for the Cabinet. From W. H. Long.

12 Charles E. Callwell, *Field-Marshal Sir Henry Wilson: His Life and Diaries*, 2 vols (London: Cassell, 1927) cited in Travis L. Crosby, *The Unknown David Lloyd George: A Statesman in Conflict* (London: I. B. Tauris, 2014), p. 278.

13 TNA, CAB 24-112, CP 1936, 'Undated' (late September/early October 1920). *Contracts for Supplies to the Soviet Government*, Memorandum by the General Staff, circulated by the Secretary of State for War.

14 TNA, CAB 24-114, CP 2099, 14 November 1920. *Russian Trade Negotiations*, Memorandum by the Secretary of State for Foreign Affairs.

15 Churchill Papers: C. 16/53. Cited in M. V. Glenny, 'The Anglo-Soviet Trade Agreement, March 1921', *Journal of Contemporary History*, 5:2 (1970), 63–82.

16 Winston Churchill, 'Bolshevism and Imperial Sedition' (speech given at the United Wards Club Luncheon, Cannon Street Hotel, London, 4 November 1920), *International Churchill Society* [online resource] (n.d.) <http://www.winstonchurchill.org/resources/speeches/1915-1929-nadir-and-recovery/bolshevism-and-imperial-sedition>, accessed 7 March 2016.

17 TNA, CAB 24-116, CP 2286, 13 December 1920. *The Russian Trade Agreement*.

18 Command Papers [Cmd. 1207] *Russian trade agreement. Trade agreement between His Britannic Majesty's government and the government of the Russian Socialist Federal Soviet Republic* (London: HMSO, 1921).

19 TNA, CAB 23, 13(21), 14 March 1921.

20 *The Times*, 29 October 1920.

21 TNA, CAB 24-155, CP 2116, 18 November 1925. RROUK no. 81. Veltheim, who was being concealed in a safe house by Rothstein, had been in the United Kingdom for about a fortnight before he was arrested.

22 Modern estimates of the actual number of deaths lie between 379 and 1,000. It is interesting to note that, while Malone cited Amritsar in support of his call for Churchill's lynching, Churchill had been explicit in his condemnation of the action of Dyer, the officer commanding the soldiers who opened fire upon the unarmed Indians, which he described as 'monstrous' and 'sinister' Hansard, HC Deb, 8 July 1920, vol. 131, col. 1725. Lloyd George had expressed the same sentiment: 'The whole country has been horrified at what took place. [There has] never been anything like it before in British history. If you are able to find anything so damning to the British reputation you have to go back centuries.' Hansard, HC Deb, 22 December 1919, vol. 123, col. 1231.

23 *The Times*, 8 November 1920.

24 The connection between the (abortive) development of the Red Officer Course, the Finnish communist Erkki Veltheim, Malone and Harold Grenfell, who stood surety for Malone (*The Times*, 10 November, 1920) after his trial, is discussed at greater length in Kevin Morgan and Tauno Saarela, 'Northern Underground Revisited: Finnish Reds and the Origins of British Communism', *European History Quarterly, 29 (April)* 1999), 179–215.

25 TNA, CAB 24-114, CP 2067, 4 November 1920. RROUK no. 79 (also reported verbatim in *The Times*, November 20 1920).

26 Ibid.

27 Morgan and Saarela, 'Northern Underground Revisited', p. 210.

28 For example see Hansard, HC Deb, 30 April 1930, vol. 238, cols 176–77 (on religious persecution); *2 March 1931, vol. 249, col. 42 (timber); 14 May 1931, vol. 252, col. 1334 (supporting the cause of Russian employees of Arcos in the UK)*.

29 *The Times*, 28 June 1919.

30 Hansard, HC Deb, 16 April 1919, vol. 114, cols 3001–2.

31 *The Times*, 1–3 December 1921.

32 See the remarks of the Earl of Onslow in 'Subversive Propaganda', Hansard, HL Deb, 15 June 1921, vol. 45, cols 547–59.

33 TNA, CAB 24-129, CP 3410, 15 October 1921. *Foreign Support for Communist Agitators in the United Kingdom*. Memorandum circulated by the Home Secretary.

Chapter 4

1 James Keir Hardie, *Karl Marx: The Man and his Message* (Manchester: National Labour Press, 1910), p. 13 (reprinted from the *Labour Leader* of August 12, 19, and 29 1910).

2 Harold Laski, *The Webbs and Soviet Communism* (Webb Memorial Lecture, 1947; London: Fabian Publications, 1947), p. 8.

3 Gerald Gould, *The Coming Revolution in Great Britain* (London: William Collins, 1920), p. 233. Gould was associate editor of Lansbury's *Daily Herald* and had led the welcome for Lansbury at the Albert Hall meeting of 19 March 1919. He was a fellow University College London (1906), and a fellow of Merton College, Oxford (1909–16).

4 *New Leader*, 24 November 1922.

5 Hardie, *Karl Marx: The Man and his Message*, p. 13.

6 *Plebs Magazine*, 1921, cited in John Simkin, 'Aneurin Bevan', *Spartacus Educational* [online resource] (September 1997, updated July 2016) <http://spartacus-educational.com/TUbevan.htm>, accessed 5 November 2015.

7 Hansard, HC Deb, 7 April 1933, vol. 276, col. 2111.

8 Karl Marx, *Communist Manifesto: Socialist Landmark: A New Appreciation Written for the Labour Party*, ed. Harold Laski (London: Allen and Unwin, 1948), dust jacket and p. 7. As noted in the text, Laski's authorship of the dust jacket text cannot be proven but, as editor of this special edition, his agreement with it is certain.

9 *The Times*, 3 August 1950.

10 Karl Marx, *The German Ideology*, cited in David McLellan, *The Thought of Karl Marx: An Introduction* (London: Macmillan, 1971), p. 36.

11 Emil Lederer, 'Communism', and G. D. H. Cole, 'Socialism' in *Encyclopaedia Britannica* (14th edn, London: Encyclopaedia Britannica, 1929).

12 Bill Jones, *The Russia Complex: The British Labour Party and the Soviet Union* (Manchester: Manchester University Press, 1977), p. 9.

13 'They are planning war against Socialist Russia because they like wars and because Russia is Socialist', *Daily Herald*, 10 August 1920, cited in L. J. Macfarlane, 'Hands off Russia: British Labour and the Russo-Polish War, 1920', *Past and Present*, 38 (December 1967), 126–52.

14 American Civil Liberties Union, *The Attempted Deportation of John Strachey* (New York: ACLU, 1935), pp. 19,22.

15 James Maxton, *Dictators and Dictatorship* (London: Independent Labour Party, 1932), reproduced in 'Maxton Papers', *Glasgow Digital Library* [online resource] (n.d.) <http://gdl.cdlr.strath.ac.uk/maxton/maxton101.htm>, accessed 6 November 2015.

16 Fred Henderson, *The Case for Socialism* (London: Clarion Press, 1908), pp. 4–5.

17 'Basis of the Fabian Society', adopted 23 May 1919 (Fabian Society Annual Report, 1919).

18 Interview with Karl Marx, *Chicago Tribune*, 5 January 1879. Marxists Internet Archive, accessed 3 November 2015.

19 Karl Marx, 'The Victory of the Counter-Revolution in Vienna', *Neue Rheinische Zeitung*, 7 November 1848, Marxists Internet Archive, https://www.marxists.org/archive/marx/works/1848/11/06.htm>, accessed 31 December 2016

20 Richard Pipes, *A Concise History of the Russian Revolution* (New York: Knopf, 1995), puts the total at nine million, while Orlando Figes, *A People's Tragedy: The Russian Revolution, 1891–1924* (London: Jonathan Cape, 1997) arrives at a figure of ten million. The difference can be broken down into approximately five million famine deaths, two million combat and civilian deaths, two million deaths from epidemics. On the choice of the word 'Russian' to describe the nationality of those believers and citizens referred to in this book, see the Preface. <http://necrometrics.com/20c5m.htm >, accessed 19 January 2017.

Chapter 5

1 James Ramsay MacDonald, *Parliament and Revolution* (Manchester: National Labour Press, 1919), p. 101.

2 Ibid.

3 Ibid., p. 98, 15.

4 Ibid., p. 91.

5 Ibid., p. 91, 98–9.

6   Ibid., p. 30.

7   Ibid., p. 20.

8   Ibid., p. 15.

9   George Lansbury, *What I Saw in Russia* (London: Parsons, 1920), p. xiii.

10 George Lansbury, 'Preface', in W. P. Coates, *More Anti-Soviet Lies Nailed* (London: Anglo-Russian Parliamentary Committee, 1933), p. 7.

11 MacDonald, *Parliament and Revolution*, p. 26.

12 Ibid., p. 20.

13 Ibid., p. 37.

14 Ibid., p. 33.

15 Ibid., p. 36.

16 Ibid., p. 22-3.

17 Ibid., p. 92.

18 Ibid., p. 70.

19 Ibid., p. 13–14. The word 'chains' is an allusion to the declaration in the *Communist Manifesto*'s 'the proletarians have nothing to lose but their chains'.

20 Ibid., p. 93.

21 Ibid., p. 82.

22 Ibid., p. 76.

23 Ibid., p. 70.

24 Ibid., p. 34–6.

25 Ibid., p. 103.

26 *The Herald*, 12 January 1918.

27 *Report of the Annual Conference Held at Leicester, April 1918* (London: Independent Labour Party, 1918), p. 58.

28 *Report of the Annual Conference Held at Scarborough, April 1931* (London: Independent Labour Party, 1931), p. 45.

29 Harold Laski, *Karl Marx: An Essay* (London: Allen & Unwin, 1925), p. 37.

30 Laski, *The Webbs and Soviet Communism*, p. 8.

31 Marx, *Communist Manifesto, Socialist Landmark*, ed. Laski. (London: Allen & Unwin) 1948.

32 *Workers' Weekly*, 20 June 1924, cited in *What They Have Said*, 2 (23 October 1925). .'TUC Library Collections' (*TUC History Online*) <http://www.unionhistory.info/http://www.unionhistory.info/generalstrike/background.php>, accessed 5 November 2015. According to the handbill, *Workers' Weekly* claimed that the statement was made at a dinner given by Joseph King in November 1918.

33 *New Leader*, 24 January 1918. Cited in Ian Bullock, *Romancing the Revolution: The Myth of Soviet Democracy and the British Left* (Edmonton, Alberta: AU Press, 2011), p. 81.

34 *The Times*, 3 December 1946.

Chapter 6

1   Dimitry V. Pospielovsky, *A History of Soviet Atheism in Theory and Practice, and the Believer*, 3 vols (London: Macmillan, 1987–88), vol. 2 (*Soviet Antireligious Campaigns and Persecutions*), ch. 3.

2   N. E. Yemelyanov, 'Оценка статистики гонений на Русскую Православную Церковь (1917–1952 годы)'

[Estimation of the Statistics of the Persecutions of the Russian Orthodox Church (1917–52)] Православный Свято-Тихоновский гуманитарный Университет [website] (2004) <http://martyrs.pstbi.ru/institut/sb/f12.htm>, accessed 21 January 2017.

3   TNA, CAB 24-127, CP 3247, 'Undated' (late August 1921). *Russian Trade Agreement.*

4   TNA, CAB 23, 93(21), 16 December 1921.

5   TNA, CAB 23, 21(22), 28 March 1922.

6   *Report of the Annual Conference Held at Leicester April, 1918*, p. 58.

7   Report by bishop Neveu, 1935, cited in Christopher Zugger, *The Forgotten: Catholics of the Soviet Empire from Lenin through Stalin* (Syracuse, NY: Syracuse University Press, 2001), p. 257.

8   *The Spectator*, 11 May 1923, p. 6.

9   'Mr. Hodgson to M. Chicherin', 30 March 1923 [Cmd. 1869] Russia no. 2 (1923). *Correspondence between His Majesty's government and the Soviet government* (London: HMSO, 1923), p. 3.

10 Soviet Note signed by G. Weinstein, 31 March 1923. [Cmd. 1869] *Russia no. 2 (1923). Correspondence between His Majesty's government and the Soviet government respecting the relations between the two governments* (London: HMSO, 1923), p. 3.

11 *Daily Herald*, 4 April 1923.

12 TNA, CAB 23, 27(23), 15 May 1923.

13 TNA, CAB 23, 23(23), 2 May 1923. Appendix 1. Also in [Cmd. 1869] *Russia No. 2 (1923)*.

14 TNA, CAB 23, 30 (23), 11 June 1923.

Chapter 7

1 *The Times*, 9 January 1924, quoting 'Labour on the threshold', MacDonald's speech at the rally in celebration of Labour's victory (Royal Albert Hall, 8 January 1924).

2 Joseph Stalin, 'The International Situation and the Defence of the U.S.S.R.' (speech of 1 August 1927), *Marxists Internet Archive* [online archive] (2009), <https://www.marxists.org/reference/archive/stalin/works/1927/07/29.htm>, accessed 21 January 2017.

3 *The Times*, 9 January 1924.

4 Victor Madeira, *Britannia and the Bear: The Anglo-Russian Intelligence Wars, 1917–1929* (Woodbridge: The Boydell Press, 2014), p. 121.

5 *Daily Herald*, 2 February 1924.

6 *Workers' Weekly*, 25 July 1924.

7 *The Times*, 7 August 1924.

8 TNA, CAB 23, 48(24).

9 Ibid. The minutes of Cabinet 48(24) of 6 August conclude with a later note 'Conversation with the Prime Minister, 22 September 1924'. This was appended to the minutes on 8 December 1924 by Sir Maurice Hankey, signed as witness by his private secretary Capt. Burgis. The note added a transcript of the conversation taken by Mr T. Jones, principal assistant secretary.

10 TNA, CAB 124-21, CP 21, 19 January 1924. RROUK no. 238.

11 An example of Campbell's writing had been included in a Cabinet intelligence report as early as 1920, in this piece from *The Worker* in late October 1920: 'Both the employed and unemployed must realise that the end of all their efforts must be to smash the power of the capitalist state, take possession of the workshops, and run them on behalf of the entire working class … [Lloyd George] and his gang are robbers and murderers … Down with the system of greedy capitalism that develops bloodmania in its dominant class!' TNA, CAB 24-114, CP 2067, 4 November 1920. RROUK no. 79. Campbell would go on to publish more than thirty books and pamphlets, including *Soviet Policy and its Critics* (London: Gollancz, 1939).

12 *The Times*, 8 October 1924.

13 Hansard, HC Deb, 8 October 1924, vol. 177, cols 581–704.

14 H. Montgomery Hyde, *Sir Patrick Hastings, His Life And Cases* (London: Heinemann, 1960), p. 150.

15 A transcript of the Zinoviev letter may be found in Foreign Office Note N 8105/108/38 and also in 'History of the Zinoviev Incident' in TNA, CAB 24-168, CP 484, 11 November 1924.

16 The exact figures for the 1924 election were: Conservatives 7,418,983 (1923: 5,286,159), Labour 5,281,626 (1923: 4,267,831), Liberal 2,818,717 (1923: 4,129,922).

17 Gill Bennett, *'A Most Extraordinary and Mysterious Business': The Zinoviev Letter of 1924* (London: Foreign & Commonwealth Office, 1999).

18 Some examples: 'MacDonald was brought down by the Zinoviev letter.' Twitter comment by George Galloway, 8 November 2015; (The 1924) 'election was lost by Labour, largely because of a red scare started in the Daily Mail around a letter, purportedly from the Russian revolutionary Zinoviev to the British Communist Party', Lindsey German (formerly of the Socialist Workers Party) 20 September 2015. <http://www.counterfire.org/history/17991-labour-a-party>, accessed 24 January 2017; Seamus Milne (appointed in 2015 as the Labour Party's executive director of strategy) claims that the Zinoviev letter 'helped bring down the first Labour government' *The Enemy Within, The Secret War Against The Miners* (3rd edn; London: Verso, 2004), p. 255. Even historians slip up on this – 'The publication of the Zinoviev Letter and the Campbell case both created enough of an uproar to ensure that MacDonald had to go to the country' Andrew Williams, *Trading with the Bolsheviks: The Politics of East-West Trade, 1920–1939* (Manchester: Manchester University Press, 1992), p. 76; Bill Jones, whose *The Russia Complex* tends to be more objective than most

about Labour's attitude to the Soviets, is mistaken too: 'A *dubious* prosecution case against the communist journalist J. R. Campbell for *allegedly* seditious writings was withdrawn at the behest of the Labour Attorney General. *MacDonald lost the resulting motion of censure*'. (My italics). *The Russia Complex* (Manchester: Manchester University Press, 1977), p. 9. In fact the case was clear-cut, not dubious, the text legally seditious, and MacDonald did not lose the censure motion.

19 Andrew Thorpe, however, to his credit, writes that the content of the Zinoviev letter 'was hardly out of line with much that the CI [Comintern] had been sending to the [CPGB] in previous months'. *The British Communist Party and Moscow, 1920–43* (Manchester: Manchester University Press, 2000), p. 80.

20 'Yet, dependent on Liberal support to remain in power, the government fell as a result of a political row about the actions of Attorney-General Sir Patrick Hastings. In the subsequent election, the Daily Mail published the infamous Zinoviev letter, a forgery which alleged there were links between Russian Communists and the British Labour Party. With an atmosphere of fervent anti-Communism, Labour lost 40 seats and the Tories were returned to power.' Anonymous, 'History of the Labour Party', *The Labour Party* [political party website] (n.d.) <http://www.labour.org.uk/pages/history-of-the-labour-party>, accessed 31 December 2016.

21 TNA, CAB 24-129, CP 3448, September 1921. MRRM no. 35. Speech to the Third Congress of the Third International (June-July 1921).

22 BEU 1924 annual report, cited in Ian Thomas, 'Confronting the Challenge of Socialism: The British Empire Union and the National Citizens' Union, 1917–1927', MPhil thesis, University of Wolverhampton, 2010, p. 119.

23 Thomas, 'Confronting the Challenge', p. 6.

24 BEU 1924 annual report, cited in Thomas, 'Confronting the Challenge', p. 29.

25 G. D. H. Cole, 'Non-Manual Trade Unionism', *North American Review*, 215 (January–June 1922), 38–45, at p. 43. Cited in Thomas, 'Confronting the Challenge', p. 80.

26 Independent Labour Party Information Committee, *Who Pays for the Attacks on Labour? An Exposure of the Blackleg Organisations and Propaganda Agencies of Big Capital* (London: Independent Labour Party, n.d. [1920]). Cited in Thomas, 'Confronting the Challenge', p. 80.

27 Thomas, 'Confronting the Challenge', p. 35.

28 Thomas, 'Confronting the Challenge', p. 35–6.

29 Thomas, 'Confronting the Challenge', and Thomas Linehan, *British Fascism 1918–39: Parties, Ideology and Culture* (Manchester: Manchester University Press, 2000).

30 *New Voice*, October 1923, p. 3. Cited in Thomas, 'Confronting the Challenge', p. 154.

31 Linehan, *British Fascism*, p. 55.

32 Thomas, 'Confronting the Challenge', p. 160.

33 Thomas, 'Confronting the Challenge', p. 164.

34 *Socialist Review*, June 1926. Cited in W. Milne-Bailey, *A Nation On Strike* (typescript, n.d. [1927?]) 'TUC Library Collections', *TUC History Online* [online resource] (n.d.) <http://www.unionhistory.info/britainatwork/emuweb/objects/nofdigi/tuc/imagedisplay.php?irn=5000446&reftable=ecatalogue&refirn=5000854/>, accessed 21 January 2017.

35 Hansard, HL Deb, 17 June 1926, vol. 64, col. 464.

36 *Report on the 22nd Annual Conference of the Labour Party, 1922* (London: Labour Party, 1922), pp. 193–6.

37 *Report of the Executive Committee to the 23rd Annual Conference, 1923* (London: Labour Party, 1923), p. 15.

38 'Correspondence on the Hunger Strike of Socialist Prisoners on Solovetsky Island' (typescript, headed 'Trades Union Congress and The Labour Party, Joint International Department', n.d. [early October 1924]) < https://contentdm.warwick.ac.uk/cdm/compoundobject/collection/russian/id/2804/rec/1>, accessed 21 January 2017.

39 *Report of the 24th Annual Conference of the Labour Party, 1924* (London: Labour Party, 1924), p. 23.

40 Ibid.

41 TUC, *Russia, The Official Report of the British Trades Union Delegation to Russia and Caucasia, Nov. and Dec., 1924* (London: TUC General Council, 1925), p. 9.

42 Ibid., p. 105.

43 F. A. Mackenzie, *The Russian Crucifixion* (London: Jarrolds, 1930), p. 84. Mackenzie says that the

figure was given to him during a conversation with the Patriarch shortly before his death in April 1925. The report was published in March.

44 TUC, *Russia, The Official Report ... 1924*, p. 171. The report was signed on p. 16–17 by Herbert Smith, Ben Tillett MP, John Turner, John Bromley, Alan Findlay, Albert Purcell (the outgoing chairman of the TUC), Fred Bramley (TUC Secretary).

45 The British Committee for the Defence of Political Prisoners in Russia published a critical reply to the TUC report. It also alleged that the authors of the report had been deceived by their hosts, and told a different side of the Butyrka visit: 'When they visited the politicals in the Butyrka prison, they did so in the company of two notorious Chekists, Deribas and Katanian ... No wonder Timofeev, one of the members of the Central Committee of the Social Revolutionary Party, was noncommittal and even austere with Messrs Purcell and Bramley who interpreted his attitude as showing that he was "dangerous to be released".' Emma Goldman (ed.), *Russia and the British Labour Delegation's Report: A Reply* (London: British Committee for the Defence of Political Prisoners in Russia, 1925), p. 26.

46 Christopher Addison et al., *Problems of a Socialist Government* (London: Gollancz, 1933), ch. 38.

47 *The Times*, 8 September 1925.

48 Joint declaration of the Anglo-Russian conference between members of the General Council International Committee of the British TUC and representatives of All-Russian Trade Union Council, London, April 6–8 1925. The TUC was represented by, among others, A. B. Swales, G. Hicks, B. Tillett, A. A. Purcell, W. Thorne MP, F. Bramley (secretary) and W. Citrine (assistant secretary).

49 Ben Tillett, *Some Russian Impressions* (London: Labour Research Department, 1925).

50 Ibid., pp. 12, 33.

51 Ibid., p. 24.

Chapter 8

1 'All told, the Arcos Raid revealed that the Soviet Union used its London trade headquarters as a base for directing subversive activities and disseminating hostile propaganda'. Harriette Flory, 'The Arcos Raid and the Rupture of Anglo-Soviet Relations', *Journal of Contemporary History*, 124 (October 1977), 707–23 at p. 708. Cited in Jennifer Betteridge, 'The Political Purposes of Surveillance: the Rupture of Diplomatic Relations with Russia, May 1927', unpublished paper (Leeds: University of Leeds, 2006), p. 7. Betteridge adds: 'Harriette Flory's account of the Arcos Raid accurately [*sic*] disputes the traditional view that raiders failed to unearth any significant documents'.

2 Hansard, HC Deb, 26 May 1927, vol. 206, cols 2195–326, 2249–50.

3 *The Times*, 11 June 1927.

4 *The Times*, 11 July 1927.

5 *The Times*, 27 July 1927.

6 *The Times*, 31 August 1927, 14 September 1927.

7 *The Times*, 21 September 1927.

8 *The Times*, 26 August 1927.

9 Hansard, HC Deb, 15 June 1927, vol. 207, cols 978–80: MPs Campbell Stephen, George Buchanan, David Kirkwood, and Ernest Thurtle (Lansbury's son-in-law). A similar defence was made of the Soviet arrests of the British Metro-Vickers engineers in 1933 by George Lansbury, among others.

10 *The Times*, 14 June 1927.

11 *The Times*, 23 June 1927.

12 *The Times*, 28 June 1927.

13 Ibid.

14 *The Times*, 30 June 1927.

15 *Anglo-Russian Joint Advisory Council, Supplementary Statement, Trade Union Congress, Edinburgh 1927* (Edinburgh: Dobson Molle, 1925), pp. 2-9.

16 *Anglo-Russian ... Supplementary Statement*, p. 11.

17 TNA, CAB 24-188, CP 246, 18 October 1927.

18 *The Times*, 16 September 1927.

19 *New Leader*, 16 September 1927.

20 *The Times*, 25 October 1927.

21 *New Leader*, 4 November 1927.

22 *New Leader*, 4 November 1927.

23 Lansbury, *My Life*, pp. 242, 245.

24 *Report of the 28th Annual Conference of the Labour Party, 1928* (London: Labour Party, 1928), p. 154.

Chapter 9

1   Tom Mahon, 'The Secret IRA-Soviet Agreement, 1925', *History Ireland* [online journal], 17:Issue 3 (May–June 2009) <http://www.historyireland.com/20th-century-contemporary-history/the-se-cret-ira-soviet-agreement-1925/>, accessed 11 February 2016.

2   [Cmd. 2682] *Communist papers. Documents selected from those obtained on the arrest of the Communist leaders on the 14th and 21st October, 1925* (London: HMSO, 1926). Letter 30, undated, 'shorthand notes to Comrade Bennett', pp. 61–32, complained that the CPGB was in considerable financial difficulties because it had only received £14,600 of its £16,000 allocation (£1.03 million) for the year.

3   Hansard, HC Deb, 23 April 1928, vol. 216, cols 630–2.

4   [Cmd. 3125] *Russian banks and communist funds. Report of an enquiry into certain transactions of the Bank for Russian Trade, Ltd., and the Moscow Narodny Bank, Ltd. Memorandum by the directors of the Moscow Narodny Bank, Ltd* (London: HMSO, 1928), p. 36.

5   His name appears on the delegates list in *Soviet Russia To-Day: the Report of the British Workers' Delegation Which Visited Soviet Russia for the Tenth Anniversary of the Revolution, November, 1927.* (London: Labour Party, 1927). Quelch's name appears in the list of delegates included at the front of the book.

6   Betteridge, 'The Political Purposes of Surveillance'.

7   N. Barou and E. F. Wise, *The Russian Cooperative Movement* (London: Moscow Narodny Bank, 1926).

8   [Cmd. 3125] *Russian banks and communist funds*, p. 36.

9   TNA, KV3/34, cited in Betteridge, 'The Political Purposes of Surveillance', p. 25.

10 Reader Bullard's diary (manuscript, private collection), entry for 15 August 1932. 'In early April the Economist published a series of letters over the signature of Frank Wise, a Labour M.P. but who is also paid £5,000 a year to represent the Russian co-operatives in England.'

11 [Cmd. 3125] *Russian banks and communist funds*, p. 50.

12 Wise published his account of the event in a full-page article in the ILP journal. He described the Revolution as 'a turning point in world history'. E. F. Wise, 'The Soviet Anniversary As I Saw It', *New Leader*, 25 November 1927, p. 6.

13 The International Committee for Political Prisoners, *Letters from Russian Prisons* (London: C. W. Daniel, 1925), p. 10.

14 *Report of the Executive Committee to the 23rd Annual Conference,1923* (London: Labour Party, 1923), p. 15.

15 Boris Pasternak, *Doctor Zhivago* (New York: Pantheon, 1958), p. 189.

16 Hansard, HC Deb, 17 July 1923, vol. 166, col. 2189. Kirkwood was a Labour MP from 1922 until 1950, ending his career ennobled as Baron Kirkwood PC.

Part II

1   Christopher Fuller, 'Some Aspects of Life in Soviet Russia (II)', *The English Review*, 54 (June 1932), 667–75. Col. Fuller travelled with Duncan Sandys, third secretary at the British Embassy in Berlin (Bullard, diary, 26 July 1931). Sandys married Winston Churchill's daughter Diana in 1935 and later became a Conservative minister. Both men were Russian speakers and able to avoid the usual closely chaperoned tours.

Chapter 10

1   Alexander Solzhenitsyn, *The Gulag Archipelago, 1918–1956: An Experiment in Literary Investigation* (trans. T. P. Whitney and H. T. Willetts), 3 vols (London: Collins/Fontana 1974), vol. 1, p. 54.

2   For further details, see Edward Radzinsky, *Stalin* (New York: Doubleday, 1996), p. 295.

3   *O priznakah kulackih hozjajstv, v kotoryh dolzhen primenjat'sja Kodeks Zakonov o trude* [On the Characteristics of Kulak Farms Subject to the Labour Code], 21 May 1929. English text in Dimitry V. Pospielovsky, *A History of Soviet Atheism*, vol. 1 (*A History of Marxist-Leninist Atheism and Soviet Antireligious Policies*), p. 44.

4   An observation originally made by E. H. Carr, *Socialism in One Country 1924–1926*, 3 vols (London: Macmillan, 1958–64) vol. 1, p. 99.

5   Stalin, 'Speech Delivered at a Conference of Marxist Students of Agrarian Questions, 27 December 1929', *Pravda*, 29 December 1929, reproduced in *Marxists Internet Archive* (2008) <https://www.marxists.org/reference/archive/stalin/works/1929/12/27.htm>, accessed 21 January 2017.

6   Ibid.

7   Stalin, 'Concerning the Policy of Eliminating of the Kulaks as a Class', *Krasnaya Zvezda*, 18, 21 January 1930, reproduced in *Marxists Internet Archive* (2005) <https://www.marxists.org/reference/archive/stalin/works/1930/01/21.htm>, accessed 21 January 2017.

8   Stalin, 'Political Report Of The Central Committee To The Sixteenth Congress Of The C.P.S.U.(B.)', *Pravda*, 29 June 1930, reproduced in *Marxists Internet Archive* (2000) <https://www.marxists.org/reference/archive/stalin/works/1930/aug/27.htm>, accessed 21 January 2017.

9   Stalin, 'Reply To Collective-Farm Comrades', *Pravda*, 3 April 1930, reproduced in *From Marx to Mao* (1988) <http://www.marx2mao.com/Stalin/RCFC30.html>, accessed 21 January 2017.

10 Vasily Grossman, *Forever Flowing* (New York: Harper & Row, 1972), p. 142ff.

11 Ibid.

12 'O meroprijatijah po likvidacii kulackih hozjajstv v rajonah sploshnoj kollektivizacii' [Measures To Liquidate Kulak Households In Regions Of Total Collectivisation], 30 January 1930, in *Tragedija sovetskoj derevni. Kollektivizacija i raskulachivanie. Dokumenty i materialy Tom 2. nojabr' 1929 — dekabr' 1930.* (Moscow: ROSSPEN, 2000), pp. 126–30, reproduced in Исторические материалы [online archive] (n.d.) <http://istmat.info/node/30863>, accessed 10 November 2016.

13 There were 140,724 'first category' arrests in 1930 and 142,993 in 1931. The precise number of executions cannot be determined. Different records were kept, the period covered by some of these overlapped, and some were inaccurate. However, it is possible to make a reasonable estimate. One source records that the number of all OGPU executions in 1930 and 1931 was 20,201 and 10,651 respectively; another states that 18,966 'first category' kulaks were shot in 1930. Given that approximately the same number of arrests were made in 1931 as in 1930, the final total probably lies between 30,000 and 40,000. (I am much indebted to Lynne Viola for most of the data reproduced in this section, which she has extracted from Russian archive material.) Lynne Viola, *The Unknown Gulag: The Lost World of Stalin's Special Settlements* (Oxford: Oxford University Press, 2007), p.30.

14 'Kartashev, an OGPU investigator, willingly spoke of his part in persecuting kulaks', Yuri Druzhnikov, *Informer 001: The Myth of Pavlik Morozov* (trans. Sonia Melnikova) (New York: Rosen, 1993), p. 89.

15 Grossman, *Forever Flowing*, p. 145.

16 Conquest, *Harvest of Sorrow*, p. 136–7.

17 The total number of kulaks and others deported was 1,804,000. Census figures in 1932 showed only 1,317,000 deportees remained, a shortfall of 487,000. Of these it is estimated that 50 per cent had escaped and 50 per cent (243,000) had perished. Nicolas Werth, *Mass Crimes under Stalin* (1930-1953), [online] (2008), <http://www.sciencespo.fr/mass-violence-war-massacre-resistance/fr/node/2653>, accessed 24 January 2017.

18 Lynne Viola, 'The Other Archipelago: Kulak Deportations to the North in 1930', *Slavic Review*, 60:4 (winter, 2001), 735.

19 Designated 'Severny Krai' on 14 January 1929, and subsequently (5 December 1936) 'Severnaya oblast'.

20 Viola, 'The Other Archipelago', p. 740.

21 Ibid., p. 739.

22 Ibid., p. 741.

23 Robert Conquest, *The Harvest of Sorrow: Soviet Collectivisation and the Terror-Famine* (London: Hutchinson, 1986), p. 138.

24 Ibid.

25 Lynne Viola 'A Tale Of Two Men; Bergavinov, Tolmachev and the Bergavinov Commission', *Europe-Asia Studies*, 52:8 (2000), 1449–66, at p. 1451.

26 V. Tendryakov, 'Death', *Moskva*, 3 (1968), cited in Conquest, *Harvest of Sorrow*, p. 138. Tendryakov was born in Vologda in 1923. The city became a transit point for the kulak contingents as they arrived in the North. The inspiration for this scene in his novella may well derive from things either seen or heard of at an impressionable age. Tendryakov's fictional 'district capital' is named 'Vokhrovo', but this is presumed to represent Vologda, the real-life regional capital in which he lived.

27 Viola, *Unknown Gulag*, p. 49.
28 Viola, 'The Other Archipelago', p. 743.
29 Ibid.
30 Enclosure no. 1 in a letter of 25 February 1931 from ambassador Frederic M. Sackett, American Embassy, Berlin, to the Hon. Secretary of State, Washington. Records of the Department of State Relating to Internal Affairs of the Soviet Union, 1930-1939, NARA T1249, 861/5017-LIVING CONDITIONS/230, reproduced in *Fold3* (n.d.) <https://www.fold3.com/image/1/32577945> , accessed 20 January 2017.
31 Boris Pasternak, *Doctor Zhivago* (New York: Pantheon, 1958), p. 452.
32 Hugh Walpole (ed.), *Out of the Deep: Letters from Soviet Timber Camps* (London: Geoffrey Bles, 1933), p. 34.
33 Ibid., p. 90.
34 *New Statesman*, 25 January 1930.
35 *Report of the Annual Conference Held at Birmingham, April 1930* (London: Independent Labour Party, 1930), pp. 74–5.
36 *New Leader*, 7 February 1930.
37 British imports accounted for one-third of all Russian timber exports. TNA, FO 371/15591, N 4364/1/38.

Chapter 11

1 Commission on the Ukraine Famine, *Investigation of the Ukrainian Famine, 1932–1933: Report to Congress*, (Washington: United States Government Printing Office, 1987), pp. 100–3. Available online at *Hathi Trust* [digital library] (n.d.) <https://catalog.hathitrust.org/Record/001299877>, accessed 3 October 2016.
2 Ibid., p. 102.
3 Ibid., p. 103.
4 Ibid.
5 *The Ukrainian Weekly*, 7 December 1986, p. 5.
6 *Investigation of the Ukrainian Famine*, p. 101.
7 *The Ukrainian Weekly*, 7 December 1986, p. 5.

Chapter 12

1 Karl Marx and Friedrich Engels, *The Communist Manifesto*. Marx and Engels cite these words as accusations raised against Communism. It is not a misquote to attribute them to Marx and Engels because the sense of the passage makes it clear that they accept them as a true representation of their position. One anti-religious quotation frequently, but wrongly, ascribed to Marx is: 'We shall do well if we stir hatred and contempt against all existing institutions; we make war against all prevailing ideas of religion, of the state, of country, of patriotism. The idea of God is the keystone of perverted civilization; the true root of liberty, of equality, of culture, is atheism.' It is in fact from Wilhelm Marr's *Secret Societies in Switzerland* – see John Rae, *Contemporary Socialism* (2nd edn; New York: Charles Scribner & Sons, 1891), p. 136. The earliest misattribution I can find, ascribing it to Marx, is in 1901 in 'Assassination The Fruit of Socialism', *Fortnightly Review*, 70:418 (1 October 1901), 571–80. It also appears in the *London Monitor and New Era*, 10 September 1910, p. 2, and again in Cyprian Leycester Drawbridge, *Anti-Christian Socialism* (London: Longmans, Green & Co., 1915), p. 32. It is now frequently attributed to Marx unquestioned.
2 Friedrich Engels, 'The Eighteenth Century', *Vorwarts*, 71 (4 September 1844), cited in *Marxists Internet Archive* (n.d.) <http://marxists.anu.edu.au/archive/marx/works/1844/condition-england/ch01.htm>, accessed 5 November 2015.
3 V. I. Lenin to Maxim Gorky, 13 or 14 November 1913 (trans. Andrew Rothstein), in Lenin, *Collected Works*, 45 vols (Moscow: Progress Publishers, 1976), vol. 35, pp. 121–4.
4 Stalin, 'Questions and Answers to American Trade Unionists: Stalin's Interview with the First American Trade Union Delegation to Soviet Russia', *Pravda*, 15 September 1927, reproduced in *Marxists Internet Archive* (2005) < https://www.marxists.org/reference/archive/stalin/works/1927/09/15.htm>, accessed 22 January 2017.
5 'The question has previously always been: What is God? And German philosophy has answered the question in this sense: God is man.' Friedrich Engels, 'Review of Past and Present by Thomas

Carlyle, London 1843', *Deutsch-Franzosische Jahrbucher*, January 1844, reproduced in *Marxists Internet Archive* (1996) <https://www.marxists.org/archive/marx/works/1844/df-jahrbucher/carlyle.htm>, accessed 22 January 2017.

6   Friedrich Engels, *Anti-Duhrung: Herr Duhrungs Revolution in Science* (1877), ch. 11, reproduced in *Marxists Internet Archive* (1996) <https://www.marxists.org/archive/marx/works/1877/anti-duhring/>, accessed 22 January 2017.

7   *Dictatorship vs Democracy, Terrorism and Communism: A Reply to Karl Kautsky* (New York: Workers Party of America, 1922), p. 63. Trotsky's words are more well known in their widely quoted modern translation, often without a source reference: 'We must put an end once and for all to the Papist-Quaker babble about the sanctity of human life.' (e.g. in Orlando Figes, *A People's Tragedy*, p. 641)

8   Lenin, 'The Tasks of the Youth Leagues' (speech at The Third All-Russia Congress of The Russian Young Communist League, 2 October 1920), *Pravda* 5-7 October 1920, reproduced in *Marxists Internet Archive*, (1999) < https://www.marxists.org/archive/lenin/works/1920/oct/02.htm > accessed 22 January 2017.

9   *The Young Guard: The Life of the Komsomol* is cited as such, with the date 1927, in *A Challenge to Christendom – Facts about the Russian Persecutions and the Communist Attitude to Religion* (London: Christian Protest Movement, 1930). LPL, Canon J. A. Douglas Papers, vol. 42, p. 211. Molodaya Gvardiya ('The Young Guard'), founded in 1922, was the magazine of the Komsomol, the Soviet political youth organisation. It is presumed that 'Life of the Komsomol' was an article in the magazine.

10   Trotsky, *Dictatorship vs Democracy*, p. 64.

11   Solzhenitsyn quotes Latsis via S. P. Melgunov, *The Red Terror in Russia* (London: J. M. Dent & Sons, 1925), who comments: 'Latsis was not original here, he simply rephrased the words of Robespierre about the mass terror: "To execute the enemies of the Fatherland, it is sufficient to establish their identities. Not punishment but elimination is required"' (Alexander Solzhenitsyn, *Dvesti let vmeste* ('Two Hundred Years Together'), p. 140–41, available in *Internet Archive* [digital archive] (n.d.) <https://archive.org/details/Solzhenitsyn200YearsTogether>. accessed 31 December 2016). Melgunov's authority comes because he was a Russian Socialist politician who saw the Revolution at first hand and then fled Russia in 1922. His book was first published in Berlin in 1923 under the title *Krasnyj terror v Rossii 1918-1923 (Красный террор в России 1918-1923)*.

12   Trotsky, *Between Red and White. A Study of Some Fundamental Questions of Revolution* (1922), ch. 4, *Marxists Internet Archive* (28 April 2007) <https://www.marxists.org/archive/trotsky/1922/red-white/ch04.htm>, accessed 2 November 2010.

13   Bullard, diary, 11 September 1932. Bullard heard of the comment from Geoffrey Wilson.

14   Lenin, 'Socialism and Religion', *Novaya Zhizn*, 28 (3 December 1905), *Marxists Internet Archive* (2000) <https://www.marxists.org/archive/lenin/works/1905/dec/03.htm >, accessed 22 January 2017.

15   Marx, 'Introduction', *Zur Kritik der Hegelschen Rechtsphilosophie* [Critique of the Hegelian Philosophy of Law] *Deutsch-Französische Jahrbücher* (7, 10 February 1844), reproduced in *Marxists Internet Archive* (February 2005; corrected 2009) <https://www.marxists.org/archive/marx/works/1843/critique-hpr/intro.htm>, accessed 2 November 2015.

16   Engels, 'Review of Past and Present'.

17   V. I. Lenin to Maxim Gorky, 13 or 14 November 1913 (trans. Andrew Rothstein), in Lenin, *Collected Works*, 45 vols (Moscow: Progress Publishers, 1976), vol. 35, pp. 121–4.

18   Bertram D. Wolfe, 'V. L. Lenin and Maxim Gorky: Study of a Stormy Friendship' in *Society and History: Essays in Honor of Karl August Wittfogel*, ed. G. L. Ulman (The Hague: Mouton, 1978), 281–310, at p. 309, n. 33.

Chapter 13

1   *New Leader*, 18 January 1929.

2   Paul Bickley, *Building Jerusalem: Christianity and the Labour Party* (Swindon: Bible Society, 2010), p. 23.

3   Tony Blair, 'Preface', in Graham Dale, *God's Politicians: The Christian Contribution to 100 Years of Labour* (London: Harper Collins, 2000), p. x.

4   Dale, *God's Politicians*, pp. 59–64. Dale describes MacDonald as a Unitarian. As Unitarians deny the central Christian doctrine of the Trinity, they are considered heterodox in Christian terms. To claim MacDonald as a Christian socialist is therefore rather tenuous.

5   Bob Holman, 'Keir Hardie', *Third Way*, November 1992, p. 23. Holman also suggests that over time Hardie became less of a churchgoer.

6   Neil Riddell, 'The Catholic Church and the Labour Party, 1918–1931', *Twentieth Century British History*, 8:2 (1977), 165–93, at p. 178.

7   Mark Bevir, 'The Labour Church Movement, 1891–1902', *Journal of British Studies*, 38 (April 1999), 217–45.

8   Ibid., p. 142.

9   Henry Pelling, *The Origins of the Labour Party, 1880-1900* (London: Macmillan, 1954); Henry Pelling, *A Short History of the Labour Party* (London: Macmillan, 1961).

10 Pelling, *The Origins of the Labour Party*, p. 125. Another scholar, Peter Catterall, concurs: 'The Liberal party was the traditional ally of the free churches'. 'Morality and Politics: The Free Churches and the Labour Party between the Wars', *Historical Journal*, 36 (1993), 667–85, at p. 667.

11 E. P. Thompson, 'Homage to Tom Maguire' in Asa Briggs and John Saville (eds), *Essays in Labour History: In Memory of G. D. H. Cole* (London: Macmillan, 1960), p. 289.

12 Leonard Smith, *Religion and the Rise of Labour: Nonconformity and the Independent Labour Movement in Lancashire and the West Riding, 1880-1914* (Keele: Ryburn, 1993), p. 30.

13 *The British Congregationalist*, 24 February 1910, cited in W. C. R. Hancock, 'No Compromise: Nonconformity and Politics 1893-1914', *Baptist Quarterly*, 36:2 (April 1995), 56–68, at p. 57.

14 Graham Johnson, 'British Social Democracy and Religion, 1881-1911', *Journal of Ecclesiastical History*, 51 (January 2000), 94–115, at p. 104.

15 E. H. Hobsbawm, *Primitive Rebels: Studies in Archaic Forms of Social Movement in the 19th and 20th Centuries* (Manchester: Manchester University Press, 1959), p. 149.

16 Catterall, 'Morality and Politics', p. 670. In apparent contradiction to this statement, Catterall includes data (table 2, p. 677) which claims that over 40 per cent of Labour MPs in 1929 were 'Nonconformist'. The source for the data is given only as 'denominational and local press of the period' and cannot be checked. It is unclear if these were active self-identifying Nonconformists or only nominal members, claiming faith in the manner many non-churchgoers describe themselves as 'C of E', or claimed as members by over-enthusiastic chapels which they formerly attended, a tendency noted by Hobsbawm (*Primitive Rebels*, p. 128) and Smith (*Religion and the Rise of Labour*, p. 11). Catterall also states that the 122 'Nonconformist' Labour MPs comprised 48.61 per cent of those elected in 1929. Parliamentary records show that 287 Labour MPs were elected in 1929, which means that the correct figure should be 42.50 per cent. 'Research Paper 04/61', *UK Election Statistics: 1918–2004* (London: House of Commons Library, 2004), p. 10.

17 Neil Riddell, 'The Catholic Church and the Labour Party'.

18 Leo XIII, *Rerum Novarum. Encyclical on Capital and Labour, 15 May 1891* (Vatican: The Holy See, 1891).

19 *The Tablet*, 15 March 1930, p. 327, cited in Riddell, 'The Catholic Church', p. 171.

20 *London Catholic Herald*, 7 May 1927, cited in Riddell, 'The Catholic Church', p. 175.

21 Pius XI, *Quadragesimo Anno. Encyclical Letter on the Reconstruction of the Social Order, 15 May 1931* (Vatican: The Holy See, 1931).

22 Hansard, HC Deb, 17 July 1929, vol. 230, col. 405.

23 Hansard, HC Deb, 26 March 1930, vol. 237, col. 541.

24 E.g. John Bromley MP: 'The Baptist sect in Russia has increased since the Revolution out of all proportions of what it was in the old days', Hansard, HC Deb, 5 November 1929, vol. 231, col. 941.

25 Hansard, HC Deb, 17 July 1929, vol. 230, col. 405.

26 Hansard, HC Deb, 24 March 1930, vol. 237, col. 63.

27 *The Times*, 30 April 1930.

28 TNA, FO 371/14842, N 1526/23/38.

29 Hansard, HC Deb, 30 April 1930, vol. 238, col. 177. If, as seems likely, Henderson did intervene in the wording of the request that Ovey report on Soviet religious persecution, this would have indicated some private awareness of the Russian Baptists' plight which he did not express in public. See 'Cypher Telegram to Sir E. Ovey No. 56', 18 February 1930. The document is unnumbered, but can be found after TNA, FO 371/14841, N 911/23/38.

30 Dale's chapter on Lansbury implies this. *God's Politicians*, p. 106–17.

31 Bickley, *Building Jerusalem*, p. 32.

32 As was Ramsay MacDonald, for whom erroneous claims of conventional religious belief have been made on account of his membership (with Lansbury) of the South Place Ethical Church. Dale, *God's Politicians*, p. 60.

33 Lansbury, *My Life*, p. 6.

34 Margaret Cole, 'Lansbury, George' in *Dictionary of Labour Biography*, ed. Bellamy, Saville et al., vol. 2, p. 215. Cole writes that Lansbury joined the Theosophists at the end of his life. Lansbury himself indicates that he was warmly disposed to Annie Besant and Theosophy from the 1890s. Lansbury, *My Life*, p. 78.

35 Lansbury, *My Life*, p. 231.

36 Ibid.: 'In 1920 [there was] complete freedom of worship and freedom of opinion and expression as long as in the practice of these there was no organized attack on the Soviet Government'.

37 'It now appears that the diamonds brought by Kamenev were disposed of by Mrs Glassman, the mother-in-law of Edgar Lansbury, and that they were actually displayed in Edgar Lansbury's house. As George Lansbury breakfasts with his son every morning it is inconceivable that he was ignorant of the transaction.' TNA, CAB 24/11, CP 1885, 23 Sept. 1920, RROUK no. 73.

38 Lansbury, *My Life*, pp. 251, 260.

39 George Lansbury, 'Preface' in W. P. Coates, *More Anti-Soviet Lies Nailed*, p. 7.

40 The argument that the Church authorities' attempt to do so amounted to 'ecclesiastical McCarthyism' seems somewhat contrived. Dianne Kirby, 'Ecclesiastical McCarthyism: Cold War Repression in the Church of England', *Contemporary British History*, 19:2 (2005), 187–203.

41 Hobsbawm, *Primitive Rebels*, p. 149.

42 Sidney Webb, 'The Basis of Socialism (Historic)' in Shaw and Webb, *Fabian Essays in Socialism* (London: Fabian Society, 1889), 30-61, p. 36.

43 *New Leader*, 21 February 1930.

44 *New Leader*, 29 November 1929.

45 Hansard, HC Deb, 7 April 1933, vol. 276 col. 2111.

46 Denis Lawton, *Education and Labour Party Ideologies, 1900–2001 and Beyond* (London: Routledge, 2005), p. 23.

47 Edward Royle, *Radicals, Secularists, and Republicans: Popular Freethought in Britain, 1866-1915* (Manchester: Manchester University Press, 1980), p. 315.

48 *The Tablet*, 8 August 1908.

49 Royle, *Radicals, Secularists, and Republicans*, p. 316.

50 *The Tablet*, 2 September 1911.

51 Charles Trevelyan to Bertrand Russell (May 1929), Trevelyan Papers, Newcastle University Library, CPT.138, cited in Riddell, *The Catholic Church*, p.184.

52 *Report of the Annual Conference, 1932* (London: Independent Labour Party, 1932).

53 S. Harrison, *Alex Gossip* (London: Lawrence and Wishart, 1962), pp. 36–7.

54 'Socialist Precepts' in *Socialist Sunday Schools: Aims, Objects and Organisation* (n.p.: National Council of British Socialist Sunday Schools, 1920), inside front cover.

55 *Socialist Sunday Schools*, pp. 12, 5, 2, 1.

56 *The Times*, 1 February 1923.

57 Tom Anderson, *How to Open and Conduct a Proletarian Sunday School* (Glasgow, n.d. [1920?]), cited in *Danger Ahead: Socialist and Proletarian Sunday Schools* (London: British Empire Union, 1922), p. 4.

58 'The Ten Proletarian Maxims' in Tom Anderson, *The Proletarian Catechism* (Glasgow: The Proletarian Press, 1931), inside front cover.

59 For example, 'The Glasgow Schools', a series of events and performances in celebration of the Socialist and Proletarian Sunday School movements, was part of the Glasgow International Festival of Visual Art, 20 April to 7 May 2012.

60 Butcher had been elevated to the House of Lords as Lord Danesfort and his bill was re-introduced there, as was The Seditious and Blasphemous Teaching to Children Bill. Hansard, HL Deb, 3 July 1924, vol. 58 cols 158–201.

61 BEU, 1924 annual report, pp. 11, 29, cited in Thomas, 'Confronting the Challenge', p. 30.

62 *Literary Guide*, April 1924.

63 'Glass Houses', *Literary Guide*, April 1930.

64 *Holmes-Laski Letters: The Correspondence of Mr. Justice Holmes and Harold J. Laski, 1916–1935*, ed. Mark De Wolfe Howe (Cambridge, Mass.: Harvard University Press, 1953), pp. 938–41.

Chapter 14

1 Lenin to Molotov (19 March 1922). *The Unknown Lenin: From the Secret Archive*, ed. Richard Pipes, David Brandenberger and Catherine A. Fitzpatrick (New Haven: Yale University Press, 1996), p. 153.
2 Yakovlev, *A Century of Violence in Soviet Russia*, p. 160.
3 *The Unknown Lenin*, p. 152.
4 Dimitry V. Pospielovsky, *The Russian Church under the Soviet Regime, 1917–1982*, 2 vols (Crestwood, NY: St Vladimir's Seminary Press, 1984), vol. 1, pp. 94–6.
5 Yakovlev, *A Century of Violence in Soviet Russia*, p. 159. Yakovlev does not name his source beyond 'an official announcement on 28th March, 1922'.
6 Pospielovsky, *A History of Soviet Atheism*, vol. 2 (*Soviet Antireligious Campaigns and Persecutions*), p. 60.
7 Yemelyanov, [Estimation of the Statistics of the Persecutions].
8 Dispatch from Ovey quoting M. Rabinovitch of the Commissariat of Trade (18 February 1930). Cited in K. Bourne, D. Cameron Watt and D. Lieven (eds), *British Documents on Foreign Affairs: Reports and Papers from the Foreign Office Confidential Print. Part II, From the First to the Second World War. Series A, The Soviet Union, 1917–1939*, 15 vols (Frederick, Md. University Publications of America, 1984–86), vol. 10 (*The Soviet Union, May 1930–December 1931*), p. 324.
9 'Instructions as to Elections' (4 November 1926), cited in Lord Charnwood (Godfrey Benson, 1st Baron Charnwood), 'Memorandum on the Oppression of Religion in Russia' (March 1931), Lambeth Palace Library, Cosmo Gordon Lang Papers, vol. 74, pp. 170–212.
10 *Bezbozhnik* [The Godless], 24 November 1929, cited in Charnwood, 'Memorandum'.
11 [Cmd. 3511] *Russia no. 1 (1930). Decree of the All-Russian Central Executive Committee and the Council of People's Commissars respecting religious associations* (London: HMSO, 1930).
12 Report of 'Father Simeon' to the CPM council meeting, 17 November 1932. LPL, Canon J. A. Douglas Papers, vol. 42, p. 233.
13 For more details, see Pospielovsky, *A History of Soviet Atheism*, vol. 2 (*Soviet Antireligious Campaigns and Persecutions*), pp. 62–3.
14 Ibid., p. 63.
15 *Information Bulletin on Religion and Morality in the USSR*, 3 (July 1930), copy in LPL, Lang Papers, vol. 74, p. 137. The work of the Information Service was partly financed by Prebendary Gough's Christian Protest Movement, which is discussed in Chapter 22.
16 Ibid.
17 Stalin, 'Questions and Answers to American Trade Unionists'.
18 Quoted by Viscount Brentford, Hansard, HL Deb, 4 December 1929, vol. 75, col. 901, and Cosmo Lang, Hansard, HL Deb, 2 April 1930, vol. 76, col. 1135.
19 Charnwood, 'Memorandum', p. 37.
20 Ibid., p. 39.
21 Conquest, *Harvest of Sorrow*, p. 375.
22 J. B. S. Haldane, 'The Alleged Persecution in Russia', *Literary Guide*, May 1930 (The *Literary Guide* was the journal of the Rationalist Press Association, London).
23 Yemelyanov, [Estimation of the Statistics of the Persecutions], and Yakovlev, *A Century of Violence in Soviet Russia*, p. 165.
24 Pospielovsky, *A History of Soviet Atheism*, vol. 2 (*Soviet Antireligious Campaigns and Persecutions*), p. 64.
25 Yakovlev, *A Century of Violence in Soviet Russia*, p. 164.
26 [On the Characteristics of Kulak Farms Subject to the Labour Code] in Dimitry V. Pospielovsky, *A History of Soviet Atheism*, vol. 1 (*A History of Marxist-Leninist Atheism and Soviet Antireligious Policies*), p. 44.

Part III

1 *Antireligious Activity in Soviet Russia – Non-Political Bulletin Based on Information Contained in the Soviet Press*, 1-2 (July 1930), p. 53. A copy of this bulletin was sent by Sir Bernard Pares to Arthur Henderson on 15 July 1930: see TNA, FO 371/14860, N 4897/23/38. Four other churches in the monastery complex were also destroyed: the Spassov (1591), Znamenskaya (1677), Tilkhvinskaya (*c*.1680), and Soshestvia Sv. Dukha (*c*.1700).

2 Ibid.

3 From *The Godless* by Scheinmann, a co-worker of Yaroslavsky's. *The Godless, c.1929* [typescript] cited in LPL, Douglas Papers, vol. 42, p. 375

4 *Report of the Annual Conference Held at Scarborough, April 1931* (London: Independent Labour Party, 1931), p. 45.

Chapter 15

1 Hansard, HC Deb, 17 July 1929, vol. 230, col. 405.

2 *Stalin's Letters to Molotov 1925–1936*, ed. Lars T. Lih, Oleg V. Naumov and Oleg V. Klevniuk (New Haven: Yale University Press, 1995), letter 47 (to Molotov, 9 September 1929), p. 177–8.

3 See, for example, Hansard, HC Deb, 26 March 1930, vol. 237, cols 526–69; HL Deb, 12 November 1930, vol. 79, cols 95–130; HC Deb, 18 May 1931, vol. 252, cols 1619–87. Complaints over Soviet wireless broadcasts to Britain are raised in TNA, FO 371/15592, N 4653/4/38, N 5061/4/38, and N 5543/4/38 – all of July 1931.

4 Madeira, *Britannia and the Bear*, p. 39; John Callaghan and Kevin Morgan, 'The Open Conspiracy of the Communist Party and the Case of W. N. Ewer, Communist and Anti-Communist', *Historical Journal*, 49:2 (2006), 549–64.

5 London School of Economics, British Library of Political and Economic Science, *Diary, correspondence and papers of Hugh Dalton, 1887–1962*. Entries for 17 and 29 June 1929.

6 Ibid., 13 July 1929.

7 Ibid., 10, 13 and 15 July 1929.

8 'Uncle asks my view of W's reliability. I say that he's all right if you want him to leak to the Russians, but not otherwise'. Ibid., 10 July 1929.

9 Hansard, HC Deb, 5 November 1929, vol. 231, col. 905.

10 *Forward*, 14 October 1922. Cited in Arthur Henry Lane, *The Alien Menace* (London: Boswell, 1934), p. vi. Also mentioned by Edward Marjoribanks MP, Hansard, HC Deb, 5 November 1929, vol. 231, col. 934.

11 Hansard, HC Deb, 5 November 1929, vol. 231, cols 941, 949.

12 A. Haycock in Hansard, HC Deb, 5 November 1929, vol. 231, cols 973–4.

13 TNA, CAB 23, 47(29), 13 November 1929.

14 TNA, CAB 23, 51(29), 3 December 1929.

15 Hansard, HC Deb, 10 December 1929, vol. 233, col. 231.

16 Ibid.

17 Hansard, HC Deb, 16 December 1929, vol. 233, cols 945–6.

18 LPL, Lang papers, vol. 73, p. 20. Letter to Evelyn Hubbard (20 October 1929).

19 LPL, Lang papers, vol. 73, p. 24. Letter to Father Timotheieff (27 November 1929).

20 Hansard, HL Deb, 4 December 1929, vol. 75, cols 899–900.

21 Hansard, HL Deb, 4 December 1929, vol. 75, col. 901. Cited by Lord Brentford, joint president of the Christian Protest Movement. The League's membership peaked at 5.6 million in 1932. In 1931, the weekly circulation of *Bezbozhnik* in the Soviet Union was 500,000.

22 *New Leader*, 9 January 1931. For more examples of Lunacharsky's vehemently anti-religious speeches, see Pospielovsky, *A History of Soviet Atheism*, vol. 1 (*History of Marxist-Leninist Atheism*), p. 52–3.

23 LPL, Lang papers, vol. 73, p. 65. Letter from Archbishop Eulogius (22 December 1929).

24 LPL, Lang papers, vol. 73, p. 31. Letter from J. H. Rushbrooke (6 December 1929).

25 London Metropolitan Archives (LMA), Brompton Parish Church Collection (BPCC), P84/TRI2/200. 'From the "News" April 23, 1897', in 'The Rev. Alfred W. Gough, The New Vicar of Brompton' [pamphlet] (c.1899), p. 3.

26 LMA/BPCC, P84/TRI2/200. 'Noted Churchman Dead' (undated, unidentified press cutting, probably early October 1931).

27 LMA/BPCC, P84/TRI2/200. Brig. Sir Henry Page-Croft MP, 'Prebendary Gough and the Empire' in *Tributes to Prebendary A. W. Gough*.

28 Alfred Gough, *The Lure of Simplicity* (London: E. Nash & Grayson, 1929), p.13.

29 LMA/BPCC, P84/TRI2/200, *Brompton Parish Church Magazine*, 564 (January 1930). This change, engineered by Gough, casts doubt upon M. Ruotsila's dismissal of Gough as the anti-Semitic 'cleric of the nascent British fascists'. M. Ruotsila, 'The Antisemitism of the Eighth Duke of

Northumberland's the *Patriot*, 1922–1930', *Journal of Contemporary History* 39:1 (2004), 179–215, at p. 88. The final prayers written for the Day of Prayer in March 1930, in which Gough played a major role, included those 'for the Jews of Russia who, with the Christian church, are suffering persecution for righteousness [*sic*] sake'. Furthermore, the Chief Rabbi was one of the vice-presidents of Gough's Christian Protest Movement and a speaker at CPM rallies. The marked contrast between benign British fascists and their violent, more extreme Italian counterparts is highlighted in Thomas Linehan, *British Fascism*, p. 55.

30 LMA/BPCC, P84/TRI2/200, *Brompton Parish Church Magazine*, 565 (February 1930).

31 LMA/BPCC, P84/TRI2/200, *Brompton Parish Church Magazine*, 564 (January 1930).]

32 LPL, Lang Papers, vol. 73, pp. 39–40. Letter to Prebendary Gough (12 December 1929).

33 LPL, Lang Papers, vol. 73, p. 55. Letter from Leonard White-Thompson, Bishop of Ely (14 December 1929).

34 LPL, Lang Papers, vol. 73, pp. 46, 56. Letter to Charles D'Arcy, the Archbishop of Armagh (13 December 1929); letter from Charles D'Arcy (14 December 1929).

35 LPL, Lang Papers, vol. 73, p. 63. Letter to Arthur Henderson (18 December 1929).

36 LPL, Lang Papers, vol. 73, p. 71. Letter from Arthur Henderson (24 December 1929).

37 LMA/BPCC, P84/TRI2/200. 'The Cross of St George' (unidentified press cutting, December 1929).

38 *Manchester Guardian*, 20 December 1929.

39 Ibid.

40 LMA/BPCC P84/TRI2/200. *Brompton Parish Church Magazine*, 567 (April 1930).

41 LPL, Lang Papers, vol. 75, p. 89. *Christian Protest Movement, Review of Four Years' Work* (London: Christian Protest Movement, 1933).

42 *The Times*, 12 February 1931.

43 How 'tireless' is evidenced from Gough's own admission, in September 1930, at which time his health had begun to fail under the strain of the work, that he had not taken a single day off during the first seven months of the campaign. LMA/BPCC P84/TRI2/200. 'Notes by the Vicar', *Brompton Parish Church Magazine*, 572 (September 1930).

Chapter 16

1 LSE/BLPES, Dalton, *Diary*, 10 June 1929.

2 Ibid., 29 June 1929.

3 Hugh Dalton, *The Capital Levy Explained* (London: Labour Publishing, 1923).

4 LSE/BLPES, Dalton, *Diary*, 8 November 1929.

5 Ibid. Osborne had also said that he would happily serve in Moscow in spite of this. Lindsay remarked that this was proof of his objectivity, but Dalton recorded that he would ensure that Henderson vetoed this appointment if it was proposed by the Foreign Office.

6 Private communications from former senior diplomats, who found Dalton's intervention surprising.

7 TNA, CAB 23, 47(29), 13 November 1929.

8 There is an interesting postscript to this affair. In 1943, lifelong Communists W. P. and Zelda Coates published *A History of Anglo-Soviet Relations*. The book is often used by unwitting historians as a handbook to the events of that time. The picture it gives, however, is frequently misleading. Kamenev was shot in 1936 and, in common with others who shared the same fate, he became a 'non-person' in the Soviet Union. See Appendix 3.

9 *Beatrice Webb's Typescript diary*, 2 June 1932 (p. 178), *LSE Digital Library* [online] (n.d.) <http://digital.library.lse.ac.uk/objects/lse:nut827hel?id=lse%3Anut827hel#page/178/mode/2up>, accessed 29 September 2016.

10 Rhea Clyman, the journalist, in conversation with Beatrice Webb. Ibid., 9 April 1932 (p. 173). <http://digital.library.lse.ac.uk/objects/lse:nut827hel/read/single#page/72/mode/2up>, accessed 3 January 2017.

11 Bullard, diary, 12 July 1933.

12 Ibid., 18 January 1932.

13 Ibid., 19 February and 14 October 1932.

14 Ibid., 16 and 17 November 1932.

15 Gareth Jones, 'Soviet Dwindling Trade', *Western Mail*, 6 April 1933, reproduced in *Gareth Richard Vaughan Jones, Hero of Ukraine (1905–1935)* [website] (n.d.) <www.garethjones.org/soviet_articles/soviet_dwindling_trade.htm>, accessed 7 December 2008.

16 Bullard, diary, 19 February1932. Walker was writing from Moscow to Bullard in Leningrad.
17 LSE/BLPES, Dalton, *Diary*, 20 March 1930.
18 Ibid., 24 March 1930.
19 His four articles were published in *New Leader* in March 1928.

Chapter 17

1 Bullard said the same, calling it 'the life of a fish in an aquarium' in his diary, 17 November 1931.
2 [Cmd. 3467] [Russia No. 2 (1929).] *Notes exchanged on the resumption of Diplomatic Relations with the USSR* (London: HMSO, January, 1930). The first protocol was signed on 3 October 1929 in Paris, and 'Notes exchanged', the final agreement, on 20 December 1929.
3 [Cmd. 1869] [Russia No. 2 (1923).] *Correspondence between His Majesty's government and the Soviet government respecting relations between the two governments* (London: HMSO, 1923), p. 4.
4 TNA FO 371/14840, N 631/23/38.
5 TNA FO 371/14841, N 1004/23/38.
6 [Cmd. 3552] *Temporary commercial agreement between the United Kingdom and Russia* (London: HMSO, 1930). It was finally signed on 16 April 1930.
7 TNA FO 371/14840, N 630/23/38.
8 Source for all statistics: Yemelyanov, [Estimation of the Statistics of the Persecutions].
9 TNA FO 371/14840, N 836/23/38.
10 TNA FO 371/14842, N 1396/23/38.

Chapter 18

1 TNA CAB 23, 10(30), 12 February 1930.
2 Hansard, HC Deb, 13 February 1930, vol. 235, col. 608.
3 Hansard, HL Deb, 13 February 1930, vol. 76, col. 588.
4 Hansard, HL Deb, *13 February 1930, vol. 76, cols 578–81.*
5 *The Diary of Beatrice Webb*, ed. N. and J. MacKenzie, 4 vols (London: Virago/London School of Economics and Political Science, 1982–85), vol. 3, p. 346.
6 TNA FO 371/14841, N 1007/23/38.
7 *Cypher Telegram to Sir E. Ovey No. 56* (18 February 1930). The document is unnumbered but can be found after TNA FO 371, N 911/23/38.
8 LSE/BLPES, Dalton, *Diary*, 18 February 1930.
9 TNA FO 371/14841, N 1256/23/38.
10 TNA FO 371/14841, N1200/23/38.
11 Beatrice was greatly taken by Sokolnikov and described him in her diary as a 'singularly sympathetic man'. *Beatrice Webb's Typescript diary*, 3 August 1930 (p. 244), *LSE Digital Library* [online] (n.d.) <http://digital.library.lse.ac.uk/objects/lse:qux395wip/read/single#page/244/mode/2up >, accessed 22 January 2017. Sokolnikov did not last long after his return to Russia. Arrested in 1936, he was imprisoned after a show trial in January 1937, and was killed in a labour camp in 1939, ostensibly by a fellow inmate, but in fact on orders from the NKVD.
12 TNA FO 371/14841, N 1200/23/38.

Chapter 19

1 TNA FO 371/14841, N 1183/23/38
2 TNA FO 371/14843, N2273/23/38.
3 Robert Conquest, *Harvest of Sorrow*, p. 136.
4 TNA FO 371/14842, N 2273/23/38.
5 Ibid.
6 TNA FO 371/14842, N 2120/23/38.
7 Durham Cathedral Library, Papers of Hensley Henson, Bishop of Durham, vol. HHH52 (1 January–31 May 1931), diary entry for Thursday, 5 February 1931.
8 Ovey's report is to be found in TNA FO 371/14842, N 1390/23/38. It is dated 24 February 1930, and was received in London on 3 March 1930.
9 LSE/BLPES, Dalton, *Diary*, 3 March 1930.
10 TNA CAB 23, 11(30), 19 February 1930.

11 A few months later, the Anglican Bishop of Korea passed through Moscow and attempted to dis-
    cuss the religious persecution with Ovey, but he appears to have been rebuffed. He reported to
    the archbishop that Ovey showed absolutely no interest in getting involved in the matter. By way
    of explanation, he added that Ovey was 'not a Churchman'. LPL, Lang Papers, vol. 74, p. 135.
    Memorandum on meeting with Bishop Embling (17 July 1930).
12 Michael Bourdeaux, *Faith on Trial in Russia* (London: Hodder & Stoughton, 1971), p. 45, 50.
13 Conquest, *Harvest of Sorrow*, p. 202.
14 Pospielovsky, *A History of Soviet Atheism*, vol. 1 (*History of Marxist-Leninist Atheism*), p. 41.
15 Chaim Lavshai, 'Minsk, Jerusalem of White Russia' (trans. Jerrold Landau), in *Minsk, ir va-em*
    ('Minsk, Jewish Mother-City'), Shlomo Even-Shoshan (ed.), 2 vols (Jerusalem: Association of
    Olim from Minsk and its Surroundings, 1975-85), vol 1, p. 148. *Yizkor Book Project* [online re-
    source] (27 March 2011) <http://www.jewishgen.org/Yizkor/minsk/min2_148.html>, accessed 20
    January 2017.
16 LSE/BLPES, Dalton, *Diary*, 19 December 1929.
17 Ibid., 11 March 1930.
18 Ibid. (undated [3–9 March 1930])
19 Hansard, HC Deb, 3 February 1930, vol. 234, col. 1474.
20 LSE/BLPES, Dalton, *Diary*, 3 March 1929.

Chapter 20
1   The CPM resolution at the first Albert Hall rally in December 1929 ran as follows: 'This meeting of
    worshippers of Almighty God vehemently protests against the persistent and cruel persecution of
    our fellow-worshippers in Russia and calls upon believers in God and lovers of liberty throughout
    the world to pray and work unceasingly for the religious freedom of the people of Russia ... [and
    that] the British Government be urged to make the strongest possible representations to the Soviet
    Government to bring this persecution to an end'. LMA/BPCC, P84/TRI2/200, *Brompton Parish
    Church Magazine*, 564 (January 1930).
2   TNA FO 371/14841, N 1016/23/38 contains the summary by ambassador Chilton in Rome to Hen-
    derson on 13 February 1930. The Pope's call for prayer was not only for Russian believers but more
    broadly for 'the release of our dear Russian people'.
3   *The Times*, 13 February 1930.
4   *The Times*, 1 March 1930.
5   Sidney Webb, 'The Basis of Socialism (Historic)', p. 36.
6   TNA, CAB 23, 11(30), 19 February 1930.
7   LPL, Lang Papers, vol. 73, p. 176. Letter to Rev. Mervyn Haigh, Lang's private secretary, from the
    Very Rev. A. C. S. Jarvis, Army Chaplain General (25 February 1930).
8   *The Times*, 3 March 1930.
9   *Daily Telegraph*, 28 February 1930.
10 LPL, Lang Papers, vol. 73, p. 191. Letter from William Temple, Archbishop of York (2 March
    1930).
11 LPL, Lang Papers, vol. 73, p. 198. Letter to Temple (5 March 1930).
12 Hansard, HC Deb, 4 March 1930, vol. 236, col. 255.
13 Hansard, HL Deb, 6 March 1930, vol. 76, cols 806–40.
14 LPL, Lang Papers, vol. 73, p. 225. Letter from Ramsay MacDonald (7 March 1930).
15 LPL, Lang Papers, vol. 73, p. 234. Letter to Ramsay MacDonald (8 March 1930).
16 *Manchester Guardian*, 17 March 1930.
17 Ibid.
18 Ibid.
19 Ibid.
20 Ibid.
21 Ibid.
22 *The Times*, 15 March 1930.
23 *Time Magazine*, 17 February 1930.
24 TNA, FO 371/14842, N 1950/23/38.
25 *The Times*, 20 February 1931.
26 *The Times*, 17 March 1931.

27 *Time Magazine*, 10 March 1931.
28 *Morning Post*, 15 July 1930.

Chapter 21

1   *The Times*, 13 February 1930.
2   *Manchester Guardian*, 28 February 1930.
3   *Information Bulletin on Religion and Morality in the USSR*, 2 (June 1930). Copy in LPL, Lang Papers, vol. 74, p. 57.
4   *The Times*, 17 March 1930.
5   *Manchester Guardian*, 10 March 1930.
6   *Manchester Guardian*, 8 March 1930.
7   *The Times*, 24 February 1930.
8   For example, the paper's dismissal of Lord Phillimore's bill (see Chapter 32) as an 'attempt to drape an ethical cloak round a purely interested motive. The Bill is just one more case of [trade] Protection masquerading as virtue'. *Manchester Guardian*, 25 June 1931.
9   *The Times*, 30 July 1930.
10 Quoted in *New Leader*, 18 May 1923, cited in F. M. Leventhal, 'H. N. Brailsford and the New Leader', *Journal of Contemporary History*, 9:1 (January 1974), 91–113, at p. 91.
11 Kingsley Martin, *Editor: A Second Volume of Autobiography* (London: Hutchinson, 1968), p. 131.
12 *The Labour Party and the I. L. P.: The Clear Issue* (London: Labour Party, 1932), p. 1.
13 W. P. Coates, 'Russian Fairy Tales – the Latest Stunt', *New Leader*, 6 (March 1931).
14 An outspoken atheist, Joad converted to Christianity at the end of his life, telling the story in *The Recovery of Belief* (London: Faber, 1952).
15 *New Leader*, 17 January 1930.
16 *New Leader*, 14 February 1930.
17 *New Leader*, 21 February 1930.
18 *Daily Herald*, 27 February 1930. At this time, the deportation of the kulaks had been proceeding for about three weeks. On 23 February, owing to the large number of frostbite cases, especially among children, the OGPU was forced temporarily to suspend its operation of transporting the exiles deep into the Urals interior. The temperature would have been -20°C (-4°F) or below.
19 Amabel Williams-Ellis, in common with a number of Soviet enthusiasts, was also a supporter of the militantly atheist Rationalist Press Association.
20 Neill Harvey-Smith, 'H. N. Brailsford' in *Dictionary of Labour Biography*, ed. Greg Rosen (London: Methuen, 2001), pp. 82–3.
21 F. M. Leventhal, 'Brailsford, Henry Noel' in *Dictionary of Labour Biography* ed. Bellamy, Saville et al., vol. 2, pp. 46–53.
22 H. N. Brailsford, 'Beating the Russian Bear: A Tory Trap for Labour', *New Leader*, 7 February 1930.
23 H. N. Brailsford, 'Russia and Religion: Exploiting the Primary Passions', *New Leader*, 21 February 1930.
24 Leventhal, 'Brailsford, Henry Noel', p. 52.
25 'An Appeal on the Campaign against Russia', *Manchester Guardian*, 16 March 1930.
26 Trotsky, *Between Red and White*, ch. 4.
27 *On the Deviations from the Party Line in the Kolkhoz Movement*, Central Committee Decree, 15 March 1930. Cited by Roy Medvedev, *Let History Judge: The Origins and Consequences of Stalinism* (New York: Columbia University Press, 1989), p. 229, and quoted by Lang, who did not mention the exact source, in Hansard, HL Deb, 2 April 1930, vol. 76, col. 1145.
28 *Pravda*, 2 March 1930.
29 Criticising apparently overzealous party officials who had been shutting churches as part of the collectivisation programme, Stalin continued: 'I say nothing of those "revolutionaries" ... who *begin* the work of organising artels [agricultural communes] by removing the bells from the churches. Just imagine, removing the church bells – how r-r-revolutionary! How could there have arisen in our midst such blockheaded exercises in "socialisation," such ludicrous attempts to overleap oneself, attempts which aim at bypassing classes and the class struggle, and which in fact bring grist to the mill of our class enemies?' 'Dizzy with Success' in *Marxists Internet Archive* (n.d.) <https://www.marxists.org/reference/archive/stalin/works/1930/03/02.htm>, accessed 1 January 2017.
30 Hansard, HL Deb, 13 February 1930, vol. 76, col, 585–6.

31 LPL, Lang Papers, vol. 74, p. 29. Enclosure with letter from W. P. Coates: *From the Press Department. Weekly Bulletin No 20. 10th April 1930* (London, Anglo-Russian Parliamentary Committee, 1930).
32 See Appendix 3.
33 TNA, FO 371/15589, N 1831/1/38. *Soviet Union Annual Report, 1930*. British Embassy, Moscow, 10 March 1931.
34 See also the case of 'Mrs Walford', otherwise Varvaria Tunikov, who married her British husband in Odessa on 8 February 1931. Hansard, HC Deb, 27 July 1931, vol. 255, cols 2071–80.

Chapter 22

1 LPL, Lang Papers, vol. 74, p. 27. Letter from Pares (7 April 1930): 'We have arranged for [Klepenin] to set up a news service in Paris which is sure to be well and accurately conducted as Klepenin will look after it himself. The Christian Protest are very generous about it and are financing it.'
2 Nicholas Klepenin, 'The War on Religion in Russia', *The Slavonic and East European Review*, 8:24 (1930), 514–32.
3 LPL, Lang Papers, vol. 73, pp. 206–13. Memorandum on meetings with Nikolai Klepenin on 6 and 11 March 1930.
4 This important typescript document is to be found in LPL, Lang Papers, vol. 74, pp. 170–212, marked only with an archivist's pencil note: 'Date 1930, Author?'. It contains a number of corrections in ink which exactly match the handwriting of the letters sent from Lord Charnwood to Lang. The document can therefore be safely identified as Charnwood's *Memorandum* of 17–21 March 1930.
5 LPL, Lang Papers, vol. 73, p. 309. Lang's letter of thanks to Lord Charnwood is dated 22 March 1930.
6 TNA, FO 371/14842, N 1979/23/38.
7 Although unsigned, it is probably written by Henderson's private secretary, Jebb. The handwriting does not match that of any of the Foreign Office civil servants who dealt with Russian matters.
8 TNA, FO 371/14842, N 1979/23/38.
9 LSE/BLPES, Dalton, *Diary*, March 20 1930.
10 Hansard, HL Deb, 2 April 1930, vol. 76, cols 1131–81.
11 TNA, FO 371/14843, N 2238/23/38.
12 Ibid.
13 TNA, FO 371/14843, N 2528/23/38.
14 TNA, FO 371/14843, N 3470/23/38.

Chapter 23

1 Medvedev. *On the Deviations from the Party Line.* Op cit.
2 LPL, Lang Papers, vol. 74, p. 110. Letter from S. M. Dawkins, secretary of the Christian Protest Movement to Rev. Mervyn Haigh, Lang's private secretary (24 June 1930).
3 LPL, Lang Papers, vol. 74, p. 107. Letter from Temple (22 June 1930).
4 LPL, Lang Papers, vol. 74, p. 135. Memorandum on meeting with Bishop Embling (17 July 1930).
5 *Morning Post*, 26 June 1930.
6 TNA, FO 371/14843, N 4358/23/38.
7 Hansard, *HC Deb, 2 July 1930, vol. 240, col. 1935.*
8 TNA, FO 371/14843, N 4358/23/38.
9 LMA/BPCC, P84/TRI2/200, *Brompton Parish Church Magazine*, 570 (July 1930).
10 *Antireligious Activity in Soviet Russia – Non-Political Bulletin Based upon Information Contained in the Soviet Press*, 1-2 (July 1930). A copy, sent to Arthur Henderson by Sir Bernard Pares on 15 July 1930, can be found in the Foreign Office archives. TNA, FO 371 14860, N 4897/23/38.
11 *Red Evening Newspaper*, 92 (19 April 1930). Cited in *Antireligious Activity in Soviet Russia*, 1-2 (July 1930), p. 19.
12 *Izvestia*, 126 (9 May 1930). Cited in *Antireligious Activity in Soviet Russia*, 1-2 (July 1930), p. 16.
13 LPL, Lang Papers, vol. 74, p. 128. Letter to Sir Bernard Pares (3 July 1930). *The Times* had reported this on 1 July 1930.
14 TNA, FO 371/14844, N 4642/23/38.
15 [Cmd. 3641] *Russia no. 2 (1930). Certain legislation respecting religion in force in the Union of Soviet Socialist Republics* (London: HMSO, 1930).
16 *Morning Post*, 15 July 1930.

Part IV

1   Letters dated January 1931 to October 1932 from kulaks deported from the Volga region and Crimea to the Northern Region timber camps, collated by the 'Baltische Russlandarbeit' (Baltic Society for Work in Russia). Published in *Out of the Deep: Letters from Soviet Timber Camps*, p. 91-94.

2   C. H. Hardy was assistant archivist at the British Embassy in Moscow. His report can be found in TNA, FO 371/14860, N 2725/75/38.

3   Deuss was Moscow correspondent for the International News Service and was reporting, to the American Embassy in Berlin, a conversation with the German Consul in Leningrad. Enclosure no. 1 in a letter of 25 February 1931 from ambassador Frederic M. Sackett, American embassy, Berlin, to the Hon. Secretary of State, Washington. Records of the Department of State Relating to Internal Affairs of the Soviet Union, 1930-1939, NARA T1249, 861/5017-LIVING CONDITIONS/230, reproduced in *Fold3* (n.d.) <https://www.fold3.com/image/1/32577945> , accessed 20 January 2017.

Chapter 24

1   TNA, FO 371/15588, N 923/1/38. Letter from 'Mr McGregor' to Arthur Henderson (3 February 1931).

2   Hansard, HL Deb, 5 February 1931, vol. 79, col. 873.

3   United States Congress Special Committee on Communist Activities in the United States, *Investigation of Communist Propaganda: Report, pursuant to H. Res. 220* (Washington: United States Government Printing Office, 1931), pp. 40–1. Also quoted by Lord Newton in Hansard, HL Deb, 5 February 1931, vol. 79, col. 846.

4   Hansard, HC Deb, 26 March 1930, vol. 237, col. 556.

5   The Solovetsky camp group population was rising so fast that even this figure was out of date. It was closer to 65,000 in 1929–30. The population of Solovetsky was 13,000 in early 1928, 22,000 in 1929, and had risen to 71,800 by January 1931. The geographical reach of the camp group also extended beyond the islands themselves, and took in the timber port and transit camp at Kem on the mainland. M. B. Smirnov et al., *Sistema ispravitel'no-trudovykh lagerei v SSSR: 1923–1960* [The System of Corrective Labour Camps in the USSR, 1923–60] (Moscow: Zven'ya, 1998), p. 395.

6   Hansard, HC *Deb, 26 March 1930, vol. 237, col. 557.*

7   TNA, FO 371/14860, N 2725/75/38.

8   TNA, CAB 24-213, CP 237, 11 July 1930. *Stowaways from Archangel*, Memorandum by Rt. Hon. J. R. Clynes, Home Secretary.

9   TNA, FO 371/14878, N 5830/1459/38.

10 Ibid.

11 TNA, FO 371/14878, N7520/1215/38.

12 Hansard, HL Deb, 12 *November 1930, vol. 79, cols 95–111.*

13 The following week in the House of Lords, the Earl of Glasgow stated that 'in Rumania and Yugo-Slavia and Hungary they have absolutely prohibited the import of all Russian goods. In France and other countries in Europe, except Finland, they have committees sitting which will not allow any Russian goods to enter without a licence. In America it is the same. We are the only country which has this laisser [*sic*] faire policy, and one simply cannot understand it.' Hansard, HL Deb, 20 November 1930, vol. 79, col. 284.

14 *Sweated Imports and International Labour Standards* (London: Labour Party, 1926). Its authors were members of the Labour Party 'Sweated Goods Committee': Rt Hon. Philip Snowden, Lord Arnold, V. Crittall, Rt Hon. Arthur Henderson, Thomas Johnson MP, George A. McEwan, Tom Shaw MP, Frank Varley MP, Rt Hon. Sidney Webb MP, Rt Hon. John Wheatley MP, Arthur Greenwood MP.

15 Hansard, HL Deb, 20 *November 1930, vol. 79, cols 277–313.*

16 TNA, FO 371/14862, N 6833/75/38.

Chapter 25

1   *The Times*, 16 December 1930.

2   *The Times*, 2 January 1931.

3   Ibid.

4   Ibid.

5   *The Times*, 3 January 1931.

6   Ibid.

7   Ibid.

8   *The Times*, 20 January 1931. There are unnumbered carbon copies of letter, dated 12-18 January, with corrections in MacDonald's own hand, in TNA, FO 371/15587, between N 180/1/38 and N198/1/38.

9   TNA, FO 371/15587, N 105/1/38.

10 TNA, FO 371/15587, N 215/1/38.

11 TNA, FO 371/15617, N 764/84/38.

12 TNA, FO 371/15588, N 604/1/38.

13 TNA, FO 371/15589, N 1144/1/38.

14 TNA, FO 371/15589, N 1144/1/38. 'Statement of Pastor Aatami Kuortti'.

15 TNA, FO 371/15588, N 604/1/38.

16 TNA, FO 371/15589, N 1144/1/38.

17 Hansard, HL Deb, *5 February 1931, vol. 79, col. 876.*

18 Ibid.

19 *The Times*, 21 January 1931.

20 'Obzatelnoya Decree No.2, Glazov Village Soviet regarding timber work by the disenfranchised', 9 February 1931. Dispatch from Ambassador F. W. B. Colman, American Embassy Riga (Latvia), 14 March 1931. U.S. State Dept. ref 861.6172/71. The ambassador added: 'this translation, which is reproduced in the enclosure without alteration, was furnished to a member of my staff by Mr Julius Wood, Moscow correspondent of the Chicago Daily News. Mr Wood stated that the original of the order, in the Russian language, was mailed anonymously to the British Embassy at Moscow presumably after having been secretly removed from the village bulletin board. Mr Wood obtained his translation from the Embassy. It is significant that some resident of this forest village in north western Russia should have been so aroused by the harsh terms of the order as to risk his or her personal safety by making away with it and mailing it to the British Embassy which, as the Soviet press had widely reported, had been refused permission to investigate labour conditions in the forest areas. The contents of the order throw a most revealing light on the manner in which Labour is now being "recruited" for work in the timber camps.' Reproduced in *Fold3* (n.d.) <https://www.fold3.com/image/1/32561072> , accessed 30 November 2015.

21 Hansard, HC Deb, 21 January 1931, vol. 247, col. 165.

22 TNA, FO371/15588, N 501/1/38.

23 'Amalgamated Society of Woodworkers Journal' (February 1931), *Forced Labour in Russia: Facts and Documents* (London: British Russian Gazette and Trade Outlook, 1931), p. 41.

24 *Forced Labour in Russia*, pp. 37–41.

Chapter 26

1   [Cmd. 3775] *Russia no. 1 (1931). A selection of documents relative to the labour legislation in force in the Union of Soviet Socialist Republics* (London: HMSO, 1931).

2   Hansard, HL Deb, 5 February 1931, vol. 79, cols 842–80.

3   E.g. The *Dundee Courier and Advertiser* (headline: 'Soviet Horrors Denounced; Bishop on our "Moral Disgrace" ') and the *Irish Times* carried reports the next day.

4   Durham, Henson Papers, HHH52. Diary entry of 6 February 1931.

5   Arthur Ponsonby, *Religion in Politics* (London: Parsons, 1921).

6   Durham, Henson Papers, HHH52. Diary entry of 23 February 1931.

7   *The Times*, 20 November 1909. It was not only a Church affair: among the hundreds present were Sir Arthur and Lady Conan Doyle and Mrs Holman Hunt, wife of the painter, and fifty MPs.

8   *The United Methodist*, 27 February 1908.

9   Oleg Khlevniuk, *The History of the Gulag: From Collectivization to the Great Terror* (New Haven: Yale University Press, 2004), p. 360–1.

10 Viola, 'The Other Archipelago', p. 735.

Chapter 27 .

1   TNA, CAB 23, 13(31), 11 February 1931.

2   TNA, FO 371/15589, N 1291/1/38.

3   Interview reported in a letter from American Consulate General Hamburg to the Hon. Secretary

of State, Washington, 21 February 1931. Records of the Department of State Relating to Internal Affairs of the Soviet Union, 1930–1939. NARA T1249, 861.5048/27. Reproduced in *Fold3* (n.d.) <https://www.fold3.com/image/1/32460410>, accessed 20 January 2017.

4 *The Times*, 6 February 1931.
5 Ibid.
6 TNA, FO 371/15589, N 1142/1/38.
7 TNA, FO 371/15588, N 951/1/38.
8 Hansard, HC Deb, 9 February 1931, vol. 248, col. 13.
9 Hansard, HC Deb, *9 February 1931, vol. 248, col. 11.*
10 Ibid.
11 On the Anglo-Russian Parliamentary Committee, see Appendix [0000]
12 Unnumbered FO minute of 11 February 1931, located after TNA, FO 371/15588, N 1008/1/38.
13 Ibid.
14 TNA, CAB 23, 13(31), 11 February 1931.
15 TNA, FO 371/15587, N 105/1/38.
16 *Forced Labour Convention*, article 1 (Geneva: International Labour Office, 1930).
17 Frederick Pollock, *The League of Nations*, 2nd ed. (London: Stevens and Sons, 1922), p.170.
18 TNA, FO 371/15588, N 1072/1/38.
19 TNA, FO 371/15589, N 1144/1/38.
20 TNA, FO 371/15588, N 1074/1/38.
21 TNA, FO 371/15589, N 1291/1/38.
22 Ibid.
23 Ibid.
24 TNA, FO 371/15589, N 1461/1/38.
25 *Manchester Guardian*, 7 March 1931.
26 TNA, FO 371/15589, N 1635/1/38.
27 Ibid. 'Use the Criminal Code against Class enemies' in *Pravda Severa* [Truth of the North], 10 January 1931. Reader Bullard wrote in his diary on 23 February 1931: 'Junius Wood, the Chicago journalist, came in for some income-tax formality. He said he got hold of three very interesting numbers of the Northern Pravda. One contained a notice giving a clear warning to kulaks that they would be shot if they ever spoke about forced labour. He got two telegrams away to U.S.A. but the *Narkomindel* [the Commissariat for Foreign Affairs] borrowed the two later papers from him because they were so interesting – and now they "can't find them".'
28 *Daily Herald*, 10 March 1931.
29 *Morning Post*, 27 February 1931.

Chapter 28

1 *The Times*, 7 March 1931.
2 G. M. Godden, 'The Commercial Conscience', *The Tablet*, 15 November 1930.
3 *Forced Labour in Russia*, p. 2.
4 *The Times*, on 21 October 1933, announced the arrival in Lithuania of some freed priests who gave the number remaining in Solovki as sixty. It seems reasonable to estimate that there were at least fifty in 1931.
5 Godden, 'The Commercial Conscience'.
6 TNA, CAB 2-17-24, CP 416, 9 December 1930. *Russian 'Dumping', Memorandum by the President of the Board of Trade.*
7 Godden, 'The Commercial Conscience'.
8 TNA, CAB 2-17-24, CP 416, 9 December 1930. *Russian 'Dumping'.* Equivalent of an increase from 47,000 imperial tons to 5.63 million.
9 Ibid.
10 Godden, 'The Commercial Conscience'.
11 On the railway sleepers, see Hansard, HC Deb, 18 May 1931, vol. 252, col. 1613; on the doors, see TNA, CAB 24-217, CP 416, 9 December 1930. *Russian 'Dumping', Memorandum by the President of the Board of Trade.*
12 'Editorial', *Timber Trades Journal*, 20 December 1930.
13 *The Times*, 20 December 1930.

14 *The Tablet*, 7 February 1931.

15 *The Tablet*, 14 February 1931.

16 *Timber Trades Journal*, 21 March 1931.

17 *The Tablet*, 28 February 1931.

18 *Manchester Guardian*, 15 April 1931.

19 TNA, FO 371/15589, N 1871/1/38.

20 *Daily Worker*, 28 February 1931.

21 *The Times*, 11 February 1931.

22 *The Times*, 26 February 1931.

23 *The Times*, 7 March 1931.

24 W. P. and Zelda Coates, *A History of Anglo-Soviet Relations*, p. 319.

25 The October 1929 edition of the *British Russian Gazette* describes him as 'of the English Steel corporation'.

26 Bullard, diary, 31 July 1931; 25 April 1934.

27 *The Second National Congress of Peace and Friendship with the USSR March 13-14, 1937* (London: Left Book Club, 1937).

28 He wrote regular letters to the press in support of Anglo-Russian trade. E.g. *Manchester Guardian*, 19 April 1931, 24 May 1931.

29 *British Russian Gazette and Trade Outlook*, 6 March 1931.

30 *Forced Labour in Russia*, p. 2.

31 *Timber Trades Journal*, 14 March 1931.

32 *Timber Trades Journal*, 21 March 1931.

33 *The Times*, 19 March 1931.

34 *Timber Trades Journal*, 28 March 1931.

35 *Timber Trades Journal*, 8 August 1931.

36 E. P. Tetsall, 'Seen on the Russian Tour. Federation Delegates Amazed at the Transformation', *Timber Trades Journal*, 8 August 1931.

37 *Daily Worker*, 18 August 1931.

38 Katharine Stewart-Murray, Duchess of Atholl, *The Conscription of a People* (London: Philip Allan, 1931), photograph facing p. 67, translation p. 195.

39 Bullard, diary, 17 February 1932.

40 Hansard, HC Deb, 3 November 1920, vol. 134, cols 412–33; HC Deb, 10 November 1920, vol. 134, cols 1204–5; HC Deb, 24 November 1920, vol. 135, cols 461–3; HC Deb, 25 November 1920, vol. 135, cols 683–4.

41 11, 15, 18, 24 and 25 February, 3 and 4 March and 15 April.

42 According to Christopher Andrew, although the KGB held a file on Wilson, they never managed to recruit him. *The Defence of the Realm: The Authorized History of MI5*, p. 416–19.

43 David Leigh, *The Wilson Plot* (London: Heinemann Mandarin, 1989), p. 64.

44 Leigh, *The Wilson Plot*, p. 196.

Chapter 29

1 The Consolidated Fund (no. 2) Bill, 25 March 1931. Hansard, HC Deb, *25 March 1931, vol. 250,* cols 422–89. The online version of Hansard does not record any Commons sittings for 25 March 25, 1931, but the debate is available in hard copy.

2 Hansard, HC Deb, 26 March 1930, vol. 237, cols 526–69.

3 TNA, FO 371/15590, N 2106/1/38.

4 *Labour Conditions in the Soviet Timber Industry (prepared with information from the Foreign Office)*, TNA, FO 371/15589, N 2085/1/38.

5 Hansard, HC Deb, *25 March 1931, vol. 250*, cols 423, 429.

6 Ibid., col. 471.

7 Ibid., col. 479.

8 Ibid., col. 460.

9 Ibid., col. 461.

10 Ibid., cols 430, 435–7.

11 Ibid., col. 463.

12 Ibid.

13 In support of his view that the testimony of escaped prisoners should be treated with scepticism, he also cited forestry expert J. F. Stewart's letter to the *Manchester Guardian*, as Strauss had done in his speech. The errors in Stewart's evidence which invalidated it are discussed in Appendix [0000].
14 Ibid., col. 449.
15 Ibid., col. 456.
16 Ibid., col. 482.
17 Ibid., col. 484. Graham prefaced his comments absolving and praising the Soviets with the words: 'We have made it perfectly clear that we are not necessarily supporters of everything that is being done in Russia at present'. The sole function of the remark appears to be to deflect criticism and, while it should be noted here for the sake of completeness, its inclusion in the main text would give a misleading impression of Graham's moderation. There was none.

Chapter 30

1   George Kitchin, *Prisoner of the OGPU* (London: Longmans, Green, 1935), p. 222, 334.
2   Ibid., pp. 259, 222–3.
3   Ibid., p. 234ff.
4   Ibid., p. 236–7.
5   TNA, FO 371/15589, N 1635/1/38.
6   Kitchin, *Prisoner of the OGPU*, p. 264–71.
7   Ibid., p. 273–81.
8   Ibid., p. 334.
9   TNA, FO 371/15590, N 2582/1/38.
10 Lynne Viola, 'A Tale of Two Men', p. 1457.
11 W. H. Chamberlin, *Russia's Iron Age* (London: Duckworth, 1935), p. 364–5.

Chapter 31

1   Hansard, *HC Deb, 21 April 1931, vol. 251, cols 807–14*.
2   Barbara Neild, 'Taylor, Robert Arthur' in *Dictionary of Labour Biography*, ed. Bellamy, Saville et al., vol. 4, p. 173–5.
3   See Appendix [0000] for an analysis of the disinformation in statements used by those opposing the protests.
4   The Papers of the Anti-Slavery Society (ASS), Bodleian Library, University of Oxford. 'Russia (forced labour in timber camps) 1930–1931'. MSS. Brit. Emp. s. 22 / G405-G408. Letter from John Harris to Sir William Henderson (22 January 1931).
5   ASS, letter, K. E. Harris to Sir Alan Pim (2 February 1931).
6   ASS, undated unsigned typescript, probably mid to late February 1931.
7   Ibid.
8   ASS, copy of a letter signed 'Hesketh' from Edward Nicholson Ltd. Stevedores, Garston, Liverpool (22 July 1930), sent to Carlyon Bellairs by Samuel Appleton on 12 February 1931.
9   ASS, letter, K. E. Harris to Sir Arthur Steel-Maitland (27 February 1931).
10 ASS, letter, Sir Austen Chamberlain to John Harris (19 February 1931).
11 ASS, typescript headed 'Russian Timber', attached to a letter from John Harris to Sir Alan Pim (25 February 1931).
12 Quoted in Sir Alan Pim and Edward Bateson, *Report on Russian Timber Camps* (London: Ernest Benn, 1931), p. 44.
13 Ibid., p. 45.
14 Ibid., p. 52.
15 Ibid., p. 121.
16 Ibid., p. 122.
17 Ibid., pp. 92-3.
18 Ibid., pp. 71–3, 83-4.
19 Ibid., pp. 109, 110.
20 Ibid., p. 130, 59.
21 Ibid., p. 119.
22 Ibid., p. 132.
23 TNA, FO 371/15590, N 3394/1/38.

24　Ibid.

25　Hansard, HC Deb, 2 June 1931, vol. 253, cols 25–6.

26　Pim and Bateson, *Report on Russian Timber Camps,* pp. 131–2.

27　Kitchin, *Prisoner of the OGPU*, p. 276.

28　The most reliable estimate, from Russian archives. Lynne Viola, *The Unknown Gulag*, p. 196.

29　Pim and Bateson, *Report on Russian Timber Camps*, p. 117.

30　*Newcastle Evening Chronicle*, 4 June 1931; *Huddersfield Daily Examiner, Liverpool Post, Notting-ham Guardian, Burton Daily Mail, Yorkshire Herald*, 5 June 1931; *Sunday Referee*, 7 June 1931; *Yorkshire Post*, 8 June 1931; *Brighton & Hove Weekly News,* 12 June 1931; *Western Daily Press*, undated. Cuttings all in ASS.

31　*Manchester Guardian*, 15 May 1931.

32　*Manchester Guardian*, 5 June 1931.

33　ASS, letter, Lord Olivier to John Harris (28 May 1931).

34　*New Statesman*, 13 June 1931.

35　*Labour Leader*, 29 May 1919.

36　*The Spectator*, 13 June 1931.

37　*New Statesman*, 4 July 1931.

Chapter 32

1　Hansard, HC Deb, 15 July 1930, vol. 241 cols 1085–6. William Graham said that only penitentia-ries, houses of correction, and prisons, not prison camps, were covered by the act.

2　Hansard, *HC Deb, 7 July 1931, vol. 254, cols 1884–5.*

3　[21 & 22 GEO. 5.] *Prevention of Imports of Products of Convict or Forced Labour*. [H.L.] A copy can be found at TNA, FO 371/ 15591, N 4364/1/38.

4　Hansard, HC Deb, 26 January 1931, vol. 247, col. 588.

5　LMA/BPCC, Holy Trinity Brompton Archive, P84/TRI2/200, unidentified newspaper cutting (May 1931?).

6　[Cmd. 3558] *International labour conference. Report to the Minister of Labour by the government dele-gates of H. M. Government in the United Kingdom of Great Britain and Northern Ireland, presented by the Minister of Labour to parliament by command of His Majesty, April 1930* (London: HMSO, 1930).

7　TNA, FO 371/15587, N 105/1/38: 'It is no doubt true that the circumstance of goods being manufac-tured by forced labour is not likely to occur in many, if in any, countries other than Soviet Russia'.

8　TNA, FO 371/15591, N 4364/1/38.

9　Professor David Northrup, author of *Indentured Labor In The Age Of Imperialism, 1834–1922* (Cambridge: Cambridge University Press, 1995). Private communication, 1 November 2009.

10　Hansard, HL Deb, 24 June 1931, vol. 81, col. 351.

11　*Manchester Guardian*, 25 June 1931 (leader comment).

Chapter 33

1　Hansard, HL Deb, *5 February 1931, vol. 79, cols 857–60.*

2　Clement Attlee, *As it Happened* (London: Heinemann, 1954), p. 107.

3　Labour Party, *General Election Manifesto*, 1931, *Labour Manifestos* [online archive] (2001) <la-bourmanifesto.com/1931/1931-labour-manifesto.shtml>, accessed 2 November 2015.

4　*The Listener*, 21 October 1931. The remark, often wrongly repeated as 'Bolshevism gone mad', has also been incorrectly attributed to MacDonald.

5　Hansard, *HC Deb, 10 November 1931, vol. 259, cols 81–90.*

6　TNA, FO 371/15591, N 7904/1/38.

7　Hansard, *HC Deb, 18 October 1932, vol. 269, cols 10–12.*

8　The Metropolitan-Vickers affair, and Labour's support for the Soviet trial, is discussed at greater length in Chapter 35.

Part V

1　Simon Hoggart and David Leigh, *Michael Foot: A Portrait* (London: Hodder & Stoughton, 1981), p. 98. Date and source of the quotation are not given.

2　Charles Trevelyan, *Soviet Russia: A Description for British Workers* (London: Gollancz, 1935), p. 38.

Chapter 34

1 Fenner Brockway, 'Chairman's Address', *Report of the Annual Conference Held at Blackpool, April 1932* (London: Independent Labour Party, 1932), p. 10.

2 George Lansbury, 'Preface' in Coates, *More Anti-Soviet Lies Nailed*, p. 7.

3 Clough and Amabel were enthusiastic pro-Soviets, Clough having travelled to Russia and written on Soviet architecture. Over the years, they encouraged a large number of similarly inclined friends, many of them Oxbridge intellectuals, to take weekend cottages on their Welsh estate. Eric Hobsbawm was one of them, as he recounts in *Interesting Times: A Twentieth-Century Life* (London: Abacus, 2003), p. 233ff.

4 L. Auerback et al., *The White Sea Canal*, ed. M. Gorky (trans. Amabel Williams-Ellis) (London: Bodley Head, 1935), p. ix-xi.

5 James Maxton, *Lenin*, p. 144.

6 Hansard, HC Deb, 7 April 1933, vol. 276, col. 2112.

7 Russian Goods (Import Prohibition) Bill on April 5, 1933. Hansard, HC Deb, 5 April 1933, vol. 276, cols 1804-5.

8 *Report of the 33rd Annual Conference of the Labour Party, 1933* (London: Labour Party, 1933), p. 230.

9 *Report of Proceedings at the 63rd Annual Trades Union Congress, 1931* (London: Cooperative Printing Society, 1931), p. 10.

10 *The Times*, 21 December 1934.

11 *The Times*, 3 January 1935.

12 Kingsley Martin, 'The Moscow Purge', *New Statesman*, 5 September 1936.

13 Several of their sad stories are told in Francis Beckett, *Stalin's British Victims* (Stroud: Sutton, 2004).

14 Kingsley Martin, review of a new edition of *Soviet Communism: A New Civilisation*, *New Statesman*, 6 November 1937.

15 The precise number of victims of Soviet repression and brutality in the gulag era has become a matter of dispute between historians, revisionists battling with their more establishment opponents. The best summary can be found in Anne Applebaum's *Gulag: A History of the Soviet Camps* (London: Allen Lane, 2003), pp. 515–22.

16 Michael Foot, 'The Road to Ruin', in E. Thomas (ed.), *Tribune 21*,1958, pp. 7–8, cited in Paul Corthorn, *In the Shadow of the Dictators: The British Left in the 1930s* (London: I. B. Tauris, 2012), p. 137.

17 Letter from Page Arnot to Pollitt (20 August 1936), cited in Paul Corthorn, 'Labour, the Left, and the Stalinist Purges of the Late 1930s', *The Historical Journal*, 48:1 (March, 2005), 179–207, at p. 187.

18 *Beatrice Webb's Typescript diary*, 28 August 1936, (p. 330), *LSE Digital Library* (n.d.) <http://digital.library.lse.ac.uk/objects/lse:qif604fiv/read/single#page/330/mode/2up>, accessed 23 January 2017

19 *Daily Herald*, 26 November 1937, cited in W. P. and Zelda Coates, *A History of Anglo-Soviet Relations*, pp. 577–8.

20 *The Times*, 10 March 1938.

Chapter 35

1 Famine estimates range from 2 to 10 million. The figure of 7,000 is calculated on the basis of two years of famine and 5 million deaths. See Dana Dalrymple, 'The Soviet Famine of 1932–1934', *Soviet Studies*, 15:3 (1964), 250–84 and 'The Soviet Famine of 1932–1934; Some Further References', *Soviet Studies*, 16:3 (1965), 471–4.

2 *Pravda*, 16 December, 1933, cited in Robert Conquest, *Harvest of Sorrow*, p. 262.

3 Dalrymple, 'The Soviet Famine of 1932-34' and 'The Soviet Famine of 1932–1934; Some Further References'. Dalrymple's figures for grain exports are 1.7 million tons in 1932 and 1.8 million in 1933. The article also reviews twenty different famine death estimates and finds that their average is 5.5 million.

4 Ibid., p. 269.

5 Bullard thought so: 'We think that the whole affair is a dodge to enable the Soviet Government to delay or refuse payment to Metro-Vickers, to whom they owe about a million and a half pounds,

and this view is supported by recent exhortations in the press, calling upon the heads of industries to try to find defects in foreign goods and demand reductions' Bullard, diary, 1 April 1933.

6   A.T. Cholerton, typescript note (private collection; his private papers remain in the possession the family).
7   Ovey quoted by Sir John Simon in Hansard, HC Deb, 5 April 1933, vol. 276, col. 1791.
8   [Cmd. 4286] *Russia no. 1 (1933). Correspondence relating to the arrest of employees of the Metropolitan-Vickers Company at Moscow* (London: HMSO, 1933). See also [Cmd. 4290] *Russia no. 2 (1933). Further correspondence relating to the arrest of employees of the Metropolitan-Vickers Company at Moscow* (London: HMSO, 1933).
9   The article is quoted by Sir John Simon in Hansard, HC Deb, 5 April 1933, vol. 276, col. 1782.
10 [Cmd. 4286], p. 13.
11 Bullard, diary, 23 March 1933.
12 Ibid., 15 April 1933.
13 Ibid., 23 March, 1 April 1933.
14 See n. 7 [0000] above. According to one report, Soviet debt of £64–5 million was due to mature in 1933, while the Russian could draw on no more than £70–5 million sterling to meet that. Anything which could either delay payment or reduce the Metro-Vickers £1.5 million debt would have been welcome. The Duchess of Atholl suggested as much: see Hansard, HC Deb, 5 July 1933, vol. 280, col. 426.
15 [Cmd. 4286] *Russia no. 1 (1933)*.
16 Hansard, HC Deb, 5 April 1933, vol. 276, col. 1805.
17 *Wrecking Activities at Power Stations in the Soviet Union*, 3 vols in 2 (Moscow, State Law Publishing House, 1933), vol. 3, p. 26; David Caute, in one of the few works on the subject of Western Soviet enthusiasts, writes of Cripps in 1936 that 'he was no Marxist and he regarded the Soviet experiment with some scepticism'. *The Fellow-Travellers* (New York: Macmillan, 1973), p. 157. While that may well have been true in 1936, little scepticism is evident in his words in the Commons debate three years earlier.
18 Dalton, diary, 20 March 1930.
19 Hansard, HC Deb, 5 April 1933, vol. 276, cols 1816–19.
20 Ibid., col. 1820.
21 Ibid., col. 1823. This last comment was to have unexpected consequences. Shortly after the debate, Maxton received a letter from Malcolm Muggeridge, which is reproduced as Document 5.
22 Ibid., col. 1840.
23 Ibid., col. 1838.
24 Ibid., col. 1846.
25 Ibid., col. 1812.
26 Lansbury, 'Preface' in W. P. and Zelda Coates, *More Anti-Soviet Lies Nailed.*
27 Hansard, HC Deb, 5 April 1933, vol. 276, col. 1851.
28 Bullard, diary, 26 April 1933.
29 Bullard, diary, 15 April 1933.
30 *The Times*, April 18, 1933.
31 Bullard, diary, 22 April 1933.
32 Bullard, diary, 15 April 1933.
33 Hansard, HL Deb, 26 April 1933, vol. 87, col. 621.
34 Bullard, diary, 6 April 1933.
35 Hansard, HL Deb, 26 April 1933, vol. 87, col. 633.
36 Ibid., col. 632.

Chapter 36

1   Deirdre Terrins and Phillip Whitehead (eds), *100 Years of Fabian Socialism 1884–1984* (London: Fabian Society, 1984), p. 3; Margaret Cole, *The Story of Fabian Socialism.*
2   Margaret Cole, 'Beatrice Webb, Obituary', *The Times*, 5 May 1943.
3   Pelling, p. 44.
4   Margaret Cole, *Beatrice Webb* (New York: Harcourt Brace, 1946), p. v.
5   Beatrice Webb, *Beatrice Webb's Diaries 1924–1932*, ed. Margaret Cole (London: Longmans, Green, 1956), entry for 14 May 1932.

6 Ibid., 18 August 1931.

7 Sidney and Beatrice Webb, *Soviet Communism: A New Civilisation?*, in the second edition of which the '?' was dropped from the title. Sidney Webb made it clear in 1936 that he felt that the question mark was superfluous in 'Soviet Communism: Its Present Position and Prospects', *International Affairs (Royal Institute of International Affairs 1931–1939)*, 15:3 (May–June 1936), 395–413.

8 Institute of Pacific Relations, *Hearings before the Subcommittee to Investigate the Administration of the Internal Security Act and Other Internal Security Laws, U. S. Senate, 82d Cong., 2d sess., part 13, 7 April 1952, p.4510* (Washington: United States Government Printing Office, 1952).

9 Beatrice Webb, *The Diary of Beatrice Webb*, vol. 4 (*The Wheel of Life', 1924–1943*), entry for 20 December 1935.

10 Ibid.

11 Ibid., 25 November 1936.

12 Special editions (typically created by including the organisation's name on the flyleaf) were commissioned by the Amalgamated Society of Woodworkers, the Cooperative Union, the Left Book Club, the London Teachers' Association, the National Association of Local Government Officials, the National Union of Distributive and Allied Workers, the National Union of General and Municipal Workers, the National Union of Journalists, the Transport and General Workers' Union, and the Workers' Educational Association, among others. Another private subscription edition was printed by the authors for members of the Labour Party.

13 Sidney and Beatrice Webb, *The Truth about Soviet Russia* (London: Longmans, Green, 1935), p. 14.

14 Ibid., p.16.

15 Yakovlev, *A Century of Violence in Soviet Russia* (New Haven: Yale University Press, 2002), p. 174.

16 Margaret Cole, *The Story of Fabian Socialism*, p. 251.

17 Review of *Soviet Communism: A New Civilisation* in *New Statesman*, 6 November 1937.

18 *New Statesman*, 22 January 1938.

19 Cole, *Beatrice Webb*, p. 205.

20 Neil Wood, *Communism and British Intellectuals* (London: Gollancz, 1959), p. 59.

21 See Chapter 35, n .1.

22 Webbs, *Soviet Communism,* pp. 258–68.

23 Ibid., p. 260.

24 Ibid., p. 262–3.

25 Ibid., p. 270.

26 Ibid., p. 268, n.

27 Ibid., p. 270.

28 Ibid., p. 268.

29 Ibid., p. 282, n.

30 Ibid., p. 557.

31 Ibid. Even as the affair was being debated in the House of Lords, the Webbs were entertaining the Soviet ambassador Ivan Maisky and his wife at their country house: 'The Maiskys spent the weekend with us, an engagement made before the episode of the arrest of the British engineers, but which we hastened to endorse when the breach came. We like both husband and wife.' *Beatrice Webb's Typescript diary*, 11 April 1933, (p. 246), *LSE Digital Library* (n.d.) <http://digital.library.lse.ac.uk/objects/lse:nut827hel/read/single#page/246/mode/2up>, accessed 22 January 2017. The next day, in the House of Lords, Sidney Webb downplayed the excesses of the OGPU by comparing them favourably with the police in two of Russia's most hated ideological enemies, Poland and America: 'I am not going here to defend the police system of Russia, except to say that private investigation in prison, though alien to our system, is not confined to Soviet Russia. It is a system which prevails nearly all over Europe, and the case of what has happened in Russia is nothing to what has happened under a similar system in Poland, and nothing to be compared to the horrible tales which we have heard on the best authority as having taken place in the United States of America.' Hansard, *HL Deb, 11 April 1933, vol. 87, col. 525.*

32 Webbs, *Soviet Communism*, p. 243.

33 Ibid., pp. 574–5.

34 Ibid., p. 594.

35 Oleg V. Khlevniuk, *The History of the Gulag*, p. 288–90.

36 Nicolas Werth, *Mass Crimes under Stalin* (1930-1953), [online] (2008), <http://www.sciencespo.fr/mass-violence-war-massacre-resistance/fr/node/2653>, accessed 24 January 2017.

37 Webbs, *Soviet Communism*, p. 263.

38 Michael Ellman, 'Stalin and the Soviet Famine of 1932–33 Revisited', *Europe-Asia Studies*, 59:4 (June 2007), 663-693, at pp. 668ff.

39 Doreen Warriner, 'Is Soviet Farming a Success?', *The New Fabian Research Bureau Quarterly*, 11 (autumn 1936), at p. 15.

40 Webbs, *Soviet Communism*, p. 261.

41 Ibid., p. 282.

42 Ibid., p. 566-567.

43 'Chamberlin is going on leave, and the Manchester Guardian have sent out a young man named Muggeridge to act for him. He was almost a communist (he is the son of a former Labour MP), but Strang says that in a very short time he has faded to a mild pink.' Bullard, diary, 17 November 1932.

44 'The Guardian wrote to say that they could not print his comments as they would then be in bad company – i.e. with the out-and-out opponents of Soviet Russia. They have always tended to toady to Russia…' Bullard, diary, 24 March 1933.

45 Letter from Malcolm Muggeridge to Gareth Jones (17 April 1933), reproduced in *Gareth Richard Vaughan Jones, Hero of Ukraine (1905–1935)* (n.d.) <http://www.garethjones.org/overview/muggeridge3.htm>, accessed 3 December 2008.

46 Ibid.

47 Beatrice Webb, *The Diary of Beatrice Webb*, vol. 4 (*The Wheel of Life', 1924–1943*), entry for 19 January 1931.

48 Ibid., 29 March 1933.

49 Ibid., 21 October 1933.

50 Ibid., 22 February 1934.

51 Ibid., 22 February 1934.

52 Ibid., 30 January 1937.

53 Ibid., 22 January 1937.

54 Ibid., 29 March 1933.

55 Ibid., 30 March 1933.

56 'Some of our conclusions about Soviet Russia', August 1932, *Beatrice Webb's Typescript diary*, (p. 196), *LSE Digital Library* (n.d.) <http://digital.library.lse.ac.uk/objects/lse:nut827hel/read/single#page/196/mode/2up>, accessed 2 January 2017.

57 Beatrice Webb, *The Diary of Beatrice Webb*, vol. 4 (*The Wheel of Life', 1924–1943*), entry for 25 November 1936.

58 Ibid., p. 16.

59 Ibid., 25 March 1943.

60 K. Muggeridge and R. Adam, *Beatrice Webb: A Life, 1858–1943* (London: Secker & Warburg, 1967), cited in John Davis, 'Webb, (Martha) Beatrice (1858–1943)', *Oxford Dictionary of National Biography* [online edn] (May 2008) <http://www.oxforddnb.com/view/article/36799>, accessed 27 March 2015.

Chapter 37

1 Tracey, *The Book of the Labour Party*, vol. 1, p. 95.

2 *New York Times*, 3 November 1950.

3 Ibid.

4 *New York Times*, 12 November 1950.

5 *The Times*, 3 November 1950.

6 Fenner Brockway, *Inside the Left: Thirty Years of Platform, Press, Prison and Parliament* (London: Allen & Unwin, 1942), p. 22.

7 Fenner Brockway, *Outside the Right: A Sequel To 'Inside The Left'* (London: Allen & Unwin, 1963), p. 83.

8 Kingsley Martin, *Father Figures: A First Volume of Autobiography, 1897–1931* (London: Hutchinson, 1966), p. 92. The original reads 'and *lose* scores of votes' but this makes no sense in the context and must be a misprint.

9 Tracey, *The Book of the Labour Party*, vol. 1, p. 95.

10 Bernard Crick, 'George Bernard Shaw' in *Dictionary of Labour Biography*, ed. G. Rosen, pp. 508.

11 http://news.bbc.co.uk/1/hi/magazine/4944100.stm [online] (28 April 2006)

12 Andrew Walker, 'Wit, Wisdom and Windows', *BBC News* [online] (26 April 2006) <http://news.bbc.co.uk/1/hi/magazine/4944100.stm>, accessed 25 September 2016.

13 Bernard Crick, 'George Bernard Shaw', p. 508.

14 Beatrice Webb, *The Diary of Beatrice Webb*, vol. 4 (*The Wheel of Life', 1924–1943*), entry for 1 July 1935.

15 George Bernard Shaw, *Prefaces* (London: Constable, 1934), p. 296.

16 Bernard Shaw, 'The Dictatorship of the Proletariat', *Labour Monthly*, 1:4 (October 1921), 297–316.

17 'Most of you will know what it means when 100 bodies lie together, when 500 are there or when there are 1,000. And … to have seen this through and – with the exception of human weakness – to have remained decent, has made us hard and is a page of glory never mentioned and never to be mentioned.' Heinrich Himmler, speech at Posen, 4 October 1943. Cited in International Military Tribunal, *Trials of the Major War Criminals before the International Military Tribunal*, 42 vols (Nuremberg: International Military Tribunal, 1947–49), vol. 29, pp. 110–73.

18 George Bernard Shaw, speech at the ILP summer school, *The Times*, 6 August 1931.

19 *Look, You Boob… ! What Bernard Shaw Told the Americans About Russia! His Famous Broadcast, 11 October 1931* (London: The Friends of the Soviet Union, 1931).

20 'Preface', *On the Rocks* (Edinburgh: R & R Clark, 1934), excerpts from pp. 3–25.

21 Michael Holroyd, *George Bernard Shaw*, 4 vols (London: Chatto & Windus, 1988–92), vol. 3 (*The Lure of Fantasy, 1918–1950*), p. 339.

22 George Bernard Shaw, 'Eugenics Education Society Lecture', *The Daily Express,* 4 March 1910, cited in Dan Stone, *Breeding Superman: Nietzsche, Race and Eugenics in Edwardian and Interwar Britain* (Liverpool: Liverpool University Press, 2002), p. 127.

23 George Bernard Shaw, 'Preface', Sidney and Beatrice Webb, *English Local Government*, 9 vols. (London: Longmans, Green, 1922), vol. 6 (*English Prisons under Local Government*), p. xxix, xxxi.

24 Ibid., p. lvi.

25 *The Listener*, 7 February 1934.

26 George Bernard Shaw, *The Intelligent Woman's Guide to Socialism and Capitalism*, pp. 423ff. The book went through reprints and new editions in 1929, 1930, 1937, 1949, 1965, 1971, 1989 and 2005.

27 H. N. Brailsford, 'Bernard Shaw's New Book – the Case for Equality', *New Leader*, 1 June 1928.

28 George Bernard Shaw, 'Questionnaire about one of Stalin's early show trials, with Shaw's autograph and typed answers'. Sotheby's, London, sale of 10 July 2003, lot 274. The catalogue gave a full description of the document, a questionnaire submitted by journalist Dorothy Royal, but the online link no longer exists and the document is now presumed to be in private hands. It was incorrectly catalogued as 1935 because it referred to the ILP appeal ('end this regime of blood') made to Stalin in 1938. See also 'How Shaw defended Stalin's mass killings', *Daily Telegraph*, 18 June 2003.

29 E.g. 'We have been behaving disgracefully with regard to Russia and have circulated the most monstrous stories', *British Russian Trade Gazette and Trade Outlook*, December 1930, p. 62.

30 George Bernard Shaw et al., 'An appeal on the "Campaign against Russia" ', *Manchester Guardian*, 16 March 1930. For full text, see Appendix 7.

31 George Bernard Shaw et al., 'Social Conditions in Russia', *Manchester Guardian*, 2 March 1933. For full text, see Appendix 8.

32 'I saw no underfed people there; and the children were remarkably plump'. Shaw, *On the Rocks*, p. 164.

33 Holroyd, *George Bernard Shaw*, vol. 3 (*The Lure of Fantasy, 1918–1950*), p. 251.

Chapter 38

1 Freda Utley, *Odyssey of a Liberal* (Washington: Washington National Press, 1970), p. 44.

2 Ibid., p. 44.

3 Freda Utley, *The Dream We Lost: Soviet Russia, Then and Now* (New York: John Day, 1940), p. 86.

4 Freda Utley, *Lost Illusion* (London: George Allen & Unwin, 1949), p. 83.

5   Utley, *Odyssey of a Liberal*, p. 86.
6   Utley, *Odyssey of a Liberal*, p. 153.
7   Ibid., p. 154.
8   Ibid., p. 156.
9   Ibid., p. 158.
10 Ibid., p. 160.
11 *Manchester Guardian*, 25 July 1931.
12 Holroyd, *Bernard Shaw*, vol. 3 (*The Lure of Fantasy, 1918–1950*), pp. 241–2.
13 *Manchester Guardian*, 3 August 1933. It was reported in the West as 'exile' but as Raisa had trav-
    elled to extensively abroad with her husband and son before the Revolution (they were in Argentina
    from 1908 to 1917) it is more probable that she was sent to the camps, not just into rural exile.
14 *Manchester Guardian*, 13 August 1931.

Chapter 39

1   Webb, *The Diary of Beatrice Webb*, vol. 4 (*The Wheel of Life', 1924–1943*), entry for 16 July 1935.
2   George Orwell, 'Letter To Humphrey House' (11 April 1940), in *The Complete Works of George
    Orwell*, ed. Peter Davison, 20 vols (London: Secker & Warburg, 1997–98), vol. 12 (*A Patriot after
    All: 1940–1941*), p. 141.
3   Geoffrey Foote, 'G. D. H. Cole', *Dictionary of Labour Biography*, ed. Greg Rosen (London:
    Methuen, 2001), p. 128
4   'G. D. H. Cole', obituary, *The Times*, 15 January 1959.
5   *The Times*, 26 January 1959.
6   *The Hindu*, 23 November 2003.
7   Max Beloff, 'The Age of Laski', *Fortnightly Review*, June 1950, 167 (1950), 378–84. More recent-
    ly Neil Riddell makes a plea for Cole to be seen alongside Laski as a major figure of the period.
    '"The Age of Cole"? G. D. H. Cole and the British Labour Movement 1929–1933' *Historical
    Journal*, 38:4 (1995), 933–57.
8   The names published in the press are: Clement Attlee, H. N. Brailsford, G. D. H. Cole, F. S. Cocks
    MP, Sir Stafford Cripps MP, P. J. Dollan, Mrs Bruce Glasier, J. F. Corrigan, T. Johnston, David
    Kirkwood MP, Harold Laski, Neil Maclean MP, William Mellor, F. Pethwick Lawrence, Arthur
    Pugh, Alfred Salter, R. H. Tawney, Sir Charles Trevelyan and E. F. Wise. *The Times*, 24 September
    and 3 October 1932.
9   'A Moscow acquaintance of Tawney's … came for a night on Friday. A clever little adventuress
    and no mistake! … She was indignant that they (the OGPU) had not let her go to Turkestan. …
    "Wise told me that he wanted to go to Turkestan. He asked me a lot of questions about my life in
    Moscow. I told him he would not be allowed to go". "I should advise you to be discreet with Mr
    Wise," said I quietly, "after all he is a salaried servant of a Russian organisation". "Oh, yes, I know
    he's 'bought'". "Not *bought* – but salaried," I repeated. "He might feel bound to report you," I
    added with a laugh and turned the conversation.' *Beatrice Webb's Typescript diary*, 9 April 1932
    (p. 70, 74), *LSE Digital Library* (n.d.) <http://digital.library.lse.ac.uk/objects/lse:nut827hel/read/
    single#page/70/mode/2up>, accessed 3 January 2017.
10 *The Times*, 18 January 1932.
11 Harold J. Laski, 'The Position and Prospects of Communism', *Foreign Affairs*, 11 (October 1932),
    93–106, at p. 104.
12 Cited in Pimlott, *Labour and the Left in the 1930s*, p. 50.
13 Anonymous, Review of 'Problems of a Socialist Government', *The Times*, 29 August 1933.
14 Ibid.
15 Ibid.
16 G. D. H. Cole, *The Intelligent Man's Review of Europe Today* (London: Gollancz, 1933), p. 658.
17 Cole, *The Intelligent Man's Review*, p. 674.
18 Ibid., p. 388.
19 *Report of the 34th Annual Conference of the Labour Party 1934* (London: Labour Party, 1934), p.
    9.
20 George Lansbury, speech at the annual conference of the Labour Party, 29 June 1923, in Keith
    Sutherland, *The Rape of the Constitution?* (Tiverton: Imprint Academic, 2000), p. 99.
21 George Lansbury, 'Preface' in W. P. Coates, *More Anti-Soviet Lies Nailed*, p. 7.

22 *British Russian Gazette and Trade Outlook* (October 1930), p. 23.

23 Harold Laski, *Democracy in Crisis* (London: Allen and Unwin, 1933), p. 87.

24 *New Statesman*, 10 September 1932.

25 Kingsley Martin, *Harold Laski, 1893–1950: A Biographical Memoir* (London: Gollancz, 1953), pp. 83–5.

26 Hansard, HC Deb, 5 April 1933, vol. 276, cols 1804–5.

27 Harold J. Laski, 'Soviet Russia, the Structure and the Spirit, the Webbs' Survey', *Manchester Guardian*, 25 November 1935, pp. 9–10.

28 Pelling, *A Short History of the Labour Party*, p. 83.

29 Walter Citrine, *I Search for Truth in Russia* (London: Routledge, 1936). p. vii.

30 Stafford Cripps, Harry Pollitt and James Maxton, *The Unity Campaign* (London: National Unity Campaign Committee, 1937), p. 1.

31 Stafford Cripps, Harry Pollitt and James Maxton, *The Unity Campaign* (London: National Unity Campaign, 1937). See also Gordon Brown, *Maxton* (Edinburgh, Mainstream, 1986, p. 272.

32 The vote to expel Cripps was carried by 2,100,000 votes to 402,000. Peter Clarke and Richard Toye, 'Cripps, Sir (Richard) Stafford (1889–1952)', *Oxford Dictionary of National Biography* [online edn] (January 2011) <http://www.oxforddnb.com/view/article/32630>, accessed 23 March 2015.

33 Hansard, HC Deb, 25 March 1931, vol. 250, col. 432.

34 G. D. H. Cole, *Europe, Russia and the Future* (New York: Macmillan, 1942) p. 9–10.

35 Andrew Thorpe, 'Stalinism and British Politics', *History*, 83 (1998), 608–27, at p. 625.

36 *Labour Monthly*, November 1937, pp. 671–2. Cited in 'Cohen, Rose', *Dictionary of Labour Biography*, ed. Bellamy, Saville et al., vol. 11, p. 38.

37 'The World of G. D. H. Cole', *New Statesman and Nation*, 25 August 1956, cited in C. Wright Mills, *The Marxists* (Harmondsworth: Pelican, 1962), p. 154. Rt Hon. Peter Shore PC (1924–2001) was a Labour MP, Cabinet minister and peer who, prior to his entry into Parliament, was the head of the Labour Party's Research Department.

38 Attlee to Laski (20 August 1945), Laski MSS, University of Hull, cited in Michael Newman, 'Laski, Harold Joseph (1893–1950)', *Oxford Dictionary of National Biography* [online edn] (January 2011) <http://www.oxforddnb.com/view/article/34412>, accessed 22 March 2015.

39 *The Times*, 11 June 1946.

40 Laski, *The Webbs and Soviet Communism*, pp.8, 11, 13.

41 The idea had been discussed for many years, but Labour had previously lacked the parliamentary majority to introduce it. As Hugh Dalton, Chancellor of the Exchequer in the 1945 Labour government, had written twenty years earlier: 'No defence can be put forward where wealth has been obtained by inheritance. No inheritor of wealth has done anything to earn it.' Cited in Tracey, *The Book of the Labour Party*, vol. 2, p.293.

42 *Socialist Landmark*, p. 101. Laski added: 'A century after its publication no one has been able seriously to controvert any of its major propositions.'

43 *The Times*, 27 and 28 November 1946.

44 Laski, *Democracy in Crisis*, p. 87.

45 *Socialist Landmark,* pp. 96–7.

46 *Beatrice Webb's Typescript diary*, 27 January 1932, (p. 24), *LSE Digital Library* (n.d.) <http://digital.library.lse.ac.uk/objects/lse:nut827hel/read/single#page/24/mode/2up>, accessed 3 January 2017. The Webbs had just hosted Dalton for a week. Her perception of his attitude, drawn from their lengthy conversations, should thus be reasonably trustworthy.

47 Bullard, diary entries for 18, 27 and 30 April 1931.

48 Lawrence Goldman, *The Life of R. H. Tawney, Socialism and History* (London: A&C Black, 2013), p. 177.

49 Ibid., p. 5.

50 Ibid., p. 278.

51 *Beatrice Webb's Typescript diary*, 8December 1935, (p. 210), *LSE Digital Library* (n.d.) http://digital.library.lse.ac.uk/objects/lse:qif604fiv/read/single#page/210/mode/2up> , accessed 22 January 2017.

52 R.H. Tawney, 'British Socialism Today', *Socialist Commentary*, June 1952, p. 339.

53 Some, such as Tony Benn and Ellen Wilkinson, on quite tenuous grounds. Dale, *God's Politicians*, pp. 118, 194.

Chapter 40

1   Christopher Andrew, 'Foreword', in Madeira, *Britannia and the Bear*, p. x.

2   Chris Wrigley, 'Bevin, Ernest (1881–1951)', *Oxford Dictionary of National Biography* [online edn] (January 2008) <http://www.oxforddnb.com/view/article/31872>, accessed 23 March 2015.

3   TNA, CAB 129-22, CP 313, 24 November 1947, *Extinction of Human Rights in Eastern Europe*; TNA, CAB 129-25, CP 72, 3 March 1948, *The Threat to Western Civilisation*; TNA, CAB 129-23, CP 7, 5 January 1948, *Review of Soviet Policy.*

4   TNA, CAB 129-22, CP 313, 24 November 1947, *Extinction of Human Rights*, p. 1.

5   TNA, CAB 23, 10/30, 12 February 1930.

6   E.g. John Bromley MP: 'The internal affairs of Russia are nothing to do with us'. Hansard, HC Deb, 5 November 1929, vol. 231, col. 949.

7   Hansard, HL Deb, 13 February 1930, vol. 76, cols 584–5.

8   Hansard, HL Deb, 25 July 1934, vol. 93, col. 1114.

9   TNA, CAB 129-22, CP 313, 24 November 1947, *Extinction of Human Rights*, p. 2.

10 TNA, CAB 129-23, CP 7, 5 January 1948, *Review of Soviet Policy*, p. 5.

11 The *Herald* article is cited in William Wainwright, *The Forced Labour Swindle* (London, British-Soviet Society, 1949). Wainwright, 'one of the Communist Party of Great Britain's most effective journalists, pamphleteers, and speakers' (*The Guardian*, 16 November 2000) rushed to reply, and in the pamphlet described the Soviet criminal legislation was 'The World's Most Humane Penal Code', and the accusations to be 'An old, old lie', pp. 4,14.

12 TNA, CAB 129-23, CP 7, 5 January 1948, *Review of Soviet Policy*, p. 1, 3, 2.

13 Ibid., p.11.

14 Ibid.

15 TNA, CAB 129-25, CP 72, 3 March 1948, *The Threat to Western Civilisation*, p. 3.

16 Paul Robeson, 'To You Beloved Comrade', *New World Review*, 21:4 (April 1953), 11–13.

Conclusion

1   The list includes: TUC presidents George Hicks MP, A. A. Purcell MP, Ben Tillett MP, John Bromley MP, Alexander Walkden MP, A. B. Swales; union leaders Robert Smillie MP, Will Lawther MP, A. J. Cook, Alex Gossip; and TUC General Secretary Fred Bramley.

2   'I believe that it is necessary to postpone process concerning Tikhon in connection with the intensity of propaganda abroad' (signed by Dzerzhinsky, Zinoviev, Kamenev, Stalin, Soglasen). 'Note by F. E. Dzerzhinsky, chairman of the GPU, at the meeting of the Politburo of the Central Committee concerning a delay in the action against Patriarch Tikhon, 21 April 1923', *Archives of the Kremlin: The Politburo and the Church, 1922-1925*, GARF, f.3, of. 60. d.25. *Historical materials* [online archive] (n.d.) <http://istmat.info/node/27756>, accessed 21 January 2017.

3   *Morning Star*, 12 April 2001.

4   Dept of State Telegram to US Embassy, Constantinople, 29 May 1915. Original reference 867.4106/67 Sent by the U.S. Dept. of State on behalf of the French Government.

5   Jonathan Davis, in John Shepherd, Jonathan Davis and Chris Wrigley, *Britain's Second Labour Government, 1929-31: A Reappraisal* (Manchester: Manchester University Press, 2011), pp. 150-169

6   Hansard, HL Deb, 1 November 1932, vol. 85, col. 940.

7   TNA, FO 371/15590, N 2582/1/38.

8   TNA, CAB 129-22, CP 313, 24 November 1947, *Extinction of Human Rights*, p. 2.

9   <http://www.bbc.co.uk/pressoffice/pressreleases/stories/2005/07_july/13/radio4.shtml> , accessed 16 January 2017

10 *Beatrice Webb's Diaries 1924–1932*, ed. M. Cole, entry for 14 May 1932.

11 It is interesting to note how many significant Soviet enthusiasts were children of the vicarage or manse: H. N. Brailsford, F. Bramley, Fenner Brockway, W. P. Crozier, Hugh Dalton, Cecil Malone, Sydney Olivier, Graham Wallas, among others.

Postscript

1   *New Statesman*, 15 March 2016.

Appendix 1

1   The details in this appendix have been taken from the database 'Zhertvy politicheskogo terrora v

SSSR' (Жертвы политического террора в CCCP) [The victims of political terror in the USSR], *Memorial* [online list] (2007) <http://lists.memo.ru/>, accessed 3 January 2017.
2 Dalton, *Diary*, 15 May 1931.
3 Andrew, *The Defence of the Realm*, p. 145.
4 Andrew Thorpe, *The British Communist Party and Moscow*, p. 43.
5 TNA, KV 2/1410-1416.
6 See Chapter 25.

Appendix 2
1 *Manchester Guardian*, 8 March 1930.
2 *Manchester Guardian*, 21 February 1930.
3 Bullard, diary, 2 February 1931.
4 Pim and Bateson, *Report on Russian Timber Camps*, p. 12.
5 Ibid., p. 100.
6 *The Spectator*, 14 November 1931.
7 *The Tablet*, 11 April 1931. The paper also reported that Harby's letter had been used by timber interests in the *Bucks Free Press* to quell unease among those in the local chair-making trade which was predominantly located in High Wycombe.
8 Statement by Aatami Kuortti, in a letter from Carlyon Bellairs to Ramsay MacDonald (6 February 1931), TNA 371/15589, N 208(x)[numeral unclear]/1/38.
9 Hansard, HC Deb, 21 April 1931, vol. 251, col. 811.
10 Hansard, HC Deb, 5 November 1929, vol. 231, cols 973–4.
11 Hansard, HC Deb, 26 November 1930, vol. 245, col. 1388.
12 *Forced Labour in Russia?*, p. 31
13 TNA, FO 371/15588, N 525/1/38.

Appendix 3
1 TNA, CAB 24-111, CP 1885, 23 September 1920.
2 The British Library, The British Library of Political Science (London School of Economics), and the library of the School of Slavonic and East European Studies.
3 Philip Grierson, *Books on Soviet Russia, 1917–1942: A Bibliography and a Guide to Reading* (London: Methuen, 1943).
4 Hansard, HL Deb, 13 February 1930, vol. 76, cols 585–6.
5 George Lansbury, 'Preface', in W. P. Coates, *More Anti-Soviet Lies Nailed*, p. 7-8.
6 Ibid., p. 9.
7 Andrew J. Williams, *Labour and Russia: The Attitude of the Labour Party to the USSR, 1924–1934* (Manchester: Manchester University Press, 1989), pp. 17, 135.
8 With the exception of E. D. Morel (who died in 1924) and Duncan Carmichael, who were only on the 1924 list, the membership remained fairly constant, according to the available lists of members in 1924, 1927 and 1930. Sources: W. P. and Zelda Coates, *History of Anglo-Soviet Relations*, p.152; LPL, Lang Papers, vol. 74, p. 29. Letter, W. P. Coates to Lang (April 10, 1930) (names on ARPC letterhead).

Appendix 4
1 See Chapter 31.
2 ASS, newspaper cutting (name and date omitted) sent to the Anti-Slavery Society investigators on 12 February 1931.
3 ASS, statement of Gordon Whitefield.

Appendix 5
1 LPL, Canon J. A. Douglas Papers, vol. 40, p. 130.

Appendix 6
1 LPL, Lang Papers, vol. 73, p. 83. The wording of a circular from the Christian Protest Movement.

Appendix 7
1 *Manchester Guardian*, 6 March 1930.

2   What the authors misleadingly left out was the context in which this figure should have been assessed: 20,000 churches (one-third) of all churches had already been closed and the process was continuing unchecked. A report by a Capt. Liddell, Metropolitan Police, Special Branch, headed 'Secret', reads: 'The following extract from an article called "Women Workers and Religious Dope", dated Moscow 9.3.30, which has been sent to the "[Daily] Worker", contains certain figures regarding the closing of churches in Soviet Russia which, owing to their source, may presumably be taken to be authentic as far as they go: out of the 65,000 churches which existed before the Revolution only 45,000 open now. Out of the 20,000 churches that have been closed down 7,000 have been turned into museums and art memorials. In Moscow out of the 1,600 churches only 700 are open whilst another 92 churches are to be closed down, on the decisions taken at workers' meetings. The big synagogue has been given to the Atheists' Society for their needs. We learn from Kharkov that 364 churches and prayer houses have been closed down in the Ukraine, on initiatives of the workers and peasants. The former churches are occupied by 120 Village Soviets, 60 schools, clubs and other cultural institutions'. FO 371/14842, N 1893/23/38, 19 March 1930.

Appendix 9

1   Glasgow City Archives, *Glasgow Digital Library* (n.d.) <http://gdl.cdlr.strath.ac.uk/maxton/maxton009.htm>, accessed 29 September 2016.

Appendix 10

1   Printed circular, a copy of which can be found at LPL, Lang Papers, vol 75, p. 56.

Appendix 11

1   LPL, Lang Papers, vol 75, pp. 119–21.

BIBLIOGRAPHY

Newspapers and periodicals

Anglo-Russian News Bulletin, Birmingham Post, Brighton & Hove Weekly News, British Russian Trade Gazette and Trade Outlook, Burton Daily Mail, Daily Express, Daily Herald, Daily Telegraph, Daily Worker, Dundee Courier and Advertiser, Evening Chronicle, Forward, Home and Empire, Huddersfield Daily Examiner, Irish Times, Liverpool Post, Manchester Guardian, Morning Post, Morning Star, New Leader, New Statesman (in the period 1931–64, *New Statesman and Nation*), *Northern Daily Mail, Northern Mail & Newcastle Chronicle, Nottingham Guardian, Scotsman, Sunday Referee, The Literary Guide, The Spectator, The Tablet, The Times, The United Methodist, Timber Trades Journal, Time Magazine, Western Daily Press, Yorkshire Herald, Yorkshire Post*

Archives

Durham, Durham Cathedral Library, *Bishop Henson Papers*. MSS Henson GB-0034-HHH 49–52.

Kew, National Archives, CAB 23, Cabinet Minutes & Conclusions.

Kew, National Archives, CAB 24, Cabinet Memoranda.

Kew, National Archives, FO 371, Foreign Office: Political Departments, General Correspondence from 1906.

London, Lambeth Palace Library, *The Papers of Cosmo Gordon Lang, Archbishop of Canterbury*. MSS Lang 73–75.

London, Lambeth Palace Library, *The Papers* of *Canon J. A. Douglas*. MSS Douglas 40.

London, London Metropolitan Archive, Records of the Parish of Holy Trinity, Brompton, *c.*1829–1981. MSS P84/TRI2.

London, London School of Economics, British Library of Political and Economic Science, *Diary, Correspondence and Papers of Hugh Dalton, 1887–1962.*

London, School of Slavonic and East European Sciences, *Sir Bernard Pares Collection*. MSS PAR/7.

Oxford, Bodleian Library, *The Papers of the Anti-Slavery Society*. MSS Brit.Emp. G405–408.

Private Collection, Reader W. Bullard, 'Diaries (Typescript Mss)'.

Private Collection, *The Papers of A. T. Cholerton*.

Command Papers

1919 [Cmd. 8] *Russia. No. 1 (1919), A collection of reports on Bolshevism in Russia.*

1920 [Cmd. 587] *Russia. No. 1 (1920). Agreement between His Majesty's government and the Soviet government of Russia for the exchange of prisoners.*

1920 [Cmd. 772] *Army. Statement of expenditure on naval and military operations in Russia, from the date of the armistice to the 31st March, 1920.*

1920 [Cmd. 818] *Army. The evacuation of North Russia, 1919.*

1921 [Cmd. 1207] *Russian trade agreement. Trade agreement between His Britannic Majesty's government and the government of the Russian Socialist Federal Soviet Republic.*

1922 [Cmd. 1602] *Russia no. 1 (1922). Correspondence with the Russian Soviet government respecting the imprisonment of Mrs. Stan Harding in Russia.*

1923 [Cmd. 1846] *Russia no. 1 (1923). Correspondence between His Majesty's government and the Soviet government respecting the murder of Mr. C. F. Davison in January 1920.*

1923 [Cmd. 1869] *Russia no. 2 (1923). Correspondence between His Majesty's government and the Soviet government respecting the relations between the two governments.*

1923 [Cmd. 1874] *Russia no. 3 (1923). Reply of Soviet government to His Majesty's government respecting the relations between the two governments.*

1923 [Cmd. 1890] *Russia no. 4 (1923). Further correspondence between His Majesty's government and the Soviet government respecting the relations between the two governments.*

1924 [Cmd. 2215] *Russia no. 1 (1924). Draft of proposed general treaty between Great Britain and Northern Ireland and the Union of Soviet Socialist Republics.*

1924 [Cmd. 2216] *Russia no. 2 (1924). Draft of proposed treaty of commerce and navigation between Great Britain and Northern Ireland and the Union of Soviet Socialist Republics.*

1924 [Cmd. 2260] *Russia no. 4 (1924). General treaty between Great Britain and Northern Ireland and the Union of Soviet Socialist Republics.*

1924 [Cmd. 2261] *Russia no. 5 (1924). Treaty of commerce and navigation between Great Britain and Northern Ireland and the Union of Soviet Socialist Republics signed at London, August 8, 1924.*

1927 [Cmd. 2822] *Russia no. 1 (1927). Note from His Majesty's government to the government of the Union of Soviet Socialist Republics respecting the relations existing between the two governments and note in reply. February 23/26, 1927.*

1927 [Cmd. 2874] *Russia no. 2 (1927). Documents illustrating the hostile activities of the Soviet government and Third International against Great Britain.*

1927 [Cmd. 2895] *Russia no. 3 (1927). Selection of papers dealing with the relations between His Majesty's government and the Soviet government 1921–1927.*

1928 [Cmd. 3125] *Russian banks and communist funds. Report of an enquiry into certain transactions of the Bank for Russian Trade, Ltd., and the Moscow Narodny Bank, Ltd. Memorandum by the directors of the Moscow Narodny Bank, Ltd.*

1929–30 [Cmd. 3418] *Russia no. 1 (1929). Correspondence regarding the resumption of relations with the government of the Union of Soviet Socialist Republics.*

1929–30 [Cmd. 3467] *Notes exchanged on the occasion of the resumption of diplomatic relations with the Union of Soviet Socialist Republics (December, 1929).*

1929–30 [Cmd. 3511] *Decree of the All-Russian Central Executive Committee and the Council of People's Commissars respecting religious associations, 8th April, 1929*

1929–30 [Cmd. 3552] *Temporary commercial agreement between the United Kingdom and Russia.*

1929–30 [Cmd. 3558] *International Labour Conference. Report to the Minister of Labour by the Government Delegates of H.M. Government.*

1929–30 [Cmd. 3583] *Temporary Fisheries agreement between the Governments of the United Kingdom and the Union of Soviet Socialist Republics (May, 1930).*

1929–30 [Cmd. 3641] *Russia no. 2 (1930). Certain legislation respecting religion in force in the Union of Soviet Socialist Republics.*

1930–31 [Cmd. 3775] *Russia no. 1 (1931). A selection of documents relative to the labour legislation in force in the Union of Soviet Socialist Republics.*

1930–31 [Cmd. 3841] *Fourteenth Session – Proposed action relating to the draft convention on forced labour (Labour Conference (International)).*

1930–31 [Cmd. 3904] *Report on the organization of the foreign trade of the Union of Soviet Socialist Republics.*

1932–33 [Cmd. 4286] *Russia no. 1 (1933). Correspondence relating to the arrest of employees of the Metropolitan-Vickers Company at Moscow.*

1932–33 [Cmd. 4290] *Russia no. 2 (1933). Further correspondence relating to the arrest of employees of the Metropolitan-Vickers Company at Moscow.*

1933–34 [Cmd. 4513] *Russia no. 1 (1934). Temporary commercial agreement between His Majesty's government in the United Kingdom and the government of the Union of Soviet Socialist Republics.*

General bibliography

Addison, Christopher, et al., *Problems of a Socialist Government* (London: Gollancz, 1933).

Aikman, David, 'The Role of Atheism in the Marxist Tradition', PhD thesis, University of Washington, 1979.

Anderson, Tom, *How to Open and Conduct a Proletarian Sunday School* (Glasgow: n.d., [1920]).

———, *John Davidson and Mary Davis: Lessons given to the Glasgow Socialist Children's School, etc.* (Reformers' Series, 7; Glasgow: Reformers' Bookstall, 1914).

———, *The Proletarian Catechism* (Glasgow: The Proletarian Press, 1931).

Andrew, Christopher M., *The Defence of the Realm: The Authorized History of MI5* (London: Penguin, 2010).

———, *KGB: The Inside Story of its Foreign Operations from Lenin to Gorbachev* (London: Hodder & Stoughton, 1990).

———, *The Mitrokhin Archive: The KGB in Europe and the West* (London: Allen Lane, 1999).

Anglo-Russian Joint Advisory Council, *Anglo-Russian Joint Advisory Council, Supplementary Statement, Trade Union Congress, Edinburgh 1927* (Edinburgh: Dobson Molle, 1925).

Anonymous, 'Communism in the United States', *Advocate of Peace through Justice*, 93 (1931), 22–4.

Anonymous, *Molodaya Gvardiya* [The Young Guard], 'The Life of the Komsomol. Collection of Articles, Lenin and Youth' (USSR: State Editions, 1927).

Anonymous, *Red Gaols: A Woman's Experiences in Russian Prisons* (trans. from Fr. O. B.) (London: Burns, Oates & Washbourne, 1935).

Anonymous, *Report of Court Proceedings in the Case of the Anti-Soviet 'Bloc of Rights and Trotskyites' heard before the Military Collegium of the Supreme Court of the U.S.S.R., Moscow, March 2–13, 1938* (Moscow: People's Commissariat of Justice of the USSR, 1938).

Anonymous, *Tragedija Sovetskoj Derevni. Kollektivizacija I Raskulachivanie* [The Tragedy of the Soviet Countryside. Collectivization and Dispossession. Documents and Materials], 5 vols (Moscow: ROSSPEN, 1999 - 2006), vol. 2.

Anonymous, *The Anti-Socialist: Organ of the National Movement against Socialism* (London: Anti-Socialist Union of Great Britain, 1909).

Anonymous, *Wrecking Activities at Power Stations in the Soviet Union* (Moscow: State Law Publishing House, 1933).

Antonov-Ovseenko, Anton, *The Time of Stalin-Portrait of a Tyranny* (1st edn, New York: Harper & Row, 1981).

Applebaum, Anne, *Gulag: A History of the Soviet Camps* (London: Allen Lane, 2003).

———, *Iron Curtain: The Crushing of Eastern Europe 1944–56* (London: Allen Lane, 2012).

Atholl, Duchess of (Katharine Stewart-Murray), *The Conscription of a People* (London: Philip Allan, 1931).

Attlee, Clement R., *As it Happened* (London: Heinemann, 1954).

Auerback, Leopold, et al., *The White Sea Canal*, ed. M. Gorky (trans. Amabel Williams-Ellis) (London: Bodley Head, 1935).

Bacon, Edwin, *The Gulag at War: Stalin's Forced Labour System in the Light of the Archives* (London: Macmillan Press/CREES, 1994).

Baikaloff, Anatole V., *In the Land of Communist Dictatorship* (London: Jonathan Cape, 1929).

Barberis, Peter, *Encyclopedia of British and Irish Political Organizations: Parties, Groups and Movements of the Twentieth Century* (London: Pinter, 2000).

Barnes, George Nicoll and International Conference on Labour and Religion London, *The Religion in the Labour Movement* (London: Holborn, 1919).

Baron, Nick, 'Conflict and Complicity: The Expansion of the Karelian Gulag, 1923–1933', *Cahiers du monde russe*, 42/2-4 (2001), 615–48.

Barou, N., and Wise, E. F., *The Russian Cooperative Movement* (London: Moscow Narodny Bank, 1926).

Barry, E. Eldon, *Nationalisation in British Politics: The Historical Background* (London: Jonathan Cape, 1965).

Bebbington, David, *Evangelicalism in Modern Britain: A History from the 1730s to the 1980s* (London: Routledge, 2005).

Beckett, Francis, *Stalin's British Victims* (Stroud: Sutton, 2004).

Bellamy, Joyce M., John Saville et al. (eds), *Dictionary of Labour Biography*, 13 vols (London: Macmillan, 1972–2010).

Beloff, Max, 'The Age of Laski', *Fortnightly Review*, 167 (1950), 378–84.

Benn, H. H., 'Judging the USSR', *Anglo-Soviet Journal,*, 2, (1941), 171–87.

Bennett, Gillian, *'A Most Extraordinary and Mysterious Business': The Zinoviev Letter of 1924* (London: Foreign & Commonwealth Office, General Services Command, 1999).

Betteridge, Jennifer, 'The Political Purposes of Surveillance', unpublished paper, University of Leeds, 2006.

Bevir, Mark, 'The Labour Church Movement, 1891–1902', *Journal of British Studies*, 38 (April 1999), 217–45.

Bickley, Paul, *Building Jerusalem? Christianity and the Labour Party* (London: Bible Society, 2010).

Bohlen, Charles E., *Witness to History, 1929–1969* (New York: Norton, 1973).

Bourdeaux, Michael, *Faith on Trial in Russia* (London: Hodder & Stoughton, 1971).

Bourne, Kenneth, Donald Cameron Watt and Dominic Lieven, *British Documents on Foreign Affairs: Reports and Papers from the Foreign Office Confidential Print. Part II, From the First to the Second World War, Series A, the Soviet Union, 1917–1939*, 15 vols (Frederick, Md.: University Publications of America, 1984–86).

Brackman, Roman, *The Secret File of Joseph Stalin: A Hidden Life* (Portland, Ore.: Frank Cass, 2000).

Briggs, Asa and John Saville, *Essays in Labour History: In Memory of G. D. H. Cole* (London: Macmillan, 1960).

British Empire Union, Research Department, *Danger Ahead: Socialist and Proletarian Sunday Schools* (London: British Empire Union, 1922).

British Russian Gazette and Trade Outlook, *Forced Labour in Russia? Facts and Documents* (London: British Russian Gazette and Trade Outlook, 1931).

British Trades Union Delegation to Russia and Caucasia, *Russia: The Official Report of the British Trades Union Delegation to Russia and Caucasia, Nov. and Dec., 1924.* (London: Trades Union Congress, General Council, 1925).

Brockway, Fenner, *Inside the Left: Thirty Years of Platform, Press, Prison and Parliament* (London: Allen & Unwin, 1942).

———, *Outside the Right: A Sequel To 'Inside The Left'* (London: Allen & Unwin, 1963).

Brown, Gordon, *Maxton* (Edinburgh: Mainstream, 1986).

Buber-Neumann, Margarete, *Under Two Dictators* (London: Gollancz, 1949).

Budenz, Louis F., *The Techniques of Communism* (New York: Arno Press, 1977)

Bullard, Reader W., *Inside Stalin's Russia: The Diaries of Reader Bullard, 1930–1934*, ed. Julian Bullard and Margaret Bullard (Charlbury: Day, 2000).

Bullock, Ian, *Romancing the Revolution: The Myth of Soviet Democracy and the British Left* (Edmonton, Alberta: AU Press, 2011).

Burleigh, Michael, *Sacred Causes: The Clash of Religion and Politics, from the Great War to the War on Terror* (New York: Harper Collins, 2007).

Busky, Donald F., *Democratic Socialism: A Global Survey* (Westport, Conn.: Praeger, 2000)

Callaghan, John, 'The Left and the "Unfinished Revolution": Bevanites and Soviet Russia in the 1950s', *Contemporary British History*, 15 (2001), 63–82.

Callaghan, John and Kevin Morgan, 'The Open Conspiracy of the Communist Party and the Case of W. N. Ewer, Communist and Anti-Communist', *The Historical Journal*, 49:2 (2006), 549–64.

Callwell, Charles E., *Field-Marshal Sir Henry Wilson: His Life And Diaries*, 2 vols (London: Cassell, 1927).

Campbell, Alan, John McIlroy and Kevin Morgan, *Party People, Communist Lives: Explorations in Biography* (London: Lawrence & Wishart, 2001).

Carlton, David, *MacDonald versus Henderson: The Foreign Policy of the Second Labour Government* (London: Macmillan, 1970).

Carr, E. H., *Socialism in One Country 1924–1926*, 3 vols (London: Macmillan, 1958–64), vol. 1.

Carynnyk, Marco, Lubomyr Y. Luciuk and Bohdan S. Kordan, *The Foreign Office and the Famine: British Documents on Ukraine and the Great Famine of 1932–1933* (Kingston, Ontario: Limestone Press, 1988).

Catterall, Peter, 'Morality and Politics: The Free Churches and the Labour Party between the Wars', *The Historical Journal*, 36 (1993), 667–85.

Caute, David, *The Fellow Travellers: A Postscript to the Enlightenment* (New York: Weidenfeld and Nicolson, 1973).

Ceadel, Martin, 'The "King and Country" Debate, 1933: Student Politics, Pacifism and the Dictators', *The Historical Journal*, 22 (1979), 397–422.

Chamberlin, W. H., *Russia's Iron Age* (London: Duckworth, 1935).

——, 'What is Happening in Russia?', *International Affairs*, 12 (1933), 187–204.

Chernavin, Vladimir, 'Life in Concentration Camps in USSR', *The Slavonic and East European Review*, 12 (1934), 387–408.

——, 'Prison Life in USSR', *The Slavonic and East European Review*, 12 (1933), 63–78.

Christian Protest Movement, *A Challenge to Christendom – Facts about the Russian Persecutions and the Communist Attitude to Religion)* (London: Christian Protest Movement, n.d. [1931?]).

——, *A World War on All Religions* (London: Christian Protest Movement, 1933).

Citrine, Walter, *In Russia Now* (London: Robert Hale, 1942).

——, *I Search for Truth in Russia* (London: Routledge, 1936).

Clapham, Barbara and Catherine Tye, *Holy Trinity Brompton: Through the Generations* (London: Holy Trinity Brompton, 2005).

Clavin, Patricia, *Securing the World Economy: The Reinvention of the League of Nations, 1920–1946* (Oxford: Oxford University Press, 2013).

Cliff, Tony, *The Labour Party: A Marxist History* (London: Bookmarks, 1988).

Coates, W. P., *Anti-Soviet Lies Nailed* (London: Anglo-Russian Parliamentary Committee, 1930).

——, *More Anti-Soviet Lies Nailed* (London: Anglo-Russian Parliamentary Committee, 1933).

——, *Religion in Tsarist and Soviet Russia* (London: Anglo-Russian Parliamentary Committee, 1927).

——, *Russia's Counter-Claims* (London: National 'Hands Off Russia' Committee, 1924).

——, Zelda K. Coates (Kahan), *A History of Anglo-Soviet Relations* (London: Lawrence and Wishart, 1943).

——, ——, and Joseph Stalin, *The Moscow Trial (January, 1937) and Two Speeches by J. Stalin* (London: The Anglo-Russian Parliamentary Committee, 1937).

Cockett, R. B., ' "In Wartime Every Objective Reporter Should Be Shot." The Experience of British Press Correspondents in Moscow, 1941–5', *Journal of Contemporary History*, 23 (1988), 515–30.

Cole, G. D. H., *Europe, Russia and the Future* (New York: Macmillan, 1942).

——, 'Non-Manual Trade Unionism', *The North American Review*, 215 (January–June 1922), 38–45.

Cole, Margaret, *The Story of Fabian Socialism* (New York: John Wiley, 1961).

Collard, Dudley, *Soviet Justice and the Trial of Radek and others* (London: Gollancz, 1937)

Commission on the Ukraine Famine, *Investigation of the Ukrainian Famine, 1932–1933: Report to Congress* (Washington: United States Government Printing Office, 1987).

Communist Party of the Soviet Union, *History of the Communist Party of the Soviet Union (Bolsheviks): Short Course* (Moscow: Red Star Press, 1939).

—— and Joseph Stalin, *Political Report to the Sixteenth Party Congress of the Russian Communist Party* (Moscow: Modern Books, 1930).

Connor, Emmet O., 'Communists, Russia, and the IRA, 1920–1923', *The Historical Journal*, 46 (2003), 115–31.

Conquest, Robert, 'In Celia's Office', *Hoover Digest*, (1999), 2, p. 3.

——, *The Great Terror: A Reassessment* (London: Hutchinson, 1990).

——, *The Harvest of Sorrow: Soviet Collectivisation and the Terror-Famine* (London: Hutchinson, 1986).

——, 'Victims of Stalinism: A Comment', *Europe-Asia Studies*, 49 (1997), 1317–19.

—— (ed.), *Religion in the USSR* (London: Bodley Head, 1968).

Conservative and Unionist Central Office, The Subversive Movements Investigation Department, *Special Issue on Slave Labour and Forced Labour in Russia* (London: Conservative and Unionist Central Office, 1931).

Corley, Felix, *Religion in the Soviet Union: An Archival Reader* (Basingstoke: Macmillan, 1996).

Corthorn, Paul, *In the Shadow of the Dictators: The British Left in the 1930s* (London: I. B. Tauris, 2012).

——, 'Labour, the Left, and the Stalinist Purges of the Late 1930s', *The Historical Journal*, 48:1 (March 2005), 179–207.

Courtois, Stéphane et al., *The Black Book of Communism: Crimes, Terror, Repression* (trans. Jonathan Murphy and Mark Kramer) (Cambridge, Mass.: Harvard University Press, 1999).

Craig, Maggie, *When the Clyde Ran Red* (Edinburgh: Mainstream Publishing, 2011).

Cripps, Richard Stafford, Harry Pollitt and James Maxton, *The Unity Campaign* (London: National Unity Campaign, 1937).

Crosby, Travis L., *The Unknown David Lloyd George: A Statesman in Conflict* (London: I.B. Tauris, 2014).

Crossman, Richard, *The God that Failed: Six Studies in Communism* (London: Hamish Hamilton, 1950).

Dallin, David J., *Forced Labour in Soviet Russia* (London: Hollis and Carter, 1948).

Dalrymple, Dana G., 'The Soviet Famine of 1932–1934', *Soviet Studies*, 15:3 (1964), 250–84.

———, 'The Soviet Famine of 1932–1934; Some Further References', *Soviet Studies*, 16:3 (1965), 471–4.

Dalton, Hugh, *The Capital Levy Explained* (London: Labour Publishing, 1923)

Davies, Andrew, *To Build a New Jerusalem: The British Labour Movement from the 1880s to the 1990s* (London: Michael Joseph, 1992).

Davis, Tracy C., *George Bernard Shaw and the Socialist Theatre* (Westport, Conn.: Praeger, 1994).

Deacon, Richard, *The British Connection: Russia's Manipulation of British Individuals and Institutions* (London: Hamish Hamilton, 1979).

Degras, Jane Tabrisky, *Calendar of Soviet Documents on Foreign Policy, 1917–1941* (London: Royal Institute of International Affairs, 1948).

———, *The Communist International 1919–1943: Documents*, 3 vols (London: Oxford University Press, 1956–65).Deli, Peter, 'The Image of the Russian Purges in the Daily Herald and the New Statesman', *Journal of Contemporary History*, 20 (1985), 261–82.

Democritus (pseud.), *Labour and Democracy: Being a Series of Open Letters to the Labour Party* (London: British Workers' League, 1916).

Deutscher, Isaac, *Stalin: A Political Biography* (Harmondsworth: Penguin, 1966).

Dilling, Elizabeth Kirkpatrick, *The Red Network: A 'Who's Who' and Handbook of Radicalism for Patriots* (Kenilworth, Ill.: Elizabeth Dilling, 1935).

Douglas, Roy, 'The National Democratic Party and the British Workers' League', *The Historical Journal*, 15 (1972), 533–52.

Drazin, Charles, *In Search of the Third Man* (London: Methuen, 1999).

Druzhnikov, Yuri, *Informer 001: The Myth of Pavlik Morozov* (trans. Sonia Melnikova) (New York: Rosen, 1993).

Duranty, Walter, *Duranty Reports Russia* (New York: The Viking Press, 1934).

———, *USSR: The Story of Soviet Russia* (Philadelphia: J. B. Lippincott, 1944).

Durham, Martin, 'British Revolutionaries and the Suppression of the Left in Lenin's Russia, 1918–1924', *Journal of Contemporary History*, 20 (1985), 203–19.

Eight Labour Members of Parliament (pseud.), *To the Workers of the World: An Appeal for Personal Religion* (London: W. A. Hammond, 1913).

Evans, Stanley, *East of Stettin-Trieste* (London: Fore Publications, 1951).

———, *Hungary's Churches Today* (London: Hungarian News and Information, 1951).

———, *Joseph Stalin: An Address Given by Rev. Stanley Evans, M.A. at a Memorial Service for Joseph Stalin at the Church of St. George, Queen Square, London, on March 13th, 1953* (London: Society of Socialist Clergy and Ministers, 1953).

———, *Russia and the Atomic Bomb* (London: British-Soviet Society, 1949).

Even-Shoshan, Shlomo (ed.), *Minsk, ir va-em* ('Minsk, Jewish Mother-City'), 2 vols (Jerusalem: Association of Olim from Minsk and its Surroundings, 1975–85).

Eyre-Todd, George, *Mobocracy; Or, Toward the Abyss* (Glasgow: Scottish Council of the National Citizens' Union, 1922).

Fabian Society, *Annual Report* (London: The Fabian Society, 1919).

Figes, Orlando, *A People's Tragedy: The Russian Revolution, 1891–1924* (London: Jonathan Cape, 1996).

Fisher, David, *A Band of Little Comrades: The Story of Socialist Sunday Schools in Edinburgh, 1905–1945* (Edinburgh: Dept of Recreation, City of Edinburgh Council, 2001).

Fleay, C., and M. L. Sanders, 'Looking into the Abyss: George Orwell at the BBC', *Journal of Contemporary History*, 24 (1989), 503–18.

Flory, Harriette, 'The Arcos Raid and the Rupture of Anglo-Soviet Relations, 1927', *Journal of Contemporary History*, 12:4 (October 1977), 707–23.

Foreign Office, *The Foreign Office List* (London: HMSO, 1930).

Fuller, Christopher, 'Some Aspects of Life in Soviet Russia (II)', *The English Review*, 54 (1932), 667–75.

Garton Ash, Timothy, 'Orwell's list', *The New York Review of Books*, 50 (2003).

Gellately, Robert, *Lenin, Stalin, and Hitler: The Age of Social Catastrophe* (New York: Vintage Books, 2008).

Gibson, Melissa, 'British Theatre and the Red Peril: The Portrayal of Communism 1917–1945, and: British Theatre Between the Wars 1918–1939 (Review)', *Theatre Journal*, 54 (2002), 659–61.

Gide, André, *Back from the U.S.S.R.* [Eng. trans. of *Retour de l'U.R.S.S.*] (trans. Dorothy Bussy) (London: Secker and Warburg, 1937).

Glenny, M. V., 'The Anglo-Soviet Trade Agreement, March 1921', *Journal of Contemporary History*, 5 (1970), 63–82.

Goldman, Emma (ed.), *Russia and the British Labour Delegation's Report: A Reply.* (London: British Committee for the Defence of Political Prisoners in Russia, 1925).

Goldman, Lawrence, *The Life of R. H. Tawney: Socialism and History* (London: Bloomsbury Academic, 2014).

Gollancz, Victor, *Russia and Ourselves* (London: Gollancz, 1941).

Goold, Neil, *The Twentieth Congress and After* (Belfast: B&ICO, 1969).

Gough, Alfred William, *The Lure of Simplicity* (London: E. Nash & Grayson, 1929).

———, *The Saving of Democracy* (London: The National Review, 1920).

Gould, Gerald, *The Coming Revolution in Great Britain* (London: William Collins, 1920).

Gregory, Paul R., and V. V Lazarev, *The Economics of Forced Labor: The Soviet Gulag* (Stanford, Calif.: Hoover Institution Press, 2003).

Grierson, Philip, *Books on Soviet Russia, 1917–1942: A Bibliography and a Guide to Reading* (London: Methuen, 1943).

Griffiths, Brian, *Morality and the Market Place* (London: Hodder & Stoughton, 1982)

Grossman, Vasily, *Forever Flowing* [Eng. trans. of Vse Techet] (New York: Harper & Row, 1972).

Gruber, Ruth, *I Went to the Soviet Arctic* (London: Gollancz, 1939).

Haldane, Charlotte, *Truth Will Out* (London: Weidenfeld and Nicolson, 1949).

Hamill, John, and Andrew Prescott, '"The Masons' Candidate": New Welcome Lodge No. 5139 and the Parliamentary Labour Party', *Labour History Review*, 71 (2006), 9–41.

Hamilton, Cicely, *Modern Russia: As Seen by an Englishwoman* (London: J. M. Dent, 1934).

Hancock, W. C. R., 'No Compromise: Nonconformity and Politics 1893–1914', *Baptist Quarterly*, 36:2 (April 1995), 56–69.

Hardie, James Keir, *Karl Marx: The Man and his Message* (Manchester: National Labour Press, 1910).

Harrison, Austin, 'The Riddle of Lord Haldane', *The English Review, 1908–1937*, 22 (1915), 215–21.

Harrison, Stanley, *Alex Gossip* (London: Lawrence and Wishart, 1962).

Haydon, Walter, *Russia as Seen by Two Tilmanstone Miners. A Record of a Tour to the Donetz Basin in Aug.–Sept., 1929* (Dover: G. W. Grigg & Son, 1929).

Haynes, John Earl, *In Denial: Historians, Communism and Espionage* (San Francisco, Calif.: Encounter Books, 2005).

Hecker, Julius Friedrich, *Religion and Communism: A Study of Religion and Atheism in Soviet Russia* (London: Chapman & Hall, 1933).

Henderson, Fred, *The Case for Socialism* (London: Clarion Press, 1908).

Herling-Grudziński, Gustaw, *A World Apart* (London: Heinemann, 1951).

Hill, Christopher, *Two Commonwealths* (London: Harrap, 1945).

Hobsbawm, E. J., *Interesting Times: A Twentieth-Century Life* (London: Abacus, 2003).

———, *Primitive Rebels: Studies in Archaic Forms of Social Movement in the 19th and 20th Centuries* (Manchester: Manchester University Press, 1959).

Hochschild, Adam, *King Leopold's Ghost: A Story of Greed, Terror, and Heroism in Colonial Africa* (London: Macmillan, 1999)

Hoggart, Simon and David Leigh, *Michael Foot: A Portrait* (London: Hodder & Stoughton, 1981).

Hollander, Paul, *Political Pilgrims: Travels of Western Intellectuals to the Soviet Union, China, and Cuba 1928–1978* (New York: Oxford University Press, 1981).

Holroyd, Michael, *Bernard Shaw*, 4 vols (London: Chatto and Windus, 1988–92), vol. 3 (*The Lure of Fantasy, 1918–1950*).

Howe, Mark De Wolfe (ed.), *Holmes-Laski Letters: The Correspondence of Mr. Justice Holmes and Harold J. Laski 1916–1935* (Cambridge, Mass.: Harvard University Press, 1953).

Hyde, H. Montgomery, *Sir Patrick Hastings: His Life and Cases* (London: Heinemann, 1960).

Independent Labour Party Information Committee, *Who Pays for the Attacks on Labour? An Exposure of the Blackleg Organisations and Propaganda Agencies of Big Capital* (London: Independent Labour Party, 1920).

Independent Labour Party, *Report of the Annual Conference Held at Leicester, April 1918* (London: Independent Labour Party, 1918).

––––––, *Report of the Annual Conference Held at Huddersfield, April 1919* (London: Independent Labour Party, 1919).

––––––, *Report of the Annual Conference Held at Birmingham, April 1930* (London: Independent Labour Party, 1930). ––––––, *Report of the Annual Conference Held at Scarborough, April 1931* (London: Independent Labour Party, 1931).

––––––, *Report of the Annual Conference Held at Blackpool, April 1932* (London: Independent Labour Party, 1932).

Institute of Pacific Relations, *Hearings before the Subcommittee to Investigate the Administration of the Internal Security Act , U. S. Senate, 82d Cong., 2d sess., part 13, 7 April 1952, p.4510* (Washington: United States Government Printing Office, 1952).

International Committee for Political Prisoners, *Letters from Russian Prisons* (London: C. W. Daniel, 1925).

International Military Tribunal, *Trials of the Major War Criminals before the International Military Tribunal*, 42 vols (Nuremberg: International Military Tribunal, 1947–49), vol. 29.

Jarman, Robert L., *Soviet Union Political Reports, 1917–1970* (Slough: Archive Editions, 2004).

Jenkins, Roy, *Churchill* (London: Macmillan, 2001).

Joad, C. E. M., *The Recovery of Belief* (London: Faber, 1952).

Johnson, Graham, 'British Social Democracy and Religion, 1881–1911', *The Journal of Ecclesiastical History*, 51 (January 2000), 94–115.

Johnson, Hewlett, *The Socialist Sixth of the World* (London: Gollancz, 1940).

Jones, Bill, *The Russia Complex: The British Labour Party and the Soviet Union* (Manchester: Manchester University Press, 1977).

Kadish, Sharman, *Bolsheviks and British Jews: The Anglo-Jewish Community, Britain and the Russian Revolution* (London: Routledge, 2013).

Kelsen, Hans, *The Communist Theory of Law* (London: Stevens & Sons, 1955).

Kern, Gary, *A Death in Washington: Walter G. Krivitsky and the Stalin Terror* (New York: Enigma, 2003).

––––––, *The Kravchenko Case: One Man's War on Stalin* (New York: Enigma Books, 2013).

Khlevniuk, Oleg V., *The History of the Gulag: From Collectivization to the Great Terror* (New Haven: Yale University Press, 2004).

––––––, *Stalin: New Biography of a Dictator* (New Haven: Yale University Press, 2015).

Kirby, Dianne, 'Anglo-American Relations and the Religious Cold War', *Journal of Transatlantic Studies*, 10 (2012), 167–81.

––––––, 'Divinely Sanctioned: The Anglo-American Cold War Alliance and the Defence of Western Civilization and Christianity, 1945–48', *Journal of Contemporary History*, 35 (2000), 385–412.

––––––, 'Ecclesiastical McCarthyism: Cold War Repression in the Church of England', *Contemporary British History*, 19:2 (2005), 187–203.

––––––, 'Harry S. Truman's International Religious Anti-Communist Front, the Archbishop of Canterbury and the 1948 Inaugural Assembly of the World Council of Churches', *Contemporary British History*, 15 (2001), 35–70.

Kitchin, George, *Prisoner of the OGPU* (London: Longmans, Green, 1935).

Kizny, Tomasz, *Gulag* (Buffalo: Firefly, 2004).

Klehr, Harvey and John Earl Haynes, *The Secret World of American Communism* (New Haven: Yale University Press, 1995).

Klepenin, Nicholas, *Anti-Religious Activity in Soviet Russia: Non-Political Bulletin Based on Information Contained in the Soviet Press*, bulletins 1–2 (1930), 5–6 (1931).

––––––, 'The Speeches of Yaroslavsky (President of the Union of the Godless)', *The Slavonic and East European Review*, 9 (1931), 536–46.

––––––, 'The War on Religion in Russia', *The Slavonic and East European Review*, 8 (1930), 514–32.

Knox, W. W., 'Religion and the Scottish Labour Movement c.1900–39', *Journal of Contemporary History*, 23 (1988), 609–30.

Koestler, Arthur, *Darkness at Noon* (London: Jonathan Cape, 1970).

Kokurin, A. I. and N. V. Petrov (eds), *GULAG 1917–1960, Dokumenty* (Moscow: Materik, 2000).

Kostiuk, Hryhory, *Stalinist Rule in the Ukraine: A Study of the Decade of Mass Terror (1929–39)* (London: Stevens Atlantic Books, 1960).

Kravchenko, Victor, *I Chose Justice* (London: Robert Hale, 1951).

———, *Kravchenko versus Moscow: The Report of the Famous Paris Case* (London: Wingate, 1950).

Krivitsky, Walter G., *I Was Stalin's Agent* (London: Hamilton, 1939).

Kuusinen, Aino, *Before and after Stalin: A Personal Account of Soviet Russia from the 1920s to the 1960s* (London: Michael Joseph, 1974).

Labour Party (Great Britain), *British Labour Delegation to Russia 1920: Report* (London: Labour Party, 1920).

———, *General Election Manifesto* (London: Labour Party, 1931).

———, *Report of the 22nd Annual Conference of the Labour Party, 1922* (London: Labour Party, 1922).

———, *Report of the 24th Annual Conference of the Labour Party, 1924* (London: Labour Party, 1924).

———, *Report of the 28th Annual Conference of the Labour Party, 1928* (London: Labour Party, 1928).

———, *Report of the 33rd Annual Conference of the Labour Party, 1933* (London: Labour Party, 1933).

———, *Report of the 34th Annual Conference of the Labour Party, 1934* (London: Labour Party, 1934).

———, *Report of the Executive Committee to the 23rd Annual Conference of the Labour Party, 1923* (London: Labour Party, 1923).

———, *Sweated Imports and International Labour Standards* (London: Labour Party, 1926).

———, *The Labour Party and the I.L.P.: The Clear Issue* (London: Labour Party, 1932).

Labour Research Department, *Soviet Russia To-Day: The Report of the British Workers' Delegation which Visited Soviet Russia for the Tenth Anniversary of the Revolution, November, 1927* (London: Labour Party, 1927).

Lane, Arthur Henry, *The Alien Menace* (London: Boswell, 1934).

Lansbury, George, *My Life* (London: Constable, 1928).

———, *What I Saw in Russia* (London: Parsons, 1920).

Lansbury, Violet, *An Englishwoman in the U.S.S.R.* (London: Putnam, 1941).

Laski, Harold J., *Democracy in Crisis* (London: Allen & Unwin, 1933).

———, *Karl Marx: An Essay* (London: Allen & Unwin, 1925)

———, *Law and Justice in Soviet Russia* (London: Hogarth Press, 1935).

———, 'The Position and Prospects of Communism', *Foreign Affairs*, 11 (1932), 93–106.

———, *The Webbs and Soviet Communism* (Webb Memorial Lecture, 1947; London: Fabian Publications, 1947).

Lawton, Denis, *Education and Labour Party Ideologies 1900–2001 and Beyond* (London: Routledge, 2005).

Leigh, David, *The Wilson Plot* (London: Heinemann Mandarin, 1989).

Lenin, Vladimir Ilyich, *On Religion* (Moscow: Progress Publishers, 1969).

———, *What is to be Done?* (Moscow: Progress Publishers, 1947).

Leo XIII, *Rerum Novarum. Encyclical on Capital and Labour, 15 May 1891* (Vatican: The Holy See, 1891).

Leonard, Raymond W., *Secret Soldiers of the Revolution: Soviet Military Intelligence, 1918–1933* (Westport, Conn.: Greenwood Press, 1999).

Leventhal, F. M., 'H. N. Brailsford and the New Leader', *Journal of Contemporary History*, 9:1 (January 1974), 91–113.

Liberman, Simon Isaevich, *Building Lenin's Russia* (Chicago: University of Chicago Press, 1945).

Lilleker, Darren G., *Against the Cold War: The History and Political Traditions of pro-Sovietism in the British Labour Party 1945–89* (London: I. B. Tauris, 2004).

Linden, Harry, 'Marx and Morality: An Impossible Synthesis?', *Theory and Society*, 13 (1984), 119–35.

Linehan, Thomas P., *British Fascism, 1918–39: Parties, Ideology and Culture* (Manchester: Manchester University Press, 2000).

London Workers' Committee, *Hands off Russia! An Urgent Appeal to the Workers of Great Britain.* (London: London Workers' Committee, 1919).

Losev, P. M., and G. I. Ragulin (eds), *Sbornik normativnykh aktov po sovetskomu ispravitel' no-tru-dovomu pravu (1917–1959)* [*A Collection of Normative Acts on Soviet Corrective Labor Law, 1917–1959*] (Moscow: Gosyurizdat, 1959).

Luboff, Edouard, *Soviet Dumping* (London: n.n., 1931).

Lyons, Eugene, *Assignment in Utopia* (New York: Harcourt Brace, 1937).

MacDonald, James Ramsay, *Parliament and Revolution* (Manchester: National Labour Press, 1919).

Macfarlane, L. J., 'Hands off Russia: British Labour and the Russo-Polish War, 1920', *Past & Present*, 38 (December 1967), 126–52.

Mackenzie, F. A., *The Russian Crucifixion* (London: Jarrolds, 1930).

Maclean, Fitzroy, *Eastern Approaches* (London: Jonathan Cape, 1949).

Madeira, Victor, *Britannia and the Bear: The Anglo-Russian Intelligence Wars, 1917–1929* (Woodbridge: Boydell Press, 2014).

Mahon, Tom, 'The Secret IRA-Soviet Agreement, 1925', *History Ireland* [online journal], 17:3 (May–June 2009), <http://www.historyireland.com/20th-century-contemporary-history/the-secret-ira-soviet-agreement-1925/>, accessed 11 February 2016.

Marquand, David, *Ramsay MacDonald* (London: Jonathan Cape, 1977).

Martin, Kingsley, *Father Figures: A First Volume of Autobiography, 1897–1931* (London: Hutchinson, 1966).

——, *Editor: A Second Volume of Autobiography, 1931–45* (London: Hutchinson, 1968).

——, *Harold Laski, 1893–1950: A Biographical Memoir* (London: Gollancz, 1953).

——, 'The Influence of the Press', *The Political Quarterly*, 1 (1930), 157–78.

Marx, Karl, *Communist Manifesto: Socialist Landmark: A New Appreciation Written for the Labour Party*, ed. Harold Laski (London: Allen and Unwin, 1948).

—— and Friedrich Engels, *Collected Works*, 50 vols (London and Moscow: Lawrence & Wishart and Progress Publishers, 1975).

Matters, Leonard W., *Through the Kara Sea* (London: Skeffington & Son, 1932)

Matthews, H. C. G, and Brian Harrison, eds., *Oxford Dictionary of National Biography* (Oxford: Oxford University Press in association with the British Academy, 2004).

Maxton, James, *Dictators and Dictatorship: (Full Report of a Speech ... to the Civil Service Clerical Association)* (London: Independent Labour Party, 1932).

——, *Lenin* (London: Daily Express Publications, 1932).

McDermott, Kevin and Barry McLoughlin, *Stalin's Terror: High Politics and Mass Repression in the Soviet Union* (Basingstoke: Palgrave Macmillan, 2004).

McKibbin, Ross, *Classes and Cultures: England, 1918–1951* (Oxford: Oxford University Press, 1998).

McLellan, David, *The Thought of Karl Marx: An Introduction* (London: Macmillan, 1971).

Medvedev, Roy A., *Let History Judge: The Origins and Consequences of Stalinism* (New York: Columbia University Press, 1989).

Melgunov, S. P., *The Red Terror in Russia* (London: Dent, 1925).

Mills, C. Wright, *The Marxists* (Harmondsworth: Penguin, 1962).

Montagu, Ivor, *Stalin: A Biographical Sketch of the Man who Leads the U.S.S.R.* (London: Communist Party of Great Britain, 1942).

Montefiore, Simon Sebag, *Stalin: The Court of the Red Tsar* (London: Weidenfeld & Nicolson, 2003).

Morgan, Kevin, *Bolshevism and the British Left*, 3 vols (London: Lawrence & Wishart, 2006–13), vols 1–2 (*Labour Legends and Russian Gold*; *The Webbs and Soviet Communism*).

—— and Tauno Saarela, 'Northern Underground Revisited: Finnish Reds and the Origins of British Communism', *European History Quarterly*, 29 (April 1999), 179–215.

Morley, Edith, et al., 'G. D. H. Cole: Tributes', *Fabian Journal*, 27 (1959), 1–6.

Morrell, Gordon W., *Britain Confronts the Stalin Revolution: Anglo-Soviet Relations and the Metro-Vickers's Crisis* (Waterloo, Ontario: Wilfrid Laurier University Press, 1995).

Moscow Patriarchate, *The Truth about Religion in Russia* (trans. Rev. E. N. C. Sergeant) (London: Hutchinson, 1944).

Mowat, Charles, 'The Fall of the Labour Government in Great Britain, August, 1931', *Huntington Library Quarterly*, 7 (1943), 353–86.

Muggeridge, Kitty, *Beatrice Webb: A Life, 1858–1943* (London: Secker & Warburg, 1967).

Muggeridge, Malcolm, *Chronicles of Wasted Time*, ed. Ian Hunter (Vancouver: Regent College Publishing, 2006).

————, 'The Great Liberal Death-Wish', *New Statesman*, 71 (1966), 331.

————, *Winter in Moscow* (London: Eyre & Spottiswode, 1934).

National Congress of Peace and Friendship with the U.S.S.R, *For Peace and Friendship* (London: Gollancz, 1937).

National Council of British Socialist Sunday Schools, *Socialist Sunday Schools: Aims, Objects and Organisation* (n.p.: National Council of British Socialist Sunday Schools, 1920).

National Union of Mineworkers. Scottish Area, *British Miners in Russia: A British Soviet Friendship Society Edition of the Report of the Delegation of the Scottish Area, National Union of Mineworkers* (London: British Soviet Friendship Society, 1950).

New Fabian Research Bureau, *Twelve Studies in Soviet Russia* (London: Gollancz, 1933).

Northrup, David A., *Indentured Labor in the Age of Imperialism, 1838–1922* (Cambridge: Cambridge University Press, 1995).

Orwell, George, *The Complete Works of George Orwell*, ed. Peter Davison, 20 vols (London: Secker & Warburg, 1997–98), vol. 12 (*A Patriot after All: 1940–1941*).

————, *Essays*, ed. Bernard Crick (London: Penguin Classics, 2000).

Paperno, Irina, 'Exhuming the Bodies of Soviet Terror', *Representations*, 75 (2001), 89–118.

Pares, Bernard, *Russia* (Harmondsworth: Penguin, 1941).

Pasternak, Boris, *Doctor Zhivago* (New York: Pantheon, 1958).

Pelling, Henry, *The British Communist Party: A Historical Profile* (London: A. & C. Black, 1975).

————, *The Origins of the Labour Party, 1880–1900* (London: Macmillan, 1954).

————, *A Short History of the Labour Party* (London: Macmillan, 1961).

Pim, Sir Alan and Edward Bateson, *Report on Russian Timber Camps* (London: Ernest Benn, 1931).

Pimlott, Ben, *Labour and the Left in the 1930s* (Cambridge: Cambridge University Press, 1977).

Pipes, Richard, *A Concise History of the Russian Revolution* (New York: Knopf, 1995).

————, 'Lenin's Gulag', *International Journal of Political Science and Development*, 2:6 (2014) 140–6.

————, David Brandenberger and Catherine A. Fitzpatrick (eds), *The Unknown Lenin: From the Secret Archive* (New Haven: Yale University Press, 1996).

Pius XI, *Quadragesimo Anno. Encyclical Letter on the Reconstruction of the Social Order, 15 May 1931* (Vatican: The Holy See, 1931).

Pohl, J. Otto, *The Stalinist Penal System: A Statistical History of Soviet Repression and Terror, 1930–1953* (Jefferson, NC: McFarland, 1997).

Ponsonby, Arthur, *Religion in Politics* (London: Parsons, 1921).

Porter, Bernard, *Critics of Empire: British Radicals and the Imperial Challenge* (London: I. B. Tauris, 2008).

Pospielovsky, Dimitry V., *A History of Soviet Atheism in Theory and Practice, and the Believer*, 3 vols (London: Macmillan, 1987–88), vols 1–2 (*A History of Marxist-Leninist Atheism and Soviet Antireligious Policies*; *Soviet Antireligious Campaigns and Persecutions*).

————, *The Russian Church under the Soviet Regime, 1917–1982*, 2 vols (Crestwood, NY: St Vladimir's Seminary Press, 1984).

Powell, David E., *Antireligious Propaganda in the Soviet Union: A Study of Mass Persuasion* (Cambridge, Mass.: MIT Press, 1975).

Pritt, Denis Noel, *Light on Moscow: Soviet Policy Analysed* (Harmondsworth: Penguin Books, 1939).

Purves-Stewart, Sir James, *A Physician's Tour in Soviet Russia* (London: George Allen & Unwin, 1933).

Radzinsky, Edvard, *Stalin* (New York: Doubleday, 1996).

Ratcliffe, Samuel Kerkham, *The Story of South Place* (London: Watts, 1955).

Rayfield, Donald, *Stalin and His Hangmen: An Authoritative Portrait of a Tyrant and Those who Served Him* (London: Penguin, 2005).

Read, Anthony, *The World on Fire: 1919 and the Battle with Bolshevism* (London: Jonathan Cape, 2008).

Reed, Douglas, *Far and Wide* (London: Jonathan Cape, 1951)

Reed, John Silas, *Ten Days that Shook the World* (New York: Boni & Liveright, 1919).

Reid, F., 'Socialist Sunday Schools in Britain, 1892–1939', *International Review of Social History*, 11 (1966), 18–47.

Riddell, Neil, '"The Age of Cole"? G. D. H. Cole and the British Labour Movement 1929–1933', *The Historical Journal*, 38 (1995), 933–957

————, 'The Catholic Church and the Labour Party, 1918–1931', *Twentieth Century British History*, 8:2 (1997), 165–93.

Robeson, Paul, 'To You Beloved Comrade', *New World Review*, 21:4 (1953), 11–13.

Rosen, Greg (ed.), *Dictionary of Labour Biography* (London: Methuen, 2001).

Rossi, Jacques, *The Gulag Handbook: An Encyclopedia Dictionary of Soviet Penitentiary Institutions and Terms Related to the Forced Labor Camps* (New York: Paragon House, 1989).

Salvemini, Gaetano, *The Attempted Deportation of John Strachey: Abstract of the Proceedings Before the District Director of Immigration at Chicago* (New York: American Civil Liberties Union, 1935).

Saville, John, *Memoirs from the Left* (London: Merlin, 2003).

Schinness, Roger, 'An Early Pilgrimage to Soviet Russia: Four Conservative M.P.s Challenge Tory Party Policy', *The Historical Journal*, 18 (1975), 623–631

Sebag Montefiore, Simon, *Young Stalin* (London: Phoenix, 2008)

Service, Robert, *Spies and Commissars: Russia and the West in the Russian Revolution* (London: Macmillan, 2011)

————, *Stalin: A Biography* (London: Macmillan, 2004)

Sevander, Mayme, *They Took My Father: Finnish Americans in Stalin's Russia* (Minneapolis: University of Minnesota Press, 2004)

Shaw, George Bernard, 'The Dictatorship of the Proletariat', *Labour Monthly*, 1 (1921), 297–316.

————, *The Intelligent Woman's Guide to Socialism, Capitalism, Sovietism and Fascism* (London: Constable, 1932).

————, *Look, You Boob… ! What Bernard Shaw Told the Americans About Russia! His Famous Broadcast, 11 October 1931* (London: The Friends of the Soviet Union, 1931).

————, *Prefaces* (London: Constable, 1934).

————, *Too True to be Good, Village Wooing, and On the Rocks: Three Plays* (London: Constable, 1934).

———— and Sidney Webb, *Fabian Essays in Socialism* (London: Fabian Society, 1889).

Sheehan, Helena, *Marxism and the Philosophy of Science: A Critical History* (Atlantic Highlands, NJ: Humanities Press, 1984).

Shepherd, John, *George Lansbury: At the Heart of Old Labour* (Oxford: Oxford University Press, 2002).

————, 'A Life on the Left: George Lansbury (1859–1940): A Case Study in Recent Labour Biography', *Labour History*, 87 (2004), 147–65.

————, Jonathan Shaw Davis and Chris Wrigley, *Britain's Second Labour Government, 1929–31: A Reappraisal* (Manchester: Manchester University Press, 2011).

Siemens, Ruth Derksen, *Remember Us: Letters from Stalin's Gulag (1930–37)* (Kitchener, Ontario: Pandora Press, 2008).

Smirnov, M. B. et al., *Sistema ispravitel'no-trudovyh lagerej v SSSR: 1923–1960* [The System of Corrective Labour Camps in the USSR, 1923–60] (Moscow: Zven'ya, 1998).

Smith, Leonard, *Religion and the Rise of Labour: Nonconformity and the Independent Labour Movement in Lancashire and the West Riding 1880–1914* (Keele: Ryburn, 1993).

Smith, Tim, Robert Perks and Graham Smith, *Ukraine's Forbidden History* (Stockport: Dewi Lewis, 1998).

Smolka, H. P., 'Arctic Siberia: Its Discovery and Development', *The Slavonic and East European Review*, 16 (1937), 60–70.

————, 'The Economic Development of the Soviet Arctic', *The Geographical Journal*, 89 (1937), 327–38.

————, *Forty Thousand against the Arctic* (rev. edn.; London: Hutchinson, 1937).

————, 'Soviet Development of the Arctic New Industries and Strategical Possibilities', *International Affairs (Royal Institute of International Affairs 1931–1939)*, 16 (1937), 564–78.Solzhenitsyn, Aleksandr Isaevich, *The Gulag Archipelago, 1918–1956: An Experiment in Literary Investigation* (trans. T. P. Whitney and H. T. Willetts) 3 vols (London: Collins/Fontana, 1974–78).

————, *Warning to the Western World* (London: Bodley Head, 1976).

South Place Ethical Society, *A Short History of the South Place Ethical Society and an Urgent Appeal.* (London: n.n., 1927).

Anonymous, *Wrecking Activities at Power Stations in the Soviet Union* (Moscow: State Law Publishing House, 1933).

Spiller, Gustav, *The Ethical Movement in Britain* (London: The Farleigh Press, 1934).

Stalin, Joseph, *Leninism* (London: George Allen & Unwin, 1928).

———, *Stalin's Letters to Molotov, 1925–1936*, ed. Lars T. Lih, Oleg V. Naumov, L. Kosheleva and O. V. Khlevniuk (New Haven: Yale University Press, 1995).

Stone, Dan, *Breeding Superman: Nietzsche, Race and Eugenics in Edwardian and Interwar Britain* (Liverpool: Liverpool University Press, 2002).

Strachey, John, *The Theory and Practice of Socialism* (London: Gollancz, 1936).

Strong, Anna Louise, *The Stalin Era* (New York: Mainstream, 1957).

Taylor, D. J., *Bright Young People: The Rise and Fall of a Generation, 1918–1939* (London: Chatto & Windus, 2007).

Taylor, S. J., *Stalin's Apologist: Walter Duranty, the New York Times's Man in Moscow* (Oxford: Oxford University Press, 1990).

Tchernavin, Tatiana, *Escape from the Soviets* (London: Hamish Hamilton, 1933).

Terrins, Deirdre and Phillip Whitehead (eds), *100 Years of Fabian Socialism 1884–1984* (London: Fabian Society, 1984).

Thomas, Ian, 'Confronting the Challenge of Socialism: The British Empire Union and the National Citizens' Union 1917–1927', MPhil thesis, University of Wolverhampton, 2010.

Thomas, Ivor, *The Socialist Tragedy* (London: Allen & Unwin, 1949).

Thompson, Noel W., *Political Economy and the Labour Party: The Economics of Democratic Socialism 1884–2005* (2nd edn; New York: Routledge, 2006).

Thorpe, Andrew, 'Arthur Henderson and the British Political Crisis of 1931', *The Historical Journal*, 31 (1988), 117–39.

———, *The British Communist Party and Moscow, 1920–43* (Manchester: Manchester University Press, 2000).

———, 'Stalinism and British Politics', *History*, 83 (1998), 608–27.

Tillett, Ben, *Some Russian Impressions* (London: Labour Research Department, 1925).

Tiltman, H. Hessell, *The Terror in Europe* (London: Jarrolds, 1931).

Timasheff, N. S., 'The Church in the Soviet Union 1917–1941', *The Russian Review*, 1 (1941), 20–30.

Tracey, Herbert, *The Book of the Labour Party, its History, Growth, Policy, and Leaders* (London: Caxton, 1925).

Trades Union Congress, *Report of Proceedings at the 57th Annual Trades Union Congress, 1925* (London: Cooperative Printing Society, 1925).

———, *Report of Proceedings at the 63rd Annual Trades Union Congress, 1931* (London: Cooperative Printing Society, 1931).

Trevelyan, Charles, *Soviet Russia: A Description for British Workers* (London: Gollancz, 1935).

Trotsky, Leon, *Between Red and White. A Study of Some Fundamental Questions of Revolution, with Particular Reference to Georgia* (London: Communist Party of Great Britain, 1922).

———, *Dictatorship vs Democracy, Terrorism and Communism: A Reply to Karl Kautsky* (New York: Workers Party of America, 1922).

Tzouliadis, Tim, *The Forsaken: From the Great Depression to the Gulags: Hope and Betrayal in Stalin's Russia* (London: Little, Brown, 2008).

Udy, Giles, 'The Christian Protest Movement, the Labour Government and Soviet Religious Repression, 1929–1931', *Journal of Ecclesiastical History*, 66 (2015), 116–39.

———, 'Civil and Religious Repression in Belarus', *Keston Newsletter*, 15 (2012), 1–12.

———, 'For Slaves: Against Labour', *Church Times* 7829 (5 April 2013), 17–18.

———, 'Lejboristy, Sovetskij Sojuz, Hristianskoe Dvizhenie Protesta Protiv Presledovanija Za Veru I Lesopoval v GULAGe, 1929–1931' *Russian Review*, 62 (2014).

———, 'See No Evil Labour, the Soviet Union, the Christian Protest Movement and the Timber Gulag, 1929–31', *Keston Newsletter*, 17 (2013), 17–30.

Ulmen, G. L. (ed.), *Society and History: Essays in Honor of Karl August Wittfogel* (The Hague: Mouton, 1978).

United States Congress Special Committee on Communist Activities in the United States, *Investigation of Communist Propaganda: Hearings before a Special Committee to Investigate Communist Activities in the United States of the House of Representatives, Seventy-First Congress, Second Session, pursuant to H. Res. 220, Providing for an Investigation of Communist Propaganda in the United States* (Washington: United States Government Printing Office, 1930).

———, *Investigation of Communist Propaganda: Report, pursuant to H. Res. 220* (Washington: United States Government Printing Office, 1931).

United States Department of State, *Soviet Active Measures: The Christian Peace Conference* (Washington: U.S. Department of State, 1985).

United States Commission on the Ukraine Famine, *Investigation of the Ukrainian Famine, 1932–1933: First Interim Report of Meetings and Hearings of and before the Commission on the Ukraine Famine, Held in 1986* (Washington: United States Government Printing Office, 1987).

United States Information Agency, *Soviet Active Measures in the 'Post-Cold War' Era 1988–1991: A Report Prepared at the Request of the United States House of Representatives Committee on Appropriations* (Washington: United States Information Agency, 1992).

Utley, Freda, *The Dream We Lost: Soviet Russia, Then and Now* (New York: John Day, 1940).

——, *Lost Illusion* (London: George Allen & Unwin, 1949).

——, *Odyssey of a Liberal* (Washington: Washington National Press, 1970).

Valeryev, N., 'It's Impossible to Forget ('Nevozmozhno Zzabyt'), *Dvinskaya Pravda*, (15 December 1992) <http://www.kotlas.org/kotlas/history/sleigh-driver.php>, accessed 9 November 2016.

Viola, Lynne, 'The Other Archipelago: Kulak Deportations to the North in 1930', *Slavic Review*, 60:4 (winter 2001), 730–55.

——, 'A Tale of Two Men: Bergavinov, Tolmachev and the Bergavinov Commission', *Europe-Asia Studies*, 52:8 (2000), 1449–66.

——, *The Unknown Gulag: The Lost World of Stalin's Special Settlements* (Oxford: Oxford University Press, 2007).

Wainwright, William, *The Forced Labour Swindle* (London: British-Soviet Society, 1949).

Walpole, Hugh (ed.), *Out of the Deep: Letters from Soviet Timber Camps* (London: Geoffrey Bles, 1933).

Walt, Stephen M., *Revolution and War* (Ithaca, NY: Cornell University Press, 2013).

Warriner, Doreen, 'Is Soviet Farming a Success?', *The New Fabian Research Bureau Quarterly* (autumn 1936).

Watson, George, *The Lost Literature of Socialism* (Cambridge: Lutterworth Press, 1998).

Webb, Beatrice, *Beatrice Webb's Diaries 1912–1924*, ed. Margaret Cole (London: Longmans, Green, 1952).

——, *Beatrice Webb's Diaries 1924–1932*, ed. Margaret Cole (London: Longmans, Green, 1956).

——, 'Beatrice Webb's Typescript Diary', *Beatrice Webb's Diaries* [LSE Digital Library] (n.d.) <http://digital.library.lse.ac.uk/collections/webb>, accessed 30 December 2016.

——, *The Diary of Beatrice Webb*, ed. Norman MacKenzie and Jeanne MacKenzie, 4 vols (London: Virago/LSE, 1982–85), vol. 4 (*The Wheel of Life (1924–1943)*).

Webb, Sidney, 'Soviet Communism: Its Present Position and Prospects', *International Affairs (Royal Institute of International Affairs 1931–1939)*, 15:3 (May–June 1936), 395–413.

—— and Beatrice Webb, *Soviet Communism: A New Civilisation* (2nd edn; London: Longmans, Green, 1937).

—— ——, *English Local Government* 9 vols (London: Longmans, Green, 1906–29), vol. 6 (*English Prisons under Local Government*).

—— ——, *The Truth about Soviet Russia* (London: Longmans, Green, 1941).

West, Nigel, *The Crown Jewels: The British Secrets Exposed by the KGB Archives* (London: Harper Collins, 1999).

——, ' "Venona": The British Dimension', *Intelligence and National Security*, 17 (2002), 117–34.

Wheatcroft, Stephen, 'The Scale and Nature of German and Soviet Repression and Mass Killings, 1930–45', *Europe-Asia Studies*, 48 (1996), 1319–53.

——, 'Victims of Stalinism and the Soviet Secret Police: The Comparability and Reliability of the Archival Data – Not the Last Word', *Europe-Asia Studies*, 51 (1999), 315–45.

Wicksteed, Alexander, *Life under the Soviets* (London: John Lane, 1928).

Williams, Andrew J., *Labour and Russia: The Attitude of the Labour Party to the USSR, 1924–1934* (Manchester: Manchester University Press, 1989).

——, 'The Labour Party's Attitude to the Soviet Union, 1927–35: An Overview with Specific Reference to Unemployment Policies and Peace', *Journal of Contemporary History*, 22 (1987), 71–90.

——, *Trading with the Bolsheviks: The Politics of East-West Trade, 1917–1939* (Manchester: Manchester University Press, 1992).

Williamson, Philip, *Stanley Baldwin: Conservative Leadership and National Values* (Cambridge: Cambridge University Press, 1999).

Wise, E. F., 'Soviet Russia's Place in World Trade', *Journal of the Royal Institute of International Affairs*, 9 (1930), 498–518.

Wood, Neil, *Communism and British Intellectuals* (London: Gollancz, 1959).

Worley, Matthew, *Labour inside the Gate: A History of the British Labour Party between the Wars* (London: I. B. Tauris, 2005).

Wrigley, Chris, *Arthur Henderson* (Political Portraits; Cardiff: University of Wales Press, 1990).

Wurmbrand, Richard, *Marx and Satan* (Bartlesville, Okla.: Living Sacrifice Book Company, 1990).

Yakovlev, Aleksandr N., *A Century of Violence in Soviet Russia* (New Haven: Yale University Press, 2002).

Yates, Edwin George, *Labour Personalities in the House of Commons* (Watford: Watford Printers, 1923).

Zagorsky, Semen O., *Wages and Regulations of Conditions of Labour in the U.S.S.R.* (Geneva: International Labour Office, 1930).

Zamoyski, Adam, *Warsaw 1920: Lenin's Failed Conquest of Europe* (London: Harper Press, 2008).

Zilliacus, Konni, *I Choose Peace* (Harmondsworth: Penguin Books, 1949).

Zugger, Christopher Lawrence, *The Forgotten: Catholics of the Soviet Empire from Lenin through Stalin* (Syracuse, NY: Syracuse University Press, 2001).

INDEX